F inan

20 095 195 15
AF845992
UNIVERSITY ... WITH...

While every care has been taken to ensure the accuracy of this work, no responsibility for loss or damage occasioned to any person acting or refraining from action as a result of any statement in it can be accepted by the authors, editors or publishers.

Finance Act Handbook 2019

Contributors

Kevin Barke
Lynnette Bober, ACA
Richard Cherrett
Helen Cox
Mike Dalton
Bill Dodwell, LLB, LLM, CTA (Fellow), ACA
Andrew Goodall
Phil Greatrex, FCA, ATII
Mark Groom
Claire Hayes
John Hayward
Barney Horn
Jo Houghton
Andrew Hubbard, BMus, PhD, CTA (Fellow), ATT (Fellow)
Lydia Hutchinson
Zigurds Kronbergs, BSc, ARCS, MA, ACA, FCCA
John Lindsay BA, FCA, FTII
Lisa Macpherson
Pete Miller, CTA (Fellow)
Ruth Newman
Hugo Powell
Lynne Poyser BMedSc (Hons), ATT, CTA
David Rudling, CTA
Ben Saunders
David Smailes, FCA
James Stewart
Matt Stringer
Edd Thompson
Helen Thompson, ACA
Mike Trotman
Kevin Walton
Richard Whitaker, TEP

Tolley®

LexisNexis UK & Worldwide

United Kingdom	RELX (UK) Limited trading as LexisNexis, 1–3 Strand, London WC2N 5JR and 9–10 St Andrew Square, Edinburgh EH2 2AF
LNUK Global Partners	LexisNexis® encompasses authoritative legal-publishing brands dating back to the 19th century including; Butterworths® in the United Kingdom, Canada, the Asia-Pacific region, Les Editions du Juris Classeur in France and Matthew Bender® worldwide. Details of LexisNexis® locations worldwide can be found at www.lexisnexis.com

© 2019 RELX (UK) Limited

Published by LexisNexis

This is a Tolley title

All rights reserved. No part of this publication may be reproduced in any material form (including photocopying or storing it in any medium by electronic means and whether or not transiently or incidentally to some other use of this publication) without the written permission of the copyright owner except in accordance with the provisions of the Copyright, Designs and Patents Act 1988 or under the terms of a licence issued by the Copyright Licensing Agency Ltd, Saffron House, 6–10 Kirby Street, London EC1N 8TS. Applications for the copyright owner's written permission to reproduce any part of this publication should be addressed to the publisher.

Warning: The doing of an unauthorised act in relation to a copyright work may result in both a civil claim for damages and criminal prosecution.

Crown copyright material is reproduced with the permission of the Controller of HMSO and the Queen's Printer for Scotland. Parliamentary copyright material is reproduced with the permission of the Controller of Her Majesty's Stationery Office on behalf of Parliament. Any European material in this work which has been reproduced from EUR-lex, the official European Communities legislation website, is European Communities copyright.

LexisNexis® and the Knowledge Burst logo are registered trademarks of Reed Elsevier Properties Inc., used under license. Butterworths and Tolley are registered trademarks of RELX (UK) Limited. Matthew Bender is a registered trademark of Matthew Bender Properties Inc. Other products and services may be trademarks or registered trademarks of their respective companies.

A CIP Catalogue record for this book is available from the British Library.

ISBN 9781474311281

Typeset by Letterpart Limited, Caterham on the Hill, Surrey CR3 5XL

Printed and bound by CPI Group (UK) Ltd, Croydon, CR0 4YY

Visit LexisNexis at www.lexisnexis.co.uk

FOREWORD

On 12 February, Her Majesty the Queen gave Royal Assent to Finance Act 2019. The new Act is 328 pages long – which sounds bad until we recall previous Finance Acts more than twice as long.

The biggest exchequer costs in the Act come from the early adoption of the £12,500 personal allowance and the £50,000 higher rate tax threshold (outside Scotland). No doubt many will welcome the income tax savings and the fact that more people are taken out of income tax (although not national insurance).

The Act contains a number of international corporate tax provisions. It imposes UK corporation tax on overseas companies based in locations with which the UK does not have a full tax treaty, where those companies derive income from intangible assets. The income charged must relate to rights to intangible property which enables, facilitates or promotes UK sales, directly or indirectly. The new tax charge replaces an even more complicated withholding tax, but is unlikely to be easy to apply. Fortunately, limiting its application to those territories where the UK does not have a full tax treaty with a non-discrimination clause will limit its overall impact.

The Act makes small changes to the UK's controlled foreign company rules to bring them in line with the EU's Anti-Tax Avoidance Directives, by specifying that the finance company exemption can only apply where the income is not related to UK activities. Adoption of the change also means that the UK's current rules now comply with EU state aid rules. There's also a change to company exit taxation from 2020, again stemming from the Directive.

There's also a change to the UK's definition of a taxable permanent establishment, by bringing the anti-fragmentation rule developed during the Base Erosion and Profit Shifting project into UK domestic law. The idea is to combine the activities carried on by a multinational to determine whether the combined whole amounts to a taxable presence. The UK has ratified the BEPS Multilateral Convention, which allows such a rule and so domestic law needed to be widened to make it effective.

After a gap of four years, qualifying expenditure on the acquisition of goodwill qualifies for intangibles allowances. The rule is tightly drawn, by limiting the amount of goodwill that qualifies to a multiple of other intangible assets acquired in the same transaction. It remains to be seen how much of a benefit this turns out to be, especially as customer-related intangibles continue to be excluded.

There's also a new capital allowance – structures and buildings allowance. Due to the pressure on parliamentary counsel from the Brexit process, the Act simply includes enabling law with the substantive provisions arriving through statutory instrument. Surprisingly, the Chancellor decided to increase the annual investment allowance for a two-year period. This costly change is likely to benefit a small number of groups. The Office of Tax Simplification identified that only 25,000 companies claimed the lower level of allowance in full – and then, not every year. Just 8,500 groups always spent at least £200,000.

Entrepreneurs' relief is the subject of a variety of changes. The relief is potentially controversial, not least due to its significant cost – some £3 billion annually. The changes require that a qualifying shareholder must hold the shares for two years instead of one and have a 5% economic interest, rather than just 5% of the share capital. However, there's a new election where the company ceases to be a personal company through a new share issue. The individual may elect to trigger a gain to which entrepreneurs' relief applies and then defer it until ultimate disposal.

It's perhaps not surprising to see that the Act contains changes to quite a few recently-introduced measures. The anti-hybrid rules, corporate interest restrictions and the corporate loss relief restrictions all see updates. Whilst it is good that changes are made, the speed with which such substantial pieces of law were introduced made it almost inevitable that there would need to be adjustments.

I would like to congratulate the publishers in preparing this book so quickly and the authors of the commentary in the speed of their analysis, which I hope will aid those charged with considering the changes introduced by this Act.

Bill Dodwell
April 2019

CONTENTS

RELEVANT DATES AND ABBREVIATIONS

29 October 2018	Budget Statement
7 November 2018	Finance Bill
12 February 2019	Royal Assent

ABV	=	alcohol by volume
ACS	=	authorised contractual schemes
ALDA 1979	=	Alcoholic Liquor Duties Act 1979
APD	=	Air Passenger Duty
ATT	=	Association of Taxation Technicians
CA 2006	=	Companies Act 2006
CAA 2001	=	Capital Allowances Act 2001
CFC	=	controlled foreign company
CGT	=	capital gains tax
Ch	=	Chapter (of a part of an Act)
CIOT	=	Chartered Institute of Taxation
CTA 2009	=	Corporation Tax Act 2009
CTA 2010	=	Corporation Tax Act 2010
DPT	=	diverted profits tax
EBITDA	=	earnings before interest, tax, depreciation and amortisation
EEA	=	European Economic Area
EU ETS	=	EU Emissions Trading Scheme
FA	=	Finance Act
HMRC	=	Her Majesty's Revenue and Customs
HRAD	=	higher rates of tax for additional dwellings
IHT	=	inheritance tax
IHTA 1984	=	Inheritance Tax Act 1984
ITA 2007	=	Income Tax Act 2007
ITEPA 2003	=	Income Tax (Earnings and Pensions) Act 2003
ITTOIA 2005	=	Income Tax (Trading and Other Income) Act 2005
LLPs	=	limited liability partnerships
OECD	=	Organisation for Economic Co-operation and Development
para	=	paragraph (of a Schedule to an Act)
PAYE	=	pay as you earn
PE	=	permanent establishment
PRT	=	petroleum revenue tax
Pt	=	part (of an Act or of a Schedule to an Act)
reg	=	regulation (of an SI)
RNRB	=	residence nil rate band
s	=	section (of an Act)
Sch	=	Schedule (to an Act)
SDIL	=	soft drinks industry levy
SI	=	Statutory Instrument (since 1948)
ss	=	sections (of an Act)
STC	=	Simon's Tax Cases
sub-para	=	sub-paragraph
sub-s	=	subsection
TCGA 1992	=	Taxation of Chargeable Gains Act 1992
TIOPA 2010	=	Taxation (International and Other Provisions) Act 2010
TMA 1970	=	Taxes Management Act 1970
TPDA 1979	=	Tobacco Products Duty Act 1979
TTH	=	transferable tax history
UK	=	United Kingdom
VATA 1994	=	Value Added Tax Act 1994
VED	=	vehicle excise duty
VERA 1994	=	Vehicle Excise and Registration Act 1994

ABOUT THE AUTHORS

Lynnette Bober, ACA

Lynnette is a chartered accountant, a Chartered Tax Adviser, and a member of the Society of Trust and Estate Practitioners. Specialising in the field of personal taxation (including remittance basis issues and offshore trust planning) she advises clients on personal and trust taxation issues. She also contributes to various technical publications and journals. Lynnette is the deputy chairman of the ICAEW Tax Faculty Private Client Committee and on a number of its subcommittees and working parties.

Lynnette Bober has written the commentary for FA 2019, s 22, Sch 7.

Richard Cherrett

Richard Cherrett is a director in Deloitte's International Markets business tax advisory group, and a fellow of the ICAEW. He advises large corporate groups on complex issues, principally the application of corporate debt and derivatives rules, and the taxation of cross-border flows.

Richard Cherrett has written the commentary for FA 2019, s 19, Sch 20.

Helen Cox

Helen Cox is a partner in the tax and private client practice at Fladgate LLP. Helen's practice area combines advising on corporate and personal taxation. She acts for a wide range of clients, including private individuals, family offices, trustees and corporate entities. Helen has particular expertise in advising on corporate structures, joint ventures, succession planning and international tax planning. Helen is a Chartered Tax Adviser and a member of the Chartered Institute of Taxation.

Helen Cox has written the commentary for FA 2019, Sch 4.

Mike Dalton

Mike Dalton is Director and Head of Stamp Taxes at Grant Thornton UK LLP. Mike is a Chartered Accountant and Chartered Tax Adviser and an active member of the Stamp Taxes Practitioners' Group. He is a member of Grant Thornton's Real Estate team and provides a wide range of clients with both stamp taxes and property tax advice.

Mike Dalton, and Hugo Powell have co-authored the commentary for FA 2019, ss 42 to 50.

Bill Dodwell, LLB, LLM, CTA (Fellow), ACA

Bill Dodwell is Tax Director at the Office of Tax Simplification and a past president of the Chartered Institute of Taxation.

Bill Dodwell has written the Foreword to the handbook.

Andrew Goodall

Andrew Goodall is a freelance writer specialising in UK tax policy, law and administration. He is a regular contributor to Tax Notes, published by Tax Analysts. His work has been published by several LexisNexis UK titles including Simon's Tax Intelligence, Tolley's Tax Guide and Tax Journal. He is a non-practising member of the Chartered Institute of Taxation.

Andrew Goodall has written the commentary for FA 2019, ss 90, 92, 93.

Phil Greatrex, FCA, ATII
Phil Greatrex is a partner in CW Energy LLP. Phil has been providing tax advice to a wide range of clients in the oil and gas sector, covering petroleum revenue tax corporation tax and supplementary charge on varied, and often complex, issues for over 30 years. He has been an active member of the UKOITC and BRINDEX tax committees for many years and has extensive experience of dealing with Treasury and HMRC in lobbying for tax changes. More recently he was a member of the expert panel advising Treasury on the options available for taxation of late life assets.

Phil Greatrex has written the commentary for FA 2019, ss 37, 38, Sch 15.

Mark Groom
Mark Groom is an employment tax partner in Deloitte's Compensation and Benefits group. He is also Vice Chairman of the Employment Taxes sub-committee of the Chartered Institute of Taxation. Mark specialises in pay and incentives, employment status and intermediaries, and benefits and expenses consulting and compliance including KYC, SAO, and HMRC investigations. He is a regular speaker at seminars and contributor to articles on employment tax matters and to HMRC consultations.

Mark Groom has advised on the commentary for FA 2019, ss 9, 10.

John Hayward
John Hayward is a former part-time self-employed pensions author. He has written for Pensions World and Tax Journal and is a member of the latter's Editorial Board. He has contributed to Butterworth's Tax Planning Service, Robin Ellison's Pensions Law and Practice, Simon's Taxes, Tolley's Finance and Law for the Older Client, Finance Act Handbook 2004 to 2018 and the ICAEW's TAXline. His specialist topics include small self-administered pension schemes and taxation aspects of all pension schemes.

John Hayward has written the commentary for FA 2019, s 11.

Barney Horn
Barney Horn is a senior Indirect Tax Partner with over 28 years of experience with HM Customs & Excise, Deloitte UK and Deloitte Australia. He advises businesses in a number of sectors but with a particular specialism in betting and gaming, hospitality and leisure. This advice covers a wide range of matters including VAT reclaims, dispute resolution including litigation, M&A and cross border supplies of goods and services.

Barney Horn has written the commentary for FA 2019, Sch 19.

Jo Houghton
Jo Houghton is a UK Chartered Accountant and Chartered Tax Adviser. She specialises in corporate tax and has worked both in industry and as a senior manager in practice with PwC. In addition, Jo has worked as a CPD tax lecturer with Mercia Group, a national training provider, where she lectured on a range of topic areas including business tax and tax accounting. Jo is currently a technical writer at LexisNexis.

Jo Houghton has written the commentary for FA 2019, ss 24, 83, 84, Sch 14.

Andrew Hubbard, BMus, PhD, CTA (Fellow), ATT (Fellow)
Andrew Hubbard is the editor-in-chief of Taxation magazine. He is a long-term contributor to Tolley's Tax Planning and Finance Act Handbook. In 2006 he won the tax writer of the year award at the Taxation Awards and is a former president of both the CIOT and the ATT. He is well known as a writer and lecturer on tax matters. He has recently retired as a partner in the Nottingham office of RSM where he specialised in tax dispute resolution and the taxation of entrepreneurial businesses. Andrew originally trained as a musician before joining the Inland Revenue as an Inspector of Taxes.

Andrew Hubbard has written the commentary for FA 2019, ss 80–82, 85–87, 95.

Lydia Hutchinson
Lydia Hutchinson has been writing on corporation tax for Simon's Taxes and TolleyGuidance since 2017. She qualified as a solicitor in 2011 having trained at Dechert, before joining the Freshfields tax team, and subsequently the tax team at Olswang (now CMS). She advised on all areas of corporate tax, as well as some aspects of tax for individuals.

Lydia Hutchinson has written the commentary for FA 2019, Sch 6.

Zigurds Kronbergs, BSc, ARCS, MA, ACA, FCCA
Zigurds Kronbergs is an experienced writer on UK, European and international tax, and is a regular contributor to several publications, including Finance Act Handbook. A specialist in tax for 40 years, he is also European Tax Coordinator for Moore Stephens Europe Ltd and the correspondent on Latvia and several UK chapters for the IBFD.

Zigurds Kronbergs has written the Introduction to FA 2019.

John Lindsay, BA, FCA, FTII
John Lindsay is a consultant in the tax department of Linklaters LLP. He advises on all corporate taxes with a focus on the taxation of capital market and securitisation transactions. John is a contributor to Simon's Taxes, Simon's Tax Planning and Tolley's Tax Planning and is also a co-author of the Taxation of Companies and Company Reconstructions (Sweet & Maxwell, 2009). He is a member of both the CIOT Technical Committee and the CIOT Corporate Tax Sub-committee and is also a member of a number of HMRC working groups.

John Lindsay has written the commentary for FA 2019, ss 28, 29, Schs 11, 12.

Lisa Macpherson
Lisa Macpherson is the Head of Tax Technical at PKF Francis Clark, supporting the firm's teams on tax policy and technical issues across its offices and also across the wider PKF network. She has more than 20 years' experience working in all areas of taxation including compliance and consultancy. For the last fifteen years Lisa has specialised in dealing with inheritance tax planning, onshore and offshore trust taxation, residence and domicile issues, capital gains tax and pre-owned assets tax for a number of high net worth clients.

Lisa Macpherson has written the commentary for FA 2019, Schs 1, 2.

Pete Miller, CTA (Fellow), Partner, The Miller Partnership
Pete Miller has worked in tax for 31 years, starting as an Inspector of Taxes where he had roles in Policy and Technical Divisions and was the Inland Revenue's expert on distributions. He spent 11 years in 'Big 4' firms, specialising in corporate transactions, before founding The Miller Partnership, which advices other advisers on transactions in securities, reorganisations, reconstructions, distributions, partnerships, Patent Box, HMRC clearances and intangible assets. Pete speaks and writes regularly on tax and is General Editor of Whiteman and Sherry on Capital Gains Tax and on Income Tax and is on the Editorial Boards of Taxation, The Tax Journal and Simon's Taxes.

Hugo Powell
Hugo Powell is a manager at Grant Thornton UK LLP. Hugo is a Chartered Accountant and a member of the CIOT. He sits in Grant Thornton's Real Estate team and provides advice to a wide range of funds and property investment companies.

Hugo Powell and Mike Dalton have co-authored the commentary for FA 2019, ss 42 to 50.

Lynne Poyser, BMedSc (Hons), ATT, CTA
Lynne Poyser is the in-house writer of the Personal Tax module of TolleyGuidance. An expert in personal taxation with over 15 years' experience, Lynne joined Tolley from BDO, where she worked in the private client team and the national tax training department, having previously worked for Grant Thornton and Arthur Andersen. Lynne has written for Taxwise 1, Taxation magazine, Tax Adviser magazine and has been a tutor for Tolley Exam Training. She is also the former Chairman of the London branch of ATT and CIOT.

Lynne Poyser has written the commentary for FA 2019, ss 1, 3–6, 11, 40.

David Rudling, CTA
David Rudling is a technical writer with LexisNexis. Before joining LexisNexis he worked for HMRC, in industry, and for a Big Four firm of accountants. He specialises in VAT and is involved in the production of De Voil Indirect Tax Service, Tolley's VAT Planning, Tolley's VAT Handbook and Tolley's VAT cases.

David has written the commentary for FA 2019, ss 51–53 and Schs 17, 18.

Ben Saunders
Ben Saunders specialises in owner-managed business tax issues. He has a wide range of experience from his time in practice, training in a mixed tax role at PKF before moving to roles advising large corporate clients at PwC and then personal tax clients at UHY. During his time at PwC Ben was part of the firm's research and development tax relief network and he went on to work as an independent adviser helping businesses claim R&D tax relief before joining Tolley. In addition to TolleyGuidance, Ben has written for Taxation magazine, Taxwise and Tolley's Tax Digest.

Ben Saunders has written the commentary for FA 2019, ss 31–35, Sch 13.

David Smailes, FCA
David Smailes is a senior tax writer on the staff of LexisNexis and is the current author of Tolley's Income Tax. His career in tax publishing has taken in many publications, and he previously worked full-time in tax practice with medium to large professional firms.

David Smailes has written the commentary for FA 2019, ss 2, 7, 8.

James Stewart
James Stewart is a senior counsel in the tax department at Taylor Wessing LLP. He works on a range of matters including commercial real estate and finance transactions, specialising in corporation tax, stamp taxes and VAT. James is a solicitor and Chartered Tax Adviser.

James Stewart has written the commentary for FA 2019, s 17, Sch 5.

Matt Stringer
Matt Stringer is the Head of International Tax at Grant Thornton UK. He has a decade of experience in large corporate and international tax, working with both inbound and outbound multinational groups. Matt has particular expertise in cross border structuring matters and the OECD BEPS initiatives, with recent experience across Diverted Profits Tax, Anti-Hybrid rules and structuring opportunities for US multinationals in light of US tax reform measures. Matt writes for Tax Adviser magazine in the UK, with recently published articles on Diverted Profits Tax, State Aid and the new UK Digital Services Tax.

Matt Stringer has written the commentary for FA 2019, ss 15, 20, Sch 3.

Edd Thompson
Edd Thompson is a Chartered Accountant and Chartered Tax Adviser. He trained and worked in a top 10 accountancy firm for a number of years where he provided indirect tax advice to a broad range of clients including large corporates, owner managed businesses, public bodies and not-for-profits. He now works for Tolley as a technical writer where he contributes to several publications including De Voil Indirect Tax Service and De Voil Indirect Tax Intelligence.

Edd Thompson has written the commentary for FA 2019, ss 54–61.

Helen Thompson, ACA
Helen Thompson is a partner in Deloitte's indirect tax practice, specialising in environmental taxes and VAT, and leads Deloitte's Environmental Taxes group. She also chaired the CIOT's Environmental Taxes Working Group from 2007–2010. Helen has extensive experience in advising businesses on their environmental tax obligations and liabilities and has provided specialist environmental due diligence services in relation to major acquisitions.

Helen Thompson and Mike Trotman have co-authored the commentary for FA 2019 ss 69–79, 91.

Mike Trotman

Mike Trotman is an associate director in Deloitte LLP with more than 25 years' experience in indirect taxation. In Deloitte Mike has provided a firm-wide resource on environmental tax matters for over 17 years. Mike is a member of the CIOT Indirect Tax Technical Sub-Committee where he focusses on environmental taxes and has been a special advisor to the devolved governments in the UK in connection with devolution of environmental taxes from central government.

Mike Trotman and Helen Thompson have co-authored the commentary for FA 2019, ss 69–79, 91.

Kevin Walton

Kevin Walton is an in-house writer with Tolley. He is the author of Tolley's Capital Gains Tax, Tolley's Corporation Tax and Tolley's Capital Allowances.

Kevin Walton has written the commentary for FA 2019, s 30.

Richard Whitaker, TEP

Richard Whitaker qualified as a solicitor in 2013 after spending 12 years in the military as a musician. Before joining Tolley, he worked in practice advising clients on Wills, trusts, estate administration and inheritance tax. Richard is a full member of the Society of Trust and Estate Practitioners (STEP) and is currently the senior examiner and a technical author for the STEP Advanced Certificate in Administration of Estates.

Richard Whitaker has written the commentary for FA 2019, s 66.

INTRODUCTION

After a brief respite in terms of a comparatively short Finance Act 2018, at least in comparison to the gargantuan tomes to which we have become accustomed in recent years, this year's Act, weighing in at over 300 pages containing 97 sections and 20 Schedules, marks a regress towards those longer statutes. Out of the 328 pages of this Act, four are devoted to a new tax (the Carbon Emissions Tax) that is contingent on an event that may never take place, while a substantial 100 pages, just under a third of the entire Act, are devoted to the extension of CGT or corporation tax to all direct and indirect disposals of UK land (whether residential or otherwise). The bulk of the remainder is spent on amendments to existing, in many cases relatively new, legislation, many of which add further complexity to what must already be one of the most voluminous tax codes in the world.

In this Introduction, capital gains tax is abbreviated throughout to 'CGT' and stamp duty reserve tax to 'SDRT'.

Royal Assent was given on 12 February 2019.

PART 1 DIRECT TAXES

Charge to tax

Section 1 imposes the charge to income tax for the year 2019/20.

Section 2 imposes the charge to corporation tax for the financial year (FY) 2020 (the year beginning 1 April 2020). The charge to corporation tax for the coming year, FY 2019, was imposed by FA 2018, s 2. As no further amendment is made to F(No 2)A 2015, s 7(1), the main rate of corporation tax for FY 2019 remains 19% and that set for FY 2020 is 17%.

Income tax rates, allowances and limits

Section 3 sets the main rates of income tax for 2019/20; these remain 20% (the basic rate), 40% (the higher rate) and 45% (the additional rate). These rates apply to the 'non-savings, non-dividend income' of taxpayers in England and Northern Ireland. The rates applicable to the 'non-savings, non-dividend income' of Scottish taxpayers for the year 2019/20 have been set by the Scottish Parliament under the Scotland Act 1998, s 80C and those for Welsh taxpayers by the National Assembly for Wales under the Government of Wales Act 2006, s 116D. The effect is that the rates for Welsh taxpayers are identical to those for taxpayers in England and Northern Ireland, but the Scottish rates are as follows:

Name of rate	Tranche of income (£)	Rate of income tax
Starter rate	0 to 2,049	19%
Scottish basic rate	2,050 to 12,444	20%
Intermediate rate	12,445 to 30,930	41%
Scottish higher rate	Above 30,930	46%

Section 4 sets the default and savings rates for the year 2019/20, leaving them at the 2018/19 levels, ie the default basic rate and the savings basic rates are 20%; the default and savings higher rates are 40%; and the default and savings additional rates are 45%. The default rates are the rates that apply to the 'non-savings, non-dividend income' of all UK taxpayers who are not subject to either the UK main rates of income tax (see s 3) or the Scottish rates of income tax (ITA 2007, s 11C – these rates currently apply to non-resident individuals). Savings rates are the rates applicable to savings income (but not dividend income).

Section 5 sets the basic-rate limit for 2019/20 at £37,500 (up from £34,500 in 2018/19) and freezes it at that level for 2020/21. Similarly, it sets the person allowance for 2019/20 at £12,500 (up from £11,850 in 2018/19) and freezes it at that level for 2020/21. As a result of the increase in the personal allowance, F(No 2)A 2015, s 4, which obliges the Chancellor of the Exchequer to have regard to the effect on a person paid at the national minimum wage of a proposal to increase the personal allowance to an amount less than £12,500 becomes redundant and is repealed, as are related provisions in that Act and in ITA 2007. The indexation provisions for the basic-rate limit (ITA 2007, s 21(3)) and the personal allowance (ITA 2007, s 57) are disapplied for the years 2019/20 and 2020/21.

Section 6 disapplies the indexation of the starting-rate limit for savings under ITA 2007, s 21(3A) and freezes the starting-rate limit at £5,000 for 2019/20.

Employment and social security income

Section 7 makes amendments to the taxation of benefits-in-kind provided under optional remuneration arrangements (OpRA) as introduced by FA 2017, s 7 and Sch 2. Under the OpRA legislation, broadly speaking, the taxable benefit is deemed to be the greater of the amount forgone by the employee and the modified cash equivalent of the benefit. By oversight, the original legislation failed to ensure that connected costs were included in the calculation of the amount forgone. These amendments are intended to correct this oversight. It is a pity that the opportunity has not also been taken to correct the lamentable misspelling of 'forgone' as 'foregone'.

ITEPA 2003, s 120A taxes the provision of a car under OpRA. It is amended by s 7(2) to provide that the tax charge is to be based on the 'total foregone [sic] amount', which is defined (by *new ITEPA 2003, s 120A(4)*) as the sum of the total amount forgone with respect to the benefit of the car itself (as heretofore) and (now) the amount forgone with respect to every other benefit connected with the car provided pursuant to optional remuneration arrangements but excluding the provision of fuel or of a driver. Consequential amendments are made (by s 7(3)) to ITEPA 2003, s 121A, which sets out the method of calculating the amount to be treated as earnings.

The intention of the amendments made to ITEPA 2003, s 132A by s 7(4) is to ensure that the amount of the deduction in respect of the employee's capital contribution to the cost of providing the car is reduced pro rata for the amount of time within the tax year during which the car is not available. Thus, the amount of the deduction is now, by virtue of *substituted ITEPA 2003, s 132A(3)* and *new ITEPA 2003, s 132A(4A) and (4B)*, to be found by first multiplying the capped deduction by the 'appropriate percentage' (as heretofore) but then multiplying the product by the 'availability factor', defined by *new ITEPA 2003, s 132A(4A)* as (Y – U)/Y, where Y is the number of days in the tax year and U is the number of days in that tax year on which the car is unavailable.

The amendments made by s 7(5) to ITEPA 2003, s 154A, which taxes the provision of a van under OpRA, mirror those made by s 7(2) to ITEPA 2003, s 120A.

Consequential amendments are made by s 7(6) to ITEPA 2003, s 239.

All the amendments made by s 7 have effect from the tax year 2019/20.

Section 8 introduces a new exemption from the benefit charge, in respect of the provision of a charging point for vehicle batteries. *New ITEPA 2003, s 237A*, inserted by s 8(1), provides that no liability to income tax shall arise in respect of the provision of vehicle-battery charging facilities at or near the workplace for a vehicle used by the employee (including use as a passenger), subject to the proviso that the facilities be generally provided to all the employees. This new exemption has retroactive effect from the tax year 2018/19.

Section 9 makes three amendments to the tax treatment of benefits-in-kind from the provision of emergency vehicles.

ITEPA 2003, s 248A has hitherto exempted the benefit derived from the private use of an emergency vehicle provided to an employee of an emergency service, provided that the terms on which it is made available prevent its private use except when the employee is on call or using it for 'on-call commuting' and the employee concerned abides by those terms. The amendment now made to that section by s 9(2) and (3) restate the exemption so that it applies where the vehicle is provided mainly for use for the employee's business travel and the terms of provision prevent its use except where the employee is on call or engaged in commuting (generally). This represents a broadening of the exemption.

Where use of an emergency vehicle extends beyond the terms in ITEPA 2003, s 248A, the benefit is one of the use of an asset without its transfer, and the charge to tax is under ITEPA 2003, s 205, on the 'annual cost' of the benefit less any deduction under ITEPA 2003, s 205A for periods when the vehicle is unavailable for private use. The 'annual cost' of the benefit is defined as the higher of the annual value of the use of the asset and the annual sums paid by the provider by way of rent or hire charge, together with the amount of any 'additional expense'. *New ITEPA 2003, s 205*(*5*), inserted by s 9(4), provides that the expense of providing fuel is not to be an additional expense for this purpose as long as no expense is incurred by the provider in respect of fuel for the employee's private use or the employee makes good all the cost of private fuel by 6 July following the tax year. *New ITEPA 2003, s 205*(*6*), also inserted by s 9(4), provides definitions.

These amendments to ITEPA 2003, ss 205 and 248A have retroactive effect from the tax year 2017/18.

The third amendment addresses the method of calculating the benefit from use of an emergency vehicle in the three tax years 2017/18 to 2019/20. The amendments made by s 9(6)–(9) provide that for this purpose, the charge to tax will be on the private-use proportion of the annual cost, defined as the proportion that private miles travelled bear to total miles. At the same time, some of the definitions in ITEPA 2003, s 205A(2) of when a vehicle is unavailable for private use are to be disregarded. The overall effect is broadly to restore the concessionary treatment of the calculation that prevailed before the changes made with effect from 6 April 2017 by FA 2017, s 8 for the three tax years in question.

Section 10 is intended to remove the requirement under ITEPA 2003, s 289A for employers to check receipts or other evidence provided by employees to justify use of HMRC's scale rates for exempting the payment or reimbursement of employees' qualifying travel or subsistence expenses. ITEPA 2003, s 289A has heretofore exempted expenses in general that are paid or reimbursed to an employee if, inter alia, checks are operated on whether the employee has in fact incurred and paid the expenditure. *New ITEPA 2003, s 289A*(*2A*), (*4A*) substitute a less rigorous checking requirement in respect of travel for which a deduction would be allowed under ITEPA 2003, Pt 5, Ch 2 or 5 and for which the employee has been paid HMRC scale rates. As from the tax year 2019/20, it will only be necessary to check that the employee has actually undertaken the travel in question. As before, the exemption will not apply where the payment is made under a salary-sacrifice scheme. *New ITEPA 2003, s 289A*(*8*) provides for regulations to be made to include overseas scale rates within the new exemption.

Section 11 addresses the exemption given under ITEPA 2003, s 307 for sums paid by employers to provide death or retirement benefits to employees or members of the employee's family or household. With effect from the tax year 2019/20, the exemption is widened to allow the employee to nominate any individual or charity as a beneficiary.

Section 12 addresses the tax treatment of certain social security benefits. Carer's allowance supplement, to be introduced by the Scottish Government, is added to those benefits taxable under ITEPA 2003, ss 660 and 661 in respect of the full amount of benefit accruing in the tax year. Seven benefits, some of them newly introduced in Scotland, namely best-start grant, discretionary housing payment, discretionary support award, funeral-expense assistance, flexible support-fund payment, payments under a council-tax reduction scheme for England, and young-carer grant are added to the list in Table B in ITEPA 2003, s 677(1) of tax-free benefits, with effect from 12 February 2019 (Royal Assent).

Chargeable gains: interests in UK land etc

Section 13, which introduces **Sch 1**, completes the inexorable drive to include direct and indirect disposals by non-residents of interests in UK land within the scope of CGT or corporation tax on chargeable gains. These provisions extend the net to disposals by non-resident companies and collective investment vehicles and disposals by non-residents generally of non-residential UK land, with effect from 6 April 2019. They also involve a fundamental rewrite of TCGA 1992, Pt 1 and the abolition of the ATED-related and NRCGT-gains regime, which now become redundant.

In the notes that follow, the designation 'existing TCGA 1992, s x' refers to the provisions of TCGA 1992 before amendment or omission by these provisions. References to the 'restatement' of an existing provision should not be taken to imply that the provision is reproduced verbatim or virtually verbatim in the corresponding new provision.

Schedule 1 consists of 3 Parts. Part 1 (paras 1–21) substitutes a *new TCGA 1992, Pt 1*; Part 2 (paras 22–119) makes consequential amendments to the rest of TCGA 1992 and other statutes; Part 3 (paras 120–126) makes commencement and transitional provisions. All told, Sch 1 runs for exactly 100 pages, or 30.5% of the entire Act.

Schedule 1, para 1 is introductory. Schedule 1, para 2 substitutes the new TCGA 1992, Pt 1. Whereas the existing Part I (sic) consists of 31 extant sections (1–14H), the new Part 1 contains 32 sections (but numbered 1–3G), subdivided into three Chapters.

The title of new TCGA 1992, Pt 1, 'CGT and corporation tax on chargeable gains' is unchanged.

New TCGA 1992, Pt 1, Ch 1, consisting of ss 1–1O, is entitled 'Capital Gains Tax'.

New TCGA 1992, s 1 substantially restates the existing TCGA 1992, s 1. However, it omits references to ATED-related and NRCGT gains and provides that corporation tax on chargeable gains is to be charged under the provisions of *new TCGA 1992, Pt 1 Ch 2*, as well as under CTA 2009, s 2 and other relevant provisions of the Corporation Tax Acts (as heretofore). *New TCGA 1992, s 1(3)* essentially restates existing TCGA 1992, s 2(2), providing that CGT is to be charged on the total amount of chargeable gains accruing to a person in a tax year after deducting the allowable losses of that year and any outstanding allowable losses from previous tax years. The other provisions of existing TCGA 1992, s 2 relating to losses are transferred to *new TCGA 1992, s 1E*.

New TCGA 1992, s 1A provides for the territorial scope of the CGT charge and largely restates existing TCGA 1992, s 2 but includes the new charging provisions on direct or indirect interests in UK land. In the case of a UK-resident person, CGT is chargeable in respect of chargeable gains accruing to that person in the tax year from the disposal of assets wherever situated, subject to further provisions in new TCGA 1992, Sch 1 (foreign gains under the remittance basis), *new TCGA 1992, s 1G* (split years), *new TCGA 1992, ss 1M* and *1N* (temporary non-residence), *new TCGA 1992, Pt 1, Ch 3* (non-UK resident companies' chargeable gains attributable to individuals) and the provisions of TCGA 1992 on non-UK resident trustees' gains attributable to individuals. In the case of a non-UK resident, *new TCGA 1992, s 1A(3)* provides that the charge to CGT is to apply in respect of disposals of:

(a) UK-situated assets having a relevant connection with a UK branch or agency,
(b) interests in UK land other than those of a UK branch or agency, and
(c) assets deriving at least 75% of their value from UK land,

providing that the person has a 'substantial indirect interest' in that UK land. Residence means residence for any part of the year and is determined by reference to FA 2013, Sch 45 (individuals), TCGA 1992, ss 62(3) (personal representatives) and 69 (trustees).

New TCGA 1992, s 1B provides for the charge to CGT on the disposals of assets of a UK branch or agency of a non-UK resident and largely restates existing TCGA 1992, s 10.

New TCGA 1992, s 1C defines what is meant by 'an interest in UK land'. The definition is taken practically unchanged from existing TCGA 1992, Sch B1, paras 2 and 3, in respect of disposals of UK residential-property interests. TCGA 1992, Sch B1 is to be omitted.

New TCGA 1992, s 1D is a new provision, relating to assets deriving 75% or more of their value from UK land. It introduces *new TCGA 1992, Sch 1A* (inserted by Sch 1, para 13), which is to determine whether an asset derives at least 75% of its value from UK land and whether the person making the disposal has the sufficient substantial indirect interest in the UK land at the time of its disposal so as to incur the charge to CGT.

New TCGA 1992, ss 1E and *1F* provide for the deduction of allowable losses. *New TCGA 1992, s 1E*(*1*) provides that, for all purposes of TCGA 1992, a loss is not an allowable loss if the corresponding gain would not have been a chargeable gain and restricts the deduction of losses from the disposal of assets in respect of which a non-resident is chargeable to chargeable gains from the disposal of other such assets. Otherwise, it largely restates some of the other loss provisions in existing TCGA 1992, s 2 not already dealt with in preceding sections.

New TCGA 1992, s 1F provides for allowable losses to be used in the way most beneficial for the taxpayer, largely restating existing TCGA 1992, s 4B, but adding the provisions in existing TCGA 1992, s 2(3), which prevent the double or further deduction of any part of an allowable loss and the deduction of any amount already relieved under the Income Tax Acts.

New TCGA 1992, s 1G provides for the treatment of gains accruing to UK-resident individuals in split years. Gains accruing to the individual in the overseas part of the year are to be chargeable to CGT only if they accrue on the disposal of assets in respect of which a non-resident would be chargeable under *new TCGA 1992, s 1A*(*3*). The only losses deductible from such gains where they arise from the disposal of a direct or indirect interest in UK land, are losses derived from the disposal of other such assets, whether or not belonging to a UK branch or agency. However, to the extent that losses accruing to the individual in the overseas part of the year are not already deducted under the preceding rule, they may be deducted without further restriction from gains accruing in the UK part of the year.

New TCGA 1992, ss 1H–1J are the rate-setting provisions, replacing existing TCGA 1992, ss 4 and 4A. There is no change in the law but the new sections are much simpler to understand and apply. Thus, *new TCGA 1992, s 1H*(*2*) provides that residential-property gains (to be defined in *new TCGA 1992, Sch 1B*, inserted by Sch 1, para 15) and carried-interest gains (defined in *new TCGA 1992, s 1H*(*9*)–(*11*)) are to be charged to CGT at a rate of 18% or 28%, whereas other chargeable gains are to be taxed at a rate of 10% or 20%. Where residential-property gains or carried-interest gains accrue to personal representatives, *new TCGA 1992, s 1H*(*5*) provides that they are to be subject to the 28% rate and *new TCGA 1992, s 1H*(*6*) provides that other gains accruing to personal representatives are to be charged at the 20% rate. Similarly, *new TCGA 1992, s 1H*(*7*) and (*8*) charge residential-property gains made by trustees at the 28% rate and other trustees' gains at 20%. Otherwise, which rate is to apply to chargeable gains is to be determined under *new TCGA 1992, s 1I*. *New TCGA 1992, s 1J* contains definitions for the purposes of *new TCGA 1992, s 1I* and restates the rules with respect to the treatment of life-insurance gains under ITTOIA 2005, ss 465 or 539 currently found in existing TCGA 1992, s 4A.

New TCGA 1992, s 1K provides for the annual exempt amount, restating the existing TCGA 1992, s 3, except for the indexation provisions, which are restated in *new TCGA 1992, s 1L*. Subject to the application in future tax years of *new TCGA 1992, s 1L*, the annual exempt amount is set at £12,000 by *new TCGA 1992, s 1K*(*2*). *New TCGA 1992, s 1K*(*8*) introduces *new TCGA 1992, Sch 1C*, which governs the application of the annual exempt amount to trustees and is inserted by Sch 1, para 16.

New TCGA 1992, ss 1M and *1N* deal with the treatment of temporary non-residents, replacing existing TCGA 1992, ss 10A and 10AA. *New TCGA 1992, s 1M* contains the main rule, while *new TCGA 1992, s 1N* prescribes the exclusions from the charge that crystallises on the temporary non-resident's return to the United Kingdom. However, those parts of existing TCGA 1992, s 10A that relate to 'section 13' gains and losses (ie the gains and losses of a non-resident closely held company attributable to its UK-resident participators) are now restated in *new TCGA 1992, s 3E*.

New TCGA 1992, s 1O is an interpretative provision relating to references to persons who are or are not 'UK-resident'.

New TCGA 1992, Pt 1, Ch 2, entitled 'Corporation tax on chargeable gains', provides for corporation tax on chargeable gains and consists of *new TCGA 1992, ss 2–2G*.

New TCGA 1992, s 2 is the main charge to corporation tax on chargeable gains, restating existing TCGA 1992, s 1(2). Thus, corporation tax is to be charged on all chargeable gains accruing to a company on the disposal of assets, as a result of CTA 2009, s 2(1) and (2). The provisions in existing TCGA 1992, s 1(2A) charging a company's ATED-related and NRCGT gains to CGT, are omitted.

New TCGA 1992, s 2A provides that the amount of chargeable gains to be included in a company's total profits for an accounting period is the total amount of chargeable gains accruing to it in that period, after deducting any allowable losses accruing to it in that period and any unused allowable losses brought forward from previous periods within which it was within the charge to corporation tax, restating existing TCGA 1992, s 8(1), omitting any reference to brought-forward NRCGT losses. *New TCGA 1992, s 2A(2)* restates existing TCGA 1992, s 8(2) using slightly different wording, providing accordingly that a loss is not allowable if the company would not have been chargeable to corporation tax on the corresponding gain.

New TCGA 1992, s 2B sets the territorial scope of the charge to corporation tax on chargeable gains. A company that is resident in the United Kingdom in an accounting period is to be chargeable to corporation tax on chargeable gains in respect of the disposal of assets wherever situated (*new TCGA 1992, s 2B(1)*), subject to the elective exemption under CTA 2009, Pt 2, Ch 3A for the profits of foreign permanent establishments (*new TCGA 1992, s 2B(2)*).

As regards companies that are not resident in the United Kingdom, they are to be chargeable to corporation tax on chargeable gains in respect of two classes of gains only.

The first class consists of chargeable gains accruing to the company on the disposal of assets having a 'relevant connection' to a UK permanent establishment of that company, accruing at a time when it has that permanent establishment and are attributable to that establishment under CTA 2009, ss 20–32 (*new TCGA 1992, s 2B(3)*). *New TCGA 1992, s 2C* contains relevant definitions.

The second class incorporates the new rule bringing into charge gains from the disposal of assets not already falling within the first class, but which are interests in UK land or assets (eg shares in a company), wherever situated, deriving at least 75% of their value from UK land, provided that the company has a 'substantial indirect interest' in that land (*new TCGA 1992, s 2B(4)*). What is an interest in UK land is defined by cross-reference to *new TCGA 1992, s 1C*. *New TCGA 1992, Sch 1A* (inserted by Sch 1, para 13) contains definitions of assets deriving at least 75% of their value from UK land and what constitutes a substantial indirect interest in such land.

New TCGA 1992, s 2C (which substantially restates existing TCGA 1992, s 10B) defines what is meant by a company's having a UK permanent establishment (UK PE) and when an asset has a 'relevant connection' with such a permanent establishment. As under existing TCGA 1992, s 10B(3), non-resident companies are excluded from the charge to corporation tax on chargeable gains under *new TCGA 1992, s 2B(3)* (assets of a UK PE, ie the first class referred to above) if they are exempt from corporation tax in the accounting period concerned under the terms of a double tax treaty. This exemption does not, however cover the new charge under *new TCGA 1992, s 2B(4)* (on interests in UK land, ie the second class referred to above).

New TCGA 1992, s 2D explains how CGT principles are to be applied in calculating the gains and losses of a company subject to corporation tax on chargeable gains. It essentially restates existing TCGA 1992, s 8(3).

New TCGA 1992, s 2E prescribes how references in the enactments relating to CGT to income tax or the Income Tax Acts are to be construed in the case of companies. It is essentially a restatement of existing TCGA 1992, s 8(4).

New TCGA 1992, s 2F, which deals with the interaction of CGT and corporation tax, is essentially a restatement of existing TCGA 1992, s 8(5).

New TCGA 1992, s 2G prescribes how the corporation tax provisions of *new TCGA 1992, Pt 1, Ch 2* are to apply where the assets of a company are vested in a liquidator and is a restatement of existing TCGA 1992, s 8(6).

New TCGA 1992, Pt 1, Ch 3, consisting of *new TCGA 1992, ss 3–3G*, deal with the attribution of the gains of non-UK resident closely held companies. The Chapter thus replaces existing TCGA 1992, ss 13, 13A, 14 and 14A.

New TCGA 1992, s 3 contains the main charging provision and is a restatement and rearrangement of the majority of existing TCGA 1992, s 13, omitting any reference to ATED-related or NRCGT gains. It is now clearly provided that *new TCGA 1992, s 3* applies only where:

- a chargeable gain accrues at any time to a 'non-UK-resident close company';
- the gain is 'connected to avoidance' (as defined in *new TCGA 1992, s 3A*) but not 'connected to a foreign trade' or 'other economically significant foreign activities' (also as defined in *new TCGA 1992, s 3A*); and
- some or all of the gain would not otherwise be chargeable to corporation tax on the company.

This is essentially a restatement of existing TCGA 1992, s 13(1) and (5). The phrase 'non-UK-resident close company' is now used to refer to a company that would be a close company if it were UK-resident (*new TCGA 1992, s 3*(*11*)).

New TCGA 1992, s 3A essentially pulls together the provisions currently found in existing TCGA 1992, s 13(5) and 13A. It defines what is meant by a gain's being 'connected to avoidance', 'connected to a foreign trade' and 'connected to other economically significant foreign activities'.

New TCGA 1992, s 3B defines what is meant by a 'participator' and a participator's interest. It essentially restates existing TCGA 1992, s 13(10B) and 13(12)–(14)).

New TCGA 1992, s 3C sets out how double taxation is to be avoided if attribution of the gain is triggered by *new TCGA 1992, s 3* and tax is paid by a person as a result. It essentially restates existing TCGA 1992, s 13(5A), (5B), (7), (7A) and (11).

New TCGA 1992, s 3D provides for the treatment of a gain apportioned to an individual who is not domiciled in the United Kingdom and to whom the remittance basis applies. It restates existing TCGA 1992, s 14A.

New TCGA 1992, s 3E provides for how a gain or loss apportionable to a temporarily non-resident individual is to be dealt with if it accrues to the company in a tax year falling wholly or partly in the period of non-residence. It restates those parts of existing TCGA 1992, s 10A that relate to 'section 13' gains and losses.

New TCGA 1992, s 3F provides for how certain provisions of TCGA 1992 are to be modified for the purposes of new TCGA 1992, s 3 in their application to non-resident companies that are members of a non-resident group of companies. It is essentially a restatement of existing TCGA 1992, s 14.

Finally, *new TCGA 1992, s 3G* 'laps up' two remaining provisions in relation to existing TCGA 1992, s 13. New TCGA 1992, s 3G(1) and (2) is a restatement of existing TCGA 1992, s 13(11) to the effect that tax payable by a person under *new TCGA 1992, s 3* but paid by the company (C) to which the gain accrues or by a company by reference to which that person is an indirect participator in C is not to be regarded as paid by the person. *New TCGA 1992, s 3G*(*3*) is a restatement of existing TCGA 1992, s 13(11A), providing that the amount of a gain or loss under *new TCGA 1992, s 3* is to be computed as if the company in question were UK-resident and chargeable to corporation tax in respect of the gain.

Since that concludes the *new TCGA 1992, Pt 1*, it follows that existing TCGA 1992, ss 2B (persons chargeable to CGT on ATED-related gains), 2C (relevant high-value disposal), 2D (the threshold amount), 2E (restriction of losses), 2F (tapering relief for gains), 14B (meaning of 'non-resident CGT disposal'), 14D (persons chargeable to CGT on NRCGT gains), 14E (further provision about use of NRCGT losses), 14F (persons not chargeable under section 14D if a claim is made), 14G (section 14F: divided companies) and 14H (section 14F: arrangements for avoiding tax) are omitted without restatement. This is consonant with the repeal of the special ATED-related and NRCGT-gain regimes, which are now subsumed in the general charge on disposals of interests in UK land.

However, existing TCGA 1992, ss 3A and 11A, which are also consequently omitted are restated elsewhere. Existing TCGA 1992, ss 3A (reporting limits) is restated (by

Sch 1, para 22) as *new TMA 1970, s 8C* and existing TCGA 1992, s 11A (visiting forces and official agents) is restated (by Sch 1, para 9) as *new TCGA 1992, ss 271ZA* and *271ZB*.

Schedule 1, para 3 repeals existing TCGA 1992, ss 16ZB, 16ZC and 16ZD, which deal with the treatment of non-domiciled individuals who have made an election under existing TCGA 1992, s 16ZA, which remains in place, for their foreign losses to be allowable losses. The provisions contained in the repealed sections are restated in *new TCGA 1992, Sch 1*, inserted by Sch 1, para 13.

Schedule 1, para 4 inserts *new TCGA 1992, s 36A*, which in turn introduces *new TCGA 1992, Sch 4AA*. Together, the new section and the new Schedule provide for the automatic rebasing (subject to an election for rebasing not to apply) of interests in UK land to their 5 April 2019 value where a direct or indirect disposal of the interest is made after that date.

Schedule 1, para 5 omits existing TCGA 1992, Pt II, Ch 5 (consisting of TCGA 1992, s 57A and Sch 4ZZA), which provides for the computation of gains and losses on relevant high-value disposals; Sch 1, para 6 omits existing TCGA 1992, Pt II, Ch 6 (consisting of TCGA 1992, s 57B and Sch 4ZZB), which provides for the computation of gains and losses on NRCGT disposals; and Sch 1, para 7 omits TCGA 1992, Pt II, Ch 7 (consisting of TCGA 1992, s 57C and Sch 4ZZC), which provides for the computation of gains and losses on disposals of residential-property interests). This is consonant with the repeal of the special ATED-related and NRCGT-gain regimes, which are now subsumed in the general charge on disposals of interests in UK land.

Schedule 1, para 8 inserts *new TCGA 1992, s 103DB*, which in turn introduces *new TCGA 1992, Sch 5AAA*. Together, the new section and the new Schedule provide for an exemption from the charge to tax on direct or indirect disposals of an interest in UK for collective investment vehicles.

Schedule 1, para 9 'rescues' the omitted existing TCGA 1992, s 11A and restates it as *new TCGA 1992, ss 271ZA* and *271ZB*. These sections exempt visiting forces and staff of designated allied headquarters from CGT to the extent that they are not considered resident for the period of their stay in the United Kingdom (*new TCGA 1992, s 271ZA*) and provide immunity from CGT to official agents of Commonwealth countries or of the Republic of Ireland (*new TCGA 1992, s 271ZB*).

Schedule 1, paras 10–12 omit existing TCGA 1992, Schs B1 (disposals of UK residential-property interests), BA1 (disposals of non-UK residential-property interests) and C1 (meaning of closely held company and widely marketed scheme for the purposes of section 14F). Some of their provisions are restated where they are relevant to the definitions of interests in UK land etc. Otherwise, their omission is consonant with the repeal of the special ATED-related and NRCGT-gain regimes, which are now subsumed in the general charge on disposals of interests in UK land.

Schedule 1, para 13 substitutes a *new TCGA 1992, Sch 1*, which brings together the detailed treatment of non-domiciled individuals on the remittance basis. *New TCGA 1992, Sch 1* consists of five paragraphs.

In a tax year in which a UK-resident but not UK-domiciled individual to whom the remittance basis applies has gains accruing to him on the disposal of foreign assets, they are treated as accruing to him for CGT purposes only to the extent, if any, to which they are remitted to the United Kingdom, in the full amount, unless they have been taken out of the charge to CGT under the split-year rule now in *new TCGA 1992, s 1G*. This provision (*new TCGA 1992, Sch 1, para 1*) is a restatement of existing TCGA 1992, s 12(1), (2), (3) and (4).

New TCGA 1992, Sch 1, para 2 is effectively a restatement of existing TCGA 1992, s 16ZB, but in a much less opaque way. It provides that where an individual under the remittance basis has made an election under TCGA 1992, s 16ZA for foreign losses to be allowable losses remits gains to the United Kingdom in a particular tax year and is hence treated as if they had accrued to him in that year, whereas they in fact accrued to him in an earlier tax year, the individual may not deduct losses of that year or any earlier year from those gains. This is not to prevent the offset of matched allowable losses against those gains. *New TCGA 1992, Sch 1, paras 3* and *4* restate the matching rules currently found in existing TCGA 1992, s 16ZC and 16ZD. *New TCGA 1992, Sch 1, para 5* contains definitions.

Schedule 1, para 14 inserts *new TCGA 1992, Sch 1A*, which contains definitions of assets deriving at least 75% of their value from UK land and what constitutes a substantial indirect interest in such land and consists of 11 paragraphs divided into four Parts. Part 1 ('Introduction') comprises paras 1 and 2; Part 2 ('Whether asset derives at least 75% of its value from UK land') comprises paras 3–7; Part 3 ('Whether person has substantial indirect interest in UK land') comprises paras 8–10 and Part 4 ('Anti-Avoidance') consists solely of para 11.

New TCGA 1992, Sch 1A, Pt 1 is introductory. *New TCGA 1992, Sch 1A, para 1* provides that the purpose of the Schedule is to determine whether an asset derives at least 75% of its value from UK land ('the property-richness test') and whether the person making the disposal of an asset has a substantial indirect interest in that land (the substantial indirect-interest test'). Both tests must be satisfied for the charge to tax to apply. *New TCGA 1992, Sch 1A, para 2* provides that the Schedule needs to be read together with *new TCGA 1992, Sch 5AAA, paras 5* (units in a CoACS are to be treated as shares for the purposes of the Schedule) and *6* (certain disposals of interests in collective investment vehicles to be treated as meeting the conditions of Part 3 of the Schedule).

New TCGA 1992, Sch 1A, para 3 provides that an asset derives at least 75% of its value from UK land if:

(a) the asset consists of a right or an interest in a company, and
(b) at the time of the disposal at least 75% of the total market value of the company's 'qualifying assets' derives directly or indirectly from interests in UK land.

Market value can be traced through any number of companies, partnerships, trusts and other entities or arrangements but not through a normal commercial loan (as defined in CTA 2010, s 158(1)(b) or 159(4)(b)). It is irrelevant under what law the entity is established and assets held by an entity must be attributed to the shareholders, partners, beneficiaries or other participants as the case may be. Exceptions are provided by *new TCGA 1992, Sch 1A, paras 5* and *6*.

New TCGA 1992, Sch 1A, para 4 defines 'qualifying assets' by exclusion. All a company's assets are qualifying assets unless excluded by that paragraph. Essentially, an asset is not a qualifying asset to the extent that it is matched to a 'related party liability', unless it is itself an interest in UK land, which is always a qualifying asset.

New TCGA 1992, Sch 1A, para 5 provides an important exception from the charge to tax on indirect disposals by non-residents of interests in UK land. The exception applies in respect of land held for trading purposes by the company an interest in which is the subject of the disposal. The exception consists of this – a disposal of a right or interest in a company is not to be regarded as a disposal of an asset deriving at least 75% of its value from UK land where 'it is reasonable to conclude that all (or all but 'low-value non-trading interests') of the interests in UK land are held for trading purposes, so far as the market value of the company's qualifying assets derives directly or indirectly from interests in UK land. An interest in UK land is held for trading purposes if and only if at the time of the disposal, it is being used in, or for the purposes of, a 'qualifying trade' or has been acquired in, or for the purposes of, such a trade. A 'qualifying trade' is a trade that:

(a) has been carried on on a commercial basis with a view to the realisation of profits by the company or a connected person for at least one year leading up to the disposal; and
(b) in respect of which it is reasonable to conclude that it will continue to be so carried on for more than an insignificant period of time.

A 'low-value non-trading interest' is an interest not used for trading purposes and whose total market value is no more than 10% of the total market value of the trading interests (i e non-trading interests in UK land must comprise no more than one-eleventh of all interests in UK land).

New TCGA 1992, Sch 1A, para 6 provides another exception, in this case for linked disposals. Where two or more linked disposals of rights or interests in different companies take place, some but not all of which would otherwise be disposals of assets deriving at least 75% of their value from UK land ('chargeable disposals'), none of them is to be treated as such a disposal, subject to the important proviso that if one company were to include all the assets of the other, a disposal of a right or interest in that company would not be a chargeable disposal. A definition is provided of when a disposal of a right or interest in one company is to be regarded for these purposes as linked with a disposal of a right or interest in another company.

New TCGA 1992, Sch 1A, para 7 defines 'interest in UK land' by cross-reference to *new TCGA 1992, s 1C.*

New TCGA 1992, Sch 1A, para 8 contains the basic rule for determining whether a person has a substantial indirect interest in UK land. The charge to tax does not apply to indirect disposals of interests in UK land, it will be remembered, unless the person making the disposal has such an interest. The rule is that a person who disposes of an asset consisting of a right or interest in a company and deriving at least 75% of its value from UK land has a substantial indirect interest in UK land if the person has, or at any time in the two years leading up to the disposal had, a '25% investment' in the company ('25% investment' is defined in *new TCGA 1992, Sch 1A, para 9*). However, if the person held that 25% investment for an insignificant proportion of the entire time within that two-year period in which he held any right or interest in the company, that ephemeral holding period does not count.

New TCGA 1992, Sch 1A, para 9 defines a '25% investment' in a company as one that:

(a) consists of possession of, or entitlement to acquire, 25% or more of the voting power;
(b) would entitle the person to receive 25% or more of the proceeds if there were a disposal of the entire equity in the company;
(c) would entitle the person to receive 25% or more of a distribution among equity holders of the income in respect of the equity in the company; or
(d) would entitle the person to receive 25% or more of the company's assets available for distribution among equity holders in any other circumstances (including a winding-up).

Equity for these purposes excludes restricted preference shares and normal commercial loans. Provision is made for companies without a share capital. *New TCGA 1992, Sch 1A, para 10* provides how rights and interests are to be attributed to a person for these purposes.

New TCGA 1992, Sch 1A, para 11 is an anti-avoidance provision. It applies to a tax advantage arising as a result wholly or partly from the application or non-application of any provision in *new TCGA 1992, Sch 1A* or from the abusive use ('contrary to [its] object and purpose') of a double tax treaty ('treaty shopping') to override such a provision, where the obtaining of that advantage was the main purpose or one of the main purposes of arrangements into which a person enters. In these circumstances, the advantage is to be counteracted, overriding, in the case of treaty shopping, the rule in TIOPA 2010, s 6(1) (that provisions in a double tax treaty override domestic law). In the case of treaty shopping, the provision applies to arrangements entry into which takes place after 21 November 2017 and in any other case, to arrangements entry into which takes place after 6 July 2018.

Schedule 1, para 15 inserts *new TCGA 1992, Sch 1B*, which contains detailed provisions relating to gains from the disposal of residential property. Such gains when they are made by an individual, it will be remembered, are subject to the higher 18% or 28% rates of CGT under *new TCGA 1992, s 1H*. The Schedule incorporates much of the material from existing TCGA 1992, Schs B1 and BA1, which are now omitted.

New TCGA 1992, Sch 1B comprises ten paragraphs.

New TCGA 1992, Sch 1B, para 1 defines a 'residential-property gain', somewhat circuitously, as so much of a chargeable gain accruing to a person on a disposal of residential property as is attributable to that property. *New TCGA 1992, Sch 1B, para 2* provides how much of a chargeable gain is to be so attributable; namely, the fraction A/B where A is the number of days in the 'applicable period' on which the land to which the disposal relates consisted or included a dwelling and B is the total number of days in the applicable period. This fraction needs to be adjusted on a just and reasonable basis when there has been mixed use of the land at any time during the applicable period. The 'applicable period' begins with the day of acquisition of the interest (or any later date on which it became chargeable) and ends with the *day before* the day of the disposal. An interest becomes chargeable from 31 March 1982 or, if the person who makes the disposal does so in a tax year in which he is non-resident or in the overseas part of a split year, from 6 April 2015. Thus, periods of ownership before 31 March 1982 will always be ignored, as will any period before 6 April 2015 if the disposal is made by a non-resident etc. *New TCGA 1992, Sch 1B, paras 1* and *2* are essentially restatements of existing TCGA 1992, Sch B1, para 1 and Sch 4ZZC, para 4.

New TCGA 1992, Sch 1B, para 3 defines what is meant by a disposal of residential property and is essentially a restatement of existing TCGA 1992, Sch B1 para 1(2) and (3). *New TCGA 1992, Sch 1B, para 4* defines an interest in land for these purposes and is essentially a restatement of existing TCGA 1992, Sch B1, paras 2 and 3.

New TCGA 1992, Sch 1B, para 5 provides the basic meaning of 'dwelling' and is a restatement of existing TCGA 1992, Sch 1B, para 4(1)–(9). *New TCGA 1992, Sch 1B, para 6* provides for circumstances in which a building that is temporarily unsuitable for use as a dwelling may, and may not, be regarded as continuing to be suitable for use as a dwelling and is a restatement of existing TCGA 1992, Sch B1 paras 4(10) and 6. *New TCGA 1992, Sch 1B, para 7* provides for circumstances in which a building that had ceased to exist or had become unsuitable for use as a result of certain works is to be regarded as having been unsuitable for use as a dwelling throughout the period of the works, and is a restatement of existing TCGA 1992, Sch B1 para 8.

New TCGA 1992, Sch 1B, para 8 provides other definitions and is a restatement of existing TCGA 1992, Sch B1 paras 7 and 10. *New TCGA 1992, Sch 1B, para 9* confers powers on the Treasury to modify the meaning of 'use as a dwelling' by regulations and is the same power heretofore conferred by existing TCGA 1992, Sch B1 para 5. *New TCGA 1992, Sch 1B, para 10* allows for further regulatory powers.

Schedule 1, para 16 inserts *new TCGA 1992, Sch 1C*, which regulates the application of the annual exempt amount in cases involving settled property and is introduced by *new TCGA 1992, s 1K(8)*. It comprises eight paragraphs and is essentially a restatement of existing TCGA 1992, Sch 1 (effectively omitted by Sch 1, para 13).

New TCGA 1992, Sch 1C, para 1 is introductory. *New TCGA 1992, Sch 1C, paras 2–4* deal with the application of the annual exempt amount to trustees of a settlement for the benefit of a disabled person and are essentially a restatement of existing TCGA 1992, Sch 1, para 1(1)–(2A). *New TCGA 1992, Sch 1C, para 5* covers other settlements and is essentially a restatement of existing TCGA 1992, Sch 1, para 2(1)–(2A). *New TCGA 1992, Sch 1C, paras 6* and *7* bring together the special rules for groups of settlements, heretofore located in existing TCGA 1992, Sch 1, paras 1(3)–(5) and 2(4)–(6). *New TCGA 1992, Sch 1C, para 8* contains the rules for sub-fund settlements resulting from an election under TCGA 1992, Sch 4ZA. This is a restatement of existing TCGA 1992, Sch 1, para 3.

Schedule 1, para 17 inserts *new TCGA 1992, Sch 4AA*, which provides for rebasing of non-residents' interests in UK land held at 5 April 2019. Rebasing is automatic, but there is provision for an election for rebasing not to apply. *New TCGA 1992, Sch 4AA* consists of 22 paragraphs, divided into five Parts. Part 1 ('Introduction') comprises para 1. Part 2 ('Indirect disposals and direct disposals not chargeable before 6 April 2019') comprises paras 2–5. Part 3 ('Direct disposals of pre-April 2015 assets fully chargeable before 6 April 2019') comprises paras 6–11. Part 4 ('Direct disposals of assets partly chargeable before 6 April 2019') comprises paras 12–15. Part 5 ('Miscellaneous') comprises paras 16–22.

New TCGA 1992, Sch 4AA, para 1 is introductory and explains that *new TCGA 1992, Sch 4AA* is to apply on the first occasion on which a person disposes of an asset that he held on 5 April 2019 such that the disposal is either a direct or indirect disposal of UK land made by a non-resident or by a UK resident in the overseas part of a split tax year. An indirect disposal of UK land is a disposal that meets both the property-richness test and the substantial indirect-interest test.

As provided by *new TCGA 1992, Sch 4AA para 2*, *new TCGA 1992, Sch 4AA, Pt 2* applies to all indirect disposals of UK land (which, by their nature, are not chargeable to tax before 6 April 2019), direct disposals of UK land that was not fully residential before 6 April 2019 and direct disposals of land by persons who were not chargeable before 6 April 2019. The legislation talks of *disposals* that are or are not 'fully residential', which seems somewhat curious. Be that as it may, a direct disposal of UK land that was not fully residential before 6 April 2019 is one made by a person during whose period of ownership (going back only as far as 6 April 2015) there was no day on which the land in question consisted of or included a dwelling. In the case of an off-plan purchase, a disposal of an interest in land is regarded as one of land that is fully residential before 6 April 2019 if at any time before 6 April 2019 the land consisted of or included a building to be constructed or adapted for use as a dwelling. A disposal is made by a person who was not chargeable before 6 April 2019 if, immediately before that date, that person was:

(a) a company that was not closely held;
(b) a 'widely marketed scheme'; or
(c) a company carrying on life-assurance business, where the interest in UK land was being held in the course of that business for the purposes of providing benefits to its policyholders.

Somewhat curiously, *new TCGA 1992, Sch 4AA, para 2*(*5*) and (*6*) refer the definitions of 'closely held company' and 'widely marketed scheme' back to existing TCGA 1992, ss 14F and 14G and Sch C1, although both of these provisions are omitted and repealed by Sch 1. One wonders why the relevant provisions were not simply reproduced in *new TCGA 1992, Sch 4AA*.

New TCGA 1992, Sch 4AA, para 3 provides that a gain or loss accruing to a disposal within *new TCGA 1992, Sch 4AA, para 2* is to be calculated on the assumption that the asset was sold on 5 April 2019 and immediately reacquired for its market value on that date. However, under *new TCGA 1992, Sch 4AA, para 4*, the person making a disposal within *new TCGA 1992, Sch 4AA, para 2* may elect for rebasing not to apply. A loss on an indirect disposal following such an election is not to be an allowable loss, however. When it is necessary to calculate how much of the gain is a residential-property gain where an election to disapply rebasing has been made, *new TCGA 1992, Sch 4AA, para 5* provides that the 'applicable period' (for which see *new TCGA 1992, Sch 1B, para 2*) runs from the date of acquisition (but no earlier than 31 March 1982) until the day before the day of disposal.

New TCGA 1992, Sch 4AA, Pt 3 applies to direct disposals of 'pre-April 2015 assets' fully chargeable before 6 April 2019. As provided by *new TCGA 1992, Sch 4AA, para 6*, an asset is a 'pre-April 2015' asset if it was in the ownership of the person making the disposal immediately before 6 April 2015. A disposal is fully residential (sic) before 6 April 2019 if the person making the disposal of the interest in UK land has owned it throughout the period beginning on 6 April 2015 and ending with the disposal and on every day in the period from 6 April 2015 to 5 April 2019, the land to which the disposal relates *consisted of* a dwelling – it is not sufficient for the land to have *included* a dwelling. In the case of an off-plan purchase, a disposal of an interest in land is regarded as one that is not fully residential before 6 April 2019 if at any time before 6 April 2019 the land did not consist of a building to be constructed or adapted for use as a dwelling – again it is insufficient for the land not to have *included* a dwelling. The rules of Part 3 do not apply to disposals by persons who were not chargeable before 6 April 2019.

When calculating a gain or loss within *new TCGA 1992, Sch 4AA, para 6*, the default position (as provided by *new TCGA 1992, Sch 4AA, para 7*) is rebasing, but this time to the 5 April 2015 value, i e the assumption that the asset was sold on 5 April 2015 and immediately reacquired for its market value on that date. Again, the person making a disposal within *new TCGA 1992, Sch 4AA, para 6* may elect for rebasing not to apply. Unlike the position with a Part 2 disposal, however, that person may choose between one of two methods of calculation – referred to as 'the retrospective basis of calculation' and 'straight-line time apportionment' respectively.

Where a person elects under *new TCGA 1992, Sch 4AA, para 8* for the retrospective basis of calculation, *new TCGA 1992, Sch 4AA, para 10* provides that, where it is necessary to calculate how much of the gain is a residential-property gain, the calculation is carried out by reference to an 'applicable period' (for which see *new*

TCGA 1992, Sch 1B, para 2) that runs from the date of acquisition (but no earlier than 31 March 1982) until the day before the day of disposal. Where, on the other hand, the person elects under *new TCGA 1992, Sch 4AA, para 9* for straight-line apportionment, only that proportion of the gain or loss accruing on the disposal that the number of days in the period of ownership falling after 5 April 2015 and including the day of disposal bear to the number of days of the entire period of ownership is taken to be the chargeable gain or allowable loss. Where it is necessary to calculate of how much of the gain is a residential-property gain, *new TCGA 1992, Sch 4AA, para 11* provides that the calculation is carried out by reference to an 'applicable period' (for which see *new TCGA 1992, Sch 1B, para 2*) that runs from 6 April 2015 until the day before the day of disposal.

New TCGA 1992, Sch 4AA, Pt 4 applies to direct disposals of assets that were partly chargeable before 6 April 2019, i e broadly, direct disposals involving land that has at some time been residential and at other times not. More particularly, *new TCGA 1992, Sch 4AA, para 12* provides that this Part applies to any direct disposal of UK land to which neither *new TCGA 1992, Sch 4AA, Part 2* nor *new TCGA 1992, Sch 4AA, Pt 3* applies but not to any disposal of an interest in UK land that was acquired after 5 April 2015 where the land consisted of a dwelling on every day during the period from acquisition to 5 April 2019. In the case of an off-plan purchase, a disposal of an interest in land is regarded as one that is not fully residential before 6 April 2019 if at any time from its acquisition to 5 April 2019 there was a day on which the land did not consist of a building to be constructed or adapted for use as a dwelling – again it is insufficient for the land not to have *included* a dwelling.

New TCGA 1992, Sch 4AA, para 13 provides for double rebasing of the asset. Thus, in calculating the gain or loss on the disposal, it is assumed that the asset was sold on 5 April 2015 (unless it was acquired after that date) and immediately reacquired for its market value on that date. There is then a further assumption that the asset was also sold on *5 April 2019* and immediately reacquired for its market value on that date. The gain or loss on this second deemed disposal is added to the gain or loss on the actual disposal.

There is an option under *new TCGA 1992, Sch 4AA, para 14* to opt that this double rebasing not apply. In that case, the retrospective basis (see under *new TCGA 1992, Sch 4AA, para 8*) applies instead. Where in that event it is necessary to calculate how much of the gain is a residential-property gain, *new TCGA 1992, Sch 4AA, para 15* provides that the calculation is carried out by reference to an 'applicable period' (for which see *new TCGA 1992, Sch 1B, para 2*) that runs from the later of the date of acquisition and 31 March 1982 until the day before the day of disposal.

New TCGA 1992, Sch 4AA, paras 16–18 deal with the situation where, after 5 April 2019, a non-resident company becomes resident or resident trustees or a resident company become non-resident. *New TCGA 1992, Sch 4AA, para 16* provides that where a company that has become UK-resident after 5 April 2019 makes a direct or indirect disposal of UK land that would otherwise have been chargeable under *new TCGA 1992, Sch 4AA*, it will still be so chargeable despite the fact that the company is now UK-resident. Under *new TCGA 1992, Sch 4AA, para 17*, where trustees who ceased to be UK-resident after 5 April 2019 make a direct or indirect disposal of UK land, they are to be exempt from any charge either under *new TCGA 1992, Sch 4AA* or under TCGA 1992, s 80(2) (the exit charge on trustees ceasing to be UK-resident). The same holds good under *new TCGA 1992, Sch 4AA, para 18* for companies that cease to be UK-resident after 5 April 2019 and make a direct or indirect disposal of UK land. They too are to be exempt from any charge either under *new TCGA 1992, Sch 4AA* or under TCGA 1992, s 185(2) or (3) (the exit charge on companies ceasing to be UK-resident).

New TCGA 1992, Sch 4AA, para 19 provides that where a gain or loss is calculated using rebasing under any of *new TCGA 1992, Sch 4AA, paras 3*, *7* or *13* and it is necessary to determine whether an asset is a wasting asset, the assumption that the asset was (re)acquired on the appropriate date is to be ignored for that purpose. *New TCGA 1992, Sch 4AA, para 20* provides that the rebasing value is to be used as the value of an asset for the purposes of capital allowances or renewals allowances and their effect on the restriction under TCGA 1992, s 41 of losses by reference to capital allowances and under TCGA 1992, s 47 on wasting-asset calculations.

Elections to disapply rebasing are to be made in an ordinary tax return or a reporting return for disposals of UK land under Sch 2. Such an election is to be irrevocable unless made in a Schedule 2 return and then revoked in an in-time ordinary tax return (*new TCGA 1992, Sch 4AA, para 21*). *New TCGA 1992, Sch 4AA, para 22* provides for interpretation.

Schedule 1, paras 18–20 omit TCGA 1992, Schs 4ZZA (gains and losses on relevant high-value disposals), 4ZZB (gains and losses on NRCGT disposals) and 4ZZC (gains and losses on disposals of residential-property disposals), consonant with the abolition of the ATED-related gains and NRCGT gains regimes.

Schedule 1, para 21 inserts *new TCGA 1992, Sch 5AAA*, which applies the new rules on indirect disposals of interests in UK land to collective investment vehicles. It consists of no less than 50 paragraphs, divided into seven Parts. Part 1 ('Introduction: key expressions') consists of paras 1–3; Part 2 ('Basic rules') consists of paras 4–7. Part 3 ('Election for transparency') comprises paras 8–11; Part 4 ('Exemption') comprises paras 12–42; Part 5 ('Reporting and payment') comprises paras 43–45; Part 6 ('General') comprises paras 44–48; and Part 7 ('Transitional provision') comprises paras 49 and 50.

New TCGA 1992, Sch 5AAA, para 1 defines 'collective investment vehicle', 'participant' and 'unit'. A collective investment vehicle (CIV) for these purposes is a collective investment scheme, an authorised investment fund (AIF), a company that is a UK REIT, or any non-resident company meeting the 'property-income condition'. A company meets the property-income condition if it satisfies all of four conditions. These are that:

(a) it is not a close company or is such only because it has a 'qualifying investor' (as defined in *new TCGA 1992, Sch 5AAA, para 46*(*3*)) as a direct or indirect participator;
(b) at least 50% of its income is income deriving from direct or indirect investments made on a long-term basis in land or in estates, interests or rights in or over land ('property income from long-term investments');
(c) it distributes all or substantially all of its property income from long-term investments on an annual basis; and
(d) it is not liable to tax on that income under the law of any jurisdiction in which it is resident.

A 'participant' is either a shareholder in the company (where the CIV is a company) or a person who becomes an owner of all or any part of the property held under the collective investment scheme or AIF. *New TCGA 1992, Sch 5AAA, para 2* defines an 'offshore CIV' as a CIV that is either:

(a) a CIV constituted as a body corporate resident outside the United Kingdom;
(b) a CIV under which property is held on trust for the participants by trustees who are not resident in the United Kingdom; or
(c) a CIV constituted under other arrangements under foreign law creating co-ownership rights.

NB: a limited-liability partnership is not regarded as a body corporate for these purposes. *New TCGA 1992, Sch 5AAA* defines a CIV as being 'UK property-rich' where, broadly, a disposal of a right or interest in it would be regarded as a disposal of an asset deriving at least 75% of its value from UK land.

The effect of *new TCGA 1992, Sch 5AAA, para 4* is that gains accruing to an offshore CIV are to be chargeable to corporation tax under the new rules (and are to be regarded as companies where they are not already companies, unless constituted by persons carrying on a trade or business in partnership) and investors are to be treated as shareholders. These rules have precedence over the rule under TCGA 1992, s 103D in respect of a CIV that is a tax-transparent fund but the rules for calculating gains on the disposal of units in such a fund are retained; nor is TCGA 1992, s 99 (unit-trust schemes) to apply. However, taxation at the level of the CIV is not to apply where an election for transparency is made under *new TCGA 1992, Sch 5AAA, para 9*. For the purposes of considering whether a non-UK resident has an interest in a UK propery-rich company, a unit in a CoACS is to be treated under *new TCGA 1992, Sch 5AAA, para 5* as if it were a share in a company.

New TCGA 1992, Sch 5AAA, para 6 provides that where a person disposes of an asset deriving at least 75% of its value from UK land in a disposal having an 'appropriate connection to a CIV', that person is to be treated as having a substantial indirect interest in that land, regardless of the extent of his interest (ie the 25% minimum threshold is overridden). Where any one of four tests is met, there is that appropriate connection. Test 1 is where the asset that is the subject of the disposal consists of a right or interest in a CIV or a company at least 50% of whose market value derives from its being a direct or indirect participant in one or more CIVs. Test 2 is met where the CIV is constituted by two or more persons carrying on a trade or business in partnership and the disposal is made by a person as a participant in that CIV. Test 3 is met where the CIV is a company and the disposal is made by it. Test 4 is met where a company (other than the CIV) makes the disposal and the CIV and one or more other CIVs that are UK property-rich have a '50% investment' (as defined) in the company.

New TCGA 1992, Sch 5AAA, para 7 allows for exceptions from the 25% override in *new TCGA 1992, Sch 5AAA, para 6* where the CIV to which the connection exists meets both of two conditions at the time of the disposal in question. The first condition is the so-called 'non-UK real-estate condition' and the second condition is the 'genuine diversity of ownership condition' or (if the CIV is a company) the 'non-close condition'. The 'non-UK real-estate condition' is met at any time if no more than 40% of the expected market value of the CIV's investments, by reference to its prospectus, is intended to derive from interests in UK land or rights or interests in UK property-rich companies. The 'genuine diversity of ownership condition' is met at any time if at that time the CIV meets the relevant conditions in the Offshore Funds (Tax) Regulations 2009 (SI 2009/3001). The 'non-close condition' is met at any time when the CIV is not a close company or is one only because it has a 'qualifying investor' as a direct or indirect participator.

New TCGA 1992, Sch 5AAA, para 8 provides for the manager of a CIV that is UK property-rich to make an election for the CIV to be transparent for the purposes of TCGA 1992. The election is only available, however, if the CIV is already transparent for the purposes of income tax. If the election is made, the CIV is to be treated as if it were and always had been a partnership. In considering whether the CIV is UK property-rich, reference may be had to its prospectus on the assumption that investments are to be made in accordance with that prospectus. *New TCGA 1992, Sch 5AAA, para 9* provides that a transparency election may only be made with the consent of all participants and must be made no later than 12 months after the CIV makes its first acquisition of an interest in UK land or a right or interest in a UK property-rich company. A transparency election is to have no effect on CIV investors who are an insurance company investing for the purposes of its long-term business (*new TCGA 1992, Sch 5AAA, para 10*). Where a transparency election applies, and as a result a participant making a disposal of his interest would be treated as making a direct disposal of a pre-April 2015 asset that was fully chargeable before 6 April 2019 (one to which *new TCGA 1992, Sch 4AA, Pt 3* applies) or a direct disposal of an asset that was partly chargeable before 6 April 2019 (one to which *new TCGA 1992, Sch 4AA, Pt 4* applies), the disposal is nevertheless to be treated as if it were a direct disposal not chargeable before 6 April 2019 (ie one to which *new TCGA 1992, Sch 4AA Pt 2* applies), so that the 5 April 2019 rebasing applies.

New TCGA 1992, Sch 5AAA, Pt 4 provides for certain CIVs to claim exemption from corporation tax on chargeable gains on all direct and indirect disposals of UK land. Under *new TCGA 1992, Sch 5AAA, para 12*, an exemption election may be made on behalf of a CIV if it is an offshore CIV that is UK property-rich and meets all the qualifying conditions set out in *new TCGA 1992, Sch 5AAA, para 13*. If the CIV is an AIF, it must also qualify as a CIV for some other reason. Such a fund is referred to as a 'qualifying fund'. An exemption election may also be made on behalf of a company that is not a CIV, wherever it is resident, if it also meets the qualifying conditions set out in *new TCGA 1992, Sch 5AAA, para 13* and, additionally, is wholly or almost wholly owned by a CIV constituted by persons carrying on a trade or business in partnership or by a CoACS and either the company or the CoACS, as the case may be, is UK property-rich. Such a company is referred to as a 'qualifying company'.

New TCGA 1992, Sch 5AAA, para 13 sets out the qualifying conditions a CIV or a company must meet to be a qualifying fund or a qualifying company. In the case of a qualifying fund, the CIV must be:

(a) a collective investment scheme meeting the genuine diversity of ownership condition; or

(b) a company (and not a deemed company under *new TCGA 1992, Sch 5AAA, para 4*) meeting the 'recognised stock-exchange condition'; or
(c) a CIV of any kind meeting both the 'UK tax condition' and the 'non-close condition'.

The genuine diversity of ownership condition and the non-close condition are as defined in *new TCGA 1992, Sch 5AAA, para 7*. The 'recognised stock-exchange condition' is that the company have ordinary share capital and that the shares forming part of that capital be regularly traded on a recognised stock exchange. The 'UK tax condition' is met if the person making the exemption election reasonably believes that if there were to be a disposal for market value of all the company's shares no more than 25% of the proceeds would be exempt from UK tax purely as a result of the provisions of a double tax treaty. In the case of a qualifying company, the qualifying conditions are that either the company meet the UK tax condition and the non-close condition or that the CIV that wholly or almost wholly owns the company meet the genuine diversity of ownership condition.

New TCGA 1992, Sch 5AAA, para 14 provides that the exemption election must be accompanied by information prescribed by HMRC concerning disposals made by participants in the relevant fund in the two years preceding the day on which the election or since its constitution if it is less than two years old at that time, where not already provided. Further prescribed information must be provided with respect to every period of account for which the election has effect, within 12 months of the end of that period. Regulations made under *new TCGA 1992, Sch 5AAA, para 15* may provide the conditions concerning the provision of documents and information. A designated HMRC officer is also to have the authority to revoke an exemption election if he considers that there is no reasonable excuse for a breach of these conditions but may waive an insignificant breach.

New TCGA 1992, Sch 5AAA, para 16 provides an exemption for certain direct or indirect disposals of UK land by a person in whom a qualifying fund or qualifying company that has made an exemption election has invested to the extent of at least 40%. The proportion of the gain that is exempt is the proportion of the qualifying fund's or qualifying company's investment in that person.

New TCGA 1992, Sch 5AAA, para 17 provides that an exemption election must be made by 'the relevant fund manager' (defined in *new TCGA 1992, Sch 5AAA, para 39*) and will apply to disposals made on or after the day specified in the notice of election. The notice may specify a day preceding the day on which the election is made but that day may be no earlier than 12 months before the election day, unless HMRC gives its consent to an earlier date. Under *new TCGA 1992, Sch 5AAA, para 18*, both the relevant fund manager and HMRC may revoke an exemption election. HMRC may do so if a designated officer considers it necessary for the protection of the public revenue. The relevant fund manager may revoke the election at any time by giving notice, with effect from a day specified in the notice. That day may precede the date of the notice, but only if HMRC consents. An HMRC revocation must state the reasons for the revocation and *new TCGA 1992, Sch 5AAA, para 19* provides for a right of appeal, to be exercised no later than 30 days of the day on which the revocation notice is given. An appeal to the Tribunal will be upheld only if the Tribunal considers that HMRC could not reasonably have been satisfied there were grounds for revocation. *New TCGA 1992, Sch 5AAA, para 20* provides that at such time as a qualifying fund or qualifying company ceases to meet any of the qualifying conditions, the election ceases to have effect from the day of cessation. The 'relevant fund manager' is defined by *new TCGA 1992, Sch 5AAA, para 39* as the manager of the 'relevant fund'. The 'relevant fund' is in turn defined by that paragraph as the CIV concerned in the case of a qualifying fund and as the CIV wholly or almost wholly owning the company in the case of a qualifying company.

New TCGA 1992, Sch 5AAA, para 21 provides that when a participant in a qualifying fund or qualifying company is about to receive a revenue payment representing value derived directly or indirectly from a direct or indirect disposal of UK land and that payment would not be subject to UK income tax or corporation tax, the participant is deemed to have made a disposal of units in the fund or rights or interests in the company immediately before the payment is made and to have reacquired them for their market value immediately after the payment is made. Similarly, when an exemption election ceases to have effect, each participant in the qualifying fund or qualifying company is deemed under *new TCGA 1992, Sch 5AAA, para 22* to have sold and immediately reacquired all the participant's units or rights or interests, as the case may be, immediately before the election ceases to have effect for their market value at that time.

New TCGA 1992, Sch 5AAA, para 23 provides how a gain arising from such a deemed disposal is to be treated. In the case of a deemed disposal when an election ceases to have effect (ie under *new TCGA 1992, Sch 5AAA, para 22*), it applies only for a cessation caused by a failure to meet the qualifying conditions, not on a revocation of the election. Where it is applicable, any gain accruing on the deemed disposal is brought into charge only when an actual disposal is made of the units or the revenue payment is received, and then only in the proportion that the consideration for the actual disposal or the amount of the receipt bears to the amount of the deemed gain. So much of the consideration or receipt as exceeds the deemed gain is ignored. If some of the deemed gain has so accrued on previous occasions, no more than 100% of the deemed gain may be treated as so accruing over all those occasions taken together. In the event of a deemed disposal under *new TCGA 1992, Sch 5AAA, para 21* (revenue payment), the remainder of the deemed gain, if not already treated as having accrued, does so only when the relevant fund is wound up. In the event of a deemed disposal under *new TCGA 1992, Sch 5AAA, para 22* (election ceasing to have effect by virtue of a breach of the qualifying conditions), the remainder of the deemed gain crystallises on the earlier of three years after the deemed disposal and the winding-up of the fund. In calculating the deemed gain, *new TCGA 1992, Sch 5AAA, para 24* provides that the deemed disponer is treated as having incurred incidental costs of disposal that could reasonably have been incurred if the deemed sale had been an actual sale.

Whenever a deemed disposal in these circumstances is treated as taking place or the remainder of the deemed gain crystallises, the relevant fund manager is required, under *new TCGA 1992, Sch 5AAA, para 25* to notify the person concerned in writing within 30 days of the deemed disposal or crystallisation. Failure to comply gives rise under *new TCGA 1992, Sch 5AAA, para 26* to a penalty not exceeding £3,000. HMRC must assess the penalty on the person or persons in default within 12 months of the day on which an officer of HMRC first becomes aware of the default. Any appeal against the penalty must be made within 30 days of the penalty notice. In the absence of an appeal, the penalty must be paid within 30 days of the penalty notice; if an appeal is lodged and the penalty is confirmed, payment is due within 30 days of the determination or withdrawal of the appeal.

New TCGA 1992, Sch 5AAA, paras 27–29 provide for instances when a temporary breach of exemption conditions is not to cause the exemption election to cease to have effect. Other than where the relevant condition that fails to be satisfied is that the CIV or appropriate entity be UK property-rich, *new TCGA 1992, Sch 5AAA, para 27* provides that the breach will not cause the election to case to have effect if the relevant fund manager expects the qualifying fund or qualifying company again to be in compliance within 30 days. This provision may be called in aid no more than four times in any period of 12 months. Under *new TCGA 1992, Sch 5AAA, para 28*, any breach of the exemption conditions will not cause the election to cease to have effect if the relevant fund manager expects the breach to last no longer than a temporary period no longer than nine months. Nevertheless, under this provision, the deemed disposal under *new TCGA 1992, Sch 5AAA, para 22* is still deemed to take place. *New TCGA 1992, Sch 5AAA, para 29* provides that if *new TCGA 1992, Sch 5AAA, para 28* has previously applied to a temporary breach, the remainder of the deemed gain does not crystallise under *new TCGA 1992, Sch 5AAA, para 23(8)* until the relevant fund is wound up.

If the exemption election is about to cease to have effect because of a breach of the exemption conditions but at that time the relevant fund manager is arranging for the relevant fund to be wound up, *new TCGA 1992, Sch 5AAA, para 30* provides that the deemed disposal under *new TCGA 1992, Sch 5AAA, para 22* is still deemed to take place but for all other purposes, the election continues to have effect until the relevant fund is wound up.

New TCGA 1992, Sch 5AAA, para 31 provides for a proportionate rebasing where a qualifying fund or qualifying company or a company covered by the exemption election made by the qualifying fund or qualifying company disposes of all of its rights or interests in another company (C) that is UK property-rich and also covered by the election. References to being covered by the election are to instances where *new TCGA 1992, Sch 5AAA, para 16* applies to the election. In these circumstances, company C is deemed to have sold the 'appropriate proportion' of every 'qualifying asset' for its market value immediately before the disposal and to have reacquired that proportion immediately thereafter. The 'appropriate proportion' for these purposes is what would be the appropriate proportion under *new TCGA 1992, Sch 5AAA, para 16* of a notional gain of £100. A 'qualifying asset' is an asset that has been held by C, the qualifying fund or qualifying company or any other company covered by the election throughout a period of one year up to the date of disposal.

New TCGA 1992, Sch 5AAA, para 32 also provides for proportionate rebasing, but in the circumstances where an exemption election has been in force for a continuous period of at least five years and either the election ceases to have effect (for reasons other than by a notice of revocation) or the relevant fund manager begins to take steps to dispose of the fund assets and wind up the fund (the 'triggering event'). In such a case, the qualifying fund or qualifying company is deemed to have sold and reacquired every asset the actual disposal of which would be a direct or indirect disposal of UK land for its market value immediately before the triggering event. In the case of any asset covered by the election for 12 months (and presumably for longer also) and held by a company, the company is to have sold the 'appropriate proportion' of that asset for its market value immediately before the triggering event and to have reacquired that proportion immediately thereafter. The 'appropriate proportion' for these purposes is again what would be the appropriate proportion under *new TCGA 1992, Sch 5AAA, para 16* of a notional gain of £100.

A simplified form of the substantial-shareholdings exemption under TCGA 1992, Sch 7AC was introduced under F(No 2)A 2017, s 28 for investing companies substantially owned by persons who are 'qualifying institutional investors'. *New TCGA 1992, Sch 5AAA, para 33* provides an exemption for disposals of units in a relevant fund by participants who are not themselves CIVs and are qualifying institutional investors for the purposes of the substantial-shareholdings exemption or who are insurance companies in defined circumstances. Gains on disposals of units in a qualifying fund or qualifying company by such persons are not to be chargeable gains. In addition, the receipt of a payment of value by such a person is not, despite the contrary provision under *new TCGA 1992, Sch 5AAA, para 21*, to give rise to a deemed disposal of an asset by that person. 'Qualifying institutional investors' for the purposes of the substantial-shareholdings exemption are pension schemes (as defined), insurance businesses (as defined), sovereign wealth funds, charities, investment funds, authorised investment funds and exempt unauthorised unit trusts (see TCGA 1992, Sch 7AC, para 30A).

New TCGA 1992, Sch 5AAA, paras 34–37 deal with the interaction of exemptions under these rules and other statutory exemptions.

New TCGA 1992, Sch 5AAA, para 34 concerns the interaction between the significant-shareholdings exemption under TCGA 1992, Sch 7AC and exemptions conferred under these rules. Under TCGA 1992, Sch 7AC, para 3A, the so-called subsidiary exemption applies where a gain or loss accrues to a company on a disposal of shares or of an interest in shares in another company (called here 'the investee company') and:

(1) the investing company meets the substantial-shareholding requirement and is not a 'disqualified listed company'; but
(2) the investee company fails the requirement under TCGA 1992, Sch 7AC, para 19 to itself be a trading company or the holding company of a trading group or trading sub-group immediately before the disposal and for the requisite period preceding the disposal; and
(3) the investing company is not a 'disqualified listed company'.

In these circumstances, where, immediately before the disposal, qualifying institutional investors own at least 25% of the ordinary share capital of the investing company, the corresponding proportion of the gain is exempt; where their ownership is 80% or more, the whole of the gain is exempt.

Where, however, the investing company has:

(a) ordinary share capital owned to any extent by one or more qualifying institutional investors;
(b) some of that ownership is traced through a qualifying fund or qualifying company having 40% or more ownership of the investing company; and
(c) some or all of that gain relates to interests in UK land so that the appropriate proportion of the gain would qualify for exemption both under these rules (by virtue of *new TCGA 1992, Sch 5AAA, para 16*(*3*)) and the substantial-shareholding rule in TCGA 1992, Sch 7AC, para 3A;

the latter is not to apply.

New TCGA 1992, Sch 5AAA, para 35 concerns direct or indirect disposals of UK land made by a company that is, or is a member of, a UK REIT. So much of the gain on such a disposal as would be exempt under the REIT rules by virtue of CTA 2010, s 535 or *new CTA 2010, s 535A* (inserted by Sch 1, para 115) but is not one that is exempt under those sections following a notice given under CTA 2010, ss 586(1) or 587(1) where the company is part of a REIT group under a joint-venture election) is not also to be exempt under these rules. The joint-venture exemption is dealt with by *new TCGA 1992, Sch 5AAA, para 36*. Where such a gain falls to be exempt as just described under the REIT rules, and the principal company of the group UK REIT is covered by an exemption election under these rules (ie under *new TCGA 1992, Sch 5AAA, para 12*) that also covers the joint-venture company, the amount of the gain that is to be exempt under these rules is the difference between two amounts. The first amount (A) is found by ignoring the REIT exemption rules (CTA 2010 Part 12) and applying these rules. The second amount (B) is found by ignoring these rules and applying the REIT exemption rules to determine how much of the gain accruing to the joint-venture company would be exempt under the REIT rules. The amount (if any) by which A exceeds B is the amount that is to be exempt under these rules. Finally, *new TCGA 1992, Sch 5AAA, para 37* deals with the interaction between these rules, the substantial-shareholding rules (TCGA 1992, Sch 7AC) and the REIT rules (CTA 2010, Part 12) in any situation not already covered in any of *new TCGA 1992, Sch 5AAA, paras 34–36*. It provides that each set of rules is to apply separately in relation to each proportion of the gain or loss to which it applies, but so as to ensure that the total proportion of the gain or loss that is to be exempt (or not allowable) is not to exceed 100%.

New TCGA 1992, Sch 5AAA, paras 38–42 contain definitions of terms appearing in *new TCGA 1992, Sch 5AAA, Pt 4*.

New TCGA 1992, Sch 5AAA, para 43 confers on HM Treasury the power to make regulations providing for managers of CIVs to provide information concerning any participants holding units the disposal of which would constitute an indirect disposal of UK land, thereby relieving the participants themselves of the obligation to provide information or documents. Under *new TCGA 1992, Sch 5AAA, para 44*, HM Treasury may make regulations allowing managers of CIVs to deduct tax on account of participants' liability to CGT or corporation tax on capital gains, whereas *new TCGA 1992, Sch 5AAA, para 45* confers a general regulatory power in respect of *new TCGA 1992, Sch 5AAA*.

New TCGA 1992, Sch 5AAA, paras 46–47 contain definitions of terms. *New TCGA 1992, Sch 5AAA, para 48* confers another regulatory power on HM Treasury, under which it may make amendments to any provision of TCGA 1992 in relation to CIVs that are UK property-rich or to direct or indirect investments by CIVs in companies that are UK property-rich.

New TCGA 1992, Sch 5AAA, paras 49 and *50* contain two transitional provisions. It will be recalled that an offshore CIV may make a transparency election under *new TCGA 1992, Sch 5AAA, para 8* within 12 months of the CIV's first acquisition of an interest in UK land or of a right or interest in a company that is UK property-rich. In the case of CIVs that were constituted before 6 April 2019, *new TCGA 1992, Sch 5AAA, para 49* permits the election to be made at any time before 6 April 2020. *New TCGA 1992, Sch 5AAA para 50* refers to the exemption election under *new TCGA 1992, Sch 5AAA, para 12*. Under *new TCGA 1992, Sch 5AAA, para 14*, such an election must be accompanied by information about disposals made by participants at any time in the two years preceding the date of the election (or since constitution if that took place less than two years before the date of the election); however, no information is to be required under this rule about disposals taking place before 6 April 2019.

Schedule 1, Pt 2 (paras 22–119) makes consequential amendments to TCGA 1992 and other statutes. They are mostly of three types. The first replaces references to NRCGT gains by references to all direct or indirect disposals of UK land. The second type replaces references to a non-resident company's being subject to CGT on gains to its being subject to corporation tax on those gains. The third type relates to the abolition of the ATED-related gains regime. Only the most significant will be discussed below.

Schedule 1, para 22 inserts *new TMA 1970, s 8C*, which prescribes new reporting requirements relating to CGT. Where an individual (1) who is not 'a remittance-basis individual' receives a notice under TMA 1970, s 8 (personal return) or 8A (trustee's return) requiring him to make a return relating to his chargeability to CGT for a particular tax year but (2) the chargeable gains accruing to him in that year do not exceed the annual exempt amount and (3) the total amount or value of the consideration the person receives for all 'chargeable disposals' of assets does not exceed four times the annual exempt amount, a statement confirming points (1) to (3) will be sufficient and a full return (as far as CGT is concerned) need not be made. A remittance-basis individual for this purpose is an individual to whom ITA 2007, s 809B applies or to whom *new TCGA 1992, Sch 1, para 2* applies because he has made an election under TCGA 1992, s 16ZA for foreign losses to be allowable losses. A 'chargeable disposal' is every disposal other than one on which any gain accruing is not a chargeable gain or a disposal between spouses or civil partners.

Schedule 1, para 26 substitutes a *new TCGA 1992, s 25ZA*, providing for the postponement of gains or losses deemed to accrue to a person by virtue of his ceasing to carry on a trade in the United Kingdom through a branch or agency (as provided under TCGA 1992, s 25(3)). Where the deemed disposal is one of an interest in UK land, the gain or loss is deemed not to accrue in that tax year but is deferred and will crystallise (in whole or in part) only when there is a subsequent actual disposal (excluding intra-group disposals to which TCGA 1992, s 171 applies) of the whole or part of the interest. However, a person who would prefer not to have the gain or loss deferred in this way may elect for the deferment rule not to apply, provided he does so within two years of the day on which the deemed disposal is considered to take place. This provision replaces the existing TCGA 1992, s 25ZA, which makes the same provision in the case of deemed NRCGT gains and losses.

Schedule 1, para 31 substitutes a *new TCGA 1992, s 80A*, which mirrors *new TCGA 1992, s 25ZA*, but relates to gains made by trustees.

Schedule 1, para 53 substitutes a *new TCGA 1992, s 159A*. Whereas the existing TCGA 1992, s 159A provides for rollover relief where the proceeds of a disposal giving rise to an NRCGT gain are invested in a 'qualifying residential-property interest', *new TCGA 1992, s 159A* provides for rollover relief where both the old and new assets are interests in UK land generally.

Schedule 1, para 57 substitutes a *new TCGA 1992, s 168A*. Whereas the existing TCGA 1992, s 168A provides for the postponement of a gain in relation to a transfer of a business asset consisting of a UK residential-property interest held over under TCGA 1992, s 165 which would otherwise crystallise on the emigration of the transferee, *new TCGA 1992, s 168A* provides for such postponement in relation to an interest in UK land generally.

Schedule 1, para 67 substitutes a *new TCGA 1992, s 187B*. Whereas the existing TCGA 1992, s 187B provides for a deferment of the exit charge under TCGA 1992, s 185 on the occasion of a company's ceasing to be UK-resident to the extent that it involves a deemed disposal of a UK residential-property interest, *new TCGA 1992, s 187B* provides for such a deferment to the extent that the charge relates to a deemed disposal of an interest in UK land generally.

Schedule 1, para 68 omits existing TCGA 1992, ss 188A–188K, which provide for the pooling of NRCGT gains and losses.

Schedule 1, para 115 inserts *new CTA 2010, s 535A* and *s 535B* into the UK REIT regime, under which where a company that is a UK REIT or is a member of a UK REIT disposes of an asset consisting of a right or interest in a another company (B) that is UK property-rich, the 'appropriate proportion' of a gain accruing to the disponer company is not to be a chargeable gain. The 'appropriate proportion' is the proportion that the value of B's assets deriving directly or indirectly from assets used for the purposes of UK property-rental business bears to the total value of B's assets at the beginning of the accounting period in which the disposal is made. *New CTA 2010, s 535B* provides that in determining the gain that is not to be a chargeable gain under *new CTA 2010, s 535A*, any 'pre-April 2019 residual business losses or deficits' that have not been deducted from other profits or gains or under previous iterations of *new CTA 2010, s 535B* may be deducted from the gain. 'Pre-April 2019 residual business losses or deficits' are allowable losses accruing on disposals made before 6 April 2019 or deficits or other losses for accounting periods ending before that date.

Schedule 1, Pt 3 (paras 120–126) contains commencements and transitional provisions. Subject to exceptions, the amendments made by Sch 1 are to have effect for CGT purposes as from the tax year 2019/20 and for the purposes of corporation tax for accounting periods beginning after 5 April 2019.

Section 14 introduces Sch 2, which provides for reporting requirements and payments on account of CGT in relation to direct or indirect disposals of UK land.

Schedule 2 entitled 'Returns for disposals of UK land etc', consists of three Parts: Part 1 ('Returns and payments on account: disposals of UK land etc') contains paras 1–17; Part 2 ('notification of chargeable amounts, amendments of returns, enquiries etc') contains paras 18–24; and Part 3 ('Consequential amendments') contains paras 25–32).

Schedule 2, para 1 provides that Sch 2 is to apply for CGT purposes to any direct or indirect disposal of UK land meeting the 'non-residence condition' made after 5 April 2019 and any other direct disposal of UK land on which a 'residential-property gain' accrues and made after that date, unless the disposal is an 'excluded disposal'. 'Any other direct disposal of UK land on which a residential-property gain accrues is such a gain made by a UK resident. These rules therefore apply as much to UK residents making such gains as they do to non-residents making director indirect disposals of UK land.

An 'excluded disposal' is any of the following:

- a no-gain, no-loss disposal;
- the grant of a lease for no premium to a person not connected with the grantor under an arm's length bargain;
- a disposal made by a charity; or
- a disposal of any pension-scheme investments.

Under Sch 2, para 2, a disposal meets the 'non-residence condition' if it is:

(a) a disposal made by a non-resident on which a gain accrues that is chargeable to tax under *new TCGA 1992, s 1A*(*3*)(*b*) or (*c*)*;*
(b) a gain made by a UK resident in the overseas part of a split year on which a gain accrues that is chargeable to tax by virtue of *new TCGA 1992, s 1A*(*3*)(*b*) or (*c*)*;* or
(c) a disposal on which a gain does not accrue but which would have been chargeable under (a) or (b) above had a gain accrued.

A 'residential-property gain' is as defined in *new TCGA 1992, Sch 1B.*

Schedule 2, para 3 provides that where a person makes a disposal to which Sch 2 applies, that person must make a return (a 'Sch 2 return') in respect of the disposal within 30 days of the day following the completion of the disposal, but if two or more such disposals are made in the same tax year, the person must make a single return with respect to all those disposals, subject to exceptions under Sch 2, paras 4, 5 or 10. This and the following provisions mirror the current regime for NRCGT returns.

Schedule 2, para 4 makes an exception from the return requirement in relation to a disposal that is 'any other direct disposal of UK land on which a residential-property gain accrues' in respect of which the person is not required to make a payment on account under Sch 2, para 6. Schedule 2, para 5 makes an exception for returns for which the filing date would otherwise fall on or after the filing date for the person's ordinary self-assessment tax return (including details of the disposal) or on or before the date on which HMRC has required the person to make such a return. Schedule 2, para 10 makes an exception in relation to disposals having an 'appropriate connection' to a CIV (as defined in *new TCGA 1992, Sch 5AAA, para 6*) and in respect of which the person would not be required to make a payment on account under Sch 2, para 6.

Schedule 2, para 6 provides for payments on account of CGT to be made by a person required to make a return under Sch 2 if at the filing date of the return, that person is 'notionally chargeable' to CGT under Sch 2, para 7, to the extent that the amount has not already become payable as a result of a previous return under Sch 2. Schedule 2, para 7 provides that a person is notionally chargeable to an amount of CGT as at the filing date for a Sch 2 return if and to the extent that he would be liable to CGT for the tax year concerned, ignoring disposals with a completion date later than the completion date of the disposal to which the Sch 2 return relates and disposals on which a gain accrues but which do not fall within Sch 2. Any unused allowable losses that have accrued on or before the completion date of the disposal to which the Sch 2 return relates may be taken into account.

Schedule 2, para 8 provides for repayments of CGT to be made if at the time that a person makes a Sch 2 return, he has already made payments on account in respect of the tax year concerned that exceed the tax notionally chargeable on the person at the filing date. The repayment is of the excess. Where a disposal has not had to be reported because it resulted in an allowable loss but would have had to be reported (as any other disposal of UK land on which a residential-property gain accrued) if a gain had been the result, may be reported under Sch 2, para 9 to secure a repayment, provided that the filing date for the return does not fall on or after the date for filing an ordinary self-assessment tax return in respect of the disposal.

Schedule 2, paras 10–12 relate to collective investment schemes (CISs) to which *new TCGA 1992, Sch 5AAA* applies. For Sch 2, para 10, see above under Sch 2, para 4. Schedule 2, para 11 applies where an offshore CIS has made a transparency election under *new TCGA 1992, Sch 5AAA para 8* and a disposal is made of property in which the scheme has invested. Where the disposal is made before the day on which the election is made and it is one in respect of which a Sch 2 return must be made, the completion date for the disposal is deemed to be the day on which the election is made. Schedule 2, para 12 applies where there is a deemed disposal under *new TCGA 1992, Sch 5AAA para 21* (participant in exempt fund receiving value) or *para 22* (exemption election ceasing to have effect) and that disposal is one in respect of which a Sch 2 return must be made. In that case, if the disposal is one from which a gain is deemed to accrue under *new TCGA 1992, Sch 5AAA para 23*, a Sch 2 return must be made in respect of each occasion (subject to the single-return rule under Sch 2, para 3(2)) on which any part of the gain is treated as accruing to the relevant person and the time of completion of the disposal is taken to be the later of the time on which the gain is deemed to accrue and the day on which the notification to participants under *new TCGA 1992, Sch 5AAA para 25* must be given. If the disposal is one from which a gain is not deemed to accrue under *new TCGA 1992, Sch 5AAA para 23*, it is treated for the purposes of Sch 2 as completed on the day on which the notification to participants under *new TCGA 1992, Sch 5AAA para 25* must be given.

Schedule 2, para 13 provides that where an option binding the grantor to sell an asset is granted, the grant is a disposal in respect of which a Sch 2 return must be made and the option is subsequently exercised so that the grant is treated under TCGA 1992, ss 144(2) or 144A(2)(b) as the same transaction as the sale, the grantor is nevertheless to remain subject to the obligation to file a Sch 2 return etc in relation to the grant.

Schedule 2, para 14 provides for the making, where necessary, of assumptions or reasonable estimates in connection with future events etc. Schedule 2, para 15 provides that where a return has been made relying on such estimates and subsequent events turn out differently, the person may file an amended return as if an additional disposal had been made incorporating that difference but otherwise in all respects the same. In these circumstances the calculation of tax notionally chargeable is made ignoring the actual disposal.

Schedule 2, para 16 provides for HMRC to prescribe the contents of a Sch 2 return and Sch 2, para 17 contains definitions.

Schedule 2, para 18 provides that a person need not give notice of chargeability to CGT under TMA 1970, s 7 in respect of a disposal if he has already made a Sch 2 return in respect of that disposal before the end of the period by which notice must be given under that section. Schedule 2, para 19 provides for amendments to be made to a Sch 2 return as they may be made to an ordinary tax return, subject to certain modifications, and Sch 2, para 20 applies the enquiry provisions to Sch 2 return, subject also to certain modifications. Schedule 2, para 21 allows for amendments to be made to a Sch 2 return while an enquiry is in progress, as provided under TMA 1970, ss 9B and 9C and certain paragraphs of TMA 1970, Sch 3ZA. Schedule 2, para 22 applies HMRC's determination provisions to Sch 2 returns subject to modifications and Sch 2, para 23 performs the same function with respect to discovery assessments. Schedule 2, para 24 provides for interpretation.

Schedule 2, paras 25–31 make consequential amendments to TMA 1970, TCGA 1992, FA 2007, Sch 24, FA 2008, Sch 36 and FA 2009, ss 101–103 and Schs 55 and 56.

Schedule 2, para 32 provides that the amendments made by Sch 2, Pt 3 (the consequential amendments) are to have effect in relation to disposals made after 5 April 2019. The substantial provisions also apply in relation to disposals made after that date (see under Sch 2, para 1). However, TMA 1970, s 12ZG, which provides for instances where advance self-assessment in respect of an NRCGT gain is not required, remains in force in relation to disposals made before 6 April 2020, although it is omitted by Sch 2, para 25(3).

International matters

Section 15 introduces Sch 3, which imposes a charge to UK income tax on certain receipts by non-UK resident persons ('offshore receipts') in respect of intangible property. There is a high de minimis threshold of £10 million of UK sales.

Schedule 3 consists of 14 paragraphs. Schedule 3, para 4 inserts the substantive provisions; the other paragraphs are introductory or make consequential amendments.

Schedule 3, para 4 inserts *new ITTOIA 2005 Part 5 Chapter 2A*, consisting of 26 sections (*new ITTOIA 2005, ss 608A–608Z*).

New ITTOIA 2005, s 608A provides that there is to be a charge to income tax on 'UK-derived amounts' arising in a tax year to a person who is neither UK-resident nor resident in a 'full-treaty territory'. 'UK-derived amount' is defined in *new ITTOIA 2005, s 608F* and 'full-treaty territory' in *new ITTOIA 2005, s 608E*.

New ITTOIA 2005, s 608B provides that tax under *new ITTOIA 2005, s 608A* is to be charged on the full amount of the UK-derived amounts arising in the tax year.

New ITTOIA 2005, s 608C provides that the person liable for the tax is to be the person receiving or entitled to receive the UK-derived amounts.

New ITTOIA 2005, s 608D defines 'residence' for these purposes by reference to the person's domicile, residence or place of management but not in respect only of income from sources there or capital situated there. Where a person is resident in a foreign jurisdiction generally under its laws, but it has no law providing for a person to be resident there for tax purposes, the person will be regarded as resident there for the purposes of these rules.

New ITTOIA 2005, s 608E defines 'full-treaty territory' as a territory that has a double tax treaty with the United Kingdom containing a non-discrimination provision.

New ITTOIA 2005, s 608F defines a 'UK-derived amount' as an amount of a revenue or capital nature receivable in respect of the enjoyment or exercise of rights constituting intangible property, the enjoyment or exercise of which (or of rights directly or indirectly derived from such rights) directly or indirectly enables, facilitates or promotes 'UK sales'. 'UK sales' are in turn defined as services, goods or other property provided in the United Kingdom or provided to persons in the United Kingdom.

New ITTOIA 2005, s 608G provides for apportionment of amounts in relation to intangible property, the enjoyment or exercise of which (or of rights directly or indirectly derived from such rights) directly or indirectly enables, facilitates or promotes 'UK sales' and anything else (whether or not other sales). In such a case, the amount chargeable to income tax is the proportion that UK sales bear to the value of all sales (where there are also other sales) or as is just and reasonable.

New ITTOIA 2005, s 608H defines intangible property for these purposes as any property except:

- tangible property;
- an estate, interest or right over land;
- a right in respect of the above;
- a financial asset or a share or other right in relation to the profits, governance or winding-up of a company; or
- any property that HM Treasury may prescribe.

New ITTOIA 2005, s 608I provides how these rules are to apply to partnerships that are regarded for tax purposes under the law of a foreign jurisdiction as an entity separate from the partners.

New ITTOIA 2005, ss 608J–608N provide for exemptions.

New ITTOIA 2005, s 608J provides that the charge to tax under *new ITTOIA 2005, s 608A* is not to apply to a person in a particular tax year if the total value of that person's UK sales in that tax year does not exceed £10 million. However, to prevent fragmentation where a person (A) or a person connected with A receives or is entitled to an amount relating wholly or partly, and directly or indirectly, to the provision of services, goods or other property constituting UK sales, the UK sales are to be regarded as A's UK sales.

New ITTOIA 2005, s 608K provides an exemption in relation to a person ('the relevant person') who is resident in a foreign territory throughout a tax year, all or substantially all of whose 'relevant activity' in relation to any intangible property to which any UK-derived amount relates is (and at all times has been) undertaken in that territory. 'Relevant activity' means anything done by any person for the purpose of creating, developing or maintaining any of the intangible property or for generating amounts relating to the enjoyment or exercise of rights constituting any of the intangible property. An additional condition is that there must be no 'relevant connection' between the intangible property and a 'related person'. Such a connection exists where any of the relevant intangible property has been directly or indirectly transferred from a person related to the relevant person, derives directly or indirectly from anything so transferred or derives directly or indirectly from intangible property held by a person related to the relevant person. *New ITTOIA 2005, s 608T* defines when persons are related for these purposes.

New ITTOIA 2005, s 608L provides a further exemption where the local tax paid in the foreign territory by the person concerned in respect of the UK-derived amounts arising in the (UK) tax year is at least 50% of the UK income tax that would be charged under these rules on those amounts, calculated on the assumption that the charge under *new ITTOIA 2005, s 608A* applies to those amounts and the person concerned is not entitled to any reliefs or allowances for the tax year. It is a further condition that the local tax is not determined under 'designer tax provisions' (provisions designed to enable persons to exercise significant control over the amount of tax that they pay).

New ITTOIA 2005, s 608M allows for the local tax amount to be apportioned between UK-derived amounts and other amounts and to be reduced by any repayments of local tax or payments in respect of credits for tax. *New ITTOIA 2005, s 608N* confers regulatory powers on HM Treasury to amend these rules.

New ITTOIA 2005, s 608O enables HMRC to recover tax charged under *new ITTOIA 2005, s 608A* on a person ('the taxpayer') for a tax year which remains unpaid for more than six months after the 'relevant date' from another person who is or was in the same 'control group' as the taxpayer at any time in the tax year. Membership of a 'control group' is defined by *new ITTOIA 2005, s 608S* as subsisting between two persons at any time if:

- they are consolidated for accounting purposes (as defined) for a period including that time;

- one of them has a '51% investment' (as defined) in the other at that time; or
- the same third person has a 51% investment in both of them at that time.

Recovery of tax from the other person is to be effected by a notice requiring that person to pay any unpaid tax and interest within 30 days of the date of the notice. These notices must be given no more than 42 months after the 'relevant date'. Where tax is determined under TMA 1970, s 28C in the absence of a return, the relevant date is the date of the determination. In the case of a late self-assessment return the relevant date is the date on which the return was delivered, and in any other case it is the date on which the outstanding tax became due and payable. There is a right of appeal against the notice. However, for the purposes of recovering unpaid tax and interest from any person whether or not pending an appeal, *new ITTOIA 2005, s 608P* provides that the amount of income tax originally assessed on the taxpayer is treated as assessed on the other person, and this deemed assessment does not entitle the other person to appeal against the original assessment on the taxpayer or against the deemed assessment.

However, *new ITTOIA 2005, s 608Q* entitles the other person to appeal against the recovery notice itself, within 30 days of the date of the notice, but only on the grounds that the other person is or was not in the same control group as the taxpayer.

New ITTOIA 2005, s 608R provides that any person who pays an amount of tax or interest in relation to a notice under *new ITTOIA 2005, s 608O* may recover that amount from the taxpayer. Any amount paid is not allowable as a deduction in calculating the other person's income, profits or losses and nor is any reimbursement treated as a receipt.

New ITTOIA 2005, s 608S defines 'control group' (see under *new ITTOIA 2005, s 608O*) and *new ITTOIA 2005, s 608T* defines 'related person' for the purposes of *new ITTOIA 2005, s 608K. New ITTOIA 2005, s 608U* defines '51% investment' (for the purposes of *new ITTOIA 2005, s 608S*) and '25% investment' for the purposes of *new ITTOIA 2005, s 608T.* New ITTOIA 2005, s 608V defines what is meant by direct or indirect participation in management, control or capital for the purposes of *new ITTOIA 2005, s 608T.*

New ITTOIA 2005, s 608W is an anti-avoidance provision. It applies to a tax advantage arising as a result wholly or partly from the non-application of any provision of the charge under *new ITTOIA 2005, s 608A* or from the abusive use ('contrary to [its] object and purpose') of a double tax treaty to override such a provision, where the obtaining of that advantage was the main purpose or one of the main purposes of arrangements into which a person enters. In these circumstances, the advantage is to be counteracted, overriding, in the case of treaty shopping, the rule in TIOPA 2010, s 6(1) (that provisions in a double tax treaty override domestic law).

New ITTOIA 2005, s 608Y provides that an appeal against a charge to income tax under *new ITTOIA 2005, s 608A* is to be ineffective in staying the payment of tax and that no agreement to postpone any of that tax or interest may be made. On a further appeal, the court or tribunal may give a direction that any tax repayable as a result of the first appeal not be repaid if necessary for the protection of the revenue.

New ITTOIA 2005, s 608Z contains definitions.

Schedule 3, paras 5–14 make consequential amendments and provide further regulatory powers.

Section 16 introduces Sch 4, which is an anti-avoidance measure intended to counteract the fragmentation of UK profits by their attribution to entities in low-tax jurisdictions. Schedule 4 consists of 12 paragraphs.

Schedule 4, para 1 is introductory. It names the parties involved in 'profit-fragmentation arrangements' at which Sch 4 is aimed as:

- a person resident in the United Kingdom ('the resident party');
- an 'overseas person or entity' ('the overseas party');
- a 'related individual', who may be the resident party, a fellow partner of the resident party or, where the resident party is a company, a participator in the resident party.

An 'overseas person or entity is a person who is resident outside the United Kingdom or a person domiciled outside the United Kingdom within the meaning of ITA 2007, s 718 or a company, partnership, trust or other entity or arrangements established or having effect under foreign law (whether or not as a legal person).

Schedule 4, para 2 defines 'profit-fragmentation arrangements', in language borrowed from transfer pricing legislation and the diverted profits tax. Thus, these are arrangements whereby:

- a provision ('the material provision') exists between the resident party (RP) and the overseas party (OP);
- as a result of the material provision, there is a transfer of value from RP to OP deriving directly or indirectly from the profits of a business chargeable to UK income tax or corporation tax;
- the value transferred is greater than it would have been if it had resulted from an arm's length provision; and
- any of the 'enjoyment conditions' (defined in Sch 4, para 4) are met in relation to a related individual.

Put briefly, value must be transferred out of a business taxable in the United Kingdom in a way such that a party related to the UK transferor may enjoy the benefits of what is transferred.

However, for arrangements to be profit-fragmentation arrangements within Sch 4, the material provision must result in a mismatch for a tax period of the resident party and it must be reasonable to conclude that the main purposes or one of the main purposes for entering into the arrangements was to obtain a tax advantage.

Schedule 4, para 3 deals with transfers of value. In determining whether value is transferred from RP to OP, account must be taken of any method, however indirect, by which any property or right is transferred or the value of any property or right is enhanced or diminished. Value is traceable through any number of persons, entities or arrangements. A non-exhaustive list of circumstances by which a transfer of value may be effective is provided by Sch 4, para 3(2). These include e g sales, contracts or other transactions made otherwise than for full consideration or for more than full consideration or the creation of an option affecting the disposition of any property or right and the giving of consideration for granting it.

Schedule 4, para 4 defines what are the enjoyment conditions that must be met in relation to a related individual for Sch 4 to apply. There are two enjoyment conditions. The first is that it is a reasonable conclusion that some or all of the value transferred relates to something done by, or any property or purported right of, the individual. The second enjoyment condition is that either of two further conditions must be met.

The first further condition is that the related individual must be able to enjoy the benefit of at least some of the value transferred. This may be in any one of five ways:

- part or all of the value transferred is dealt with by any person so that it enures to the benefit of the individual at some time;
- part or all of the value transferred operates to increase the value of any assets held by, or for the benefit of, the individual;
- the individual receives, or is entitled to receive, any benefit provided, or to be provided, out of all or part of the value transferred;
- as a result of the exercise or successive exercise of one or more powers, the individual may become entitled to the beneficial enjoyment of part or all of the value transferred; or
- whether alone or acting together with others, the individual is able directly or indirectly to control the application of part or all of the value transferred.

The second (and alternative) further condition is that (it is reasonable to conclude that) the individual (whether alone or acting together with others) has procured the transfer of value from RP to OP in such a way as to avoid meeting any of the five above tests.

Schedule 4, para 5 defines the circumstances in which a tax mismatch for a 'tax period' of RP results. The provision closely matches the equivalent definition of a tax mismatch for the purposes of diverted profits tax in FA 2015, s 107.

Broadly, there is such a mismatch where in relation to a 'relevant tax' there is in that period, either or both:

- an increase in RP's deductible expenses; or
- a reduction in RP's taxable income;

and it is at the same time reasonable to conclude that:

- the resulting reduction in the tax payable by RP exceeds the increase in the relevant tax(es) payable by OP for the corresponding period; and
- that additional tax is not at least 80% of the reduction in RP's tax payable ('the 80% payment test').

A 'tax period' of RP means a tax year or, if it is a company, an accounting period of RP. A corresponding period for OP is either a period coinciding with RP's tax period or a notional period for the purposes of relevant taxes that would coincide with RP's tax period.

Exceptions are provided where the mismatch arises solely as a reason of employer pension contributions, payments to charities, payments to persons enjoying sovereign immunity or payments to certain offshore funds or authorised investment funds meeting the genuine diversity of income condition or in which at least 75% of the investors are the payees just mentioned.

'Relevant taxes' are income tax, corporation tax on income, the banking surcharge under CTA 2010, s 269DA, the supplementary charge on ring-fence trades under CTA 2010, s 330(1) and any non-UK tax on income.

Schedule 4, para 6 makes provisions supplementing Sch 4, para 5 and provides how RP's tax reduction and OP's additional tax payable are to be calculated. The language follows very closely that of FA 2015 s 108, which serves the same function in relation to a tax mismatch for the purposes of diverted profits tax.

Schedule 4, para 7 provides for adjustments to be made to counteract any tax advantage arising from profit-fragmentation arrangements. The adjustments must relate to RP's expenses, income, profits or losses for the tax period in which the value is transferred and must be based on what the value transferred would have been under arm's length terms.

Schedule 4, para 8 provides for RP to lodge a claim for consequential adjustments if the result of the counteractive adjustments under Sch 4, para 7 result in an element of double taxation. Schedule 4, para 9 provides that any amounts directly or indirectly paid to meet or reimburse the cost of tax charged by virtue of Sch 4, para 7 are not to be taken into account in calculating income, profits or losses for any tax purposes. Schedule 4, para 10 clarifies that references to a person's expenses, income, profits or losses or to adjustments thereto include references to that person's share of a partnership's expenses etc if the person is a member of the partnership. Schedule 4, para 11 defines further terms.

Schedule 4, para 12 provides that Sch 4 has effect for the purposes of income tax in relation to any value transferred after 5 April 2019 and for the purposes of corporation tax in relation to any value transferred after 31 March 2019.

Section 17 introduces Sch 5, which provides for non-resident companies carrying on a UK property business to be chargeable to corporation tax on the profits of such a business, on profits consisting of other UK property income and on profits arising from certain loan relationships and derivative contracts. Non-resident companies carrying on a business in the United Kingdom otherwise than through a UK permanent establishment have hitherto been chargeable to income tax, unless the business was a trade of dealing in or developing UK land.

Schedule 5 consists of 50 paragraphs, divided into three Parts. Part 1 (paras 1–5) extends the scope of the charge to corporation tax; Part 2 (paras 6–34) makes supplementary and consequential amendments; Part 3 (paras 35–50) makes detailed commencement and transitional provisions.

Schedule 5, para 1 introduces amendments to be made to CTA 2009, s 5, which provides for the territorial scope of the charge to corporation tax. Schedule 5, paras 2–4 make those amendments, so that the relevant parts of it now reads as follows:

'5 Territorial scope of charge

...

(2) A non-UK resident company is within the charge to corporation tax only if—

- it carries on a trade of dealing in or developing UK land (see section 5B),
- it carries on a trade in the United kingdom (other than a trade of dealing in or developing UK land) through a permanent establishment in the United Kingdom,
- it carries on a UK property business, or
- it has other UK property income.

...

(3A) A non-UK resident company which carries on a UK property business is chargeable to corporation tax on income on all its profits that are—

- profits of that business, or
- profits arising from loan relationships or derivative contracts that the company is a party to for the purposes of that business.

(3B) A non-UK resident company which has other UK property income is chargeable to corporation tax on income on all its profits that—

- consist of that income, or
- are profits arising from loan relationships or derivative contracts that the company is a party to for the purposes of enabling it to generate that income.

...

(5) In this Part "other property income" means income dealt with by any of the following Chapters of Part 4—

- Chapter 7 (rent receivable in connection with a UK section 39(4) concern;
- Chapter 8 (rent receivable for UK electric-line wayleaves;
- Chapter 9 (post-cessation receipts arising from a UK property business).'

Schedule 5, paras 6–34 make supplementary and consequential amendments to FA 1998, FA 2004, ITTOIA 2005, ITA 2007, CTA 2009, CTA 2010 and TIOPA 2010. Only the most significant of these will be discussed below.

FA 2004, s 55 (one of those provisions one almost forgets is still there) provides that a company must give notice to HMRC of the beginning of its first accounting period and of the beginning of any other accounting period that does not immediately follow the previous accounting period. Schedule 5, para 7 inserts *new FA 2004, s 55A*, waiving the requirement to give notice under FA 2004, s 55 if the company reasonably expects that all the income on which it will be chargeable to corporation tax for that period will consist of payments on which it will suffer deduction at source of income tax and that it will have no chargeable gains. If that reasonable expectation cannot be held for any subsequent period, it is to be treated as not immediately following the previous period and thus require a notice to be given to HMRC in respect of it under FA 2004, s 55.

Within the intangible assets regime of CTA 2009, Pt 8, an election may be made under CTA 2009, s 792 to transfer a degrouping charge to another group company. CTA 2009, s 793 provides that such an election may only be made if the transferee company is either UK-resident or carries on a trade in the United Kingdom through a permanent establishment (PE) and is not exempt from corporation tax in respect of the PE's income or chargeable gains by virtue of a double tax treaty. Schedule 5, para 24 adds two further possibilities for the transferee company by inserting *new CTA 2009, s 793*(*3A*) *and* (*3B*). The first is that it may also be a company carrying on a trade of dealing in or developing UK land and is not exempt from corporation tax in respect of the profits of that trade by virtue of a double tax treaty. The second is that the transferee company may be carrying on a UK property business and not be exempt from corporation tax in respect of the profits of that business by virtue of a double tax treaty. Schedule 5, para 25 inserts *new CTA 2009, s 793A*. This provides that in respect of a UK-resident transferee company, the degrouping charge or the part specified in the election is to be treated as accruing to the transferee company immediately before the transferor company leaves the group as a non-trading credit.

If, on the other hand, the transferee company is a non-resident company carrying on a trade in the United Kingdom through a PE, the degrouping charge or the part specified in the election is to be treated as accruing to the transferee company immediately before the transferor company leaves the group as a non-trading credit and to have accrued in respect of an asset held for the purposes of a UK PE of the transferee company. However, if the transferee company is carrying on a trade of dealing in or developing UK land, the degrouping charge or the part specified in the election is to be treated as accruing to the transferee company immediately before the transferor company leaves the group as a credit in respect of an asset held for the purposes of the trade of dealing in or developing UK land. Finally, if the transferee company is carrying on a UK property business, the degrouping charge or the part specified in the election is to be treated as accruing to the transferee company immediately before the transferor company leaves the group as a credit in respect of an asset held for the purposes of the UK property business.

Schedule 5, para 35 provides that Sch 5 is to come into force on 6 April 2020 ('the commencement date'), subject to several transitional provisions. Schedule 5, para 36 provides for any straddling periods to be divided into two notional accounting periods, one ending on 5 April 2020 and the other beginning on 6 April 2020. Schedule 5, paras 37–44 provide for the extent to which property-business losses, profits and losses from loan relationships and derivative contracts remain allowable or chargeable after the transition from income tax to corporation tax. Schedule 5, para 45 provides that assets held by a non-resident company for the purposes of its UK property business or for enabling it to generate other UK property income which become chargeable intangible assets upon entry into corporation tax are to be treated as acquired on the commencement date for their accounting value on that date. Schedule 5, para 46 provides when a degrouping election under CTA 2009, s 792 may or may not be made when either new CTA 2009, s 793(3A) or (3B) (inserted by Sch 5, para 24) applies to the transferee company at a particular time preceding the commencement date. Schedule 5, para 47 prevents a claim under CTA 2009, s 1147(7) for corporation tax relief for expenditure on contaminated or derelict land incurred by a non-resident company before it begins to carry on a UK property business at any time after the commencement date. Schedule 5, para 48 provides that the instalment payment regulations (SI 1998/3175) are not to apply to a company for the accounting period deemed to begin when the company comes within the charge to corporation tax.

Schedule 5, para 49 is an anti-avoidance provision. Where after 28 October 2018, a company enters into an arrangement the main purpose or one of the main purposes of which is to secure a tax advantage related to the coming into force of these rules (Sch 5) for any person, that advantage is to be counteracted, unless, as provided by Sch 5, para 50, the arrangements involve the taking of solely ordinary commercial steps in accordance with a generally prevailing commercial practice and the tax advantage obtained is a relief expressly conferred by the corporate interest-restriction rules of TIOPA 2010, Pt 10 with the policy objectives of which this is wholly consistent.

Section 18 introduces Sch 6, which makes amendments to diverted profits tax (DPT) as charged under FA 2015, Pt 3. The main purpose of the amendments is to close tax-planning opportunities. Schedule 6 comprises 12 paragraphs.

Schedule 6, para 1 is introductory. Schedule 6, paras 2–5 are largely restructuring amendments affecting FA 2015, ss 82–85, intended to clarify the operation of the charge to tax under the first charging arm of DPT, i e where (as determined under either FA 2015, s 80 or 81) entities or transactions lacking economic substance are involved. By inserting *new FA 2015, s 85(7)*, Sch 6 para 5(6) makes it clear that, in calculating the 'notional additional amount' by reference to which taxable diverted profits are calculated and 'the actual provision condition' (see FA 2015, s 82(7)) is not met, no account is to be taken of any adjustment that either the transfer-pricing rules of TIOPA 2010, Pt 4 or any other provision require to be made to the results of 'the material provision'.

The second charging arm of DPT is defined in FA 2015, s 86 and involves the avoidance of a UK taxable presence in the form of a UK permanent establishment (PE) by a foreign company. FA 2015, s 88 introduces how the taxable diverted profits of the foreign company are to be calculated in these circumstances. *New FA 2015, s 88(5B) and (5C)*, inserted by Sch 6 para 6, provide explicitly that in calculating the 'notional PE profits' of the 'avoided PE' no account is to be taken of any transfer-pricing adjustments that TIOPA 2010, Pt 4 requires to be made to the results of any provision made or imposed between the foreign company and the avoided PE if those adjustments are not taken into account in the avoided PE's company tax return at any time before the end of the 'review period' (which is the period of 12 months beginning immediately after any DPT charged becomes due and payable, which is 30 days after the charging notice).

Schedule 6, para 7 inserts *new FA 2015, s 111A*, which provides that a reference in FA 2015, ss 82 or 88 to any adjustments that the transfer-pricing rules of TIOPA 2010, Pt 4 require to be made to the results of any provision includes a reference to an adjustment that any other enactment requires to be made to those results if, and to the extent that, the absence of that other adjustment would have resulted in a transfer-pricing adjustment.

Schedule 6, para 8 provides that the preceding amendments are to have effect in relation to accounting periods beginning after 28 October 2018.

Under FA 2015, s 93, if an officer of HMRC believes that taxable diverted profits have arisen to a company, the officer must send the company a preliminary notice stating the amount of the proposed charge to DPT and how it has been calculated. Such a notice may be sent no later than 24 months after the end of the relevant accounting period. Schedule 6, para 9 amends FA 2015, s 93(5) to substitute a different (extended deadline) for cases where the first charging arm of DPT applies, i e where entities or transactions lacking economic substance are involved so that either FA 2015, s 80 or s 81 applies. Where that is the case, a preliminary notice may now be sent at any time until the expiry of six months after the last day on which the company's company tax return for the relevant accounting period can be amended. Under FA 1998, Sch 18, para 15, amendments may normally be made at any time up to 12 months after the filing date. The deadline for preliminary notices where FA 2015, s 86 applies (avoided PE) remains 24 months after the relevant accounting period.

Schedule 6, para 10 inserts *new FA 2015, s 100A*, which provides that where a company has definitively become liable to pay an amount of DPT, it cannot also be chargeable to corporation tax for the same accounting period on that amount if it has failed before the end of the 'review period' (for which see under Sch 6 para 6) to take it into account in an assessment to corporation tax for that accounting period. This effectively prevents double taxation to both DPT and corporation tax and has effect for accounting periods beginning after 31 March 2015 (therefore from the inception of DPT).

Schedule 6, para 11 extends the life of the review period (for which see under Sch 6 para 6) from 12 months to 15 months from the date on which DPT becomes due and payable.

Schedule 6, para 12 inserts *new FA 2015, ss 101A* and *101B*. *New FA 2015, s 101A* extends the period during which a company to which a DPT charging notice has been issued by virtue of FA 2015, ss 80 or 81 may amend its company tax return so as to reduce its taxable diverted profits to include the first 12 months of the review period. *New FA 2015, s 101B* does likewise for companies to which a DPT charging notice has been issued by virtue of FA 2015, s 86. The new sections have effect from 12 February 2019.

Section 19 makes technical amendments to the hybrid and other mismatches regime of TIOPA 2010, Pt 6A. The amendments ensure the regime is fully compliant with the EU's ATAD (Anti-Tax Avoidance Directive), Council Directive (EU) 2016/1164, as amended by Council Directive (EU) 2017/952 – an irony, perhaps, in view of what is consuming most of Parliament's time. They also provide a new exemption for certain types of regulatory capital.

TIOPA 2010, Pt 6A, Ch 8 (TIOPA 2010, ss 259H–259HC) are intended to counteract deduction/non-inclusion mismatches arising from payments or quasi-payments where the payer is within the charge to corporation tax because a payee is a multinational company (MNC).

TIOPA 2010, s 259HA prescribes five conditions (A to E) all of which must be met for Chapter 8 to apply. Condition C (as prescribed by TIOPA 2010, s 259HA(5)) is that the payer must be within the charge to corporation tax for the payment period (the payer's taxable period in which a deduction for the payment would fall to be made). Section 19(2) substitutes a *new TIOPA 2010, s 259HA(5)*, which now provides an alternative situation in which Condition C may be met. That situation is where the payee MNC is resident in the United Kingdom for the payment period and under the law of its parent jurisdiction it is regarded as carrying on a business in another jurisdiction ('the PE jurisdiction') through a permanent establishment (PE) in that jurisdiction *but* is not regarded as doing so under the law of the PE jurisdiction.

Section 19(3) makes a consequential substitution of the relevant counteraction provision, TIOPA 2010, s 259HC. Hitherto, it has simply provided that, for corporation tax purposes, the deduction that may be made from the payer's income for the payment period is reduced by an amount equal to the MNC's deduction/non-inclusion mismatch. *New TIOPA 2010, s 259HC* now provides that where the new alternative Condition C situation (as inserted by s 19(2)) applies, an amount equal to the MNC's deduction/non-inclusion mismatch is to be treated as income of the MNC arising in the United Kingdom (and nowhere else) for the payment period. Where Condition C is met as heretofore (because the payer is UK-resident), the counteraction is as before.

These two amendments are to have effect in relation to payments made after 31 December 2019 and quasi-payments in relation to which the payment period begins after that date. Section 19(6) provides for apportionment of amounts in respect of straddling periods.

TIOPA 2010, s 259N defines what is meant by 'financial instrument' for the purposes of the hybrid and other mismatch rules. Certain categories of instrument are taken out of the definition and hence their use falls outside the rules. TIOPA 2010, s 259N(3)(b) currently exempts regulatory capital securities within the Regulatory Capital Securities Regulations 2013 (SI 2013/3209). Amendments made by s 19(4) remove the reference to this SI (which is revoked by Sch 20, para 1) but substitute a reference to any regulations that may be made for this purpose. These new regulations may have retroactive effect but not to a time before 1 January 2019.

Section 20 makes technical amendments to the CFC legislation in TIOPA 2010, Pt 9A. They too are made to ensure compliance with ATAD (see under s 19).

TIOPA 2010, Pt 9A, Ch 9 (TIOPA 2010, ss 371IA–371IJ) provide for the exemption of 'qualifying loan-relationship profits' from the CFC rules ('the finance-company exemption'). TIOPA 2010, s 371IA(4) defines 'qualifying loan-relationship profits' as the CFC's profits from all of its qualifying loan relationships taken together. Section 20(2) amends TIOPA 2010, s 371IA(4) so as to limit the exemption to so much of those profits as are non-trading finance profits derived from capital investment in the United Kingdom (as defined by TIOPA 2010, s 371EC as falling within the CFC charge gateway for non-trading finance profits) but are not generated by 'UK activities' (as defined by TIOPA 2010, s 371EB).

TIOPA 2010, Pt 9A, Ch 18 (TIOPA 2010, ss 371RA–371RF) defines what is meant by 'control' under the CFC rules. Section 20(4) inserts *new TIOPA 2010, s 371RG* to include companies in which a UK-resident company has more than a '50% investment' within the CFC net.

Under *new TIOPA 2010, s 371RG(1)*, a non-resident company is a CFC (if it would not otherwise be) if a UK-resident company (alone or together with associated enterprises) directly or indirectly has more than a 50% investment in that non-resident company.

A UK-resident company has an associated enterprise if that enterprise has directly or indirectly a 25% investment in the company (or vice versa) or another person directly or indirectly has a 25% investment in both. Both '25% investment' and '50% investment' take their definitions from TIOPA 2010, s 259ND.

These amendments have effect for CFC accounting periods beginning after 31 December 2018, with provision for straddling periods.

Section 21 amends the definition of 'permanent establishment' (PE) in CTA 2010, Pt 24 Chapter 2 with respect to preparatory or auxiliary activities as part of the BEPS programme.

Under the OECD Model Treaty, certain preparatory and auxiliary activities are not to constitute a foreign company's PE in the home jurisdiction. The interpretation of this exception in UK law is reflected in CTA 2010, s 1143, which provides that a company is not to be regarded as having a PE in a territory by reason of the fact that it maintains a fixed place of business for carrying on activities or an agent carrying on activities on its behalf if, in relation to the business of the company as a whole, those activities are only of a 'preparatory or auxiliary character' (as defined in TIOPA 2010, s 1143(3)).

The amendments made by s 21 are intended to deny this exception if those activities are part of a 'fragmented business operation'. *New TIOPA 2010, s 1143*(*2A*) and (*2B*), inserted by s 21(3), provide three conditions that must be met for activities to be part of a fragmented business operation. These are that:

- the company or a person closely related to the company carries them on at one or at different places in the same territory;
- they constitute complementary functions that are part of a cohesive business operation and either:
  - the overall activity resulting from the combination of these functions is not activity that is solely of a preparatory or auxiliary nature; or
  - the company or a closely related person has a PE in the territory by reason of carrying on any of those functions.

A person who is not a company is to be treated as having a PE in a particular territory if, if that person were a company, the person would have a PE there. Closely related persons are defined in *new CTA 2010, s 1143*(*2D*).

The amendments made by s 21 have effect for accounting periods beginning after 31 December 2018, with provision for straddling periods.

Section 22 introduces Sch 7, which provides for CGT exit charges incurred under TCGA 1992, s 80 by trustees ceasing to be UK-resident to be deferred and paid in six equal annual instalments. This measure has been taken in response to the judgment of the Court of Justice of the European Union (CJEU) in *Trustees of the P Panayi Accumulation & Maintenance Settlements* (C-646/15), [2017] STC 2495, delivered in September 2017. Briefly put, the CJEU in that case held that where the trustees of a settlement were treated as a single and continuing body of persons, distinct from persons who may be trustees from time to time, the right to freedom of establishment applied to those trustees, and hence that the exit charge had in their case also to allow for deferment of the tax payable. Schedule 7, which consists of seven paragraphs, also provides for similar deferment plans for persons resident in another EEA member state who incur a UK exit charge under TCGA 1992, s 25(1) or (3) on the deemed disposal of chargeable assets that are taken outside the UK tax net.

Reminder: the EEA (European Economic Area) consists of the 28 EU Member States plus Iceland, Liechtenstein and Norway. If and when the United Kingdom leaves the European Union, it will also cease to be an EEA member state.

Schedule 7, para 1 inserts *new TMA 1970, s 59BB*, which introduces *new TMA 1970, Sch 3ZAA*, which is to provide for the CGT exit charge uncured under either TCGA 1992, s 25 or TCGA 1992, s 80 to be paid by instalments. *New TMA 1970, Sch 3ZAA* comprises ten paragraphs.

New TMA 1970, Sch 3ZAA, para 1 is introductory and provides that agreements to pay by instalments are to be called 'CGT exit-charge payment plans', abbreviated here to 'CGTEXCPPs'.

New TMA 1970, Sch 3ZAA, paras 2 and *3* prescribe who is to be eligible to enter into such plans. *New TMA 1970, Sch 3ZAA, para 2* applies to persons resident in another EEA state who are deemed to make a market-value disposal and reacquisition of chargeable assets when either those assets cease to be situated in the United Kingdom because they are held for the purposes of a trade carried on in the United Kingdom through a branch or agency and the person ceases to carry on that trade in the United Kingdom (under TCGA 1992, s 25(3)) or the chargeable asset becomes situated outside the United Kingdom for some other reason (under TCGA 1992, s 25(1)). Exploration or exploitation assets are excluded from the exit charge under

TCGA 1992, s 25. In these circumstances, the person is eligible to enter into a CGTEXCPP in relation to any one or more of the assets concerned if, at the time of the event triggering the exit charge:

- the person had a right to freedom of establishment under TFEU art 49 or Article 31 of the EEA Agreement; and
- at any time after that event the person carries on a trade in an EEA state other than the United Kingdom through a branch or agency and the asset(s) is/are held for the purposes of the trade or of the branch or agency.

New TMA 1970, Sch 3ZAA, para 3 applies to the relevant trustees of a settlement who cease to be resident in the United Kingdom and are thereby deemed under TCGA 1992, s 80(2) to make a market-value disposal and reacquisition of all the assets constituting settled property of the settlement. In these circumstances, the trustees are eligible to enter into a CGTEXCPP in relation to any one or more of the assets concerned if, at the time of they ceased to be resident:

- the trustees had a right to freedom of establishment under TFEU art 49 or Article 31 of the EEA Agreement;
- immediately before that time the trustees used the asset(s) for an 'economically significant activity' (as defined by TCGA 1992, s 13A(4)) carried on in the United Kingdom; and
- immediately after that time, the trustees become resident in another EEA member state and use the asset(s) for an economically significant activity carried on there.

New TMA 1970, Sch 3ZAA, para 4 provides that a CGTEXCPP plan need not extend to the whole of the exit charge attributable to the asset(s) included in the plan but may also apply to part only of the charge. Thus, not only does a CGTEXCPP not need to cover all of the assets involved; it also does not need to cover all of the CGT in respect of the assets selected for the plan.

New TMA 1970, Sch 3ZAA, para 5 provides that under a CGTEXCPP, the tax deferred must be paid in six equal annual instalments, the first of which is to be due on the day on which the exit charge would otherwise be payable in full under TMA 1970, s 59B, and the remainder due on each of the next five anniversaries of that date.

New TMA 1970, Sch 3ZAA, para 6 provides that the taxpayer(s) concerned must apply to HMRC if they wish to enter into a CGTEXCPP, provide the required information and receive HMRC approval. The application must be made before the day on which the exit charge would otherwise be payable in full under TMA 1970, s 59B. A plan will be void if the event triggering the exit charge is part of arrangements the main purpose or one of the main purposes of which is to defer payment of the charge or the information provided by the taxpayer does not fully and accurately disclose all facts and considerations material to HMRC's decision to approve or withhold approval.

New TMA 1970, Sch 3ZAA, para 7 provides for the content of the plan. *New TMA 1970, Sch 3ZAA para 8* provides that the exit charge deferred under the plan remains due and payable under TMA 1970, s 59B and therefore carries interest as if it had not been entered into. The requisite amount of interest is payable with each instalment. HMRC may not seek payment of any of the deferred charge other than in accordance with the plan and may reimburse to the taxpayer any amounts of the charge paid or paid on account before the plan took effect.

New TMA 1970, Sch 3ZAA, para 9 provides that if a double tax treaty treats a person at any time as resident in a territory outside the EEA, the person shall also be so treated for the purposes of these rules. *New TMA 1970, Sch 3ZAA, para 10* contains definitions.

Schedule 7, para 3 inserts failure to pay an amount of exit charge payable under a CGTEXCPP on time into the penalty provisions of FA 2009, Sch 56. Schedule 7, paras 4–6 make consequential amendments.

Schedule 7, para 7 provides that *new TMA 1970, s 59BB* and *new TMA 1970, Sch 3ZAA* are to have effect in relation to payments of CGT that a person is liable to make as a result of events triggering an exit charge and occurring after 5 April 2019. Schedule 7, paras 3–6 must therefore have effect from 12 February 2019 (Royal Assent).

Section 23 introduces Sch 8, which makes amendments to the existing rules concerning exit-charge payment plans in respect of corporation tax (abbreviated here to 'CTEXCPPs') in TMA 1970, Sch 3ZB. Of most significance is the elimination of the option of the so-called realisation method for paying the deferred corporation tax exit charge. Schedule 8 comprises three Parts and 12 paragraphs in all. Schedule 8 Part 1 (paras 1–8) amends the provisions relating to CTEXCPPs themselves; Part 2 (paras 9 and 10) repeals certain existing postponement provisions; Part 3 (paras 11 and 12) alters the treatment of assets subject to EU exit charges.

Schedule 8, para 1 is introductory. Schedule 8, para 2 limits the application of the eligibility to enter into a CTEXCPP to a company that is resident not in any other EEA state but only in those EEA states ('relevant EEA states') that have concluded an agreement on mutual assistance for the recovery of tax equivalent to the MARD (Council Directive 2001/24/EU).

TMA 1970, Sch 3ZA, para 4 prescribes the circumstances in which a non-resident company with a UK permanent establishment (PE) may enter into a CTEXCPP. One of the necessary circumstances is that a 'PE qualifying event' must have occurred in respect of any of the company's assets or liabilities. A 'PE qualifying event' occurs when three conditions are met:

- an event occurs triggering a deemed disposal and reacquisition of the asset or liability or a valuation of the asset under specified exit-charge provisions;
- the event occurs during the migration accounting period (the accounting period in which the asset or the company transfer their residence from the United Kingdom) or causes the migration accounting period to come to an end; and
- at the time of the event the company is not treated under the terms of a double tax treaty as resident in a territory outside the EEA.

The amendment made by Sch 8, para 3(2) adds a fourth condition: that immediately after the event the asset or liability is held or owed by the company for the purposes of a PE in a relevant EEA state or held or owed by the company otherwise than for the purpose of a PE but the company is resident in a relevant EEA state.

Schedule 8, paras 4 and 5 make amendments consequential on the removal of the option to choose the 'realisation method' of payment under a CTEXCPP.

Hitherto, companies entering into a CTEXCPP have been able to choose between two methods of payment – the 'standard instalment method' under which payment of the deferred tax is made in six equal annual instalments and the realisation method, under which payment is made on the earliest of (a) an actual disposal of the asset or liability; (b) the 10th anniversary of the end of the migration period; and (c) the company's becoming insolvent or entering liquidation or administration or an equivalent procedure under foreign law.

The amendments made by Sch 8 para 6 remove the option for the realisation method and restate the new rules by omitting existing TMA 1970, Sch 3ZA, paras 11–17 and replacing them by *new TMA 1970, Sch 3ZA, paras 11–14*.

New TMA 1970, Sch 3ZA, para 11 provides for a single payment method under a CTEXCPP. That is for payment in six equal annual instalments, with the first being due on the first day after the expiry of nine months following the end of the migration accounting period, and the remainder due on each of the next five anniversaries of that day.

New TMA 1970, Sch 3ZA, para 12 provides that if certain events occur, the whole balance of tax due must be paid when the next instalment would otherwise be due, notwithstanding the terms of the CTEXCPP. Those events are: (a) the company's becoming insolvent or entering liquidation or administration or an equivalent procedure under foreign law; (b) the company's ceasing to be resident in a relevant EEA state without becoming resident in another such state; or (c) the company's failure to pay any instalment due within a 12-month period thereafter.

New TMA 1970, Sch 3ZA, paras 13 and *14* prescribe other 'trigger events', the occurrence of which will cause a further amount of deferred tax to become due and payable. *New TMA 1970, Sch 3ZA, para 13* applies on the first occurrence of a trigger event in relation to an exit-charge asset or liability during the 'instalments period'. The 'instalments period' begins immediately after a company ceases to be resident in the United Kingdom or (in the case of a non-resident company with a UK PE) immediately after the PE qualifying event occurs in relation to an asset or liability and ends on the day on which the final instalment is due. The trigger event at issue in the case of:

(a) the CGT exit charge under TCGA 1992, s 25 with respect to an asset ('a TCGA asset');
(b) trading stock requiring to be valued by virtue of CTA 2009, ss 41(2)(b) and 162 where a company ceases to be within the charge to corporation tax; or
(c) an intangible-asset exit charge under CTA 2009, s 859 on a non-resident company where an asset ceases to be a chargeable intangible asset other than by realisation;

is the disposal of the asset or ceasing to hold it for the purposes of a business carried on by the company in a relevant EEA state and not immediately thereafter coming to hold it for the purposes of another such business.

With respect to the exit charge under CTA 2009, s 334 on an asset or liability representing a loan relationship of a non-resident company which ceases to be held for the purposes of its UK PE and the equivalent exit charge under CTA 2009, s 610 when a right or liability under a derivative contract ceases to be so held (a 'financial asset'), a trigger event occurs when the company either ceases to be a party to the loan relationship or derivative contract or ceases to be such a party for the purposes of a business it carries on in a relevant EEC state and does not immediately thereafter begin to be a party to it for the purposes of another such business.

When any of these trigger events occurs, the amount of deferred tax that becomes due is given by the formula:

$$(A-B)\times\frac{O}{T}$$

where A is the amount of deferred tax attributable to the exit-charge asset or liability, B is the amount of deferred tax that has previously become due on a partial trigger event under *new TMA 1970, Sch 3ZA, para 14* in relation to the same asset or liability, O is the amount of deferred tax outstanding on the occurrence of the event and T is the total amount of deferred tax.

New TMA 1970, Sch 3ZA, para 14 applies on the occurrence of a 'partial trigger event' in relation to an exit-charge asset or liability during an instalments period before any [full] trigger event has occurred in relation to the same asset or liability in that period.

In the case of a TCGA asset or trading stock, a partial trigger event occurs when the company disposes of part, but not all, of the asset. In the case of a financial asset, a partial trigger event occurs when there is a disposal of a right or liability under the loan relationship or derivative contract amounting to a 'related transaction' (as defined in CTA 2009, s 304 or 596, respectively). In the case of an intangible asset, a partial trigger event occurs when there is a transaction resulting in a reduction of its accounting value without its ceasing to be recognised in the company's balance sheet.

The amount of tax due on the occurrence of a partial trigger event is a just and reasonable proportion of the tax that wold have been due on a full trigger event.

Schedule 8, para 7 makes a consequential amendment. Schedule 8, para 8 provides that the amendments made by Sch 8, Pt 1 (except by Sch 8, para 7) are to have effect for accounting periods ending after 31 December 2019.

Schedule 8, para 9 repeals TCGA 1992, s 187, which allows a company that is a 75% subsidiary of a UK-resident parent company to postpone the exit charge on cessation of residence subject to its crystallisation in the hands of the parent if the non-resident company disposes of the asset in question within the next six years. Schedule 8, para 10 repeals CTA 2009, ss 860–862, which perform the same function in respect of a migrating company's chargeable intangible assets.

The repeals have effect for companies ceasing to be resident after 31 December 2019.

Schedule 8, paras 11–12 have effect in the reverse situation where an immigrating company comes within the charge to corporation tax having suffered an exit charge in another EU Member State. They allow the company to 'step up' the value of the relevant asset to its market value at the time of entry into the UK tax system. They have effect in relation to assets that become chargeable assets or chargeable intangible assets at any time after 31 December 2019.

Schedule 8, para 11 inserts *new TCGA 1992, s 184J*. This provides that where a company becomes resident in the United Kingdom or where a non-resident company begins to hold an asset for the purposes of a trade it carries on in the United Kingdom through a PE, so that the asset becomes a chargeable asset and by virtue of that event the company suffers an 'EU exit charge' in relation to the asset, the company is to be treated as having acquired the asset for its market value at the time it became a chargeable asset.

For these purposes, an asset is a chargeable asset if the company would be chargeable to corporation tax on any gain from its disposal. An 'EU exit charge' is a charge to tax under the law of an EU Member State made in accordance with the EU Anti-Tax Avoidance Directive (Directive (EU) 2016/1164).

Schedule 8, para 12 inserts new TCGA 1992, s 863A, which performs exactly the same function in respect of a company's chargeable intangible asset. That is to say, it provides that where a company becomes resident in the United Kingdom or where a non-resident company begins to hold an intangible asset for the purposes of a trade it carries on in the United Kingdom through a PE, so that the asset becomes a chargeable intangible asset and by virtue of that event the company suffers an 'EU exit charge' in relation to the asset, the company is to be treated as having acquired the asset for its market value at the time it became a chargeable intangible asset.

Section 24 makes technical amendments to the meaning of 'UK-related company' under the group-relief provisions of CTA 2010. The amendments are made in connection with the 'migration' of a non-resident company's UK property business from income tax to corporation tax. As a corollary, it has been decided to treat such a non-resident company as a UK member of a group of companies so that it may claim and surrender losses from and to other members of the group.

Accordingly, the existing definitions of 'UK-related company' in both CTA 2010, s 134 (group relief) and s 188CJ (group relief for carried-forward losses), which are identical, are amended to include non-UK resident companies within the charge to corporation tax, rather than, as hitherto, non-resident companies carrying on a trade in the United Kingdom through a permanent establishment. The amendments have retroactive effect from 5 July 2016.

Section 25 introduces Sch 9, which provides for the tax amortisation of goodwill and certain similar assets at a straight-line rate of 6.5% per annum. Schedule 9 consists of seven paragraphs.

Schedule 9, para 1 is introductory and Sch 9, paras 2–5 make consequential amendments. Schedule 9, para 6 inserts *new CTA 2009 Part 8 Chapter 15A* into the chargeable intangible assets regime. *New CTA 2009, Pt 8, Ch 15A* comprises 16 sections (*new CTA 2009, ss 879A–879P*).

New CTA 2009, s 879A introduces the Chapter as containing special rules for bringing debits into account by a company for tax purposes in respect of 'relevant assets'. Those assets are:

- goodwill in a business or part of a business;
- an intangible fixed asset that consists of information relating to customers or potential customers of a business or part of a business;
- an intangible fixed asset that consists of a relationship (whether contractual or not) between a person carrying on a business and one or more customers of that business or part of that business;

- an unregistered trade mark or other sign used in the course of a business or part of a business and;
- a licence or other right in respect of an asset within any of the above.

New CTA 2009, s 879B provides that where a company acquires or creates a relevant asset after 31 March 2019, it is to be treated as having made an election under CTA 2009, s 730 to write down the cost of the asset for tax purposes at a fixed rate. That rate is set at 6.5%, subject to amendment at any time by regulations.

New CTA 2009, s 879C prohibits the bringing into account of a debit by way of amortisation (under CTA 2009, Pt 8, Ch 3) in respect of a 'pre-FA 2019 relevant asset', as defined by *new CTA 2009, ss 879D–879H*. A debit that the company brings into account on the realisation of a pre-FA 2019 relevant asset under CTA 2009, Pt 8, Ch 4 is to be treated as a non-trading debit.

New CTA 2009, s 879D defines the first case in which a relevant asset is a pre-FA 2019 asset. This is where the company acquired or created the asset in the period from 8 July 2015 to 31 March 2019 and the asset was a chargeable intangible asset of the company at any time in the period from 29 October 2018 to 31 March 2019.

New CTA 2009, s 879E defines the second case in which a relevant asset is a pre-FA 2019 asset. This is where another company:

- acquired or created the asset in the period from 8 July 2015 to 31 March 2019;
- the asset was a chargeable intangible asset of that other company at any time in the period from 29 October 2018 to 31 March 2019; and
- the company in question acquired the asset after 31 March 2019 from a related party (as defined), except in circumstances labelled 'Case A' and 'Case B'.

Case A is where the company in question acquired the asset from another company that was within the charge to corporation tax at the time and the asset was not a pre-FA 2019 asset of that other company immediately before the acquisition.

Case B is where the company in question acquired the asset from an intermediary that itself acquired the asset after 31 March 2019 from a third person who:

- was not at the time of the intermediary's acquisition a related party of the intermediary or (where the intermediary is not a company) of a company of which the intermediary was a related person; and
- is not, at the time of the acquisition by the company in question a related party of that company

New *CTA 2009, s 879F* defines the third case in which a relevant asset is a pre-FA 2019 asset. This is where:

- the relevant asset was created after 28 October 2018;
- the company acquired the relevant asset after 31 March 2019 from a person ('the transferor') who was a related party at the time of the acquisition;
- the value of the asset derives wholly or partly from another asset; and
- that other asset meets the 'preserved-status condition' (as defined in new *CTA 2009, s 879G*).

Where the value of the asset derives partly from another asset, it is to be treated for these purposes as if it comprised two separate assets, one representing the derived value and the other the remaining value.

New CTA 2009, s 879G provides for two instances in which the preserved-status condition is met. The first is where the other asset was:

- acquired or created by a company in the period from 8 July 2015 to 31 March 2019; and
- a chargeable intangible asset of that company at any time in the period from 29 October 2018 to 31 March 2019 when that company and the company in question were related parties or that company and the transferor were related parties.

The second instance is where the asset was a pre-FA 2019 asset of a company (A) at any time in the period from 1 April 2019 until its acquisition by the company in question from the transferor at a time when A and the company in question, or A and the transferor, were related parties.

New *CTA 2009, s 879H* defines the fourth case in which a relevant asset is a pre-FA 2019 asset. This is where the company in question acquired the asset after 31 March 2019 as a consequence directly or indirectly or otherwise in connection with the disposal of a relevant asset by another person and that asset would have been a pre-FA 2019 relevant asset of the company in question had the other person transferred it to the company in question at the time of the disposal.

New CTA 2009, s 879I provides for another bar on tax amortisation of a relevant asset. In this instance, the bar also applies to bringing a debit into account under CTA 2009, Pt 8, Ch 15 on a change in accounting policy. The bar applies if the company in question:

- either acquires the asset after 31 March 2019 otherwise than as part of the acquisition of a business;
- or does acquire it as part of the acquisition of a business but does not acquire any 'qualifying IP assets' of the business for continuous use in the course of the business.

A debit that the company brings into account on the realisation of the relevant asset under CTA 2009, Pt 8, Ch 4 is to be treated as a non-trading debit. *New CTA 2009, s 879J* defines 'qualifying IP asset' as an intangible fixed asset that meets both of two conditions. The first condition is that the asset is a patent, registered design, copyright or design right or plant breeder's right or a right under Plant Varieties Act 1997, s 7 or a similar foreign right or a licence or other right in respect of the preceding assets. The second condition is that the asset is, in the hands of the company in question, not to any extent an excluded asset under CTA 2009, Pt 8, Ch 10 nor a pre-FA 2002 asset (as defined by CTA 2009, s 881).

A further bar on tax amortisation of a relevant asset is introduced by *new CTA 2009, s 879K*. As with *new CTA 2009, s 879I*, the bar also extends to bringing a debit into account under CTA 2009, Pt 8, Ch 15 on a change in accounting policy. The bar applies where the company acquires the relevant asset after 31 March 2019 directly or indirectly from an individual or a firm ('the transferor') and the 'related-party condition' is met but the 'third-party acquisition condition' *is not met*.

The 'related party condition is met at any time where the transferor (if an individual) is a related party of the company at that time or (if a firm) where any individual who is a member of the transferor is a related party at that time.

The third-party acquisition condition is met where (if the relevant asset is goodwill) the transferor acquired all or part of the 'relevant business' in one or more 'third-party acquisitions' as part of which the transferor acquired goodwill and the relevant asset is acquired by the company as part of an acquisition of all the relevant business. If the relevant asset is not goodwill, on the other hand, the third-party acquisition condition is met where the transferor acquired the relevant asset in a third-party acquisition and the relevant asset is acquired by the company as part of an acquisition of all the relevant business.

A debit that the company brings into account on the realisation of the relevant asset under CTA 2009, Pt 8, Ch 4 is to be treated as a non-trading debit.

New CTA 2009, s 879L defines 'relevant business' and 'third-party acquisition'. The 'relevant business' is that business or part of that business with respect to which an asset is a relevant asset, as defined in *new CTA 2009, s 879A*. A 'third-party acquisition' is, essentially an acquisition by the transferor from a non-related party.

New CTA 2009, ss 879M–879O impose partial restrictions on amortisation and other debits. *New CTA 2009, s 879M* provides that these restrictions are to apply in cases where the relevant asset is acquired after 31 March 2019 as part of the acquisition of a business under which the company also acquires 'qualifying IP assets' (as defined in new CTA 2009, s 879J) for use continuously in the course of the business and the expenditure incurred by the company on the acquisition of the asset concerned and any other relevant assets ('B') is more than six times the expenditure ('A') it incurs on the acquisition of the qualifying IP assets (or, mathematically, where $6A < B$). However, if debits in respect of the asset already fall to be restricted under either *new CTA 2009, s 879C* (because it is a pre-FA 2019 relevant asset) or *s 879K* (acquisitions from related parties), those provisions have precedence.

New CTA 2009, s 879N provides for a further instance where partial restrictions on debits are to apply. These resemble the restrictions imposed by *new CTA 2009, s 879K* on acquisitions from related parties but are not mirror images of one another. They apply where the company acquires the relevant asset after 31 March 2019 directly or indirectly from an individual or a firm ('the transferor') , the 'related-party condition' is met *and* the 'third-party acquisition condition' is met, but the expenditure ('B') incurred by the company on the acquisition of the relevant asset and capitalised for accounting purposes, or recognised in determining the company's taxable profit without being capitalised, is greater than the 'relevant accounting value' of third-party acquisitions ('A'). The related-party condition and the third-party acquisition condition are as defined by *new CTA 2009, s 879K*.

Where the relevant asset is goodwill, the 'relevant accounting value' of third-party acquisitions is the notional accounting value of the goodwill acquired under previous third-party acquisitions and where the relevant asset is not goodwill, the 'relevant accounting value' of third-party acquisitions is the notional accounting value of the relevant asset. Notional accounting value is what the accounting value of an asset would have been in GAAP-compliant accounts drawn up by the transferor immediately before the relevant asset was acquired by the company on the basis that the relevant business (see *new CTA 2009, s 879L*) was a going concern.

However, if debits in respect of the asset already fall to be restricted under either *new CTA 2009, s 879C* (because it is a pre-FA 2019 relevant asset) or *s 879I* (no business or no qualifying IP assets acquired), those provisions have precedence.

New CTA 2009, s 879O quantifies the partial restriction where either of new *CTA 2009, s 879M* or *879N* applies. In the case of amortisation debits under CTA 2009, Pt 8, Ch 3 or debits on a change of accounting policy under CTA 2009, Pt 8, Ch 15, the debit is restricted to D x RA, where D is the debit that would otherwise be brought into account (disregarding any previous applications of this section) and RA is 'the relevant amount'. Where only *new CTA 2009, s 879M* applies, RA is 6A/B (see under that section); where only *new CTA 2009, s 879N* applies, RA is A/B (see under that section). Where both sections apply, RA is the product of the two fractions.

Where the company needs to bring a debit into account in these circumstances under CTA 2009, Pt 8, Ch 4, due to a realisation of the asset, it must bring two debits into account. The realisation debit is to be D x RA, where D is again the debit that would otherwise be brought into account under that Chapter (disregarding any previous applications of this section) and RA is as above. The company must also bring into account a non-trading debit of D – TD, where TD is the amount of the restricted Chapter 4 debit (ie what remains of D after deducting the restricted realisation debit).

New CTA 2009, s 879P defines when a company can be said to acquire a relevant asset if it does so under an unconditional contractual obligation. In such a case, the date of acquisition is taken to be the later of the date on which the company became subject to that obligation and the date on which the obligation became unconditional.

Schedule 9, para 7 provides that the amendment made by Sch 9 have effect in relation to accounting periods beginning after 31 March 2019, with provision for straddling periods.

Section 26 makes further amendments to the intangible fixed assets regime of CTA 2009, Pt 8, to provide that the degrouping charge under CTA 2009, s 780 is not to apply where the company holding the transferred asset leaves a group as a result of a 'relevant share disposal'. The intention behind the amendments is not to discourage commercially motivated mergers and acquisitions. The exception is enacted by *new CTA 2009, s 782A*, inserted by s 26(3), which also defines a 'relevant share disposal' as a disposal of shares in respect of which the company would not be chargeable to corporation tax in respect of any gain accruing on the disposal because it is a disposal qualifying for the significant-shareholdings exemption under TCGA 1992, Sch 7AC, para 1, providing only that the disposal is not part of an arrangement for the recipient of the shares to dispose of them in turn to a third party.

Amendments made to CTA 2009, s 785 clarify the circumstances in which a degrouping charge arises under CTA 2009, s 785(3) (crystallisation of a deferred degrouping charge where a company leaves a group because the principal company becomes a member of a second group; the charge crystallises if within six years of that event, the company holding the transferred asset leaves the second group). They also provide that the degrouping charge under CTA 2009, s 785 is not to apply if the company leaves the group as a result of a relevant share disposal under *new CTA 2009, s 782A*. These amendments have effect for relevant events occurring after 6 November 2018.

Section 27 introduces Sch 10, which amends the legislation on carried-forward losses introduced by F(No 2)A 2017 with effect from 1 April 2017. Schedule 10 comprises 32 paragraphs.

Schedule 10, paras 1–6, **13** and **14** omit the need to modify various provisions in relation to insurance companies carrying on basic life-assurance and general annuity business (BLAGAB). These omissions are consequential on the consolidation and modification of how the various loss restrictions and restrictions on the use of carried-forward losses apply to these companies. Schedule 10, para 7 omits CTA 2010, s 269ZE, which has hitherto determined how restrictions on deductions from total profits apply to insurance companies.

New CTA 2010, s 269ZFA, inserted by Sch 10, para 8, contains the new definition of 'relevant profits', by reference to which the maximum deduction from total profits may be made in respect of losses. The (different) definition was previously to be found in CTA 2010, s 269ZD(5), omitted by Sch 10, para 6(4).

'Relevant profits' of a company for an accounting period are its 'qualifying profits' for that period, less its 'deductions allowance' for that period. The deductions allowance is as defined in CTA 2010, s 269ZD(6). 'Qualifying profits' are the company's modified total profits, less the sum of any amounts ('in-year reliefs') that could be relieved against those total profits on the assumption that the total profits are to be calculated with the modifications set out in CTA 2010, s 269ZF(4). Those modifications are to ignore certain income and refrain from making certain deductions. For a full explanation of these modifications, readers should refer to the notes on CTA 2010, s 269ZF in the *Finance Acts Handbook 2017*, page 183.

New CTA 2010, s 269ZFB, inserted by Sch 10, para 9, constitutes the consolidated and modified provision for determining the taxable total profits for an accounting period of an insurance company carrying on basic life-assurance and general annuity business. Under CTA 2010, s 269ZD(7), the cap on relevant deductions that a company may make from total profits in arriving at its taxable total profits does not apply where the company's total profits (as modified) are not greater than nil. For insurance companies carrying on BLAGAB, total profits as modified are (a) not to ignore income from distributions referable to BLAGAB unless they are treated as distributions solely by virtue of an election under CTA 2009, s 931R to treat distributions that would otherwise be exempt as not exempt and (b) not to ignore any I – E income, except for the policyholders' share of that income.

Similarly, references in the new definition of relevant profits in *new CTA 2010, s 269ZFA* to modified total profits and to the amounts that could be relieved against those total profits are themselves to be modified as explained in the previous paragraph.

Schedule 10, paras 10, **11** and **16–19** make amendments consequential on the omission by Sch 10, para 20 of FA 2012, ss 124D and 124E, relating to insurance companies.

Schedule 10, para 12 amends CTA 2010, s 269ZV so as to prevent the allocation to a company of a share of the deductions allowance from a group of which it is the ultimate parent (as defined by CTA 2010, s 269ZZB(3)) if it is also a member of another group.

Schedule 10, para 20 omits FA 2012, ss 124D and 124E. These were provisions inserted in the insurance companies code by F(No 2)A 2017, Sch 4, paras 24 and 26, to align the provisions for relief for BLAGAB trade losses against total profits with the reform of corporate loss reliefs generally. As a consequence of the modifications now made by Sch 10 to the treatment of insurance companies with BLAGAB described above, both CTA 2010, s 124D, which restricts the total amount of deductions an insurance company may make in any later period to the 'relevant maximum', and CTA 2010, s 124E, which excludes the shock loss of a Solvency 2 insurance company from those restrictions, are now redundant.

Schedule 10, para 21 substitutes a *new CTA 2010, s 45G*, which provides for the allocation of terminal loss relief to periods falling partly within and partly outside the three-year terminal-loss period. The existing CTA 2010, s 45G, inserted by F(No 2)A 2017 Sch 4, para 11, simply provides for a pro-rata allocation of the profits available for set-off. So, for example, if only three months of a particular 12-month accounting period ('the straddling period') fall within the three years ending with the end of the terminal period, the proportion of 'relevant profits' of the straddling period available for terminal-loss relief are three-twelfths. 'Relevant profits' are as defined in CTA 2010, s 45F(7), namely the company's total profits where the loss was carried forward under CTA 2010, s 45A ('post-1 April 2017 trade losses) but trading profits where the loss was carried forward under CTA 2010, s 45 ('pre-1 April 2017 trade losses) or CTA 2010, s 45B (losses for which s 45A is not available). Because pro-rata trading profits and pro-rata total profits were calculated separately, this allowed for a total deduction greater than the appropriate pro-rata amount of total profits of the straddling period. The *new CTA 2010, s 45G* accordingly imposes a further cap, namely that the sum of deductions from trading profits and from total profits may not exceed the appropriate pro-rata amount of total profits.

Schedule 10, paras 22–25 address the treatment of carried-forward losses. Schedule 10, para 22 is introductory. Schedule 10, para 23 amends CTA 2010, s 188BG(3) by adding prior-period BLAGAB trade losses carried forward under FA 2012 s 124A(2) or 124C(3) to the types of loss that a Solvency 2 insurance company may not surrender in a claim for group relief to the extent that the loss is a shock loss.

CTA 2010, s 188DB places a general limitation on all group-relief claims for carried-forward losses under CTA 2010, s 188CB. These are claims where the companies are in a group relationship or where the claimant company is owned by a consortium and the surrendering company is a member of the consortium or a member of the same group as the link company. It provides that the amount of group relief for carried-forward losses to be given on a claim under CTA 2010, s 188CB is to be limited to the smaller of (a) the unused part of the surrenderable amounts (as defined in CTA 2010, s 188DC) and (b) the difference between (i) the claimant company's 'relevant maximum for the overlapping period' (as defined in CTA 2010, s 188DD) and (ii) the amount of previously claimed group relief for carried-forward losses for the overlapping period (as defined in CTA 2010, s 188DE). CTA 2010, s 188DD provides a limit in these circumstances on the amount of profits against which group relief for carried-forward losses may be allowed; that limit is the company's 'relevant profits', where these are less than the amount of the company's deductions allowance (as calculated under CTA 2010, s 269ZD(5)).

The amendment now made to CTA 2010, s 188DD by Schedule 10, para 24 substitutes 'qualifying profits' for 'relevant profits'. 'Qualifying profits' are as defined in *new CTA 2010, s 269ZFA* (inserted by Sch 10, para 8).

Schedule 10, para 25 makes the same amendments in respect of claims for carried-forward losses under CTA 2010, s 188CC. These are claims under consortium conditions 3 or 4, i e where the surrendering company is owned by a consortium and the claimant company is either a member of the consortium or a member of the link company's group.

Schedule 10, paras 26–30 correct references to the anti-avoidance provisions on transferred trades contained in CTA 2010 Part 22 Chapter 1 to include references to that Chapter as amended and expanded by F(No 2)A 2017, Sch 4, paras 61–68 in the following provisions: CTA 2010, s 357JI(2), which deals with transfers of trade without a change of ownership where the Northern Ireland rate of corporation tax (yet to take effect) is involved and CTA 2010, s 676, which restricts the use of trading losses in certain circumstances on a change in ownership as part of a company reconstruction. Schedule 10, para 28 also adds losses carried forward under CTA 2010, ss 45A, 45B, 303B, 303C and 303D to the losses restricted under that section.

Schedule 10, para 29 amends CTA 2010, s 676AF, which imposes restriction on the use of carried-forward post-1 April losses on a change of ownership. The amendment prevents losses incurred by another company ('the predecessor company') and transferred to the company whose trade is subsequently transferred ('the transferee company') in an accounting period before the change of ownership from being deducted under any of CTA 2010, ss 45A, 45F or 303C (as applied by virtue of CTA 2010, Pt 22, Ch 1) from 'affected profits' (as defined in CTA 2010, s 676AE) arising after the change.

Schedule 10, para 30 makes a similar amendment to CTA 2010, s 676BC. That section restricts relief under CTA 2010, ss 45A, 45F and 303C and FA 2012 s 124B for trade losses made by a company in the trade before a change in its ownership. In the circumstances defined in the section, a loss made in an accounting period beginning before the change in ownership may not be deducted under any of the sections mentioned above from so much of the company's total profits of an accounting period ending after the change in ownership as represents the 'relevant gain' (as defined in CTA 2010, s 676BE). As now amended, CTA 2010, s 676BC provides also that losses incurred by the predecessor company and transferred to the transferee company before the change in ownership may not be deducted under any of CTA 2010, ss 45A, 45F or 303C (as applied by virtue of CTA 2010, Pt 22, Ch 1) from so much of the total profits of the company arising in an accounting period after the change as represent the relevant gain.

Schedule 10, para 31 corrects technical errors in CTA 2010, s 730C.

Schedule 10, para 32 provides that the amendments made by Sch 10 are to have effect in relation to accounting periods beginning on or after a relevant date. That date is 1 April 2017 for the amendments made by Sch 10, paras 24 and 25; 6 July 2018 for the amendments made by Sch 10, paras 1–11, 13 and 14; and 1 April 2019 as regards the remaining amendments.

Section 28 introduces Sch 11, which amends the legislation in TIOPA 2010 Part 10 relating to the corporate-interest restriction, introduced a bare two years ago. Schedule 11 comprises 27 paragraphs.

Schedule 11, para 1 is introductory. Schedule 11, para 2 inserts *new TIOPA 2010, s 391A*. This provides that where interest or other financing costs are capitalised in the carrying value of an intangible fixed asset for the purposes of the intangible assets regime in CTA 2009 Part 8, the exclusivity rule in CTA 2009, s 906(1) is not to have effect with regard to amounts of interest brought into account under the loan-relationships or derivative-contracts rule, so that these amounts are not to be overlooked in determining tax-interest expense or tax-interest income.

Schedule 11, para 3 inserts *new TIOPA 2010, s 395A*. This provides that where, as part of a 'qualifying takeover', one company ceases to be the ultimate parent of one worldwide group ('the old group') and another company becomes the ultimate parent of a new worldwide group, the old group's interest allowance may be transferred across to the new group. A 'qualifying takeover' is one as a result of which the change of ownership of the ultimate parent of the old group may be disregarded under CTA 2010, s 724A.

Schedule 11, para 4 inserts *new TIOPA 2010, s 400A*, which is the parallel provision to *new TIOPA 2010, s 395A* and allows the carry-forward from the old group to the new group of the old group's excess debt cap for the period of account ending immediately before the qualifying takeover.

TIOPA 2010, s 410 defines the net group-interest expense of a worldwide group for a period of account ('the relevant period of account') as A – B, where A is the sum of 'relevant expense amounts' (payments of interest etc) recognised in the group's financial statements as items of profit or loss and B is the sum of 'relevant income amounts' (receipts of interest etc) recognised in the group's financial statements as items of profit or loss. A is to include capitalised expenses in relation to an asset *other than* a 'relevant asset' (defined in TIOPA 2010, s 417) where part or all of the asset's carrying value is written down, and B is to include capitalised income in the same circumstances. The amendment now made to TIOPA 2010, s 410 by Sch 11, para 5 makes it clear that any amounts of capitalised expenses or capitalised income that would have been so included if the section had applied to relevant assets *are not to be included* under TIOPA 2010, s 410.

TIOPA 2010, s 413 defines 'adjusted net group-interest expense' ('ANGIE') of a worldwide group, used in the calculation under TIOPA 2010, s 400 of the fixed-ratio debt cap, for a period of account as A + B – C, where A is the net group-interest expense, B the sum of 'upward adjustments' and C the sum of 'downward adjustments'. Upward adjustments and downward adjustments largely adjust for capitalised interest and other items included in the carrying value of assets or liabilities. The intention is that capitalised interest is included in ANGIE when capitalised and excluded when written down. The amendments now made to TIOPA 2010, s 413 by Sch 11, para 6 restrict those assets and liabilities to 'non-financial' assets and liabilities. Assets and liabilities are 'non-financial' if they are not a financial asset or liability for accounting purposes or, in the case of a liability, where it is in respect of a share issued by a company.

TIOPA 2010, s 423 provides for the effect of an interest-allowance (alternative calculation) election on the calculation of ANGIE. When this election, made under TIOPA 2010, Sch 7A para 16, is in force, the calculation of ANGIE under TIOPA 2010, s 413 (see immediately above) is modified, by deleting the provisions concerning capitalised interest. However, the amendments now made by Sch 11, para 7 ensure that where a 'GAAP-taxable asset' (as defined) is also a 'relevant asset' (as defined in TIOPA 2010, s 417), upward adjustments and downward adjustments are to include amounts written down in respect of previously capitalised relevant expense and income amounts.

Schedule 11, para 8 makes further tweaks to TIOPA 2010, s 413. The calculation of the upward adjustment is now to include so-called release credits (credits on release of connected companies' debts) that CTA 2009, ss 358 or 359 do not allow to be brought into account for the purposes of corporation tax. Similarly, the calculation of the downward adjustment is now to include 'release debits' (debits for impaired or released connected companies' debts) that CTA 2009, s 354 does not allow to be brought into account for the purposes of corporation tax.

Schedule 11, para 9 inserts *new TIOPA 2010, s 424A*. This provides that when an interest allowance (alternative calculation) election is in force, the calculation under TIOPA 2010, s 416 of group-EBITDA should be adjusted to exclude from the group's profit before tax amounts representing employee remuneration remaining unpaid nine months after the end of the period of account in which they are recognised. As a corollary, when those amounts come to be paid, they are to be included in the group's profit before tax for the period of account in which they are paid.

Schedule 11, para 10 amends TIOPA 2010, s 426, which provides for the effect of an interest-allowance (alternative calculation) election on the calculation of the group's profit before tax with respect to changes in accounting policy. When this election is in force, the financial statements of the group are to be subject to the adjustments that would be made to them under the existing UK provisions on change of accounting policy if the group were a company within the charge to corporation tax. The amendments now made by Sch 11, para 10 ensure that these rules apply in relation to property businesses also. They also make it clear that for the purposes of the interest-restriction rules, only actual changes of accounting policy need to be taken into account.

Schedule 11, para 11 amends TIOPA 2010, s 427, which provides for the adjustments that need to be made when an interest allowance (non-consolidated investment) election, made under new TIOPA 2010, Sch 7A para 17, is in force. The adjusted net group-interest expense (ANGIE) of the worldwide group is to be treated as increased by the appropriate proportion of the ANGIE of each associated worldwide group. The 'qualifying net group-interest expense of the worldwide group' (QNGIE), as defined in TIOPA 2010, s 414, is to be treated as increased by the appropriate proportion of the QNGIE of each associated worldwide group. The group-EBITDA of the worldwide group is to be treated as increased by the appropriate proportion of the group-EBITDA of each associated worldwide group. The 'appropriate proportion' is the proportion of the profits or losses of the associated worldwide group to which the worldwide group is entitled. The amendment now made by Sch 11, para 11 provides that these increases are to be made as part of the single calculation under TIOPA 2010, ss 413(1) and 414(1).

Schedule 11, para 12 amends TIOPA 2010, s 433, which sets out the requirements for a company to be a 'qualifying infrastructure company. These are:

(a) meeting the public-infrastructure income test;
(b) meeting the public-infrastructure assets test;

(c) that the company is fully taxed in the United Kingdom; and
(d) that the company makes an election.

Test (b) is met if all or all but an insignificant proportion of the total value of the company's assets derives from (1) tangible assets related to qualifying infrastructure activities; (2) service-concession arrangements in respect of assets related to qualifying infrastructure activities; (3) financial assets to which the company is a party in order for it or another qualifying infrastructure company to carry out qualifying infrastructure activities; (4) shares in a qualifying infrastructure company; or (5) loan relationships or other financing arrangements to which the only other party is a qualifying infrastructure company.

The amendment now made by Sch 11, para 12 adds two further ways of meeting the public-infrastructure assets test (Test (b) above). These are that all or all but an insignificant proportion of the total value of the company's assets derives from (6) assets held for a pension scheme providing benefits for persons employees in carrying on qualifying infrastructure activities by the company or another associated qualifying infrastructure company or (7) assets in respect of deferred tax to the extent this is attributable to qualifying infrastructure activities carried on by the company or another associated qualifying infrastructure company.

TIOPA 2010, s 438 provides that certain amounts arising to a qualifying infrastructure company in an accounting period are not to be regarded as tax-interest amounts. These include amounts in respect of a 'qualifying old loan relationship'. In all cases, amounts cannot be excluded unless the recourse of each creditor is limited to income or assets of a qualifying infrastructure company or shares in or debt issued by a qualifying infrastructure company. TIOPA 2010, s 439 defines a qualifying old loan relationship as one the company entered into before 13 May 2016, at which time at least 80% of the total value of the company's future 'qualifying infrastructure receipts' for the qualifying period was highly predictable by reference to qualifying public contracts. 'Qualifying infrastructure receipts' are defined as receipts arising from qualifying infrastructure activities carried on by the company and the appropriate proportion of the receipts arising from qualifying infrastructure activities carried on by another company in which the first company has an interest by way of shares and loans. Schedule 11, para 13 amends the definition of 'qualifying infrastructure receipts' in TIOPA 2010, s 439(3) to exclude amounts representing the reimbursement of expenses incurred by either company.

Schedule 11, para 14 amends TIOPA 2010, s 452, which applies to REITs, and provides that the exempt property-rental business and the residual business of the REIT are to be treated as separate members of the worldwide group. In addition, the assumption is made that the profits of the property-rental business are not exempt from corporation tax for the purposes of calculating tax-interest and tax EBITDA. It prescribes how the restricted interest is to be allocated between these companies and facilitates the carry-forward of excess amounts. The amendments made by Sch 11, para 14 clarify that CTA 2010, s 599 (which prescribes how the profits of a REIT are to be calculated) is not to apply in determining what amounts relating to a REIT should be included in calculating the corporate-interest restriction (CIR). This has the result that interest or other financing amounts in the REIT's property-rental business are to be subject to the CIR rules. *New TIOPA 2010, s 452*(*4A*), inserted by Sch 11, para 14(3), provides that where an amount is charged on the notional residual-business company to corporation tax under CTA 2010, s 543 (because the REIT's interest-cover ratio has fallen below 1.25), that amount is to be treated as a tax-interest income amount under TIOPA 2010, s 385, thereby avoiding a double restriction. Finally, another amendment provides expressly that any allocated disallowance for the property-rental business under the CIR rules must be taken into account under CTA 2010, s 530 to determine the amount that the REIT must distribute.

Schedule 11, paras 15–18 amend the rules for interest-restriction returns in TIOPA 2010, Sch 7A. Schedule 11, para 15 extends the time limit for appointing, or revoking the appointment of, a reporting company from six months to 12 months. Schedule 11, para 16 ensures that the extension of the appointment or revocation period cannot further delay the filing date for the return. Schedule 11, para 17 inserts new TIOPA 2010, Sch 7A para 7A, which provides that where there is a takeover, so that a period of account of the worldwide group ends solely because the ultimate parent company becomes a member of a different worldwide group within 12 months of the beginning of the period of account in question, the filing date need be no earlier than 24 months after the beginning of that period. Schedule 11, para 18 empowers HMRC to specify additional information to be included in an interest-restriction return.

Schedule 11, paras 19–21 make consequential amendments. Schedule 11, paras 22–26 provide different commencement dates. Schedule 11, para 27 provides that groups that made an interest-allowance (alternative calculation) election before 7 November 2018 in respect of any period of account ending before that date may revoke the election at any time before 12 May 2019 (three months after the day of Royal Assent). This measure is intended to help groups that might otherwise be disadvantaged as a result of the introduction of *new TIOPA 2010, s 424A* (employee remuneration unpaid for more than nine months) by Sch 11, para 9.

Section 29 introduces Sch 12, which amends the loan-relationships legislation in CTA 2009 Part 5 to prevent a tax mismatch where two linked loan relationships would otherwise be taxed on a different basis (eg because one falls within the hybrid-mismatch rules). Schedule 12 is a comparatively short Schedule, comprising just five paragraphs.

Schedule 12, para 1 inserts *new CTA 2009, s 352B.* This applies where a company has two loan relationships, one to which CTA 2009, s 349 applies, ie it is a 'connected companies relationship' to which the amortised-cost basis applies, and the other (referred to as 'the external loan relationship') to which CTA 2009, s 349 does not apply and which is a debtor relationship dealt with on the basis of fair-value accounting, and there is a 'qualifying link' between the external loan relationship and one or more of the company's other loan relationships. A 'connected companies relationship' is defined in CTA 2009, s 348 as a debtor relationship of a company with a connection to another company that stands in the position of a creditor as respects the debt in question or as a creditor relationship of a company with a connection to another company that stands in the position of a debtor as respects the debt in question.

A 'qualifying link' exists where each of the linked relationships is a connected companies relationship to which CTA 2009, s 349 applies and, taking both or all of the loan relationships together, the money received by the company under the external loan relationship is wholly or mainly used to lend money under those other loan relationships.

In these circumstances, the debits and credits that are to be brought into account under the loan-relationships rules in respect of the external loan relationship must be determined on an amortised-cost basis (as for the first relationship).

If, furthermore, the company has a hedging relationship between a derivative contract ('the hedging instrument') and the liability under the external loan relationship, the company may adjust the carrying value of the external loan relationship when applying the amortised-cost basis on the assumption that the hedging instrument is a fair-value hedge of the loan relationship.

Schedule 12, para 2 makes a consequential amendment. Schedule 12, para 3 provides that the amendments made by Sch 12 are to have effect for accounting periods beginning after 31 December 2018, with provision for straddling periods. Schedule 12, para 4 provides that where the tax-adjusted carrying value for the loan relationship as at 31 December 2018 differs from its tax-adjusted carrying value on 1 January 2019, the difference is to be brought into account in the accounting period beginning on 1 January 2019 as a debit or credit in the same way as a debit or credit is brought into account in determining the company's profit or loss for that period in accordance with GAAP.

Schedule 12, para 5 empowers HM Treasury to amend *new CTA 2009, s 352B* by regulations at any time before 1 January 2020.

Capital allowances

Section 30 paves the way for the introduction of the new capital allowance for construction expenditure on buildings and structures by way of regulations amending CAA 2001 where (a) expenditure is incurred after 28 October 2018 on the construction of a building; (b) the building is in 'qualifying use'; and (c) the expenditure incurred on the construction of the building, or other expenditure, is 'qualifying expenditure'. The section goes on to provide in some detail what the regulations must contain and provide for.

Section 31 reduces the rate of writing-down allowance on special-rate expenditure under CAA 2001, Pt 2, Ch 10A from 8% to 6% and makes consequential amendments. The reduction is to have effect from 1 April 2019 for the purposes of corporation tax and from 6 April 2019 for the purposes of income tax. For chargeable periods straddling those dates, a hybrid time-apportioned rate applies.

Section 32 makes yet another amendment to the annual investment allowance, despite the promise of stability made when setting the limit at £200,000 *indefinitely* by virtue of F(No 2)A 2015. Nevertheless, s 32 provides for another temporary increase in the maximum allowance to £1 million, for the two years ending 31 December 2020. **Schedule 13**, introduced by s 32(2), provides for straddling-period calculations. Schedule 13 has just three paragraphs.

Schedule 13, para 1 deals with chargeable periods straddling 1 January 2019, when the maximum increases. The straddling period is to be divided into two notional periods, one ending on 31 December 2018 (maximum allowance £200,000) and the other beginning on 1 January 2019 (maximum allowance £1,000,000). The maximum allowance for the straddling period is to be the sum of the maxima for the separate periods, but the maximum allowance for expenditure in the first deemed period is not to exceed what it would have been had the increase to £1,000,000 not been made.

Schedule 13, para 2 deals with chargeable periods straddling 1 January 2021, when the maximum falls back to £200,000. The straddling period is to be divided into two notional periods, one ending on 31 December 2020 (maximum allowance £1,000,000) and the other beginning on 1 January 2021 (maximum allowance £200,000). The maximum allowance for the straddling period is to be the sum of the maxima for the separate periods, but the maximum allowance for expenditure in the the second deemed period is not to exceed the maximum for that second period.

Schedule 13, para 3 provides for the case where restrictions apply under CAA 2001, s 51K on the operation of the annual investment allowance.

Section 33 abolishes the 100% first-year allowances under CAA 2001, ss 45A–45C for energy-saving plant or machinery and under CAA 2001, ss 45H–45J for environmentally beneficial plant or machinery, with effect from 1 April 2020 (corporation tax) or 6 April 2020 (income tax). It also abolishes from that date the associated tax credits under CAA 2001, s 262A and Sch A1. Consequential amendments are made to other provisions.

Section 34, by contrast, extends the life of the first-year allowance under CAA 2001, s 45EA for electric-vehicle charge points, from 31 March or 5 April 2019 to 31 March 2023 or 5 April 2023, respectively.

Section 35 amends CAA 2001, ss 21(4) and 22(4) to ensure that the exceptions provided by CAA 2001, s 23 from the exclusions from plant and machinery allowances under CAA 2001 Part 2 for the expenditure on buildings, structures etc listed in CAA 2001, ss 21 and 22 are not to enable allowances to be claimed on costs relating to the excluded assets. The amendments are deemed always to have had effect but will not affect claims made before 29 October 2018.

Leases

Section 36 introduces Sch 14, which amends the provisions in CAA 2001, ITTOIA 2005, ITA 2007, CTA 2010 and TIOPA 2010 dealing with leases, to ensure continuity following the adoption of IFRS (International Financial Reporting Standard) 16 or FRS (Financial Reporting Standard) 101. Schedule 14 has 19 paragraphs, divided into three Parts. Part 1 (paras 1–6) deals with the taxation of finance leases; Part 2 (paras 7–10) deals with the treatment for capital allowance purposes of long funding leases; Part 3 (paras 11–19) deals with the effect of changes to accounting standards and related tax adjustments.

These changes are necessary because entities applying IFRSs or FRS 101 are required to adopt IFRS 16 (the leasing standard) for periods of account beginning after 31 December 2018 and, under IFRS 16, the distinction between an operating lease and a finance lease is removed for lessees (but not lessors). Under IFRS 16, lessees are required to recognise all leases on their balance sheet, except for a few excluded leases. Under FRS 102, the main financial reporting standard applicable in the United Kingdom and the Republic of Ireland, the distinction is maintained.

Schedule 14, para 1 amends CAA 2001, Pt 2, namely ss 67, 70E, 70YA, 70YI and 228J. CAA 2001, s 67 broadly provides that persons who are lessees under a finance lease or purchasing an asset under a hire-purchase contract are to be treated for the purpose of capital allowances as the owner of the asset and hence entitled to claim capital allowances. The amendment made to CAA 2001, s 67 by Sch 14 para 1(2) inserts reference to a 'right-of-use lease' in addition to a finance lease. A 'right-of-use lease' is defined in CAA 2001, s 70YI (as amended by Sch 14, para 1(5)) as a lease in respect of which a 'right-of-use asset' falls or would fall to be recognised under GAAP in the lessee's accounts at the commencement date of the leaser or would fall to be so recognised if the lessee had not granted a sublease of the asset. A right-of-use asset under IFRS 16 or FRS 101 is a lessee's right to use an asset over the life of a lease. The asset is calculated as the initial amount of the lease liability, plus any lease payments made to the lessor before the lease commencement date, plus any initial direct costs incurred, minus any lease incentives received. References to 'right-of-use leases are also added to CAA 2001, s 70YA (which provides for the consequences of a change in the accountancy qualification of a long funding lease) by Sch 14, para 1(4) wherever the words 'or an operating lease' occur.

CAA 2001, s 70E defines disposal events and disposal values in relation to lessees under a long funding lease. Schedule 14, para 1(2) adds 'interest expenses' to finance charges as items that fall to be excluded from the 'qualifying amount' under CAA 2001, s 70E(2C).

Further amendments made to CAA 2001, s 70YA provide that there is not to be a requirement for a deemed disposal and reacquisition where a long funding lease is reclassified (under a so-called relevant change of classification) for accountancy purposes resulting from the adoption of a different accounting standard or a change to an accounting standard in the two cases (Case 1 and Case 2) there specified. Schedule 14, para 1(4)(e) adds a Case 3, which is a situation where the lease in question is a right-of-use lease that is a long funding lease immediately before it is reclassified but becomes a lease that is not a right-of-use lease and which falls or would fall to be treated in the accounts under GAAP as not a finance lease. In such a case, there would be a deemed disposal and reacquisition.

CAA 2001, s 70YI is the section containing general definitions for the provisions on long funding leases. Schedule 14, para 1(5) inserts new definitions the need for which arises from the other amendments made by Sch 14, para 1 and amends the existing definition of 'long funding finance lease' to include not only a long funding lease meeting the finance-lease test by virtue of CAA 2001, s 70N(1)(a) but also a right-of-use lease that is a long funding lease meeting the lease-payments test in CAA 2001, s 70O or the useful-economic-life test in CAA 2001, s 70P but is not a lease that was a long funding operating lease before a relevant change of classification. The effect of this is to 'grandfather' long funding operating leases where the lessee changes the accounting standard applicable to the lease.

CAA 2001, s 228J provides for restrictions on deductions a lessee-back may make under an operating lease following a sale and finance lease-back or a lease and finance lease-back under which some or all of the plant or machinery in question becomes the subject of an operating sublease back to the same lessee-back or to a connected person. One of the conditions for the section to apply is that the sublease is an operating lease (i e that it is not accounted for by the lessee as a finance lease). CAA 2001, s 228J(7) defines for these purposes when a lease *is* accounted for as a finance lease (so that the section would not apply). The amendment now made to CAA 2001, s 228J(7) provides that a lease is also to be regarded as accounted for as a finance lease if the lessee is a lessee under a right-of-use lease and the lease would fall to be treated in the lessee's accounts as a finance lease if the lessee were required under GAAP to determine whether the lease fell to be so treated.

Schedule 14, para 2 makes amendments to ITTOIA 2005.

ITTOIA 2005, s 148G provides for a cap on the deductions in respect of amounts payable under a lease that a lessee of plant or machinery under a long funding finance lease may make in calculating the profits of his trade, profession or vocation for the purposes of income tax. Those deductions may not exceed the amounts that fall or would fall to be shown in the lessee's accounts as finance charges. The amendment made by Sch 14, para 2(2) adds interest expenses as an alternative capping amount.

New ITTOIA 2005, s 148GA, inserted by Sch 14, para 2(3) provides for the treatment of lessees under a long funding finance lease that is a right-of-use lease. It applies where for any part of a period of account there is a change in the amounts payable under such a lease and, as a result of the change, there is in accordance with GAAP a remeasurement under IFRS 16 of the lease liability shown in the lessee's accounts or a deduction is shown other than as an interest expense under the lease or as an amount of depreciation or impairment in respect of the right-of-use asset arising from the lease. In such circumstances, the lessee may adjust the deductions cap under ITTOIA 2005, s 148G upwards or downwards by the amount of the increase or decrease resulting from the remeasurement or deduction. However, no such adjustment is to be made if the remeasurement or deduction results in enhanced capital expenditure under CAA 2001, s 70D.

Schedule 14, para 3 amends ITA 2007, s 809BZN, which forms part of the anti-avoidance provisions in ITA 2007, Pt 13, Ch 5B against structured finance arrangements, under which a person ('the borrower') receives money or another asset ('the loan') from another person ('the lender'), the borrower or a person connected with the borrower disposes of an asset ('the security') to or for the benefit of the lender or a person connected with the lender, and the lender or a person connected with the lender is entitled to payments in respect of the security. The security is a type of asset from which there is a predictable income stream and the loan is usually equal in amount to the present value of the future income that the lender will now receive, so that the lender receives interest and amounts that repay the principal. There are also likely to be arrangements such as options, under which the asset and income reverts to the borrower at the end of the arrangements. The intention is that the borrower will claim that the income arising during the period of the arrangement is not taxable on him because he has disposed of the asset, albeit temporarily. It will also be claimed that the lump sum is a capital receipt either giving rise to a capital gain or is not taxable at all. The aim of the arrangements is to give effective tax relief to the borrower not only for the finance charge (i e interest) but also the principal of the loan.

The legislation identifies three different types of arrangements, referred to as a 'finance arrangement code'. ITA 2007, s 809BZN provides exceptions from the application of the Chapter. The amendment made by Sch 14, para 3 provides for an additional exception where the arrangement is a right-of-use lease (as defined in CAA 2001, s 70YI as amended by Sch 14, para 1(5)) and the borrower would not have accounted for the arrangement as a finance lease or loan in accordance with GAAP if he had been so required.

Schedule 14, para 4 amends provisions in CTA 2010.

CTA 2010, s 288, deals with sale and lease-back arrangements under a ring-fence oil trade. It provides that where the lessee-back uses an asset for the purposes of a ring-fence trade carried on by him within two years of the original sale, expenditure the lessee incurs on the asset that falls under GAAP to be treated by the lessee as a finance charge, or (in the case of a long funding operating lease) to be deducted in calculating the lessee's profits, is not to be allowable as a deduction in calculating the profits of the ring-fence trade. The amendment now made to CTA 2010, s 288 by Sch 14 para 4(2) adds two further categories of expenditure to be so disallowed. These are (a) expenditure falling to be treated as an interest expense where it would fall to be treated as a finance charge if the lessee were required under GAAP to determine whether it should be so treated and (b) where the lease-back is a right-of-use lease that is a long funding finance lease and falls to be treated under GAAP as an interest expense in the lessee's accounts.

CTA 2010, s 331 defines 'financing costs' for the purposes of the supplementary charge under CTA 2010, Pt 8, Ch 5A on ring-fence trades. The amendments now made to CTA 2010, s 331 by Sch 14, para 4(3) add to the definition costs falling under GAAP to be treated in the accounts of the company as an interest expense where the company is a lessee under a right-of-use lease that is a long funding finance lease and add to the definition of a finance lease a right-of-use lease that would fall to be treated in the accounts of the lessee or a connected person as a finance lease.

Schedule 14, para 4(5) inserts *new CTA 2010, s 377A*, which is the parallel provision for the purposes of corporation tax to *new ITTOIA 2005, s 148GA* (inserted by Sch 14, para 2(3)). Accordingly, *new CTA 2010, s 377A* provides for the treatment of lessees under a long funding finance lease that is a right-of-use lease. It applies where for any part of a period of account there is a change in the amounts payable under such a lease and, as a result of the change, there is in accordance with GAAP a remeasurement under IFRS 16 of the lease liability shown in the lessee company's accounts or a deduction is shown other than as an interest expense under the lease or as an amount of depreciation or impairment in respect of the right-of-use asset arising from the lease. In such circumstances, in calculating its profits for the period of account, the lessee company may adjust the deductions cap under CTA 2010, s 377 (which is the parallel provision to ITTOIA 2005, s 148G) upwards or downwards by the amount of the increase or decrease resulting from the remeasurement or deduction. However, no such adjustment is to be made if the remeasurement or deduction results in enhanced capital expenditure under CAA 2001, s 70D.

Schedule 14, para 4(9) amends CTA 2010, s 771, which is the parallel provision to ITA 2007, s 809BZN. Thus, it is part of the anti-avoidance provisions against structured finance arrangements in CTA 2010, Pt 16, Ch 2 and provides exceptions from the application of the Chapter. The amendment made by Sch 14, para 4(9) provides for an additional exception where the arrangement is a right-of-use lease (as defined in CAA 2001, s 70YI as amended by Sch 14, para 1(5)) and the borrower would not have accounted for the arrangement as a finance lease or loan in accordance with GAAP if it had been so required.

Schedule 14, para 5 substitutes a new definition for 'finance lease' in TIOPA 2010, s 494, which provides definitions for the purposes of the corporate-interest-restriction rules and inserts a definition of 'right-of-use lease'.

Schedule 14, para 6 provides that the amendments made by Sch 14, Pt 1 are to have effect in relation to periods of account beginning after 31 December 2018.

Schedule 14 Part 2 (paras 7–10) amend the rules relating to long funding leases under the plant and machinery code for capital allowances in CAA 2001 Part 2.

Schedule 14, para 7 is introductory. Schedule 14, para 8 amends the definition of a short lease in CAA 2001, s 70I. The amendments extend the maximum term of a short lease from five to seven years and repeal the conditions that made certain leases with terms of between five and seven years also short leases. It also makes consequential amendments to CAA 2001, s 70YF (which defines what is meant by the term of a lease) and to CAA 2001, s 220 (which provides for allocation of expenditure to a chargeable period, as part of the anti-avoidance provisions of CAA 2001, Pt 2, Ch 17).

CAA 2001, s 70O sets out the lease-payments test, which is one of the defining tests for a funding lease. Where the interest rate implicit in the lease cannot be determined by reference to GAAP or normal commercial criteria, it has hitherto provided that the temporal discount rate under FA 2005 s 70 be used instead. The amendment now made to CAA 2001, s 70O by Sch 14, para 9 replaces the temporal discount rate by a rate that is 1% above LIBOR.

Schedule 14, para 10 provides that the amendments made by Sch 14, Pt 2 are to have effect in relation to leases entry into which takes place after 31 December 2018.

Schedule 14 Part 3 (paras 11–19) provides for a new treatment for tax purposes of adjustments made on the adoption of IFRS 16.

Schedule 14, para 11 repeals FA 2011, s 53. This section broadly provides that, with some exceptions, any changes made after 31 December 2010 in the accounting standards for leases are to be ignored for tax purposes where they abolish the distinction between operating and finance leases. That section is now repealed for periods of account beginning after 31 December 2018 and replaced by transitional provisions contained in Sch 14, paras 12–17.

Schedule 14, paras 12 is introductory and provides for modifications of the 'change-of-basis provisions' in ITTOIA 2005, Pt 2, Ch 17 and Pt 3, Ch 7 and CTA 2009, Pt 3, Ch 14 and ss 261 and 262 in relation to periods of account of a lessee beginning after 31 December 2018 where the lease is one:

- in respect of which a right-of-use asset falls or would fall to be recognised in the lessee's accounts for accounting purposes under GAAP for any period of account whenever beginning; and
- that would not fall to be treated in those accounts as a finance lease if the lessee were required under GAAP to determine whether the lease would fall to be so treated.

The ITTOIA 2005, Pt 2, Ch 17 change-of-basis provisions (abbreviated here to 'COB provisions') apply where a person changes the basis on which profits of a trade, profession or vocation are calculated for the purposes of income tax, either because of a change of accounting policy or a change in the tax adjustments applied. The ITTOIA 2005, Pt 3, Ch 7 provisions perform the like function for a change in the basis on which the profits of a property business are calculated. The CTA 2009 COB provisions mirror the ITTOIA 2005 provisions for the purposes of corporation tax.

Schedule 14, para 13 applies to cases where a right-of-use asset is or would be first recognised for accounting purposes in a period of account of the lessee beginning after 31 December 2018. This first period of recognition is referred to as 'the first period of account'. It provides that any adjustment income or adjustment expense or any receipt or expense treated by the COB provisions as arising in consequence of a change of accounting policy (in this case particularly, the transition to IFRS 16) resulting in that first recognition is to be treated for tax purposes as arising over a 'spreading period' to be determined under a five-step process.

Step 1 requires the lessee to calculate for each lease the amount by which the credits exceed the debits (or vice versa) and credits brought into account. These are the credits and debits which are taken under GAAP to equity as adjustments in the lessee's accounts and are in consequence of the transition to IFRS 16.

Step 2 requires the lessee to calculate a percentage for each lease ('the relevant percentage') by dividing the amount under Step 1 for that lease by the total amounts for the lessee for all leases found under Step 1 (treating such amounts as positive amounts) and multiplying by 100.

Step 3 requires the lessee to multiply the relevant percentage found under Step 2 by the remaining period outstanding in days of the lease term as at the date of transition (the date on which the first period of account begins). The term of the lease is determined in accordance with GAAP as it applies for the first period of account.

Step 4 requires the lessee to find the sum of the amounts calculated under Step 3. This will result in the weighted average or weighted mean of remaining periods of the leases affected by IFRS 16 transitional accounting adjustments taken to equity.

Step 5 defines the spreading period as the number of days found under Step 4 beginning with the day on which the first period of account begins.

Schedule 14, para 14 provides for instances where the right-of-use asset falls or would fall to be first recognised for a period of account earlier than 'the first period of account' (which cannot be one beginning before 1 January 2019). In such a case, the COB provisions and the provisions of Sch 14, Pt 3 are to have effect as if the change of accounting policy had taken place in the first period of account.

Schedule 14, para 15 applies where a lease or part of a lease is transferred during the spreading period to a person ('the transferee') who is connected to the lessee in circumstances where it is reasonable to suppose that the transfer is not part of a tax-avoidance arrangement. In such circumstances, the spreading arrangement under Sch 14, para 13 continues in the hands of the transferee for the remainder of the spreading period.

Schedule 14, para 16 applies where the lessee permanently ceases to carry on activities chargeable to income tax or corporation tax before the spreading period has expired and there is no transferee to whom to transfer the remainder of the adjustment amount. In such a case, that remainder is treated as arising to the lessee immediately before the cessation.

Schedule 14, para 17 provides that the above provisions apply in the same way to a portfolio of leases having similar characteristics.

TIOPA 2010, s 426 (part of the corporate-interest-restriction rules – 'CIR rules') provides for the effect of an interest allowance (alternative calculation) election on the calculation of the group's profit before tax with respect to certain changes in accounting policy listed in that section. When this election is in force, the financial statements of the group are to be subject to the adjustments that would be made to them under those changes if the group were a company within the charge to corporation tax. Schedule 14, para 18 amends TIOPA 2010, s 426 to add the transitional adjustments under Sch 14, paras 12–17 ('the above provisions') to the list of specified changes.

Schedule 14, para 19 provides for the effect on the CIR rules of certain transitional adjustments arising on the repeal of FA 2011 s 53 and changes in accounting policy arising on the adoption of IFRS 16. It applies to lessee companies where:

- adjustments are made for the purposes of corporation tax for a period of account beginning after 31 December 2018 by way of a receipt or expense arising from the effect of the corporation tax change of basis (COB) provisions referred to in Sch 14, para 12;
- the receipt or expense is treated as arising to the company as a consequence of a change of accounting policy relating to a lease in respect of which the company is a lessee;
- under the change of accounting policy, the lease, having previously been treated as a finance lease would now be treated as a right-of-use lease were it not for the fact that it is either a short lease or the leased asset is a low-value asset.

In these circumstances, if the adjustment is brought into account as an expense, it is not to be a tax-interest expense amount within the meaning of TIOPA 2010, s 382 and if the adjustment is brought into account as a receipt, it is not to be treated as a tax-interest income amount within the meaning of TIOPA 2010, s 385.

Oil activities and petroleum revenue tax

Sections 37 and 38 provide further relief for companies with North Sea oil and gas operations as they come to decommission oil fields.

Section 37 introduces Sch 15, which provides for an oil company to transfer a portion of its historic profits and the tax paid on those profits to another company to which it sells an oil licence. The purchasing company may then be able to claim a repayment of the tax paid by the vendor company in certain circumstances when the purchasing company decommissions the oil field.

Schedule 15 has no less than 108 paragraphs, divided into 15 Parts.

Schedule 15, Pt 1 (paras 1 and 2) provides for an election to transfer a tax history. Schedule 15, paras 1 and 2 provide that Sch 15 is to apply where the Oil and Gas Authority gives consent after 31 October 2018 for a company ('the seller') to sell an interest in a UK oil licence to another company ('the purchaser') and, at any time on or after the 'licence-transfer date' (defined in Sch 15, para 101 as the date of completion of the sale of the interest in the transferred oil field) the seller and the purchaser make a joint election ('the TTH election') in respect of that interest ('the TTH asset') in a transferred oil field lying within the area of the licence. Under the TTH election, an amount ('the total TTH amount') of the seller's ring-fence profits is treated as if it were instead an amount of the purchaser's profits. The election also has effect to treat the corresponding amount of the seller's adjusted ring-fence profits for the purposes of the supplementary charge under CTA 2010, Pt 8, Ch 6 as if they were instead the buyer's adjusted ring-fence profits.

Schedule 15, Pt 2 (paras 3–14) make provision concerning the total TTH amount. Schedule 15, para 3 provides that the total TTH amount may comprise both an amount representing the seller's 'eligible ring-fence profits' for the 'reference accounting period' and amounts representing the seller's eligible ring-fence profits for any number of preceding accounting periods ending after 16 April 2002 specified by the seller and purchaser. 'Eligible ring-fence profits' are defined in Sch 15, para 13 and the 'reference accounting period' of the seller is defined in Sch 15, para 102 as the accounting period that is the seller's most recent qualifying accounting period in respect of which the 'amendment period' has ended, as at the licence-transfer date. The 'amendment period' is itself defined as the period of 12 months beginning with the filing date for the company tax return for the accounting period concerned.

Schedule 15, para 4 restricts the total TTH amount to the lower of (a) the 'uplifted decommissioning costs estimate' in relation to the TTH asset and (b) the total amount of the seller's 'eligible ring-fence profits' for the period beginning on 17 April 2002 and ending at the end of the seller's 'reference accounting period'.

Schedule 15, paras 5–9 prescribe the steps that need to be taken to arrive at the uplifted decommissioning costs estimate referred to in Sch 15, para 4. Step 1 is to determine the 'transferred proportion of the net cost amount' (as defined in Sch 15, paras 6 and 7). Step 2 is to allocate the 'relevant proportion' of the amount found by Step 1 to the TTH asset (as defined by Sch 15, para 8). Step 3 is to adjust the allocated amount found under Step 2 as required by Sch 15, para 9. Finally, Step 4 is to double the adjusted amount as found under Step 3. The result is the uplifted decommissioning costs estimate.

Schedule 15, para 6 provides that the 'net cost amount' is the 'appropriate DSA estimate' (i e the estimate approved for the purposes of the decommissioning security agreement (DSA)) of the decommissioning costs for the TTH oil field. It also provides which estimate of the decommissioning costs to use when there is more than one such estimate in the 12 months ending on the date on which the TTH election is made (or, where the hive-down condition in Sch 15, para 56 is met, the date on which the seller and the purchaser cease to be associated). Schedule 15, para 7 defines the 'transferred proportion of the net cost amount' as the proportion of the decommissioning costs for which the seller is responsible if the DSA is entered into before the sale of the interest or as the proportion of the decommissioning costs for which the purchaser is responsible if the DSA is entered into on or after the sale of the interest. Schedule 15, para 8 defines the 'relevant proportion' of the 'transferred proportion of the net cost amount' as the proportion that the TTH asset bears to the seller's other interests in the TTH oil field (if the DSA is entered into before the sale of the sold interest) or as the proportion that the TTH asset bears to the purchaser's other interests in the TTH oil field (if the DSA is entered into on or after the sale of the sold interest). Schedule 15, para 9 sets out the adjustments that must be made to the amount allocated under Sch 15, para 8. Schedule 15, para 10 defines what is meant by a decommissioning security agreement and a qualifying decommissioning security agreement.

Schedule 15, para 11 provides that the total TTH amount may not include eligible ring-fence profits for a particular accounting period other than the reference accounting period unless it also includes the eligible ring-fence profits for the next accounting period in respect of which the seller has eligible ring-fence profits.

Schedule 15, para 12 provides that, except for the earliest accounting period for which there is a 'transferred profits amount', the whole of the seller's eligible ring-fence profits for an accounting period must be the 'transferred profits amount' for that period. 'Transferred profits amount' is defined in Sch 15, para 107 as the amount of the seller's ring-fence profits transferred to form part of the total TTH amount. With respect to the earliest period, the transferred profits amount must also be the whole of the seller's eligible ring-fence profits, subject to the proviso that it may not exceed the TTH balance, which is the total TTH amount, less the transferred profits amounts for each later accounting period.

Schedule 15, para 13 contains the key definition of what constitutes the seller's eligible ring-fence profits of a particular accounting period. These are the profits of its ring-fence trade on which corporation tax has been charged at the main ring-fence rate (30%), in respect of which no marginal relief under CTA 2010, ss 279B or 279C applies, and in respect of which the seller's liability to corporation tax has been fully discharged. It also provides that the same ring-fence profits cannot be included in more than one TTH election. Schedule 15, para 14 provides that eligible ring-fence profits for an accounting period straddling 17 April 2002 are to be apportioned on a *pro rata temporis* basis.

Schedule 15, Pt 3 (paras 15–22) deal with the effect of a successful TTH election on the seller. Schedule 15, para 15 is introductory.

Schedule 15, para 16 prevents the seller from claiming carry-back relief under CTA 2010, s 37(3)(b) for a trade loss against any part of its total profits of a pre-transfer period that have been transferred under a TTH election. It does likewise in respect of a claim under CTA 2010, s 42 for carry-back relief in respect of losses from a ring-fence trade. A pre-transfer period is defined by Sch 15, para 104 as the reference accounting period and any previous accounting period.

Schedule 15, para 17 provides that transferred profits are to be disregarded for the purposes of any claim to relief from, or repayment of, corporation tax.

Schedule 15, para 18 provides that if at any time after the licence-transfer date, the seller's eligible ring-fence profits of a pre-transfer period are revised downwards to an amount lower than the transferred profits of that period, it is to be treated as incurring a ring-fence loss in that period of an amount equal to the deficit. That amount is not to be disregarded under Sch 15, para 17.

Schedule 15, paras 19–22 apply to the supplementary charge on ring-fence profits. Schedule 15, para 19 is introductory. Schedule 15, para 20 provides that the amount of 'transferred adjusted ring-fence profits' for any accounting period out of which profits have been transferred carries no entitlement to a repayment of the supplementary charge and defines those profits as the amount of the seller's eligible adjusted ring-fence profits of the period (or the relevant proportion in the case of the earliest period).

Schedule 15, para 21 provides that the amount of the 'ARFP component' for each accounting period in which there are transferred profits is to be disregarded for the purposes of loss relief under CTA 2010 Part 4 and the oil-activities provisions of CTA 2010 Part 8. The 'ARFP component' is defined as the sum of (a) any financing costs for the period left out of account under CTA 2010, s 330 when calculating the seller's adjusted ring-fence profits and (b) reductions of the seller's adjusted ring-fence profits under any of CTA 2010, ss 332E (investment allowance), 356D (onshore allowance) or 356JG (cluster-area allowance). However, the ARFP component is not to be disregarded when determining the seller's eligible adjusted ring-fence profits for the purposes of Sch 15. Schedule 15, para 22 provides definitions, including that for 'eligible adjusted ring-fence profits'. These are, in line with the definition of 'eligible ring-fence profits' in Sch 15, para 13, the adjusted profits of its ring-fence trade on which the supplementary charge under CTA 2010, s 330 has been charged and in respect of which the seller's liability to the supplementary charge has been fully discharged.

Schedule 15, Pt 4 (paras 23–29) deal with the effect of a successful TTH election on the purchaser. Schedule 15, paras 23 and 24 provide that Schedule 15 Part 4 applies where, following a successful TTH election, the winning of oil from the TTH oil field has permanently ceased and in a 'post-acquisition accounting period', the purchaser makes a 'decommissioning loss' in the ring-fence trade and holds an 'activated TTH amount'. A decommissioning loss is a loss for which the purchaser claims carry-back relief for a terminal loss under CTA 2010, ss 39, 40 or 42. A 'post-acquisition accounting period' is defined in Sch 15, para 105(2) as the first accounting period after the purchaser's reference period, any subsequent accounting period and any notional accounting period under CAA 2001, s 165 (general decommissioning expenditure after ceasing ring-fence trade) or s 416ZA (mineral allowances: expenditure on site restoration in a ring-fence trade). An 'activated TTH amount' is as determined under Sch 15, Pts 5 and 6.

Schedule 15, para 25 provides that in the circumstances prescribed by Sch 15, paras 23 and 24, the purchaser's total profits (against which the decommissioning loss is to be set, under either CTA 2010, s 37(3)(b) or s 42, for a pre-acquisition period are to be treated as increased by any activated TTH amount allocated to that period under Sch 15, para 44, but only to the extent that the loss involved in the claim exceeds the total profits.

Schedule 15, para 26 allows for repayment of the supplementary charge where there is a decommissioning loss in a pre-acquisition period and the purchaser's total profits include an activated TTH amount. The repayment is calculated on the presumption that supplementary charge had been charged under CTA 2010, s 330 on the 'activated ARFP amount' (for which see Sch 15, para 53) and paid by the purchaser and the 'transferred adjusted ring-fence profits' had been recalculated as required under Sch 15, para 50. Schedule 15, para 27 defines the 'transferred adjusted ring-fence profits' as the 'transferred adjusted ring-fence profits amount' (as defined in Sch 15, para 20) for the accounting period of the seller coinciding with the pre-acquisition period of the purchaser. Where there is no such coincident period, the overlapping proportion of those profits is taken. Schedule 15, para 28 provides that for the purposes of repaying excess corporation tax, the corporation tax and supplementary charge paid by the seller on the activated transferred profits is to be treated as having been paid by the purchaser.

Schedule 15, para 29 provides that any enquiry into a tax return for an accounting period in which a claim for relief is made under CTA 2010, s 37 in respect of a decommissioning loss may extend to the 'decommissioning expenditure amount' attributable to the TTH oil field for any period, the 'tracked' profit or loss attributable to the TTH asset for any period and to whether a 'TTH activation event' had occurred in relation to the TTH asset. The 'decommissioning expenditure amount' is defined in Sch 15, para 31; the 'tracked' profit or loss is defined in Sch 15, para 64 and a 'TTH activation event' in Sch 15, para 30.

Schedule 15, Pt 5 (paras 30–35) explains 'TTH activation'. Schedule 15, para 30 defines a 'TTH activation event' as an event that occurs where both of two conditions are met:

- the winning of oil from the TTH oil field has permanently ceased; and
- at the end of a post-acquisition period of the purchaser, the 'total decommissioning expenditure amount' exceeds the 'total net-profits amount'.

The 'total decommissioning expenditure amount' is the 'relevant proportion' of the sum of the 'decommissioning expenditure amounts' (as defined in Sch 15, para 31) attributable to the TTH oil field for each period that is a pre-acquisition period until the end of the pre-acquisition period in question. The 'relevant proportion' is the proportion that the interest in the TTH oil field (the TTH asset) bears to the purchaser's other interests in the TTH oil field. The 'total net profits amount' is the sum of the 'tracked' profits or losses attributable to the TTH asset over the same period of time.

Schedule 15, para 31 defines the 'decommissioning expenditure amount' attributable to a TTH oil field for an accounting period as the sum of the 'special allowance amount', the 'post-cessation expenditure amount' and the 'restoration expenditure amount' attributable to the field for that period. Schedule 15, para 32 defines the 'special allowance amount' as the amount of any special allowances made to the purchaser under CAA 2001, s 164 (general decommissioning expenditure before ceasing ring-fence trade) to the extent that they relate to expenditure incurred on decommissioning plant or machinery that was used wholly or partly in direct connection with the TTH oil field. Schedule 15, para 33 defines the 'post-cessation expenditure amount' as the amount of any allowances under CAA 2001, s 165 (general decommissioning expenditure after ceasing ring-fence trade) to the extent that they relate to expenditure incurred on decommissioning plant or machinery that was used wholly or partly in direct connection with the TTH oil field. Schedule 15, para 34 defines the 'restoration expenditure amount' as the amount of any allowances made to the purchaser under CAA 2001, s 416ZA (mineral allowances: expenditure on site restoration in a ring-fence trade) to the extent that they relate to expenditure incurred on the restoration of a site used in relation to the TTH oil field. Schedule 15, para 35 requires that any apportionment of amounts under Sch 15, paras 32, 33 or 34 between the TTH oil field and any other oil field or part thereof must be made on a basis that is just and reasonable.

Schedule 15, Pt 6 (paras 36–49) provides for how an 'activated TTH amount' is to be allocated. Schedule 15, para 36 provides that Sch 15, Pt 6 is to apply when a TTH activation event (see Sch 15, para 30) occurs in relation to a TTH asset. Schedule 15, para 37 defines the terms 'first activation period' and 'post-activation period'. The 'first activation period' is the first accounting period of the purchaser in which a TTH activation event occurs and a 'post-activation period' as any subsequent accounting period.

Schedule 15, para 38 defines the 'total activated TTH amount' held by the purchaser for a loss period that is the first activation period as the lower of (a) the amount by which the total decommissioning expenditure amount' (as defined in Sch 15, para 30) exceeds the 'total net-profits amount' (also as defined Sch 15, para 30) at the end of that period and (b) the total TTH amount (as defined in Sch 15, para 2). Schedule 15, para 39 defines the 'total activated TTH amount' for any post-activation period as the lower of (a) the 'adjusted activated TTH amount' (as defined in Sch 15, paras 40–41), and (b) 'the closing balance of the total TTH amount' at the end of the preceding accounting period (as defined in Sch 15, para 49).

Schedule 15, para 40 provides that where, in any post-activation period, there is an excess of the 'relevant proportion' (as defined in Sch 15, para 30) of the decommissioning expenditure amount' (defined by Sch 15, para 31) attributable to the TTH oil field for that period (as a result of incurring further decommissioning costs in that period) over any 'tracked' profits or losses attributable to the TTH asset for that period, the 'additional activated TTH amount' for that post-activation period is the amount of that excess. It also defines the 'adjusted activated TTH amount' as the total of (a) the closing balance of activated TTH for the immediately preceding accounting period and (b) the additional activated TTH amount in that period.

Schedule 15, para 41 provides that where, in a post-activation period, the 'tracked' profit or loss amount attributable to the TTH asset is greater than the relevant proportion of the decommissioning expenditure amount attributable to the TTH oil field for that period (for which see Sch 15, para 40), there is a 'TTH reduction amount' equal to the excess. If that TTH reduction amount is less than the 'closing balance amount' (the 'closing balance of activated TTH' (for which see Sch 15, para 48) for the accounting period immediately beforehand), the 'adjusted activated TTH amount' is equal to the difference. If the TTH reduction amount is equal to or greater than the closing balance amount, the adjusted activated TTH amount is nil.

Schedule 15, para 42 provides that where neither Sch 15, para 40 nor Sch 15, para 41 applies (i e there are no further decommissioning costs incurred in relation to the TTH asset, and no further 'tracked' profits or losses made), the 'adjusted activated TTH amount' is the closing balance of activated TTH for the immediately preceding accounting period, or nil if the closing balance is nil or negative.

Schedule 15, para 43 introduces Sch 15, para 44, which sets out the process for allocating activated TTH to an accounting period, in order to effect the enhanced loss relief available under Sch 15, para 25. Schedule 15, para 44 sets out the four-step process for allocating the 'total activated TTH amount' (as defined in Sch 15, paras 38 and 39) for a loss period to pre-acquisition periods of the purchaser.

Step 1 is to take the most recent pre-acquisition accounting period for which there is an 'unused transferred profits amount' (as defined in Sch 15, paras 45 and 46) greater than nil.

Step 2 is to allocate to that pre-acquisition accounting period an amount equal to the lower of (a) the unused transferred profits amount and (b) the total activated TTH amount held by the purchaser for the loss period.

Step 3 is to allocate to the next most recent pre-acquisition accounting period an amount equal to the lower of (a) the transferred profits amount for that period and (b) the 'available activated TTH amount' (defined in Sch 15, para 47) for the loss period.

Step 4 is to repeat Step 3 (taking later periods before earlier periods) until the amount referred to in Step 3 is exhausted.

Schedule 15, para 45 defines the transferred profits amount for an accounting period of the purchaser as either (a) the transferred profits of the coinciding accounting period of the seller or (b) where there is no such directly coinciding accounting period of the seller, the overlapping proportion of the transferred profits amount for each accounting period of the seller that overlaps with the purchaser's pre-acquisition period concerned. Schedule 15, para 46 goes on to define the 'unused transferred profits amount' for a pre-acquisition period as the transferred profits amount for that period less any amounts previously applied in accordance with Sch 15, para 25.

Schedule 15, para 47 defines the 'available activated TTH amount' held by the purchaser for the loss period as the total activated TTH amount (as defined in Sch 15, paras 38 and 39) held by the purchaser for that period, less any amounts previously allocated to a subsequent pre-acquisition accounting period in accordance with Sch 15, para 44.

Schedule 15, para 48 defines the 'closing balance of activated TTH' (referred to in Sch 15, para 41) for the first activation period or a post-acquisition period as the total activated TTH amount held by the purchaser for that period, less any amounts against which losses have already been set in accordance with Sch 15, para 25. However, if the period in question is a post-acquisition period for which the TTH reduction amount is not less than the closing balance amount (so that Sch 15, para 41(4) applies), the closing balance of activated TTH for the period is the negative amount found by deducting the TTH reduction amount for that period (see Sch 15, para 41) from the closing balance of activated TTH for the immediately preceding period.

Schedule 15, para 49 defines the 'closing balance of the total TTH amount' (referred to in Sch 15, para 39) as the total TTH amount less any TTH amounts against which losses have already been set in accordance with Sch 15, para 25.

Schedule 15, Pt 7 (paras 50–55) provides for the recalculation of adjusted ring-fence profits for the purpose of repaying the supplementary charge as required by Sch 15, para 26.

Schedule 15, para 50 provides that 'the recalculated transferred adjusted ring-fence profits amount' for a pre-acquisition accounting period is the aggregate of (a) the 'reduced ARFP amount' (defined by Sch 15, paras 51 and 52) and (b) the adjusted finance-cost amount' (defined by Sch 15, para 55) for the loss period referred to in Sch 15, para 26. If this produces a negative amount, 'the recalculated transferred adjusted ring-fence profits amount' is taken to be nil. Schedule 15, para 51 defines the 'reduced ARFP amount' for a pre-acquisition accounting period as the 'activated ARFP amount' (as defined in Sch 15, para 53) for that period, as reduced by the amount of activated transferred profits applied under Sch 15, para 25 for the loss period referred to in Sch 15, para 26. However, where in any pre-acquisition period the rate of the supplementary charge was greater than 20% (as it was for accounting periods beginning after 23 March 2011 and before 1 January 2015), Sch 15, para 52 provides that the reduced ARFP amount' is instead the amount found by adding the activated ARFP amount for the period and the 'ARFP uplift amount' (as defined in Sch 15, para 55) and then deducting from that sum the amount applied under Sch 15, para 25. Schedule 15, para 53 defines the 'activated ARFP amount' as:

$$\frac{A}{T} \times ARFP$$

where A is the amount applied under Sch 15, para 25; T is the unused transferred profits amount (as defined by Sch 15, para 46) for that period and ARFP is the amount of the transferred adjusted ring-fence profits as determined under Sch 15, para 27, reduced by any earlier claims (the total of the activated ARFP for the particular pre-acquisition accounting period applied for each earlier repayment). The 'ARFP uplift amount' for a pre-acquisition accounting period is defined by Sch 15, para 54 as:

$$\frac{SC - 20\%}{SC} \times A$$

where SC is the rate of the supplementary charge for the pre-acquisition period and A is again the amount applied under Sch 15, para 25. Schedule 15, para 55 defines the 'adjusted finance-cost amount' (see Sch 15, para 50) as:

$$\frac{A}{L} \times FC$$

where A has the same meaning as above, L is the amount of the decommissioning loss in the loss period and FC is the lower of (a) the financing costs left out of account in calculating the company's adjusted ring-fence profits under CA 2010, s 330 and (b) the amount of the purchaser's loss in the ring-fence trade for the loss period.

Schedule 15, Pt 8 (paras 56–60) sets out the conditions and procedure for the making of a TTH election.

Schedule 15, para 56 provides that a TTH election may only be made if the seller and the purchaser are not associated with one another on the licence-transfer date unless one out of two further conditions is met. Those two conditions are 'the corporate-restructuring condition' and 'the hive-down condition'.

The corporate-restructuring condition is met where the seller and the purchaser are associated with one another on the licence-transfer date and either they make, within the permitted period, a third-party election in respect of the TTH asset or they make a hive-down election in respect of that asset. A third-party election may only be made between companies that are not associated with one another at that time (although they are associated at the licence-transfer date) and the permitted period is the 90 days immediately preceding or immediately following the licence-transfer date.

The hive-down election may only be made if the hive-down condition is met and the permitted period for making the election is the 180 days immediately preceding the licence-transfer date. The hive-down condition is met where the seller and the purchaser are associated with one another on the licence-transfer date but within 90 days of that date, the purchaser ceases to be associated with the seller and any other company associated with the seller. The definition of associated companies is that found in CTA 2010, s 271.

Schedule 15, para 57 provides that a seller may not make a TTH election if it is a party to a decommissioning relief agreement under FA 2013, s 80 unless the agreement provides for the total TTH amount to be disregarded when calculating any 'reference amount' referred to in that section.

Schedule 15, para 58 provides that a TTH election may only be made in the 90 days immediately following the licence-transfer date or, if later, by 1 June 2019.

Schedule 15, para 59 empowers HMRC to specify the form and content of a TTH election. Schedule 15, para 60 amends the time limits under TMA 1970, Sch 1A para 5 within which HMRC may open an enquiry if either the corporate-restructuring condition or the hive-down condition is met.

Schedule 15, Pt 9 (paras 61–70) sets out the procedure for HMRC approval of a TTH election and its subsequent monitoring.

Schedule 15, para 61 provides that a TTH election is to be approved by an officer of HMRC, by giving notice of approval to the seller and the purchaser and Sch 15, para 62 provides that if an election is not so approved, but HMRC does not open an enquiry into the election within the permitted time, the election is deemed to have been approved.

Schedule 15, para 63 requires the purchaser, once the TTH election has been approved, to comply with the 'profit-tracking requirements' and to keep such records as HMRC may require. Schedule 15, para 64 provides that for each accounting period in which the election has effect, the purchaser complies with the profit-tracking requirement if it submits a statement of the 'tracked' profit or loss alongside its corporation tax return. The 'tracked' profit or loss amount for an accounting period is the amount of profit or loss attributable to the TTH asset, excluding the 'relevant proportion' (see Sch 15, para 30) of the decommissioning expenditure amount attributable to the TTH oil field for that period. Schedule 15, para 65 requires the tracked profit or loss amount to be calculated on a basis that justly and reasonably apportions receipts, expenses, assets and liabilities of the purchaser. Under Sch 15, para 66, the purchaser must in each period after the transfer and before the filing date of its company tax return notify HMRC of the name of its 'senior tracking officer' ('STO'), who must ensure the purchaser complies with the profit-tracking requirement and certify to HMRC that it has done so. Schedule 15, para 67 sets out that the STO must be a director, manager, secretary or other person managing or purporting to manage the purchaser company's affairs. Schedule 15, para 68 provides that the STO may be charged a penalty of £5,000 if he or she fails without reasonable excuse to comply with the requirements in Sch 15, para 66. A penalty of £5,000 may also be charged on the purchaser if it fails to notify HMRC who its STO is for any accounting period. Schedule 15, para 69 provides that a penalty under Sch 15, para 68 must be assessed within six months of the date when the failure first comes to the attention of an officer of HMRC and no more than six years after the filing date of the purchaser's tax return for the tracking period. Schedule 15, para 70 provides that penalties charged under Sch 15, para 68 must be paid within 30 days of the issue of the penalty notice. If an appeal is made against the penalty, payment must be made within 30 days of the determination or withdrawal of the appeal. A penalty is enforceable as if it were income tax or corporation tax charged in an assessment and due and payable.

Schedule 15, Pt 10 (paras 71 and 72) prescribe the effective date of a TTH election and how it may be withdrawn.

Schedule 15, para 71 provides that a TTH election is to have effect from the licence-transfer date and that it continues indefinitely as far as the seller is concerned but may be withdrawn by HMRC as regards the purchaser. Schedule 15, para 72 entitles HMRC to revoke the election with respect to the purchaser if the purchase persistently fails without reasonable excuse to comply with the conditions specified in Sch 15, para 63. In these circumstances, it ceases to have effect in relation to the purchaser's accounting period in which the notice of revocation is given but does not affect any relief given previously under Sch 15, paras 25 or 26.

Schedule 15, Pt 11 (paras 73–75) provides for the effect of inaccuracies on a TTH election. Schedule 15, para 73 provides that a penalty may be charged on the seller if an inaccurate TTH election is submitted. The penalty is to be a geared penalty under FA 2007, Sch 24 with reference to the 'potential lost revenue', which is fixed at 10% of the amount by which the total TTH amount is overstated. Schedule 15, para 74 allows HMRC to amend a TTH election by giving notice to the purchaser if the election is discovered to be inaccurate. However, the power to make an amendment may only be exercised if at the time the election was approved, an officer of HMRC could not reasonably have been aware, based on the information made available, that the amount stated was incorrect; nor may an amendment be made more than 12 months after information justifying the correction first comes to the officer's attention. Schedule 15, para 75 provides that an amendment under Sch 15, para 74 is not to interfere with claims already made by the purchaser under which an activated transferred-profits amount has been applied in a loss-relief claim under Sch 15, para 25.

Schedule 15, Pt 12 (paras 76–80) deals with capital gains. Schedule 15, para 76 provides that the transfer of tax history between the seller and the purchaser is not to constitute the disposal or acquisition of an asset for the purposes of TCGA 1992 nor the disposal or acquisition of an intangible fixed asset for the purposes of CTA 2009, Pt 8 (the intangible fixed-assets code). Schedule 15, para 77 provides that any consideration attributed to the transfer of tax history under a joint election is to be treated as part of the consideration for the disposal of the licence interest for chargeable gains and mineral-extraction capital allowance purposes. Schedule 15, para 78 requires any value attributable to the transfer of tax history to be included when calculating the market value of the licence interest for the purposes of TCGA 1992, s 17 (market value rule for non-arm's length and certain other disposals) and for CAA 2001, Pt 5 (mineral-extraction allowances) if the disposal value of the licence interest is the market value of the licence interest at the time of the disposal. Schedule 15, para 79 provides that the transfer of tax history is to be treated as included in any reference to the disposal of a licence interest where there is an oil-licence swap for the purposes of TCGA 1992, ss 195A–196. Schedule 15, para 80 defines what is meant by the transfer of tax history for the purposes Sch 15, Pt 12.

Schedule 15, Pt 13 (paras 81–91) provides for the consequences of an onward sale by the original purchaser of the licence interest when a TTH election is in force between the original seller and the original purchaser.

Schedule 15, para 81 provides that Sch 15, Part 13 ('the onward-sale provisions') is to apply where the purchaser ('the first purchaser') of an interest ('the first TTH asset') in a TTH oil field has made a joint TTH election ('the first TTH election') with the original seller and the first purchaser subsequently sells on an interest in a UK oil licence that applies to the area that includes the TTH oil field to another company ('the second purchaser') and the first purchaser and the second purchaser jointly make another TTH election ('the subsequent TTH election') in respect of an interest ('the subsequent TTH asset') in the TTH oil field.

Schedule 15, para 82 provides that where the original purchaser has other interests in the transferred oil licence, for the purposes of the onward-sale provisions interests acquired by the original purchaser later are to be treated as being transferred to the new purchaser before interests acquired earlier by the first purchaser.

Schedule 15, para 83 provides that any amount of tax history that was transferred under the original election from the seller to the first purchaser ('the original TTH amount') is to be treated as being part of the first purchaser's eligible ring-fence profits and so can be transferred to the second purchaser on the onward sale of the TTH asset. However, this only applies insofar as the transferred tax history has not already been activated and allocated to a pre-acquisition accounting period (ie the original TTH amount is transferable only in respect of any pre-acquisition accounting period of the first purchaser for which there is, immediately before the effective date of the subsequent TTH election, an unused transferred amount – such an accounting period is referred to as a 'relevant accounting period'). Where only part of the first TTH asset is transferred to the second purchaser (ie the first TTH asset is not the same as the subsequent TTH asset), only the corresponding proportion of the first TTH amount may be transferred.

Schedule 15, para 84 provides that where there is an onward sale, the unused transferred-profits amounts of each relevant accounting period cease to be available to the first purchaser for the purposes of the first election.

Schedule 15, para 85 provides that the first purchaser and the second purchaser may elect at the time of their TTH election that the rules set out in Sch 15, paras 86 and 87 for the treatment of the transferred TTH amount are not to apply.

Unless they so elect, Sch 15, para 86 has effect to alter the normal rules in Sch 15, paras 11 (consecutive accounting periods) and 12 (transferred profits amount). The result is that Sch 15, para 11 should be construed so as to read that the total TTH amount may not include an amount representing the original TTH amount for a particular accounting period unless it also includes an amount representing the original TTH amount for the next following relevant accounting period, but where the original TTH amount exceeds the total TTH amount, the transferred profits amount for the earliest relevant accounting period must be set at the total TTH amount, less the transferred profits amount for later relevant accounting periods. 'Relevant accounting period' is as defined by Sch 15, para 83. As regards the rule in Sch 15, para 12, this should be construed so as to provide that, except for the earliest accounting period for which there is a 'transferred profits amount' by reason of the first purchaser's eligible ring-fence profits for that period, the whole of the first purchaser's eligible ring-fence profits for an accounting period must be the transferred profits amount for that period. With respect to that earliest period, the transferred profits amount must also be the whole of the first purchaser's eligible ring-fence profits, subject to the proviso that this may not exceed the TTH balance, which is the total TTH amount, less the transferred profits amounts for each relevant accounting period.

Schedule 15, para 87 provides that for the purposes of the subsequent TTH election, references to the purchaser in Sch 15, para 30 and 31 are to be taken to include references to the first purchaser. However, references in Sch 15, paras 83–86 and 89 to an amount of the first purchaser's eligible ring-fence profits are not to include references to an original TTH amount.

The result of all this is that, unless the election mentioned in Sch 15, para 85 is made, amounts of transferred tax history from the first election that are treated as being part of the first purchaser's eligible ring-fence profits are transferred to the second purchaser in priority to the first purchaser's own eligible ring-fence profits.

Where the first purchaser and the second purchaser do make the election under Sch 15, para 85(2), and the total TTH amount in relation to the subsequent TTH election exceeds the total amount of the first purchaser's eligible ring-fence profits for both (a) the accounting period that is, at the licence-transfer date for the subsequent TTH election, the first purchaser's most recent qualifying accounting period (for which see Sch 15, para 11) in respect of which the amendment period has ended (for which see under Sch 15, para 3) and (b) each earlier accounting period that is a post-acquisition accounting period of the first purchaser in relation to the first TTH election, Sch 15, para 88 provides that for the purposes of the subsequent TTH election, references to the purchaser in Sch 15, para 30 and 31 are to be taken to include references to the first purchaser, but references to the first purchaser's eligible ring-fence profits in Sch 15, para 83 (and immediately above in the qualifying condition for these rules to apply) are not to include references to an original TTH amount.

Schedule 15, para 89 provides that for the purposes of the subsequent TTH election as it relates to the supplementary charge, the TTH rules in Sch 15 are to apply as if the transferred adjusted ring-fence profits amount for each relevant accounting period or, if the first TTH asset is not the same as the subsequent TTH asset, the 'relevant proportion' of that amount for that period, were an amount of the first purchaser's eligible adjusted ring-fence profits for that period. The 'relevant proportion' here is the proportion that the subsequent TTH asset bears to the first TTH asset.

Schedule 15, para 90 provides that where, after the effective date of the subsequent TTH election, the first purchaser continues to be liable for some or all of the decommissioning costs of the subsequent TTH asset, for the purposes of the tracking requirements for the subsequent TTH election, Sch 15, para 65 should be read so as to require the tracked profit or loss amount to be calculated on a basis that justly and reasonably apportions receipts, expenses, assets and liabilities of the second purchaser.

Schedule 15, para 91 provides that the onward-sale rules in Sch 15, Pt 13 shall also apply mutatis mutandis to further sales of the subsequent TTH asset by the second and subsequent purchasers.

Schedule 15, Pt 14 (paras 92–96) deals with miscellaneous matters. Schedule 15, para 92 allows the seller and the purchaser to make a single TTH election where interests in two or more oil licences are sold at the same time and as a result the purchaser acquires more than one interest in the same oil field. Schedule 15, para 93 makes provision for how to allocate activated TTH amounts held by a purchaser in a loss period where more than one election has been made in respect of the same TTH asset.

Schedule 15, para 94 makes provision for appeals to be made against decisions to charge a penalty on an STO under Sch 15, para 68, to revoke a TTH election under Sch 15, para 72 and to amend a TTH election under Sch 15, para 74. Appeals must be made in writing to an officer of HMRC within 30 days of the issue of the penalty notice and state the grounds of appeal. The Tribunal may overturn the decision that is the subject of the appeal or confirm it; or, in the case of an appeal against an amendment, substitute another decision that an officer of HMRC had power to make. Where the Tribunal cancels a decision to revoke a TTH election, the election is treated as having had continuing effect throughout.

Schedule 15, para 95 is an anti-avoidance provision. It allows an officer of HMRC to amend an election or amend or disallow a claim if certain arrangements have been entered into to counteract the effect of those arrangements. The arrangements in question are arrangements designed to secure an entitlement to repayment of tax or an earlier repayment of tax than would otherwise have been the case, or otherwise circumvent the intended limits of the legislation.

Schedule 15, para 96 provides that loss relief may not be given to two different persons in respect of the same amount of the seller's ring-fence profits or adjusted ring-fence profits.

Schedule 15 Part 15 (paras 97–108) provides interpretations and definitions.

Section 38 amends OTA 1975 in order to allow participators in oil fields to obtain PRT relief for decommissioning expenditure incurred or funded by the previous holder of the interest in the oil field. It should therefore be seen as a companion piece to Sch 15.

New OTA 1975, Sch 3, para 11A, inserted by s 38(2), applies where a participator in an oil field ('the old participator') transfers all or part of an interest in the field to another person ('the new participator') and the Oil and Gas Authority (OGA) consents to that transfer at any time after 31 October 2018.

OTA 1975, Sch 3, para 8(1) provides for a disregard of any expenditure to the extent that it is directly or indirectly met, inter alia, by any other person ('the subsidy rule'). *New OTA 1975, Sch 3, para 11A(2)* overrides that disregard in respect of any decommissioning expenditure incurred by the new participator and met directly or indirectly out of a payment from the old participator. Furthermore, any decommissioning expenditure incurred by the old participator after the end of the 'transfer period' is to be treated as if it had been incurred by the new participator and the subsidy rule is to be disregarded for that expenditure also. The 'transfer period' is defined in FA 1980, Sch 17, para 1(3) as the chargeable period in which the transfer takes place.

Where the old participator has made more than transfer of interests in the same oil field and some of those transfers received OGA consent before 1 November 2018, these rules are to apply to a just and reasonable proportion of any decommissioning expenditure met or incurred by the old participator in relation to the field.

These rules are also to apply mutatis mutandis to further transfers of interest by new participators and apply with effect from 12 February 2019.

Miscellaneous reliefs

Section 39 introduces **Sch 16**, which makes various changes to the rules of entrepreneurs' relief under TCGA 1992, Pt 5, Ch 3. The changes include both restrictive measures (eg requiring claimants to have an interest in the business for a longer period of time) and relieving measures (eg where the individual's shareholding is diluted below 5%).

Schedule 16 comprises four paragraphs.

Schedule 16, para 1 amends TCGA 1992, s 169I to increase the minimum period for which an individual must have held an interest in the business to qualify for entrepreneurs' relief from one year to two. Consequential amendments are made to TCGA 1992, ss 169J, 169K, 169O and Sch 7ZA. Schedule 16, para 1(2)(d) also inserts new TCGA 1992, s 169I(7ZA) and (7ZB).

TCGA 1992, s 169I defines what is a material disposal of business assets qualifying for entrepreneurs' relief. Where the disposal is one of shares or securities (or interests in shares or securities) in a company, such a disposal must meet one of four conditions (A to D). Condition B is that throughout the period of two years (as now amended) ending with either the date on which the company ceases to be a trading company without continuing to be or becoming a member of a trading group or ceases to be a member of a trading group without continuing to be or becoming a trading company, the company must (a) be the individual's personal company which is either a trading company or the holding company of a trading group and (b) the individual must be an officer or employee of the company or of one or more companies in the trading group. The new subsections provide that these conditions (a) and (b) are also to be satisfied where there has been a prior issue of shares in the company to the individual following a 'relevant business transfer' and any of the issued shares constitute or otherwise form part of the shares subject to the disposal. A 'relevant business transfer' is a transfer of a business as a going concern (together with the whole of the assets of the business, or the whole without cash) wholly or partly in exchange for shares.

TCGA 1992, s 169K sets out what is a disposal associated with a relevant material disposal qualifying for entrepreneurs' relief. These disposals are of assets used in the business but owned personally by the individual. One of the conditions that must be met (although it is not sufficient for the disposal to be a qualifying disposal), referred to as Condition A2, is that the individual must make a material disposal of shares in a company, at least some of which must be ordinary shares, and, at the date of the disposal, the ordinary shares involved constitute at least 5% of the company's ordinary share capital and carry at least 5% of the voting rights in the company, absent 'share-purchase arrangements'. Schedule 16, para 2(2) amends this condition so that it now stipulates that, additionally, the company must be the individual's personal company (as defined by the amended TCGA 1992, s 169S).

TCGA 1992, ss 169L and 169LA set out what disposals of 'relevant business assets' qualify for entrepreneurs' relief where the qualifying business disposal is not a disposal of shares or securities (or interests in shares or securities). TCGA 1992, s 169LA specifies the circumstances in which a disposal of goodwill transferred to a close company is excluded from being the disposal of a relevant business asset. The test for exclusion has heretofore been that, immediately after the disposal, the individual and any relevant connected person together still own at least 5% of the ordinary share capital of, or hold at least 5% of the voting rights in (a) the close-company transferee, or (b) any company that is a fellow member of a group to which the close company belongs. This test is now amended by Sch 16, para 2(3) to require that immediately after the disposal, the individual meet any of the 'personal-company conditions' in relation to the close company or any company that is a fellow member of a group to which the close company belongs. The 'personal-company conditions' are the specified conditions in TCGA 1992, s 169S as amended by Sch 16, para 2(4) and as modified by *new TCGA 1992, s 169LA(1ZB)*.

TCGA 1992, s 169S(3) defines a personal company. Hitherto, a company has been an individual's personal company if the individual holds at least 5% of the company's ordinary share capital and at least 5% of the voting rights are exercisable by the individual by virtue of that holding. That definition is now extended by Sch 16, para 2(4) to include two additional tests, at least one of which must be met for the company to be an individual's personal company. These tests are that, by virtue of the individual's holding of ordinary shares, (a) the individual is beneficially entitled to at least 5% of the profits available for distribution to equity holders and, on a winding-up, to at least 5% of the assets so available; or (b) in the event of a disposal of the whole of the company's ordinary share capital, the individual would be beneficially entitled to at least 5% of the proceeds. Modifications, assumptions and provisos in relation to these tests are included in *new TCGA 1992, s 169S(3A)–(3E)*.

Schedule 16, para 3 inserts *new TCGA 1992, Pt V, Ch 3A*, which makes entrepreneurs' relief available in certain instances where a company ceases to be an individual's personal company. *New TCGA 1992, Pt V, Ch 3A* comprises seven sections (*new TCGA 1992, ss 169SB–169SH*).

New TCGA 1992, s 169SB explains that Chapter 3A provides for claims to entrepreneurs' relief in cases where it would otherwise be unavailable because a company ceases to be an individual's personal company. The overall scheme of the new provisions is the option of making two elections – the first being for there to be a deemed market-value disposal and reacquisition at the point when the company ceases to be the individual's personal company and the second to defer the resulting chargeable gain or allowable loss to an actual disposal of shares.

New TCGA 1992, s 169SC provides for the first election, which may be made if two conditions are met. The first condition is that, as a result of a 'relevant share issue', the company ceases to be the individual's personal company. A 'relevant share issue' is a share issue by the company for consideration consisting wholly of cash, for genuine commercial reasons, by way of subscription and not as part of a tax-avoidance arrangement. The second condition is that, had the individual disposed of all his shares or securities in the company immediately before the relevant share issue, the disposal would have been a material disposal of business assets (hence eligible for entrepreneurs' relief). It is part of this second condition that the hypothetical disposal would have been for the 'relevant value' of the shares and securities. This is defined as, in respect of shares, the appropriate proportion of the market value of the whole of the share capital and in respect of securities their market value.

Where these two conditions are satisfied, the individual may elect to be treated as if he had made a disposal of his entire holding immediately before the relevant share issue for its relevant value and immediately thereafter reacquired it for the same value.

New TCGA 1992, s 169SD provides that an individual who has made the first election (under *new TCGA 1992, s 169SC*) may also make a second election to defer the chargeable gain or allowable loss until the individual actually disposes of all or any part of the shares or securities. In such an event, if the second election has been made, there is a three-step process for calculating the chargeable gain treated as accruing to the individual on a subsequent disposal.

Step 1 is to attribute the notional gain on the notional disposal under *new TCGA 1992, s 169SC* to each of the classes of shares or securities involved, by reference to the proportion that the gains accruing on that disposal within each class bears to the total amount of gains accruing on the notional disposal.

Step 2 is further to attribute the amount attributed to each class under Step 1 to the shares or securities involved in the actual disposal, by reference to their nominal values.

Step 3 is to add together all the amounts found under Step 2, but, taking into account previous actual disposals, capping it at the total gain or loss attributed to that class.

A special rule in *new TCGA 1992, s 169SD(3)* applies if the actual disposal is a capital distribution under TCGA 1992, s 122.

New TCGA 1992, s 169SE provides for the situation where following a second election there is a reorganisation, conversion or reconstruction to which TCGA 1992, s 116 applies so that all or part of the new holding consists of qualifying corporate bonds. On a subsequent disposal of the new asset, (a) a calculation must be made of the chargeable gain that would have been treated as accruing to the individual on the deemed disposal of the old asset immediately before the reorganisation etc; (b) the whole or a corresponding part of that gain is to be treated as accruing on the subsequent disposal of all or part of the new asset, in addition to any gain or loss that actually accrues on the disposal and any chargeable gain treated as accruing under TCGA 1992, s 116(10)(b); and (c) on that subsequent disposal, the exemption under TCGA 1992, s 115 on the disposal of qualifying corporate bonds is to apply only in relation to any gain that actually accrues and not to any gain treated as accruing under (b).

New TCGA 1992, s 169SF provides for the situation where following a second election there is a reorganisation of share capital to which TCGA 1992, ss 127–130 apply. Where a deferred gain is treated as accruing on a subsequent disposal of the new holding, any apportionment of the gain between shares and securities comprised in the new holding is to be made in the same proportions as those by reference to which the acquisition costs of the original shares are apportionable under the reorganisation rules. Where, under TCGA 1992, s 128(3), the individual is treated as making a disposal of the original shares because he receives consideration other than the new holding for the original shares, that deemed disposal is also so treated under *new TCGA 1992, s 169SD.*

New TCGA 1992, s 169SG provides that an election under *new TCGA 1992, s 169SC* or *169SD* is irrevocable. An election under *new TCGA 1992, s 169SC* must be made by the first anniversary of the 31 January immediately following the tax year in which the notional disposal is made, whereas an election under *new TCGA 1992, s 169SD* must be made no later than four years after the end of that tax year.

New TCGA 1992, s 169SH provides how claims for entrepreneurs' relief under this Chapter are to be made, following an election under *new TCGA 1992, s 169SD.* The claim for relief must be made by the first anniversary of the 31 January immediately following the tax year in which the subsequent (actual) disposal is made.

Schedule 16, para 4 provides for commencement. In general, the amendments made by Sch 16 are to apply to disposals made after 5 April 2019. However, the extension of the minimum holding period from one to two years is not to apply in relation to a disposal where the time at which the business ceases to be carried on is before 29 October 2018, nor to a disposal where the date on which the company ceases to be a trading company without continuing to be or becoming a member of a trading group or ceases to be a member of a trading group without continuing to be a trading company is before 29 October 2018. The additional requirements relating to beneficial ownership introduced by Sch 16, para 2 are to apply, with certain exceptions, to disposals made after 28 October 2018. The new extension to entrepreneurs' relief introduced by Sch 16, para 3 is to have effect in relation to relevant share issues taking place after 5 April 2019.

Section 40 amends the restrictions placed by ITA 2007, s 418 and CTA 2010, s 197 on associated benefits for charitable donations to qualify for Gift Aid. Heretofore, the qualifying conditions have been breached if either of two conditions, A or B, has been met. Condition A is that the benefits associated with the gift exceed (1) 25% of the amount of the gift if that amount is £100 or less; (2) £25, if the amount of the gift is more than £100 but not more than £1,000; and (3) 5% of the amount of the gift if that amount is more than £1,000. These limits are now amended to read: (1) 25% of the amount of the gift if that amount is £100 or less; and (2) the sum of £25 and 5% of the amount of the excess if the amount of the gift exceeds £100. Thus, for a gift of £2,000, the benefit must now not exceed (£25 + 5% x (£2,000 – £100)) = £120, whereas previously, the benefit must not have exceeded £100 (5% of £2,000). Condition B remains unchanged. These amendments have effect for gifts or payments made after 5 April 2019.

Section 41 increases the non-primary purpose small-trading tax exemption for charitable companies and charitable trusts. ITA 2007, s 528 and CTA 2010, s 482 are amended to provide that the charity's trading-income resources and miscellaneous incoming resources (as defined) must not exceed or be expected to exceed 25% of the lower of total incoming resources and £80,000, but in all cases, there is to be a 'safe harbour' of £8,000. These monetary amounts have previously been £50,000 and £5,000, respectively. These amendments have effect from the tax year 2019/20 for charitable trusts and for accounting periods beginning after 31 March 2019 for charitable companies.

PART 2 OTHER TAXES

Stamp duty land tax

Section 42 provides new reliefs from stamp duty land tax (SDLT) to first-time buyers under a shared-ownership scheme.

First-time buyer's relief from SDLT was introduced in relation to land transactions with an effective date after 21 November 2017. The relief is also available where the purchase is made under a shared-ownership scheme, but only where the purchaser makes a 'market-value election' under FA 2003, Sch 9, paras 2 or 4, under which SDLT is payable on the grant of the lease on the full market value of the property. The alternative to making a market-value election is for the purchaser to pay SDLT on the initial grant of the lease and on any further purchases of an interest in the freehold. Where the freeholding is purchased in stages, with a corresponding reduction in the rent payable, this is known as 'staircasing'. If the election is not made, FA 2003, Sch 9, para 16 denies first-time buyer's relief on the acquisition of the lease and on any further acquisition of equity.

Section 42(3) inserts *new FA 2003, Sch 9, para 15*, which provides that where a shared-ownership lease is granted allowing for staircasing transactions and a market-value election is made, when a first-time buyer claims first-time buyer's relief under FA 2003, Sch 6ZA para 1 in respect of the grant of the lease, the rent payable under the lease will also be exempt from tax, as well as the premium, as at present.

Section 42(4) inserts *new FA 2003, Sch 9, paras 15A* and *15B*, which provide for first-time buyer's relief under shared-ownership schemes where no market-value election is made.

New FA 2003, Sch 9, para 15A provides that where a shared-ownership lease is granted but no market-value election is made under FA 2003, Sch 9, para 2 (no staircasing) or para 4 (staircasing allowed), and a claim is made for first-time buyer's relief on the first transaction (the grant of the lease), the net value of the rental payments under the lease is also be exempt from SDLT. Exemption for the premium (which will reflect the market value of the initial equity being purchased) is now also to be available, by virtue of the amendments being made to FA 2003, Sch 9, para 16 by s 42(6).

New FA 2003, Sch 9, para 15B provides equivalent relief to first-time buyers under a shared-ownership trust. Where on the declaration of the trust, no market-value election under FA 2003, Sch 9, para 9 is made, and a claim is made for first-time buyer's relief, the net value of the rent-equivalent payments under the trust will also be exempt from SDLT. Exemption for the initial capital payable on the declaration is now also to be available, by virtue of the amendments being made to FA 2003, Sch 9, para 16 by s 42(6).

The amendments made to FA 2003, Sch 9, para 16 by s 42(6) limit the denial of first-time buyer's relief to staircasing transactions (the acquisition of additional equity under either a shared-ownership lease or shared-ownership trust).

The amendments made by s 42 are to have effect for transactions with an effective date after 28 October 2018 and any transaction with an earlier effective date in respect of which a land-transaction return had not been made by 29 October 2018.

Section 43 extends the time limit for repayment claims in respect of land transactions that would have qualified for relief under the amendments made by s 42 had they been in force at the time.

Claims for the repayment of tax may be made until 29 October 2019 in respect of two types of land transaction and must be made by way of an amendment to the land-transaction return.

The first type of transaction is one in respect of which the amount of tax chargeable would have been less had the amendment made by s 42(3) (the insertion of *new FA 2003, Sch 9, para 15*) been in force from the effective date of the transaction. The second type of transaction is one in respect of which first-time buyer's relief could not have been claimed at the time but could have been claimed if the amendments made by s 42(4)–(6) (the insertion of *new FA 2003, Sch 9, paras 15A* and *15B* and the amendments to FA 2003, Sch 9, para 16) had been in force from the effective date of the transaction and a claim for first-time buyer's relief had been made.

Section 44 makes two amendments to the rules on the higher rates of SDLT for additional dwellings etc in FA 2003, Sch 4ZA.

FA 2003, Sch 4ZA, para 2 introduces the definitions of what is meant by a 'higher-rates transaction', on which the higher rates are payable. In each case, the main subject-matter of the transaction must be a major interest in one or more dwellings. Section 44(2) amends FA 2003, Sch 4ZA, para 2 to make it clear that an undivided share in a major interest (such as a tenancy in common) is itself a major interest.

Where individuals buy a new dwelling that is intended as a replacement for their only or main residence, the higher rates are not applied, provided that, inter alia and broadly, the replacement dwelling is bought within three years of the disposal of the old or the old dwelling is sold within three years of the purchase of the new. Under FA 2003, Sch 4ZA, para 8(3), in the latter case (ie the sale of the old residence after the purchase of the replacement residence), the amendment to the land-transaction return by virtue of which a claim to repayment of the additional tax is made must be within the later of (a) three months of the effective date of the sale of the old residence and (b) 12 months of the filing date for the original return. The amendment now made to FA 2003, Sch 4ZA, para 8(3) by s 44(4) is to substitute a new time limit, namely the later of (a) 12 months of the effective date of the sale of the old residence and (b) 12 months of the filing date for the original return.

The amendment made with respect to a major interest is to have effect in relation to any land transaction with an effective date after 28 October 2018. The amendment made to the time limit for the amendment return is to have effect for a 'subsequent transaction' (the sale of the old residence) with an effective date after 28 October 2018.

Section 45 introduces a new exemption from SDLT for financial institutions in resolution. *New FA 2003, s 66A*, inserted by s 45(1), provides exemption from charge for a land transaction effected by an instrument specified in *new FA 2003, s 66A(2)* or by an instrument made under such a specified instrument. The exemption concerns transfers of land following the exercise of certain resolution powers under the special-resolution régime for failing financial institutions under the Banking Act 2009. The exemption is to have effect in relation to land transactions with an effective date after 11 February 2019.

Section 46 makes a major change to the time limit for filing a land-transaction return, reducing it in most cases from 30 days after the effective date to 14 days after the effective date.

The provisions in respect of which the 14-day limit is now to apply instead of the former 30-day limit are:

- FA 2003, s 76(1), which imposes the duty on the purchaser to deliver a land-transaction return in relation to a notifiable transaction.
- FA 2003, s 80(2), which requires a return to be made if a transaction that was not previously notifiable becomes notifiable because a contingency ceases or consideration is ascertained ('new information').
  NB: where a transaction was previously notified but a further return is required as a result of the new information (because tax, or additional tax, becomes payable), the limit remains 30 days.
- FA 2003, s 81A(1), under which a return or further return is required as a consequence of a later linked transaction.
  NB: where the effect of the later transaction is that a further return is required following an earlier notified transaction (because tax, or additional tax, becomes payable), the limit remains 30 days from the effective date of the later transaction.
- FA 2003, Sch 17A para 3(3), as substituted by s 46(8), under which a transaction becomes notifiable because a lease continues for a period or further period of one year after a fixed term.
  NB: where the effect of the continuation is that a further return is required following an earlier notified transaction (because tax, or additional tax, becomes payable), the limit remains 30 days after the end of the one-year period.
- FA 2003, Sch 17A, para 4(3), as substituted by s 46(8), under which a transaction becomes notifiable because a lease continues after a deemed fixed term.
  NB: where the effect of the continuation is that a further return is required following an earlier notified transaction (because tax, or additional tax, becomes payable), the limit remains 30 days after the end of the deemed term.
- FA 2003, Sch 17A, para 8(3), as substituted by s 46(8), under which a transaction becomes notifiable because the rent paid or payable in respect of the first five years of a lease ceases to be uncertain or the fifth year of the term is reached at a later date.
  NB: where the effect of the cessation of the uncertainty is that a further return is required following an earlier notified transaction (because tax, or additional tax, becomes payable), the limit remains 30 days after the end of the fifth year or the earlier cessation of uncertainty.
- FA 2009 Sch 61, para 7(5), as amended by s 46(9), under which, following withdrawal of relief from the first transaction using alternative-finance investment bonds, interest is to run as from the end of a period of 14 days (previously 30) after the effective date of the first transaction.
  NB: the time limit for delivering the further return remains 30 days after the disqualifying event.
- FA 2009, Sch 61, para 20(3), as amended by s 46(9), under which relief withdrawn from first and second transactions using alternative-finance investment bonds where bond-holder acquires control of the underlying asset within 14 days (previously 30) of the effective date of the first transaction.

FA 2003, s 81 prescribes time limits for the delivery of further returns required after a particular relief is withdrawn on the occurrence of a disqualifying event. The general time limit for these further returns remains 30 days from the date of the disqualifying event, but in respect of certain reliefs, the 30 days are measured from the 'relevant date', defined in FA 2003, s 81(1B). The amendments made by s 46(4) add two further definitions of the relevant date, relating to relief for acquisitions under a regulated home-reversion plan and for acquisitions by a management company of a flat for occupation by a caretaker.

FA 2003, s 86 provides for the payment of tax. The default rule is that tax must be paid no later than the filing date for the land-transaction return. FA 2003, s 86(2) provides that where tax becomes payable because certain reliefs are withdrawn, that tax must be paid no later than the filing date for the return relating to the withdrawal. The amendment made by s 46(6) adds the withdrawal of relief from the application of the 15% higher-rates charge in certain cases relating to property businesses, farmhouses etc to the list in FA 2003, s 86(2).

FA 2003, s 87(1) provides that interest is payable on any unpaid tax from the end of the 30-day period from the 'relevant date' (defined in FA 2003, s 87(3)). This remains the default rule; however, new FA 2003, s 87(1A), inserted by s 46(7), provides that where a return has to be delivered within 14 days of the relevant date and that date is defined in respect of tax payable under FA 2003, s 81A, certain events in relation to leases under FA 2003, Sch 17A or in any case that is not specified under FA 2003, s 87(3), interest on unpaid tax is to run from the end of that 14-day period.

The amendments made by s 46 are to have effect for any land transaction with an effective date after 28 February 2019 and any land transaction with an earlier effective date but which becomes notifiable after 28 February 2019.

Stamp duty and SDRT

Section 47 has effect for stamp duty and imposes a new rule for valuing consideration on transfers of listed securities between connected persons.

It applies where an instrument transfers listed securities to a company or to the nominee of a company and the transferor is either connected with the company or is the nominee of a person connected with the company.

'Listed securities' are defined as stock or marketable securities that are regularly traded on a regulated market, a multilateral trading facility or a recognised foreign exchange, as defined in FA 1986, s 80B.

When such a transfer takes place for consideration in money or any stock or security or of the assumption or release of debt within SA 1891, s 57, the value of the consideration is to be treated for all purposes of the charge to stamp duty as the higher of (a) the value of the listed securities being transferred and (b) the amount or value of the consideration.

Where the consideration takes some other form or there is no consideration at all, the transfer is to be treated as taking place for consideration in money equal to the value of the listed securities.

In either case. the value of listed securities is to be taken to be the price that they might reasonably be expected to fetch on a sale in the open market at the date of execution of the transfer instrument.

HM Treasury is given the power to exempt certain cases from the application of s 47.

Section 47 is to have effect in relation to instruments executed after 28 October 2018.

Section 48 performs the like function for the purposes of SDRT.

It applies where:

- a person connected with a company or that person's nominee agrees to transfer listed securities to that company or that company's nominee (whether or not for consideration); or
- that person or that person's nominee transfers listed securities to that company or that company's nominee for consideration in money or money's worth.

'Listed securities' are defined as for s 47.

For the purposes of the principal charge to SDRT under FA 1986, s 87, where the agreement is one to transfer securities for consideration in money or money's worth, the value of that consideration is to be treated as equal to the higher of (a) the value of the listed securities at the time the agreement is made and (b) the amount or value of the consideration.

Where the consideration takes some other form or there is no consideration at all, the agreement is to be treated as made for consideration in money equal to the value of the listed securities at the time the agreement is made.

For the purposes of the SDRT charge under FA 1986, s 93 on transfers into a depositary-receipt system or the charge under FA 1986, s 96 on transfers into clearance services, the transfer is to be treated as being for consideration in money equal to the value of the securities at the time of transfer if the amount of consideration actually passing is less than that value.

In all cases, the value of listed securities at any time is to be taken to be the price that they might reasonably be expected to fetch on a sale in the open market at that time.

HM Treasury is given the power to exempt certain cases from the application of s 48.

For the purposes of the principal charge, s 48 is to have effect in relation to agreements to transfer securities made after 28 October 2018, and to conditional agreements made on or before that date but in respect of which the condition becomes satisfied after that date. For the purposes of the depositary-receipts charge and the clearance-services charges, s 48 is to have effect for transfers taking place after 28 October 2018, whenever the arrangement to transfer may have been made.

Section 49 is the equivalent for stamp duty of s 45 and confers exemption for transfers of stock or marketable securities in connection with financial institutions in resolution.

New FA 1986, s 85A, inserted by s 49(1) provides that stamp duty is not to be chargeable on the transfer of stock or marketable securities by an instrument specified in *new FA 1986, s 85A(2)* or by an instrument made under such a specified instrument. NB: the instruments specified for the purposes of this section are not necessarily identical to, and are greater in number than, the instruments specified in *new FA 2003, s 66A* for the purposes of stamp duty land tax.

The amendment made by s 49 are to have effect for instruments executed after 11 February 2019.

Section 50 makes a technical amendment to FA 2001, s 95, which confers exemption on share incentive plans under ITEPA 2003, s 488. It deletes the word 'approved' from the title of the section and replaces the reference in FA 2001, s 95(3) to 'an approved share incentive plan' by a reference to 'a Schedule 2 SIP', with effect from 6 April 2014. The amendment is necessary following the removal of the requirement for HMRC to approve such plans.

Value added tax

Section 51 makes a minor amendment to VATA 1994, s 55A.

VATA 1994, s 55A provides for the reverse charge to apply in certain circumstances to supplies of goods or services of the kind commonly used in missing trade intra-Community fraud. Under VATA 1994, s 55A(3), the recipient of the affected supplies must account for VAT on those supplies if their total value exceeds £1,000 in a given month. In order to relieve the regulatory burdens on small businesses that may arise as a consequence, *new VATA 1994, s 55A(9A)*, inserted by s 51, empowers HM Treasury to make an order modifying the application of VATA 1994, s 55A(3) in relation to any specified description of goods or services. The amendment is to have effect from 12 February 2019.

Section 52 introduces Sch 17, which amends the VAT treatment of vouchers, transposing into UK law Council Directive (EU) 2016/1065. Schedule 17 comprises six paragraphs.

Schedule 17, para 1 is introductory. Schedule 17, para 2 amends VATA 1994, s 51B, which introduces VATA 1994, Sch 10A, providing for the treatment of face-value vouchers. The amendments have the effect that VATA 1994, Sch 10A is now to have effect solely for face-value vouchers issued before 1 January 2019.

Schedule 17, para 3 inserts *new VATA 1994, ss 51C* and *51D*.

New VATA 1994, s 51C introduces *new VATA 1994, Sch 10B*, which is to make provision for the VAT treatment of vouchers (as defined by that Schedule) issued after 31 December 2018.

New VATA 1994, s 51D provides for the treatment of postage stamps. Its introduction is necessary due to the fact that postage stamps have hitherto been treated under VATA 1994, Sch 10A as a variety of face-value voucher but are expressly excluded from the definition of 'voucher' under *new VATA 1994, Sch 10B*. Under VATA 1994, Sch 10A para 5, consideration for the supply of a postage stamp is disregarded for all purposes of VAT, except to the extent that the consideration exceeds its face value, in which case the excess consideration is a standard-rated supply of services. For postage stamps issued after 31 December 2018, new *VATA 1994, s 51D* replicates this treatment, as it provides that the issue of a postage stamp and any subsequent transfer of it is to be a supply of services, the consideration for which is to be disregarded for all purposes of VAT except to the extent that it exceeds the face value of the stamp.

Schedule 17, para 4 makes a consequential amendment to the title of VATA 1994, Sch 10A.

Schedule 17, para 5 inserts *new VATA 1994, Sch 10B*, which comprises 11 paragraphs. It makes a distinction between 'single-purpose vouchers' and 'multi-purpose vouchers', for which separate special rules are provided.

New VATA 1994, Sch 10B, para 1 defines the concept of 'voucher' as an instrument in physical or electronic form in relation to which three conditions are met.

The first condition is that one or more persons must be under an obligation to accept the voucher as consideration for the provision of goods or services. The second condition is that either those goods or services or the persons who are under that obligation, or both, must be limited and stated on or recorded in the voucher or the terms and conditions governing its use. The third condition is that the voucher must be transferable by gift (whether or not also for consideration). Three types of instrument are expressly excluded from the definition of 'voucher': discount vouchers, tickets and postage stamps.

New VATA 1994, Sch 10B, para 2 defines related expressions.

New VATA 1994, Sch 10B, para 3 sets out the general rule for the treatment of vouchers, which is that the issue and any subsequent transfer of a voucher is to be treated as a supply of the goods or services for which the voucher may be accepted as consideration ('relevant goods or services'). Such a supply is referred to as a 'paragraph 3 supply'.

New VATA 1994, Sch 10B, paras 4 and *5* provide special rules for 'single-purpose vouchers'.

New VATA 1994, Sch 10B, para 4 defines a 'single-purpose voucher' as a voucher in relation to which it is known at the time of its issue both what is to be the place of supply of the relevant goods or services and the single supply category into which that supply falls (i e standard-rated, reduced-rated, zero-rated or exempt or outside the scope).

New VATA 1994, Sch 10B, para 5 provides that when a single-purpose voucher is accepted as consideration for the provision of relevant goods or services, that provision is not to be a supply of goods or services for VAT purposes. However, where the person who provides those goods or services is not the person who issued the voucher, the provider is to be treated as having made a supply of those goods or services to the issuer.

New VATA 1994, Sch 10B, paras 6–8 provide special rules for 'multi-purpose vouchers'.

New VATA 1994, Sch 10B, para 6 defines a multi-purpose voucher by exception as a voucher that is not a single-purpose voucher.

New VATA 1994, Sch 10B, para 7 provides that any consideration for the issue or subsequent transfer of a multi-purpose voucher is to be disregarded for VAT purposes, nor is the paragraph 3 supply itself to give rise to allowable input tax under VATA 1994, s 26.

New VATA 1994, Sch 10B, para 8 provides that when a multi-purpose voucher is accepted as consideration for the provision of relevant goods or services, that provision is to be treated as a supply (in contrast to the treatment of a single-purpose voucher under *new VAT 1994, Sch 10B para 5*) and the value of that supply is to depend on whether the supplier knows what the consideration was for the most recent transfer of the voucher for consideration. If the supplier knows that consideration, the value of his supply is the amount of that consideration, net of VAT. For example, if the supply is standard-rated, and the consideration for the most recent transfer of the voucher was £10, the value of the supply is £8. If the supplier does not know the amount of the consideration for the most recent transfer of the voucher for consideration, the value of the supply is to be the face value of the voucher, net of VAT.

New VATA 1994, Sch 10B, para 9 provides for the involvement of intermediaries. Where a voucher is issued or transferred by an agent acting in his own name, the paragraph 3 supply is not to be treated as a supply under VATA 1994, s 47(3) if it otherwise would be. VATA 1994, s 47(3) provides that where services (other than electronically supplied services and telecommunications services) are supplied through an agent acting in his own name, HMRC may treat the supply as both made to and by the agent. Nevertheless, that paragraph 3 supply is in every case to be treated as both a supply to and by the agent.

New VATA 1994, Sch 10B, para 10 provides that any services additional to the issue or transfer of a voucher provided by the issuer or the transferor are not to be subject to these rules.

New VATA 1994, Sch 10B, para 11 provides that where both a supply of goods or services to a person and the issue or transfer of a voucher to that person form part of a single composite transaction, the paragraph 3 supply (the supply of relevant goods or services treated as made on the issue and any subsequent transfer of the voucher) is to be treated as made for no consideration if the total consideration for the composite transaction is not different or not significantly different from what it would have been if the voucher had not been issued or transferred.

Section 52(6) makes a consequential amendment to the VAT Regulations (to SI 1995/2518 reg 38ZA(2)).

Section 53 introduces Sch 18, which extends the eligibility for joining a VAT group beyond bodies corporate. Hitherto, UK law has limited membership of a VAT group to bodies corporate, but in the joined cases of *Larentia + Minerva* (Case C-108/14) and *Marenave Schiffahrts AG* (Case C-109/14), delivered on 16 July 2015, the Court of Justice of the European Union held that Member States are precluded from preserving the right to form a VAT group solely for entities with legal personality and linked to the controlling company in a relationship of subordination, unless these requirements were proportionate and necessary to combat abuse. Following consultation, the legislation has now been enacted, nearly four years down the line and within a few weeks of the United Kingdom's likely exit from the European Union, allowing entities other than bodies corporate to join a VAT group but retaining a strict holding-company control requirement. Even so, Schedule 18 is not to take effect until a day to be appointed.

Schedule 18 comprises 15 paragraphs, divided into two Parts. Part 1 (paras 1 and 2) makes the substantive amendments; Part 2 (paras 3–15) makes consequential amendments.

Schedule 18, para 1 amends VATA 1994, s 43A, which defines eligibility for membership of a VAT group. *New VATA 1994, s 43A(4)* and *(5)*, inserted by Sch 18, para 1(4), extend eligibility beyond bodies corporate to individuals and partnerships in defined circumstances.

An individual who carries on a business is to be eligible to be treated as a member of a group together with one or more UK bodies corporate on condition that the individual controls the UK body corporate or all the UK bodies corporate and is established, or has a fixed establishment, in the United Kingdom in relation to the business he carries on.

Two or more 'relevant persons' carrying on a business in partnership are to be eligible to be treated as members of a group together with one or more UK bodies corporate on condition that the partnership controls the UK body corporate or all the UK bodies corporate and is established, or has a fixed establishment, in the United Kingdom in relation to the business it carries on.

A UK body corporate is defined as a body corporate established, or having a fixed establishment, in the United Kingdom. A 'relevant person' may be an individual, a body corporate or a Scottish partnership.

New VATA 1994, s 43AZA, inserted by Sch 18, para 2, defines what is meant by 'control' for the purposes of VATA 1994, s 43A. A body corporate ('X') is to be regarded as controlling a UK body corporate ('UKCo') if (a) X is empowered by statute to control UKCo's activities or (b) X is UKCo's holding company. An individual is to be regarded as controlling UKCo if that individual, were he to be a company, would be UKCo's holding company. Likewise, a partnership is to be regarded as controlling UKCo if that partnership, were it to be a company, would be UKCo's holding company. The definition of 'holding company' is to be that in Companies Act 2006, s 1159 and Sch 6. *New VATA 1994, s 43AZA* is essentially a restatement of what was previously VATA 1994, s 43A(2) and (3), omitted by Sch 18, para 1(3), supplemented by the definition of control by a partnership.

Schedule 18, Pt 2 makes consequential amendments throughout VATA 1994, chiefly substituting references to bodies corporate by references to persons and similar.

Alcohol

Section 54 amends ALDA 1979, s 62(1A)(a) to increase the rate of alcoholic liquor duty on sparkling cider of a strength exceeding 5.5% abv from £279.46 to £288.10 per hectolitre; this is an increase of 3.09%. It also substitutes the Table in ALDA 1979, Sch 1, Pt 1, imposing new rates of duty per hectolitre on wine or made-wine of a strength not exceeding 22%. The amendments made by s 52 are to have effect from 1 February 2019.

Section 55 introduces a new alcoholic liquor duty band and rate for mid-strength cider. Mid-strength cider is defined by new ALDA 1979, s 62B(4)(aa), inserted by s 55(3)(e)(iii), as cider that is not sparkling and is of a strength of not less than 6.9% abv but not exceeding 7.5% abv. Hitherto, for the purposes of alcoholic liquor duty on still (non-sparkling) cider, there have been just two duty bands – the first of a strength not exceeding 7.5% abv ('standard cider') and the second of a strength exceeding 7.5% abv ('strong cider'). The rate of duty on mid-strength cider is set at £50.71 per hectolitre. The rate of duty on standard cider (now still cider of a strength less than 6.9% abv) remains £61.04 per hectolitre and that on strong cider (still cider of a strength exceeding 7.5% abv but less than 8.5% abv) remains £40.38 per hectolitre.

Consequential amendments are made to ALDA 1979, s 62B, which has hitherto defined 'strong cider' and is now also to define 'mid-strength cider'. All amendments made by s 55 are to have effect from 1 February 2019.

Tobacco

Section 56 increases the rate of tobacco products duty, substituting the Table in TPDA 1979, Sch 1. The products affected are cigarettes, cigars, hand-rolling tobacco and other smoking tobacco and chewing tobacco and the increases are approximately 5.09%. The new rates are to have effect from 18:00 hrs on 29 October 2018.

Section 57 introduces a new dutiable category of tobacco product, namely tobacco for heating. This is a type of tobacco designed to be heated so as to produce nicotine-infused vapour for smoking. The rate of duty on tobacco for heating is to be set at £234.65 per kilogram and consequential amendments are made to TPDA 1979. However, the definition of this product and details of the charge to duty are delegated to regulations, which are yet to be made.

Vehicle duties

Section 58 makes amendments to VERA 1994, generally increasing rates of vehicle excise duty.

The general rates in VERA 1994, Sch 1, para 1 on vehicles not covered elsewhere are increased from £155 to £160 (where the engine cylinder capacity does not exceed 1549 cc) and from £255 to £265 (where the engine cylinder capacity exceeds 1549 cc).

The graduated rates of duty under VERA 1994, Sch 1, para 1B for light passenger vehicles registered before 1 April 2017 are amended, increasing all but the two lowest rates so that they now range from £20 to £570 (previously £20 to £550).

The graduated rates of duty under VERA 1994, Sch 1, para 1GC (Tables 1 and 2) for the first licence of a light passenger vehicle registered after 31 March 2017 are amended, increasing in Table 1 all but the two lowest rates so that they now range from £10 to £2135 (previously £10 to £2070) and in Table 2 all but the lowest rate so that they now range from £25 to £2135 (previously £25 to £2070).

Rates charged in VERA 1994, Sch 1, paras 1GD, 1GE, 1J and 2(1) are also increased.

All amendments made by s 58 are to have effect for licences taken out after 31 March 2019.

Section 59 introduces an exemption from vehicle excise duty for taxis capable of zero emissions. The amendments made exclude the application under to VERA 1994 Sch 1, para 1GE of the higher rates of duty on vehicles with a price exceeding £40,000 in respect of taxis that are capable of zero emissions when they are first registered under either VERA 1994 or foreign law, but details are to be left to regulations. The exemption is to apply to qualifying vehicles first registered after 31 March 2019 but also to vehicles first registered no earlier than 1 April 2017, from the date from which the licence is first renewed on or after that date.

Section 60 introduces a lower rate of HGV road-user levy under HGVA 2013 for vehicles meeting the latest Euro 6 emissions standard and a higher rate for those that do not.

Section 60(4) inserts *new HGVA 2013, s 7(2A)*, which provides that a rebate entitlement is also to arise where levy has been paid at the rate applicable to vehicles not meeting Euro 6 emissions standards when they come to meet them.

Section 60(6) replaces Table 1 in HGVA 2013, Sch 1, para 5 by *new Tables 1* and 1A. *New Table 1* now provides new rates for vehicles meeting Euro 6 emissions standards for the existing bands A to E(T), ranging from a yearly rate of £76.50 for Band A to £747.00 for Band E(T). *New Table 1A* sets rates for vehicles not meeting Euro 6 emission standards for the same bands, ranging from a yearly rate of £102.00 for Band A to £996.00 for Band E(T). Rates of levy under the previous Table 1 ranged from £85.00 to £830.00, by way of comparison.

Consequential amendments are made to other provisions of HGVA 2013 and VERA 1994 and the HGV Road User Levy (Rate for Prescribed Vehicles) Regulations 2018 are revoked.

The amendments made to HGVA 2013 and the revocation of the regulations are to have effect in relation to levy that becomes due and payable after 31 January 2019 and paid after that date. The amendments made to VERA 1994 are to have effect in relation to licences taken out after 31 January 2019.

Air passenger duty

Section 61 increases the long-haul rates of air passenger duty under FA 1994, s 30(4A) from £78 to £80 for standard-class travel and from £172 to £176, with effect in relation to the carriage of passengers beginning after 31 March 2020. The rates applicable between 1 April 2019 and 31 March 2020 are £78 and £156, respectively.

Gaming

Section 62 increases the rate of remote gaming duty under FA 2014, s 155(3) from 15% to 21% of the gaming provider's profits on remote gaming for an accounting period, with effect for accounting periods beginning after 31 March 2019, with provision for straddling periods.

Section 63 introduces **Sch 19**, which introduces changes to the administration of gaming duty. Schedule 19 comprises eight paragraphs.

Schedule 19, para 1 amends FA 1997, s 11 in consequence of the change to permissible accounting periods to be introduced under FA 1997, Sch 1, para 9 as amended by Sch 18, para 2. Hitherto, accounting periods for gaming duty have been six-month periods beginning on 1 April and 1 October (FA 1997, s 15(3)), although duty payers have been able to agree six-month periods beginning on other dates with HMRC. Under the amended provisions, duty payers will be able to agree 'alternative accounting periods' shorter or longer than six months to a limited extent but may also have other accounting periods imposed on them. Accordingly, *new FA 1997,* *s 11(4A)–(4B)*, inserted by Sch 19, para 1(3), provide for adjusting the duty rate bands in the Table in FA 1997, s 11(2) by multiplying them by the fraction A/B, where A is the number of days in the alternative accounting period and B the number of days in the period that would have been the accounting period (or, where the alternative accounting period spans more than one such period, the first of those periods).

Schedule 19, para 2 makes provision for the new alternative accounting periods, by substituting *new FA 1997, Sch 1, para 9(1)–(1F)* for the existing FA 1997, Sch 1, para 9(1).

Where HMRC and every 'relevant person' now so agree, the gaming-duty provisions of FA 1997 are to have effect in relation to accounting periods which may either be six-month periods beginning on any date or periods beginning on any date which are longer or shorter than six months, but approximately equivalent to periods of six months in weeks.

However, where HMRC has reason to believe that there is a risk to the revenue, it may impose accounting periods shorter than six months and periods beginning other than on 1 April and 1 October and impose or agree transitional accounting periods where a premises ceases to trade or alternative periods begin or cease to have effect.

The review and appeal procedures under FA 1994, ss 13A–16 are to apply in respect of decisions by HMRC to refuse a request for alternative accounting periods and a direction to impose such periods.

Schedule 19, para 3 makes a consequential amendment.

FA 1997, s 11(8) defines gross gaming yield (by reference to which the duty rate bands are set) for any accounting period to be the aggregate of the gaming receipts from the premises for that period and the 'banker's profits' from gaming where the provider of the premises or a person acting on his behalf acts as banker in relation to any dutiable gaming taking place on the premises. 'Banker's profits' are defined in FA 1997, s 11(10). The amendments now made by Sch 19, para 4 substitute *new FA 1997, s 11(10)* and *(10ZA)* for the existing FA 1997, s 11(10). The effect of the amendments is to provide that where the gross gaming yield (GGY) for any premises in an accounting period is a negative amount, the GGY is to be taken as nil and the negative amount may be carried forward to reduce the GGY for those premises for later periods.

Schedule 19, paras 5 and **6** amend FA 1997, s 12 and the Gaming Duty Regulations 1997 (SI 1997/2196) so as to remove HMRC's power to require payments on account of gaming duty and the associated administrative provisions.

Schedule 19, para 7 provides that the amendments made by Sch 19 are to come into force on 1 October 2019, but Sch 19, para 8 makes transitional provisions where there is an agreement in force for an alternative accounting period straddling 30 September 2019.

Environmental taxes

Section 64 amends the climate change levy exemption for mineralogical and metallurgical processes.

The amendments now made to FA 2000, Sch 6, para 12A have the effect that the exemption need no longer apply only where the taxable commodity is supplied to the person who uses it in a mineralogical or metallurgical process. It is now to be sufficient that the supply is made for use in such a process. They also amend the definition of 'mineralogical process' to mean a process falling within Division 23 of NACE Rev 2.

The amendments made by s 64 are to have effect from 12 February 2019.

Section 65 increases the rates of landfill tax under FA 1996, s 42. The standard rate is to be increased from £88.95 to £91.35 per whole tonne and the reduced rate from £2.80 to £2.90. These amendments are to have effect for disposals made after 31 March 2019.

Inheritance tax

Section 66 makes technical amendments to the IHT provisions relating to the residence nil-rate band with a view to clarifying the downsizing provisions and the definition of 'inheriting' property for the purposes of the residence nil-rate band in IHTA 1984, ss 8A–8M.

IHTA 1984, s 8D(5)(e) defines the abbreviation 'VT' as standing for the value transferred by the *chargeable transfer* [author's italics] under [IHTA 1984] section 4 on the person's death. The amendments now made by s 66(2) to IHTA 1984, s 8FA (2)(b) and 8FA(5) replace 'VT', wherever it occurs there by 'the value transferred by the *transfer of value* [author's italics] under [IHTA 1984] section 4 on the person's death', thus correcting the error. 'VT' remains as 'VT' in the remaining parts of IHTA 1984, s 8FA, where it is indeed the chargeable transfer that is intended. The amendments now made by s 66(3) to Step 2 in IHTA 1984, s 8FE(9) perform the same function. The amendment made by s 66(4) to IHTA 1984, s 8E(1) add the words 'on the person's death' to complete the same expression in that provision.

IHTA 1984 s 8J defines the meaning of 'inherited' for these provisions. IHTA 1984, s 8J(6) provides that where the property inherited from the deceased person forms part of that person's estate immediately before his death because it forms part of a gift with reservation under FA 1986, s 102(3) previously made by the deceased person, the person inheriting inherits the property if he was the person to whom the gift was made. The amendment now made by s 66(5) to IHTA 1984, s 8J(6) expressly disapplies IHTA 1984, s 8J(2)–(5) and restates the provision to state that where the property inherited from the deceased person forms part of that person's estate immediately before his death because it forms part of a gift with reservation under FA 1986, s 102(3) previously made by the deceased person, the person inheriting inherits the property if the property originally comprised in the gift became comprised in the estate of the person inheriting on the making of the disposal.

The amendments made by s 66 are to have effect in relation to deaths after 29 October 2018.

Soft drinks industry levy

Section 67 brings certain penalties relating to the soft drinks industry levy into the harmonised penalty regimes of FA 2009, Schs 55 and 56.

Soft drinks industry levy is an indirect tax introduced under FA 2017, Pt 2, with effect from 6 April 2018. The Soft Drinks Industry Levy Regulations, SI 2018/41 reg 21, made under FA 2017, s 52, requires a liable person to make returns within 30 days of the end of each accounting period. Penalties for failure to make such a return are chargeable under FA 2009, Sch 55, by virtue of Item 13A in the Table in FA 2009, Sch 55, para 1(5), with effect from 6 April 2018, by virtue of SI 2018/468.

The amendment made by s 67(1) to F(No 3)A 2010, Sch 10, para 7, which prospectively inserts *new FA 2009, Sch 55, paras 13A–13J*, inserts a reference to Item 13A in *new FA 2009, Sch 55, para 13A(1)*. *New FA 2009, Sch 55, paras 13A–13J* provide for the amount of penalties to be charged for the failure to make returns for period of between two and six months. Section 67(2) provides for all the prospective amendments to be made to FA 2009, Sch 55 by F(No 3)A 2010 (as amended by s 66(1)) to have effect for the purposes of the soft drinks industry levy from 12 February 2019.

FA 2009, Sch 56 provides for penalties to be made for failure to pay tax on time. Item 11ZA in the Table in FA 2009, Sch 56, para 1(4), which relates to penalties for failure to pay the levy on time, was inserted with effect from 6 April 2018 by virtue of SI 2018/467. However, the amendments to be made to FA 2009, Sch 56 by F(No 3)A 2010, Sch 11 have yet to be given effect. Section 67(3) amends the text to be substituted for existing FA 2009, Sch 56, para 3(1)(a) by F(No 3)A 2010, Sch 11, para 5(3) to include a reference to Item 11ZA. This will enable the amount of the penalty to be set.

Section 68 makes amendments in relation to the soft drinks industry levy that the Isle of Man Government intends to introduce there with effect from 1 April 2019.

Section 68(1) amends the Isle of Man Act 1979, s 1(1) to add the new Manx levy and the UK levy to the list of 'common duties' as defined in that Act.

Section 68(3) inserts *new FA 2017, s 58A*, the object of which is to prevent double taxation, and which applies where chargeable soft drinks are imported into the United Kingdom from the Isle of Man and a charge to the Manx levy arises in relation to those drinks. If the rate of the Manx levy is not less than the UK rate, the importation is not to be treated under FA 2017, s 33 as a chargeable event for the purposes of the UK levy. If the rate of the Manx levy is less than the UK rate, the amount of the UK levy charged in relation to the soft drinks is to be reduced by the amount of the Manx levy.

For the purposes of the tax credits available under FA 2017, s 39 and SI 2018/41, Pt 6 on the export of chargeable soft drinks, exports to the Isle of Man are not to qualify for credits.

Consequential amendments are made to FA 2017, ss 33 and 39.

The amendments made by s 68 are to have effect from 1 April 2019.

PART 3 CARBON EMISSIONS TAX

Introductory

Sections 69 to 79 pave the way for the introduction of a new tax, carbon emissions tax, the detail of which is to be left to regulations. The current intention is that the tax is to be introduced only if the United Kingdom leaves the European Union without a withdrawal agreement.

Section 69 provides that a tax to be known as 'carbon emissions tax' is to be charged in accordance with FA 2019, Pt 3 and that HMRC is to be responsible for its collection and management.

Charge to tax

Section 70 provides that carbon emissions tax (abbreviated here to 'CET') is to be charged in relation to a 'regulated installation' if the amount of reported carbon emissions for a reporting period exceeds the 'emissions allowance' for that period. The amount of 'taxable carbon emissions' is to be the amount of the excess. The rate of CET is to be £16 per tonne of carbon dioxide equivalent (abbreviated here to 'CO_2 equivalent').

Section 71 defines 'reported carbon emissions' in relation to an installation for a reporting period as the total amount of emissions from the installation, in tonnes of CO_2 equivalent as stated in the 'emissions determination' or the latest such determination or, in the absence of a determination, in the 'emissions report' for that period. 'Emissions determination' is defined as the regulator's estimate of the total amount of emissions from the installation for the period, determined in accordance with article 70 of the Monitoring and Reporting Regulation (Commission Regulation (EU) No 601/2012) or the Greenhouse Gas Emissions Trading Scheme Regulations 2012 (SI 2012/3038), reg 44.

Section 72 defines 'emissions report' and 'reporting period'. The emissions report is the report of emissions submitted to the regulator in order to comply with the monitoring and reporting requirements (or the monitoring and reporting conditions for an 'excluded installation') or with a requirement of a notice of surrender or of a revocation notice. The 'reporting period' is a 'scheme year' or such shorter period for which an emissions report is required by a notice of surrender or a revocation notice.

Section 73 defines 'emissions allowance', which is to be expressed in tonnes of CO_2 equivalent.

Section 74 provides that CET is to be payable in relation to an installation by the person who is the permit holder for the installation at the end of the reporting date. The 'reporting date' is defined as the day on which the emissions report for a reporting period has to be submitted to the regulator under the Emissions Regulations.

Administration etc

Section 75 confers on HMRC the power to make regulations concerning the matters specified.

Section 76 inserts CET into the list of taxes in PCTA 1968, s 1 in relation to which temporary statutory effect may be given by House of Commons resolutions and a consequential amendment is made to regulation 52 of the Emissions Regulations. The European Union (Withdrawal) Act 2018 is not to apply for the purposes of CET in relation to any rights, powers, liabilities, obligations, restrictions, remedies and procedures so far as they arise under Council Directive 2008/118/EC (general excise-duty arrangements) or Council Directive 2003/96/EC on the Community framework for the taxation of energy products and electricity. It also provides for additional regulatory powers.

General

Section 77 provides for interpretation.

Section 78 provides for further regulations to be made under ss 73, 75 or 76.

Section 79 provides for commencement (which is to be from an appointed day) and transitional provisions.

PART 4 ADMINISTRATION AND ENFORCEMENT

Time limits for assessments etc

Section 80 amends TMA 1970 in relation to offshore income or gains to increase time limits for assessment.

Section 80(2) inserts *new TMA 1970, s 36A*, which applies where there is a loss of income tax or CGT where the lost tax involves an offshore matter or an offshore transfer making the lost tax significantly harder to identify. It provides that an assessment may be made on the taxpayer at any time within 12 years of the end of the year of assessment to which the lost tax relates, subject to TMA 1970, s 36(1A), which sets an overall time limit of 20 years for assessments where the loss of tax was brought about carelessly or deliberately.

Section 80(3)–(6) define in which circumstances lost income tax or CGT involves an offshore matter or an offshore transfer and cites instances in which an offshore transfer makes lost tax significantly harder to identify.

Section 80(7) provides that an assessment under s 80(2) may not be made if within the time limit, HMRC has received 'relevant overseas information' on the basis of which it could reasonably have been expected to become aware of the lost tax and it was reasonable to expect the assessment to have been made before that time limit.

Section 80(9) prevents the making of an assessment under s 80(2) to the extent that liability to the lost tax arises as a result of transfer pricing adjustments under TIOPA 2010, Pt 4.

The amendments made by s 80 are to have effect in relation to assessments made on a person relating to the year of assessment 2013/14 and subsequent years where the loss of tax is brought about carelessly and relating to the 2015/16 year of assessment and subsequent years in any other case.

Section 81 performs the same function as s 80 in relation to inheritance tax.

Section 81(3) inserts *new IHTA 1984, s 240B*, which applies where there is a loss of inheritance tax in relation to a chargeable transfer where the lost tax involves an offshore matter or an offshore transfer making the lost tax significantly harder to identify. It provides that proceedings to recover the lost tax may be brought at any time within 12 years (rather than the normal four years) of the later of the two dates in IHTA 1984, s 240(2)(a) and (b). Those dates are: (a) the date on which the payment or the last instalment payment of tax was made and accepted and (b) the date on which the tax or the last instalment became due.

The amendments made by s 81 are to have effect in relation to chargeable transfers made after 31 March 2013 where the loss of tax is brought about carelessly and to transfers made after 31 March 2015 in any other case.

Security deposits

Section 82 inserts *new FA 2004, s 70A* and *new FA 1998, Sch 18, reg 88A*, which confer on HMRC the power to make regulations requiring persons to give security for construction-industry scheme deductions and liabilities to corporation tax, respectively, where HMRC considers it necessary for the protection of the revenue.

International agreements

Section 83 introduces statutory powers to implement Council Directive (EU) 2017/1852 on tax-dispute resolution mechanisms in the European Union.

It inserts *new TIOPA 2010, ss 128A–128C*.

New TIOPA 2010, s 128A empowers HM Treasury to make regulations in relation to the Directive. *New TIOPA 2010, s 128B* enables HMRC to give effect to any agreements, decisions or opinions that anything in regulations under *new TIOPA 2010, s 128A* may require. *New TIOPA 2010, s 128C* provides for any necessary disclosures in relation to the instruments, agreements or arrangements to which reference is made in *new TIOPA 2010, s 128A(1)*.

Section 84 confers the power on HM Treasury to make regulations requiring disclosure of information concerning certain cross-border tax arrangements to HMRC and constitutes the implementation of Council Directive 2018/822 amending Directive 2011/16/EU on the mandatory automatic exchange of tax information. It also paves the way for regulations to ensure compliance with arrangements specified in an Order in Council made under FA 2006, s 173, which could include the OECD's model mandatory disclosure rules.

Section 84(8) and (9) provide that no regulations may be made under s 84 unless the Chancellor of the Exchequer has reported to the House of Commons how powers under s 84 may be exercised if the United Kingdom should leave the European Union without ratification of a negotiated withdrawal agreement and a framework for its future relationship ('no-deal Brexit') as well as with such agreements in place.

Payment of unlawful advance corporation tax

Sections 85 and 86 are intended to address uncertainty that has arisen following the Supreme Court's decision in the test case *Prudential Assurance Co Ltd v HMRC* (2018 UKSC 39). This was a test case in the controlled foreign company (CFC) and dividend GLO, which concerns the tax treatment of UK-resident companies that received dividends from overseas portfolio shareholdings.

On receiving dividends from a UK-resident company, a UK-resident recipient was exempt from corporation tax, and (prior to 1999) would receive a tax credit equal to the amount of ACT (advance corporation tax) that the distributing company had paid on the distribution. In contrast, up until 2009, a UK-resident company receiving dividends from an overseas company was subject to corporation tax. Furthermore, it did not receive a tax credit on the dividends other than for withholding tax under the appropriate double tax treaty. The essential elements of this system were found to be in breach of European law.

Prudential brought a claim to recover corporation tax and ACT levied contrary to EU law, seeking compound interest on the various categories of overpaid tax.

Whereas the Supreme Court upheld Prudential's right to a credit for UK corporation tax on foreign dividend income at the nominal tax rate of the jurisdiction of the paying company, it also held, overturning its previous decision in *Sempra Metals v IRC* [2007] UKHL 34, that the taxpayer was not entitled to compound interest in respect of tax that was levied in breach of EU law and that a claim in restitution did not lie to recover lawful ACT that was set against unlawful mainstream corporation tax.

Section 85 is an attempt to reconcile the interests of taxpayers and the public purse by providing for a form of quasi-interest to apply to outstanding litigation where, on any date before 12 December 2012, a person started proceedings against HMRC including a claim arising out of a 'relevant payment' and the claim is yet to be settled, discontinued or finally determined.

A 'relevant payment' is defined as a payment of unlawful ACT made by the claimant after 31 December 1996 or in the six years immediately preceding the starting date of the proceedings in question and that was set off or wholly or partly repaid before the proceedings were started.

In these circumstances, s 85 provides that the claimant is to be entitled to an order requiring HMRC to pay him 'the principal amount' and simple interest. The 'principal amount' is an amount equal to the interest that would have accrued if simple interest had been due on the relevant payment at the 'appropriate rate' for the period beginning with the date the payment was made and ending on the date of set-off or repayment of the unlawful ACT. In addition, simple interest at the 'appropriate rate' is to be due to the claimant from the date the appropriate-rate period ends and ending with the date the principal amount is paid.

Section 85(4) sets out what the appropriate rate per annum is, beginning with 1 October 1993. That rate is, in fact, the statutory rate of interest on overpaid tax for the appropriate time. Any interest or 'repayment supplement' already paid by HMRC together with the repayment of the unlawful ACT is to be deducted from the principal amount.

Section 86 clarifies that nothing in s 85 is to be construed as limiting the remedies a court may award in respect of the claim in s 85, but that a person who has already obtained a remedy for the loss of use of money in respect of a relevant payment under s 85 is not to be entitled to an order under s 85 and that, on the other hand, a person who has obtained an order under s 85 is not to be entitled to any other remedy for the loss of use of money in respect of the relevant payment. The payment of interest or of repayment supplement by HMRC is not to be regarded as such a remedy. Amounts paid by HMRC under s 85 are not to be subject to income tax or corporation tax.

Voluntary returns

Section 87 is intended to put on a statutory footing HMRC's practice on treating voluntary returns. In a nutshell, where a taxpayer has filed a tax return without having received a statutory notice requiring him to deliver a return, HMRC has historically treated such a return as if it had been delivered in compliance with such a notice. This practice has recently been found by the First-Tier Tribunal as unlawful. An appeal is in progress, but s 87 intends to make HMRC's practice both retrospectively and prospectively lawful.

Section 87(1) inserts *new TMA 1970, s 12D*, which is to apply where:

- a person delivers a 'purported return' under TMA 1970, ss 8 (personal returns), 8A (trustee's returns) or 12AA (partnership returns) without having received a notice to do so under the relevant section; and
- HMRC treats the return as a return made and delivered in compliance with such a notice.

Where this is the case, the relevant notice is to be treated as having been given to the person on the day the return was delivered, and the return is to be treated as having been made and delivered in compliance with that notice for all purposes of the Tax Acts.

A 'purported return' is a return in a form and delivered in a way that a corresponding return could have been made and delivered in response to the relevant notice and purports to be a return under the relevant section. Nothing in s 87, however, is to affect the statutory time limits under TMA 1970, ss 34–36 for assessments or self-assessments nor any other provision of the Tax Acts specifying a period for making or delivering assessments to income tax or CGT.

Section 87(2) inserts *new FA 1998, Sch 18, para 20A*, the parallel provisions for the purposes of company tax returns.

Section 87(3) and (4) provide that the amendments made by s 87 are to be treated as always having been in force, but are not to apply in relation to a purported return where a person has made an appeal under the Taxes Acts or a claim for judicial review before 29 October 2018 on grounds consisting of or including that the purported return was not a valid return under the relevant section.

Interest

FA 1989, s 178(1) provides for rates of interest on unpaid and overpaid tax to be set in relation to the provisions listed in FA 1989, s 178(2) but those rates may only be given effect by an order (an Appointed Day Order) made by statutory instrument under FA 1989, s 178(7) appointing a day from which that rate is to apply.

Section 88 amends the law retrospectively to remove the need for an Appointed Day Order before interest may be charged or repaid.

Section 88(1) provides that, where before 12 February 2019 regulations under FA 1989, s 178(1) provide for a rate of interest for the purposes of the specified provisions but no order was made under FA 1989, s 178(7) appointing the appropriate day, the rate is to have effect for any period of time beginning on or after the day on which the regulations came into force, whether or not such an order was made.

Section 88(2) removes the need for an Appointed Day Order, without affecting such orders as have already been made.

Section 88(3) and (6) provide that FA 2009, s 101 is to have effect for charging interest on:

- penalties under FA 2014, Sch 35, para 11 for the promoters of tax avoidance schemes;
- penalties under FA 2009, Sch 55, paras 6B–6D for failure to make real-time PAYE returns;
- penalties under FA 2009, Sch 56, paras 5–8 for failure to make payments on time in relation to PAYE and Construction Industry Scheme amounts; and
- penalties under FA 2014, s 208 for failure to take corrective action in respect to follower notices and FA 2014, s 226 for failure to pay under accelerated payment notices and partner payment notices where the penalties relate to PAYE.

The latter three amendments are to be treated as having come into force on 6 May 2014.

Section 88(4) amends the Taxes (Interest Rate) Regulations 1989 (SI 1989/1297) and inserts new SI 1989/1297, reg 5A, which provides that the rate of interest on unpaid diverted profits tax is to be 3% per annum for the period from 1 October 2015 to 5 April 2017 and 2.5% per annum thereafter.

PART 5 MISCELLANEOUS AND FINAL

Regulatory capital securities

Section 89 introduces Sch 20, which revokes the previous rules in relation to regulatory capital securities and makes new rules in relation to 'hybrid capital instruments'. The intention is to secure that payments of interest arising from hybrid capital instruments (debt instruments having certain equity-like features) are deductible from the issuer's taxable profits. The resulting uncertainty as to interest deductibility has hitherto been addressed for the financial sector by the Taxation of Regulatory Capital Securities Regulations 2013 (SI 2013/3209), as amended.

From June 2018, banks have been permitted to issue types of hybrid capital instruments not covered by those regulations. The opportunity has now been taken to review the treatment of such instruments across all sectors.

Schedule 20 has 21 paragraphs, divided into three Parts. Part 1 (para 1) revokes existing regulations. Part 2 (paras 2–19) introduces the new rules for the purposes of income tax, CGT and corporation tax and provide for commencement. Part 3 (paras 20 and 21) introduces the new rules for the purposes of stamp duty and SDRT and provides for commencement.

Schedule 20, para 1 revokes SI 2013/3209 and the amending order, SI 2015/2056.

Schedule 20, para 2 inserts *new CTA 2009, s 420A*, which applies where a loan relationship is a 'hybrid capital instrument' (as defined in *new CTA 2009, s 475C*, inserted by Sch 20, para 3) for an accounting period of the debtor.

New CTA 2009, s 420A(*2*) provides that 'qualifying amounts' payable on a hybrid capital instrument are not to be treated as distributions for the purposes of the Corporation Tax Acts. A 'qualifying amount' is defined as any amount payable under a hybrid capital instrument that would otherwise be a distribution by virtue of the ability to defer or cancel interest. A hybrid capital instrument is not to be identified as an equity note for the purposes of *new CTA 2010, s 1015*(*1A*), inserted by Sch 20, para 4.

Schedule 20, para 3 inserts *new CTA 2009, s 475C*, which defines what is meant by a 'hybrid capital instrument'. This is an instrument that entitles the debtor to cancel or defer a payment of interest but has no other significant equity features. In order for an instrument to be treated as such, the debtor must make an election under this section to that effect.

An instrument is to be treated as having 'no other significant equity features' if it does not have features conferring voting rights in the debtor; the right to exercise a dominant influence over the debtor; the ability to alter the amount of the debt except in 'write-down events ' or 'conversion events' in qualifying cases; and any provision for the creditor to receive more than principal plus interest, except in 'conversion events' in qualifying cases.

New CTA 2009, s 475C(*3*)(*b*) defines what is meant by the right to exercise a dominant influence over the debtor. *New CTA 2009, s 475C*(*4*) defines a 'write-down event' as a permanent release or temporary write-down of all or part of the debt, whether this is exercisable by the debtor, arises from a condition within the instrument, or otherwise. *New CTA 2009, s 475C*(*5*) defines a 'conversion event' as the conversion of the loan relationship into the debtor's, or its quoted parent's, ordinary share capital. *New CTA 2009, s 475C*(*6*) defines a 'qualifying case' as one where the provision for write-down or conversion applies only when the debtor is approaching insolvency or where the provision is included solely because of a need to comply with a regulatory or other legal requirement. An instrument that contains a temporary write-down provision may be a qualifying case provided that when written back up, the amount of the debt may not be increased above its original amount.

New CTA 2009, s 475C(*8*) provides that any election for a loan relationship to be a hybrid capital instrument is to be irrevocable, must be made within six months of the issue of the instrument, and has effect for all subsequent accounting periods. However, for loan relationships entered into before 1 January 2019, the election may be made at any time before 1 October 2019.

New CTA 2009, s 475C(*9*) is an anti-avoidance provision that invalidates the election if the company is party to the hybrid capital instrument as a result of an arrangement with a main purpose of securing a tax advantage.

Schedule 20, para 4 inserts *new CTA 2010, s 1015*(*1A*), providing that hybrid capital instruments are not to be treated as special securities by reason of condition E of CTA 2010, s 1015. This ensures that amounts payable on a hybrid capital instrument cannot be treated as distributions for the purposes of the Corporation Tax Acts by virtue of being equity notes.

Schedule 20, para 5 inserts *new CTA 2009, s 320B*. This applies where an amount in respect of a hybrid capital instrument is recognised under GAAP in equity or shareholders' funds and not as an item of profit or loss or as an item of other comprehensive income. The amount so identified is to be brought into account in the same way (and subject to the same rules) as if it were an amount recognised as an item of profit or loss for the period in accordance with GAAP. Any exchange gains or losses on the hybrid capital instrument are excluded from this treatment.

Schedule 20, para 6 amends CTA 2010, s 162 to include a hybrid commercial instrument as a normal commercial loan within that section.

Schedule 20, paras 7–9 make consequential amendments.

Schedule 20, paras 10–15 provide for commencement in relation to corporation tax. The default rule is that the provision made by Sch 20, paras 1–4 and 6, so far as they relate to corporation tax, and the amendments made by Sch 20, paras 5–7 and 9 are to have effect in relation to accounting periods beginning after 31 December 2018, with provision for straddling periods. However, there are transitional provisions for instruments to which the Regulatory Capital Security Regulations 2013 applied on 31 December 2018 ('transitional qualifying instruments'), extending in certain cases to 31 December 2023.

Schedule 20, paras 16–18 provide for commencement in relation to income tax and CGT. The default rule is that the provision made by Sch 20, paras 1–4 is to have effect for the purposes of income tax in relation to payments made after 31 December 2019. However, the revocation made by Sch 20, para 1 (of the Regulatory Capital Securities Regulations 2013 as amended) is not to apply to the exception from the duty to deduct income tax on certain payments in respect of regulatory capital securities, where those payments are before 12 February 2019. Furthermore, there is also to be a specified period for continuity of treatment of transitional qualifying instruments that have previously been excepted from the duty to deduct income tax from yearly interest and payments, and from payments made on building society securities so that they retain the exception for payments made before 1 January 2024.

Schedule 20, para 17 provides that the revocation made by Sch 20, para 1 is to apply to disposals taking place after 31 December 2018 for the purposes of CGT. Schedule 20, para 18 provides that the amendment made by Sch 20, para 6 to the definition of 'normal commercial loan', is to apply, so far as it relates to the definition of 'corporate bonds' in TCGA 1992, s 117(1), to disposals of such bonds after 31 December 2018.

Schedule 20, para 19 empowers HM Treasury to amend *new CTA 2009, s 475C* by regulations.

Schedule 20, para 20 provides that the transfer of a hybrid capital instrument is to be exempt from all stamp duties. It further provides that the revocation made by Sch 20, para 1 and the exemption conferred by Sch 20, para 20 are to apply for stamp duty in relation to instruments executed after 11 February 2019 and for SDRT, to agreements to transfer securities to those made after that date and also to earlier conditional agreements in respect of which the condition becomes satisfied after that date.

EU withdrawal

Section 90 confers on HM Treasury the power to make minor consequential amendments to such provisions in tax legislation that it considers to be appropriate in relation to the United Kingdom's likely exit from the European Union.

Preparatory expenditure

Section 91 entitles the Secretary of State to incur preparatory expenditure for the introduction of an emissions-reduction trading scheme, allocating emissions allowances under the Climate Change Act 2008, Sch 2, para 5.

Reviews

Sections 92–95 are provisions originating from Opposition amendments to the Finance Bill. They were intended primarily as a political tool to curtail the powers of the Chancellor of the Exchequer in the event of a 'no-deal' withdrawal from the European Union and call him to account to the House of Commons. However, s 94 is the response to the Government's decision to defer the introduction of new limits on stakes under remote gambling terminals and s 95 is a response to the continuing controversy surrounding the retroactive effect of the provisions on disguised loans.

Section 92 provides that the Chancellor of the Exchequer must review the impact of the anti-avoidance provisions there specified and report to the House on that review within six months of Royal Assent (ie before 13 August 2019). The review must have regard to their impact on child poverty, households at different levels of income, people with protected characteristics and different parts of the United Kingdom and different regions of England.

Section 93 provides that the Chancellor of the Exchequer must review the effectiveness of the provisions specified (which are the same as those specified in s 92) and report to the House on that review within six months of Royal Assent (ie before 13 August 2019). The review must have particular regard to their effect in reducing tax avoidance and evasion, in inducing new anti-avoidance measures unanticipated by FA 2019 and estimates of their efficacy in reducing the tax gap for each year from 2018/19 to 2028/29.

Section 94 provides that the Chancellor of the Exchequer must review the effects on public health of the gaming-duty provisions of s 62 and Sch 19 and report to the House on that review within six months of Royal Assent (ie before 13 August 2019). The review must consider the effects of those provisions in reducing the negative effects on public health of gambling and the implications for the public finances of those effects of those provision and the operation of the law relating to remote gaming duty and gaming duty if those provisions were not given effect.

Section 95 provides that the Chancellor of the Exchequer must review the effects of the changes made by the offshore matters and transfers provisions of ss 80 and 81 and report to the House on that review no later than 30 March 2019. The review must include a comparison of the time limit on proceedings for the recovery of lost tax involving an offshore matter with other time limits for the recovery of lost tax, including those under F(No 2)A 2017, Schs 11 and 12 (the so-called disguised-loans provisions).

Other

Section 96 provides a key to interpretation of abbreviations of enactments used in the Act and **s 97** gives the short title.

Zigurds G Kronbergs

March 2019

FINANCE ACT 2019

2019 Chapter 1

ARRANGEMENT OF SECTIONS

PART 1—DIRECT TAXES

An Act to grant certain duties, to alter other duties, and to amend the law relating to the national debt and the public revenue, and to make further provision in connection with finance.

[12th February 2019]

PART 1
DIRECT TAXES

Charge to tax

1 Income tax charge for tax year 2019–20

Income tax is charged for the tax year 2019–20.

COMMENTARY ON SECTION 1

Section 1 imposes the charge to income tax for 2019/20. Income tax is an annual tax, and the charge must be renewed by statute each year (ITA 2007, s 4).

2 Corporation tax charge for financial year 2020

Corporation tax is charged for the financial year 2020.

COMMENTARY ON SECTION 2

Corporation tax is charged on profits of companies for any financial year for which an Act so provides (CTA 2009, s 2(1)). FA 2019, s 2 imposes the charge to corporation tax for financial year 2020, ie the twelve months beginning 1 April 2020.

The *rate* of corporation tax for financial year 2020 has already been set at 17% (F(No 2)A 2015, s 7(2) as amended by FA 2016, s 46).

Income tax rates, allowances and limits

3 Main rates of income tax for tax year 2019–20

For the tax year 2019–20 the main rates of income tax are as follows—

(a) the basic rate is 20%;
(b) the higher rate is 40%;
(c) the additional rate is 45%.

COMMENTARY ON SECTION 3

Section 3 sets out the main rates at which income tax is charged for 2019/20. These are unchanged from 2018/19, so the basic rate is 20%, the higher rate is 40% and the additional rate is 45% (ITA 2007, s 6(1), (2)).

The main rates apply to an individual who is resident in the UK and is not subject to the Scottish rates of income tax or the Welsh rates of income tax (ITA 2007, ss 6(3), 11A, 11B). The Welsh rates of income tax are effective from 2019/20 onwards. The main rates apply to all of the individual's taxable income apart from savings income and dividend income, each of which have their own rates (see ITA 2007, ss 7, 7A, 8 and the commentary under section 4 below).

The Scottish rates of income tax for 2019/20 also remain the same as in 2018/19, so the starter rate is 19%, the basic rate is 20%, the intermediate rate is 21%, the higher rate is 41% and the top rate is 46%. The rates are set via a resolution in the Scottish Parliament and apply to Scottish taxpayers, as defined under Scotland Act 1998, ss 80D, 80E.

The Welsh rates of income tax for 2019/20 remain the same as the UK rates, ie the basic rate is 20%, the higher rate is 40% and the additional rate is 45%. Unlike in Scotland, where the Scottish Parliament has the power to set income tax bands as well as rates, the Welsh Parliament only has limited powers to set its own basic rate, higher rate and additional rate. The rates are set via a resolution in the Welsh Parliament and apply to Welsh taxpayers, as defined under Government of Wales Act 2006, ss 116E, 116G.

4 Default and savings rates of income tax for tax year 2019–20

(1) For the tax year 2019–20 the default rates of income tax are as follows—

(a) the default basic rate is 20%;
(b) the default higher rate is 40%;
(c) the default additional rate is 45%.

(2) For the tax year 2019–20 the savings rates of income tax are as follows—

(a) the savings basic rate is 20%;
(b) the savings higher rate is 40%;
(c) the savings additional rate is 45%.

COMMENTARY ON SECTION 4

Section 4(1) provides that for 2019/20 the default basic rate is 20%, the default higher rate is 40%, and the default additional rate is 45% (ITA 2007, s 6C). This means that the default rates for 2019/20 are the same as the main rates of income tax.

The default rates of income tax apply to the non-savings and non-dividend income of taxpayers who are not subject to either the UK main rates of income tax, the Scottish rates of income tax or the Welsh rates of income tax (ITA 2007, s 11C). These include trustees (other than where the trust rates in ITA 2007, s 9 apply) and non-UK resident individuals.

Section 4(2) provides that for 2019/20 the savings basic rate is 20%, the savings higher rate is 40%, and the savings additional rate is 45% (ITA 2007, s 7A).

The savings rates are charged on the savings income of any individual liable to UK income tax (including Scottish and Welsh taxpayers and non-UK residents) (ITA 2007, s 11D). Savings income is defined in ITA 2007, s 18. Generally speaking, savings income is treated as the highest part of an individual's total income apart from dividend income (subject to the ordering rules in ITA 2007, s 1012) (ITA 2007, s 16).

The savings rates have effect only after the starting rate for savings and the savings nil rate have been applied (ITA 2007, ss 12, 12A).

---

5 Basic rate limit and personal allowance

(1) For the tax years 2019–20 and 2020–21, the amount specified in section 10(5) of ITA 2007 (basic rate limit) is "£37,500".

(2) For the tax years 2019–20 and 2020–21, the amount specified in section 35(1) of ITA 2007 (personal allowance) is "£12,500".

(3) In consequence of the amendment made by subsection (2), omit section 4 of F(No 2)A 2015 (which has effect only if the personal allowance is less than £12,500).

(4) Omit the following (which relate to the link between the personal allowance and the national minimum wage)—

(a) sections 57(8), 57A and 1014(5)(b)(iia) of ITA 2007, and
(b) section 3 of F(No 2)A 2015.

(5) In consequence of the provision made by this section—

(a) section 21 of ITA 2007 (indexation of basic rate limit and starting rate limit for savings) does not apply in relation to the basic rate limit, and
(b) section 57 of ITA 2007 (indexation of allowances) does not apply in relation to the amount specified in section 35(1) of that Act,

for the tax years 2019–20 and 2020–21.

COMMENTARY ON SECTION 5

Section 5(1) sets the basic rate limit at £37,500 for 2019/20 and 2020/21. As a consequence, section 5(5)(a) disapplies the automatic indexation of the basic rate limit for those tax years. The basic rate limit was £34,500 for 2018/19, so this is a significant increase to the limit.

The basic rate limit applies for the purposes of the main basic rate, the default basic rate, the savings basic rate, the dividend ordinary rate and the Welsh basic rate. The limit for the Scottish basic rate, which applies to non-savings non-dividend income of Scottish taxpayers, is set by the Scottish Government. For the definition of a Scottish taxpayer, see Scotland Act 1998, ss 80D, 80E.

This means that the higher rate threshold in 2019/20 and 2020/21 is £50,000 (personal allowance of £12,500 plus basic rate limit of £37,500). Note that the higher rate threshold for the non-savings non-dividend income of Scottish taxpayers is £43,430 in 2019/20 (personal allowance of £12,500 plus intermediate rate limit of £30,930). The Scottish tax band limits are set via a resolution in the Scottish Parliament.

Section 5(2) sets the personal allowance at £12,500 for 2019/20 and 2020/21 (ITA 2007, s 35). As a consequence, section 5(5)(b) disapplies the automatic indexation of the allowance for those tax years. The personal allowance was £11,850 for 2018/19, so this is a significant increase to the personal allowance and represents a fulfilment of a Conservative Party manifesto promise.

As a result of the increase to the personal allowance, the amount of the transferable tax allowance (also known as the marriage allowance) is £1,250 for 2019/20 and 2020/21 (ITA 2007, s 55B(4), (5)).

Section 5(3), (4) repeals various sections in ITA 2007 and F(No 2)A 2015 which linked the amount of the personal allowance to the yearly equivalent of the adult national minimum wage.

6 Starting rate limit for savings for tax year 2019–20

Section 21 of ITA 2007 (indexation) does not apply in relation to the starting rate limit for savings for the tax year 2019–20 (so that the starting rate limit for savings remains at £5,000 for that tax year).

COMMENTARY ON SECTION 6

Section 6 disapplies the indexation uplift in ITA 2007, s 21 from the starting rate limit for savings. It sets the starting rate limit for 2019/20 at £5,000, the same as for 2018/19 (ITA 2007, s 12). The starting rate for savings remains 0% in 2019/20 and applies before considering the savings nil rate (ITA 2007, ss 7, 12A).

Employment and social security income

7 Optional remuneration arrangements: arrangements for cars and vans

(1) ITEPA 2003 is amended as follows.

(2) In section 120A (optional remuneration arrangements: benefit of a car)—

(a) in subsection (3)(b), for the words from "the amount" to "year is" substitute "the total foregone amount in connection with the car for the tax year is", and

(b) after subsection (3) insert—

"(4) In this section, and in section 121A, the total foregone amount in connection with the car for a tax year is the total of—

(a) the amount foregone (see section 69B) with respect to the benefit of the car for that year, and

(b) the amount foregone (see section 69B) with respect to each other benefit that—

(i) is connected with the car,

(ii) is provided in that year for the employee, or a member of the employee's household, pursuant to optional remuneration arrangements, and

(iii) is neither the provision of a driver nor the provision of fuel."

(3) In section 121A (optional remuneration arrangements: method of calculating relevant amount)—

(a) in subsection (1), for step 1 substitute—

"Step 1

Take the total foregone amount in connection with the car for the tax year (see section 120A(4)).", and

(b) in subsection (2)—

(i) for ""amount foregone" under" substitute ""total foregone amount" for the purposes of", and

(ii) for "the benefit of the car" substitute "a benefit mentioned in section 120A(4)(a) or (b)".

(4) In section 132A (capital contributions by employee: optional remuneration arrangements)—

(a) for subsection (3) substitute—

"(3) The amount of the deduction allowed in any tax year is found by—

(a) first multiplying the capped amount by the appropriate percentage, and
(b) then multiplying the result by the availability factor.", and

(b) after subsection (4) insert—

"(4A) For the purposes of subsection (3), "the availability factor" is given by the formula—

(Y – U) / Y

where—

Y is the number of days in the tax year, and
U is the number of days in the tax year on which the car is unavailable.

(4B) For the purposes of subsection (4A), the car is unavailable on any day if the day—

(a) falls before the first day on which the car is available to the employee,
(b) falls after the last day on which the car is available to the employee, or
(c) falls within a period of 30 days or more throughout which the car is not available to the employee."

(5) In section 154A (optional remuneration arrangements: benefit of a van)—

(a) in subsection (2)(b), for the words from "the amount" to "section 69B)" substitute "the total foregone amount in connection with the van",
(b) in subsection (3), for step 1 substitute—

"Step 1
Take the total foregone amount in connection with the van for the tax year.",

(c) in subsection (7), for "the benefit of the van" substitute "a benefit mentioned in subsection (8)(a) or (b)", and
(d) after subsection (7) insert—

"(8) In this section the total foregone amount in connection with the van for a tax year is the total of—

(a) the amount foregone (see section 69B) with respect to the benefit of the van for that year, and
(b) the amount foregone (see section 69B) with respect to each other benefit that—
(i) is connected with the van,
(ii) is provided in that year for the employee, or a member of the employee's household, pursuant to optional remuneration arrangements, and
(iii) is neither the provision of a driver nor the provision of fuel."

(6) In section 239 (exemptions for payments and benefits relating to taxable cars, vans and exempt HGVs), in subsection (3)—

(a) after "by virtue of" insert "section 120A (optional remuneration arrangements: benefit of a car),", and
(b) before "or section 160" insert ", section 154A (optional remuneration arrangements: benefit of a van)".

(7) The amendments made by this section have effect for the tax year 2019–20 and subsequent tax years.

COMMENTARY ON SECTION 7

The rules covering optional remuneration arrangements (also known in practice as salary sacrifice arrangements) are in ITEPA 2003, ss 69A, 69B, introduced by FA 2017, Sch 2. In their application to company cars and vans they generally have effect for 2017/18 onwards but are delayed until 2021/22 where the arrangements themselves were in place before 6 April 2017. If pre-6 April 2017 arrangements are varied or renewed, the transitional protection ceases and the optional remuneration rules then take effect. Cars with a CO_2 emissions figure not exceeding 75g/km fall outside the optional remuneration rules altogether.

Broadly, the optional remuneration rules operate by comparing the amount of earnings forgone (the salary sacrificed) with the amount that would normally be charged by reference to the cash equivalent of the benefit. The employee is then taxed on the higher figure. Two anomalies have been discovered which have the result that like was not being compared with like. Section 7 corrects these anomalies as described below. The corrections have effect for 2019/20 onwards (though not so as to bring the optional remuneration rules into play any sooner than would otherwise be the case as regards pre-6 April 2017 arrangements).

Firstly, it is established law (ITEPA 2003, s 239) that the cash equivalent of a company car covers all expenses incurred in connection with the vehicle, other than the provision of fuel and of a driver (which are taxed under separate rules). Examples of such connected expenses include insurance, servicing, vehicle tax and breakdown recovery (HMRC Employment Income Manual EIM44105). The amount forgone under optional remuneration arrangements should therefore include amounts forgone in respect of connected expenses as well as the car itself but did not previously do so. Section 7 amends this by additionally bringing into account the amount forgone with respect to any benefit that is connected with the car, is provided in the tax year for the employee (or a member of the employee's household) pursuant to optional remuneration arrangements, and is neither the provision of a driver nor the provision of fuel.

The same considerations apply to company vans, and section 7 makes a similar amendment to those rules.

Secondly, in calculating the cash equivalent of a company car the deduction available under ITEPA 2003, s 132 for employee capital contributions to the car (up to a maximum of £5,000) is made before the cash equivalent is reduced under ITEPA 2003, s 143 for periods during which the car is unavailable to the employee. In calculating the amount forgone under optional remuneration arrangements, capital contributions were previously deductible without regard to periods of unavailability. Section 7 corrects this by requiring the capital contributions themselves (capped at £5,000) to be reduced to take account of any such periods.

8 Exemption for benefit in form of vehicle-battery charging at workplace

(1) In Chapter 3 of Part 4 of ITEPA 2003 (employment income: travel-related exemptions), after section 237 insert—

"237A Vehicle-battery charging

(1) No liability to income tax arises in respect of the provision, at or near an employee's workplace, of facilities for charging a battery of a vehicle used by the employee (including a vehicle used by the employee as a passenger).

(2) Subsection (1) applies only if the facilities are made available generally to the employer's employees at that workplace.

(3) In this section—

"facilities"—

(a) includes electricity, but

(b) does not include workplace parking,

"taxable", in relation to a car or van, has the meaning given by section 239(6),

"vehicle" means a vehicle—

(a) to which Chapter 2 applies (see section 235), and

(b) which is neither a taxable car nor a taxable van, and

"workplace parking" has the meaning given by section 237(3)."

(2) The amendment made by subsection (1) has effect for the tax year 2018–19 and subsequent tax years.

COMMENTARY ON SECTION 8

With backdated effect for 2018/19 onwards, section 8 inserts a new ITEPA 2003, s 237A which removes the charge to income tax on facilities (including electricity) provided for charging a battery of a vehicle used by an employee. This is intended to encourage employers to provide charging facilities for all-electric and plug-in hybrid vehicles.

The charging facilities must be at or near the employee's workplace; this is generally interpreted by HMRC as meaning at or within a reasonable distance from the place of work, having regard to the nature of the locality. The facilities must be available generally to all the employer's employees at the workplace in question. The exemption applies equally if the vehicle using the facilities is used by the employee as a passenger. It does not apply to the provision of workplace parking.

Taxable cars and vans, ie company cars and vans within the charge to tax as a benefit in kind, are excluded from this exemption, but this is only because the provision of charging facilities is already exempt for these vehicles by virtue of ITEPA 2003, s 239(4). In the absence of the exemption introduced by section 8, charging facilities for vehicles other than taxable cars and vans would incur a tax charge under ITEPA 2003, Pt 3, Ch 10 (taxable benefits: residual liability to charge).

9 Exemptions relating to emergency vehicles

(1) Section 248A of ITEPA 2003 (emergency vehicles) is amended in accordance with subsections (2) and (3).

(2) In subsection (1)—

- (a) in paragraph (a), for "for the person's private use" substitute "mainly for use for the person's business travel";
- (b) in paragraph (b), omit "engaged in on-call".

(3) In subsection (8)—

- (a) in the opening words, omit "engaged in on-call";
- (b) in paragraph (a), for "it" substitute "the vehicle";
- (c) omit paragraph (b) (and the "and" before it).

(4) In section 205 of ITEPA 2003 (cost of the benefit: asset made available without transfer), after subsection (4) insert—

> "(5) Where the asset is an emergency vehicle, the expense of providing fuel for it in a tax year is not an additional expense by virtue of subsection (4) so long as—
>
> - (a) the person incurring that expense incurs no expense in that tax year in the provision of fuel for the vehicle which is used for the employee's private travel ("private fuel expense"), or
> - (b) all private fuel expense that the person does incur in that tax year is made good by the employee on or before 6 July following the tax year.
>
> (6) For the purposes of this section—
>
> "emergency vehicle" has the same meaning as in section 248A;
> "fuel" includes electrical energy;
> "private travel" means travelling the expenses of which, if incurred and paid by the employee, would not be deductible under Chapter 2 or 5 of Part 5."

(5) The amendments made by subsections (1) to (4) have effect for the tax year 2017–18 and subsequent tax years.

(6) For the tax year 2017–18, the tax year 2018–19 and the tax year 2019–20, sections 205 and 205A of ITEPA 2003 (taxable benefits: assets made available without transfer) have effect, where the asset mentioned in section 205(1)(a) is an emergency vehicle, with the modifications in subsections (7) and (8).

(7) Section 205(1C) has effect as if—

- (a) in paragraph (a), at the beginning, there were inserted "the private use proportion of";
- (b) after paragraph (b), and on a new line, there were inserted—

(8) Section 205A(2) has effect as if paragraphs (c) and (d) were omitted.

(9) For the purposes of subsection (6), "emergency vehicle" has the same meaning as in section 248A of ITEPA 2003.

COMMENTARY ON SECTION 9

Prior to this change in legislation, where an emergency vehicle was made available to a person employed in an emergency service for their private use, no liability to income tax arises under Chapter 6 (Cars, Vans and Related Benefits) and Chapter 10 (Residual Liability to Charge) of Part 3, ITEPA 2003, provided that certain conditions were met.

Prior to the FA 2019 changes, the exemption only applied if private use was prohibited other than when an employee was on call or engaged in on-call commuting, and provided that there was no actual private use other than in those circumstances. HMRC had had an informal practice where a car was occasionally used in a way that would not qualify for exemption of allowing for an apportionment of any benefit in kind charge so that only any private use was taxed. This practice ceased with changes to the 'use of assets' legislation in FA 2017, leaving affected employees with a potentially significant increase in tax liabilities virtually overnight.

Recognising that the emergency services require flexibility to maintain fast response times, it seems counterproductive if a tax charge on private use discourages employees from taking emergency vehicles home. To address this, the principal changes being introduced by s 9 are to:

(a) allow ordinary commuting in an emergency vehicle, regardless of on-call use. Note that other types of private use are not permitted e g weekly shopping trips or use on holidays;
(b) ignore fuel provided for emergency vehicles as an 'additional expense' when calculating benefits arising under Chapter 10, retrospective back to 6 April 2017; and
(c) dampen the effect of the changes to Chapter 10 made in Finance Act 2017, as they would otherwise apply to the private use of emergency vehicles, through transitional provisions applicable between 6 April 2017 and 5 April 2020.

Where emergency services currently allow employees to use emergency vehicles for private use other than commuting (e g cars with concealed blue lights), the employer/employee will need to decide whether to accept the higher tax charge from 6 April 2020 or whether to vary the contractual arrangements to restrict private use to commuting only.

ITEPA 2003, s 248A

To achieve the above objectives, the condition for exemption in s 248A(1)(a) will apply where the vehicle is provided *mainly for* private use, and s 248A(1)(b) is extended to apply when the person is on call *or commuting*, rather than engaged in on-call commuting.

ITEPA 2003, s 205 (as regards the private use of emergency vehicles)

Chapter 10 charges tax on the annual value of an asset made available for use (e g the higher of the hire charge to those providing the asset (if any)); or, 20% of its market value when first provided as an employer-related benefit or in the case of land, its annual rental value *plus* the amount of any additional expenses.

In the case of emergency vehicles, sub-s (7) provides a form of transitional relief for tax years from 2017/18 to 2019/20. Instead of calculating the private use benefit under normal rules by reference to the annual cost of the benefit, ITEPA 2003, s 205(1C) is amended so that the tax charge only arises on the *private use proportion* of the annual cost, by pro-rating the annual cost by reference to actual private miles travelled. Note that this transitional provision falls away from April 2020.

ITEPA 2003, s 205A (as regards periods unavailable)

When considering days when an emergency vehicle can be taken to be unavailable for private use, sub-s (8) removes ITEPA 2003, s 205A(2)(c) and (d), so that it is not necessary to consider whether a vehicle is fit for purpose for more than 12 hours during any particular day, or whether the vehicle is used solely for business purposes on that day.

ITEPA 2003, s 205 (as regards fuel)

The addition of new ITEPA 2003, s 205(5) and (6) removes fuel provided for an emergency vehicle from being an 'additional expense' under s 205(4), provided that either no fuel is provided for private use or, if it is, the cost of providing that private fuel is fully reimbursed by the employee by 6 July following the tax year concerned. This change applies for all tax years from 2017/18.

10 Exemption for expenses related to travel

(1) Section 289A of ITEPA 2003 (exemption for paid or reimbursed expenses) is amended as follows.

(2) After subsection (2) insert—

"(2A) No liability to income tax arises in respect of an amount paid or reimbursed by a person ("the payer") to an employee (whether or not an employee of the payer) for expenses in the course of qualifying travel if—

(a) the amount has been calculated and paid or reimbursed in accordance with regulations made by the Commissioners for Her Majesty's Revenue and Customs,

(b) the payment or reimbursement is not provided pursuant to relevant salary sacrifice arrangements, and

(c) condition C is met."

(3) After subsection (4) insert—

"(4A) Condition C is that—

(a) the payer or another person operates a system for checking that the employee has undertaken the qualifying travel in relation to which the amount is paid or reimbursed, and

(b) neither the payer nor any other person operating the system knows or suspects, or could reasonably be expected to know or suspect, that the travel was not undertaken."

(4) In subsection (5)—

(a) for ""Relevant" substitute "In this section "relevant", and

(b) before "in respect of" insert "for or".

(5) After subsection (5) insert—

"(5A) In this section "qualifying travel" means travel for which a deduction from the employee's earnings would be allowed under Chapter 2 or 5 of Part 5."

(6) In subsection (6), for "this section" substitute "subsection (2)".

(7) In subsection (7), after "subsection" insert "(2A)(a) or".

(8) After subsection (7) insert—

"(8) Regulations made under subsection (2A)(a) may contain provision about calculating amounts that is framed by reference to rates (for expenses) published from time to time by the Commissioners for Her Majesty's Revenue and Customs."

(9) The amendments made by this section have effect for the tax year 2019–20 and subsequent tax years.

(10) For the tax year 2019–20 and subsequent tax years, the Income Tax (Approved Expenses) Regulations 2015 (SI 2015/1948)—

(a) have effect as if made under section 289A(2A)(a) of ITEPA 2003 (and may be revoked, or amended, accordingly), and

(b) have effect as if in regulation 2(1)—

(i) the reference to section 289A of ITEPA 2003 were to section 289A(2A)(a) of that Act,

(ii) for the words "in an approved way" there were substituted "in accordance with these regulations", and

(iii) the words "purchased by the employee" were omitted.

COMMENTARY ON SECTION 10

These measures will be warmly welcomed by employers as a practical step forward in the simplification of the taxation of travel and subsistence expenses with effect from 6 April 2019.

In short, the new provisions enable employers to reimburse an employee's qualifying subsistence expenses when travelling for work using HMRC's benchmark scale rates, without having to carry out random checks on employees for evidence of expenditure incurred. Secondly, overseas scale rates for accommodation and subsistence have now also been brought within the statutory framework, also without a requirement to check evidence of amounts spent. For both benchmark scale rates and overseas scale rates, employers only need to check that employees are undertaking qualifying business travel, rather than check for evidence of expenses incurred.

NB employers reimbursing expenses at their own bespoke rates must still carry out random checks on expenditure actually incurred.

ITEPA 2003, s 289A(2A)

New s 289A(2A) brings overseas scale rates into the statutory exemption. The conditions are (a) the amount has been calculated or paid in accordance with HMRC Regulations (see below); (b) the amount is not provided pursuant to relevant salary sacrifice arrangements; and (c) new condition C is met.

ITEPA 2003, s 289A(4A)

New condition C is inserted at s 289A(4A), which only requires a system for checking that the employee has *undertaken the qualifying travel* in relation to which the amount is paid or reimbursed (not a system to check the actual expenditure incurred).

ITEPA 2003, s 289A(5A)

Qualifying travel is defined in new s 289A(5A) as travel for which a deduction from the employee's earnings would be allowed under Chapter 2 or 5 of Part 5. Those provisions primarily incorporate the 'wholly, exclusively and necessarily' rule for expenses in ITEPA 2003, s 336, and the rules on permanent and temporary workplaces and overseas travel which we all know and love.

On this point it is worth remembering that no deduction is allowed where ITEPA 2003, s 339A applies, whether expenses are reimbursed on an actual basis or using benchmark scale rates. This is relevant to engagements through intermediaries which are treated as separate employments under s 339A(2) so that travel to those engagements will normally be ordinary commuting, although travel in the course of those engagements (aka 'work travel') should still qualify for relief.

Income Tax (Approved Expenses) Regulations 2015 (SI 2015/1948)

Section 10(10) ensures that the current benchmark scale rates set out in SI 2015/1948 fall within the new rules.

The Income Tax (Approved Expenses) (Amendment) Regulations 2019 (SI 2019/358)

These are new regulations made under ITEPA 2003, s 289A(2A) and pave the way for overseas scale rates to be incorporated within SI 2015/1948 and so to fall under the new rules for payments made from 6 April 2019.

---

11 Beneficiaries of tax-exempt employer-provided pension benefits

(1) In section 307(2) of ITEPA 2003 ("death or retirement benefit" is a benefit for employee or others on employee's retirement or death), for "or a member of the employee's family or household" substitute ", or paid or given in respect of the employee to any other individual or to a charity,".

(2) The amendment made by subsection (1) has effect for the tax year 2019–20 and subsequent tax years.

COMMENTARY ON SECTION 11

The Chancellor announced at Autumn Budget 2017 that the tax exemption for death in service benefits would be widened. At that time and up to 5 April 2019 when an employer provides death in service benefits through a life assurance policy or provides retirement benefits via a qualifying relevant overseas pension scheme (QROPS), the employee will usually name a beneficiary to receive any payment due on their death and may be able to name a beneficiary to receive their retirement benefits. Any premiums paid into such schemes by the employer are only tax exempt if the named beneficiary of the employee's death or retirement benefits is the employee so far as retirement benefits are concerned, a member of the employee's family, or a member of their household. The definitions of family and household only cover: spouse, civil partners, parents, children and dependents, domestic staff and the employee's guests.

Section 11 widens the scope of the exemption from 6 April 2019 allowing employees to name any individual or a charity, as the beneficiary of the employee's death in service or retirement benefits. In addition employees will not be liable to income tax as a benefit in kind on contributions paid in these circumstances. This extension of the exemption allows employees to nominate their preferred recipient regardless of their relationship to employees in law. This will ensure that employees throughout the workforce are treated fairly and proportionately with employees in marriages or with close family. The exemption also allows employees to nominate a registered charity thus being consistent with existing government policy of providing tax relief on charitable donations.

Section 11(1) introduces amendments to ITEPA 2003, s 307(2) widening the scope of the exemption to allow an employee to name any individual, or a charity, as the beneficiary of their death in service or retirement benefits. Consequently, an employee will not be liable to income tax as a benefit in kind on contributions paid by their employer in these circumstances. Section 11(2) provides for the amendments in section 11(1) to apply to tax years 2019/20 et seq.

12 Tax treatment of social security income

(1) Part 10 of ITEPA 2003 (social security income) is amended as follows.

(2) In Table A in section 660 (taxable UK benefits), at the appropriate place insert—

"Carer's allowance supplement	SS(S)A 2018	Sections 24 and 28"

(3) In section 658 (amount charged to tax), in subsection (4), after "carer's allowance," insert "carer's allowance supplement,".

(4) In section 661 (taxable social security income), in subsection (1), after "carer's allowance," insert "carer's allowance supplement,".

(5) In Part 1 of Table B in section 677(1) (UK social security benefits wholly exempt from tax: benefits payable under primary legislation), insert each of the following at the appropriate place—

"Best start grant	SS(S)A 2018	Sections 24 and 32"
"Discretionary housing payment	SS(S)A 2018	Section 88"
"Discretionary support award	DSR(NI) 2016	Regulation 2"
"Funeral expense assistance	SS(S)A 2018	Sections 24 and 34"
"Flexible support fund payment	ETA 1973	Section 2"
"Payment under a council tax reduction scheme: England	LGFA 1992	Section 13A(2)"
"Young carer grant	SS(S)A 2018	Sections 24 and 28"

(6) In the heading of Part 1 of Table B in section 677(1), after "Northern Ireland welfare supplementary payments" insert "etc".

(7) In Part 2 of Table B in section 677(1) (UK social security benefits wholly exempt from tax: benefits payable under regulations), insert each of the following at the appropriate place—

"Discretionary housing payment	CSPSSA 2000	Section 69"
"Payment under a council tax reduction scheme: Wales	LGFA 1992	Section 13A(4)"

(8) In Part 1 of Schedule 1 to ITEPA 2003 (abbreviations of Acts and instruments), insert each of the following at the appropriate place—

"LGFA 1992	Local Government Finance Act 1992"
"CSPSSA 2000	Child Support, Pensions and Social Security Act 2000"
"DSR(NI) 2016	Discretionary Support Regulations (Northern Ireland) 2016 (SR (NI) 2016 No 270)"
"SS(S)A 2018	Social Security (Scotland) Act 2018"

COMMENTARY ON SECTION 12

Section 12 provides whether newly introduced state benefits are taxable or non-taxable via the amendment of ITEPA 2003, ss 658, 660, 661, 677. Many of these new benefits have been or will be introduced by the Scottish Government.

The carer's allowance supplement is taxable as income on the accruals basis, meaning that it is the amount that is due for the tax year that is subject to income tax, irrespective of whether it is actually paid (ITEPA 2003, ss 660, 661). This benefit is payable twice a year to carers living in Scotland who also receive a carer's allowance and was introduced in 2018, with the first payment made in December 2018 (SS(S)A 2018, ss 24, 28). As the benefit is taxable on the accruals basis, rather than the receipts basis, this means that any payments accrued in 2018/19 are taxable, even those received prior to Royal Assent. The carer's allowance supplement is neither savings income nor dividend income, meaning that the Scottish rates of income tax apply to this amount (as this benefit is only paid to carers living in Scotland, meaning they will be considered as Scottish taxpayers under Scotland Act 1998, ss 80D, 80E).

The following state benefits are not taxable (ITEPA 2003, s 677):

- best start grant—payable to individuals living in Scotland, this covers a range of grants including the pregnancy and baby payment (introduced in 2018/19), the early learning payment, the school age payment and best start foods payment (all expected to be introduced in 2019)
- discretionary housing payment—payable to those living in England, Wales or Scotland, although the Scottish benefit was introduced under separate legislation. This benefit is designed to help those whose benefits do not cover their housing costs (rent, deposit, moving costs) and the decision on whether to award the benefit and how much to award is devolved to the local council
- discretionary support award—payable to those living in Northern Ireland in a crisis situation, this benefit is wider than the discretionary housing payment that is available to those living in the rest of the home nations, and is in the form of a grant or an interest-free loan
- funeral expense assistance—payable to those living in Scotland to reduce funeral poverty, this benefit is expected to be introduced in 2019
- flexible support fund payment—a little known discretionary benefit payable through the Jobcentre Plus to those living in England, Wales and Scotland in receipt of other benefits, this can be used for various costs including travel to interviews, childcare and clothing for work
- payment under a council tax reduction scheme: England and Wales—rather than a payment, the benefit is via a reduction in the council tax bill and is payable to those on low incomes
- young carer grant—payable to those aged 16–18 living in Scotland who do not qualify for the carer's allowance, this benefit is expected to be introduced in 2019

As reproduced in the explanatory notes accompanying the Finance Bill, the fiscal framework (see bit.ly/2BrpJLv) in relation to benefits introduced by the Scottish Government states 'any new benefits or discretionary payments introduced by the Scottish Government will not be deemed to be income for tax purposes, unless topping up a benefit which is deemed taxable such as carer's allowance'. However the fiscal framework does not carry the force of law and so the primary legislation in ITEPA 2003 must be amended to clarify the income tax treatment of Scottish state benefits.

Chargeable gains: interests in UK land etc

13 Disposals by non-UK residents etc

(1) Schedule 1 substitutes a new Part 1 of TCGA 1992 which—

(a) extends the cases in which gains accruing to persons not resident in the United Kingdom are chargeable to tax, and

(b) abolishes the specific charge to tax on ATED-related chargeable gains.

(2) Schedule 1 also—

(a) repeals other provisions contained in the previous version of Part 1 of TCGA 1992 or in Part 2 of that Act and restates their effect in rewritten form (whether in the new Part 1 or elsewhere),

(b) makes provision in relation to collective investment vehicles that (directly or indirectly) hold interests in land in the United Kingdom, and
(c) makes provision connected with the matters mentioned in subsection (1) or this subsection.

14 Disposals of UK land etc: payments on account of capital gains tax

(1) Schedule 2 makes provision for the purposes of capital gains tax requiring returns, and payments on account of that tax, to be made where there is—
(a) any direct or indirect disposal of UK land which meets the non-residence condition (whether or not a gain accrues), or
(b) any other direct disposal of UK land on which a residential property gain accrues.

(2) Subsection (1) is to be read as if contained in Part 1 of that Schedule.

International matters

15 Offshore receipts in respect of intangible property

Schedule 3 contains provision about offshore receipts in respect of intangible property.

16 Avoidance involving profit fragmentation arrangements

Schedule 4 contains provision about profit fragmentation arrangements.

17 Non-UK resident companies carrying on UK property businesses etc

Schedule 5 contains provision for non-UK resident companies to be chargeable to corporation tax on—
(a) profits of UK property businesses,
(b) profits consisting of other UK property income, and
(c) profits arising from certain loan relationships and derivative contracts.

18 Diverted profits tax

Schedule 6 contains provision about diverted profits tax.

19 Hybrid and other mismatches: scope of Chapter 8 and "financial instrument"

(1) Part 6A of TIOPA 2010 (hybrid and other mismatches) is amended as follows.

(2) In section 259HA (circumstances in which Chapter 8 applies)—
(a) for subsection (5) substitute—

"(5) Condition C is that—
(a) the payer is within the charge to corporation tax for the payment period, or
(b) the multinational company—
(i) is UK resident for the payment period, and
(ii) under the law of the parent jurisdiction, is regarded as carrying on a business in the PE jurisdiction through a permanent establishment in that territory but, under the law of the PE jurisdiction, is not regarded as doing so.", and

(b) in subsection (9)(a), for "company" substitute "payee".

(3) For section 259HC (counteraction of the multinational payee deduction/non-inclusion mismatch) substitute—

"259HC Counteraction of the multinational payee deduction/non-inclusion mismatch

For corporation tax purposes—
(a) if paragraph (b) of Condition C in subsection (5) of section 259HA is met, an amount equal to the multinational payee deduction/non-inclusion mismatch mentioned in subsection (6) of that section is to be treated as income arising to the multinational company in the United Kingdom (and nowhere else) for the payment period, and

(b) in any other case, the relevant deduction that may be deducted from the payer's income for that period is to be reduced by that amount."

(4) In section 259N (meaning of "financial instrument")—

(a) in subsection (3), for paragraph (b) substitute—

"(b) anything of a description specified in regulations made by the Treasury.", and

(b) omit subsection (4).

(5) The amendments made by subsections (2)(a) and (3) have effect in relation to—

(a) payments made on or after 1 January 2020, and

(b) quasi-payments in relation to which the payment period begins on or after that date.

(6) For the purposes of subsection (5)(b), where a payment period begins before 1 January 2020 and ends after that date ("the straddling period")—

(a) so much of the straddling period as falls before that date, and so much of it as falls on or after that date, are to be treated as separate taxable periods, and

(b) if it is necessary to apportion an amount for the straddling period to the two separate taxable periods, it is to be apportioned—

(i) on a time basis according to the respective length of the separate taxable periods, or

(ii) if that would produce a result that is unjust or unreasonable, on a just and reasonable basis.

(7) The amendment made by subsection (2)(b) is to be regarded as always having had effect.

(8) The first regulations under section 259N(3)(b) may have effect in relation to times before they come into force, but not times before 1 January 2019.

(9) Until those regulations come into force section 259N continues to have effect (other than for the purposes of making those regulations) as if—

(a) the amendments made by subsection (4) had not been made, and

(b) the Taxation of Regulatory Capital Securities Regulations 2013 (SI 2013/3209) had not been revoked by paragraph 1 of Schedule 20 to this Act.

COMMENTARY ON SECTION 19

Section 19 makes two changes to TIOPA 2010, Pt 6A ('Hybrid and other mismatches'), primarily driven by the requirements of EU Council Directive 2016/1164 as amended by EU Council Directive 2017/952 (more commonly known as the EU 'Anti-Tax Avoidance Directives' 1 and 2 respectively). Anti-Tax Avoidance Directive 2 in particular requires EU member states to introduce comprehensive hybrid mismatch rules. The vast majority of those requirements are already considered to be satisfied by existing TIOPA 2010, Pt 6A, but these 'minor amendments' are seen as necessary to satisfy specific aspects.

TIOPA 2010, Pt 6A, Ch 8: Multinational payee deduction/non-inclusion mismatches

Chapter 8 contains the provisions dealing with deduction/non-inclusion mismatches arising by reason of a payee being a multinational company (broadly a company resident in one territory, but considered as carrying on business through a permanent establishment in another territory).

TIOPA 2010, s 259HA sets out the five conditions A to E to be met for Chapter 8 to apply. Condition C in existing s 259HA is that 'the payer is within the charge to corporation tax for the payment period'. That is, Chapter 8 is only relevant where UK corporation tax relief would, disregarding Chapter 8 and certain other stated hybrid rules, be available to a payer for a payment made to a multinational company. Condition C is now expanded to apply in situations (irrespective of the tax position of the payer) where a multinational company payee is a UK resident company, and it has a disregarded permanent establishment (ie under UK principles it has a permanent establishment in another territory, but under the law of that other territory there is no permanent establishment).

This amendment appears to be prompted by Article 9(5) of the Anti-Tax Avoidance Directive (following amendment by Anti-Tax Avoidance Directive 2), which explicitly deals with 'disregarded permanent establishment income', and requires counteraction in the member state in which the recipient is resident.

Thus, Chapter 8 following this change will be capable of applying to impose taxable income on UK resident multinational payees, as well as to deny corporation tax relief for UK deductions of payers for payments made to multinational payees. Accordingly, TIOPA 2010, s 259HC dealing with the counteraction mechanism is also expanded to deal with this. For this new situation covered in s 259HA, the amount of the multinational payee deduction/non-inclusion mismatch (as defined in TIOPA 2010, s 259HB) is treated as income arising to the multinational payee in the UK. It is notable that no amendment is made to Chapter 8 in order to specify how this income should be categorised for UK corporation tax purposes – in contrast to other chapters containing income inclusion counteraction provisions such as Chapters 3, 4 and 7. These other chapters state that such counteraction income is chargeable under CTA 2009, Pt 10, Ch 8 (i e 'miscellaneous income').

These changes to Chapter 8 have a commencement date of 1 January 2020, which is aligned with the requirements of the Anti-Tax Avoidance Directives 1 and 2. There are straddling period provisions to apportion amounts to notional periods either side of this date. The apportionment methodology is on a time basis by default, with a possible just and reasonable override.

TIOPA 2010, Pt 6A, Ch 14: Interpretation

Separately, a small amendment is made to the definition of 'financial instrument' in TIOPA 2010, s 259N (the concept principally being relevant in determining whether and when Chapters 3 or 4 may apply). The amendment is to omit the exclusion for 'regulatory capital securities' in the definition of 'financial instrument', on the basis that the regulations defining 'regulatory capital securities' (SI 2013/3209) have been revoked by Schedule 20 of Finance Act 2019 (and replaced with 'hybrid capital instrument' rules). Provision is made instead for 'anything of a description specified in regulations made by the Treasury' to be excluded from the scope of the definition of 'financial instrument'. Until any new regulations come into effect, the exemption for any instrument which would have been a regulatory capital security under SI 2013/3209 (had it not been revoked) will remain in place.

---

20 Controlled foreign companies: finance company exemption and control

(1) Part 9A of TIOPA 2010 (controlled foreign companies) is amended as follows.

(2) In section 371IA (exemptions for profits from qualifying loan relationships), in subsection (4), for the words from "the profits" to the end substitute

> "so much of the profits of all its qualifying loan relationships taken together as are non-trading finance profits which—
>
> (a) fall within section 371EC (capital investment from the UK), and
> (b) do not fall within section 371EB (UK activities)."

(3) In section 371RA (overview of Chapter 18), in subsection (2), for "Section 371RC sets" substitute "Sections 371RC and 371RG set".

(4) After section 371RF insert—

> **"371RG Companies in which a UK resident company has more than a 50% investment**
>
> (1) If a UK resident company (whether alone or together with any associated enterprises) directly or indirectly has more than a 50% investment in a non-UK resident company, the non-UK resident company is to be taken to be a CFC (if it would not otherwise be).
>
> (2) A person ("P") is an "associated enterprise" in relation to a UK resident company if—
>
> (a) P directly or indirectly has a 25% investment in the company (or vice versa), or
> (b) another person directly or indirectly has a 25% investment in each of P and the company.
>
> (3) Section 259ND (meaning of "50% investment" and "25% investment") applies for the purposes of determining for the purposes of this section—

(a) whether a person has "more than a 50% investment" in another person, and

(b) whether a person has a "25% investment" in another person,

and, accordingly, references in section 259ND to "X%" are to be read as references to more than 50% or to 25% (as appropriate) and references in that section to "X% or more" are to be read as references to more than 50% or to 25% or more (as appropriate)."

(5) The amendments made by this section have effect in relation to accounting periods of CFCs beginning on or after 1 January 2019.

(6) For the purposes of subsection (5), if a CFC has an accounting period beginning before, and ending on or after, that date ("the straddling period")—

(a) so much of the straddling period as falls before that date, and so much of it as falls on or after that date, are treated as separate accounting periods, and

(b) if it is necessary to apportion an amount for the straddling period to the two separate periods, it is to be apportioned—

(i) on a time basis according to the respective length of the separate periods, or

(ii) if that would produce a result that is unjust or unreasonable, on a just and reasonable basis.

(7) In this section "CFC" has the same meaning as in Part 9A of TIOPA 2010.

COMMENTARY ON SECTION 20

Section 20 contains two notable changes to UK taxation of Controlled Foreign Companies ('CFCs'), both of which take effect from January 1, 2019.

The current UK CFC rules were included in Finance Act 2012 following a significant re-write of older provisions. The overarching aim of the CFC rules is to deal with profits which have been artificially diverted from the UK to another, lower taxed jurisdiction. These amendments to the UK's CFC regime have been introduced to ensure that the UK rules are fully compliant with the requirements of Council Directive (EU) 2016/1164, commonly referred to as the EU Anti-Tax Avoidance Directive.

Subsection (2) amends TIOPA 2010, s 371IA, which concerns an exemption from the CFC charge for profits from certain qualifying loan relationships. For some background: where a CFC has non-trading finance profits, TIOPA 2010, Pt 9A, Ch 5 is considered to determine the taxability of these profits. Broadly, profits may fall within Chapter 5 and therefore become taxable at the UK level where they are (a) derived from capital which has been contributed from the UK, or (b) can be traced to UK activities, i e UK significant people functions.

If the finance profits fall to be taxable, Chapter 9 of the rules could then be considered, which may act to exempt some or all profits that meet certain qualifying conditions. Chapter 9 is otherwise known as the finance company exemption and is currently the subject of a European Commission State Aid investigation.

Subsection (2) removes the ability to access the finance company exemption where profits can be traced to UK activities. Only non-trading finance profits which have been derived from capital contributed from the UK (and not traced to UK activities) may fall within the exemption. Any association of the overseas finance profits with UK activities would render the exemption invalid.

Groups with non-trading finance profits in a CFC and any UK treasury activity or key decision makers will now need to undertake an analysis of the activities and decisions which led to the derivation of those profits. This may have not been undertaken previously due to reliance on the finance company exemption.

This change is noteworthy for several reasons. It adds pressure to better understand the value drivers behind financing profits, who manages the assets and risks, and accordingly how profits should be split between jurisdictions. This is certainly the direction of travel across the globe as regards transfer pricing of financial transactions. There is also an interesting political angle regarding both Brexit and the European Commission's State Aid investigation into the finance company exemption regime. There is no indication that this change would be unwound following Brexit, however it is driven from both European Law and potentially in response to the European Commission challenge.

Subsection (4) inserts TIOPA 2010, s 371RG which widens the scope of entities which are defined as a CFC for UK purposes.

For the UK CFC rules to be of relevance for an entity, that entity needs to be both 'controlled' by UK persons, and 'foreign' in its tax residence. TIOPA 2010, ss 371RA–371RF contain various provisions to consider in identifying who controls a foreign company.

Subsection (4) adds a further leg to the definition of control for these purposes. Previously, only ownership of UK resident persons was considered in determining control of a non-resident company. From January 1, 2019, any UK resident company must aggregate its ownership of any non-resident investments with the ownership of any associated enterprises (including non-UK persons) in determining if their ownership exceeds 50%. Where this is the case, that company is a CFC, even if UK ownership is minimal.

Foreign controlled groups with split shareholding structures will need to review the impact of this change. Wholly owned group companies with any element of UK ownership are now likely to meet the CFC definition.

---

21 Permanent establishments: preparatory or auxiliary activities

(1) Section 1143 of CTA 2010 (permanent establishments: preparatory or auxiliary activities) is amended as follows.

(2) In subsection (2), at the end insert "and are not part of a fragmented business operation".

(3) After subsection (2) insert—

"(2A) Activities are "part of a fragmented business operation" if—

(a) they are carried on (whether at the same place or at different places in the same territory) by the company or a person closely related to the company,

(b) they constitute complementary functions that are part of a cohesive business operation, and

(c) subsection (2B) applies.

(2B) This subsection applies if—

(a) the overall activity resulting from the combination of the functions mentioned in subsection (2A)(b) is not activity that is only of a preparatory or auxiliary character, or

(b) the company or a person closely related to the company has a permanent establishment in the territory by reason of carrying on any of those functions.

(2C) A person who is not a company is to be treated for the purposes of subsection (2B)(b) as having a permanent establishment in a territory if, were the person a company, the person would have a permanent establishment in the territory.

(2D) For the purposes of this section, one person ("A") is closely related to another person ("B") if—

(a) A is able to secure that B acts in accordance with A's wishes (or vice versa),

(b) B can reasonably be expected to act, or typically acts, in accordance with A's wishes (or vice versa),

(c) a third person is able to secure that A and B act in accordance with the third person's wishes,

(d) A and B can reasonably be expected to act, or typically act, in accordance with a third person's wishes, or

(e) the 50% investment condition is met in relation to A and B.

(2E) The 50% investment condition is met in relation to A and B if—

(a) A has a 50% investment in B (or vice versa), or

(b) a third person has a 50% investment in each of A and B,

and section 259ND of TIOPA 2010 (meaning of "50% investment") applies for the purposes of determining whether a person has a "50% investment".

(4) In subsection (3), for "For this purpose" substitute "In this section".

(5) The amendments made by this section have effect in relation to accounting periods beginning on or after 1 January 2019.

(6) For the purposes of subsection (5), if a company has an accounting period beginning before, and ending on or after, that date ("the straddling period")—

- (a) so much of the straddling period as falls before that date, and so much of it as falls on or after that date, are treated as separate accounting periods, and
- (b) if it is necessary to apportion an amount for the straddling period to the two separate periods, it is to be apportioned—
  - (i) on a time basis according to the respective length of the separate periods, or
  - (ii) if that would produce a result that is unjust or unreasonable, on a just and reasonable basis.

COMMENTARY ON SECTION 21

CTA 2010, s 1143 provides that a non-UK resident company will not be treated as having a permanent establishment in the UK as a result of conducting preparatory or auxiliary activities in the UK. CTA 2010, s 1143 is amended by FA 2019, s 21 to provide that it will not apply where the activities are part of a fragmented business operation. This will be the case where the activities carried on in the UK by the person, or a person closely related to the person, constitute complementary functions that are part of a cohesive business operation and either:

- judged as a whole the overall activities are not of a preparatory or auxiliary character, or
- the company or a person closely related to the company has a permanent establishment in the UK by reason of carrying on any of those functions.

The definition of 'closely related' is set out in a new CTA 2010, s 1143(2D), (2E).

The amendments introduced by section 21 have effect in relation to accounting periods beginning on or after 1 January 2019. Where a company has an accounting period that straddled this date the accounting period is split into two deemed periods, with the second period starting on 1 January 2019. Amounts are apportioned between the two deemed periods on a time basis unless such method of apportionment would work unjustly or unreasonably, in which case a just and reasonable basis is to be used.

This amendment tracks amendments proposed under article 13.4(b) of the OECD 'Multilateral Convention to Implement Tax Treaty Related Measures to Prevent Base Erosion and Profit Shifting'.

---

22 Payment of CGT exit charges

Schedule 7 contains provision about CGT exit charge payment plans.

23 Corporation tax exit charges

Schedule 8—

- (a) amends provisions concerning CT exit charge payment plans,
- (b) repeals certain provisions that enable the postponement of exit charges, and
- (c) contains amendments concerning the treatment of assets that are the subject of EU exit charges.

COMMENTARY ON SECTION 23

Section 23 introduces Schedule 8 which has three parts. Part 1 amends the rules in Schedule 3ZB of TMA 1970 for postponement corporation tax exit charges when a company ceases to be UK resident. Part 2 repeals TCGA 1992, s 187 and makes consequential amendments. Part 3 introduces a new rule for assets coming into the UK corporation tax regimes.

The changes are designed to implement the EU anti-tax avoidance directive.

---

24 Group relief etc: meaning of "UK related" company

(1) In section 134 of CTA 2010 (group relief: meaning of "UK related" company) in paragraph (b) for the words from "carrying on" to the end substitute "within the charge to corporation tax".

(2) In section 188CJ of CTA 2010 (group relief for carried-forward losses: meaning of "UK related" company) in paragraph (b) for the words from "carrying on" to the end substitute "within the charge to corporation tax".

(3) The amendments made by this section have effect for the purpose of determining whether a company is a UK related company at any time on or after 5 July 2016.

(4) In its application in relation to a claim for group relief or group relief for carried-forward losses made in reliance on this section, paragraph 74 of Schedule 18 to FA 1998 (time limit for claims) has effect as if the list of dates in sub-paragraph (1) of that paragraph included 31 December 2019.

COMMENTARY ON SECTION 24

Section 24 extends the definition of 'UK related' company for the purposes of group relief to include non-UK resident companies that are within the charge to corporation tax.

For the purposes of group relief claims (for current year relief and carried forward relief), both the surrendering company and the claimant company must be members of the same group of companies and also a UK resident company or a non-UK resident company carrying on a trade in the UK through a permanent establishment, for the accounting period specified in the claim.

Subsections 24(1)–(3) amend the wording 'a UK permanent establishment' in CTA 2010, s 134(b) and CTA 2010, s 188CJ(b) to being 'within the charge to corporation tax' retrospectively to any time on or after 5 July 2016. This allows non-UK resident companies that are subject to corporation tax on transactions in UK land under CTA 2010, ss 356OA–356OT (Part 8ZB), to be able to claim group relief as these rules were introduced for disposals on or after 5 July 2016.

Subsection 24(4) extends the time limit for a group relief claim (both current and carried forward relief) which relies on the FA 2019 amendment to 31 December 2019. The amendment will also mean non-UK resident companies with UK property gains and income, that are chargeable to corporation tax from 6 April 2019 and 2020 respectively, can claim group relief.

Corporation tax: miscellaneous

25 Intangible fixed assets: restrictions on goodwill and certain other assets

Schedule 9 contains provision about the debits to be brought into account for corporation tax purposes in respect of goodwill and certain other assets.

26 Intangible fixed assets: exceptions to degrouping charges etc

(1) Part 8 of CTA 2009 (intangible fixed assets) is amended as follows.

(2) In section 780 (deemed realisation etc on company leaving group) in subsection (5) (exceptions) after paragraph (a) insert—

"(aa) section 782A (company leaving group because of relevant share disposal),".

(3) After section 782 insert—

"782A Company leaving group because of relevant share disposal

(1) Section 780 does not apply if a company ceases to be a member of a group because of a relevant disposal of shares by another company.

(2) A disposal of shares by a company is "relevant" if—

(a) the company would not be chargeable to corporation tax in respect of any gain accruing on the disposal by reason of the exemption conferred by paragraph 1 of Schedule 7AC to TCGA 1992 (assuming the company was within the charge to corporation tax), and

(b) the disposal is not part of an arrangement under which the recipient of the shares is to dispose of any of them to another person.

(3) For the purposes of subsection (2)(a) ignore paragraph 6 of Schedule 7AC to TCGA 1992 (cases in which exemptions do not apply)."

(4) In section 785 (principal company becoming member of another group)—

(a) in subsection (2)(b) for the words from "both" to "effective 51%" substitute "a relevant", and

(b) after subsection (2) insert—

"(2A) For the purposes of subsection (2)(b) the transferee is a "relevant subsidiary" of a member of the second group ("A") if, but for sections 767 to 770, the transferee would be a member of another group of which A would be the principal company.

(2B) Subsection (2) does not apply if the transferee ceases to meet the qualifying condition by reason of a relevant disposal of shares by another company (within the meaning given by section 782A(2))."

(5) The amendments made by this section have effect in relation to a company that ceases to be a member of a group or ceases to meet the condition in section 785(2)(b) of CTA 2009 (as amended by subsection (4)) on or after 7 November 2018.

(6) In its application in relation to a company that ceases to be a member of a group or ceases to meet the condition in section 785(2)(b) of CTA 2009 before 21 December 2018, section 782A of CTA 2009 has effect as if subsection (3) of that section was omitted.

COMMENTARY ON SECTION 26

Section 26 amends the degrouping rules for intangible fixed assets in CTA 2009 Pt 8 to bring them into line with the effect of the degrouping rules for chargeable assets after their amendment by FA 2011. The new provision simply says that no degrouping charge arises where a company leaves a group holding an intangible fixed asset that has been transferred to it from another group company within the last six years, so long as the degrouping event is, itself, exempt from corporation tax on gains under the provisions of the substantial shareholding exemption (TCGA 1992, Sch 7AC).

The provisions relating to disposals out of a second group that the original group has become a member of are also amended to ensure that no degrouping charge arises if a company is sold out of that second group within six years of the transfer of intangible fixed assets, so long as this disposal from the second group qualifies for the substantial shareholding exemption.

The new rule does not apply where the disposal is part of an arrangement where the recipient is to dispose of them to another person. The Explanatory Notes say that this is intended to prevent the exception from applying where there are 'arrangements involving a series of disposals where the requirement [that the substantial shareholding exemption be available] is not met in relation to every disposal.' It's not clear how this meaning is imported to the words of the legislation which simply refers to the disposal not being 'part of an arrangement under which the recipient of the shares is to dispose of them to another person.'

In contrast to the rules for capital gains degrouping, there is no deemed disposal or acquisition of the intangible fixed assets in these circumstances, so the asset is not rebased for tax purposes.

The new rules apply to companies that cease to be a member of the group on or after 7 November 2018.

Some degrouping events occur under circumstances where the substantial shareholding exemption cannot apply because a company leaves the group in a transaction which is deemed to occur at no gain or no loss, and such transactions are excluded from the exemption. This would apply, for example, to a company that leaves a group as part of a scheme of reconstruction. In determining whether the substantial shareholding exemption would apply to a degrouping for the purpose of this new rule, this restriction on the availability of the substantial shareholding exemption is ignored, which ensures that a degrouping charge is not accidentally triggered by a reconstruction, for example, simply because the substantial shareholding exemption cannot apply to that transaction.

This provision only applies from 21 December 2018.

---

27 Corporation tax relief for carried-forward losses

Schedule 10 makes provision about corporation tax relief for losses and other amounts that are carried forward.

28 Corporate interest restriction

Schedule 11 contains provision amending Part 10 of TIOPA 2010 (corporate interest restriction).

29 Debtor relationships of company where money lent to connected companies

Schedule 12 makes provision for preventing a mismatch for corporation tax purposes in a case where—

(a) a company has a debtor relationship which is dealt with in its accounts on the basis of fair value accounting, and

(b) the money it receives under that relationship is wholly or mainly used to lend money to companies that are connected with it (and, accordingly, those creditor relationships are required to be dealt with for corporation tax purposes on an amortised cost basis of accounting).

Capital allowances

30 Construction expenditure on buildings and structures

(1) The Treasury may by regulations amend CAA 2001 so as to provide for allowances under that Act to be available where—

(a) expenditure has been incurred, on or after 29 October 2018, on the construction of a building,

(b) the building is in qualifying use, and

(c) the expenditure incurred on the construction of the building, or other expenditure, is qualifying expenditure.

(2) Regulations under this section ("the regulations") must—

(a) specify what is qualifying use;

(b) specify what is qualifying expenditure;

(c) provide for a writing-down allowance to be available at an annual rate of 2% of the qualifying expenditure;

(d) specify the persons to whom allowances may be made;

(e) make provision about how effect is to be given to allowances.

(3) The regulations must secure that—

(a) allowances are not available for expenditure on the acquisition of land or rights in or over land;

(b) qualifying use is restricted to use for prescribed business purposes.

(4) The regulations may provide for allowances not to be available or to be restricted—

(a) in the case of a building that is wholly or partly used as a dwelling-house or for purposes that are ancillary to the purposes of a dwelling-house;

(b) in respect of a building that is used wholly or partly for holiday or overnight accommodation of a prescribed kind;

(c) in respect of a building that is only partly in qualifying use or in respect of periods when a building is not in qualifying use;

(d) in prescribed cases or circumstances.

(5) The regulations may provide that if a person incurs expenditure for the purposes of a qualifying activity before (but not more than 7 years before) the date on which the person starts to carry on that activity, the expenditure is to be treated as if it were incurred by the person on that date.

(6) The regulations may provide that if—

(a) allowances have been available to a person (A) in respect of expenditure on the construction of a building, and

(b) A sells A's interest in the building to another person (B),

allowances are available to B in respect of the residue of the qualifying expenditure.

(7) The regulations may make provision about leases, including provision for the grant of a lease to be treated in prescribed circumstances in the same way as the sale of the grantor's interest.

(8) The regulations may make—

(a) provision under which expenditure is apportioned;

(b) provision for balancing adjustments (and about how effect is to be given to them);

(c) provision for qualifying expenditure to be written off;

(d) special provision about highway undertakings;
(e) provision about additional VAT liability and additional VAT rebate (within the meaning given by section 547 of CAA 2001);
(f) anti-avoidance provision;
(g) supplementary or incidental provision;
(h) consequential provision (including provision amending enactments other than CAA 2001).

(9) The regulations may make transitional provision, including provision under which expenditure incurred on or after 29 October 2018 is treated as incurred before that date—

(a) where the expenditure is associated or connected with expenditure incurred before that date,
(b) where the expenditure relates to a contract entered into before that date, or
(c) in other prescribed cases.

(10) Subsections (2) to (9) are not to be read as limiting subsection (1).

(11) A statutory instrument containing the regulations may not be made unless a draft of the instrument has been laid before and approved by a resolution of the House of Commons.

(12) A reference in this section to expenditure on the construction of a building includes a reference to capital expenditure—

(a) on repairs to the building, or
(b) on the renovation or conversion of the building.

(13) In this section—

"building" includes structure;
"dwelling-house" has the meaning given by the regulations;
"prescribed" means prescribed by the regulations.

COMMENTARY ON SECTION 30

Section 30 provides the Treasury with a power to make regulations by statutory instrument to introduce a new capital allowance code for expenditure on the construction of certain structures and buildings incurred on or after 29 October 2018.

The Office of Tax Simplification recommended widening the scope of capital allowances in its report of June 2018, 'Accounting depreciation or capital allowances? Simplifying tax relief for tangible fixed assets' and the new code is being introduced in response to its recommendations. The aim is to stimulate investment in buildings and other structures intended for commercial use.

HMRC published a Technical Note on 29 October 2018 outlining the proposed scheme and seeking views on some aspects of the proposals (see www.gov.uk/government/publications/capital-allowances-for-structures-and-buildings-technical-note). A draft statutory instrument was published on 13 March 2019 (see www.gov.uk/government/consultations/draft-legislation-detailing-a-new-capital-allowance-for-new-non-residential-structures-and-buildings) incorporating changes resulting from the consultation on the Technical Note proposals.

The main features of the proposed allowances, as set out in the draft statutory instrument, are as follows:

- Allowances will be available for capital expenditure on structures and buildings brought into use for the purposes of a trade, profession or vocation, a UK or overseas ordinary property business, a concern within ITOIA 2005, s 12(4) or CTA 2009, s 39(4) (mines, transport undertakings etc) or managing the investments of a company with investment business.
- Structures and buildings include offices, retail and wholesale premises, walls, bridges, tunnels, factories and warehouses. Residential property and other buildings that function as dwellings, such as school and military accommodation, will not qualify.
- Structures and buildings in the UK and overseas will qualify, provided that the business is within the charge to UK tax. Relief will not be available for structures or buildings where a contract for the construction works was entered into before 29 October 2018.
- Qualifying expenditure will include only the net direct costs related to physically preparing the site and constructing the asset. The cost of the land or of land alterations are excluded. Capital expenditure on renovations or conversions of existing commercial structures or buildings will, however, also qualify.

- If a structure or building is acquired from a developer, the expenditure will be apportioned to exclude the value of the land.
- Writing-down allowances of 2% of the qualifying expenditure will be given on a straight-line basis over a 50-year period, stating when the structure or building is first brought into use.
- Where a structure or building is divided into separate parts, some of which qualify, an appropriate proportion of expenditure will qualify for relief.
- No balancing adjustments will be made. Where the relevant interest in an asset that has qualified for relief is sold, the new owner will be able to claim the annual allowance for the remaining part of the 50-year period if it is used for a qualifying activity. The allowance for the period in which the disposal takes place will be apportioned between the seller and the buyer.
- The grant of a lease will result in the transfer of future allowances only if the effective duration of the lease is at least 35 years and the market value of the retained interest in the structure or building is less than one-third of the capital sum given as consideration for the lease.
- A claim for the allowance can only be made from when a structure or building first comes into use.
- No allowances will be given unless the requirement for an allowance statement is met. A written statement must be made before a claim for allowances is first made and must include details of the date of construction, the amount of qualifying expenditure and the date on which the structure or building is first brought into use. Where allowances are to be transferred on the sale of the asset, the buyer must obtain the allowance statement from the seller.
- If a structure or building becomes a dwelling, allowances will no longer be available.
- Where a structure or building subsequently undergoes renovation or other capital works, the expenditure will qualify for allowances, but as a separate allowance with a new 50-year period.
- Allowances will continue to be given during a period of disuse of the structure or building.
- If a structure or building is demolished allowances will cease but, relief from tax on capital gains will be available for expenditure on which allowances would still potentially have been due but for the demolition.
- Integral features and fixtures will continue to be dealt with under the plant and machinery code.

---

31 Special rate expenditure on plant and machinery

(1) Part 2 of CAA 2001 (plant and machinery allowances) is amended as follows.

(2) In section 104D(1) (writing-down allowances in respect of special rate expenditure) for "8%" substitute "6%".

(3) Accordingly, in—

(a) section 56(2)(a),
(b) the heading of section 104D, and
(c) section 104E(1)(a),

for "8%" substitute "6%".

(4) The amendments made by subsections (2) and (3) have effect in relation to chargeable periods beginning on or after the relevant day.

(5) In relation to a chargeable period that begins before and ends on or after the relevant day, section 104D(1) of CAA 2001 has effect as if the reference to 8% was a reference to X%.

(6) For the purposes of subsection (5), X is—

$$(8 \times (BRD / CP)) + (6 \times (ARD / CP))$$

where—

BRD is the number of days in the chargeable period before the relevant day,
ARD is the number of days in the chargeable period on or after the relevant day, and
CP is the number of days in the chargeable period.

(7) Where X would be a figure with more than 2 decimal places it is to be rounded up to the nearest second decimal place.

(8) In this section "the relevant day" is—

(a) for corporation tax purposes, 1 April 2019, and
(b) for income tax purposes, 6 April 2019.

COMMENTARY ON SECTION 31

The special rate of writing-down allowances applies to expenditure on certain assets. These assets are listed in CAA 2001, s 104A and include long-life assets, integral features and cars which do not qualify for the main rate of writing-down allowances, due to not qualifying as cars with low CO_2 emissions.

Section 31 reduces writing-down allowances for special rate expenditure from 8% to 6%. This takes effect for corporation tax purposes from 1 April 2019 and from 6 April 2019 onwards for income tax purposes.

Where a chargeable period includes the change of rate, a hybrid rate is to be used. This rate is calculated in accordance with subsections (6) and (7). The hybrid rate is the result of strict time apportionment between the two rates and must be calculated according to the number of days at each rate, with the resulting percentage rounded to two decimal places.

32 Temporary increase in annual investment allowance

(1) In relation to expenditure incurred during the period of two years beginning with 1 January 2019, section 51A of CAA 2001 (entitlement to annual investment allowance) has effect as if in subsection (5) the amount specified as the maximum allowance were £1,000,000.

(2) Schedule 13 contains provision about chargeable periods which straddle 1 January 2019 or 1 January 2021.

COMMENTARY ON SECTION 32

The annual investment allowance (AIA) provides 100% relief on certain capital expenditure up to an annual maximum. Qualifying expenditure is defined in CAA 2001, ss 38A and 38B, but includes plant and machinery, integral features and long-life assets, with exceptions such as for cars, assets previously used for private purposes and assets subject to a long lease under a sale and leaseback arrangement. An AIA is shared between companies in a group and those under common control. The maximum AIA, prior to changes by Finance Act 2019, was £200,000.

Section 32 increases the annual investment allowance to £1,000,000 with effect for the two-year period from 1 January 2019 to 31 December 2020. This is subject to a number of rules concerning how the AIA is calculated where a person's chargeable period includes the change in rate. Where a business does not have a 31 December year-end, the transitional rules set out in Sch 13 apply.

33 First-year allowances and first-year tax credits

(1) In Part 2 of CAA 2001 (plant and machinery allowances), the following provisions are repealed—

(a) sections 45A to 45C (energy-saving plant or machinery),
(b) sections 45H to 45J (environmentally beneficial plant or machinery), and
(c) section 262A and Schedule A1 (first-year tax credits).

(2) In consequence of subsection (1)—

(a) in TMA 1970, in the second column of the Table in section 98, in the entry relating to requirements imposed by provisions of CAA 2001, omit "45B(5) and (6)," and ", 45I(5) and (6)",
(b) in CAA 2001—
  (i) in section 2(3), for "262A" substitute "262",
  (ii) in section 3—
    (a) in subsection (1), omit ", and no first-year tax credit is to be paid under Schedule A1,", and
    (b) omit subsection (2B),
  (iii) in the list in section 39, omit—
    (a) the entry relating to section 45A, and
    (b) the entry relating to section 45H,

(iv) in section 46—

(a) in the list in subsection (1), omit the entry relating to section 45A and the entry relating to section 45H, and

(b) omit subsections (5) and (6), and

(v) in the table in section 52(3), omit—

(a) the entry relating to expenditure qualifying under section 45A, and

(b) the entry relating to expenditure qualifying under section 45H, and

(c) the following provisions are repealed—

(i) in FA 2001, section 65 and Schedule 17,

(ii) in FA 2003, paragraphs 2(c), 3, 4(1)(c) and (2) and 5 to 7 of Schedule 30,

(iii) in FA 2006, paragraph 11 of Schedule 9,

(iv) in FA 2008, section 79 and Schedule 25,

(v) in CTA 2009, paragraph 521 of Schedule 1,

(vi) in CTA 2010, paragraph 364 of Schedule 1,

(vii) in FA 2011, paragraph 12(16) of Schedule 14,

(viii) in the Welfare Reform Act 2012—

(a) paragraph 14 of Schedule 3, and

(b) in the table in Part 1 of Schedule 4, the entry relating to CAA 2001,

(ix) in FA 2012—

(a) section 45(2) and (3), and

(b) paragraph 106 of Schedule 16,

(x) in FA 2013—

(a) section 67,

(b) section 68(2), and

(c) paragraph 6 of Schedule 18,

(xi) in FA 2014, paragraph 7 of Schedule 4,

(xii) in FA 2016, paragraph 7 of Schedule 8,

(xiii) in F(No 2)A 2017—

(a) paragraph 126 of Schedule 4, and

(b) paragraph 7 of Schedule 6, and

(xiv) in FA 2018, section 29.

(3) The following orders were made under powers contained in provisions repealed by subsection (1) and are therefore revoked—

(a) the Capital Allowances (Environmentally Beneficial Plant and Machinery) Order 2003 (SI 2003/2076), and

(b) any instrument amending that order.

(4) The Capital Allowances (Energy-saving Plant and Machinery) Order 2018 (SI 2018/268) is revoked.

(5) The amendments made by this section have effect in relation to expenditure incurred on or after—

(a) for corporation tax purposes, 1 April 2020, and

(b) for income tax purposes, 6 April 2020.

COMMENTARY ON SECTION 33

Section 33 repeals the first-year allowance (FYA) of 100% for expenditure on energy-saving plant and machinery and environmentally beneficial plant and machinery. Furthermore, it also removes the availability of a first-year tax credit (FYTC) for corporation tax losses arising as a result of FYAs. These changes come into effect on 1 April 2020 for corporation tax purposes and 6 April 2020 for income tax purposes.

While this removes a number of FYA measures, there will continue to be FYAs available on certain expenditure following April 2020. This expenditure includes that incurred on cars with low emissions of carbon dioxide, zero-emission goods vehicles, electric vehicle charge points and plant and machinery used in a ring-fence trade. These FYAs are unaffected by this provision.

No FYTCs will be available beyond 1 April 2020 as CAA 2001, Sch A1 is repealed. However, as FYTCs were only available on surrendered losses arising due to FYAs on energy-saving or environmentally beneficial plant and machinery, this legislation would have been rendered redundant.

34 First-year allowance: expenditure on electric vehicle charge points

In section 45EA of CAA 2001 (expenditure on plant or machinery for electric vehicle charging point), in subsection (3) (the relevant period) for "2019", in both places it occurs, substitute "2023".

COMMENTARY ON SECTION 34

Section 34 extends the availability of a first-year allowance (FYA) on expenditure on electric vehicle charge points. Prior to this change, FYAs were only available on quality expenditure incurred on or before 31 March 2019 (corporation tax) and 5 April 2019 (income tax).

FYAs on qualifying expenditure incurred in providing electric vehicle charge points will now be available on expenditure incurred on or before 31 March 2023 (corporation tax) and 5 April 2019 (income tax).

35 Qualifying expenditure: buildings, structures and land

(1) Chapter 3 of Part 2 of CAA 2001 (qualifying expenditure) is amended as follows.

(2) In each of sections 21 and 22 (buildings, structures, assets and works), at the end of subsection (4) insert "(but any reference in list C in subsection (4) of that section to "plant" does not include anything where expenditure on its provision is excluded by this section)".

(3) The amendments made by this section—

- (a) are treated as always having had effect, but
- (b) do not have effect in relation to claims for capital allowances made before 29 October 2018.

COMMENTARY ON SECTION 35

Section 35 makes a minor amendment to the operation of lists A, B and C within CAA 2001, ss 21 to 23. Lists A and B both list items which are ineligible for plant and machinery writing-down allowances. Both state that 'expenditure on the provision of plant or machinery does not include expenditure on the provision of' listed items. List A pertains to buildings and list B pertains to structures, assets and works.

List C in CAA 2001, s 23 overrides lists A and B, effectively listing items on which expenditure on the provision of qualifies as plant and machinery for capital allowance purposes. In two places, list C mentions plant, one of which is the alteration of land only for the installation of plant. Because of the structure of the legislation and the wording of sections 21 and 22, this allows the alteration of land only to install plant to qualify as plant and machinery, even where the plant being installed has been disallowed by virtue of list A or B.

This anomaly can be seen in the recent first-tier tribunal case of *SSE Generation Limited v HMRC* [2018] UKFTT 416 (TC). In this case, a company successfully claimed the cost of alteration of land because the plant being installed, an aqueduct, met the normal, common law definition of being plant, despite the fact that expenditure on the aqueduct itself was excluded from being expenditure on plant and machinery for capital allowance purposes. By virtue of list C, expenditure on the alteration of land to install plant, was considered to be expenditure on plant or machinery.

Section 35 makes clear that where an item is included in either list A or B, it is not to be considered plant for the purpose of list C. This change is effective for claims for capital allowances made on or after 29 October 2018, even where expenditure occurred before this date. No historic claims akin to the *SSE Generation Ltd* case may be made as of that date.

Leases

36 Changes to accounting standards etc

Schedule 14 contains provision relating to the taxation of leases.

Oil activities and petroleum revenue tax

37 Oil activities: transferable tax history

Schedule 15 makes provision for a company which sells an interest in an oil licence and a company which buys that interest to make a joint election for an amount of the seller's profits to be treated, in accordance with the provisions of the Schedule, as if it were an amount of the purchaser's profits.

COMMENTARY ON SECTION 37

Section 37 introduces the Sch 15 provisions for the parties to the transfer of an oil licence to elect jointly that an amount of the seller's profits and associated corporation tax and supplementary charge payments will be treated as the purchaser's profits and tax paid.

Section 37 and Sch 15 affect UK oil and gas companies with activities subject to the provisions of CTA 2010, s 279 (the ring fence trade) on the transfer of an interest in an oil field for which the Oil and Gas Authority gives consent on or after 1 November 2018. The effect is to introduce the option to effectively transfer tax history from the seller to the purchaser to enable the purchaser to obtain effective relief, in the form of tax repayment, for decommissioning expenditure.

The measure is introduced as a reaction to the industry's request for the removal of obstacles to the transfer of late life oil and gas interests in the UK and the UK continental shelf (UKCS).

The effective transfer of the seller's history gives a potential entitlement to a tax repayment to the purchaser which would not otherwise have been available. Without the option to transfer tax history, potential purchasers of oil and gas interests in the UK and UKCS without past profits from such activities, were at a disadvantage compared to those with such history. The 'transferable tax history' in s 37 and Sch 15 aims to remove this disadvantage.

38 Petroleum revenue tax: post-transfer decommissioning expenditure

(1) Schedule 3 to OTA 1975 (petroleum revenue tax: miscellaneous provisions) is amended in accordance with this section.

(2) After paragraph 11 insert—

"*Transfers of interests in oil fields: post-transfer decommissioning expenditure*

11A (1) This paragraph applies if—

(a) there is, for the purposes of Schedule 17 to FA 1980, a transfer by a participator in an oil field of the whole or part of an interest in the field, and

(b) on or after 1 November 2018, the OGA gives consent for the transfer.

(2) Paragraph 8(1) (certain subsidised expenditure to be disregarded) does not apply to any decommissioning expenditure that—

(a) is incurred by the new participator, and

(b) has been, or is to be, met directly or indirectly out of a payment made by the old participator.

(3) Sub-paragraph (4) applies if, at the end of the transfer period, the old participator is no longer a licensee or a participator in respect of any licensed area wholly or partly included in the oil field.

(4) Decommissioning expenditure that is incurred by the old participator, after the end of the transfer period, is to be treated for the purposes of this Act as having been incurred by the new participator (and paragraph 8(1) does not apply to any such expenditure).

(5) If the old participator has transferred the whole or part of another interest in the oil field to the new participator, but the condition in sub-paragraph (1)(b) was not met

in respect of the transfer, references in sub-paragraphs (2) and (4) to decommissioning expenditure are references to such proportion of that expenditure as is just and reasonable.

(6) In this paragraph—

(a) "decommissioning expenditure" means—

(i) expenditure that is incurred, in relation to the oil field mentioned in sub-paragraph (1)(a), for a purpose within section 3(1)(i) or (j) (decommissioning or restoration), and

(ii) is allowable under that section;

(b) "the old participator", "the new participator" and "the transfer period" have the same meaning as in Schedule 17 to FA 1980 (see paragraph 1(3) of that Schedule).

(7) If there is, for the purposes of Schedule 17 to FA 1980, a subsequent transfer of the whole or part of an interest in the oil field mentioned in sub-paragraph (1)(a), references in this paragraph to "the old participator" include references to each participator whose interest, or part of it, in the oil field is the subject of a transfer to which this paragraph applies."

(3) In paragraph 8, at the end insert—

"(3) This paragraph is subject to paragraph 11A (transfers of interests in oil fields: post-transfer decommissioning expenditure)."

COMMENTARY ON SECTION 38

Section 38 introduces amendments to the Oil Taxation Act 1975 (OTA 1975), which concerns petroleum revenue tax (PRT), so that for transfer of oil field interests for which the Oil and Gas Authority gives consent on or after 1 November 2018, the purchasers of interests may obtain relief for PRT purposes where a previous owner bears the costs of decommissioning assets used in respect of that field interest.

Hitherto the PRT rules on decommissioning expenditure incurred in respect of an oil field where the cost was not ultimately borne by the person with the relevant field interest did not operate in the same way as the rules for corporation tax, and there was no relief for PRT purposes in respect of such expenditure.

Section 38 reflects the policy of removing obstacles to the transfer of late life oil fields where the difficulty arises from the arrangements for decommissioning.

Subsections (2) and (3) insert a new para 11A into OTA 1975, Sch 3 which sets out the limited precedence of the new paragraph over the general rules on subsidised expenditure.

Miscellaneous reliefs

39 Entrepreneurs' relief

Schedule 16 contains provision amending Part 5 of TCGA 1992 (transfer of business assets, entrepreneurs' relief and investors' relief) in connection with entrepreneurs' relief.

40 Gift aid etc: restrictions on associated benefits

(1) In section 418 of ITA 2007 (gifts to charities by individuals: restrictions on associated benefits) in subsection (2) (the variable limit) for paragraphs (a) to (c) substitute—

"(a) in a case where the amount of the gift is £100 or less, 25% of that amount, and

(b) in a case where the amount of the gift exceeds £100, the sum of £25 and 5% of the amount of the excess."

(2) The amendment made by subsection (1) has effect in relation to gifts made on or after 6 April 2019.

(3) In section 197 of CTA 2010 (payments to charities by companies: restrictions on associated benefits) in subsection (2) (the variable limit) for paragraphs (a) to (c) substitute—

"(a) in a case where the amount of the payment is £100 or less, 25% of that amount, and

(b) in a case where the amount of the payment exceeds £100, the sum of £25 and 5% of the amount of the excess."

(4) The amendment made by subsection (3) has effect in relation to payments made on or after 6 April 2019.

COMMENTARY ON SECTION 40

Section 40 amends the amount of the benefit the donor (or any person connected with the donor) can receive from the charity or anyone associated with the charity before tax relief is withdrawn (ITA 2007, ss 417–418; CTA 2010, ss 195–197, 201). If the limit is exceeded, the donation does not qualify for tax relief, meaning that no deduction from total profits is available to corporate donors and no gift aid is available to individual donors and the charity must refund any tax repayment received from HMRC on the gift. The definition of connected is found in ITA 2007, ss 993, 994 for individual donors and in CTA 2010, ss 1176, 1122 for corporate donors.

For donations made on or after 6 April 2019, the maximum benefit:

- for gifts of £100 or less is 25% of the amount of the gift (no change from the pre-6 April 2019 rules)
- for gifts of more than £100 is £25 plus 5% of the additional amount donated above £100 (prior to 6 April 2019 the maximum benefit for a gift between £100 and £1,000 was £25 and the maximum benefit for a gift of over £1,000 was 5% of the amount gifted)

Note that 6 April 2019 is the operative date for donations by both individuals and companies.

There are no other changes to the existing associated benefit rules, meaning that if the benefit is linked to a period of less than 12 months the annual equivalent must be found and the maximum total benefit that may be received in any tax year (individuals) or accounting period (companies) is £2,500 (ITA 2007, ss 418, 419, 420; CTA 2010, ss 197, 198). As far as individuals are concerned, as a general rule rights of admission are ignored for the purposes of the associated benefits limits (ITA 2007, s 420).

The associated benefits limits were changed following a call for evidence in 2015 and a subsequent consultation (see bit.ly/2ShX0D7) in order to simplify the rules and smooth out the limits while at the same time ensuring minimal systems disruption for charities. A two threshold option was preferred by respondents over a single threshold or the existing three threshold system. The introduction of the changes was delayed until April 2019 in order to give charities time to prepare.

---

41 Charities: exemption for small trades etc

(1) In section 528 of ITA 2007 (exemption for small trades of charitable trust: condition that trading incoming resources etc do not exceed requisite limit) in subsection (6)(b) (the requisite limit)—

(a) for "£5,000" substitute £8,000", and
(b) for "£50,000" substitute "£80,000".

(2) The amendments made by subsection (1) have effect for the tax year 2019–20 and subsequent tax years.

(3) Section 482 of CTA 2010 (exemption for small trades of charitable company: condition that trading incoming resources etc do not exceed requisite limit) is amended as follows.

(4) In subsection (6)(b) (the requisite limit)—

(a) for "£5,000" substitute "£8,000", and
(b) for "£50,000" substitute "£80,000".

(5) In subsection (7)—

(a) for "£5,000" substitute £8,000", and
(b) for "£50,000" substitute "£80,000".

(6) The amendments made by subsections (3) to (5) have effect in relation to accounting periods beginning on or after 1 April 2019.

COMMENTARY ON SECTION 41

A statutory exemption applies to the profits of small trading carried on by a charitable company or charitable trust that are not otherwise exempt, provided the profits are applied solely for the purposes of the charity.

Section 41 amends CTA 2010, s 482 and ITA 2007, s 528 to increase the monetary limits, such that the exemption will apply provided that the charity's gross income for the chargeable period does not exceed (or, at the beginning of that period, is not reasonably expected to exceed) the greater of:

- £8,000, and
- the lesser of £80,000 and 25% of the charity's incoming resources for that period

The amendments have effect in relation to accounting periods beginning on or after 1 April 2019 (corporation tax) and for tax years 2019/20 onwards (income tax).

PART 2

OTHER TAXES

Stamp duty land tax

42 Relief for first-time buyers in cases of shared ownership

(1) Schedule 9 to FA 2003 (stamp duty land tax: shared ownership leases etc) is amended as follows.

(2) In paragraph 4 (shared ownership lease: election where staircasing allowed), after sub-paragraph (4) insert—

> "(4A) See paragraph 15 for further provision in connection with relief for first-time buyers."

(3) After paragraph 14 insert—

> *"Relief for first-time buyers: shared ownership lease where election made*
>
> **15** Where—
>
> (a) paragraph 4 applies, and
> (b) relief is claimed under paragraph 1 of Schedule 6ZA in respect of the grant of the lease concerned,
>
> no tax is chargeable in respect of so much of the chargeable consideration for the grant as consists of rent."

(4) After paragraph 15 (as inserted by subsection (3)) insert—

> *"Relief for first-time buyers: shared ownership lease where no election made*
>
> **15A** (1) This paragraph applies where—
>
> (a) a shared ownership lease is granted, and
> (b) no election is made for tax to be charged in accordance with paragraph 2 or 4.
>
> (2) For the purpose of determining whether the second condition in paragraph 1 of Schedule 6ZA is met in respect of the grant, the chargeable consideration for the grant is to be treated as being the amount stated in the lease in accordance with paragraph 2(2)(e) or paragraph 4(2)(e)(i) or (ii).
>
> (3) If relief is claimed in respect of the grant under paragraph 1 of Schedule 6ZA no tax is chargeable in respect of so much of the chargeable consideration for the grant as consists of rent.
>
> (4) In this paragraph "shared ownership lease" has the same meaning as in paragraph 4A.
>
> *Relief for first-time buyers: shared ownership trust where no election made*
>
> **15B** (1) This paragraph applies where—
>
> (a) a shared ownership trust is declared, and
> (b) no election is made for tax to be charged in accordance with paragraph 9.

(2) For the purpose of determining whether the second condition in paragraph 1 of Schedule 6ZA is met in respect of the declaration, the chargeable consideration for the declaration is to be treated as being the sum specified in the trust in accordance with paragraph 7(4)(f).

(3) If relief is claimed in respect of the declaration under paragraph 1 of Schedule 6ZA no tax is chargeable in respect of any rent-equivalent payment treated by reason of paragraph 11(b) as rent."

(5) For the italic cross-heading before paragraph 16 substitute "No relief for first-time buyers for staircasing transactions etc".

(6) In paragraph 16 (cases where first-time buyer's relief is not available)—

- (a) in sub-paragraph (1), omit paragraphs (a), (b) and (d) (but not "or" at the end of paragraph (d)), and
- (b) in sub-paragraph (2), omit paragraphs (a) and (c) (but not "or" at the end of paragraph (c)).

(7) The amendments made by this section have effect in relation to—

- (a) any land transaction of which the effective date is on or after 29 October 2018, and
- (b) any land transaction of which the effective date is before 29 October 2018 and in respect of which a land transaction return has not been given by that date.

COMMENTARY ON SECTION 42

SDLT relief for first-time buyers claimed under Sch 6ZA, para 1, First-time Buyer's Relief (FTBR), was re-introduced at the Autumn Budget 2017 and applies where the purchaser is a first-time buyer buying their first home and the relevant consideration for the dwelling is no more than £500,000.

In the context of a qualifying shared ownership scheme, FTBR was only available if a market value election under Sch 9, para 4 had been made. This meant that, in practice, shared ownership buyers could be in a less advantageous position in respect of the SDLT cost on acquiring their home when compared with outright buyers acquiring for the same initial cash sum.

Section 42 introduces an amendment to FA 2003, Sch 9 to extend the availability of first-time buyer's relief, and removes the pre-requisite requirement to make the market value election. Furthermore, the amendment extends the relief such that any rental payment should not form part of the chargeable consideration.

FTBR: shared ownership lease where election made

New para 15 applies where a market value election is made under Sch 9, para 4 and FTBR is claimed. It states where FTBR is claimed no SDLT will be due on rent payable under a shared ownership lease.

FTBR: shared ownership lease or trust where no election made

New para 15A applies where a shared ownership lease is granted, but no market value election has been made. This will result in the purchaser instead opting to pay the SDLT in stages. This paragraph extends the availability of FTBR to the first tranche payment for the lease, provided the market value of the property is eligible for the second condition of Sch 6ZA, para 1, ie does not exceed £500,000.

Furthermore, when FTBR is claimed no SDLT will be due on rent payable under a shared ownership lease.

New para 15B replicates para 15A but applies to shared ownerships trusts where a shared ownership trust is declared and no election is made.

Staged transactions

The legislation continues to omit the availability of FTBR in a case where no market value election is made and a further equity acquisition is made. However, no SDLT charge should result in practice until the occupant makes a further acquisition to take their total equity stake to over 80%. FTBR is preserved on the initial payment, but is not available on the subsequent payment taking the stake over 80%.

Timing

The amendments outlined above, will apply to any land transaction with an effective date of 29 October 2018 or after, or any land transaction where the effective date precedes 29 October 2018 but a land transaction return has not been submitted by that date.

Effect of the change: practical points

Where an individual who qualifies for FTBR enters into a qualifying shared ownership scheme, a market election should normally be made for any property with a market value up to £300,000, on the basis that no SDLT should in practice be payable, or should ever be payable in the event of a staged transaction.

Where the value of the property is between £300,000 and £500,000 a decision needs to be made as to whether to make the market value election or not. As FTBR is only available on the first land transaction (ie the initial payment), that decision will be partly determined by whether a future chargeable land transaction is likely to take place ie a staircasing agreement where the buyer extends their interest to 80% or more, and whether such a future transaction would give rise to a higher amount of SDLT.

Illustrative example of benefit of changes

If we consider the following example:

> *Market Value: £400,000*
>
> *Initial tranche: £200,000*
>
> If a market value election were made and FTBR claimed, the SDLT liability would be £5,000 (£100,000 @ 5%), and no further SDLT would be payable on future transactions.
>
> Were no market value election to be made, the position *prior to the change* would have resulted (in the absence of FTBR being available) in SDLT on the initial tranche being (£200,000 – £125,000) at 2% = £1,500, a considerably lower sum.
>
> The availability of FTBR on the first tranche will now result in the SDLT liability of the initial tranche being £nil.
>
> However, no FTBR would be available on a subsequent acquisition. In practice no further SDLT would be due until the buyer acquired an interest which took their stake over 80%.
>
> If the remaining 50% interest were acquired for £200,000, then the SDLT due on that acquisition (which is treated as linked with the original grant in determining the effective rate of SDLT) would be £200,000/£400,000 × SDLT on £400,000 = 50% × £10,000 = £5,000.
>
> Therefore in this example there is clearly no benefit in making the market value election. However, there may be other cases (probably quite uncommon) where a market value election could lead to an overall lower level of SDLT.

---

43 Repayment to first-time buyers in cases of shared ownership

(1) Until 29 October 2019, a claim for the repayment of tax may be made in respect of a land transaction within subsection (2) or (3).

(2) A transaction is within this subsection if the amount of tax chargeable in respect of the transaction would have been less had the amendment made by section 42(3) been in force from the effective date of the transaction.

(3) A transaction is within this subsection if first-time buyer's relief—

- (a) could not have been claimed for the transaction, but
- (b) could have been claimed had the amendments made by section 42(4), (5) and (6) been in force from the effective date of the transaction.

(4) Where a claim is made under this section, HMRC must repay—

- (a) in a case where the transaction is within subsection (2), so much of the tax paid as exceeds the amount that would have been chargeable had the amendment made by section 42(3) been in force from the effective date of the transaction, and
- (b) in a case where the transaction is within subsection (3), so much of the tax paid as exceeds the amount that would have been chargeable had the

amendments made by section 42(4), (5) and (6) been in force from the effective date of the transaction and had a claim for first-time buyer's relief been made.

(5) A claim under this section must be made by amendment of the land transaction return.

(6) Sub-paragraphs (2A) and (3) of paragraph 6 of Schedule 10 to FA 2003 do not apply in the case of an amendment of a land transaction return made for the purpose of making a claim under this section.

(7) In this section—

- (a) the expressions used have the same meaning as in Part 4 of FA 2003;
- (b) "first-time buyer's relief" means relief under Schedule 6ZA to FA 2003.

COMMENTARY ON SECTION 43

This section allows a claim for a repayment of tax to be made in respect of a land transaction where the amount of tax chargeable in respect of the transaction would have been less had the amendment to availability of FTBR in cases of shared ownership been enacted. A claim can be made until 29 October 2019.

Where a claim is made, HMRC must repay the difference between the amount of tax paid, and the amount of tax that would have been chargeable if the amendments outlined above had been available at the point of the transaction.

There is therefore a limited window of opportunity for those first-time buyers of shared ownership dwellings who have 'lost out' compared to outright purchasers to seek a refund of SDLT.

---

44 Higher rates of tax for additional dwellings etc

(1) Schedule 4ZA to FA 2003 (stamp duty land tax: higher rates for additional dwellings and dwellings purchased by companies) is amended as follows.

(2) In paragraph 2 (meaning of "higher rates transaction" etc) after sub-paragraph (4) insert—

> "(5) References in this Schedule to a major interest in a dwelling include an undivided share in a major interest in a dwelling."

(3) The amendment made by subsection (2) has effect in relation to any land transaction of which the effective date is on or after 29 October 2018.

(4) In paragraph 8(3) (period during which land transaction return may be amended to take account of subsequent disposal of main residence) for the words from "whichever" to the end substitute "the period of 12 months beginning with—

- (a) the effective date of the subsequent transaction, or
- (b) if later, the filing date for the return."

(5) The amendment made by subsection (4) has effect in a case where the effective date of the subsequent transaction is on or after 29 October 2018.

COMMENTARY ON SECTION 44

The higher rates of tax for additional dwellings (HRAD), introduced at the 2016 Finance Act, apply generally to purchasers of a major interest in a dwelling who are not individuals and to individuals who already own residential property.

There is a key exemption which applies, broadly, where an individual is replacing their main residence.

This section clarifies the meaning of a 'major interest' to put it beyond doubt that it includes the acquisition of an undivided share in a freehold or leasehold estate.

This section also extends the time allowed to claim a refund in respect of the higher rates of tax following the disposal of a main residence.

HRAD: 'Major interest' in land

The design of the HRAD legislation attempted to capture only meaningful purchases of residential property – and was therefore drafted to exclude transactions involving a minor interest in land, for example a right of way or right of light. However, the unclear drafting of the meaning of a major interest provoked a debate between professional advisers and HMRC as to whether an undivided share of a property (such as an interest as tenant in common) should be considered a 'major interest' for the purposes of HRAD.

HMRC has publicly stated it has always viewed that the HRAD should be applicable to the acquisition of an undivided share of residential property. However, s 44(2) clarifies its view and ensures that an undivided share is reflected in the current legislation as a major interest for the purposes of HRAD through new para 2(5) to FA 2003, Sch 4ZA. The formal change is effective for transactions with an effective date of on or after 29 October 2018.

HRAD: Time limit for an amended SDLT return

In addition, s 44(4) amends Sch 4ZA to increase the time limit allowed to successfully reclaim the HRAD in the context of the disposal of a main residence after the acquisition of a new main residence.

In practice, where the replacement main residence is acquired prior to the disposal of the previous main residence the purchased dwelling would be subject to the higher rates of SDLT at the date the transaction occurs. Following the disposal of the previous main residence the purchaser must amend the original land transaction return in order to reclaim the additional tax. This revision of the legislation means that the reclaim must now be made by the later of:

- 12 months from selling the old home (formerly this was only 3 months) and
- the filing date for the SDLT return

This amendment has effect where the disposal of the previous main residence occurs on or after 29 October 2018.

---

45 Exemption in respect of financial institutions in resolution

(1) In FA 2003, after section 66 insert—

"66A Resolution of financial institutions

(1) A land transaction is exempt from charge if it is effected by—

(a) an instrument listed in subsection (2), or

(b) an instrument made under an instrument listed in subsection (2).

(2) The instruments are—

(a) a property transfer instrument made in accordance with section 12(2) of the Banking Act 2009 (transfer to a bridge bank),

(b) a property transfer instrument made in accordance with section 12ZA(3) of that Act (transfer to asset management vehicle),

(c) a supplemental property transfer instrument made in accordance with section 42(2) of that Act where the original instrument was made in accordance with section 12(2), 12ZA(3) or 41A(2) of that Act,

(d) a property transfer instrument made in accordance with section 41A(2) of that Act (transfer of property subsequent to resolution instrument),

(e) a bridge bank supplemental property transfer instrument made in accordance with section 44D(2) of that Act,

(f) a property transfer order made in accordance with section 45(2) of that Act (temporary public ownership: property transfer), or

(g) a third-country instrument made in accordance with section 89H(2) or 89I(4) of that Act.

(3) References in subsection (2) to a provision of the Banking Act 2009 include references to that provision as applied by or under any other provision of that Act (including where it is applied with modifications or in a substituted form)."

(2) The amendment made by this section has effect in relation to any land transaction the effective date of which is on or after the day on which this Act is passed.

COMMENTARY ON SECTION 45

The Banking Act 2009 (BA 2009) ensures that the Bank of England has special resolution powers to manage a failing financial institution in an orderly way. The purpose of the Banking Act 2009 was to minimise disruption to the economy and protect financial stability, depositors and the taxpayer.

Under BA 2009, the Bank of England may arrange a transfer of property, which may include land held by the failing institution, to a temporary holding entity appointed by the Bank of England or to a temporary public body. Until this amendment, such a transaction would have been subject to SDLT calculated at the appropriate rate(s) by reference to consideration given.

However, this section introduces an exemption from SDLT on land transactions following exercise of certain resolution stabilisation powers. By doing so, HMRC intends to simplify the process of resolving a failing financial institution by ensuring that an exemption from SDLT is available at the time of resolution announcement.

The exemption

Section 45 inserts new FA 2003, s 66A. The legislation provides that a land transaction effected by or made under a property transfer instrument under one of the relevant sections of BA 2009 is exempt from an SDLT charge.

The exemption from SDLT applies to the transactions that fall within a number of circumstances set out in detail in the law, and are not repeated here.

The legislation cross refers to and needs to be read in conjunction with BA 2009.

This section applies to qualifying land transactions with an effective date which is on or after 12 February 2019.

46 Changes to periods for delivering returns and paying tax

(1) FA 2003 is amended as follows.

(2) In section 76(1) (duty to deliver land transaction return), for "30 days" substitute "14 days".

(3) For section 80(2) (adjustment where contingency ceases or consideration is ascertained) substitute—

"(2) If the effect of the new information is that a transaction becomes notifiable, the purchaser must make a return to HMRC within 14 days.

(2A) If the effect of the new information is that—

(a) tax is payable in respect of a transaction where none was payable before and subsection (2) does not apply, or

(b) additional tax is payable in respect of a transaction,

the purchaser must make a further return to HMRC within 30 days.

(2B) For the purposes of subsections (2) and (2A), any tax or additional tax payable is calculated according to the effective date of the transaction.

(2C) If a purchaser is required to make a return under subsection (2) or a further return under subsection (2A)—

(a) that return must contain a self-assessment of the tax chargeable in respect of the transaction on the basis of the information contained in the return, and

(b) the tax or additional tax payable must be paid not later than the filing date for that return."

(4) In section 81 (further return where relief withdrawn)—

(a) in subsection (1B)—

(i) after paragraph (c) insert—

"(ca) in the case of relief under paragraph 5CA of that Schedule (acquisition under a regulated home reversion plan), the first day in the period mentioned in paragraph 5IA(2) of that Schedule on which the purchaser holds the higher threshold interest otherwise than for the purposes of the regulated home reversion plan, unless paragraph 5IA(3)(a) and (b) applies;", and

(ii) after paragraph (d) insert—

"(da) in the case of relief under paragraph 5EA of that Schedule (acquisition by management company of flat for occupation by caretaker), the first day in the period mentioned in paragraph 5JA(2) of that Schedule on which the purchaser holds the higher threshold interest otherwise than for the purpose of making the flat available for use as caretaker accommodation;", and

(b) in subsection (2A), after "subsection (1)" insert "or (1A)".

(5) For section 81A(1) (return or further return in consequence of later linked transaction) substitute—

"(1) Where the effect of a transaction ("the later transaction") that is linked to an earlier transaction is that the earlier transaction becomes notifiable, the purchaser under the earlier transaction must deliver a return in respect of that transaction before the end of the period of 14 days after the effective date of the later transaction.

(1A) Where the effect of a transaction ("the later transaction") that is linked to an earlier transaction is that—

(a) tax is payable in respect of the earlier transaction where none was payable before and subsection (1) does not apply, or
(b) additional tax is payable in respect of the earlier transaction,

the purchaser under the earlier transaction must deliver a further return in respect of that transaction before the end of the period of 30 days after the effective date of the later transaction.

(1B) For the purposes of subsections (1) and (1A), any tax or additional tax payable is calculated according to the effective date of the earlier transaction.

(1C) Where a purchaser is required to deliver a return under subsection (1) or a further return under subsection (1A)—

(a) that return must include a self-assessment of the amount of tax chargeable as a result of the later transaction, and
(b) the tax or additional tax payable must be paid not later than the filing date for that return."

(6) In section 86(2) (payment of tax), before paragraph (a) insert—

"(za) any of paragraphs 5G to 5K of Schedule 4A (higher rate for certain transactions),".

(7) In section 87 (interest on unpaid tax)—

(a) after subsection (1) insert—

"(1A) But where the relevant date is determined by subsection (3)(aa), (aaa), (ab) or (c), and a return is required to be delivered before the end of the period of 14 days after that relevant date, interest is instead payable on the amount of any unpaid tax from the end of that period until the tax is paid.",

(b) in subsection (2), after "subsection (1)" insert "or (1A)", and
(c) in subsection (3), before paragraph (a) insert—

"(za) in the case of an amount payable because relief is withdrawn under any of paragraphs 5G to 5K of Schedule 4A (higher rate for certain transactions), the date which is the relevant date for the purposes of section 81(1A);".

(8) In Schedule 17A (further provisions relating to leases)—

(a) for paragraph 3(3) substitute—

"(3) Where the effect of sub-paragraph (2) in relation to the continuation of the lease for a period (or further period) of one year after the end of a fixed term is that a transaction becomes notifiable, the purchaser must deliver a return in respect of that transaction before the end of the period of 14 days after the end of that one year period.

(3ZA) Where the effect of sub-paragraph (2) in relation to the continuation of the lease for a period (or further period) of one year after the end of a fixed term is that—

(a) tax is payable in respect of a transaction where none was payable before and sub-paragraph (3) does not apply, or
(b) additional tax is payable in respect of a transaction,

the purchaser must deliver a further return in respect of that transaction before the end of the period of 30 days after the end of that one year period.

(3ZB) For the purposes of sub-paragraphs (3) and (3ZA), any tax or additional tax payable is calculated according to the effective date of the transaction.

(3ZC) Where a purchaser is required to deliver a return under sub-paragraph (3) or a further return under sub-paragraph (3ZA)—

(a) that return must include a self-assessment of the amount of tax chargeable in respect of the transaction on the basis of the information contained in the return, and

(b) the tax or additional tax payable must be paid not later than the filing date for that return.",

(b) for paragraph 4(3) substitute—

"(3) Where the effect of sub-paragraph (1) in relation to the continuation of the lease after the end of a deemed fixed term is that a transaction becomes notifiable, the purchaser must deliver a return in respect of that transaction before the end of the period of 14 days after the end of that term.

(3A) Where the effect of sub-paragraph (1) in relation to the continuation of the lease after the end of a deemed fixed term is that—

(a) tax is payable in respect of a transaction where none was payable before and sub-paragraph (3) does not apply, or

(b) additional tax is payable in respect of a transaction,

the purchaser must deliver a further return in respect of that transaction before the end of the period of 30 days after the end of that term.

(3B) For the purposes of sub-paragraphs (3) and (3A), any tax or additional tax payable is calculated according to the effective date of the transaction.

(3C) Where a purchaser is required to deliver a return under sub-paragraph (3) or a further return under sub-paragraph (3A)—

(a) that return must include a self-assessment of the amount of tax chargeable in respect of the transaction on the basis of the information contained in the return, and

(b) the tax or additional tax payable must be paid not later than the filing date for that return.", and

(c) for paragraph 8(3) substitute—

"(3) If the result as regards the rent paid or payable in respect of the first five years of the term of the lease is that a transaction becomes notifiable, the purchaser must make a return to HMRC within 14 days of the date referred to in sub-paragraph (1)(a) or (b).

(3A) If the result as regards the rent paid or payable in respect of the first five years of the term of the lease is that—

(a) tax is payable in respect of a transaction where none was payable before and sub-paragraph (3) does not apply, or

(b) additional tax is payable in respect of a transaction,

the purchaser must make a further return to HMRC within 30 days of the date referred to in sub-paragraph (1)(a) or (b).

(3B) If a purchaser is required to make a return under sub-paragraph (3) or a further return under sub-paragraph (3A)—

(a) that return must contain a self-assessment of the tax chargeable in respect of the transaction on the basis of the information contained in the return,

(b) the tax so chargeable is to be calculated by reference to the rates in force at the effective date of the transaction, and

(c) the tax or additional tax payable must be paid not later than the filing date for that return."

(9) In Schedule 61 to FA 2009 (alternative finance investment bonds)—

(a) in paragraph 7(5) (interest due on first transaction where relief is withdrawn) for "30 days" substitute "14 days", and

(b) in paragraph 20(3)(a) (no relief where bond-holder acquires control of underlying asset) for "30 days" substitute "14 days".

(10) The amendments made by this section are to be treated as having effect in relation to—

(a) any land transaction with an effective date on or after 1 March 2019, and

(b) any land transaction with an effective date before 1 March 2019 which becomes notifiable on or after 1 March 2019.

COMMENTARY ON SECTION 46

Section 46 reduces the time limit that purchasers have to file a SDLT return and pay the tax due, in most circumstances, from 30 days after the effective date of the transaction to 14 days. It applies to transactions to purchase land in England and Northern Ireland with an effective date on or after 1 March 2019 and to earlier transactions which become notifiable on or after that date (such as where there is a later linked transaction).

HMRC believes that these changes should increase the efficiency of the SDLT system. It notes that the majority of land transaction returns are already completed within 14 days and as such does not envisage an increased burden on the taxpayer. However, in complex cases, and where there is a need to approach HMRC in advance of the filing date, this accelerated deadline may cause some problems in practice.

Basic changes to period to deliver returns and pay tax

The most apparent change, an amendment to FA 2003, s 76(1), is that there is now a duty to deliver a land transaction return within 14 days after the effective date of the transaction. However, the change to the period to deliver returns also applies to certain other cases for which there is a requirement to deliver returns.

On the basis the return must be accompanied by a self-assessment of the tax and payment of the amount chargeable, this amendment effectively reduces the time limit to pay the tax due to 14 days.

Furthermore, where an event takes place and has the effect of making a previous land transaction notifiable, the deadline to submit a return (and pay any SDLT arising) has been reduced to 14 days following the relevant date of the specific event. However, where the original land transaction was previously notifiable, the period for which a return must be submitted and SDLT paid remains 30 days. The relevant circumstances affected are outlined below.

Similarly, interest on tax unpaid will now be calculated with reference to the amended filing deadlines. This section provides that where the 14 day time limit applies, interest on any unpaid tax will run from the end of that period until the date the tax is paid.

Contingent, uncertain or unascertainable consideration

In a case where consideration at the time of the land transaction was contingent, uncertain or unascertainable there is a continuing responsibility to deliver an amended return at the point in time the consideration ceases to be contingent or becomes ascertainable and as a result there is a change to the chargeable consideration.

Section 46(3) amends FA 2003, s 80(2), which applies to an adjustment where a contingency ceases or consideration is ascertained, and in effect reduces the time limit to submit the land transaction to 14 days in cases where a transaction was not previously notifiable.

However, where a transaction was previously notified but as a result of the new information, a further return is required, the 30 day time limit continues to apply.

It should be noted that where an application is to be made to HMRC under FA 2003, s 90 for permission to defer the payment of SDLT on contingent or uncertain consideration, then the changes to the deadline for submission of the SDLT return will require such an application to be made within 14 days of the effective date of the land transaction. This is an important practical point which could easily be overlooked.

Further return where relief withdrawn

Although s 46(4) introduces some additional provisions which define the relevant date for relief claw-back events for the purposes of the 15% higher rate of SDLT under FA 2003, Sch 4A, all time limits for filing amended returns which are triggered by the withdrawal of reliefs set out in s 81 remain at 30 days from the relevant date.

Linked transactions

If the transaction forms part of a number of linked transactions the relevant consideration is the total of the chargeable consideration for all the linked transactions. Transactions are 'linked' if they form part of a single scheme, arrangement or series of transactions between the same vendor and purchaser or persons connected with them.

Where a return is required following a later linked transaction where an earlier transaction was not previously notifiable, the time limit for filing a return is reduced to 14 days

However, if the earlier transaction was notifiable, the deadline to submit a further return following a later linked transaction occurring remains 30 days.

Further provisions relating to leases

Schedule 17A contains special provisions in situations where leases continue after a fixed term; are considered to have an indefinite term; or where rent is uncertain. Following the pattern set out above, if the circumstances result in a land transaction becoming notifiable the deadline to submit a return becomes 14 days.

For example, if a lease is deemed to grow in term by 12 months and this results in the land transaction becoming notifiable, where it previously was not (for example where the term becomes seven years or the net present value of the rent is sufficient to give rise to an actual SDLT charge), then the purchaser must make a return to HMRC within 14 days of the date of the deemed extended lease term.

However, if the original transaction was notifiable, and the circumstances result in an obligation to amend the return which had been previously notified, then the deadline for filing remains at 30 days.

Stamp duty and SDRT

47 Stamp duty: transfers of listed securities and connected persons

(1) This section applies if—

(a) an instrument transfers listed securities to a company or a company's nominee (whether or not for consideration), and

(b) the person transferring the securities is connected with the company or is the nominee of a person connected with the company.

(2) "Listed securities" are stock or marketable securities which are regularly traded on—

(a) a regulated market,

(b) a multilateral trading facility, or

(c) a recognised foreign exchange,

and expressions used in paragraphs (a) to (c) have the same meaning as in section 80B of FA 1986 (intermediaries: supplementary).

(3) For the purposes of the enactments relating to stamp duty—

(a) in a case where listed securities are transferred for consideration which consists of money or any stock or security, or to which section 57 of the Stamp Act 1891 applies, the amount or value of the consideration is to be treated as being equal to—

(i) the amount or value of the consideration for the transfer, or

(ii) if higher, the value of the listed securities;

(b) in any other case, the transfer of listed securities effected by the instrument is to be treated as being for an amount of consideration in money equal to the value of the listed securities.

(4) For the purposes of subsection (3)—

(a) "the enactments relating to stamp duty" means the Stamp Act 1891 and any enactment amending that Act or that is to be construed as one with that Act, and

(b) the value of listed securities is to be taken to be the price which they might reasonably be expected to fetch on a sale in the open market at the date the instrument is executed.

(5) Section 1122 of CTA 2010 (connected persons) has effect for the purposes of this section.

(6) The Treasury may by regulations made by statutory instrument provide for this section not to apply in relation to particular cases.

(7) Regulations under subsection (6) may have effect in relation to instruments executed before the regulations come into force.

(8) A statutory instrument containing regulations under subsection (6) is subject to annulment in pursuance of a resolution of the House of Commons.

(9) This section is to be construed as one with the Stamp Act 1891.

(10) This section has effect in relation to instruments executed on or after 29 October 2018.

COMMENTARY ON SECTION 47

Section 47 provides for what HMRC has described as a targeted market value rule for stamp duty on instruments transferring listed securities to connected companies or the nominee for such a connected company. Listed securities are stock or marketable securities that are regularly traded on a regulated market, multilateral trading facility or recognised foreign exchange. Section 1122 of the Corporation Taxes Act 2010 has effect for the purposes of determining whether the transferee is a connected company. The section applies to instruments executed on or after 29 October 2018.

For such transfers, the consideration chargeable to stamp duty is the higher of the consideration (if any) actually given for the transfer or the market value of the listed securities. This is achieved by s 47(3) which applies where the instrument would be regarded as a conveyance on sale according to common law and recognised stamp duty principles (because there is consideration consisting of cash, shares or debt) and s 47(4) which seems to deem an instrument that would not otherwise be a sale on general principles (e g because the consideration consists of something else such as a chose in action or there is no consideration at all) to be a sale for an amount equivalent of the market value of the securities.

The market value of the listed securities is to be determined at the time the instrument of transfer is executed.

HMRC has not provided any kind of description of the avoidance activity that the targeted market value rule was directed at.

It should be remembered that there is a general exemption from stamp duty (and SDRT) for documents (and agreements) transferring shares which are traded on regulated growth markets like AIM.

A consultation was published on 7 November 2018 relating to the stamp taxes on shares consideration rules, which, inter alia, is considering extending the market value rules introduced by s 47 (and s 48 – see below) to unlisted securities and to connected party transfers other than to companies. This consultation is also considering adopting the SDRT definition of 'money or money's worth' definition of consideration for stamp duty purposes (one of the recommendations made by the OTS in 2017) and aligning the stamp duty and SDRT treatment of contingent, uncertain and unascertainable consideration. The stated aims of the consultation are (1) to simplify the stamp taxes rules applicable to shares and (2) to prevent contrived arrangements being used to avoid stamp taxes on share transactions. It looks likely that if the proposals suggested by the consultation are introduced they will bring a considerable degree of extra complexity to the stamp taxes code and it is regrettable that HMRC has not provided any kind of description at all of the contrived arrangements at which the new provisions are directed.

---

48 SDRT: listed securities and connected persons

(1) This section applies if a person is connected with a company and—

- (a) the person or the person's nominee agrees to transfer listed securities to the company or the company's nominee (whether or not for consideration), or
- (b) the person or the person's nominee transfers such securities to the company or the company's nominee for consideration in money or money's worth.

(2) "Listed securities" are chargeable securities which are regularly traded on—

- (a) a regulated market,
- (b) a multilateral trading facility, or
- (c) a recognised foreign exchange,

and expressions used in paragraphs (a) to (c) have the same meaning as in section 88B of FA 1986 (intermediaries: supplementary).

(3) For the purposes of stamp duty reserve tax chargeable under section 87 of FA 1986 (the principal charge)—

(a) in a case where the agreement is one to transfer listed securities for consideration in money or money's worth, the amount or value of the consideration is to be treated as being equal to—

(i) the amount or value of the consideration for the transfer, or

(ii) if higher, the value of the listed securities at the time the agreement is made;

(b) in any other case, the agrement to transfer listed securities is to be treated as being one for an amount of consideration in money equal to the value of the listed securities at the time the agreement is made.

(4) Subsection (5) has effect for the purposes of stamp duty reserve tax chargeable under section 93 (depositary receipts) or 96 (clearance services) of FA 1986.

(5) If the amount or value of the consideration for any transfer of listed securities is less than the value of those securities at the time they are transferred, the transfer is to be treated as being for an amount of consideration in money equal to that value.

(6) For the purposes of this section, the value of listed securities at any time is the price which they might reasonably be expected to fetch on a sale in the open market at that time.

(7) Section 1122 of CTA 2010 (connected persons) has effect for the purposes of this section.

(8) The Treasury may by regulations made by statutory instrument provide for this section not to apply in relation to particular cases.

(9) Regulations under subsection (8) may have effect in relation to transactions entered into before the regulations come into force.

(10) A statutory instrument containing regulations under subsection (8) is subject to annulment in pursuance of a resolution of the House of Commons.

(11) This section is to be construed as one with Part 4 of FA 1986.

(12) This section has effect—

(a) in relation to the charge to tax under section 87 of FA 1986 where—

(i) the agreement to transfer securities is conditional and the condition is satisfied on or after 29 October 2018, or

(ii) in any other case, the agreement is made on or after that date;

(b) in relation to the charge to tax under section 93 or 96 of that Act, where the transfer is on or after 29 October 2018 (whenever the arrangement was made).

COMMENTARY ON SECTION 48

This section provides equivalent provisions for the charge to SDRT on agreements to transfer chargeable securities under FA 1986 to those described above under the commentary on s 47 in relation to stamp duty.

More specifically, where a person agrees to transfer listed securities to a connected company (or nominee for such a connected company) for a consideration in money or money's worth, the amount of the consideration for the purposes of the principal 0.5% charge under FA 1986, s 87 will be the higher of the amount agreed to be paid or the market value of the listed securities at the time the agreement is made. Again, as with the new stamp duty rule, the section extends the concept of chargeable consideration to cover the situation where there is no money or money's worth consideration, providing that the market value will apply there too.

Subsections (4) and (5) provide that the higher of market value or actual consideration rule will also apply for the purposes of the special (higher 1.5%) rate of SDRT which is chargeable on the transfer of securities into depositary receipt or clearance service mechanisms imposed by FA 1986, ss 93 and 96. It is a general requirement for the new market value rule to apply that the agreement must be to transfer to a connected company or a nominee for a connected company so presumably the person providing the depositary receipt or clearance services (or their nominee) would themselves have to be connected with the transferor for market value to be substituted.

Section 48 contains equivalent boilerplate provisions to those described above for s 47 in relation to the meanings of 'connected', 'listed securities' and the effective date for the application of the new rules.

49 Stamp duty: exemption in respect of financial institutions in resolution

(1) In FA 1986, after section 85 insert—

"Resolution of financial institutions

85A Resolution of financial institutions

(1) Stamp duty is not chargeable on the transfer of stock or marketable securities by—

(a) an instrument listed in subsection (2), or
(b) an instrument made under an instrument listed in subsection (2).

(2) The instruments are—

(a) a mandatory reduction instrument made in accordance with section 6B of the Banking Act 2009 (mandatory write-down, conversion etc of capital instruments),
(b) a share transfer instrument or property transfer instrument made in accordance with section 12(2) of that Act (transfer to a bridge bank),
(c) a property transfer instrument made in accordance with section 12ZA(3) of that Act (transfer to asset management vehicle),
(d) a resolution instrument made in accordance with section 12A of that Act (bail-in),
(e) a share transfer order or share transfer instrument made in accordance with section 13(2) of that Act (share transfer),
(f) a supplemental share transfer instrument made in accordance with section 26 of that Act, where the original instrument was made in accordance with section 12(2) or 13(2) of that Act,
(g) a supplemental share transfer order made in accordance with section 27 of that Act,
(h) a property transfer instrument made in accordance with section 41A(2) of that Act (transfer of property subsequent to resolution instrument),
(i) a supplemental property transfer instrument made in accordance with section 42(2) of that Act where the original instrument was made in accordance with section 12(2), 12ZA(3) or 41A(2) of that Act,
(j) a bridge bank supplemental property transfer instrument made in accordance with section 44D(2) of that Act,
(k) a property transfer order made in accordance with section 45(2) of that Act,
(l) a supplemental resolution instrument made in accordance with section 48U(2) of that Act,
(m) an onward transfer resolution instrument made in accordance with section 48V of that Act in the circumstances set out in subsection (3),
(n) an order under section 85 of that Act (temporary public ownership: building societies), or
(o) a third-country instrument made in accordance with section 89H(2) or 89I(4) of that Act.

(3) The circumstances referred to in subsection (2)(m) are that the transfer—

(a) is to a person within section 67(6), (7) or (8) or section 70(6), (7) or (8) of this Act (depositary receipt issuers, clearance services), and
(b) is made by way of compensation to a creditor of the financial institution in respect of which the original instrument (within the meaning of section 48V of the Banking Act 2009) was made.

(4) References in this section to a provision of the Banking Act 2009 include references to that provision as applied by or under any other provision of that Act (including where it is applied with modifications or in a substituted form)."

(2) The amendment made by this section has effect in relation to instruments—

(a) within section 85A(2) of FA 1986, or
(b) made under an instrument within section 85A(2) of FA 1986,

which are executed on or after the day on which this Act is passed.

COMMENTARY ON SECTION 49

This section introduces a new FA 1986, s 85A. It exempts certain instruments which transfer shares from failing financial institutions to public bodies and creditors from charges to stamp duty. The measure takes effect from 12 February 2019. A complete list of the instruments which will be exempt from charge is set out in subsections (2) and (3).

50 Stamp duty and SDRT: exemptions in respect of share incentive plans

(1) In section 95 of FA 2001 (exemptions in relation to approved share incentive plans)—

(a) in subsections (1) and (2), and in the heading, omit "approved", and
(b) in subsection (3), for "an approved share incentive plan" substitute "a Schedule 2 SIP".

(2) The amendments made by subsection (1) are to be treated as having effect from 6 April 2014.

COMMENTARY ON SECTION 50

This section amends FA 2001, s 95 to ensure that relief is available for self-certified SIPs. The provision is effective from 6 April 2014.

Until 2014, tax advantaged share schemes, such as SIPs, had to be approved by HMRC before an employer could begin to operate them. Therefore, SIPs were referred to as 'approved share incentive plans' in legislation. In 2014, amendments to the legislation meant that SIPs no longer had to be approved by HMRC before an employer could operate them, and could be 'self-certified'.

Relief is available so that stamp duty and stamp duty reserve tax would not be due when shares in a SIP are transferred by the trustees to the employee. This long-standing relief was introduced to prevent a double charge arising. The legislation detailing this relief, however, was not amended to reflect the ability to self-certify SIPs.

The amendment removes any references to 'approved share incentive plans' or 'approved SIPs' and replaces them with 'Schedule 2 SIPs'. This should ensure consistency across all legislation for share incentive plans and confirms that the existing stamp duty relief continues to apply to them.

Value added tax

51 Duty of customers to account for tax on supplies

In section 55A of VATA 1994 (customers to account for tax on certain supplies of goods or services), after subsection (9) insert—

"(9A) An order made under subsection (9) may modify the application of subsection (3) in relation to any description of goods or services specified in the order."

COMMENTARY ON SECTION 51

This section inserts a new sub-s (9A) into VATA 1994, s 55A with effect from 12 February 2019.

Section 55A is an anti-fraud measure which prevents the supplier charging VAT on a supply and disappearing without accounting for that VAT to HMRC. It does this by switching the liability to account for VAT on certain specified supplies from the supplier to the customer. 'Specified supplies' means supplies of goods or services specified in an order made under VATA 1994, s 55A(9).

This accounting treatment is known as the 'reverse charge'.

The new sub-s (9A) allows an order made under sub-s (9) to modify the application of sub-s (3). That sub-section requires that the value of the supplies accounted for under the reverse charge be included in the customer's turnover for the purposes of the VAT registration limits in VATA 1994, Sch 1 (taxable supplies made by a person established in the UK) or Sch 1A (taxable supplies made by a person not established in the UK).

Thus an order made under sub-s (9) may, from 12 February 2019, provide for the value of specified reverse charge supplies to be disregarded in determining whether a business making supplies in the UK is liable to be registered for UK VAT.

52 Treatment of vouchers

Schedule 17 makes provision about the VAT treatment of vouchers.

53 Groups: eligibility

(1) Schedule 18 contains provision about the eligibility of individuals and partnerships to be treated as members of a group for the purposes of value added tax.

(2) That Schedule comes into force on such day as the Treasury may by regulations made by statutory instrument appoint.

Alcohol

54 Rates of duty on cider, wine and made-wine

(1) ALDA 1979 is amended as follows.

(2) In section 62(1A) (rates of duty on cider) in paragraph (a) (rate of duty on sparkling cider of a strength exceeding 5.5%), for "£279.46" substitute "£288.10".

(3) For Part 1 of the table in Schedule 1 substitute—

"WINE OR MADE-WINE OF A STRENGTH NOT EXCEEDING 22%

Description of wine or made-wine	*Rates of duty per hectolitre £*
Wine or made-wine of a strength not exceeding 4%	91.68
Wine or made-wine of a strength exceeding 4% but not exceeding 5.5%	126.08
Wine or made-wine of a strength exceeding 5.5% but not exceeding 15% and not being sparkling	297.57
Sparkling wine or sparkling made-wine of a strength exceeding 5.5% but less than 8.5%	288.10
Sparkling wine or sparkling made-wine of a strength of at least 8.5% but not exceeding 15%	381.15
Wine or made-wine of a strength exceeding 15% but not exceeding 22%	396.72

(4) The amendments made by this section are treated as having come into force on 1 February 2019.

COMMENTARY ON SECTION 54

Section 54 increases the rates of excise duty on certain cider, wine and made-wine.

Sections 54(2) and 54(3) increase the rates of excise duty on cider exceeding 5.5% abv but less than 8.5% abv and wine and made-wine at or below 22% abv in line with the retail price index (RPI) through amendments to the Alcoholic Liquor Duties Act (ALDA) 1979, s 62(1A) and Sch 1.

Section 54(4) provides for these amendments to be treated as having come into force on 1 February 2019.

The amendments do not affect the rates of duty on beer, spirits, wine and made-wine exceeding 22%, still cider and perry, and sparkling cider and perry not exceeding 5.5% abv.

55 Excise duty on mid-strength cider

(1) ALDA 1979 is amended as follows.

(2) In section 62(1A) (rates of excise duty on cider)—

(a) omit the "and" at the end of paragraph (b), and
(b) after paragraph (b) insert—

"(ba) £50.71 per hectolitre in the case of cider of a strength of not less than 6.9 per cent but not exceeding 7.5 per cent which is not sparkling cider; and".

(3) In section 62B (cider labelled as strong cider)—

(a) in the heading, after "strong cider" insert "or mid-strength cider",

(b) in subsection (1)—

(i) in the opening words, after "standard cider" insert "or mid-strength cider",

(ii) for paragraph (a) substitute—

"(a) is in a container which is up-labelled as a container of strong cider, or",

(iii) in paragraph (b), for "an up-labelled container" substitute "a container which is up-labelled as a container of strong cider,", and

(iv) in the words after paragraph (b), after "standard cider" insert "or mid-strength cider",

(c) after subsection (1), insert—

"(1A) For the purposes of this Act, any liquor which would apart from this section be standard cider and which—

(a) is in a container which is up-labelled as a container of mid-strength cider, or

(b) has, at any time after 31 January 2019 when it was in the United Kingdom, been in a container which is up-labelled as a container of mid-strength cider,

shall be deemed to be mid-strength cider, and not standard cider.",

(d) for subsection (2) substitute—

"(2) Accordingly, references in this Act to making cider include references to—

(a) putting standard or mid-strength cider in a container which is up-labelled as a container of strong cider;

(b) causing a container in which there is standard or mid-strength cider to be up-labelled as a container of strong cider;

(c) putting standard cider in a container which is up-labelled as a container of mid-strength cider; or

(d) causing a container in which there is standard cider to be up-labelled as a container of mid-strength cider.",

(e) in subsection (4)—

(i) in paragraph (a), for "not exceeding 7.5 per cent" substitute "of less than 6.9 per cent",

(ii) omit the "and" at the end of that paragraph, and

(iii) after paragraph (a), insert—

"(aa) "mid-strength cider" means cider which is not sparkling and is of a strength of not less than 6.9 per cent but not exceeding 7.5 per cent; and",

(f) in subsection (5), in the opening words, after "up-labelled" insert "as a container of strong cider", and

(g) after subsection (6), insert—

"(7) For the purposes of this section a container is up-labelled as a container of mid-strength cider if there is anything on—

(a) the container itself,

(b) a label or leaflet attached to or used with the container, or

(c) any packaging used for or in association with the container,

which states or tends to suggest that the strength of any liquor in that container falls within the mid-strength cider strength range.

(8) For the purposes of subsection (7), a strength falls within the mid-strength cider strength range if it is not less than 6.9 per cent but does not exceed 7.5 per cent.

(9) Where liquor is no longer in a container which is an up-labelled container, and it falls within subsection (1)(b) and within subsection (1A)(b), then it is deemed to be cider of the strength range stated or suggested by the labelling for the up-labelled container in which it was first contained.

(10) For the purposes of subsection (9)—

(a) an "up-labelled container" means—
  (i) a container which is up-labelled as a container of strong cider as mentioned in subsection (1)(b), or
  (ii) a container which is up-labelled as a container of mid-strength cider as mentioned in subsection (1A)(b), and

(b) references to the labelling for any container are references to anything on—
  (i) the container itself,
  (ii) a label or leaflet attached to or used with the container, or
  (iii) any packaging used for or in association with the container."

(4) The amendments made by this section are to be treated as having come into force on 1 February 2019.

COMMENTARY ON SECTION 55

Section 55 introduces a new band and rate of excise duty on mid-strength cider.

Section 55(2) amends the Alcoholic Liquor Duties Act (ALDA) 1979 to introduce a new band and rate in ALDA 1979, s 62(1A) for still cider of a strength of at least 6.9% but not exceeding 7.5% abv. The rate of excise duty is £50.71 per hectolitre.

Section 55(3) amends ALDA 1979, s 62B in respect of 'up-labelling' such that the provisions reflect the introduction of the new band and rate for still cider in ALDA 1979, s 62(1A).

Section 55(4) provides for the amendments in the section to be treated as having come into force on 1 February 2019.

Tobacco

56 Rates

(1) TPDA 1979 is amended as follows.

(2) For the table in Schedule 1 substitute—

"TABLE

1 Cigarettes	An amount equal to the higher of— (a)16.5% of the retail price plus £228.29 per thousand cigarettes, or (b)£293.95 per thousand cigarettes.
2 Cigars	£284.76 per kilogram
3 Hand-rolling tobacco	£234.65 per kilogram
4 Other smoking tobacco and chewing tobacco	£125.20 per kilogram"

(3) The amendment made by this section is treated as having come into force at 6pm on 29 October 2018.

COMMENTARY ON SECTION 56

Section 56 increases the rates of excise duty on tobacco products.

Section 56(2) makes amendments to the Tobacco Products Duty Act (TPDA) 1979, Sch 1 by substituting the existing table of rates of excise duty on tobacco products for a new table of rates. The effect of this change is to increase excise duty on all tobacco products by 2% above RPI. This change also affects the Minimum Excise Tax on cigarettes which is increased from £280.15 to £293.95 per 1000 cigarettes.

Section 56(3) provides for the amendment to TPDA 1979, Sch 1 to be treated as having come into force at 6pm on 29 October 2018.

This change is made in an effort to support the Government's public health objectives.

57 Tobacco for heating

(1) TPDA 1979 is amended as follows.

(2) In section 1 (tobacco products), in subsection (1)—

(a) in paragraph (d), omit the final "and";
(b) after paragraph (e) insert "and

(f) tobacco for heating,".

(3) In that section, in subsection (3), for "and chewing tobacco" substitute ", chewing tobacco and tobacco for heating".

(4) In the table in Schedule 1 (as substituted by section 56), at the end insert—

"5 Tobacco for heating	£234.65 per kilogram"

(5) The Commissioners for Her Majesty's Revenue and Customs may by regulations made by statutory instrument make consequential, supplementary, incidental or transitional provision in relation to the provision made by subsections (2) to (4) (including provision amending any enactment).

(6) A statutory instrument containing regulations under subsection (5) is subject to annulment in pursuance of a resolution of the House of Commons.

(7) The amendments made by subsections (2) and (4) come into force on such day as the Treasury may by regulations made by statutory instrument appoint.

COMMENTARY ON SECTION 57

Section 57 introduces a new category of tobacco and a new rate of duty on this category.

Section 57(2) amends the Tobacco Products Duty Act (TPDA) 1979, s 1 by introducing a new category of tobacco: 'tobacco for heating'.

Section 57(3) amends TPDA 1979, s 1 by adding tobacco for heating as a category for the purposes of the Tobacco Products (Descriptions of Products) Order 2003.

Section 57(4) amends TPDA 1979, Sch 1 such that the rate of excise duty for the new category of tobacco for heating is set at £234.65 per kilogram.

Sections 57(5) and 57(6) provide the ability to make changes to regulations which are consequential on the new tobacco for heating category and set out the procedure for so doing.

Section 57(7) provides for the new duty category and rate to be brought into force by regulations made by statutory instrument.

The amendments in this section (and the new category and rate) seek to provide greater clarity to manufacturers and consumers on the tax treatment of tobacco for heating and follow a period of consultation between March and June 2017 on the tax treatment of tobacco designed for heating.

Vehicle duties

58 VED: rates for light passenger vehicles, light goods vehicles, motorcycles etc

(1) Schedule 1 to VERA 1994 (annual rates of vehicle excise duty) is amended as follows.

(2) In paragraph 1 (general rate)—

(a) in sub-paragraph (2) (vehicle not covered elsewhere in Schedule with engine cylinder capacity exceeding 1,549cc), for "£255" substitute "£265", and
(b) in sub-paragraph (2A) (vehicle not covered elsewhere in Schedule with engine cylinder capacity not exceeding 1,549cc), for "£155" substitute "£160".

(3) In paragraph 1B (graduated rates for light passenger vehicles registered before 1 April 2017)—

(a) for the Table substitute—

"*CO2 emissions figure*		*Rate*	
(1)	*(2)*	*(3)*	*(4)*
Exceeding	*Not exceeding*	*Reduced rate*	*Standard rate*
g/km	*g/km*	*£*	*£*
100	110	10	20
110	120	20	30
120	130	115	125
130	140	135	145
140	150	150	160
150	165	190	200
165	175	225	235
175	185	250	260
185	200	290	300
200	225	315	325
225	255	545	555
255	—	560	570

(b) in the sentence immediately following the Table, for paragraphs (a) and (b) substitute—

"(a) in column (3), in the last two rows, "315" were substituted for "545" and "560", and

(b) in column (4), in the last two rows, "325" were substituted for "555" and "570"."

(4) In paragraph 1GC (graduated rates for first licence for light passenger vehicles registered on or after 1 April 2017)—

(a) for Table 1 (vehicles other than higher rate diesel vehicles) substitute—

"*CO2 emissions figure*		*Rate*	
(1)	*(2)*	*(3)*	*(4)*
Exceeding	*Not exceeding*	*Reduced rate*	*Standard rate*
g/km	*g/km*	*£*	*£*
0	50	0	10
50	75	15	25
75	90	100	110
90	100	120	130
100	110	140	150
110	130	160	170
130	150	200	210
150	170	520	530
170	190	845	855
190	225	1270	1280
225	255	1805	1815
255	—	2125	2135

(b) for Table 2 (higher rate diesel vehicles) substitute—

"*CO2 emissions figure*		*Rate*
(1)	*(2)*	*(3)*
Exceeding	*Not exceeding*	*Rate*
g/km	*g/km*	*£*
0	50	25
50	75	110
75	90	130

"CO2 emissions figure		*Rate*
(1)	*(2)*	*(3)*
Exceeding	*Not exceeding*	*Rate*
g/km	*g/km*	*£*
90	100	150
100	110	170
110	130	210
130	150	530
150	170	855
170	190	1280
190	225	1815
225	255	2135
255	—	2135

(5) In paragraph 1GD (rates for any other licence for light passenger vehicles registered on or after 1 April 2017), in sub-paragraph (1)—

- (a) in paragraph (a) (the reduced rate) for "£130" substitute "£135", and
- (b) in paragraph (b) (the standard rate) for "£140" substitute "£145".

(6) In paragraph 1GE (rates for light passenger vehicles registered on or after 1 April 2017 with a price exceeding £40,000), in sub-paragraph (4) for "£310" substitute "£320".

(7) In paragraph 1J (rates for light goods vehicles), in paragraph (a) for "£250" substitute "£260".

(8) In paragraph 2(1) (rates for motorcycles)—

- (a) in paragraph (a) for "£19" substitute "£20",
- (b) in paragraph (b) for "£42" substitute "£43",
- (c) in paragraph (c) for "£64" substitute "£66", and
- (d) in paragraph (d) for "£88" substitute "£91".

(9) The amendments made by this section have effect in relation to licences taken out on or after 1 April 2019.

COMMENTARY ON SECTION 58

Section 58 makes amendments to a number of rates of Vehicle Excise Duty (VED) in the Vehicle Excise and Registration Act 1994 (VERA), Sch 1.

Section 58(2) increases the rates of vehicles first registered before March 2001 with an engine capacity exceeding 1,549cc from £255 to £265. It also increases the rates of vehicles first registered before March 2001 with an engine capacity not exceeding 1,549cc from £155 to £160.

Section 58(3) substitutes new VED rates for light passenger vehicles first registered between 1 March 2001 and 31 March 2017 in VERA 1994, Sch 1 para 1B. The reduced rate applies to alternatively fuelled light passenger vehicles, including those powered by bioethanol and liquid petroleum gas and hybrids.

Section 58(4) amends VED rates on the first vehicle licence for light passenger vehicles first registered on or after 1 April 2017 by substituting Table 1 and Table 2 in VERA 1994, Sch 1 para 1GC. Table 1 includes the standard rate and reduced rate. Table 2 includes the rates for higher rate diesel vehicles, applying to light passenger vehicles which are propelled by diesel and do not meet the Euro 6d emissions standard.

Section 58(5) increases the rate of duty applicable to light passenger vehicles first registered on or after 1 April 2017 from the second vehicle licence onwards in VERA 1994, Sch 1 para 1GD. The reduced rate of duty is increased from £130 to £135 per annum. The standard rate of duty is increased from £140 to £145 per annum.

Section 58(6) increases the higher rate of duty applicable to light passenger vehicles with a price exceeding £40,000 from £310 to £320 in VERA 1994, Sch 1 para 1GE.

Section 58(7) increases VED rates on some light goods vehicles first registered on or after March 2001 from £250 to £260 in VERA 1994, Sch 1 para 1J.

Section 58(8) increases VED rates on motorcycles weighing no more than 450 kilograms unladen. The rate of duty increases as follows:

- from £19 to £20 for motorcycles with an engine size not over 150cc;
- from £42 to £43 for motorcycles with an engine size of over 150cc but not more than 400cc;
- from £64 to £66 for motorcycles with an engine size of over 400cc but not more than 600cc;
- from £88 to £91 for motorcycles with an engine size of over 600cc, motor tricycles with an engine size over 150cc and trade licences for motorcycles.

Section 58(9) provides for the changes in rates to take effect in relation to vehicle licenses taken out on or after 1 April 2019.

59 VED: taxis capable of zero emissions

(1) Part 1AA of Schedule 1 to VERA 1994 (annual rates of duty: light passenger vehicles first registered on or after 1 April 2017) is amended as follows.

(2) In paragraph 1GE (higher rates for vehicles with price above £40,000), after sub-paragraph (4) insert—

> "(5) Sub-paragraphs (2) and (4) do not apply to a vehicle if when it is first registered, whether that is under this Act or under the law of a country or territory outside the United Kingdom, it is a taxi capable of zero emissions (see paragraph 1GG)."

(3) After paragraph 1GF insert—

> *"Meaning of "taxi capable of zero emissions"*
>
> **1GG** (1) The Secretary of State may by regulations make provision about the meaning of "taxi capable of zero emissions" in paragraph 1GE.
>
> (2) In the following provisions of this paragraph "regulations" means regulations under sub-paragraph (1).
>
> (3) Regulations may (in particular) make provision of any one or more of the following kinds—
>
> (a) that a vehicle is a taxi capable of zero emissions if the vehicle is of a description specified in regulations;
> (b) that a vehicle is at any particular time a taxi capable of zero emissions if the vehicle is of a model specified at that time in a list maintained by the Secretary of State;
> (c) that a vehicle is a taxi capable of zero emissions if conditions specified in regulations are met.
>
> (4) Where regulations make provision of the kind mentioned in sub-paragraph (3)(b)—
>
> (a) regulations may (in particular) provide that a model of vehicle may be specified in the list only if it appears to the Secretary of State that vehicles of that model are of a description specified in regulations;
> (b) regulations must provide for publication of the list;
> (c) regulations may allow a model of vehicle to be included in the list with backdated effect.
>
> (5) A description of a kind mentioned in sub-paragraph (3)(a) or (4)(a) may be framed (in particular) by reference to a scheme, or an instrument or other document, as it has effect from time to time.
>
> (6) Regulations made before 1 April 2020 that do not increase the amount of vehicle excise duty for which any person is liable may have effect in relation to vehicle licences taken out at times before the regulations come into force (including times before the regulations are made)."

(4) The amendments made by this section have effect in relation to licences taken out on or after 1 April 2019.

(5) The new paragraph 1GE(5) has effect, in the case of a vehicle first registered in the two years beginning with 1 April 2017, as if the reference to when the vehicle is first registered were to the start of the first period beginning on or after 1 April 2019 for which a vehicle licence for the vehicle is taken out.

COMMENTARY ON SECTION 59

Section 59 introduces an exemption from the VED supplement for taxis capable of zero emissions with a list price above £40,000.

Section 59(2) introduces a new exemption to the VED supplement in VERA 1994, Sch 1 para 1GE. The exemption is for taxis capable of zero emissions.

Section 59(3) adds a new paragraph 1GA to VERA 1994 which covers the meaning of 'taxi capable of zero emissions'. In particular, it provides that the Secretary of State for Transport may make regulations defining a zero emissions capable taxi and how those regulations might define a taxi capable of zero admissions. This may include a list of eligible taxis.

Section 59(4) provides for the exemption to have effect in relation to licences taken out on or after 1 April 2019.

Section 59(5) sets out a transitional provision for eligible taxis first registered from 1 April 2017 which will become exempt from the VED supplement when their VED is renewed on or after 1 April 2019.

The provisions in this section seek to address the fact that most new purpose-built capable taxis are currently liable to pay the VED supplement as they have a list price of over £40,000. This is to be contrasted with drivers of other vehicles used as taxis or private hire vehicles who have many choices of vehicle that cost less than £40,000 and hence are not caught by the VED supplement. This discrepancy is addressed by introducing an exemption to the supplement for taxis capable of zero emissions.

60 HGV road user levy

(1) The HGV Road User Levy Act 2013 is amended in accordance with subsections (2) to (6).

(2) In section 5(5) (payment of levy for UK heavy goods vehicles) for "in Schedule 1" substitute "or Table 1A in Schedule 1 (depending on which of those Tables applies to the vehicle)".

(3) In section 6(4) (payment of levy for non-UK heavy goods vehicles) for "in Schedule 1" substitute "or Table 1A in Schedule 1 (depending on which of those Tables applies to the vehicle)".

(4) In section 7 (rebate of levy), after subsection (2) insert—

"(2A) A rebate entitlement also arises where—

(a) HGV road user levy has been paid in respect of a vehicle at the rate applicable to a vehicle that does not meet Euro 6 emissions standards, and

(b) the vehicle becomes a vehicle that meets those standards."

(5) In section 19 (interpretation)—

(a) in subsection (3)—

(i) in paragraph (b), for "under section 7" substitute "as a result of an entitlement arising under section 7(2)", and

(ii) after paragraph (b) insert—

"(c) where a person receives a rebate of levy in respect of a vehicle as a result of an entitlement arising under section 7(2A), the person is treated as not having paid levy in respect of the vehicle for the period starting with the first day of the month after the month in which the application for a rebate was made and ending with the end of the levy period.", and

(b) after subsection (3), insert—

"(4) For the purposes of subsection (3)(c), a month starts on the day of the month on which the levy period started."

(6) In Schedule 1 (rates of HGV road user levy)—

(a) for paragraph 1 substitute—

"1 (1) Table 1 applies to a heavy goods vehicle that meets Euro 6 emissions standards.

(2) Table 1A applies to a heavy goods vehicle that does not meet Euro 6 emissions standards.

(3) Tables 1 and 1A set out the rates of levy for each of the Bands given by Tables 2 to 5 and by paragraph 4.";

(b) in paragraph 5, after paragraph (b) insert—

"(c) a heavy goods vehicle meets Euro 6 emissions standards if it complies with the emission limits set out in Annex 1 of Regulation (EC) No 595/2009 of the European Parliament and of the Council of 18th June 2009 on type approval of motor vehicles and engines with respect to emissions from heavy duty vehicles (Euro VI) and on access to repair and maintenance information.";

(c) for Table 1 substitute—

"TABLE 1: VEHICLES MEETING EURO 6 EMISSIONS STANDARDS—RATES FOR EACH BAND

Band	*Daily rate*	*Weekly rate*	*Monthly rate*	*Half-yearly rate*	*Yearly rate*
A	£1.53	£3.83	£7.65	£45.90	£76.50
B	£1.89	£4.73	£9.45	£56.70	£94.50
C	£4.32	£10.80	£21.60	£129.60	£216.00
D	£6.30	£15.75	£31.50	£189.00	£315.00
E	£9.00	£28.80	£57.60	£345.60	£576.00
F	£9.00	£36.45	£72.90	£437.40	£729.00
G	£9.00	£45.00	£90.00	£540.00	£900.00
B(T)	£2.43	£6.08	£12.15	£72.90	£121.50
C(T)	£5.58	£13.95	£27.90	£167.40	£279.00
D(T)	£8.10	£20.25	£40.50	£243.00	£405.00
E(T)	£9.00	£37.35	£74.70	£448.20	£747.00

TABLE 1A: VEHICLES NOT MEETING EURO 6 EMISSIONS STANDARDS—RATES FOR EACH BAND

Band	*Daily rate*	*Weekly rate*	*Monthly rate*	*Half-yearly rate*	*Yearly rate*
A	£2.04	£5.10	£10.20	£61.20	£102.00
B	£2.52	£6.30	£12.60	£75.60	£126.00
C	£5.76	£14.40	£28.80	£172.80	£288.00
D	£8.40	£21.00	£42.00	£252.00	£420.00
E	£10.00	£38.40	£76.80	£460.80	£768.00
F	£10.00	£48.60	£97.20	£583.20	£972.00
G	£10.00	£60.00	£120.00	£720.00	£1,200.00
B(T)	£3.24	£8.10	£16.20	£97.20	£162.00
C(T)	£7.44	£18.60	£37.20	£223.20	£372.00
D(T)	£10.00	£27.00	£54.00	£324.00	£540.00
E(T)	£10.00	£49.80	£99.60	£597.60	£996.00

(7) The HGV Road User Levy (Rate for Prescribed Vehicles) Regulations 2018 (SI 2018/417) are revoked.

(8) In section 19 of VERA 1994 (rebates)—

(a) in subsection (3), after paragraph (g) insert—

"(h) a relevant application for a vehicle licence for the vehicle has been received by the Secretary of State.",

(b) after subsection (3ZA) insert—

"(3ZB) An application for a vehicle licence is a relevant application for the purposes of subsection (3)(h) if—

(a) there is an unexpired licence for the vehicle in respect of which the application is made,

(b) when the unexpired licence was taken out, the vehicle was chargeable to

HGV road user levy under section 5 of the HGV Road User Levy Act 2013 at a rate applicable to a vehicle that does not meet Euro 6 emissions standards, and

(c) the vehicle now meets those standards, and an application for a rebate of HGV road user levy has been made under section 7 of that Act as a result of an entitlement arising under subsection (2A) of that section.",

(c) in subsection (7), after "rebate conditions" insert "(other than the condition in subsection (3)(h))", and

(d) after subsection (7) insert—

"(7A) Where the rebate condition in subsection (3)(h) is satisfied in relation to a licence, the licence ceases to be in force immediately before the first day of the period for which the relevant person is treated as not having paid levy in respect of the vehicle as a result of section 19(3)(c) of the HGV Road User Levy Act 2013."

(9) The amendments and revocation made by subsections (1) to (7) are to be treated as having effect in relation to HGV road user levy that—

(a) becomes due on or after 1 February 2019, and

(b) is paid on or after that date.

(10) The amendments made by subsection (8) are to be treated as having effect in relation to licences taken out on or after 1 February 2019.

COMMENTARY ON SECTION 60

Section 60 introduces a lower rate of HGV road user levy for vehicles that meet the latest Euro 6 emissions standard and a higher rate for vehicles that do not meet this standard.

Sections 60(2) and 60(3) amend the HGV Road User Levy Act 2013, ss 5(5) and 6(4) to make references to a new Table 1A which will contain the new lower rates for Euro 6 HGVs.

Section 60(4) amends the HGV Road User Levy Act 2013, s 7 to provide for the levy to be rebated where a vehicle is upgraded to comply with Euro 6 standards. Section 60(5) then amends the HGV Road User Levy Act 2013, s 19 in relation to the time at which the levy is considered unpaid following the granting of this rebate. It provides that for the purpose of calculating when the levy is unpaid regard is to be had to the actual day of the month upon which the previous levy period had started. It follows that months, for the purposes of the provision, would be dictated by that day. When a rebate was sought, the new levy would be due on the first day following that day of the month.

Section 60(6) inserts new criteria, describing which rates apply to which vehicles, into the HGV Road User Levy Act 2013, Sch 1. It provides for rates in Table 1 to apply to vehicles meeting the Euro 6 emissions standards and the new Table 1A to apply to other vehicles paying the levy. The existing Table 1 is replaced with a new table of rates and the new Table 1A. The section also inserts a definition of the Euro 6 standard.

Section 60(7) revokes the HGV Road User Levy (Rate for Prescribed Vehicles) Regulations 2018 (SI 2018/417). These regulations introduced the lower rate for Euro 6 vehicles but are no longer required as they are superseded by the provisions in this section.

The amendments made by section 60(1)–(7) are to be treated as having effect in relation to HGV road user levy that becomes due on or after 1 February 2019 and is paid on or after that date as a result of Section 60(9).

Section 60(8) amends VERA 1994, s 19 so that VED is to be rebated in the same circumstances and at the same time as the HGV levy. This is because for UK vehicles the levy and VED are administered using the same system and must both apply for the same time periods. The section also provides that a VED rebate can only apply when the vehicle operator takes out a new vehicle licence for the period immediately following the rebate such that no gap arises between vehicle licences. These amendments are to be treated as having effect in relation to licences taken out on or after 1 February 2019 as a result of Section 60(10).

Air passenger duty

61 Rates of duty from 1 April 2020

(1) In section 30 of FA 1994 (air passenger duty: rates), in subsection (4A) (long haul rates of duty)—

(a) in paragraph (a) for "£78" substitute "£80", and
(b) in paragraph (b) for "£172" substitute "£176".

(2) Those amendments have effect in relation to the carriage of passengers beginning on or after 1 April 2020.

COMMENTARY ON SECTION 61

Section 61 makes changes to the rates of Air Passenger Duty (APD) for flights to Band B destinations.

Section 61(1) makes changes to FA 1994, s 30 which sets out the rates of APD. Reduced rates are increased from £78 to £80 and standard rates are increased from £172 to £176. These increases are in line with the retail price index (RPI).

Section 61(2) provides that the new rates of APD apply to the carriage of passengers beginning on or after 1 April 2020.

The rates of APD for flights to Band A destinations are unchanged.

Gaming

62 Remote gaming duty: rate

(1) In section 155(3) of FA 2014 (rate of remote gaming duty) for "15%" substitute "21%".

(2) That amendment has effect in relation to accounting periods beginning on or after 1 April 2019.

(3) The amount of remote gaming duty charged in respect of an accounting period that begins before and ends on or after 1 April 2019 is the sum of—

(a) the amount of that duty that would have been charged in respect of the accounting period had it consisted only of those days within the period that fell before that date, and
(b) the amount of that duty that would have been charged in respect of the accounting period had it consisted only of those days within the period that fell on or after that date and had the amendment made by subsection (1) had effect in relation to it.

COMMENTARY ON SECTION 62

Section 62 raises the rate of remote gaming duty under FA 2014, s 155(3) from 15% to 21%. The increases have effect from 1 April 2019 for accounting periods beginning on or after this date. The amount charged for an accounting period that begins before and ends on or after 1 April 2019 is the sum of—

(a) the amount (at 15%) that would have been charged had it consisted only of those days within the period that fell before that date, and
(b) the amount (at 21%) that would have been charged had it consisted only of those days within the period that fell on or after that date.

The increase had originally been planned to take effect from 1 October 2019 but was brought forward to 1 April 2019, to coincide with the reduction in the maximum stake for fixed-odds betting terminals (FOBTs). On 14 November 2018, in a written ministerial statement, Jeremy Wright, Secretary of State for Digital, Culture, Media and Sport, noted that 'the Government decided to cut the maximum stake for fixed odds betting terminals to £2 [from £100] to help stop extreme losses by those who can least afford it and protect the most vulnerable in our society'. The April 2019 rate increase aims to mitigate the impact on the public finances of the reduction in the maximum stake for FOBTs.

63 Gaming duty

Schedule 19 contains provision about gaming duty.

Environmental taxes

64 Climate change levy: exemption for mineralogical and metallurgical processes

(1) Paragraph 12A of Schedule 6 to FA 2000 (exemption: mineralogical and metallurgical processes) is amended as follows.

(2) In sub-paragraph (1)—

(a) omit "to a person", and
(b) omit "by the person".

(3) In sub-paragraph (2), for the words from "has the same meaning" to the end substitute "means a process falling within Division 23 of NACE Rev 2."

(4) In sub-paragraph (4), the words after paragraph (c) become sub-paragraph (4A).

(5) In that sub-paragraph, for "sub-paragraph" substitute "paragraph".

COMMENTARY ON SECTION 64

Section 64 amends FA 2000, Sch 6, para 12A which sets out the exemption from climate change levy for energy used in mineralogical and metallurgical processes. The exemption in para 12A(1) refers to a taxable commodity supplied 'to a person', where that commodity is to be used 'by the person' in the relevant process. This wording inadvertently excludes from the exemption tenanted businesses which carry out mineralogical and metallurgical processes, because they receive their energy via a landlord rather than directly from an energy utility.

Subsection (2) removes reference to 'to a person' and 'by the person' from para 12A(1) to clarify that the landlord is entitled to claim the exemption on behalf of a tenant.

Subsection (3) amends the definition of 'mineralogical process' in para 12A(2), so that the definition is based on NACE Rev 2 (the European system for classification of economic activities) rather than Article 2(4)(b) of the Energy Taxation Directive (2003/96/EC). This change aligns the definition with that of 'metallurgical process' which has been based on NACE Rev 2 since the exemption was introduced in April 2014, and preserves the effect of the exemption after Brexit.

The s 64 changes have effect from 12 February 2019.

65 Landfill tax rates

(1) Section 42 of FA 1996 (amount of landfill tax) is amended as follows.

(2) In subsection (1)(a) (standard rate), for "£88.95" substitute "£91.35".

(3) In subsection (2) (reduced rate for certain disposals), in the words after paragraph (b)—

(a) for "£88.95" substitute "£91.35", and
(b) for "£2.80" substitute "£2.90".

(4) The amendments made by this section have effect in relation to disposals made (or treated as made) on or after 1 April 2019.

COMMENTARY ON SECTION 65

Section 65 increases the standard rate of landfill tax under FA 1996, s 42 from '£88.95' to '£91.35' per tonne, and the reduced rate for certain disposals from '£2.80' to '£2.90' per tonne. The increases have effect in relation to disposals made (or treated as made) on or after 1 April 2019.

Inheritance tax

66 Residence nil-rate band

(1) IHTA 1984 is amended as follows.

(2) In section 8FA(2)(b) and (5) (conditions for entitlement to downsizing addition), for "VT", in each place it occurs, substitute "the value transferred by the transfer of value under section 4 on the person's death".

(3) In section 8FE(9) (calculation of downsizing addition in section 8FA cases), in Step 2, for "VT" substitute "the value transferred by the transfer of value under section 4 on the person's death".

(4) In section 8E(1) (which, in relation to the person mentioned in section 8D(1), refers to the transfer of value under section 4), after "section 4" insert "on the person's death".

(5) In section 8J(6) (meaning of "inherited": property disposed of before death by gift subject to a reservation), for the words after "by way of" substitute "gift—

(a) subsections (2) to (5) do not apply, and

(b) B inherits the property if the property originally comprised in the gift became comprised in B's estate on the making of the disposal."

(6) The amendments made by this section apply for the purpose of calculating the amount of the charge to inheritance tax under section 4 of IHTA 1984 on a person's death if the person dies after 29 October 2018.

COMMENTARY ON SECTION 66

The residence nil rate band (RNRB) was introduced on 6 April 2017 as a way of alleviating the IHT burden by recognising the fact that many estates contained valuable residences. It has suffered much criticism across the industry for a number of reasons – many regard it as unnecessarily complicated and others suggest that it discriminates against those without children.

Very broadly, the RNRB is an additional nil rate band given to an estate where a residence passes to direct descendants.

Section 66 makes technical tweaks to two parts of the RNRB provisions, closing possible loopholes – the operation of the downsizing provisions and the interaction with the gifts with reservation of benefit (GWR) rules.

The downsizing provisions

The provisions of IHTA 1984, ss 8FA–8FE operate to give some benefit to estates where the deceased sold a qualifying residence or downsized.

Where the deceased leaves some or all of a qualifying residence to a direct descendant *and* the value of the residence is less than a former residence (sold on or after 8 July 2015), some credit may be given for this lost value. This is called the 'lost relievable amount' and is calculated by way of a formula contained in IHTA 1984, s 8FE(9).

The calculation is made with reference to a value 'VT' which is the chargeable value transferred as a result of the death. The legislation has amended this (for the purposes of calculating the lost relievable amount where a person has downsized) to mean the value transferred on death. This distinction means that the value could be different if part of the residence is left to exempt beneficiaries, such as the spouse.

A simple example, using the formula contained in s 8FE(9) will illustrate this point:

Example

Bernard, a bachelor, sold his £400k residence in 2016 and bought a small flat. He married Louise in 2018 and died in March 2019.

His estate consisted of his flat (£120k) and £1m of investments.

His will directs that his estate passes to his wife Louise (80%) and his daughter Marion (20%).

The maximum RNRB that could be available on Bernard's death is £125,00. However, this is restricted to the value of the residence passing to Marion. Therefore the amount of RNRB available on Bernard's death (before any downsizing addition) is: 120,000 (value of flat) × 20% = £24,000

What is the downsizing addition under the old rules?

Step 1: Express the former residence as a percentage of the former RNRB: (400,000 / 100,000) × 100 = 100% (capped)

Step 2: Express the value of the residence on death *attributable to the chargeable estate* as a percentage of the RNRB on death: (24,000 / 125,000) × 100 = 19.2%

Step 3: Take the difference between the two percentages (100 – 19.2) = 80.8%.

Therefore the downsizing addition is 80.8% × 125,000 = £101,000. This is limited to the value of the remaining assets passing to a direct descendant (Marion). As Marion is receiving £200k (£20% × £1m) then this is not an issue.

Bernard's executors have a total RNRB of (24,000 + 101,000) = 125,000.

How does this change under the new rules?

Step 1: Express the former residence as a percentage of the former RNRB: (400,000 / 100,000) × 100 = 100% (capped)

Step 2: Express the value of the residence on death *attributable to the whole estate* as a percentage of the RNRB on death: (120,000 / 125,000) × 100 = 96%

Step 3: Take the difference between the two percentages (100 – 96) = 4%.

Therefore the downsizing addition is 4% × 125,000 = £5,000.

Bernard's executors have a total RNRB of (24,000 + 5,000) = 29,000.

Despite these changes it is not imagined that many estates will fall foul of these new rules, given the fairly limited circumstances within which they will arise.

The GWR provisions

Where a person makes a gift of their residence in their lifetime and the residence forms part of their estate (due to the GWR provisions), the RNRB might be available if the original recipient was the direct descendant.

A potential loophole emerged whereby an individual could dispose of a residence to trustees and retain the benefit of the RNRB if the trustee was a direct descendant.

Section 66(5) amends IHTA 1984, s 8J(6) so that the direct descendant of the lifetime gift must receive the residence *beneficially*. This will prevent the residence from attracting the RNRB where the lifetime gift was to a trust. The possible exception could be a bare trust (which is not a trust for tax purposes) or a disabled person's trust (which imposes a beneficial interest on the beneficiary).

Operative date

The changes, for both provisions, will have effect for deaths applying on or after 29 October 2018.

Soft drinks industry levy

67 Application of penalty provisions

(1) In Schedule 10 to F(No 3)A 2010 (which prospectively amends Schedule 55 to FA 2009 (penalties for failure to make returns etc)) in paragraph 7, in the inserted paragraph 13A(1), after "7B" insert ", 13A".

(2) The amendments to Schedule 55 to FA 2009 made by Schedule 10 to F(No 3)A 2010 (including the amendment made by subsection (1)) are taken to have come into force for the purposes of soft drinks industry levy on the day on which this section comes into force.

(3) In Schedule 11 to F(No 3)A 2010 (which prospectively amends Schedule 56 to FA 2009 (penalties for failure to make payments)) in paragraph 5(3), in the substituted text of paragraph 3(1)(a) of Schedule 56 to FA 2009, for "11" substitute "11ZA".

COMMENTARY ON SECTION 67

Section 67 makes a number of changes to bring soft drinks industry levy (SDIL) into the following penalties rules—

1. FA 2009 Sch 55 – penalties for failure to submit returns on time; and
2. FA 2009 Sch 56 – failure to pay tax on time.

1. Penalties for late returns

The practical effect of this change is that penalties can be raised on businesses which do not file SDIL returns on time. This change applies from 12 February 2019.

Background

Finance (No 3) Act 2010, Sch 10 makes various amendments to FA 2009, Sch 55. Schedule 55 sets out penalties payable for failures to submit returns on time across a range of taxes (specified in the table in Sch 55, para 1). The Sch 10 amendments will generally be brought into force from a future date.

Specifically, Sch 10, para 7 will insert a new para 13A into FA 2009, Sch 55. Paragraph 13A will introduce a new structure for penalties for the late filing of certain returns which relate to a period of between two and six months.

How is this affected by s 67?

The effect of the sub-s (1) amendment is as follows—

1. A reference to 'item 13A' is inserted into FA 2009, Sch 55, para 13A. 'Item 13A' is the entry in the table in Sch 55, para 1 relating to the SDIL return.
2. This means that SDIL returns are included in the new penalty rules for periods of between two and six months.

Subsection (2) brings all of the Sch 10 amendments to FA 2009, Sch 55 into force from 12 February 2019 for the purposes of SDIL only.

This enables penalties to be raised against businesses registered for SDIL which fail to submit a quarterly return by the due date.

2. Penalties for failure to make payments of tax

The practical effect of this change (when brought into force), will be to enable penalties to be raised for the non-payment of SDIL under the structure in FA 2009, Sch 56, para 3.

Background

Finance (No 3) Act 2010, Sch 11 makes various amendments to FA 2009, Sch 56. Schedule 56 sets out penalties for failures to pay an amount of tax on time. The taxes covered are set out in the table in Sch 56, para 1, with SDIL included as item 11ZA.

FA 2009, Sch 56, para 3 provides that, for all taxes, with certain exceptions (corporation tax and monthly payments under PAYE or the construction industry scheme or apprenticeship levy regulations) escalating penalties are chargeable at a fixed rate based on the amount of tax unpaid at any of the three statutory dates—

(a) at the penalty date (normally 30 days after the due date for payment), 5% of the unpaid tax;
(b) five months after the penalty date, 5% of any remaining unpaid tax; and
(c) 11 months after the penalty date, 5% of any remaining unpaid tax.

Schedule 11, para 5 updates references in FA 2009, Sch 56, para 3 to include income tax and CGT under 'simple assessments' (item 1A in the table in Sch 56, para 1), and VAT instalment payments (item 6B) and to ensure that other taxes, in relation to which para 3 has not yet been brought into force, are specifically excluded.

Generally, the Sch 11 amendments have not yet been brought into force.

How is this affected by s 67?

The effect of the change made by sub-s (3) is as follows—

1. A reference to 'item 11ZA' is inserted into FA 2009, Sch 56, para 3(1)(a).
2. This means that, when Sch 11 is eventually brought into force, SDIL will be included in the list of taxes in relation to which the penalty rules in para 3 apply.

The explanatory notes to the Finance Bill explain that 'this ensures that a penalty can still be raised for non-payment of any SDIL due in the event that certain provisions within F(No 3)A 2010 are enacted'.

---

68 Isle of Man

(1) In section 1(1) of the Isle of Man Act 1979 (common duties), at the end insert—

"(f) soft drinks industry levy chargeable under the law of the United Kingdom or the Isle of Man."

(2) Part 2 of FA 2017 (soft drinks industry levy) is amended in accordance with subsections (3) and (4).

(3) After section 58 insert—

"58A Isle of Man: import and export of chargeable soft drinks

(1) Subsections (2) and (3) apply if—

(a) chargeable soft drinks are imported into the United Kingdom from the Isle of Man, and
(b) a charge to soft drinks industry levy (the "corresponding charge") arises in relation to the soft drinks under the law of the Isle of Man.

(2) If the corresponding charge arises at a rate equal to, or greater than, the UK rate, the soft drinks are not to be treated as being imported into the United Kingdom for the purposes of section 33 (chargeable events: imported soft drinks).

(3) If the corresponding charge arises at a rate lower than the UK rate, the amount of soft drinks industry levy charged under this Part in relation to the soft drinks is to be reduced by an amount equal to the corresponding charge.

(4) In this section "the UK rate", in relation to chargeable soft drinks, is the rate of soft drinks industry levy that would (apart from this section) be chargeable in relation to the soft drinks under this Part.

(5) For the purposes of section 39(1)(a) (tax credits: exported soft drinks) or regulations made under that provision, chargeable soft drinks are not to be treated as being exported from the United Kingdom if the soft drinks are exported to the Isle of Man."

(4) At the end of section 33, insert—

"(10) This section is subject to section 58A (Isle of Man: import and export of chargeable soft drinks)."

(5) In section 39, after subsection (5) insert—

"(5A) This section is subject to section 58A (Isle of Man: import and export of chargeable soft drinks)."

(6) This section comes into force on 1 April 2019.

COMMENTARY ON SECTION 68

Section 68 allows the movement of levy-paid soft drinks between the UK and Isle of Man to be treated as neither an import nor an export for the purposes of soft drinks industry levy (SDIL). Subsection (3) inserts a new FA 2017, s 58A which provides the following—

- movements of chargeable soft drinks from the Isle of Man to the UK do not trigger a chargeable event under FA 2017, s 33 if Manx SDIL of an equal or greater amount to UK SDIL has already been paid in relation to those drinks;
- if, however, the amount of Manx SDIL paid is less than UK SDIL, a chargeable event will be triggered and UK SDIL will be payable to make up the shortfall; and
- movements of chargeable soft drinks from the UK to the Isle of Man do not attract an export credit under FA 2017, s 39(1)(a) or under the Soft Drinks Industry Levy Regulations, SI 2018/41.

Sub-s (1) adds SDIL and Manx SDIL to the list of common duties in the Isle of Man Act 1979, s 1(1).

The changes come into force on 1 April 2019.

The Isle of Man Treasury confirmed on 20 February 2019 that Manx SDIL would be introduced on 1 April 2019.

Note also that the following instruments will provide for a UK-Crown Dependencies Customs Union after Brexit—

- Crown Dependencies Customs Union (Guernsey) (EU Exit) Order, SI 2019/254;
- Crown Dependencies Customs Union (Jersey) (EU Exit) Order, SI 2019/256; and
- Crown Dependencies Customs Union (Isle of Man) (EU Exit) Order, SI 2019/257.

The Orders are expected to come into force either on Exit Day or, if a transition period is agreed, at the end of that period.

PART 3

CARBON EMISSIONS TAX

Introductory

69 Carbon emissions tax

(1) A tax called "carbon emissions tax" is to be charged in accordance with this Part.

(2) The Commissioners are responsible for the collection and management of carbon emissions tax.

COMMENTARY ON SECTION 69

Part 3 introduces legislation for a carbon emissions tax that would be brought into force only if the UK leaves the EU without an agreement regarding the UK's continued participation in the EU Emissions Trading Scheme ('EU ETS'), or an arrangement whereby a new, UK Emissions Trading Scheme is allowed to participate in the EU ETS. A 'no deal' scenario would see the UK being wholly excluded from participating in the EU ETS.

The EU ETS requires operators of stationary installations (mainly in sectors engaged in power generation, industrial scale manufacturing, food processing and certain public sector facilities) throughout the EU to obtain relevant permits and to report annually how many tonnes of greenhouse gasses they have emitted.

The EU ETS has been part of the Government's strategy to establish a minimum price for carbon in the UK and to support the UK's legally binding objective to meeting carbon reduction targets. It has also generated revenue for the Government from the auctioning of EU Allowances (EUAs) to participants in the scheme who are required to hold adequate allowances to meet the level of their emissions.

Announced in the 2018 Budget, a carbon emissions tax is to be introduced with a view to meeting the UK's objectives under EU ETS. The tax would continue to apply to the stationary installations requiring a permit under the EU ETS and will also continue to rely on the system currently used to monitor, report and verify emissions for EU ETS purposes.

Current EU ETS participants would be set annual emissions allowances for each installation. Emissions in excess of this allowance will be taxed at a rate of £16 per tonne for the period from 1 April (at the earliest) 2019 to the end of the first tax period 31 December 2019. Thereafter, tax periods will be calendar years. The rate may change in future periods.

The introduction of the tax will be preceded by a consultation during 2019 about detailed plans, and secondary legislation would be laid in early 2020.

Section 69(1) and (2) introduce the tax and set out that HMRC would be responsible for its collection and management.

Charge to tax

70 Charge to carbon emissions tax

(1) Carbon emissions tax is charged, in relation to a regulated installation, if the amount of reported carbon emissions for a reporting period exceeds the emissions allowance for the period.

(2) The amount of "taxable carbon emissions" in relation to the installation for the reporting period is the amount of the excess.

(3) Carbon emissions tax is charged on taxable carbon emissions at the rate of £16 per tonne of carbon dioxide equivalent.

COMMENTARY ON SECTION 70

Subsections (1)–(3) set out that the tax will apply to regulated installations only if the reported carbon emissions exceed the emissions allowance set for the installation in the tax period, and that tax at a rate of £16 per tonne will be applied to excess emissions.

---

71 "Reported carbon emissions"

(1) The amount of "reported carbon emissions" in relation to an installation for a reporting period is the total amount of emissions from the installation, in tonnes of carbon dioxide equivalent, that is stated—

(a) in the emissions determination (or, if there is more than one, the latest emissions determination) for the period, or

(b) if there is no such determination, in the emissions report for the period.

(2) In subsection (1), "emissions determination" means the regulator's estimate of the total amount of emissions from the installation for the period, determined in accordance with—

(a) article 70 of the Monitoring and Reporting Regulation, or
(b) regulation 44 of the Emissions Regulations.

COMMENTARY ON SECTION 71

Subsections (1) and (2) establish that the emissions allowance for each installation is established by reference to the regulatory determination made for EU ETS. In the case of installations covered by EU ETS, this will be the determination made by the regulator and in the case of the installations using the EU ETS simplified reporting scheme, this will be by reference to the simplified scheme's emissions report for the previous year.

---

72 "Emissions report" and "reporting period"

(1) In this Part, "emissions report" means a report of emissions that is submitted to the regulator for the purpose of complying with—

(a) the monitoring and reporting requirements or, in the case of an excluded installation, the monitoring and reporting conditions, or
(b) a requirement of a notice of surrender or of a revocation notice.

(2) "Reporting period", in relation to a regulated installation, means—

(a) a scheme year, or
(b) such shorter period for which an emissions report for the installation is required by a notice of surrender or a revocation notice.

COMMENTARY ON SECTION 72

Section 72 sets out that these terms have the same meaning for carbon emissions tax as they do for reporting under EU ETS.

---

73 "Emissions allowance"

The "emissions allowance", in relation to an installation for a reporting period, is the amount of emissions, in tonnes of carbon dioxide equivalent, specified by or under, or determined in accordance with, regulations made by the Commissioners under this section.

COMMENTARY ON SECTION 73

The emissions allowance is critical for establishing the amount of excess emissions that will be taxed at £16 per tonne. Section 73 defines that the allowance will be expressed in units of carbon dioxide equivalent, such that the tax will also apply to greenhouse gasses other than carbon dioxide.

---

74 Liability to pay carbon emissions tax

(1) Carbon emissions tax in relation to an installation is payable by the person who, at the end of the reporting date, holds the permit for the installation.

(2) The "reporting date", in relation to a reporting period, means the day on which the emissions report for that period is required to be submitted to the regulator under the Emissions Regulations.

COMMENTARY ON SECTION 74

Subsection (1) clarifies that the person liable for any carbon emissions tax arising will be the permit holder for the relevant installation at the end of the tax reporting period. The permit holder would normally also be the operator of the installation. This is in line with the responsible person for the purposes of EU ETS.

Subsection (2) aligns 'reporting date' for the purpose of emissions, with the current requirements to report emissions to the regulator.

Administration etc

75 Power to make further provision about carbon emissions tax

(1) The Commissioners may by regulations—

(a) make provision about the assessment, payment, collection and recovery of carbon emissions tax, including provision about the recovery of overpayments;

(b) require persons to keep, for purposes connected with carbon emissions tax, records of specified matters, and to preserve those records for a specified period;

(c) make provision for the review of, and a right of appeal against, specified decisions of HMRC in connection with carbon emissions tax;

(d) make provision about the enforcement of carbon emissions tax;

(e) permit or require the sharing of information between HMRC, authorities and regulators for purposes in connection with carbon emissions tax;

(f) make provision about the form, manner and content of any notice, application or other communication with HMRC in connection with carbon emissions tax (including provision about communications in electronic form);

(g) make provision in relation to cases where an individual liable for carbon emissions tax dies or becomes incapacitated, or where a person (whether or not an individual) is subject to an insolvency procedure.

(2) The Commissioners may by regulations make provision for purposes in connection with carbon emissions tax—

(a) about the submission of emissions reports to a regulator;

(b) about emissions determinations, including provision permitting or requiring a regulator to make an emissions determination in specified circumstances;

(c) specifying conditions to be included in a permit granted by a regulator;

(d) for the review of, and a right of appeal against, specified decisions of a regulator;

(e) about the performance of a function of a regulator;

(f) about the form, manner and content of any notice, application or other communication with a regulator (including provision about communications in electronic form).

(3) Regulations under this section may, in particular—

(a) make provision that is equivalent to, or applies with or without modification, any provision of an enactment relating to tax;

(b) amend the Monitoring and Reporting Regulation or the Verification Regulation.

COMMENTARY ON SECTION 75

Subsections (1), (2) and (3) establish HMRC's powers to make regulations for managing carbon emissions tax along the same lines as other taxes, including regulations for making assessments, record keeping, appeal rights, tax debt enforcement, and other administrative requirements. Given that operation and calculation of the tax will rely in part on emissions permits, emissions reports and other technical matters under the authority of the regulator, these subsections also allow for regulations to make provisions for reference to these areas for the purposes of managing the tax.

Regulations will not be laid until early 2020 – if at all – and subsequent to the end of the first reporting period for the tax (31 December 2019).

---

76 Consequential provision

(1) In section 1 of the Provisional Collection of Taxes Act 1968 (temporary statutory effect of House of Commons resolutions), in subsection (1), after "petroleum revenue tax" insert ", carbon emissions tax,".

(2) In regulation 52 of the Emissions Regulations (penalty for carrying out a regulated activity without a permit), after paragraph (2) insert—

"(2A) In paragraph (2), the reference to "costs" includes a reference to carbon emissions tax."

(3) Section 4(1) of the European Union (Withdrawal) Act 2018 does not apply, for the purposes of carbon emissions tax, in relation to any rights, powers, liabilities, obligations, restrictions, remedies and procedures so far as they arise under—

(a) Council Directive 2008/118/EC of 16 December 2008 concerning the general arrangements for excise duty, or

(b) Council Directive 2003/96/EC of 27 October 2003 restructuring the Community framework for the taxation of energy products and electricity.

(4) The Commissioners may by regulations make such provision as they consider appropriate in consequence of this Part.

(5) Regulations under subsection (4) may amend, repeal or revoke any enactment (whenever passed or made).

COMMENTARY ON SECTION 76

Subsection (1) – if enacted, carbon emissions tax will be a new tax. As such it is necessary to make changes to other tax legislation (including the Provisional Collection of Taxes Act 1968) and sections of the emissions regulations to take into account the cost of the tax when calculating the value of penalties imposed in respect of installations that have failed permit emission requirements.

Subsection (2) will amend the method of calculating the value of a civil penalty where a regulated activity has been performed without a suitable permit. The penalty is calculated by reference to the costs avoided and this subsection will have the effect of replacing the cost of emissions avoided with the value of carbon emissions tax avoided when calculating this civil penalty under the Greenhouse Gas Emissions Trading Scheme Regulations 2012 (SI 2012/3038).

Subsection (3) will prevent any direct effect on carbon emissions tax of EU directives for excise duties and energy products that might otherwise have an effect under the terms of the European Union (Withdrawal) Act 2018.

Subsections (4) and (5) provide HMRC with the power to change, repeal or revoke regulations where it feels it necessary to do so.

General

77 Interpretation

(1) In this Part—

"the Commissioners" means the Commissioners for Her Majesty's Revenue and Customs;

"emissions allowance" has the meaning given by section 73;

"emissions determination" has the meaning given by section 71;

"the Emissions Regulations" means the Greenhouse Gas Emissions Trading Scheme Regulations 2012 (SI 2012/3038);

"emissions report" has the meaning given by section 72;

"enactment" includes an enactment contained in subordinate legislation within the meaning of the Interpretation Act 1978;

"HMRC" means Her Majesty's Revenue and Customs;

"installation" has the meaning given by regulation 3 of the Emissions Regulations (and references to an installation include references to an offshore installation, as defined in those Regulations);

"the Monitoring and Reporting Regulation" means Commission Regulation (EU) No 601/2012 of 21 June 2012 on the monitoring and reporting of greenhouse gas emissions pursuant to Directive 2003/87/EC of the European Parliament and of the Council (as amended from time to time);

"operator" has the meaning given by regulation 3 of the Emissions Regulations (as read with Schedule 1 to those Regulations);

"reporting period" has the meaning given by section 72 (subject to section 79(4));

"specified" means specified in regulations under this Part;

"the Verification Regulation" means Commission Regulation (EU) No 600/2012 of 21 June 2012 on the verification of greenhouse gas emission reports and tonne-kilometre reports and the accreditation of verifiers pursuant to Directive 2003/87/EC of the European Parliament and of the Council (as amended from time to time).

(2) In this Part, the following terms have the meaning given by regulation 3 of the Emissions Regulations—

"authority",
"emissions",
"excluded installation",
"monitoring and reporting conditions",
"monitoring and reporting requirements",
"notice of surrender",
"permit",
"regulator",
"revocation notice",
"scheme year", and
"tonne of carbon dioxide equivalent".

(3) An "installation" is a "regulated installation" for a reporting period if, at any time during the period, the operator holds a permit for the installation.

(4) References in this Part to the Verification Regulation or the Monitoring and Reporting Regulation include references to any EU regulation which replaces either of them and forms part of the law of the United Kingdom as a result of section 3 of the European Union (Withdrawal) Act 2018 (and accordingly the reference in section 71(2)(a) to article 70 of the Monitoring and Reporting Regulation includes a reference to the corresponding provision in any such replacement of that Regulation).

COMMENTARY ON SECTION 77

Section 77 defines various terms within Part 3 of the Act.

Subsection (4) addresses the possibility that there may be changes to EU legislation for monitoring and reporting EU emissions before the implementation of carbon emissions tax, and requires that where this happens carbon emissions tax regulations will refer to the changed EU regulations where it would otherwise impact on the tax.

---

78 Regulations

(1) Regulations under section 73, 75 or 76 may—

- (a) make provision conferring functions or discretions on an authority, a regulator or any other person;
- (b) impose charges as a means of recovering costs incurred by a person in exercising a function conferred under the regulations;
- (c) make provision by reference to matters determined or published by HMRC, the Secretary of State, an authority or a regulator (whether before or after the regulations are made);
- (d) make different provision for different purposes;
- (e) include incidental, consequential, supplementary, transitional or transitory provision.

(2) Regulations under this Part are to be made by statutory instrument.

(3) A statutory instrument containing regulations under section 76(4) that makes provision amending or repealing any provision of an Act of Parliament may not be made unless a draft of the instrument has been laid before and approved by a resolution of the House of Commons.

(4) Any other statutory instrument containing regulations under this Part is subject to annulment in pursuance of a resolution of the House of Commons.

(5) But subsection (4) does not apply to a statutory instrument containing only regulations under section 79 (commencement).

79 Commencement and transitional provision

(1) This Part comes into force on such day as the Commissioners may by regulations appoint.

(2) Regulations under subsection (1) may—

- (a) appoint different days for different purposes;
- (b) include transitional or transitory provision.

(3) Section 72(2) (reporting period) is subject to subsection (4).

(4) For the purposes of the application of this Part in relation to the scheme year 2019, the "reporting period", in relation to a regulated installation, means—

- (a) the period beginning with 1 April 2019 and ending with 31 December 2019, or
- (b) such shorter period beginning on or after 1 April 2019 for which an emissions report is required by a notice of surrender or a revocation notice.

(5) For the purposes of the scheme year 2019, the provisions of the Emissions Regulations, the Monitoring and Reporting Regulation and the Verification Regulation apply, and anything done under those provisions has effect—

- (a) as if, for the purposes of reporting or determining emissions from an installation, references to a period corresponding to a scheme year were references to the reporting period for 2019 (and accordingly as if references to a period beginning with 1 January were references to a period beginning with 1 April 2019), and
- (b) with such other modifications as are necessary for the purposes of the charge to carbon emissions tax for a reporting period beginning in 2019.

COMMENTARY ON SECTION 79

If carbon emissions tax is implemented, it will need to come into force shortly after EU exit (originally expected to be 1 April 2019). The reporting periods for EU ETS are calendar years, so by commencing on 1 April 2019 the first period for carbon emissions tax would have been only 9 months – shorter than the 12 months EU ETS reporting period for 2019. This section provides for this variance in the first accounting period for carbon emissions tax. It also provides for HMRC appointing any other day for the tax to commence to accommodate a later EU exit date.

PART 4

ADMINISTRATION AND ENFORCEMENT

Time limits for assessments etc

80 Offshore matters or transfers: income tax and capital gains tax

(1) TMA 1970 is amended as follows.

(2) After section 36 insert—

"36A Loss of tax involving offshore matter or offshore transfer

(1) This section applies in a case involving a loss of income tax or capital gains tax, where—

- (a) the lost tax involves an offshore matter, or
- (b) the lost tax involves an offshore transfer which makes the lost tax significantly harder to identify.

(2) An assessment on a person ("the taxpayer") may be made at any time not more than 12 years after the end of the year of assessment to which the lost tax relates.

This is subject to section 36(1A) above and any other provision of the Taxes Acts allowing a longer period.

(3) Lost income tax or capital gains tax "involves an offshore matter" if it is charged on or by reference to—

- (a) income arising from a source in a territory outside the United Kingdom,
- (b) assets situated or held in a territory outside the United Kingdom,
- (c) income or assets received in a territory outside the United Kingdom,
- (d) activities carried on wholly or mainly in a territory outside the United Kingdom, or
- (e) anything having effect as if it were income, assets or activities of a kind described above.

(4) Lost income tax or capital gains tax "involves an offshore transfer" if—

- (a) it does not involve an offshore matter, and
- (b) the income or the proceeds of the disposal on or by reference to which it is charged, or any part of the income or proceeds, is transferred to a territory outside the United Kingdom before the relevant date.

(5) In subsection (4)—

"relevant date" means—

(a) in a case where the taxpayer (or a person acting on the taxpayer's behalf) delivered a return under the Taxes Acts to HMRC for the year of assessment to which the lost tax relates and in which information relating to the lost tax was required to be provided, the date on which the return was delivered, and

(b) in any other case, 31 January in the year of assessment after that to which the lost tax relates;

references to income or proceeds transferred include references to assets derived from or representing the income or proceeds.

(6) Where lost tax involves an offshore transfer, the cases in which the transfer makes the lost tax significantly harder to identify include any case where, because of the transfer—

(a) HMRC was significantly less likely to become aware of the lost tax, or

(b) HMRC was likely to become aware of the lost tax only at a significantly later time.

(7) But an assessment may not be made under subsection (2) if—

(a) before the time limit that would otherwise apply for making the assessment, HMRC received relevant overseas information on the basis of which HMRC could reasonably have been expected to become aware of the lost tax, and

(b) it was reasonable to expect the assessment to be made before that time limit.

(8) In subsection (7)(a) "relevant overseas information" means information which is provided to HMRC by an authority in a territory outside the United Kingdom under—

(a) any provision of EU law relating to any tax, or

(b) an agreement to which the United Kingdom and that territory are parties, with or without other parties.

(9) An assessment may also not be made under subsection (2) to the extent that liability to the lost tax arises as a result of an adjustment under Part 4 of TIOPA 2010 (transfer pricing adjustments).

(10) In this section "assets" has the meaning given in section 21(1) of the 1992 Act, but also includes sterling.

(11) Section 36(2) to (3A) applies for the purposes of this section (as if references to section 36(1) or (1A) were to subsection (1) of this section).""

(3) In section 37A (effect of assessment where allowances transferred), after "or (1A)" insert "or 36A".

(4) In section 40 (personal representatives), in subsection (1), for "or 36" substitute ", 36 or 36A".

(5) The amendments made by this section have effect—

(a) in relation to assessments on a person relating to the 2013–14 year of assessment and subsequent years of assessment, where the loss of tax is brought about carelessly by that person or by a person acting on that person's behalf, and

(b) in any other case, in relation to assessments relating to the 2015–16 year of assessment and subsequent years of assessment.

COMMENTARY ON SECTION 80

The Government announced in Budget 2017 that the assessing time limits which apply to offshore non-compliance will be extended. This is part of HMRC's continuing attack on offshore non-compliance but is specifically designed to enable HMRC to have time to examine all of the information which is available to it under the various Automatic Exchange of Information Agreements which it has entered into. The basic time limit for assessment for certain offshore matters not involving deliberate behaviour is increased to 12 years, although the time limit in relation to deliberate understatement remains at 20 years. The new time limits are being introduced gradually so that no year which is out of time for assessment under the existing rules will retrospectively be brought back into time.

Section 80(1) introduces amendments to TMA 1970. Subsection (2) introduces a new TMA 1970, s 36A.

New TMA 1970, s 36A: Loss of tax involving offshore matter or offshore transfer

TMA 1970, s 36A applies where there is a loss of income tax or capital gains tax where the lost tax involves either an offshore matter or involves an offshore transfer which makes the lost tax significantly harder to identify. These terms are defined later in the section.

Under TMA 1970, s 36A(2) where sub-s (1) applies an assessment may be made on a taxpayer at any time not more than 12 years after the end of the year of assessment to which the lost tax relates. However if any provision of the Taxes Acts allows a longer period in which to make an assessment that longer period overrides this 12-year period. This preserves the existing 20-year limit for assessment where there has been deliberate behaviour.

TMA 1970, s 36A(3) defines what is meant by lost income tax or capital gains tax which involved an offshore matter. There is a very wide definition with sub-s (3)(e) having the effect of a catch all.

TMA 1970, s 36A(4) defines an offshore transfer. An offshore transfer does not involve an offshore matter but the income or disposal proceeds is transferred from the UK before the relevant date. In other words, income or gains which derive from the UK are within the scope of the extended time limit if they are transferred abroad.

TMA 1970, s 36A(5) provides that relevant date means the date on which a return relating to the lost tax was delivered to HMRC. If no return was delivered the date is 31 January following the year of assessment to which the lost tax relates.

TMA 1970, s 36A(6) explains that cases which make the lost tax significantly harder to identify include cases where HMRC was significantly less likely to become aware of the lost tax or HMRC was likely to become aware of the lost tax only at a significantly later time.

TMA 1970, s 36A(7) provides that HMRC may not use the extended assessing powers under sub-s (2) where before the normal assessing time limit HMRC received relevant overseas information on the basis of which it could reasonably have been expected to become aware of the lost tax and it was reasonable to expect the assessment to be made before that time limit. It is likely that this provision will lead to disputes over what level of information it was reasonable for HMRC to have been aware of. Although the legislation is very different it may well be the case that some of the arguments made in discovery cases about the level of knowledge and awareness of HMRC officers may also be used in this context.

TMA 1970, s 36A(8) defines relevant overseas information.

Under TMA 1970, s 36A(9) no adjustment may be made under sub-s (2) above to the extent that the loss of tax arises from a transfer pricing adjustment – in other words the transfer pricing rules take priority.

TMA 1970, s 36A(1) and (11) are minor drafting amendments.

Section 80(3), (4) are minor drafting amendments.

Section 80(5) sets out the commencement provisions. The new provisions take effect in relation to assessments for 2015/16 and subsequent years. However where there is a loss of tax attributable to a person acting carelessly (or by a person acting on his behalf) the provisions apply for assessment for the year 2013/14 onwards. The effect of this is that no year of assessment which was out of time prior to the passing of this act retrospectively come back in time as a result of the changes introduced by this section.

81 Offshore matters or transfers: inheritance tax

(1) IHTA 1984 is amended as follows.

(2) In section 240 (underpayments), in subsection (3), at the end insert "and to section 240B (underpayments involving offshore matter etc)."

(3) After section 240A insert—

"240B Underpayments involving offshore matters etc

(1) This section applies in a case within section 240(2) which involves a loss of tax in relation to a chargeable transfer, where—

(a) the lost tax involves an offshore matter, or
(b) the lost tax involves an offshore transfer which makes the lost tax significantly harder to identify.

(2) Proceedings for the recovery of the lost tax may be brought at any time not more than 12 years after the later of the dates in section 240(2)(a) and (b).

(3) Lost tax "involves an offshore matter" if it is charged on or by reference to property which is situated or held in a territory outside the United Kingdom at, or immediately after, the time of the chargeable transfer.

(4) Lost tax "involves an offshore transfer" if—

(a) it does not involve an offshore matter, and
(b) the property is transferred to a territory outside the United Kingdom at a relevant time.

(5) In subsection (4)(b) "relevant time" means a time after the chargeable transfer but before—

(a) the date on which an account under section 216 is delivered to HMRC in relation to the chargeable transfer, or
(b) any later date on which an account under section 217 is so delivered.

(6) Where lost tax involves an offshore transfer, the cases in which the transfer makes the lost tax significantly harder to identify include any case where, because of the transfer—

(a) HMRC was significantly less likely to become aware of the lost tax, or
(b) HMRC was likely to become aware of the lost tax only at a significantly later time.

(7) But proceedings may not be brought under this section if—

(a) before the last date on which the proceedings could otherwise be brought, HMRC received relevant overseas information on the basis of which HMRC could reasonably have been expected to become aware of the lost tax, and
(b) it was reasonable to expect the proceedings to be brought before that date.

(8) In subsection (7)(a) "relevant overseas information" means information which is provided to HMRC by an authority in a territory outside the United Kingdom under—

(a) any provision of EU law relating to any tax, or
(b) an agreement to which the United Kingdom and that territory are parties, with or without other parties.

(9) This section is subject to any provision of this Act which allows for a longer period for the bringing of proceedings."

(4) The amendments made by this section have effect—

(a) in a case involving loss of tax brought about carelessly by a person liable for the tax (or a person acting on behalf of such a person), in relation to chargeable transfers taking place on or after 1 April 2013, and
(b) in any other case, in relation to chargeable transfers taking place on or after 1 April 2015.

(5) Section 240(8) of IHTA 1984 applies to the reference to "person liable for the tax" in subsection (4)(a).

COMMENTARY ON SECTION 81

Section 81 provides for extended time limits for inheritance tax recovery relating to offshore matters. The broad principle of a 12-year time limit which applies under new s 36A above will also apply for inheritance tax, but because of the way in which time limits for inheritance tax operate it is couched in different language.

Subsection (1) introduces amendments to IHTA 1984. Subsection (2) is a minor drafting amendment.

Subsection (3) is the substantive section. It introduces a new IHTA 1984 s 240B.

New IHTA 1984 s 240B(1) states that the section applies where there is a loss of tax involving an offshore matter or an offshore transfer which makes the loss of tax significantly harder to identify

IHTA 1984 s 240B(2) allows proceedings for the recovery of the lost tax to be brought at any time not more than 12 years after the dates in s 240(2)(a) and (b). Those are, respectively, the dates on which tax was paid and accepted (in the case of instalments the date of the last payment of instalments) and the date on which the tax (or last instalment) was due.

Under IHTA 1984 s 240B(3) lost tax involves an offshore matter if it is charged on (or by reference to) property held outside the UK at, or immediately after, the time of the chargeable transfer.

IHTA 1984 s 240B(4) states that lost tax involves an offshore transfer if it does not involve an offshore matter but the property was transferred outside the UK at a relevant time.

IHTA 1984 s 240B(5) provides that relevant time is a time after the chargeable transfer but before the date on which an account is delivered to HMRC under ss 216 or 217. Section 216 is the normal rule for delivery of accounts: s 217 is the rule which applies when a defective account is provided to HMRC – a corrected account is due within six months of making the discovery that the account was defective.

IHTA 1984 s 240B(6) explains what is meant by cases where the loss of tax is significantly harder to identify. It uses the same test as in TMA 1970, s 36A above for income and capital gains tax.

IHTA 1984 s 240B(7) places a restriction on the use of the new extended time limits. No proceeding can be brought under this section if, before the last date on which proceeding could otherwise have been brought, HMRC has received relevant overseas information on the basis of which it could reasonably have been expected to become aware of the lost tax, or it was reasonable to expect the proceedings to be brought before that date.

IHTA 1984 s 240B(8) defines relevant overseas information.

Under IHTA 1984 s 240B(9) this section is subject to any other provision of IHTA 1984 which allows for a longer period for bringing proceedings.

Subsection (4) sets out the commencement rules. The default position is that the new rules apply to chargeable transfers taking place on or after 1 April 2015. However, in a case of a loss of tax brought about by a person acting carelessly (or by a person so acting on his behalf) the rules apply to chargeable transfers taking place on or after 1 April 2013.

Subsection (5) is a minor drafting amendment.

Security deposits

82 Construction industry scheme and corporation tax etc

(1) In Chapter 3 of Part 3 of FA 2004 (construction industry scheme)—

(a) in the italic heading before section 69, after "returns" insert ", security";

(b) after section 70 insert—

"70A Security for payments to HMRC

(1) The Commissioners for Her Majesty's Revenue and Customs may by regulations make provision for and in connection with requiring the giving, by prescribed persons and in prescribed circumstances, of security for the payment of amounts that a person is or may be liable to pay to the Commissioners under this Chapter.

(2) Regulations under this section must provide that security may be required only where an officer of Revenue and Customs considers it necessary for the protection of the revenue.

(3) Regulations under this section must provide for a right of appeal against—

(a) decisions to require security to be given;

(b) decisions as to the amount, terms or duration of any security required.

(4) A person commits an offence if—

(a) the person fails to comply with a requirement to give security that is imposed by regulations under this section, and

(b) the failure continues for such period as is prescribed.

(5) A person who commits an offence under subsection (4) is liable on summary conviction—

(a) in England and Wales, to a fine;
(b) in Scotland or Northern Ireland, to a fine not exceeding level 5 on the standard scale.

(6) In this section—

"prescribed" means prescribed in regulations under this section;
"security" includes further security."

(2) In Schedule 18 to FA 1998 (company tax returns, assessments and related matters), after paragraph 88 insert—

"Security for payments

88A (1) The Commissioners for Her Majesty's Revenue and Customs may by regulations make provision for and in connection with requiring the giving, by prescribed persons and in prescribed circumstances, of security for the payment of tax that a company is or may be liable to pay.

(2) Regulations under this paragraph must provide that security may be required only where an officer of Revenue and Customs considers it necessary for the protection of the revenue.

(3) Regulations under this paragraph must provide for a right of appeal against—

(a) decisions to require security to be given;
(b) decisions as to the amount, terms or duration of any security required.

(4) A person commits an offence if—

(a) the person fails to comply with a requirement to give security that is imposed by regulations under this paragraph, and
(b) the failure continues for such period as is prescribed.

(5) A person who commits an offence under sub-paragraph (4) is liable on summary conviction—

(a) in England and Wales, to a fine;
(b) in Scotland or Northern Ireland, to a fine not exceeding level 5 on the standard scale.

(6) In this paragraph—

"prescribed" means prescribed in regulations under this paragraph;
"security" includes further security."

(3) In section 684(4A) of ITEPA 2003 (failure to comply with requirement under PAYE regulations to give security), for "on summary conviction to a fine not exceeding level 5 on the standard scale" substitute

"on summary conviction—

(a) in England and Wales, to a fine;
(b) in Scotland or Northern Ireland, to a fine not exceeding level 5 on the standard scale".

COMMENTARY ON SECTION 82

In cases of significant non-compliance or phoenixism HMRC has the power to require taxpayers to make a security deposit, ie an upfront payment of cash, against future liabilities to tax. This means that if there is a subsequent default HMRC's position is protected because it already holds funds which can be used to meet the liability. Currently the security deposit rules apply to:

- VAT,
- Pay as You Earn (PAYE)
- National Insurance Contributions (NICs),
- Landfill Tax,
- Aggregates Levy,
- Climate Change Levy,
- Insurance Premium Tax and
- certain Gambling Duties.

HMRC issued a consultation document in March 2018 which discussed extending the security deposit regime to payments under the subcontractors' scheme and to corporation tax. Following the consultation a decision was taken to make this extension and s 82 contains the relevant legislation.

Subsection (1)(a) is a minor drafting amendment.

Subsection (1)(b) introduces a new s 70A into FA 2004, Pt 3, Ch 3 (construction industry scheme).

New FA 2004, s 70A: Security for payment to HMRC

Under FA 2004, s 70A(1) HMRC is given the power to make regulations for payments of security in prescribed circumstances.

FA 2004, s 70A(2) states that Regulations must provide that security is only required when an officer of HMRC considers it necessary for the protection of the revenue.

FA 2004, s 70A(3) states that Regulations must give a right of appeal both against the decision to require security and the amount, terms and duration of any such security.

FA 2004, s 70A(4) provides that where a person fails to give security imposed by regulations and the failure continues for a prescribed period that person commits an offence.

Under FA 2004, s 70A(5) a person who commits an offence under (4) above is liable on summary conviction to a fine – in Scotland or Northern Ireland the fine must not exceed level 5 on the standard scale. The effect of this is that the amount of the fine is unlimited.

FA 2004, s 70A(6) states that 'Prescribed' means prescribed under this section; 'security' includes further security.

Subsection (2) introduces a new para 88A into FA 1998, Sch 18, which is the main section dealing with company returns, assessments and related matters.

The provisions of new para 88A are in all material terms identical to those in new s 70A above and no separate commentary on them is required.

Subsection (3) is a separate provision which aligns the maximum fine for failure to comply with PAYE security with the new fines for failure to comply with construction industry scheme or corporation tax security.

Draft regulations for both the construction industry scheme and for corporation tax were published for consultation on 14 January 2019 (https://www.gov.uk/government/consultations/the-income-tax-construction-industry-scheme-amendment-and-the-corporation-tax-security-for-payments-regulations-2019).

They have now been finalised and come into effect 6 April 2019 (SI 2019/384).

International agreements

83 Resolution of double taxation disputes

In Chapter 2 of Part 2 of TIOPA 2010 (double taxation relief: miscellaneous provisions) after section 128 insert—

"International dispute-resolution instruments and agreements

128A Power by regulations to give effect to international obligations etc

(1) The Treasury may make regulations for, or in connection with, giving effect to or enabling effect to be given to—

- (a) Council Directive (EU) 2017/1852 of 10 October 2017 on tax dispute resolution mechanisms in the European Union ("the Directive");
- (b) any instrument modifying or supplementing the Directive;
- (c) any international agreements or arrangements that deal with—
  - (i) matters dealt with by the Directive,
  - (ii) matters that are similar to any of those dealt with by the Directive, or
  - (iii) any other matters that relate to or are connected with the resolution of disputes in relation to double taxation arrangements.

(2) The provision that may be made by regulations under this section includes (in particular)—

- (a) provision as to the effect of any arrangements that the Commissioners for

Her Majesty's Revenue and Customs may make with authorities of territories outside the United Kingdom;

(b) provision conferring or imposing functions, rights or obligations, or authorising the conferral or imposition of functions, rights or obligations, on a person (including a commission, tribunal or court);

(c) provision under which the Commissioners or other persons may exercise discretions;

(d) provision about procedure in relation to the resolution of disputes;

(e) provision about costs, expenses and fees;

(f) provision imposing penalties or creating criminal offences;

(g) provision about appeals;

(h) provision about the form and manner in which, or time within which, things are to be done;

(i) provision supplementing section 128B.

(3) The regulations may—

(a) make provision having effect in relation to periods before the regulations come into force;

(b) make provision by reference to an instrument or document as it has effect from time to time;

(c) make provision about things done, or to be done, in territories outside the United Kingdom;

(d) make different provision for different purposes;

(e) make consequential, incidental, supplemental, transitional, transitory or saving provision;

(f) make provision amending, repealing, revoking or disapplying, or modifying the effect of, any enactment (whenever passed or made).

(4) The regulations may not create a criminal offence punishable on indictment with imprisonment for more than two years.

(5) Regulations under this section containing anything that amends or repeals a provision of primary legislation may not be made unless a draft of the regulations has been laid before, and approved by a resolution of, the House of Commons.

In this subsection "primary legislation" means—

(a) an Act,

(b) an Act of the Scottish Parliament,

(c) a Measure or Act of the National Assembly for Wales, or

(d) Northern Ireland legislation.

(6) In subsections (2) and (3) and sections 128B and 128C, a reference to a commission, tribunal, court or other person includes a reference to a commission, tribunal, court or other person in a territory outside the United Kingdom.

128B Giving effect to requirements under section 128A regulations

(1) Subsection (2) applies if anything in regulations under section 128A requires the Commissioners for Her Majesty's Revenue and Customs to give effect to an agreement, decision or opinion made or given by—

(a) the Commissioners (or their authorised representative),

(b) the competent authority of a territory outside the United Kingdom, or

(c) any commission, tribunal, court or other person.

(2) The Commissioners are to give effect to the agreement, decision or opinion despite anything in any enactment, and any such adjustment as is appropriate in consequence may be made.

(3) An adjustment under subsection (2) may be made by way of discharge or repayment of tax, the allowance of credit against tax payable in the United Kingdom, the making of an assessment or otherwise.

128C Disclosure under international obligations etc

(1) The obligation as to secrecy imposed by any enactment does not prevent—

(a) the Commissioners for Her Majesty's Revenue and Customs,

(b) a person who is or was an authorised Revenue and Customs official,

(c) a person who is or was a member of a committee or other body established by the Commissioners for Her Majesty's Revenue and Customs (or jointly by the Commissioners and an authority of a territory outside the United Kingdom), or

(d) a person specified, or of a description specified, in regulations made by the Treasury,

from disclosing information required to be disclosed under a relevant instrument or agreement in pursuance of a request made by any person.

(2) In this section—

"relevant instrument or agreement" means an instrument, agreement or arrangement referred to, or of a kind referred to, in section 128A(1);

"Revenue and Customs official" means—

(a) a Commissioner for Her Majesty's Revenue and Customs;
(b) an officer of Revenue and Customs;
(c) a person acting on behalf of the Commissioners for Her Majesty's Revenue and Customs;
(d) a person acting on behalf of an officer of Revenue and Customs."

COMMENTARY ON SECTION 83

Section 83 introduces statutory powers to implement the EU directive on tax dispute resolution mechanisms in the European Union and other similar international agreements.

Following a recent review, it was concluded that the mechanisms provided for in bilateral tax treaties and in the EU convention on the elimination of double taxation, known as the EU Arbitration Convention (90/463/EEC), might not result in double taxation disputes being resolved in a timely manner.

As a result, the European Council adopted Council Directive (EU) 2017/1852 on 10 October 2017 regarding tax dispute resolution mechanisms in the EU. The directive seeks to establish an effective regime for the resolution of tax disputes, and to minimise the risk of double taxation for businesses operating across borders.

Member states are required to comply with the provisions of the directive by 30 June 2019. This section sets out enabling provisions to allow the UK Government to achieve this requirement by amending TIOPA 2010, Pt 2, Ch 2, and issuing regulations. These provisions will have effect from the date of Royal Assent.

84 International tax enforcement: disclosable arrangements

(1) The Treasury may, for the purpose of securing compliance with an obligation of the government of the United Kingdom under an international tax provision, make regulations requiring persons who participate in arrangements of a description specified in the regulations to disclose information about those arrangements.

(2) Regulations under this section may—

(a) require information to be disclosed in such form and manner, and at such intervals, as may be specified in the regulations;
(b) require persons to disclose information about arrangements that they participated in before (as well as after) the coming into force of this section;
(c) provide for the imposition of penalties in respect of a contravention of, or non-compliance with, a requirement of the regulations, including provision about appeals in relation to the imposition of a penalty;
(d) make different provision for different purposes.

(3) For the purposes of subsections (1) and (2)—

"arrangements" includes any scheme, transaction or series of transactions;

"participate", in relation to arrangements, includes being involved in, or facilitating, the arrangements in any way (for example, by receiving any benefit from them or by designing, marketing or providing services in connection with them, or arranging for others to do so);

"international tax provision" means any provision of—

(a) any arrangements specified in an Order in Council made under section 173 of FA 2006 (international tax enforcement arrangements), or
(b) Council Directive 2011/16/EU of 15 February 2011 on administrative

cooperation in the field of taxation and repealing Directive 77/799/EEC, as amended from time to time.

(4) Regulations under this section may make consequential, supplementary, incidental, transitional or saving provision (and may do so by amending, repealing or revoking an enactment whenever passed or made).

(5) Regulations under this section are to be made by statutory instrument.

(6) A statutory instrument containing regulations under this section which amend or repeal an enactment contained in an Act may not be made unless a draft of the instrument has been laid before, and approved by resolution of, the House of Commons.

(7) A statutory instrument containing any other regulations under this section is subject to annulment in pursuance of a resolution of the House of Commons.

(8) No regulations may be made under this section unless the Chancellor of the Exchequer has laid before the House of Commons a report on how the powers in this section are to be exercised in each of the scenarios in subsection (9).

(9) The scenarios to be considered in the report under subsection (8) are—

(a) if either—

(i) a negotiated withdrawal agreement, or

(ii) a framework for the future relationship with the European Union,

has not been ratified under section 13 of the European Union (Withdrawal) Act 2018 at the time of the United Kingdom ceasing to be a member of the European Union, and

(b) if both—

(i) a negotiated withdrawal agreement, and

(ii) a framework for the future relationship with the European Union,

have been ratified under section 13 of the European Union (Withdrawal) Act 2018 at the time of the United Kingdom ceasing to be a member of the European Union.

COMMENTARY ON SECTION 84

Section 84 gives HM Treasury a power to make regulations to require disclosure of information about certain cross-border tax arrangements to HMRC to give effect to international rules. These provisions have effect from the date of Royal Assent.

This is in response to the publication of EU directive 2018/882/EU, commonly referred to as 'DAC 6', (amending the 2011 Directive on Administrative Cooperation (2011/16/EU)). The directive requires the disclosure of information on potentially aggressive tax planning cross-border arrangements by intermediaries, or individual or corporate taxpayers, to the relevant tax authorities. For a cross-border arrangement to be notifiable it must meet one of the hallmarks specified in the directive. Notification will need to be made within 30 days and once notified the information will automatically be exchanged between other member states.

The regulations will also permit the implementation of new Organisation for Economic Co-operation and Development (OECD) model mandatory disclosure rules, should the decision be taken to implement those.

Subsections 84(8) and (9) state that any regulations introduced by this section are subject to a report by the Chancellor on the impact of having or not having a negotiated settlement for the withdrawal of the UK from the EU.

Payment of unlawful advance corporation tax

85 Interest in respect of unlawful ACT

(1) This section applies where—

(a) on any date before 12 December 2012, a person started proceedings against the Commissioners in the High Court or the Court of Session,

(b) the proceedings include a claim arising out of a relevant payment, and

(c) the claim has not been settled, discontinued or finally determined.

(2) "Relevant payment" means a payment of unlawful ACT that—

(a) was made by the person on or after 1 January 1996 or in the period of 6 years ending immediately before the date the proceedings were started, and

(b) was set off or repaid (wholly or in part) before the proceedings were started.

(3) The person is entitled to an order requiring the Commissioners to pay to the person—

(a) an amount ("the principal amount") equal to the amount of interest that would have accrued if simple interest had accrued on the relevant payment at the appropriate rate for the period beginning with the date the payment was made and ending with—

(i) the date as regards which the unlawful ACT was set off, or

(ii) the date the unlawful ACT was repaid, and

(b) simple interest at the appropriate rate on the principal amount for the period beginning with the day after the date mentioned in paragraph (a)(i) or (ii) and ending with the date the principal amount is paid.

(4) "The appropriate rate" is, in relation to any day, the rate specified in the following table in respect of that day.

Period	*Rate per year (%)*
1 October 1993 to 31 March 1997	8
1 April 1997 to 5 January 1999	6
6 January 1999 to 5 March 1999	5
6 March 1999 to 5 February 2000	4
6 February 2000 to 5 May 2001	5
6 May 2001 to 5 November 2001	4
6 November 2001 to 5 August 2003	3
6 August 2003 to 5 December 2003	2
6 December 2003 to 5 September 2004	3
6 September 2004 to 5 September 2005	4
6 September 2005 to 5 September 2006	3
6 September 2006 to 5 August 2007	4
6 August 2007 to 5 January 2008	5
6 January 2008 to 5 November 2008	4
6 November 2008 to 5 December 2008	3
6 December 2008 to 5 January 2009	2
6 January 2009 to 26 January 2009	1
27 January 2009 to 29 October 2018	0.5
30 October 2018 onwards	0.5 or such other rate as the Treasury may by regulations specify in respect of a period specified in the regulations

(5) Where the unlawful ACT was repaid, any amount of interest or repayment supplement paid by the Commissioners on the making of the repayment is to be deducted from the principal amount (and subsection (3)(b) has effect accordingly).

(6) Where part of the unlawful ACT has been set off or repaid at one time, and part of it has been set off or repaid at another time or has not been set off or repaid, for the purposes of this section treat each part as a separate payment.

(7) In this section—

"the Commissioners" means the Commissioners for Her Majesty's Revenue and Customs (or, in relation to any time before the commencement of section 5 of the Commissioners for Revenue and Customs Act 2005, the Commissioners of Inland Revenue);

"set off or repaid": references to a payment of unlawful ACT being set off or repaid are—

(a) to it being set against a liability to corporation tax of any person, or

(b) to it being repaid by the Commissioners;

"settled" means settled by agreement;

"unlawful ACT" means advance corporation tax that was unlawfully levied.

(8) The Treasury may by regulations substitute for the date for the time being specified in subsection (1)(a) such later date as they consider appropriate.

(9) Regulations under this section are to be made by statutory instrument.

(10) A statutory instrument containing regulations under this section is subject to annulment in pursuance of a resolution of the House of Commons.

COMMENTARY ON SECTION 85

This may possibly be the final piece of the jigsaw in what has been an extremely long-running dispute over the UK's regime for charging ACT on dividends and its compatibility with European Law. Certain aspects of the ACT regime were found to be incompatible and the question then arose as to whether or not (to simply a highly complex issue of general law) interest on repayments of unlawfully demanded ACT should attract compound interest on the basis that this was a restitutionary remedy for unjust enrichment. In the *Prudential Assurance* case ([2018] UKSC 39, [2018] STC 1657) the Supreme Court decided that there was no right to compound interest but did not determine a method under which interest should be calculated. In order to deal with the uncertainty thus created s 85 sets out a statutory basis under which interest should be calculated on repayments of ACT.

Subsection (1) states that the section applies where a person started proceedings against HMRC in the High Court or Court of Session before 12 December 2012, the proceedings included a claim arising out of a relevant payment and the claim has not been settled, discontinued or finally determined.

Subsection (2) defines a relevant payment as a payment of unlawful ACT that was made on or after 1 January 1996 or in the period of six years before the proceedings were started and was set off or repaid (in whole or in part) before the proceedings started.

Subsection (3) provides that where these conditions apply the person is entitled to an order requiring repayment of amount (described as the principal amount) equal to the amount of simple interest at the appropriate rate for the period from the beginning of the date the relevant payment was made and ending on the date on which the unlawful ACT was set off or repaid. In addition the person is entitled to simple interest at the appropriate rate on the principal amount from the date on which the ACT was set off or repaid until the date on which the principal amount was paid.

There are thus two interest calculations. The first is for the period from the date of the payment of the ACT to the date on which is was set off or repaid. That interest payment is itself then subject to simple interest until it is actually paid to the taxpayer.

Subsection (4) sets out the appropriate rate.

Under sub-s (5), if interest or repayment supplement was paid by HMRC when the unlawful ACT was repaid that amount is deducted from the principal amount (including for the purpose of computing the interest payable on the principal amount). In other words there is no double counting of interest.

Subsection (6) states that where ACT has been repaid (or set off) at different times each such repayment is treated separately for the purpose of calculating the interest due under this section.

Subsection (7) defines certain terms used in this section.

Subsection (8) states that the Treasury may substitute a later date for the date given in sub-s (1)(a) above but does not have power to substitute an earlier date.

Under sub-s (9) Regulations under this section are to be made by statutory instrument.

Subsection (10) stipulates that any statutory instrument under this section is subject to annulment by the House of Commons.

86 Section 85: supplementary

(1) This section supplements section 85.

(2) Nothing in section 85 limits the remedies that a court may award in respect of the claim.

(3) However—

- (a) a person is not entitled to an order under section 85 in respect of a relevant payment if the person has obtained any other relevant remedy in respect of the relevant payment, and
- (b) a person who has obtained an order under section 85 in respect of a relevant payment is not entitled to any other relevant remedy in respect of the relevant payment.

(4) In subsection (3) "relevant remedy" means a remedy for the loss of use of the amount of the relevant payment during the period mentioned in section 85(3)(a) (or during some similar period).

(5) Any interest or repayment supplement paid by the Commissioners on the making of—

(a) a repayment of a relevant payment, or

(b) a repayment of corporation tax occurring as a result of a relevant payment,

is not regarded as a relevant remedy in respect of the relevant payment.

(6) Where the right to bring a claim arising out of a payment of unlawful ACT has been transferred from the person who made the payment ("the payor") to another person ("the successor")—

(a) in section 85(1) the reference to "a person" is to the payor or the successor;

(b) in section 85(2) the reference to "the person" is to the payor;

(c) in section 85(3) the reference to "the person" is to the successor.

(7) Any amount paid by the Commissioners to a person on a day by virtue of section 85 is to be brought into account when calculating, for tax purposes, the profits (or income) of the person for any period which includes that day.

COMMENTARY ON SECTION 86

This section contains provisions supplementing s 85.

Subsection (2) provides that s 85 does not limit the remedies which a court may award in respect of a claim.

Under sub-s (3) Orders under s 85 and other remedies are alternatives. A person who has the benefit of an order under s 85 cannot also pursue an alternative remedy, and vice versa.

Subsection (4) defines a relevant remedy for the purposes of sub-s (3) as a remedy for the loss of the use of the amount of relevant payment during the period mentions in s 85(3)(a) or some similar period.

Subsection (5) makes it clear that any repayment supplement on a relevant payment or on a related repayment of corporation tax is not a relevant remedy. Without this rule a person would not be entitled to repayment supplement because it would fall foul of the rule in sub-s (3) that only one form of remedy can be allowed.

Subsection (6) allows claims to be made by a successor of the person who made the original ACT payment.

Subsection (7) makes it clear that any amount paid under s 85 is a taxable receipt of the period in which the payment was made.

Voluntary returns

87 Voluntary returns

(1) In Part 2 of TMA 1970 (returns of income and gains), after section 12C insert—

"*Voluntary returns*

12D Returns made otherwise than pursuant to a notice

(1) This section applies where—

(a) a person delivers a purported return ("the relevant return") under section 8, 8A or 12AA ("the relevant section") for a year of assessment or other period ("the relevant period"),

(b) no notice under the relevant section has been given to the person in respect of the relevant period, and

(c) HMRC treats the relevant return as a return made and delivered in pursuance of such a notice.

(2) For the purposes of the Taxes Acts—

(a) treat a relevant notice as having been given to the person on the day the relevant return was delivered, and

(b) treat the relevant return as having been made and delivered in pursuance of that notice (and, accordingly, treat it as if it were a return under the relevant section).

(3) "Relevant notice" means—

(a) in relation to section 8 or 8A, a notice under that section in respect of the relevant period;

(b) in relation to section 12AA, a notice under section 12AA(3) requiring the person to deliver a return in respect of the relevant period, on or before the day the relevant return was delivered (or, if later, the earliest day that could be specified under section 12AA).

(4) In subsection (1)(a) "purported return" means anything that—

(a) is in a form, and is delivered in a way, that a corresponding return could have been made and delivered had a relevant notice been given, and

(b) purports to be a return under the relevant section.

(5) Nothing in this section affects sections 34 to 36 or any other provisions of the Taxes Acts specifying a period for the making or delivering of any assessment (including self-assessment) to income tax or capital gains tax."

(2) In Schedule 18 to FA 1998 (company tax returns etc) at the end of Part 2 insert—

"Voluntary returns

20A (1) This paragraph applies where—

(a) a company delivers a purported return ("the relevant return") for a period ("the relevant period"),

(b) no notice under paragraph 3 has been given to the company in respect of the relevant period, and

(c) Her Majesty's Revenue and Customs treats the relevant return as a return made and delivered in pursuance of such a notice.

(2) For the purposes of the Taxes Acts—

(a) treat a relevant notice as having been given to the company on the day the relevant return was delivered, and

(b) treat the relevant return as having been made and delivered in pursuance of that notice (and, accordingly, treat it as if it were a company tax return under paragraph 3).

(3) "Relevant notice" means a notice under paragraph 3 requiring the company to deliver a return for the relevant period.

(4) In sub-paragraph (1)(a) "purported return" means anything that—

(a) is in a form, and is delivered in a way, that a corresponding return could have been made and delivered had a relevant notice been given, and

(b) purports to be a company tax return.

(5) Nothing in this paragraph affects paragraph 46 or any other provisions of the Taxes Acts specifying a time limit for the making of an assessment."

(3) The amendments made by this section are treated as always having been in force.

(4) However, those amendments do not apply in relation to a purported return delivered by a person if, before 29 October 2018—

(a) the person made an appeal under the Taxes Acts, or a claim for judicial review, and

(b) the ground (or one of the grounds) for the making of the appeal or claim was that the purported return was not a return under section 8, 8A or 12AA of TMA 1970 or paragraph 3 of Schedule 18 to FA 1998 because no relevant notice was given.

(5) The Treasury may by regulations—

(a) make such amendments of relevant tax legislation as they consider appropriate in consequence of subsection (1) or (2);

(b) make such amendments of section 12D of TMA 1970 (inserted by subsection (1) of this section) as they consider appropriate in connection with the coming into force of section 61 of, and Schedule 14 to, F(No 2)A 2017 (digital reporting and record keeping for income tax etc).

(6) In subsection (5)(a) "relevant tax legislation" means—

(a) TMA 1970,

(b) Schedule 18 to FA 1998, or

(c) any other enactment relating to income tax, corporation tax or capital gains tax.

(7) Regulations under this section are to be made by statutory instrument.

(8) A statutory instrument containing regulations under this section is subject to annulment in pursuance of a resolution of the House of Commons.

COMMENTARY ON SECTION 87

In a number of recent cases the First-tier tribunal has concluded that a return submitted voluntarily without a notice to file having been issued is not a valid return for the purposes of TMA 1970, s 8. See for example *Patel* ([2018] UKFTT 185 (TC); [2018] SFTD 1000) and *Revell* ([2016] UKFTT 97 (TC), [2016] SFTD 618) HMRC revealed in the latter case that it receives on average 350,000 voluntary returns each year and its practice has always been to treat these as if they had been made in response to a formal notice. Section 87 gives HMRC the legal authority to continue this practice.

Subsection (1) introduces a new TMA 1970, s 12D.

TMA 1970, s 12D(1) states that this section applies where a person delivers a return (described as a 'purported return') under s 8 (individuals), s 8A (trustees) or s 12AA (partnerships) despite no notice for file having been issued by HMRC and HMRC treats the return as if it were made under the relevant notice.

TMA 1970, s 12D(2) provides that for all purposes of the Taxes Acts the person is to be treated as having been given a notice to file on the day that the return was delivered and the return is treated as having been made in response to that notice.

TMA 1970, s 12D(3) defines a relevant notice as a notice under ss 8 or 8A , or in respect of a notice under s 12AA, a notice under s 12AA(3) requiring a person to deliver a return.

TMA 1970, s 12D(4) defines a purported return as one which is in a form that the corresponding return could have been made and delivered if a notice had been given and which purports to be a return under the relevant section. This does in effect mean that the section will only apply when somebody delivers voluntarily a return which corresponds with the official return form – for example by printing off a copy of an official return. A person who simply sends HMRC a letter containing information about his or her tax affairs will not be treated as having made a return under this section.

Under TMA 1970, s 12D(5) this section does not affect the rules within TMA 1970, ss 34–36 or any other provisions of the Taxes Acts specifying the time limit for the making of an assessment, including a self-assessment.

Subsection (2) introduces a new para 20A into FA 1998, Sch 18.

FA 1998, Sch 18, para 20A(1)–(5) mirror new TMA 1970 s 12D(1)–(5) for corporation tax purposes.

Subsection (3) states that the amendments made by this section are treated as always having been in force. Thus the legislation is retrospective back to the introduction of self-assessment in 1996/97.

Under sub-s (4) these amendments do not apply in a case where a person delivered a purported return before 29 October 2018 and that person made an appeal, or a claim for judicial review, on the basis the purported return was not a return under the relevant section because no notice was given. This would mean, for example, that somebody who had submitted a voluntary return before 29 October 2018 would still be able to challenge HMRC's imposition of penalties for late filing.

Subsection (5) provides that The Treasury is given wide powers to make amendments to relevant tax legislation which it considers appropriate in consequence of sub-ss (1) or (2) above, including amendments to TMA 1970, s 12D (digital record keeping).

Subsection (6) defines terms for the purposes of this section. Subsection (7) states that Regulations under this section may be made by statutory instrument. Under sub-s (8), any statutory instrument laid under this section is subject to annulment by a resolution of the House of Commons.

Interest

88 Interest under section 178 of FA 1989 and section 101 of FA 2009

(1) Where, before the day on which this Act is passed—

(a) regulations under subsection (1) of section 178 of FA 1989 provide for a rate of interest for the purposes of an enactment to which that section applies, but
(b) no order was made under subsection (7) of that section appointing a day for that enactment,

the rate has effect for any period of time beginning on or after the day on which the regulations came into force even though no such order was made.

(2) In section 178 of FA 1989 (setting of rates of interest)—

(a) in subsection (2), omit paragraph (u);
(b) in subsection (3)(f), after "provide that" insert "rates or";
(c) omit subsection (7) (but this repeal does not affect any order already made under that subsection).

(3) In Schedule 35 to FA 2014 (promoters of tax avoidance schemes), in paragraph 11 (interest on penalties)—

(a) in sub-paragraph (1), for the words from "at the rate" to the end substitute "in accordance with section 101 of FA 2009";
(b) omit sub-paragraph (2).

(4) In the Taxes (Interest Rate) Regulations 1989 (SI 1989/1297)—

(a) in regulation 3(1), after paragraph (e) insert—

"(f) section 14(4) of the Ports Act 1991 (for any period of time beginning on or after the day on which the Finance Act 2019 is passed), and
(g) paragraph 8 of Schedule 1 to the Employment Act 2002 (for any period of time beginning on or after the day on which the Finance Act 2019 is passed),";

(b) after regulation 5 insert—

"5A Applicable rate of interest for diverted profits tax

For the purposes of section 79 of the Finance Act 2015, the rate applicable under section 178 of the Finance Act 1989 is—

(a) 3% per annum for the period beginning with 1 October 2015 and ending with 5 April 2017, and
(b) 2.5% per annum thereafter."

(5) Regulations under section 178(1) of FA 1989 may revoke or amend the provision made in the Taxes (Interest Rate) Regulations 1989 by subsection (4).

(6) Section 101 of FA 2009 is to be regarded as having come into force on 6 May 2014 for the purposes of—

(a) penalties under paragraphs 6B to 6D of Schedule 55 to FA 2009, in the case of returns falling within item 4 in the Table in paragraph 1 of that Schedule (real time information for PAYE);
(b) penalties under paragraphs 5 to 8 of Schedule 56 to FA 2009, in the case of payments of tax falling within item 2 or 4 of the Table in paragraph 1 of that Schedule (PAYE and CIS amounts);
(c) a penalty under section 208 or 226 of FA 2014 (penalties relating to follower notices, accelerated payment notices and partner payment notices), where the penalty relates to income tax payable under PAYE regulations.

COMMENTARY ON SECTION 88

This section removes the need for an appointed day order to activate interest rates for the various taxes and purposes set out in FA 1989, s 178. Interest can instead be charged from the date the regulations setting the various interest rates come into force.

This applies to those 'enactments' set out in s 178(2) for which an interest rate has been provided by regulations, but an appointed day order has not been made.

This will affect the following enactments set out in s 178(2):

- Stamp Act 1891, s 15A (stamping of instruments after execution)
- TMA 1970, s 87A (interest on overdue corporation tax)
- TCGA 1992, s 283 (repayment supplements)
- TA 1988, s 826 (interest on tax overpaid)

- FA 2003, ss 87, 88, 89 (stamp duty land tax: interest on unpaid tax, penalties and repayments)

This will have the effect of retrospectively setting interest rates. Although the Taxes (Interest Rate) Regulations, SI 1989/1297, which set out the respective rates of interest under FA 1989, s 178, came into force on 18 August 1989, several amending regulations have since been made, suggesting that the effective dates will follow the later regulations.

Interest on late payment of the levy on sale of securities under the Ports Act 1991 and of penalties for failure to comply with disclosure under the Employment Act 2002 are also, from Royal Assent (12 February 2019), added to the list of enactments set out in FA 1989, s 178(2).

This section also makes separate provision for interest in relation to:

- penalties for promoters of tax avoidance schemes, and
- diverted profits tax

Promoters of tax avoidance schemes – interest on penalties is, from Royal Assent (12 February 2019), now governed by the harmonised interest rate regime. Previously it fell within the ambit of FA 1989, s 178.

Diverted profits tax – interest on late paid tax is charged at 2.5% per annum from 6 April 2017 (3% per annum for the period from 1 October 2015 to 5 April 2017).

Finally, the section makes amendments to ensure that interest provisions in relation to certain penalties regarding PAYE are implemented correctly. It has retrospective effect where necessary.

PART 5

MISCELLANEOUS AND FINAL

Regulatory capital securities

89 Regulatory capital securities and hybrid capital instruments

Schedule 20—

(a) makes provision revoking the previous rules that applied in relation to regulatory capital securities, and

(b) makes new provision in relation to hybrid capital instruments.

EU withdrawal

90 Minor amendments in consequence of EU withdrawal

(1) The Treasury may by regulations make such provision as they consider appropriate—

(a) for the purpose of maintaining the effect of any relevant tax legislation on the withdrawal of the United Kingdom from the EU (and, accordingly, on the United Kingdom ceasing to be an EEA state);

(b) for the purposes of any relevant tax, in connection with any provision made by regulations under section 8 of the European Union (Withdrawal) Act 2018 (power to remedy deficiencies);

(c) in connection with any reference in relevant tax legislation to euros;

(d) amending paragraph 2(4) of Schedule 5 to FA 1997 (indirect taxes: overpayments etc) for the purposes of removing the reference to EU legislation;

(e) amending section 173 of FA 2006 (international tax enforcement) to permit the disclosure of information to the Commissioners by other public authorities and by the Commissioners (subject to conditions about its use) to persons outside the United Kingdom.

(2) The regulations may—

(a) amend any enactment;

(b) contain incidental, transitional or saving provision;

(c) make different provision for different purposes.

(3) Where—

(a) regulations under this section are made after exit day, and

(b) a provision of the regulations is made by virtue of any of paragraphs (a) to (d) of subsection (1), the regulations may provide that the provision has effect from exit day.

(4) Regulations under this section are to be made by statutory instrument.

(5) A statutory instrument containing regulations under this section is subject to annulment in pursuance of a resolution of the House of Commons.

(6) In this section—

"the Commissioners" means the Commissioners for Her Majesty's Revenue and Customs;
"enactment" includes an enactment comprised in subordinate legislation;
"relevant tax" means any tax (including stamp duty) except—

(a) value added tax,
(b) any duty of customs, or
(c) any excise duty under the Alcoholic Liquor Duties Act 1979, the Hydrocarbon Oil Duties Act 1979 or the Tobacco Products Duty Act 1979;

"relevant tax legislation" means any enactment relating to a relevant tax.

(7) The provisions of this section only come into force if—

(a) a negotiated withdrawal agreement and a framework for the future relationship have been approved by a resolution of the House of Commons on a motion moved by a Minister of the Crown for the purposes of section 13(1)(b) of the European Union (Withdrawal) Act 2018, or
(b) the Prime Minister has notified the President of the European Council, in accordance with Article 50(3) of the Treaty on European Union, of the United Kingdom's request to extend the period in which the Treaties shall still apply to the United Kingdom, or
(c) leaving the European Union without a withdrawal agreement and a framework for the future relationship has been approved by a resolution of the House of Commons on a motion moved by a Minister of the Crown.

COMMENTARY ON SECTION 90

Section 90 will allow the Treasury to make regulations to amend tax law to reflect the United Kingdom's exit from the EU. The new power will allow 'small, essential changes' to maintain the effect of tax legislation in the event of a no-deal Brexit, the Government said at Budget 2018.

Subsection (1) provides that the Treasury may use the power to make provision in connection with regulations made under European Union (Withdrawal) Act 2018, s 8 (dealing with deficiencies arising from withdrawal); to replace references to euros with references to sterling; to replace a reference to EU legislation in FA 1997, Sch 5, para 2(4) (indirect tax overpayments); and to allow HMRC to continue to exchange information in accordance with FA 2016, s 173.

Subsection (2) provides that the regulations may amend any enactment; contain incidental, transitional or saving provision; or make different provision for different purposes. Subsections (3)–(6) set out commencement provisions and definitions, and provide for the regulations to be made under a statutory instrument subject to annulment under the 'negative procedure'. The new power extends to any 'relevant tax', as defined in subsection (6). VAT and customs duties are excluded.

Robert Jenrick, Exchequer Secretary to the Treasury, stressed in a House of Commons debate on 19 November 2018 that the new power was not being taken in order to do 'anything other than ensure that existing tax legislation continues to have effect in the event of no deal'. It would not be used to change tax policy or the tax paid by taxpayers, he said. The Government published (see https://tinyurl.com/y67m342l) on 27 November 2018 a list of regulations that it intended to make under the new power.

MPs voted on 8 January 2019 to back a cross-party amendment restricting the Treasury's new power. The vote showed MPs' determination to prevent a no-deal Brexit, Labour MP Yvette Cooper said, while the Government argued that the amendment would merely make Britain 'somewhat less prepared' for such an outcome.

The amendment inserted subsection (7), providing that the provisions of section 90 would come into force only if:

(a) MPs approved a negotiated withdrawal agreement and a framework for the future relationship with the EU; or
(b) the Prime Minister requested an extension of the 'article 50' period, which was due to end on 29 March 2019; or
(c) a no-deal Brexit was approved by MPs by means of a House of Commons resolution on a government motion.

During the 8 January debate Cooper noted (http://bit.ly/2U1Biz7) that, in the event of deadlock in the House of Commons, subsection (7)(b) would allow the Government to use the new power. The Prime Minister wrote (http://bit.ly/2I2fS3o) to the President of the European Council on 20 March requesting an extension of the article 50 period to 30 June. The European Council agreed (http://bit.ly/2G325Yj) on 21 March to an extension (a) until 22 May if the House of Commons approved the November 2018 withdrawal agreement by 29 March, or (b) until 12 April (but the Council indicated that it expected the UK to 'indicate a way forward' before 12 April for its consideration). MPs rejected the withdrawal agreement for a third time on 29 March, and at the time of writing they had not reached a consensus on a way forward.

Preparatory expenditure

91 Emissions reduction trading scheme: preparatory expenditure

(1) The Secretary of State may incur expenditure in preparing for the introduction of a scheme for charges to be imposed for the allocation of emissions allowances.

(2) In subsection (1), "emissions allowance" means an allowance under paragraph 5 of Schedule 2 to the Climate Change Act 2008 relating to a trading scheme dealt with under Part 1 of that Schedule (schemes limiting activities relating to emissions of greenhouse gas).

COMMENTARY ON SECTION 91

The introduction of a carbon emissions tax in place of the EU ETS, will give rise to government costs including costs relating to the implementation of processes to allocate emissions allowances for permitted installations. This section allows the Secretary of State to draw in funds to achieve this.

Reviews

92 Impact analyses of the anti-avoidance provisions of this Act

(1) The Chancellor of the Exchequer must review the impact of—

(a) section 15 and Schedule 3,
(b) section 16 and Schedule 4,
(c) sections 19 and 20,
(d) section 22 and Schedule 7,
(e) section 23 and Schedule 8,
(f) sections 47 and 48, and
(g) section 84,

of this Act in accordance with this section and lay a report of that review before the House of Commons within six months of the passing of this Act.

(2) A review under this section must consider the impact of those provisions on—

(a) child poverty,
(b) households at different levels of income,
(c) people with protected characteristics (within the meaning of the Equality Act 2010), and
(d) different parts of the United Kingdom and different regions of England.

(3) In this section—

"parts of the United Kingdom" means—

(a) England,
(b) Scotland,
(c) Wales, and
(d) Northern Ireland;

"regions of England" has the same meaning as that used by the Office for National Statistics.

COMMENTARY ON SECTION 92

Section 92 requires the Chancellor to review the impact of specified provisions of FA 2019, most of which deal with international matters, and report to MPs on the outcome of that review within six months of Royal Assent. The review must consider the impact of those provisions on child poverty; households at different levels of income; people with protected characteristics within the meaning of the anti-discrimination provisions in Equality Act 2010; and the nations and regions of the United Kingdom. The provisions are:

- s 15, Sch 3 – offshore receipts in respect of intangible property;
- s 16, Sch 4 – avoidance involving profit fragmentation arrangements;
- ss 19, 20 – hybrid and other mismatches, and controlled foreign companies;
- s 22, Sch 7 – payment of CGT exit charges;
- s 23, Sch 8 – corporation tax exit charges;
- ss 46, 47 – changes to periods for delivering returns etc, and stamp duty;
- s 83 – resolution of double taxation disputes.

The Labour Party tabled this measure, as new clause 5 to the Bill, in November 2018. While the Government did not oppose it, Financial Secretary to the Treasury Mel Stride noted that tax information and impact notes published alongside the measures 'already set out the impact of anti-avoidance measures in the Bill on those sharing protected characteristics'. Labour MP Anneliese Dodds, however, said the clause was directed at the distributional impact of the tax measures, which she described as a 'government blank spot'. Dodds said an equality impact assessment was necessary because of 'the continuing leakage from our tax system owing to avoidance as well as evasion'. A failure to deal with avoidance, she argued, 'has put pressure on the rest of the tax system, which … has been exacerbated by unnecessary tax cuts to the very best-off people and to profitable corporations'.

HMRC and HM Treasury published on 13 March two reports 'fulfilling the obligations' under ss 92 and 93. The reviews, set out in annex B of a joint document 'Tackling tax avoidance, evasion and other forms of non-compliance', (see https://tinyurl.com/y2yhbct9) were published before some of the provisions took effect, prompting the ICAEW Tax Faculty to observe (http://bit.ly/2IgSKgP) that MPs would be 'disappointed in this response: by reporting on the measures before they have been introduced, the Chancellor has outwitted them'.

93 Review of effectiveness of provisions on tax avoidance

(1) The Chancellor of the Exchequer must review the effectiveness of the provisions of this Act relating to tax avoidance and lay a report of that review before the House of Commons within six months of the passing of this Act.

(2) In this section, "the provisions of this Act relating to tax avoidance" means—

(a) section 15 and Schedule 3,
(b) section 16 and Schedule 4,
(c) sections 19 and 20,
(d) section 22 and Schedule 7,
(e) section 23 and Schedule 8,
(f) sections 47 and 48,
(g) section 84.

(3) A review under this section must consider in particular—

(a) the effects of those provisions in reducing tax avoidance and evasion,
(b) the effect of those provisions in inducing new tax avoidance measures unanticipated by the Act, and
(c) estimates of the efficacy of the provisions in reducing the tax gap in each tax year from 2018–19 to 2028–29.

COMMENTARY ON SECTION 93

Section 93 requires the Chancellor to review the effectiveness of several provisions of FA 2019, and report to MPs on the outcome of that review within six months of Royal Assent. The review must consider in particular the effects of those provisions in reducing tax avoidance and evasion; the effect of those provisions in 'inducing new tax avoidance measures unanticipated by the Act'; and estimates of the efficacy of the provisions in reducing the tax gap in each tax year from 2018/19 to 2028/29. The provisions are those subject to the section 92 review:

- s 15, Sch 3 – offshore receipts in respect of intangible property;
- s 16, Sch 4 – avoidance involving profit fragmentation arrangements;
- ss 19, 20 – hybrid and other mismatches, and controlled foreign companies;
- s 22, Sch 7 – payment of CGT exit charges;
- s 23, Sch 8 – corporation tax exit charges;
- ss 46, 47 – changes to periods for delivering returns etc, and stamp duty;
- s 83 – resolution of double taxation disputes.

The Scottish National Party tabled this measure, as new clause 14 to the Bill, in November 2018. The Government did not oppose it, even though Financial Secretary to the Treasury Mel Stride said the review was unnecessary. 'The Government keeps all taxes under review and will continue to measure and publish annual statistics on the tax gap,' he said.

See the commentary under s 92 regarding the Government's reviews published on 13 March, stated to be 'fulfilling the obligations' under ss 92 and 93.

94 Review of public health effects of gaming provisions

(1) The Chancellor of the Exchequer must review the public health effects of the provisions of section 62 of and Schedule 19 to this Act and lay a report of that review before the House of Commons within six months of the passing of this Act.

(2) A review under this section must consider—

(a) the effects of those provisions in reducing the negative public health effects of gambling, and

(b) the implications for the public finances of the public health effects of—

(i) those provisions,

(ii) the operation of the law relating to remote gaming duty and gaming duty if those provisions were not given effect.

COMMENTARY ON SECTION 94

Section 94 requires the Chancellor to review the impact of specified provisions of FA 2019 and report to MPs on the outcome of that review within six months of Royal Assent. The review must consider the public health effects of gaming provisions with particular reference to the effects of those provisions with regards to:

- reducing the negative public health effects of gambling, and
- the implications for the public finances of the public health effects of those provisions and the operation of the law relating to remote gaming duty and gaming duty if those provisions were not given effect.

The provisions are:

Section 62 – Remote gaming duty: rate

Schedule 19 – Gaming Duty.

95 Review of changes made by sections 80 and 81

(1) The Chancellor of the Exchequer must review the effects of the changes made by sections 80 and 81 to TMA 1970 and IHTA 1984, and lay a report on that review before the House of Commons not later than 30 March 2019.

(2) The review under this section must include a comparison of the time limit on proceedings for the recovery of lost tax that involves an offshore matter with other time limits on proceedings for the recovery of lost tax, including, but not limited to, those provided for by Schedules 11 and 12 to the F(No 2)A 2017.

(3) The review under this section must also consider the extent to which provisions equivalent to section 36A(7)(b) of TMA 1970 (relating to reasonable expectations) apply to the application of other time limits.

COMMENTARY ON SECTION 95

Although this section refers to changes made by ss 80 and 81 it is really about the loan charge introduced in F(No 2)A 2017. During the final stages of the Finance Bill process many MPs expressed concerns about the effect of the loan charge, and in particular the fact that it appeared to operate retrospectively, in that it brought into charge loans from Employee Benefit Trusts and similar structures which had been made many years ago, often at a time when the normal assessing time limits would have prevented assessment being raised. MPs drew a comparison between the new offshore time limit of 12 years in ss 80 and 81 of this Act and the fact that the loan charge applies to loans made up to 20 years ago (the cut-off date being 6 April 1999). The Minister did not accept that the legislation was retrospective but agreed to accept this new section, which requires a review to be made, into the Act. Because the loan charge was not legislated for in this Finance Act the normal conventions of Parliamentary procedure meant that a review of the charge could not be included in the Act on a stand-alone basis. This is why the section requires a review of ss 80 and 81 to be made and for the review to compare the operation of those sections with the operation of the time limits applying to the loan charge.

Subsection (1) provides that the Chancellor is required to review the effects of the changes made by s 80 and s 81and lay a report of that review before the House of Commons by 30 March 2019.

Subsection (2) states that the review must include a comparison of the time limits for the recovery of tax related to offshore matters in the above section with other time limits that apply to the recovery of lost taxes, in particular, though not restricted to, the time limits applying to the loan charge.

Under sub-s (3) the review must also consider the extent to which provisions equivalent to TMA 1970, s 36A(7)(b) apply to the application of other time limits. That section is the provision within the new 12-year time limit for offshore matters which prevents an assessment being made within those limits if HMRC could reasonably have been expected to become aware of the lost tax or if it was reasonable to expect an assessment to be made before that time limit. What lies behind this particular subsection is concerns that in some cases HMRC was well aware of loan arrangements but did nothing within normal time limits to challenge their effectiveness and therefore it is wrong in principle for HMRC to have a second bite of the cherry by invoking the loan charge. At the time of writing the Chancellor has not published the review.

Other

96 Interpretation

In this Act the following abbreviations are references to the following Acts.

ALDA 1979	Alcoholic Liquor Duties Act 1979
CAA 2001	Capital Allowances Act 2001
CTA 2009	Corporation Tax Act 2009
CTA 2010	Corporation Tax Act 2010
FA, followed by a year	Finance Act of that year
F(No 2)A, followed by a year	Finance (No 2) Act of that year
F(No 3)A, followed by a year	Finance (No 3) Act of that year
IHTA 1984	Inheritance Tax Act 1984
ITA 2007	Income Tax Act 2007
ITEPA 2003	Income Tax (Earnings and Pensions) Act 2003
ITTOIA 2005	Income Tax (Trading and Other Income) Act 2005
OTA 1975	Oil Taxation Act 1975
TCGA 1992	Taxation of Chargeable Gains Act 1992
TIOPA 2010	Taxation (International and Other Provisions) Act 2010
TMA 1970	Taxes Management Act 1970
TPDA 1979	Tobacco Products Duty Act 1979
VATA 1994	Value Added Tax Act 1994
VERA 1994	Vehicle Excise and Registration Act 1994

97 Short title

This Act may be cited as the Finance Act 2019.

SCHEDULE 1

CHARGEABLE GAINS ACCRUING TO NON-RESIDENTS ETC

Section 13

PART 1

EXTENDING CASES IN WHICH NON-RESIDENTS ARE CHARGED TO TAX ETC

1 TCGA 1992 is amended as follows.

2 For the sections contained in Part 1 substitute—

"PART 1

CAPITAL GAINS TAX AND CORPORATION TAX ON CHARGEABLE GAINS

Chapter 1

Capital Gains Tax

Charge to capital gains tax

1 Capital gains tax

(1) Capital gains tax is charged for a tax year on chargeable gains accruing in the year to a person on the disposal of assets.

(2) As a result of section 4 of CTA 2009, capital gains tax is not charged on gains accruing to a company, but corporation tax is chargeable instead in accordance with—

(a) section 2 of CTA 2009,

(b) Chapter 2 of this Part, and

(c) other relevant provisions of the Corporation Tax Acts.

(3) Capital gains tax is charged on the total amount of chargeable gains accruing to a person in a tax year after deducting—

(a) any allowable losses accruing to the person in the tax year, and

(b) so far as not previously deducted under this subsection, any allowable losses accruing to the person in any previous tax year.

Territorial scope of charge

1A Territorial scope

(1) A person who is UK resident for a tax year is chargeable to capital gains tax on chargeable gains accruing to the person in the tax year on the disposal of assets wherever situated.

(2) In the case of individuals who are UK resident for a tax year, see also—

(a) Schedule 1 (foreign gains accruing to individuals to whom the remittance basis applies),

(b) section 1G (cases where the tax year is a split year),

(c) sections 1M and 1N (temporary periods of non-residence),

(d) Chapter 3 (gains of non-UK resident close companies attributed to individuals), and

(e) sections 86, 87, 87K, 87L and 89(2) (gains of non-UK resident trustees attributed to individuals).

(3) A person who is not UK resident for a tax year is chargeable to capital gains tax on chargeable gains accruing to the person in the tax year on the disposal of—

(a) assets situated in the United Kingdom that have a relevant connection to the person's UK branch or agency and are disposed of at a time when the person has that branch or agency (see section 1B),

(b) assets not within paragraph (a) that are interests in UK land (see section 1C), and

(c) assets (wherever situated) not within paragraph (a) or (b) that derive at least 75% of their value from UK land where the person has a substantial indirect interest in that land (see section 1D and Schedule 1A).

(4) For the purposes of this Chapter a person is "UK resident" for a tax year if the person is resident in the United Kingdom during any part of the tax year.

(5) For the relevant residence rules—

(a) in the case of individuals, see Schedule 45 to the Finance Act 2013 (which provides that individuals meeting the applicable tests for a tax year are taken to be resident for the whole of the year),

(b) in the case of the personal representatives of deceased individuals, see section 62(3), and

(c) in the case of trustees of settlements, see section 69.

1B Non-UK residents: UK branch or agency

(1) For the purposes of section 1A(3)(a) a person has a UK branch or agency at any time if, at that time, the person carries on a trade, profession or vocation in the United Kingdom through a branch or agency there.

(2) For the purposes of section 1A(3)(a) an asset has a relevant connection to a person's UK branch or agency if—

(a) it is, or was, used in or for the purposes of the trade, profession or vocation at or before the time of the disposal,

(b) it is, or was, used or held for the purposes of the branch or agency at or before that time, or

(c) it is acquired for use by or for the purposes of the branch or agency.

(3) Section 1A(3)(a) does not apply to a person who, as a result of Part 2 of TIOPA 2010 (double taxation arrangements), is exempt from income tax for the tax year in respect of the profits or gains of the branch or agency.

(4) In the case of a profession or vocation carried on by a person, an asset does not have a relevant connection to the person's UK branch or agency if—

(a) the asset was only used in or for the purposes of the profession or vocation before 14 March 1989, or

(b) the asset was only used or held for the purposes of the branch or agency before that date.

(5) In this Act, unless the context otherwise requires, "branch or agency"—

(a) means any factorship, agency, receivership, branch or management, but

(b) does not include any person within any of the exemptions under sections 835G to 835K of ITA 2007 (persons who are not UK representatives).

1C Non-UK residents: disposing of an "interest in UK land"

(1) For the purposes of section 1A(3)(b) an "interest in UK land" means—

(a) an estate, interest, right or power in or over land in the United Kingdom, or

(b) the benefit of an obligation, restriction or condition affecting the value of an estate, interest, right or power in or over land in the United Kingdom,

other than an excluded interest.

(2) The following interests are "excluded interests"—

(a) any interest or right held for securing the payment of money or the performance of any other obligation,

(b) a licence to use or occupy land,

(c) in England and Wales or Northern Ireland, a tenancy at will or an advowson, franchise or manor, and

(d) such other descriptions of interest or right in relation to land in the United Kingdom as may be specified in regulations made by the Treasury.

(3) An interest or right is not within subsection (2)(a) if it is—

(a) a rentcharge, or

(b) in Scotland, a feu duty or a payment mentioned in section 56(1) of the Abolition of Feudal Tenure etc (Scotland) Act 2000.

(4) The grant of an option by a person binding the person to dispose of an interest in UK land is (so far as it would not otherwise be the case) regarded as a disposal of an interest in UK land by the person for the purposes of section 1A(3)(b).

(5) This does not affect the operation of section 144 in relation to the grant of the option (or otherwise).

(6) In this section—

"franchise" means a grant from the Crown such as the right to hold a market or fair, or the right to take tolls, and

"land" includes—

(a) buildings and structures, and

(b) land under the sea or otherwise covered by water.

1D Non-UK residents: assets deriving 75% of value from UK land etc

(1) For the purposes of section 1A(3)(c) the following questions are determined in accordance with the provision made by Schedule 1A—

(a) whether the asset being disposed of derives at least 75% of its value from UK land, and

(b) whether the person making the disposal has a substantial indirect interest in the UK land at the time of the disposal.

(2) The provision made by Schedule 1A is not to be taken as affecting the meaning of "substantial" in other contexts.

Deduction of allowable losses

1E Losses deductible only when within scope of tax etc

(1) A loss is not an allowable loss if it accrues in a tax year at a time when, had a gain accrued instead, the gain would not have been chargeable to capital gains tax under this Act for the tax year (and see also sections 16(2) and 16A).

(2) In addition, the only allowable losses that qualify for deduction from chargeable gains under section 1A(3) (non-UK residents) are those accruing to the person on disposals of assets within that subsection.

(3) An allowable loss counts for the purposes of subsection (2) even if it accrues in a tax year in which the person was UK resident.

(4) No allowable losses may be deducted from chargeable gains treated as accruing to an individual as a result of section 87, 87K, 87L or 89(2) (read, where appropriate, with section 1M).

(5) If—

(a) amounts (or elements of amounts) treated as accruing to an individual as a result of section 86 relate to different settlements, and

(b) the deduction of allowable losses does not reduce the amounts or elements to nil,

the deduction applicable to each amount is the proportion that the amount concerned bears to the total of the amounts.

(6) The deduction of allowable losses also has effect subject to Schedule 1 (UK resident individuals not domiciled in UK).

(7) For the only case in which an allowable loss accruing in a tax year may be carried back to an earlier tax year, see section 62 (death).

1F Allowable losses to be used in most beneficial way etc

(1) Allowable losses may (subject to express provision to the contrary) be deducted from gains in whichever way is most beneficial to a person chargeable to capital gains tax.

(2) Accordingly, an allowable loss may be deducted from a chargeable gain irrespective of the rate of tax at which the gain would otherwise have been charged.

(3) Allowable losses that are deducted from gains may not be deducted any further than is necessary to eliminate the gains.

(4) No part of an allowable loss may be relieved under this Act more than once.

(5) So far as an amount has been relieved under the Income Tax Acts, it may not be further relieved under this Act.

UK resident individuals with split tax years

1G Gains accruing to UK resident individuals in split years

(1) If, as respects any individual, a tax year is a split year, sections 1A(1) and 1E have effect subject to the modifications made by this section.

(2) Gains accruing to the individual in the overseas part of the tax year are chargeable to capital gains tax only if they accrue on the disposal of assets within section 1A(3).

(3) Losses are deductible from gains accruing to the individual in the overseas part of the tax year on the disposal of assets within section 1A(3)(b) or (c) only if the losses accrue to the individual on the disposal of—

(a) assets that are within section 1A(3)(b) or (c), or
(b) assets that would be within section 1A(3)(b) or (c) if they did not have a relevant connection to the individual's UK branch or agency.

(4) But losses accruing in the overseas part of the tax year on disposals of assets within section 1A(3)(b) or (c) are (so far as not deducted as mentioned in subsection (3)) deductible from gains accruing in the UK part of the tax year.

Rates of CGT

1H The main rates of CGT

(1) This section makes provision about the rates at which capital gains tax is charged but has effect subject to—

(a) section 169N (entrepreneurs' relief: rate of 10%), and
(b) section 169VC (investors' relief: rate of 10%).

(2) Chargeable gains accruing in a tax year to an individual that are—

(a) residential property gains (see Schedule 1B), or
(b) carried interest gains (see subsections (9) to (11)),

are charged to capital gains tax at a rate of 18% or 28%.

(3) Other chargeable gains accruing in a tax year to an individual are charged to capital gains tax at a rate of 10% or 20%.

(4) The question as to which of the rates applies to the gains concerned is determined by section 1I (income taxed at higher rates or gains exceeding unused basic rate band).

(5) Chargeable gains accruing in a tax year to the personal representatives of a deceased individual that are—

(a) residential property gains, or
(b) carried interest gains,

are charged to capital gains tax at a rate of 28%.

(6) Other chargeable gains accruing in a tax year to the personal representatives of a deceased individual are charged to capital gains tax at a rate of 20%.

(7) Residential property gains accruing in a tax year to the trustees of a settlement are charged to capital gains tax at a rate of 28%.

(8) Other chargeable gains accruing in a tax year to the trustees of a settlement are charged to capital gains tax at a rate of 20%.

(9) For the purposes of this section chargeable gains are "carried interest gains" if they accrue to an individual ("X")—

(a) under section 103KA(2) or (3) (investment management services), or
(b) as a result of carried interest arising to X under arrangements not involving a partnership under which X performs investment management services directly or indirectly in respect of an investment scheme.

(10) A gain is not a carried interest gain under subsection (9)(b) if the carried interest constitutes a co-investment repayment or return.

(11) Expressions used in subsection (9) or (10) have the same meaning as they have in Chapter 5 of Part 3.

1I Income taxed at higher rates or gains exceeding unused basic rate band

(1) If any of an individual's income for a tax year is chargeable to income tax at a higher income tax rate, gains accruing to the individual in the tax year are charged—

(a) at the rate of 28%(if they are residential property gains or carried interest gains), or
(b) at the rate of 20% (if they are other kinds of gains).

(2) If—

(a) none of an individual's income for a tax year is chargeable to income tax at a higher income tax rate, but
(b) the individual is chargeable to capital gains tax for the tax year on an amount that exceeds the unused part of the individual's basic rate band,

the excess ("the higher rate excess") is charged at the rate of 28%(so far as comprising residential property gains or carried interest gains) or at the rate of 20% (so far as comprising other kinds of gains).

(3) The remainder of this section sets out special rules which apply depending on the nature of the gains within subsection (2)(b).

(4) If—

(a) the gains consist of or include gains ("entrepreneur or investor gains") chargeable at the rate of 10% under section 169N(3) or 169VC(2), and
(b) the total amount of the entrepreneur or investor gains exceeds the unused part of the individual's basic rate band,

that unused part is used fully against those gains.

(5) The effect of so doing is that other gains comprised in the higher rate excess are then charged—

(a) at the rate of 28%(if they are residential property gains or carried interest gains), or
(b) at the rate of 20% (if they are other kinds of gains).

(6) If the total amount of the entrepreneur or investor gains does not exceed the unused part of the individual's basic rate band—

(a) so much of that unused part as is equal to that total amount is used against those gains, and
(b) accordingly, the higher rate excess consists only of gains other than entrepreneur or investor gains.

(7) The individual may allocate so much of the unused part of the individual's basic rate band as then remains to—

(a) any residential property gains or carried interest gains, or
(b) any other gains.

(8) The effect of the allocation is that the gains to which the allocation is made are charged—

(a) at the rate of 18%(if they are residential property gains or carried interest gains), or
(b) at the rate of 10% (if they are other kinds of gains).

(9) Any gains to which no allocation is made are charged—

(a) at the rate of 28%(if they are residential property gains or carried interest gains), or
(b) at the rate of 20% (if they are other kinds of gains).

1J Section 1I: definitions and other supplementary provision

(1) For the purposes of section 1I—

a "higher income tax rate" means—

(a) the higher rate or the default higher rate,
(b) the savings higher rate, or
(c) the dividend upper rate, and

"the unused part of the individual's basic rate band" means the amount by which the basic rate limit exceeds the individual's Step 3 income.

(2) If an individual is entitled to relief for a tax year under section 539 of ITTOIA 2005 (contracts for life insurance) by reference to the amount of a deficiency, the individual's Step 3 income for the tax year is treated for the purposes of this section as reduced by the amount of the deficiency.

(3) If, as a result of section 669(1) and (2) of ITTOIA 2005 (inheritance tax on accrued income), there is a reduction in the residuary income of an estate for a tax year that reduces an individual's income by any amount, the individual's Step 3 income for the tax year is treated for the purposes of this section as reduced by the amount of that reduction in the individual's income.

(4) If an individual has life insurance gains for a tax year, the individual's Step 3 income for the tax year is treated for the purposes of this section as if the amount of those gains were limited to—

(a) the annual equivalent within the meaning of section 536(1) of ITTOIA 2005, or

(b) the total annual equivalent within the meaning of section 537 of that Act,

as the case may be.

(5) If—

(a) an individual has life insurance gains for a tax year,

(b) relief is given under section 535 of ITTOIA 2005 for the tax year, and

(c) the calculation under section 536(1) or 537 of that Act for the tax year does not involve the higher rate,

the individual is treated for the purposes of section 1I as if none of the individual's income were chargeable to income tax at the higher rate, the default higher rate or the dividend upper rate.

(6) In the application of section 1I in the case of any individual it is to be assumed that the individual is not a Scottish or Welsh taxpayer.

(7) In this section—

"the individual's Step 3 income" means so much of the individual's total income for the tax year as is left after taking Step 3 under section 23 of ITA 2007 (income tax liability calculation), and

"life insurance gains", in relation to an individual, means the amount or amounts treated as the individual's income as a result of section 465 of ITTOIA 2005 (gains from contracts for life insurance).

(8) Expressions used in this section which have a meaning when used in the Income Tax Acts have the same meaning in this section.

Annual exempt amount

1K Annual exempt amount

(1) If an individual is (or, apart from this section, would be) chargeable to capital gains tax for a tax year on chargeable gains, the annual exempt amount for the year is to be deducted from those gains (but no further than necessary to eliminate them).

(2) The annual exempt amount for a tax year is £12,000.

(3) The annual exempt amount may not be deducted from chargeable gains to which paragraph 2 of Schedule 1 applies (foreign gains of non-UK domiciled individuals accruing in one year and remitted in later year).

(4) The deduction of the annual exempt amount—

(a) is made after the deduction of allowable losses accruing in the tax year, but

(b) is made before the deduction of allowable losses accruing in a previous tax year or, if section 62 applies, in a subsequent tax year.

(5) The annual exempt amount may be deducted from gains in whatever way is most beneficial to a person chargeable to capital gains tax (irrespective of the rate of tax at which the gains would otherwise have been charged).

(6) An individual is not entitled to an annual exempt amount for a tax year if section 809B of ITA 2007 (claim for remittance basis) applies to the individual for the year.

(7) For the tax year in which an individual dies and for the next two tax years, this section applies to the individual's personal representatives as if references to the individual were to those personal representatives.

(8) This section applies in relation to trustees in accordance with the provision made by Schedule 1C.

1L Increasing annual exempt amount to reflect increases in CPI

(1) If the consumer prices index for the September before the start of a tax year is higher than it was for the previous September—

(a) the annual exempt amount is increased by the same percentage as the rise in that index (rounded up to the nearest £100), and

(b) section 1K(2) has effect for the tax year (and subsequent tax years) as if it referred to the increased amount.

(2) If, as a result of this section, the annual exempt amount for a tax year increases, the Treasury must before the start of the tax year make an order showing the increased amount.

Temporary periods of non-residence

1M Temporary non-residents

(1) If, in the case of the disposal of an asset by an individual who is temporarily non-resident—

(a) a gain or loss accrues to the individual in the temporary period of non-residence, and
(b) the asset is not excluded from this subsection by section 1N (certain assets acquired in that period),

the gain or loss is treated instead as accruing to the individual in the period of return.

(2) If—

(a) a gain is, as a result of subsection (1), treated as accruing to an individual in a tax year for which the remittance basis applies to the individual,
(b) the tax year consists of or includes the period of return, and
(c) the gain was remitted to the United Kingdom in the temporary period of non-residence,

the gain is treated instead as remitted to the United Kingdom in the period of return.

(3) If—

(a) an individual is temporarily non-resident, and
(b) a gain would, as a result of section 86, have accrued to the individual in a tax year falling wholly or partly in the temporary period of non-residence if the individual had been resident in the United Kingdom for that year,

the gain is treated instead as accruing to the individual in the period of return (but see also section 86A).

(4) Nothing in any double taxation arrangements prevents a charge to capital gains tax arising as a result of this section.

(5) Nothing in this section is to affect a gain or loss which, apart from this section, would be chargeable to capital gains tax or would be an allowable loss.

(6) For the purposes of this section each of the following expressions has the meaning given by Part 4 of Schedule 45 to the Finance Act 2013 (statutory residence test: anti-avoidance)—

"the period of return"
"temporarily non-resident"
"the temporary period of non-residence".

(7) In this section the reference to "the remittance basis" applying to an individual for a tax year is to section 809B, 809D or 809E of ITA 2007 applying to the individual for the year.

1N Section 1M(1): assets acquired in temporary period of non-residence

(1) An asset is excluded from section 1M(1) if—

(a) it was acquired by the individual in the temporary period of non-residence,
(b) the acquisition was otherwise than by means of a disqualifying no gain/no loss disposal,
(c) there is no reduction in the consideration for the acquisition under section 23(4)(b) or (5)(b), 152(1)(b), 153(1)(b), 162(3)(b) or 247(2)(b) or (3)(b) by reference to a UK resident disposal, and
(d) the asset is not an interest created by or arising under a settlement.

(2) This exclusion does not apply in the case of an asset ("the new asset") if—

(a) on a disposal of the new asset a gain or loss is treated as a result of 116(10) or (11), 134 or 154(2) or (4) as accruing (ignoring section 1M),
(b) the gain or loss is calculated by reference to another asset ("the old asset"), and

(c) the new asset is one that meets the conditions for exclusion but the old asset does not.

(3) For the purposes of this section "a UK resident disposal" means a disposal by a person ("P") of an asset which was acquired by P at a time when—

(a) P was resident in the United Kingdom, and
(b) P was not Treaty non-resident.

(4) For the purposes of this section "a disqualifying no gain/no loss disposal" means a UK resident disposal to which section 58, 73 or 258(4) applies.

Interpretation

1O Definitions used in Chapter

In this Chapter any reference to a person who is, or is not, "UK resident" is to be read in accordance with section 1A(4).

Chapter 2

Corporation Tax on Chargeable Gains

Corporation tax on chargeable gains: the general scheme

2 Corporation tax on chargeable gains

(1) As a result of section 2(1) and (2) of CTA 2009, corporation tax is charged on chargeable gains accruing to a company on the disposal of assets.

(2) The charge to corporation tax on chargeable gains has effect in accordance with this Act and all other relevant provisions of the Corporation Tax Acts.

2A Company's total profits to include chargeable gains

(1) The amount of chargeable gains to be included in a company's total profits for an accounting period is the total amount of chargeable gains accruing to the company in the period after deducting—

(a) any allowable losses accruing to the company in the period, and
(b) so far as not previously deducted under this subsection, any allowable losses previously accruing to the company while it was within the charge to corporation tax.

(2) For the purposes of corporation tax on gains "allowable loss" does not include a loss accruing to a company if, had a gain accrued, the company would not have been chargeable to corporation tax on the gain.

Territorial scope

2B Territorial scope of charge to corporation tax on chargeable gains

(1) A company which is resident in the United Kingdom in an accounting period is chargeable to corporation tax on chargeable gains accruing to the company in the period on the disposal of assets wherever situated.

(2) This is subject to Chapter 3A of Part 2 of CTA 2009 (exemption from charge in respect of profits of foreign permanent establishments).

(3) A company which is not resident in the United Kingdom is chargeable to corporation tax on chargeable gains that—

(a) accrue to the company on the disposal of assets situated in the United Kingdom that have a relevant connection to the company's UK permanent establishment (see section 2C),
(b) accrue at a time when it has that permanent establishment, and
(c) are, in accordance with sections 20 to 32 of CTA 2009, attributable to that permanent establishment.

(4) In addition, a company which is not resident in the United Kingdom is chargeable to corporation tax on chargeable gains accruing to the company on the disposal of assets not within subsection (3) that are—

(a) interests in UK land, or

(b) assets (wherever situated) not within paragraph (a) that derive at least 75% of their value from UK land where the company has a substantial indirect interest in that land.

(5) Section 1C applies for the purposes of subsection (4)(a) as it applies for the purposes of section 1A(3)(b) (disposing of interests in UK land).

(6) The reference in subsection (4)(b) to assets deriving at least 75% of their value from UK land where the company has a substantial indirect interest in that land is to be read in accordance with Schedule 1A.

2C Non-UK resident company with UK permanent establishment

(1) For the purposes of section 2B(3) a company has a UK permanent establishment at any time if, at that time, the company carries on a trade in the United Kingdom through a permanent establishment there.

(2) For the purposes of section 2B(3) an asset has a relevant connection to a company's UK permanent establishment if—

(a) it is, or was, used in or for the purposes of the trade at or before the time of the disposal,

(b) it is, or was, used or held for the purposes of the permanent establishment at or before that time, or

(c) it is acquired for use by or for the purposes of the permanent establishment.

(3) Section 2B(3) does not apply to a company which, as a result of Part 2 of TIOPA 2010 (double taxation arrangements), is exempt from corporation tax for the accounting period in respect of the profits of the permanent establishment.

(4) In the case of the long-term business of an overseas life insurance company, subsection (2) has effect as if for paragraph (b) there were substituted—

"(b) it is, or was, used or held for the purposes of the permanent establishment at or before that time (irrespective of where it is situated at that time),".

(5) In this section references to a trade include an office and references to carrying on a trade include holding an office.

Application of CGT principles etc

2D Application of CGT principles in calculating gains and losses

(1) The total amount of chargeable gains to be included in a company's total profits for an accounting period is calculated for corporation tax purposes in accordance with capital gains tax principles.

(2) All of the following questions are determined in accordance with the enactments relating to capital gains tax as if accounting periods were tax years—

(a) any question as to the amounts to be, or not to be, taken into account as chargeable gains or allowable losses,

(b) any question as to the amounts to be, or not to be, taken into account in calculating gains or losses,

(c) any question as to the amounts charged to tax as a company's gains, and

(d) any question as to the time when any amount is treated as accruing.

(3) This section is subject to any provision made elsewhere by the Corporation Tax Acts.

2E References to income tax or Income Tax Acts in case of companies

(1) If the CGT enactments contain any reference to—

(a) income tax, or

(b) the Income Tax Acts,

the reference is, in relation to a company, to be read as a reference to corporation tax or the Corporation Tax Acts.

(2) But—

(a) this does not affect references to income tax in section 39(2), and

(b) so far as the CGT enactments operate by reference to matters of any specified description, account is to be taken for corporation tax purposes of matters of that description confined to companies but not of any confined to individuals.

(3) In this section "the CGT enactments" means the enactments relating to capital gains tax.

2F Interaction of capital gains tax and corporation tax

(1) This Act as it has effect in accordance with this Chapter is not to be affected in its operation by the fact that capital gains tax and corporation tax are distinct taxes.

(2) But this Act is, so far as it is consistent with the Corporation Tax Acts, to apply in relation to capital gains tax and corporation tax on gains as if they were one tax.

(3) Accordingly, a matter which in a case involving two individuals is relevant to both of them in relation to capital gains tax is in a similar case involving an individual and a company—

(a) relevant to the individual in relation to capital gains tax, and
(b) relevant to the company in relation to corporation tax.

Supplementary

2G Assets of a company vested in a liquidator

(1) If assets of a company are vested in a liquidator—

(a) this Chapter, and
(b) the enactments applied by this Chapter,

apply as if the assets were vested in the company and as if the acts of the liquidator in relation to the assets were the company's acts.

(2) Accordingly, acquisitions from or disposals to the liquidator by the company are ignored.

(3) The assets may be vested in the liquidator under section 145 of the Insolvency Act 1986 or Article 123 of the Insolvency (Northern Ireland) Order 1989 or otherwise.

Chapter 3

Attribution of Gains of Non-UK Resident Close Companies

Gains of non-UK resident companies not otherwise chargeable

3 Gains attributed to UK resident individuals etc

(1) This section applies if—

(a) a chargeable gain accrues at any time to a non-UK resident close company,
(b) the gain is connected to avoidance (see section 3A),
(c) the gain is not connected to a foreign trade or other economically significant foreign activities (see section 3A), and
(d) apart from this section, some or all of the gain would not be chargeable to corporation tax on the company.

(2) So much of the gain as would not otherwise be so chargeable is apportioned among participators, or indirect participators, in the company—

(a) who are resident in the United Kingdom at that time, or
(b) who are trustees of a settlement and are not resident in the United Kingdom at that time.

(3) The proportion of the amount of the gain to be apportioned to each person corresponds to the extent of the person's interest in the company as a participator or indirect participator.

(4) The amount apportioned to each person is treated as a chargeable gain accruing to the person.

(5) No apportionment of any part of a gain is made to an individual if—

(a) the gain accrues in a tax year which, as respects the individual, is a split year, and
(b) the gain accrues in the overseas part of the year.

(6) No apportionment of any part of a gain is made to a person if the total amount that would, apart from this subsection, be apportioned to—

(a) the person, and

(b) persons connected to the person,

is 25% or less of the amount of the gain falling to be apportioned.

(7) A person ("P") is an "indirect participator" in a company ("A") if—

(a) another company ("B") which is a non-UK resident close company is a participator in A, and

(b) P is a participator in B or P is a participator in a third non-UK resident close company which is participator in B,

and so on through any number of non-UK resident close companies that are participators in other non-UK resident close companies.

(8) P's interest as an indirect participator in A in the case of any gain is determined by—

(a) apportioning the gain among the participators in A according to the extent of their respective interests as participators, and

(b) then further apportioning the gain apportioned to B among the participators in B according to the extent of their respective interests as participators, and so on through other companies.

(9) So far as it would go to reduce or extinguish chargeable gains accruing, as a result of this section, to a person in a chargeable period, this section applies to a loss accruing to the company on the disposal of an asset in that period as it would apply if there had been a gain.

(10) But—

(a) this only applies in relation to that person, and

(b) this section does not otherwise apply in relation to losses accruing to the company.

(11) In this section "a non-UK resident close company" means a company—

(a) which is not resident in the United Kingdom, and

(b) which would be a close company if it were resident in the United Kingdom.

3A Gains connected to avoidance or foreign activities etc

(1) A gain accruing to a company on the disposal of an asset is taken to be "connected to avoidance" unless it is shown that neither—

(a) the disposal of the asset by the company, nor

(b) the acquisition or holding of the asset by the company,

formed part of a scheme or arrangements of which the main purpose, or one of the main purposes, was avoidance of liability to capital gains tax or corporation tax.

(2) A gain is "connected to a foreign trade" if it accrues on the disposal of an asset used only—

(a) for the purposes of a trade carried on by the company wholly outside the United Kingdom, or

(b) for the purposes of the foreign part of a trade carried on by the company partly within, and partly outside, the United Kingdom,

and the reference here to the foreign part of a trade is to the part of the trade carried on outside the United Kingdom.

(3) For this purpose an asset is to be regarded as used only for the purposes of a trade carried on by the company wholly outside the United Kingdom if—

(a) the asset is accommodation, or an interest or right in accommodation, situated outside the United Kingdom, and

(b) the accommodation has for each relevant period been furnished holiday accommodation of which a person has made a commercial letting.

(4) Each of the following is a "relevant period"—

(a) the period of 12 months ending with the date of the disposal and each of the two preceding periods of 12 months, or

(b) if the company has beneficially owned the accommodation (or interest or right) for more than 36 months, the period of 12 months ending with the date of the disposal and each of the preceding periods of 12 months throughout which the company had that beneficial ownership.

(5) The reference in this section to the commercial letting of furnished holiday accommodation is to be read in accordance with Chapter 6 of Part 4 of CTA 2009, but as if—

(a) sections 266, 268 and 268A were omitted, and

(b) the reference to an accounting period in section 267(1) were to a relevant period.

(6) A gain accruing on the disposal of an asset is "connected to other economically significant foreign activities" if—

(a) the asset is used only for the purposes of activities carried on by the company wholly or mainly outside the United Kingdom,

(b) the activities consist of the provision of goods or services on a commercial basis, and

(c) the activities also satisfy the staff, premises and economic value test.

(7) Activities satisfy the staff, premises and economic value test if they involve—

(a) the use of employees, agents or contractors of the company in numbers, and with competence and authority, commensurate with the size and nature of the activities,

(b) the use of premises and equipment commensurate with the size and nature of the activities, and

(c) the addition of economic value by the company to the persons to whom the goods or services are provided commensurate with the size and nature of the activities.

(8) This section applies for the purposes of section 3(1)(b) and (c).

3B Participators and their interests

(1) "Participator" has the meaning given by section 454 of CTA 2010.

(2) Any reference to a person's interest as a participator in a company is to the interest in it represented by all the factors by reference to which the person is a participator.

(3) Any reference to the extent of a person's interest as a participator in a company is to such proportion of the interests as participators of all of the company's participators as, on a just and reasonable basis, is represented by that interest.

(4) If—

(a) the interest of a person in a company is wholly or partly represented by an interest under a settlement ("the beneficial interest"), and

(b) the beneficial interest is the factor (or one of them) by reference to which the person would, apart from this subsection, have an interest as a participator in the company,

that interest as a participator is, so far as represented by the beneficial interest, to be treated instead as the interest of the trustees of the settlement.

(5) If—

(a) exempt assets of a pension scheme are taken into account in ascertaining a person's interest as a participator in a company, and

(b) if those assets were ignored, an amount in respect of a gain accruing to the company would not be apportioned to the person as a result of section 3,

no amount in the respect of the gain is to be apportioned to the person as a result of that section.

(6) For this purpose—

(a) "assets of a pension scheme" means assets held for the purposes of a fund or scheme to which section 271(1)(c) or (1A) applies, and

(b) those assets are "exempt" if, at the time when the gain accrues, a disposal of those assets would be exempt from tax as a result of either of those provisions.

(7) This section applies for the purposes of section 3.

Prevention of multiple charges

3C Prevention of double UK taxation

(1) If—

(a) an amount of tax is paid by a person as a result of section 3 in respect of a gain, and
(b) there is a distribution of an amount in respect of the gain before the end of the relevant period,

the amount of tax is applied so as to reduce or extinguish any liability of the person to tax in respect of the distribution.

(2) For the purposes of subsection (1)—

(a) the distribution is one made by way of dividend or distribution of capital or on the dissolution of the company,
(b) the tax in respect of the distribution is income tax, corporation tax or capital gains tax, and
(c) in determining the liability to tax of any individual in respect of any distribution for a tax year it is to be assumed that the distribution is the highest part of the individual's income for the year.

(3) For the purposes of subsection (1) "the relevant period" means the period of 3 years from the end of whichever of the following periods is earlier—

(a) the period of account of the company in which the gain accrued, and
(b) the period of 12 months beginning with the date on which the gain accrued.

(4) The amount of tax paid by a person as a result of section 3 is allowable as a deduction in calculating a chargeable gain accruing on the disposal by the person of any asset representing the person's interest as a participator in the company.

(5) An amount of tax—

(a) is not to be used more than once under this section (whether to reduce or extinguish a liability or as a deduction or a combination of those things), and
(b) is not to be applied if it is reimbursed by the company.

Non-UK domiciled individuals and temporary non-residents

3D Non-UK domiciled individuals

(1) This section applies if, as a result of section 3, an amount in respect of a gain accruing to a company in a tax year is apportioned to an individual who is not domiciled in the United Kingdom in that year.

(2) The apportioned amount is regarded for the purposes of paragraph 1 of Schedule 1 as accruing on a disposal of a foreign asset if the asset disposed of by the company is a foreign asset (but not otherwise).

(3) For the purposes of Chapter A1 of Part 14 of ITA 2007 (remittance basis)—

(a) treat any consideration obtained by the company on the disposal of the asset as deriving from the apportioned amount, and
(b) if that consideration is less than the market value of the asset, treat the asset as deriving from the apportioned amount.

(4) The apportioned amount may not be reduced or extinguished by a loss under section 3 if—

(a) the apportioned amount is regarded for the purposes of paragraph 1 of Schedule 1 as accruing on a disposal of a foreign asset,
(b) the remittance basis applies to the individual for the tax year in question, and
(c) any of the apportioned amount is remitted to the United Kingdom in a subsequent tax year.

(5) Paragraph 5 of Schedule 1 applies for the purposes of this section as it applies for the purposes of that Schedule.

3E Temporary non-residents

(1) This section applies if—

(a) an individual is temporarily non-resident, and
(b) a gain or loss accrues to a company in a tax year falling wholly or partly in the temporary period of non-residence.

(2) So much of the gain as would, as a result of section 3, have been treated as accruing to the individual in the tax year if the residence assumption were made is to be treated as accruing to the individual in the period of return.

(3) But if—

(a) the remittance basis applies to the individual for the tax year that comprises or includes the period of return, and
(b) any part of the gain has not been remitted to the United Kingdom before the period of the return,

subsection (2) has effect subject to the further application of Schedule 1 (as read with section 3D) in relation to that part of the gain.

(4) Paragraph 5 of Schedule 1 applies for the purposes of subsection (3) as it applies for the purposes of that Schedule.

(5) So much of the loss accruing in the tax year as would, in accordance with section 3(9), have reduced or extinguished a gain treated as accruing to the individual in that year as a result of section 3 if the residence assumption were made is to be treated as accruing to the individual in the period of return.

(6) For the purposes of this section the "residence assumption" is—

(a) that the individual was resident in the United Kingdom for the tax year in which the gain or loss accrued to the company, and
(b) that the tax year was not a split year as respects the individual.

(7) Nothing in any double taxation arrangements prevents a charge to capital gains tax arising as a result of this section.

(8) For the purposes of this section each of the following expressions has the meaning given by Part 4 of Schedule 45 to the Finance Act 2013 (statutory residence test: anti-avoidance)—

"the period of return"
"temporarily non-resident"
"the temporary period of non-residence".

Application to groups

3F Non-resident groups of companies

(1) This section applies, for the purposes of section 3, certain provisions of this Act (modified as mentioned below) in relation to non-resident companies which are members of a non-resident group of companies.

(2) The applied provisions are—

(a) section 41(8),
(b) section 171 but as if subsections (1)(b) and (1A) were omitted,
(c) section 173 but as if "to which this section applies" in subsections (1)(a) and (2)(a) were omitted, as if "such" in subsections (1)(c) and (2)(c) were omitted and as if subsection (3) were omitted,
(d) section 174(4) but as if "at a time when both were members of the group" were substituted for "in a transfer to which section 171(1) applied",
(e) section 175(1) but as if "to which this section applies" were omitted, and
(f) section 179 but as if subsections (1)(b) and (1A) were omitted, as if for any reference to a group of companies there were substituted a reference to a non-resident group of companies and as if for any reference to a company there were substituted a reference to a non-resident company.

(3) In this section—

"non-resident company" means a company which is not resident in the United Kingdom,
"non-resident group of companies"—

(a) in the case of a group none of whose members are resident in the United Kingdom, means that group, and
(b) in the case of a group some of whose members are not resident in the United Kingdom, means the members which are not resident in the United Kingdom, and

"group" is to be read in accordance with section 170.

Supplementary

3G Supplementary provisions

(1) If tax payable by a person ("P") as a result of section 3 is paid by—

(a) the company ("C") to which the gain accrues, or

(b) a company by reference to which P is regarded as an indirect participator in C,

the amount paid is not a payment to P for tax purposes.

(2) The reference here to tax purposes is to the purposes of income tax, capital gains tax or corporation tax.

(3) For the purposes of section 3 the amount of a gain or loss accruing to a company is calculated as if the company were a company resident in the United Kingdom chargeable to corporation tax on the gain."

3 Omit sections 16ZB to 16ZD (losses of non-UK domiciled individuals).

4 After section 36 insert—

"Re-basing for non-residents for UK land etc held on 5 April 2019

36A Re-basing in relation to direct or indirect disposals of UK land

Schedule 4AA makes provision for the re-basing of assets where—

(a) the assets are held on 5 April 2019,

(b) there is a disposal after that date, and

(c) the disposal is a direct or indirect disposal of UK land (within the meaning of that Schedule)."

5 Omit Chapter 5 of Part 2 (computation of gains and losses: relevant high value disposals).

6 Omit Chapter 6 of Part 2 (computation of gains and losses: non-resident CGT disposals).

7 Omit Chapter 7 of Part 2 (computation of gains and losses: disposals of residential property interests).

8 After section 103DA insert—

"103DB UK property rich collective investment vehicles etc

Schedule 5AAA makes provision in relation to collective investment vehicles where the property which is the subject of or held by the vehicles consists of or includes direct or indirect interests in land in the United Kingdom."

9 After section 271 insert—

"Visiting forces and official agents etc

271ZA Visiting forces and staff of designated allied headquarters

(1) This section applies for the purposes of capital gains tax if section 833 of ITA 2007 (visiting forces and staff of designated allied headquarters) applies to an individual throughout a period.

(2) The period is not a period of residence in the United Kingdom.

(3) The period does not create a change of the individual's residence or domicile.

271ZB Official agents of Commonwealth countries or Republic of Ireland etc

(1) An individual who is entitled to immunity from income tax as a result of section 841 of ITA 2007 (official agents of Commonwealth countries or Republic of Ireland etc) is entitled to the same immunity from capital gains tax as that to which a member of the staff of a mission is entitled under the Diplomatic Privileges Act 1964.

(2) The reference here to a member of the staff of a mission is to be read in accordance with the Diplomatic Privileges Act 1964."

10 Omit Schedule B1 (disposals of UK residential property interests).

11 Omit Schedule BA1 (disposals of non-UK residential property interests).

12 Omit Schedule C1 (section 14F: meaning of "closely-held company" and "widely-marketed scheme").

13 For Schedule 1 substitute—

"SCHEDULE 1

UK RESIDENT INDIVIDUALS NOT DOMICILED IN UK

Foreign gains treated as accruing when remitted to UK

1 (1) This paragraph applies in the case of an individual to whom the remittance basis applies for a tax year if—

(a) in that year the individual disposes of foreign assets,
(b) chargeable gains accrue to the individual on the disposal of those assets, and
(c) the gains are not taken outside the charge to capital gains tax as a result of section 1G (cases where tax year is a split year).

(2) The gains are treated as accruing to the individual only so far as, and at the time when, they are remitted to the United Kingdom.

(3) The amount treated as accruing is equal to the full amount remitted to the United Kingdom at that time.

Use of allowable losses against foreign gains remitted in later year

2 (1) This paragraph applies if—

(a) gains are treated as accruing to an individual in a tax year as a result of paragraph 1,
(b) the tax year is later than the one ("the actual year of accrual") in which those gains actually accrued to the individual, and
(c) an election under section 16ZA (election for foreign losses to be allowable losses) has effect for both the tax year and the actual year of accrual.

(2) No allowable losses may be deducted under section 1 from the gains.

(3) This prohibition—

(a) applies regardless of whether or not the allowable losses accrue on disposals of foreign assets, but
(b) does not prevent the prior application of paragraph 3(3) in relation to the gains (which contains a rule for reducing the amount of the gains by reference to losses).

Matching rules for relieving allowable losses

3 (1) This paragraph applies in the case of an individual for a tax year if—

(a) the remittance basis applies to the individual for the tax year, and
(b) an election under section 16ZA has effect for the tax year.

(2) Allowable losses accruing to the individual must be matched to chargeable gains accruing to the individual in accordance with paragraph 4.

(3) If allowable losses are matched to chargeable gains accruing on disposals of foreign assets—

(a) which actually accrue in the tax year, but
(b) which are, as a result of paragraph 1, treated as not accruing in the tax year,

the amount of those gains is reduced by the matched amount (and the allowable losses are reduced accordingly).

(4) So far as allowable losses are matched to other chargeable gains, they are deducted from chargeable gains accruing to the individual in the tax year.

(5) This is subject to—

(a) paragraph 2 (no use of allowable losses against foreign gains remitted in later year), and
(b) section 1E(4) (prohibition of deduction of losses from gains treated as accruing under section 87, 87K, 87L or 89(2)).

Rules for matching losses to chargeable gains

4 (1) This paragraph explains how, for the purposes of paragraph 3, allowable losses are matched to chargeable gains in the case of an individual to whom that paragraph applies for a tax year.

(2) The losses are matched to the gains in the following order—

first, gains actually accruing to the individual in the tax year on the disposal of foreign assets so far as they are remitted to the United Kingdom in the tax year;

second, gains actually accruing to the individual in the tax year on the disposal of foreign assets so far as they are not remitted to the United Kingdom in the tax year;

third, any other gains accruing to the individual in the tax year.

(3) If the tax year is a split year, the matching under the first and second steps is to be done by reference to the extent to which the gains are, or are not, remitted in the UK part of the year.

(4) If there are losses to be matched to gains under the second step but the losses are insufficient to eliminate the gains—

(a) the losses are to be matched against gains accruing on the most recent day first (and then the next most recent day and so on until none of the losses remain), and

(b) if losses cannot be matched fully against gains accruing on a particular day, the appropriate portion of the losses is matched against each of the gains.

(5) "The appropriate portion" means the amount of each gain accruing on the day divided by the total amount of all of the gains accruing on the day.

Definitions

5 (1) For the purposes of this Schedule "foreign asset" means an asset situated outside the United Kingdom.

(2) For the purposes of this Schedule any reference to "the remittance basis" applying to an individual for a tax year is to section 809B, 809D or 809E of ITA 2007 applying to the individual for the year.

(3) For the purposes of this Schedule any question as to whether, and when, amounts are "remitted to the United Kingdom" is determined in accordance with the rules in Chapter A1 of Part 14 of ITA 2007."

14 After Schedule 1 insert—

"SCHEDULE 1A

ASSETS DERIVING 75% OF VALUE FROM UK LAND ETC

PART 1

INTRODUCTION

1 This Schedule makes provision, for the purposes of section 1A(3)(c) or 2B(4)(b), for determining in the case of any disposal of any asset—

(a) whether the asset derives at least 75% of its value from UK land (see Part 2 of this Schedule), and

(b) whether the person making the disposal has a substantial indirect interest in the UK land (see Part 3 of this Schedule).

2 The provision made by this Schedule needs to be read together with—

(a) paragraph 5 of Schedule 5AAA (which treats units in a CoACS as shares for the purposes of this Schedule), and

(b) paragraph 6 of that Schedule (which treats certain disposals of interests in collective investment vehicles as meeting the conditions in Part 3 of this Schedule).

PART 2

WHETHER ASSET DERIVES AT LEAST 75% OF ITS VALUE FROM UK LAND

The basic rule

3 (1) An asset derives at least 75% of its value from UK land if—

(a) the asset consists of a right or an interest in a company, and

(b) at the time of the disposal, at least 75% of the total market value of the company's qualifying assets derives (directly or indirectly) from interests in UK land.

(2) Market value may be traced through any number of companies, partnerships, trusts and other entities or arrangements but may not be traced through a normal commercial loan.

(3) It is irrelevant whether the law under which a company, partnership, trust or other entity or an arrangement is established or has effect is—

(a) the law of any part of the United Kingdom, or
(b) the law of any territory outside the United Kingdom.

(4) The assets held by a company, partnership or trust or other entity or arrangement must be attributed to the shareholders, partners, beneficiaries or other participants at each stage in whatever way is appropriate in the circumstances.

(5) For the purposes of this paragraph—

"normal commercial loan" means a loan which is a normal commercial loan for the purposes of section 158(1)(b) or 159(4)(b) of CTA 2010, and
"qualifying assets" has the meaning given by paragraph 4.

(6) The provision made by this paragraph is subject to exceptions provided by—

(a) paragraph 5 (interests in UK land used for trading purposes), and
(b) paragraph 6 (certain disposals of rights or interests in connected companies).

Meaning of "qualifying assets"

4 (1) Subject as follows, all of the assets of the company are qualifying assets.

(2) An asset of the company is not a qualifying asset so far as it is matched to a related party liability.

(3) But an interest in UK land is a qualifying asset of the company even if it is matched to any extent to a related party liability.

(4) An asset of the company is matched to a related party liability if—

(a) the asset consists of a right under a transaction (for example, a right under a loan relationship or derivative contract),
(b) the right entitles the company to require another person to meet a liability arising under the transaction, and
(c) the other person is relevant to the paragraph 3 tracing exercise or is a related party of the company on the day of the disposal.

(5) For the purposes of this paragraph a person is relevant to the paragraph 3 tracing exercise if—

(a) the person has assets that fall to be taken into account in the tracing exercise mentioned in paragraph 3, or
(b) the person has obligations (whether as a trustee or otherwise) in relation to the holding of assets comprised in any trust or other arrangement that fall to be taken into account in that exercise.

(6) Whether, for the purposes of this paragraph, a person is a related party of the company on any day is determined in accordance with the rules in Part 8ZB of CTA 2010 but as if, in section 356OT(4) of that Act, the words ", within the period of 6 months beginning with that day" were omitted.

(7) In this paragraph a liability includes a contingent liability (such as one arising as a result of the giving of a guarantee, indemnity or other form of financial assistance).

Exception in relation to interests in UK land used for trading purposes

5 (1) A disposal of a right or interest in a company is not to be regarded as a disposal of an asset deriving at least 75% of its value from UK land if it is reasonable to conclude that, so far as the market value of the company's qualifying assets derives (directly or indirectly) from interests in UK land—

(a) all of the interests in UK land are used for trading purposes, or
(b) all of the interests in UK land would be used for those purposes if low-value non-trade interests in UK land were left out of account.

(2) An interest in UK land is "used for trading purposes" for the purposes of this paragraph if (and only if), at the time of the disposal—

(a) it is being used in, or for the purposes of, a qualifying trade, or
(b) it has been acquired for use in, or for the purposes of, a qualifying trade.

(3) A trade is a "qualifying" trade for the purposes of this paragraph if—

(a) it has been carried on by the company, or by a person connected with the company, throughout the period of one year ending with the time of the disposal on a commercial basis with a view to the realisation of profits, and

(b) it is reasonable to conclude that the trade will continue to be carried on (for more than an insignificant period of time) on a commercial basis with a view to the realisation of profits.

(4) For the purposes of this paragraph, "low-value non-trade interests in UK land" means interests in UK land—

(a) which are not used for trading purposes, and

(b) the total market value of which is, at the time of the disposal, no more than 10% of the total market value at that time of the interests in UK land that are used for trading purposes.

Exception for certain disposals of rights or interests under same arrangements etc

6 (1) This paragraph applies if—

(a) there are two or more disposals of rights or interests in companies,

(b) the disposals are linked with each other,

(c) some but not all of the disposals would, apart from this paragraph, be disposals of assets deriving at least 75% of their value from UK land, and

(d) if one of the companies included all of the assets of the others, a disposal of a right or interest in it would not be a disposal of an asset deriving at least 75% of its value from UK land.

(2) None of the disposals are to be regarded as disposals of assets deriving at least 75% of their value from UK land.

(3) In determining whether the condition in sub-paragraph (1)(d) is met in the case of a disposal of a right or interest in a company, it is to be assumed that, for the purposes of paragraph 4, each of the other companies in which rights or interest are disposed of is (so far as this would not otherwise be the case) a related party of the company on the day of the disposal.

(4) For the purposes of this paragraph a disposal of a right or interest in a company is linked with a disposal of a right or interest in another company if—

(a) the disposals are made under the same arrangements,

(b) the disposals are made by the same person or by persons connected with each other,

(c) the disposals are made to the same person or to persons connected with each other, and

(d) in the case of each disposal, the person making the disposal is connected with the company in which the right or interest is disposed of.

(5) For the purposes of this paragraph, the question whether or not a person is connected with another is to be determined immediately before the arrangements are entered into.

(6) Section 286 (connected persons: interpretation) has effect for the purposes of this paragraph as if, in subsection (4), the words "Except in relation to acquisitions or disposals of partnership assets pursuant to bona fide commercial arrangements," were omitted.

Meaning of "interest in UK land"

7 For the purposes of this Part of this Schedule "interest in UK land" has the meaning given by section 1C.

PART 3

WHETHER PERSON HAS SUBSTANTIAL INDIRECT INTEREST IN UK LAND

Basic rule

8 (1) If—

(a) a person disposes of an asset consisting of a right or an interest in a company, and

(b) the asset derives at least 75% of its value from UK land,

the person has a substantial indirect interest in UK land if, at any time in the period of 2 years ending with the time of the disposal, the person has a 25% investment in the company.

(2) But a person is not to be regarded as having a 25% investment in the company at times falling in the person's qualifying ownership period if, having regard to the length of that period, the times (taken as whole) constitute an insignificant proportion of that period.

(3) The "person's qualifying ownership period" means the period throughout which the person has held an asset consisting of a right or an interest in the company, but excluding times that fall before the beginning of the 2 year period mentioned in sub-paragraph (1).

Meaning of "25% investment"

9 (1) A person ("P") has a 25% investment in a company ("C") if—

(a) P possesses or is entitled to acquire 25% or more of the voting power in C,
(b) in the event of a disposal of the whole of the equity in C, P would receive 25% or more of the proceeds,
(c) in the event that the income in respect of the equity in C were distributed among the equity holders in C, P would receive 25% or more of the amount so distributed, or
(d) in the event of a winding-up of C or in any other circumstances, P would receive 25% or more of C's assets which would then be available for distribution among the equity holders in C in respect of the equity in C.

(2) In this paragraph references to the equity in C are to—

(a) the shares in C other than restricted preference shares, or
(b) loans to C other than normal commercial loans.

(3) For this purpose "shares in C" includes—

(a) stock, and
(b) any other interests of members in C.

(4) For the purposes of this paragraph a person is an equity holder in C if the person possesses any of the equity in C.

(5) For the purposes of this paragraph—

"normal commercial loan" means a loan which is a normal commercial loan for the purposes of section 158(1)(b) or 159(4)(b) of CTA 2010, and

"restricted preference shares" means shares which are restricted preference shares for the purposes of section 160 of CTA 2010.

(6) In a case where C is a company which does not have share capital, in applying for the purposes of this paragraph the definitions of "normal commercial loan" and "restricted preference shares"—

(a) sections 160(2) to (7) and 161 to 164 of CTA 2010, and
(b) any other relevant provisions of that Act,

have effect with the necessary modifications.

(7) In this paragraph references to a person receiving any proceeds, amount or assets include—

(a) the direct or indirect receipt of the proceeds, amount or assets, and
(b) the direct or indirect application of the proceeds, amount or assets for the person's benefit,

and it does not matter whether the receipt or application is at the time of the disposal, distribution, winding-up or other circumstances or at a later time.

(8) If—

(a) there is a direct receipt or direct application of any proceeds, amount or assets by or for the benefit of a person ("A"), and
(b) another person ("B") directly or indirectly owns a percentage of the equity in A,

there is, for the purposes of sub-paragraph (7), an indirect receipt or indirect application of that percentage of the proceeds, amount or assets by or for the benefit of B.

(9) For this purpose the percentage of the equity in A directly or indirectly owned by B is to be determined by applying the rules in sections 1155 to 1157 of CTA 2010 with such modifications (if any) as may be necessary.

(10) Sub-paragraph (7) is not to result in a person being regarded as having a 25% investment in another person merely as a result of their being parties to a normal commercial loan.

(11) Any reference in this paragraph, in the case of a person who is a member of a partnership, to the proceeds, amount or assets of the person includes the person's share of the proceeds, amount or assets of the partnership (apportioning those things between the partners on a just and reasonable basis).

Attribution of rights and interests

10 (1) In determining for the purposes of paragraph 9 the investment that a person ("P") has in a company, P is to be taken to have all of the rights and interests of any person connected with P.

(2) A person is not to be regarded as connected with another person for the purposes of this paragraph merely as a result of their being parties to a loan that is a normal commercial loan for the purposes of paragraph 9.

(3) Section 286 (connected persons: interpretation) has effect for the purposes of this paragraph—

(a) as if, in subsection (2), for the words from ", or is a relative" to the end there were substituted "or is a lineal ancestor or lineal descendant of the individual or of the individual's spouse or civil partner", and

(b) as if subsections (4) and (8) were omitted.

PART 4

ANTI-AVOIDANCE

11 (1) This paragraph applies if a person has entered into any arrangements the main purpose, or one of the main purposes, of which is to obtain a tax advantage for the person as a result (wholly or partly) of—

(a) a provision of this Schedule applying or not applying, or

(b) double taxation arrangements having effect despite a provision of this Schedule in a case where the advantage is contrary to the object and purpose of the double taxation arrangements.

(2) The tax advantage is to be counteracted by the making of such adjustments as are just and reasonable.

(3) The adjustments may be made (whether by an officer of Revenue and Customs or the person) by way of an assessment, the modification of an assessment, amendment or disallowance of a claim, or otherwise.

(4) The counteraction has effect in a treaty shopping case regardless of section 6(1) of TIOPA 2010.

(5) This paragraph applies by reference to—

(a) arrangements entered into on or after 22 November 2017 in a treaty shopping case, and

(b) arrangements entered into on or after 6 July 2018 in any other case.

(6) In this paragraph—

"arrangements" (except in the expression "double taxation arrangements") includes any agreement, understanding, scheme, transaction or series of transactions (whether or not legally enforceable),

"double taxation arrangements" means arrangements that have effect under section 2(1) of TIOPA 2010,

"tax" means capital gains tax or corporation tax,

"tax advantage" includes—

(a) relief or increased relief from tax,

(b) repayment or increased repayment of tax,

(c) avoidance or reduction of a charge to tax or an assessment to tax,

(d) avoidance of a possible assessment to tax,

(e) deferral of a payment of tax or advancement of a repayment of tax, and

(f) avoidance of an obligation to deduct or account for tax, and

"treaty shopping case" means a case where this paragraph applies as a result of sub-paragraph (1)(b)."

15 After Schedule 1A insert—

"SCHEDULE 1B

RESIDENTIAL PROPERTY GAINS

Meaning of "residential property gain"

1 (1) For the purposes of Chapter 1 of Part 1 "residential property gain" means so much of a chargeable gain accruing to a person on a disposal of residential property as, in accordance with paragraph 2, is attributable to that property.

(2) The question whether or not a person disposes of residential property is determined in accordance with paragraphs 3 to 7.

Attribution of gain to residential property

2 (1) The proportion of a chargeable gain attributable to residential property is equal to—

(a) the relevant fraction of the gain, and
(b) if there has been mixed use of the land to which the disposal relates on one or more days in the applicable period, the relevant fraction of the gain as adjusted, on a just and reasonable basis, to take account of the mixed use on the day or days.

(2) The relevant fraction is A/B where—

A is the number of days in the applicable period on which the land to which the disposal relates consists of or includes a dwelling, and
B is the total number of days in the applicable period.

(3) There is mixed use of land on any day on which the land consists of—

(a) one or more dwellings, and
(b) other land.

(4) If the disposal is of an interest in land subsisting under a contract for the acquisition of land consisting of or including a building that is to be constructed or adapted for use as a dwelling, that land is taken to consist of or include a dwelling throughout the applicable period.

(5) In this paragraph "the applicable period" means the period—

(a) beginning with the day on which the person making the disposal acquired the interest in land being disposed of or, if later, the day from which the interest in land became chargeable, and
(b) ending with the day before the day on which the disposal occurs.

(6) For the purposes of this paragraph an interest in land became "chargeable"—

(a) in any case where the disposal is of an interest in land in the United Kingdom—
 (i) by a person in a tax year in which the person is not UK resident, or
 (ii) by a person in the overseas part of a tax year which is, as respects the person, a split year,

 from 6 April 2015, and
(b) in any other case, from 31 March 1982.

(7) If the interest in land disposed of by the person results from interests in land acquired by the person at different times, the person is regarded for the purposes of this paragraph as having acquired the interest disposed of at the time of the first acquisition.

Disposing of residential property

3 (1) For the purposes of this Schedule a person "disposes of residential property" if the person disposes of an interest in land in a case where—

(a) the land consisted of or included a dwelling at any time falling on or after the date on which the applicable period begins,
(b) the interest in land subsisted for the benefit of land that consisted of or included a dwelling at any time falling on or after that date, or
(c) the interest in land subsists under a contract for the acquisition of land consisting of or including a building that is to be constructed or adapted for use as a dwelling.

(2) No account is to be taken for the purposes of this paragraph of any time falling on (or after) the day on which the disposal is made.

Interest in land

4 (1) For the purposes of this Schedule an "interest in land" means—

(a) an estate, interest, right or power in or over land, or
(b) the benefit of an obligation, restriction or condition affecting the value of an estate, interest, right or power in or over land,

other than an excluded interest.

(2) The following interests are "excluded interests"—

(a) any interest or right held for securing the payment of money or the performance of any other obligation,

(b) a licence to use or occupy land,

(c) in relation to land in England and Wales or Northern Ireland, a tenancy at will or an advowson, franchise or manor, and

(d) such other descriptions of interest or right in relation to land as may be specified in regulations made by the Treasury.

(3) An interest or right is not within sub-paragraph (2)(a) if it is—

(a) a rentcharge, or

(b) in relation to land in Scotland, a feu duty or a payment mentioned in section 56(1) of the Abolition of Feudal Tenure etc (Scotland) Act 2000.

(4) The grant of an option by a person binding the person to dispose of an interest in land is (so far as it would not otherwise be the case) regarded as a disposal of an interest in land by the person for the purposes of this Schedule.

(5) This does not affect the operation of section 144 in relation to the grant of the option (or otherwise).

(6) In applying the domestic concepts of law mentioned in this paragraph to land outside the United Kingdom, this paragraph is to be read so as to produce the result most closely corresponding with that produced in relation to land in the United Kingdom.

(7) In this paragraph—

"franchise" means a grant from the Crown such as the right to hold a market or fair, or the right to take tolls, and

"land" includes—

(a) buildings and structures, and

(b) land under the sea or otherwise covered by water.

Dwelling: basic meaning

5 (1) For the purposes of this Schedule a building is a dwelling at any time when—

(a) it is used, or suitable for use, as a dwelling, or

(b) it is in the process of being constructed or adapted for use as a dwelling,

and, in each case, it is not an institutional building.

(2) Land that at any time is, or is intended to be, occupied or enjoyed with a dwelling as a garden or grounds (including any building or structure) is taken to be part of the dwelling at that time.

(3) A building is an institutional building if—

(a) it is used as residential accommodation for school pupils,

(b) it is used as residential accommodation for members of the armed forces,

(c) it is used as a home or other institution providing residential accommodation for children,

(d) it is used as a home or other institution providing residential accommodation with personal care for persons in need of personal care because of old age, disability, past or present dependence on alcohol or drugs or past or present mental disorder,

(e) it is used as a hospital or hospice,

(f) it is used as a prison or similar establishment,

(g) it is used as a hotel or inn or similar establishment,

(h) it is otherwise used, or suitable for use, as an institution that is the sole or main residence of its residents,

(i) it falls within—

(i) paragraph 4 of Schedule 14 to the Housing Act 2004 (buildings in England or Wales occupied by students and managed or controlled by educational establishment etc), or

(ii) any provision having effect in Scotland or Northern Ireland that is designated by regulations made by the Treasury as provision corresponding to paragraph 4 of that Schedule, or

(j) it qualifies in accordance with the next sub-paragraph as student accommodation.

(4) A building qualifies as student accommodation in accordance with this sub-paragraph at any time if the time falls in a tax year in which—

(a) the accommodation provided by the building includes at least 15 bedrooms,

(b) the accommodation is purpose-built, or is converted, for occupation by students, and

(c) the accommodation is occupied by students on at least 165 days.

(5) Accommodation is to be regarded as occupied by persons as students if they occupy it wholly or mainly for undertaking a course of education (otherwise than as school pupils).

Building temporarily unsuitable for use as a dwelling

6 (1) A building is treated for the purposes of paragraph 5 as continuing to be suitable for use as a dwelling at any time when it has become temporarily unsuitable for use as a dwelling.

(2) There is an exception to this rule if—

(a) the temporary unsuitability resulted from accidental damage to the building, and

(b) the damage resulted in the building becoming unsuitable for use as a dwelling for a period of at least 90 consecutive days ("the 90 day period").

(3) This exception does not apply if the damage occurred in the course of work that—

(a) was being done for the purpose of altering the building, and

(b) itself involved, or could be expected to involve, making the building unsuitable for use as a dwelling for at least 30 consecutive days.

(4) If the exception applies, work done in the 90 day period to restore the building to suitability for use as a dwelling is not to count for the purposes of paragraph 5 as constructing or adapting the building for use as a dwelling.

(5) For the purposes of this paragraph—

(a) references to accidental damage include damage otherwise caused by events beyond the control of the person disposing of the interest in land,

(b) references to alteration of a building include its partial demolition, and

(c) the 90 day period does not include the day of the disposal (or later days).

(6) For the purposes of this paragraph a building's unsuitability for use as a dwelling is not regarded as temporary if paragraph 7 applies (disposal of a building that has undergone works).

Disposal of a building that has undergone works

7 (1) If—

(a) a person disposes of an interest in land on which a building has been suitable for use as a dwelling, and

(b) as a result of qualifying works, the building has, at or before the time of completion of the disposal, ceased to exist or become unsuitable for use as a dwelling,

the building is to be regarded for the purposes of paragraph 5 as unsuitable for use as a dwelling throughout the works period.

(2) For the purposes of this paragraph works are "qualifying" works if—

(a) any planning permission or development consent required for the works, or for any change of use with which they are associated, has been granted (whether before or after completion), and

(b) the works have been carried out in accordance with the permission or consent.

(3) In this paragraph "the works period" means—

(a) the period when the works were in progress, and

(b) such period (if any) ending immediately before the start of the works throughout which the building was, for reasons connected with the works, not used as dwelling.

(4) If at any time when qualifying works are in progress—

(a) the building was undergoing any other work, or put to any other use, in relation to which planning permission or development consent was required but has not (at any time) been granted, or

(b) anything else was being done in contravention of a condition or requirement attached to a planning permission or development consent relating to the building,

the works period does not include that time.

(5) If sub-paragraph (1) would have applied but for the fact that, at the completion of the disposal, the works are not qualifying works, the works are regarded as not affecting the building's suitability for use as a dwelling at any time before the disposal.

Other definitions

8 (1) For the purposes of this Schedule a building is regarded as ceasing to exist from the time when either—

(a) it has been demolished completely to ground level, or
(b) it has been demolished to ground level except for a single facade (or a double facade if it is on a corner site) the retention of which is a condition or requirement of planning permission or development consent.

(2) For the purposes of this Schedule the completion of the disposal of an interest in land is regarded as occurring—

(a) at the time of the disposal, or
(b) if the disposal is under a contract which is completed by a conveyance, transfer or other instrument, at the time when the instrument takes effect.

(3) In this Schedule—

"building" includes a part of a building,

"development consent" means—

(a) in the case of land in the United Kingdom, development consent under the Planning Act 2008, and
(b) in the case of land outside the United Kingdom, consent corresponding to development consent under that Act, and

"planning permission"—

(a) in the case of land in England or Wales, has the meaning given by section 336(1) of the Town and Country Planning Act 1990,
(b) in the case of land in Scotland, has the meaning given by section 227(1) of the Town and Country Planning (Scotland) Act 1997,
(c) in the case of land in Northern Ireland, has the meaning given by Article 2(2) of the Planning (Northern Ireland) Order 1991, and
(d) in the case of land outside the United Kingdom, means permission corresponding to any planning permission in relation to land anywhere in the United Kingdom.

Power to modify meaning of "use as a dwelling"

9 (1) The Treasury may by regulations amend this Schedule for the purpose of clarifying or changing the cases where a building is, or is not, to be regarded as being used, or suitable for use, as a dwelling.

(2) The provision that may be made by the regulations includes (for example) provision omitting or adding cases where a building is, or is not, to be regarded as being used, or suitable for use, as a dwelling.

Regulations

10 Regulations under any provision of this Schedule may make incidental, consequential, supplementary or transitional provision or savings."

16 After Schedule 1B insert—

"SCHEDULE 1C

ANNUAL EXEMPT AMOUNT IN CASES INVOLVING SETTLED PROPERTY

Introductory

1 (1) This Schedule provides for the application of section 1K (in some cases with modifications) in relation to the trustees of a settlement for a tax year.

(2) The application of this Schedule depends on (among other things) whether or not—

(a) a settlement is for the benefit of a disabled person, and

(b) a settlement is a qualifying UK settlement.

(3) For the definitions of those expressions, see paragraphs 3 and 7 respectively.

(4) In this Schedule any reference to the application of section 1K in relation to an individual for a tax year is to its application in relation to an individual who is resident and domiciled in the United Kingdom for the year.

Settlements for the benefit of disabled persons

2 (1) In the case of a settlement for the benefit of a disabled person for a tax year, section 1K applies in relation to the trustees of the settlement for the year as it applies in relation to an individual for the year.

(2) This paragraph needs to be read with—

(a) paragraph 6 (cases where settlement is a qualifying UK settlement comprised in a group), and

(b) paragraph 8 (sub-fund settlements).

3 (1) A settlement is a "settlement for the benefit of a disabled person" for a tax year if, for the whole or part of that year, settled property is held on trusts which secure that, during the lifetime of a disabled person, the property and income tests are met.

(2) The property test is met if any of the property which is applied for the benefit of a beneficiary is applied for the disabled person's benefit.

(3) The income test is met if either—

(a) the disabled person is entitled to all of the income (if any) arising from any of the property, or

(b) if any income arising from any of the property is applied for the benefit of a beneficiary, it is applied for the disabled person's benefit.

(4) A settlement is not prevented from being a settlement for the benefit of a disabled person for a tax year just because—

(a) the trustees have power to apply amounts (of any nature) not exceeding the de minimis threshold for that year,

(b) the trustees have the powers of advancement conferred by section 32 of the Trustee Act 1925 or section 33 of the Trustee Act (Northern Ireland) 1958,

(c) the trustees have those powers but free from, or subject to a less restrictive limitation than, the limitation imposed by—

(i) proviso (a) of section 32(1) of the Trustee Act 1925, or

(ii) section 33(1)(a) of the Trustee Act (Northern Ireland) 1958, or

(d) the trustees have powers to the same effect as the powers mentioned in paragraph (b) or (c).

(5) For the purposes of sub-paragraph (4)(a) "the de minimis threshold" means—

(a) £3,000, or

(b) 3% of the maximum value of the settled property during the tax year,

whichever is the lower.

(6) In this paragraph "disabled person" has the meaning given by Schedule 1A to the Finance Act 2005.

(7) If the income from settled property is held for the benefit of a disabled person ("D") on trusts of the kind described in section 33 of the Trustee Act 1925 (protective trusts), the reference in this paragraph to D's lifetime is to be read as a reference to the period during which the income is held on trust for D.

(8) This paragraph applies for the purposes of this Schedule.

4 (1) The Treasury may by order—

(a) specify circumstances in which paragraph 3(4)(a) is, or is not, to apply, and

(b) amend the definition of "the de minimis threshold" in paragraph 3(5).

(2) The order may—

(a) make different provision for different purposes, and

(b) contain transitional and saving provision.

(3) A statutory instrument containing an order under this paragraph which reduces the annual exempt amount in any case may not be made unless a draft of the instrument has been laid before, and approved by a resolution of, the House of Commons.

Other settlements

5 (1) This paragraph applies if settlement is not a settlement for the benefit of a disabled person for a tax year.

(2) Section 1K applies in relation to the trustees of the settlement for the year as it applies in relation to an individual for the year but as if the annual exempt amount for the year were one-half of the amount available for the individual for the year.

(3) This paragraph needs to be read be with—

(a) paragraph 6 (cases where settlement is qualifying UK settlement comprised in a group), and

(b) paragraph 8 (sub-fund settlements).

Special rules for qualifying UK settlements comprised in groups

6 (1) This paragraph reduces the annual exempt amount for trustees of a settlement for a tax year if the settlement is one of two or more qualifying UK settlements comprised in a group.

(2) In the case of a settlement for the benefit of a disabled person for the year, the annual exempt amount for the year is to be reduced so that it is equal to—

(a) one-tenth of an individual's amount for that year, or

(b) the amount resulting from dividing the individual's amount for that year by the number of settlements in the group,

whichever is the greater.

(3) In the case of any other settlement, the annual exempt amount for the year is to be reduced so that it is equal to—

(a) one-tenth of an individual's amount for that year, or

(b) the amount resulting from dividing half of an individual's amount for that year by the number of settlements in the group,

whichever is the greater.

(4) In this paragraph "an individual's amount", in relation to a tax year, means the annual exempt amount applying to an individual for the year under section 1K.

(5) For the purposes of this paragraph all qualifying UK settlements in relation to which the same person is the settlor constitute a group.

(6) If—

(a) two or more persons are settlors in relation to a settlement, and

(b) a settlement is consequently comprised in two or more groups comprising different numbers of settlement,

sub-paragraphs (2)(b) and (3)(b) have effect by reference to the largest group.

7 (1) In this Schedule "qualifying UK settlement", in relation to a tax year, means any settlement in relation to which both of the following conditions are met—

(a) the trustees of the settlement are resident in the United Kingdom during any part of the tax year, and

(b) the property comprised in the settlement is not held for a charitable or pensions purpose.

(2) Property comprised in a settlement is held for a charitable purpose if (and only if)—

(a) it is held for charitable purposes only, and

(b) it cannot become applicable for other purposes.

(3) Property comprised in a settlement is held for a pensions purpose if (and only if) it is held for the purposes of—

(a) a registered pension scheme,

(b) a superannuation fund to which section 615(3) of the Taxes Act applies, or

(c) an occupational pension scheme (within the meaning of section 150(5) of the Finance Act 2004) that is not a registered pension scheme.

(4) For this purposes of any provision of this Schedule other than paragraph 8 a settlement is not a qualifying UK settlement if—

(a) in the case of one for the benefit of a disabled person, it was made before 10 March 1981, or

(b) in any other case, it was made before 6 June 1978.

Special rules for principal settlements and sub-funds

8 (1) This paragraph—

(a) applies if the trustees of a settlement ("the principal settlement") have made an election under paragraph 1 of Schedule 4ZA the effect of which is that one or more other settlements ("sub-fund settlements") are treated as created, and

(b) provides for the annual exempt for the trustees of each of the affected settlements to be determined by reference to the assumed annual amount.

(2) For this purposes of this paragraph—

(a) the principal settlement and each of the sub-fund settlements is an "affected settlement", and

(b) the "assumed annual amount" means the amount which would be the annual exempt for the trustees of the principal settlement on the assumption that no election had been made under paragraph 1 of Schedule 4ZA.

(3) The annual exempt amount for the trustees of each of the affected settlements is the assumed annual amount unless there are two or more qualifying UK settlements in the affected settlements.

(4) In that case, the annual exempt amount for the trustees of each of the affected settlements is the assumed annual amount divided by the number of qualifying UK settlements in the affected settlements."

17 After Schedule 4 insert—

"SCHEDULE 4AA

RE-BASING FOR NON-RESIDENTS IN RESPECT OF UK LAND ETC HELD ON 5 APRIL 2019

PART 1

INTRODUCTION

1 (1) Part 2, 3 or 4 of this Schedule applies on the first occasion on which a person disposes of an asset that the person held on 5 April 2019 where—

(a) the disposal is either a direct or indirect disposal of UK land, and

(b) the disposal is made by a non-resident or a UK resident in the overseas part of a tax year.

(2) See also paragraph 16 (non-UK resident company holding UK land becoming resident in UK after 5 April 2019).

(3) For the purposes of this Schedule—

(a) a disposal is a "direct disposal of UK land" if it is a disposal of an interest in UK land, and

(b) a disposal by a person is an "indirect disposal of UK land" if it is a disposal of an asset (other than an interest in UK land) deriving at least 75% of its value from UK land where the person has a substantial indirect interest in that land.

(4) For the purposes of this paragraph, the disposal is made by a non-resident or a UK resident in the overseas part of a tax year if it is—

(a) a disposal on which a gain accrues that falls to be dealt with by section 1A(3) because the asset disposed of is within paragraph (b) or (c) of that subsection,

(b) a disposal on which a gain accrues that falls to be dealt with by section 1A(1) in accordance with section 1G(2) because the asset disposed of is within section 1A(3)(b) or (c),

(c) a disposal on which a gain accrues that falls to be dealt with by section 2B(4), or

(d) a disposal of an asset on which a gain does not accrue but which, had a gain accrued, would fall to be dealt with as mentioned in any of the preceding paragraphs of this sub-paragraph.

PART 2

INDIRECT DISPOSALS AND DIRECT DISPOSALS NOT CHARGEABLE BEFORE 6 APRIL 2019

Introduction

2 (1) This Part of this Schedule applies to—

(a) all indirect disposals of UK land,

(b) direct disposals of UK land that were not fully residential before 6 April 2019, and

(c) direct disposals of UK land by persons who were not chargeable before 6 April 2019.

(2) For the purposes of this paragraph a direct disposal of UK land made by a person was "not fully residential before 6 April 2019" if in the period—

(a) beginning with the day on which the person acquired the interest in land being disposed of or, if later, 6 April 2015, and

(b) ending with 5 April 2019,

there was no day on which the land to which the disposal relates consisted of or included a dwelling.

(3) If the disposal is of an interest in land subsisting under a contract for the acquisition of land that, at any time before 6 April 2019, consisted of or included a building to be constructed or adapted for use as a dwelling, the disposal is taken to be fully residential before that date.

(4) For the purposes of this paragraph, a disposal is made by a person who was not chargeable before 6 April 2019 if, immediately before that date, the person was—

(a) a company which was not a closely-held company (see sub-paragraph (5)),

(b) a widely-marketed scheme (see sub-paragraph (6)), or

(c) a company carrying on life assurance business (as defined in section 56 of the Finance Act 2012) where the interest in UK land was, immediately before that date, held for the purpose of providing benefits to policyholders in the course of that business.

(5) The question as to whether a company is "a closely-held company" is determined in accordance with Part 1 of Schedule C1; but if—

(a) the company is a divided company within the meaning of section 14G, and

(b) the company would not otherwise be regarded as a closely-held company,

the company is to be so regarded if the conditions in subsection (3) of that section are met.

(6) A person is a "widely-marketed scheme" if—

(a) the person is a scheme within the meaning of section 14F, and

(b) condition A or B in that section is met,

reading the reference in subsection (8)(a) of that section to the non-resident CGT disposal as a reference to the disposal mentioned in paragraph 1(1).

(7) In determining for the purposes of this paragraph whether or not—

(a) a person is a closely-held company, or

(b) a person is a widely-marketed scheme,

arrangements are to be ignored if the main purpose of, or one of the main purposes of, them is to secure a tax advantage as a result of the person not being a closely-held company or the person being a widely-marketed scheme.

(8) In this paragraph—

(a) "arrangements" and "tax advantage" have the same meaning as in section 16A, and

(b) any reference to section 14F, 14G or Schedule C1 are to those provisions as they had effect on 5 April 2019 (before their repeal by Schedule 1 to the Finance Act 2019).

Re-basing to 5 April 2019

3 (1) In calculating the gain or loss accruing on the disposal it is be assumed that the asset was on 5 April 2019 sold by the person, and immediately reacquired by the person, at its market value on that date.

(2) This paragraph has effect subject to any election made by the person under paragraph 4 (retrospective basis of calculation).

Election for retrospective basis of calculation

4 (1) The person may make an election under this paragraph for the assumption that the asset is sold and reacquired as mentioned in paragraph 3 not to apply.

(2) If, in the case of an indirect disposal of UK land—

(a) a person makes an election under this paragraph, and
(b) a loss accrues on the disposal,

the loss is not an allowable loss.

Calculation of residential property gain if election made under paragraph 4

5 (1) This paragraph applies if—

(a) a person makes an election under paragraph 4 in respect of a disposal on which a gain accrues, and
(b) it is necessary to determine, in accordance with Schedule 1B, how much of the gain is a residential property gain.

(2) Paragraph 2 of Schedule 1B has effect as if—

(a) sub-paragraphs (5) and (6) of that paragraph were omitted, and
(b) in that paragraph, "the applicable period" had the definition given by the next sub-paragraph.

(3) "The applicable period" means the period—

(a) beginning with the day on which the person acquired the interest in land being disposed of or, if later, 31 March 1982, and
(b) ending with the day before the day on which the disposal is made.

PART 3

DIRECT DISPOSALS OF PRE-APRIL 2015 ASSETS FULLY CHARGEABLE BEFORE 6 APRIL 2019

Introduction

6 (1) This Part of this Schedule applies to any direct disposal of UK land if—

(a) the person held the interest in UK land being disposed of throughout the period beginning with 6 April 2015 and ending with the disposal, and
(b) the disposal was fully residential before 6 April 2019.

(2) For this purpose a direct disposal of UK land made by a person is "fully residential before 6 April 2019" if in the period—

(a) beginning with 6 April 2015, and
(b) ending with 5 April 2019,

every day on which the land to which the disposal relates consisted of a dwelling.

(3) If the disposal is of an interest in land subsisting under a contract for the acquisition of land that, at any time in that period, did not consist of a building to be constructed or adapted for use as a dwelling, the disposal is taken to be not fully residential before 6 April 2019.

(4) This Part of this Schedule does not apply to a direct disposal of UK land made by a person who was not chargeable before 6 April 2019, as determined for the purposes of paragraph 2.

Re-basing to 5 April 2015

7 (1) In calculating the gain or loss accruing on the disposal it is be assumed that the asset was on 5 April 2015 sold by the person, and immediately reacquired by the person, at its market value on that date.

(2) This paragraph has effect subject to any election made by the person under either—

(a) paragraph 8 (retrospective basis of calculation), or
(b) paragraph 9 (straight-line time apportionment),

(and an election may be made under only one of those paragraphs).

Election for retrospective basis of calculation

8 The person may make an election under this paragraph for the assumption that the asset is sold and reacquired as mentioned in paragraph 7 not to apply.

Election for straight-line time apportionment

9 (1) The person may make an election under this paragraph—

(a) for the assumption that the asset is sold and reacquired as mentioned in paragraph 7 not to apply, and

(b) for the gain or loss accruing on the disposal to be apportioned so that only the post-5 April 2015 proportion of it is treated as accruing on the disposal.

(2) The "post-5 April 2015 proportion" is the proportion that the days in the post-5 April 2015 period bear to the days in the ownership period.

(3) For this purpose—

"the post-5 April 2015 period" means the day beginning with 6 April 2015 and ending with the day on which the disposal is made, and

"the ownership period" means the period beginning with the day on which the person acquired the interest disposed of or, if later, 31 March 1982 and ending with the day on which the disposal is made.

Calculation of residential property gain if election made under paragraph 8 or 9

10 (1) This paragraph applies if—

(a) a person makes an election under paragraph 8 in respect of a disposal on which a gain accrues, and

(b) it is necessary to determine, in accordance with Schedule 1B, how much of the gain is a residential property gain.

(2) Paragraph 2 of Schedule 1B has effect as if—

(a) sub-paragraphs (5) and (6) of that paragraph were omitted, and

(b) in that paragraph, "the applicable period" had the definition given by the next sub-paragraph.

(3) "The applicable period" means the period—

(a) beginning with the day on which the person acquired the interest in land being disposed of or, if later, 31 March 1982, and

(b) ending with the day before the day on which the disposal is made.

11 (1) This paragraph applies if—

(a) a person makes an election under paragraph 9 in respect of a disposal on which a gain accrues, and

(b) it is necessary to determine, in accordance with Schedule 1B, how much of the gain is a residential property gain.

(2) Paragraph 2 of Schedule 1B has effect as if—

(a) sub-paragraphs (5) and (6) of that paragraph were omitted, and

(b) in that paragraph, "the applicable period" had the definition given by the next sub-paragraph.

(3) "The applicable period" means the period—

(a) beginning with 6 April 2015, and

(b) ending with the day before the day on which the disposal is made.

PART 4

DIRECT DISPOSALS OF ASSETS PARTLY CHARGEABLE BEFORE 6 APRIL 2019

Introduction

12 (1) This Part of this Schedule applies to any direct disposal of UK land if—

(a) neither Part 2 nor Part 3 of this Schedule applies to the disposal, and

(b) the interest in UK land being disposed of was not a post-April 2015 asset that was fully residential before 6 April 2019.

(2) For this purpose—

(a) the interest in UK land being disposed of is a "post-April 2015 asset" if it was acquired by the person after 5 April 2015, and

(b) the asset "was fully residential before 6 April 2019" if, in the period beginning with the day on which it was acquired and ending with 5 April 2019, every day on which the land to which the disposal relates consisted of a dwelling.

(3) If the disposal is of an interest in land subsisting under a contract for the acquisition of land that, at any time in that period, did not consist of a building to be constructed or adapted for use as a dwelling, the disposal is taken to be not fully residential before 6 April 2019.

Re-basing to 5 April 2015 and 5 April 2019

13 (1) In calculating the gain or loss accruing on the disposal ("the actual disposal") it is be assumed that—

(a) the asset was on 5 April 2015 sold by the person, and immediately reacquired by the person, at its market value on that date (but see sub-paragraph (3)), and

(b) in addition, the asset was on 5 April 2019 sold by the person, and immediately reacquired by the person, at its market value on that date.

(2) In the case of the assumed sale on 5 April 2019, the gain or loss accruing on that sale is treated as accruing on the actual disposal (in addition to the gain or loss that actually accrues on the actual disposal).

(3) If the asset was acquired by the person after 5 April 2015, the assumption that it is sold, and immediately reacquired, on 5 April 2015 is not to apply.

(4) This paragraph has effect subject to any election made by the person under paragraph 14 (retrospective basis of calculation).

Election for retrospective basis of calculation

14 The person may make an election under this paragraph for the assumptions that the asset is sold and reacquired as mentioned in paragraph 13 not to apply.

Calculation of residential property gain if election made under paragraph 14

15 (1) This paragraph applies if—

(a) a person makes an election under paragraph 14 in respect of a disposal on which a gain accrues, and

(b) it is necessary to determine, in accordance with Schedule 1B, how much of the gain is a residential property gain.

(2) Paragraph 2 of Schedule 1B has effect as if—

(a) sub-paragraphs (5) and (6) of that paragraph were omitted, and

(b) in that paragraph, "the applicable period" had the definition given by the next sub-paragraph.

(3) "The applicable period" means the period—

(a) beginning with the day on which the person acquired the interest in land being disposed of or, if later, 31 March 1982, and

(b) ending with the day before the day on which the disposal is made.

PART 5

MISCELLANEOUS

Companies with UK land becoming UK resident after 5 April 2019

16 (1) This paragraph applies in any case where—

(a) a company becomes resident in the United Kingdom after 5 April 2019,

(b) the company makes a direct or indirect disposal of UK land after that date, and

(c) (ignoring this paragraph) Part 2, 3 or 4 of this Schedule would have applied to the disposal but for the fact that it is made at a time when the company is resident in the United Kingdom.

(2) In that case, Part 2, 3 or 4 of this Schedule applies in relation to the disposal (regardless of paragraph 1(1)(b)).

Persons with UK land ceasing to be UK resident after 5 April 2019

17 (1) This paragraph applies in any case where—

(a) the trustees of a settlement cease to be resident in the United Kingdom after 5 April 2019,

(b) after that date the trustees dispose of an asset held by them on that date, and

(c) the disposal is a direct or indirect disposal of UK land.

(2) Nothing in Part 2, 3 or 4 of this Schedule applies to the disposal.

(3) The asset that is disposed of is excepted from the application of section 80(2) (deemed disposal of assets on trustees ceasing to be resident in UK).

18 (1) This paragraph applies in any case where—

(a) a company ceases to be resident in the United Kingdom after 5 April 2019,

(b) after that date the company disposes of an asset held by it on that date, and

(c) the disposal is a direct or indirect disposal of UK land.

(2) Nothing in Part 2, 3 or 4 of this Schedule applies to the disposal.

(3) The asset that is disposed of is excepted from the application of section 185(2) and (3) (deemed disposal of assets on company ceasing to be resident in UK).

Wasting assets

19 (1) This paragraph applies if, in calculating a gain or loss accruing to a person in a case where paragraph 3, 7 or 13 is applicable, it is necessary to make a wasting asset determination in relation to the asset disposed of.

(2) The assumption that the asset was acquired on a date mentioned in paragraph 3, 7 or 13 (as the case may be) is to be ignored in making that determination.

(3) In this paragraph "a wasting asset determination" means a determination whether or not an asset is a wasting asset, as defined for the purposes of Chapter 2 of Part 2 of this Act.

Capital allowances

20 (1) This paragraph applies if, in calculating a gain or loss accruing to a person in a case where paragraph 3, 7 or 13 is applicable, it is to be assumed that the asset disposed of was acquired on a particular date for a consideration equal to its market value on that date.

(2) For the purposes of that calculation—

(a) section 41 (restriction of losses by reference to capital allowances and renewals allowances), and

(b) section 47 (wasting assets qualifying for capital allowances),

are to apply in relation to any allowance made in respect of the expenditure actually incurred in acquiring or providing the asset as if it were made in respect of the expenditure assumed to have been incurred.

(3) In this paragraph "allowance" means any capital allowance or renewals allowance.

Making of elections

21 (1) An election under any provision of this Schedule must (regardless of section 42(2) of the Management Act) be made by being included in a relevant return relating to the disposal.

(2) For the purposes of this paragraph a "relevant return" means—

(a) an ordinary tax return, or

(b) a return under Schedule 2 to the Finance Act 2019.

(3) An election under any provision of this Schedule which is made by being included in a return under Schedule 2 to the Finance Act 2019 may be subsequently revoked by provision included in an ordinary tax return which is delivered on or before the filing date for the ordinary tax return.

(4) Subject to that, an election under any provision of this Schedule is irrevocable.

(5) All such adjustments are to be made, whether by way of discharge or repayment of tax, the making of assessments or otherwise, as are required to give effect to an election under any provision of this Schedule.

(6) For the purposes of this paragraph, in the case of a person other than a company—

"ordinary tax return" means a return under section 8 or 8A of the Management Act, and

"the filing date", in relation to that return, has the meaning given by section 9A(6) of that Act.

(7) For the purposes of this paragraph, in the case of a company—

"ordinary tax return" means a company tax return under Schedule 18 to the Finance Act 1998, and

"the filing date", in relation to that return, has the meaning given by paragraph 14 of that Schedule.

(8) For the purposes of this paragraph—

(a) the reference to an election being included in a relevant return includes its being included as a result of an amendment of the return, and

(b) the reference to the revocation of an election being included in an ordinary tax return includes its being included as a result of an amendment of the return.

Interpretation

22 (1) In this Schedule—

(a) any reference to an interest in UK land is to be read in accordance with section 1C (and any reference to land is to be read in accordance with that section), and

(b) any reference to an asset (other than an interest in UK land) deriving at least 75% of its value from UK land where a person has a substantial indirect interest in that land is to be read in accordance with Schedule 1A.

(2) If an interest in UK land disposed of by a person results from interests in UK land acquired by the person at different times, the person is regarded for the purposes of this Schedule as having acquired the interest disposed of at the time of the first acquisition.

(3) For the purposes of this Schedule, whether a building is a dwelling is determined in accordance with Schedule 1B."

18 Omit Schedule 4ZZA (relevant high value disposals: gains and losses).

19 Omit Schedule 4ZZB (non-resident CGT disposals: gains and losses).

20 Omit Schedule 4ZZC (disposals of residential property interests: gains and losses).

21 After Schedule 5A insert—

"SCHEDULE 5AAA

UK PROPERTY RICH COLLECTIVE INVESTMENT VEHICLES ETC

PART 1

INTRODUCTION: KEY EXPRESSIONS

Meaning of "collective investment vehicle", "participant" and "unit"

1 (1) In this Schedule "collective investment vehicle" means—

(a) a collective investment scheme,

(b) an AIF,

(c) a company which is a UK REIT, or

(d) a company which is resident outside the United Kingdom and meets the property income condition.

(2) A company meets the property income condition if—

(a) it is not a close company or is a close company but only because it has a qualifying investor as a direct or indirect participator,

(b) at least half of its income is property income from long-term investments,

(c) it distributes all, or substantially all, of its property income from long-term investments and does so on an annual basis, and

(d) it is not liable to tax on that income under the law of any territory in which it is resident.

(3) Paragraph 46 (meaning of "close company", "qualifying investor" and "direct or indirect participator") applies for the purposes of sub-paragraph (2)(a).

(4) For the purposes of sub-paragraph (2) "property income from long-term investments" means income deriving from direct or indirect investments in—

(a) land, or

(b) estates, interests or rights in or over land,

which are made on a long-term basis.

(5) In this Schedule "participant" means—

(a) in relation to a collective investment scheme or an AIF, a person who takes part in the arrangements or undertaking constituting the scheme or AIF, whether by becoming the owner of, or of any part of, the property that is the subject of or held by the arrangements or undertaking or otherwise, or

(b) in relation to a company within (1)(c) or (d), a shareholder in the company.

(6) In this Schedule "unit" means—

(a) in the case of a collective investment scheme or an AIF, the rights or interests (however described) of the participant in the scheme or AIF, or
(b) in the case of a company within (1)(c) or (d), a share in the company.

(7) In this paragraph—

"AIF" has the meaning given by regulation 3 of the Alternative Investment Fund Managers Regulations 2013, and
"UK REIT" has the same meaning as in Part 12 of CTA 2010.

Meaning of "offshore collective investment vehicle"

2 (1) In this Schedule "offshore collective investment vehicle" means—

(a) a collective investment vehicle constituted as a body corporate resident outside the United Kingdom,
(b) a collective investment vehicle under which property is held on trust for the participants where the trustees of the property are not resident in the United Kingdom, or
(c) a collective investment vehicle constituted by other arrangements that create rights in the nature of co-ownership where the arrangements take effect as a result of the law of a territory outside the United Kingdom.

(2) In this paragraph—

"body corporate" does not include a limited liability partnership, and
"co-ownership" is not restricted to the meaning of that term in the law of any part of the United Kingdom.

Meaning of a collective investment vehicle being "UK property rich" etc

3 (1) For the purposes of this Schedule the question whether a collective investment vehicle is "UK property rich" at any time is determined by applying the rules in Part 2 of Schedule 1A on the following assumptions.

(2) The assumptions are—

(a) that (so far as this would not otherwise be the case) the vehicle were a company, and
(b) that a disposal were made at that time of a right or interest in that company.

(3) If that disposal would be regarded for the purposes of Schedule 1A as a disposal of an asset deriving at least 75% of its value from UK land, the vehicle is regarded for the purposes of this Schedule as being UK property rich at that time.

(4) For the purposes of this Schedule the question whether a company is "UK property rich" at any time is determined by applying the rules in Part 2 of Schedule 1A on the assumption that a disposal were made at that time of a right or interest in the company.

(5) If that disposal would be regarded for the purposes of Schedule 1A as a disposal of an asset deriving at least 75% of its value from UK land, the company is regarded for the purposes of this Schedule as being UK property rich at that time.

PART 2

BASIC RULES

Application of Act to offshore CIV

4 (1) This paragraph applies to an offshore collective investment vehicle—

(a) which is not a company, and
(b) which is not constituted by two or more persons carrying on a trade or business in partnership.

(2) It is to be assumed that, for relevant purposes—

(a) the vehicle is a company, and
(b) the rights of the participants are shares in that company.

(3) The reference here to "relevant purposes" means—

(a) the purposes of this Schedule, and
(b) the purpose of applying section 1A(3)(b) or (c) or 2B(4) (and the other provisions of this or any other Act so far as relevant to their application) in relation to the vehicle.

(4) This paragraph does not apply to a collective investment vehicle in relation to which an election has effect under Part 3 of this Schedule (election for transparency).

(5) This paragraph applies in relation to a collective investment vehicle to which section 103D applies (tax transparent funds) but does not affect the operation of the rules set out in—

(a) section 103D(4) to (9) (calculation of gains on disposal of units etc), or
(b) section 103DA (share pooling etc).

(6) If this paragraph applies in relation to a collective investment vehicle, section 99 (application of Act to unit trust schemes) does not apply in relation to the scheme.

Units in a CoACS treated as shares in a company

5 (1) This paragraph applies to a unit in an authorised contractual scheme which is a co-ownership scheme where, as a result of the application of section 103D (application of Act to tax transparent funds), the unit is treated as an asset for the purposes of this Act.

(2) The asset is treated for the purposes of Schedule 1A as if it were a share in a company.

Disposals by non-UK residents

6 (1) This paragraph applies if—

(a) a person disposes of an asset that derives at least 75% of its value from UK land (as determined in accordance with Part 2 of Schedule 1A), and
(b) the disposal has an appropriate connection to a collective investment vehicle (see sub-paragraphs (3) to (6) for the cases in which this test is met).

(2) For the purposes of section 1A(3)(c) or 2B(4)(b) (disposals by non-UK residents of assets deriving 75% of value from UK land etc), the person is treated as having a substantial indirect interest in the UK land at the time of the disposal.

(3) A disposal has an appropriate connection to a collective investment vehicle if the asset disposed of consists of a right or interest in—

(a) a collective investment vehicle, or
(b) a company at least half of whose market value derives from its being a direct or indirect participant in one or more collective investment vehicles.

(4) A disposal has an appropriate connection to a collective investment vehicle if—

(a) the vehicle is constituted by two or more persons carrying on a trade or business in partnership, and
(b) the disposal is made by a person as a participant in the vehicle.

(5) A disposal has an appropriate connection to a collective investment vehicle if the vehicle is a company and the disposal is made by it.

(6) A disposal has an appropriate connection to a collective investment vehicle if—

(a) a company (which is not the vehicle) makes the disposal, and
(b) the vehicle, and one or more other collective investment vehicles that are UK property rich, have a 50% investment in the company.

(7) Collective investment vehicles have a 50% investment in a company if, applying the rule in paragraph 9 (but without regard to paragraph 10) of Schedule 1A as if references to 25% were references to 50%, the vehicles would be regarded as having a 50% investment in the company at the time of the disposal.

(8) For this purpose the collective investment schemes are to be regarded as if they were a single person.

(9) This paragraph is subject to paragraph 7 (collective investment vehicles expected to have no more than 40% investments in UK land).

7 (1) This paragraph applies to a disposal which would otherwise have an appropriate connection to a collective investment vehicle as a result of paragraph 6(3), (5) or (6).

(2) A disposal does not have an appropriate connection to a collective investment vehicle if, at the time of the disposal, the vehicle mentioned in paragraph 6(3)(a) or (5) or (6), or each of the vehicles mentioned in paragraph 6(3)(b), meets—

(a) the non-UK real estate condition, and
(b) the genuine diversity of ownership condition or, if the vehicle is a company, the non-close condition.

(3) If—

(a) a disposal is made as mentioned in paragraph 6(6), and
(b) the vehicle mentioned there is constituted by two or more persons carrying on a trade or business in partnership,

the condition in sub-paragraph (2)(b) is taken to be met if the company mentioned in paragraph 6(6) meets the non-close condition.

(4) A vehicle meets the non-UK real estate condition at any time if, by reference to the prospectus for the vehicle as the prospectus has effect at that time, no more than 40% of the expected market value of the vehicle's investments is intended to derive from investments consisting of—

(a) interests in UK land, or
(b) rights or interests in companies which are UK property rich.

(5) A vehicle meets the genuine diversity of ownership condition at any time if, at that time—

(a) it meets conditions A to C of regulation 75 of the Offshore Funds (Tax) Regulations 2009, or
(b) it meets the condition in regulation 75(5) of those Regulations,

and those Regulations apply for the purposes of this sub-paragraph as if any collective investment vehicle which is not an offshore fund were regarded as an offshore fund.

(6) A company meets the non-close condition at any time if, at that time, it—

(a) is not a close company, or
(b) is a close company but only because it has a qualifying investor as a direct or indirect participator.

(7) Paragraph 46 (meaning of "close company", "qualifying investor" and "direct or indirect participator") applies for the purposes of sub-paragraph (6).

PART 3

ELECTION FOR TRANSPARENCY

Election for collective investment vehicle to be treated as partnership

8 (1) This paragraph applies to an offshore collective investment vehicle—

(a) which is UK property rich, and
(b) which is transparent for income tax purposes otherwise than as a result of being constituted by two or more persons carrying on a trade or business in partnership.

(2) The manager of the vehicle may make an election for the vehicle to be treated for the purposes of—

(a) this Act, and
(b) the Management Act, and any other provision of the Corporation Tax Acts, so far as relating to the taxation of chargeable gains,

as if, in relation to all times on and after its constitution, it were to be regarded as a partnership.

(3) Accordingly, as a result of sub-paragraph (2)(b), it follows that, in applying rules such as section 1154 of CTA 2010 (meaning of "75% subsidiary" etc) for the purposes of Part 12 of that Act (Real Estate Investment Trusts) so far as relating to the taxation of chargeable gains, the vehicle is to be regarded as a partnership.

(4) In the case of section 12AA of the Management Act as it applies as a result of sub-paragraph (2), a notice under subsection (2) or (3) of that section may be given to the manager of the vehicle.

(5) The election has effect whether or not the vehicle would, but for the making of the election, be regarded as a person chargeable to capital gains tax or corporation tax on chargeable gains.

(6) For the purposes of this paragraph whether or not an offshore collective investment vehicle is regarded as being UK property rich may be determined by reference to the prospectus for the vehicle on the assumption that investments are made by the vehicle in accordance with the prospectus.

(7) For the purposes of this paragraph a collective investment vehicle is "transparent for income tax purposes" if, on the assumption that there are participants who are individuals resident in the United Kingdom, any sums which form part of the income of the vehicle—

(a) would be chargeable to income tax on those assumed participants under a provision specified in section 830(2) of ITTOIA 2005 in respect of such of those sums as would be referable to their interests, or

(b) if any of that income is derived from assets within the United Kingdom, would be so chargeable had the assets been outside the United Kingdom.

(8) If an election is made under this paragraph in relation to a collective investment vehicle—

(a) section 99 (application of Act to unit trust schemes) does not apply in relation to the vehicle, and

(b) section 103D (tax transparent funds) does not apply in relation to the vehicle.

Further provision about election

9 (1) An election under paragraph 8 in relation to an offshore collective investment vehicle—

(a) has effect only if the participants in the vehicle at the time at which it is made have consented to the making of the election,

(b) must be made by notice given to an officer of Revenue and Customs, and

(c) must be made before the end of the period of 12 months beginning with the relevant acquisition date.

(2) For this purpose "the relevant acquisition date" means the earliest date on which—

(a) an interest in UK land, or

(b) a right or interest in a company that is UK property rich,

forms part of the property that is the subject of or held by the vehicle.

(3) An election under paragraph 8 is irrevocable.

Units in CIVs held by life insurance companies

10 (1) This paragraph applies if an election under paragraph 8 has effect in relation to an offshore collective investment vehicle.

(2) The election is treated as having no effect for the purposes of this Act in relation to any units in the vehicle which are held by an insurance company for the purposes of its long-term business.

Relationship to re-basing rules under Schedule 4AA for non-UK residents

11 (1) This paragraph applies if—

(a) an election under paragraph 8 has effect in relation to an offshore collective investment vehicle, and

(b) as a result of the election, Part 3 or 4 of Schedule 4AA would (but for this paragraph) apply in relation to a disposal made by a participant in the vehicle.

(2) The disposal is to be regarded for the purposes of Schedule 4AA as if it were one to which Part 2 of that Schedule applies.

PART 4

EXEMPTION

Exemption for qualifying offshore CIV that is UK property rich etc

12 (1) An election may be made for a collective investment vehicle, or a company which is not a collective investment vehicle, to be exempt from corporation tax on chargeable gains accruing to it on—

(a) all direct disposals of UK land, and

(b) all indirect disposals of UK land.

(2) An election may be made in respect of a collective investment vehicle if each of the following entitlement conditions is met—

(a) the vehicle is offshore,

(b) the vehicle is a company (whether as a result of paragraph 4 or otherwise),

(c) the vehicle is UK property rich,
(d) the vehicle meets all of the qualifying conditions set out in paragraph 13, and
(e) if the vehicle is an AIF, it would also meet the definition of a collective investment vehicle for another reason.

(3) An election may be made in respect of a company which is not a collective investment vehicle if each of the following entitlement conditions is met—

(a) the company is wholly (or almost wholly) owned by a collective investment scheme which is constituted by two or more persons carrying on a trade or business in partnership or is constituted by a CoACS,
(b) the appropriate entity is UK property rich, and
(c) the company meets all of the qualifying conditions set out in paragraph 13,

and it does not matter where the company is resident.

(4) In sub-paragraph (3)(b) the "appropriate entity" means—

(a) in a case where the collective investment scheme is constituted by two or more persons carrying on a trade or business in partnership, the company, and
(b) in a case where the collective investment scheme is constituted by a CoACS, the CoACS.

(5) If an election is made under this paragraph in respect of a collective investment vehicle—

(a) the vehicle is referred to in this Part of this Schedule as "a qualifying fund", and
(b) any reference in this Part of this Schedule to a qualifying fund, in relation to any time after the election is made (including any time after the election ceases to have effect), is to be read as a reference to the arrangements, undertaking or company which met the definition of collective investment vehicle when the election was made.

(6) If an election is made under this paragraph in respect of a company which is not a collective investment vehicle—

(a) the company is referred to in this Part of this Schedule as "a qualifying company", and
(b) any reference in this Part of this Schedule to a qualifying company, in relation to any time after the election is made (including any time after the election ceases to have effect), is to be read as a reference to the company.

(7) Section 103D (application of Act to tax transparent funds) does not apply for the purpose of determining whether sub-paragraph (3)(a) applies.

(8) In this paragraph—

"AIF" has the meaning given by regulation 3 of the Alternative Investment Fund Managers Regulations 2013, and

"CoACS" means an authorised contractual scheme which is a co-ownership scheme.

Qualifying conditions and information provided to HMRC

13 (1) For the purposes of paragraph 12(2), a collective investment vehicle meets the qualifying conditions in this paragraph at any time if, at that time—

(a) it is a collective investment scheme and it meets the genuine diversity of ownership condition,
(b) it is a company (otherwise than as a result of paragraph 4) and it meets the recognised stock exchange condition and the non-close condition, or
(c) it is a collective investment vehicle (of any kind) and it meets the UK tax condition and the non-close condition.

(2) For the purposes of paragraph 12(3), a company which is not a collective investment vehicle meets the qualifying conditions in this paragraph at any time if, at that time, either—

(a) the company meets the UK tax condition and the non-close condition, or
(b) the collective investment scheme which wholly (or almost wholly) owns the company meets the genuine diversity of ownership condition.

(3) For the purposes of this paragraph a collective investment scheme meets the genuine diversity of ownership condition at any time if, at that time—

(a) it meets conditions A to C of regulation 75 of the Offshore Funds (Tax) Regulations 2009, or
(b) it meets the condition in regulation 75(5) of those Regulations,

and those Regulations apply for the purposes of this sub-paragraph as if any collective investment scheme which is not an offshore fund were regarded as an offshore fund.

(4) For the purposes of this paragraph a company meets the recognised stock exchange condition at any time if, at that time—

(a) it has ordinary share capital, and
(b) the shares forming part of its ordinary share capital are regularly traded on a recognised stock exchange.

(5) For the purposes of this paragraph a company meets the non-close condition at any time if, at that time, it—

(a) is not a close company, or
(b) is a close company but only because it has a qualifying investor as a direct or indirect participator.

(6) Paragraph 46 (meaning of "close company", "qualifying investor" and "direct or indirect participator") applies for the purposes of sub-paragraph (5).

(7) For the purposes of this paragraph a company meets the UK tax condition at any time if, on the assumption that all of the shares in it were disposed of for their market value at that time, the person making the election reasonably considers at that time that, as a result solely of double taxation arrangements, no more than 25% of the total proceeds would fall to be left out of account for the purposes of this Act.

14 (1) An election under paragraph 12 has effect only if it is accompanied by information of such description as may be specified by an officer of Revenue and Customs about disposals made by participants in the relevant fund at any time in—

(a) the period of two years ending with the day before the day on which the election is made, or
(b) if shorter, the period beginning with the constitution of the relevant fund and ending with the day before the day on which the election is made.

(2) Information is not required by sub-paragraph (1) to accompany the election so far as—

(a) it has already been provided to an officer of Revenue and Customs in a form and manner, and at times, specified by an officer of Revenue and Customs, and
(b) the election sets out those occasions on which the information has been so provided.

15 (1) An election under paragraph 12 has effect subject to such conditions as to the provision of information or documents to an officer of Revenue and Customs as may be specified by an officer of Revenue and Customs.

(2) The information or documents must be provided to an officer of Revenue and Customs in respect of every period of account of the relevant fund which ends at a time when the election has effect.

(3) The information or documents must be provided to an officer of Revenue and Customs within the period of 12 months from the end of the period of account.

(4) The conditions as to the provision of information or documents may include—

(a) conditions relating to the participants in the relevant fund, and
(b) conditions requiring information or documents in respect of the operation of any provision of this Schedule (or any provision of this Act relevant to this Schedule).

(5) In the case of an election under paragraph 12—

(a) a designated HMRC officer may revoke the election if, in the officer's opinion, there has been, without reasonable excuse, a breach of any provision made by or under this paragraph, but
(b) an officer of Revenue and Customs (whether or not designated) may waive a breach of any provision made by or under this paragraph if, in the officer's opinion, there is no reasonable excuse for the breach but, having regard to all the circumstances, the breach is nonetheless insignificant.

(6) The circumstances to which the officer may have regard in determining whether a breach is insignificant include the number and seriousness of previous breaches.

(7) In this paragraph "period of account", in relation to the relevant fund, means any period for which accounts of the relevant fund are drawn up.

(8) If the period of account would otherwise be longer than 12 months, the period of account is to be treated for the purposes of this paragraph as split into more than one period of account, and—

- (a) the first deemed period of account is to be 12 months long, and
- (b) any subsequent deemed period of account is to start when the previous deemed period of account ends and is to end 12 months later or, if earlier, when the actual period of account ends.

Exemption for direct or indirect disposals of UK land by persons in which fund invests

16 (1) This paragraph applies if—

- (a) an election under paragraph 12 has been made in respect of a qualifying fund or qualifying company ("Q"),
- (b) Q is UK property rich by reference (wholly or partly) to particular interests in UK land ("the relevant UK property"), and
- (c) a person other than Q makes a disposal at a time when the election has effect.

(2) If—

- (a) the disposal is a direct disposal of any of the relevant UK property by a person, and
- (b) immediately before the disposal, Q has a 40% investment in the person,

the appropriate proportion of any gain accruing to the person on the disposal is not a chargeable gain.

(3) If the disposal is an indirect disposal of UK land in a case where—

- (a) the interests in UK land in question consist of or include any of the relevant UK property, and
- (b) immediately before the disposal, Q has a 40% investment in the company in question,

the appropriate proportion of any gain accruing to the person on the disposal is not a chargeable gain.

(4) For the purposes of this paragraph the "appropriate proportion" means the proportion that so much of the consideration for the disposal as forms part (directly or indirectly) of the assets of Q bears to the total consideration for the disposal.

(5) For the purposes of this paragraph a person has a 40% investment in a company if, applying the rule in paragraph 9 (but without regard to paragraph 10) of Schedule 1A as if references to 25% were references to 40%, the person would be regarded as having a 40% investment in the company immediately before the disposal.

(6) In this paragraph—

"the interests in UK land in question" means the interests in UK land taken into account in determining whether the disposal is an indirect disposal of UK land, and

"the company in question", in relation to a disposal of a right or interest in a company by the person, means that company.

(7) If an officer of Revenue and Customs considers that the operation of this paragraph would otherwise result in the total proportion of a gain that is not a chargeable gain exceeding the whole of the gain, the officer may make such adjustments to the appropriate proportion of a gain accruing to any person as the officer considers just and reasonable to prevent that result.

Making of election and period for which it has effect

17 (1) An election under paragraph 12—

- (a) must be made by the relevant fund manager, and
- (b) must be made by notice given to an officer of Revenue and Customs.

(2) An election under paragraph 12 must specify the day from which it is to have effect.

(3) The election has effect in relation to disposals on or after the day specified in the election.

(4) A day may be specified in the election even if it falls before the day on which the election is made.

(5) But a day that falls more than 12 months before the day on which the election is made may be specified only if an officer of Revenue and Customs consents.

(6) For this purpose—

(a) consent may be given generally (for example, by describing, in a notice published by an officer of Revenue and Customs, cases in which consent is deemed to be given), or

(b) consent may be given in relation to particular cases.

Revocation of election

18 (1) In addition to the case set out in paragraph 15(5)(a), a designated HMRC officer may revoke an election under paragraph 12 if, in order to safeguard the public revenue, the officer considers it is appropriate to revoke the election.

(2) In the case of an election under paragraph 12 which is revoked by a designated HMRC officer (whether under this paragraph or paragraph 15), the revocation must be made by notice given by a designated HMRC officer to the relevant fund manager.

(3) The relevant fund manager may revoke an election under paragraph 12 by giving notice of the revocation to an officer of Revenue and Customs.

(4) A notice of revocation of an election under paragraph 12 must specify the day from which the election is to cease to have effect.

(5) The election ceases to have effect in relation to disposals made on or after the day specified in the notice of revocation.

(6) The relevant fund manager may specify a day in a notice of revocation even if the day falls before the day on which the notice is given but only if an officer of Revenue and Customs consent.

(7) For this purpose—

(a) consent may be given generally (for example, by describing, in a notice published by an officer of Revenue and Customs, cases in which consent is deemed to be given), or

(b) consent may be given in relation to particular cases.

19 (1) A notice of revocation given by a designated HMRC officer under paragraph 15 or 18 must state the grounds for revoking the election under paragraph 12.

(2) The relevant fund manager may bring an appeal against the revocation of the election.

(3) The appeal must be made by notice given to the designated HMRC officer during the period of 30 days beginning with the day on which the notice of revocation is given.

(4) In the case of an appeal which is notified to the tribunal (see Part 5 of the Management Act), the tribunal must not allow the appeal unless it considers that a designated HMRC officer could not reasonably have been satisfied that there were grounds for revoking the election.

Qualifying fund or company ceasing to meet applicable exemption conditions

20 (1) This paragraph applies if—

(a) an election under paragraph 12 has been made at any time in respect of a qualifying fund or qualifying company, and

(b) at any subsequent time, the qualifying fund or qualifying company ceases to meet the applicable exemption conditions.

(2) The election ceases to have effect from that subsequent time in relation to disposals made at or after that time.

(3) This paragraph needs to be read with—

(a) paragraph 27 (temporary period of no more than 30 days during which certain of applicable exemption conditions not met),

(b) paragraph 28 (temporary period of no more than 9 months during which applicable exemption conditions not met), and

(c) paragraph 30 (steps taken by relevant fund manager to wind up relevant fund).

Deemed disposal: payments not otherwise taxable where value derived from direct or indirect disposals of UK land

21 (1) This paragraph applies if—

(a) an election under paragraph 12 that has been made in respect of a qualifying fund or qualifying company has effect at any time,

(b) a participant in the relevant fund is entitled to receive an amount at that time ("the relevant time") which represents, in substance, value derived (directly or indirectly) from a direct disposal of UK land or from the UK land component of an indirect disposal of UK land, and

(c) the amount is regarded as being of a revenue nature and does not fall to be taken into account for the purposes of income tax or corporation tax on income.

(2) In the case of an election made in respect of a qualifying fund, the participant in the relevant fund is deemed for the purposes of this Act—

(a) to have sold its units in the relevant fund immediately before the relevant time at their market value immediately before that time, and

(b) to have reacquired those units immediately after the relevant time at their market value immediately after that time.

(3) In the case of an election made in respect of a qualifying company, the participant in the relevant fund is deemed for the purposes of this Act—

(a) to have sold its rights and interests in the company immediately before the relevant time at their market value immediately before that time, and

(b) to have reacquired those rights and interests immediately after the relevant time at their market value immediately after that time.

(4) In this paragraph "the UK land component" of an indirect disposal of UK land means the interests in UK land taken into account in determining whether the disposal is an indirect disposal of UK land.

Deemed disposal if election ceases to have effect

22 (1) This paragraph applies if at any time an election which has been made under paragraph 12 in respect of a qualifying fund or qualifying company ceases to have effect.

(2) In the case of an election made in respect of a qualifying fund, each participant in the relevant fund is deemed for the purposes of this Act—

(a) to have sold its units in the relevant fund immediately before that time, and

(b) to have immediately reacquired those rights and interests,

at their market value immediately before that time.

(3) In the case of an election made in respect of a qualifying company, each participant in the relevant fund is deemed for the purposes of this Act—

(a) to have sold its rights and interests in the company immediately before that time, and

(b) to have immediately reacquired those rights and interests,

at their market value immediately before that time.

Gains accruing on disposals under paragraph 21 or 22

23 (1) This paragraph applies if a disposal of an asset is deemed to have been made by a person at any time under—

(a) paragraph 21, or

(b) paragraph 22 but only as a result of paragraph 20 (qualifying fund or qualifying company ceasing to meet the applicable exemption conditions).

(2) Any gain ("the deemed gain") accruing to the person on the disposal is treated as accruing to the person in accordance with the rules set out in the remainder of this paragraph.

(3) If, at the time of the deemed disposal or a subsequent time—

(a) the person actually disposes of a unit in the relevant fund, or

(b) the person receives an amount of a kind mentioned in paragraph 21(1),

the appropriate portion of the deemed gain is treated as accruing to the person at the time of the actual disposal or the time of the receipt.

(4) For this purpose "the appropriate portion" means the proportion which—

(a) the consideration for the actual disposal, or

(b) the amount of the receipt,

bears to the amount of the deemed gain.

(5) If some of the deemed gain has accrued on one or more previous occasions, the appropriate portion is restricted so that, when added to the appropriate portion or portions on the previous occasion or occasions, it does not exceed 100%.

(6) In determining the appropriate proportion, so much (if any) of the consideration for the actual disposal or the amount of the receipt as exceeds the amount of the deemed gain is to be ignored.

(7) In the case of a disposal under paragraph 21, the remainder of the deemed gain is treated as accruing to the person (unless the whole amount has already accrued) when the relevant fund is wound up.

(8) In the case of a disposal under paragraph 22, the remainder of the deemed gain is treated as accruing to the person (unless the whole amount has already accrued) at—

(a) the end of the period of three years beginning with the time of the deemed disposal, or

(b) if earlier, when the relevant fund is wound up.

Relief for expenses in the case of deemed disposals under paragraph 21 or 22

24 (1) This paragraph applies if a disposal is deemed to have been made by a person as a result of paragraph 21 or 22.

(2) The person is treated for the purposes of section 38(1)(c) as having incurred incidental costs of making the deemed disposal equal to the notional costs.

(3) The reference here to the notional costs is to the incidental costs —

(a) which the person would reasonably have expected to have incurred if the deemed sale under paragraph 21 or 22 had been an actual sale, and

(b) which would have been allowable under section 38(1)(c) if there had been an actual sale.

Notification to participants in relation to deemed disposals under paragraph 21 or 22

25 (1) This paragraph applies if—

(a) a disposal is deemed to have been made by a person under paragraph 21,

(b) a disposal is deemed to have been made by a person under paragraph 22 as a result of the revocation of an election, or

(c) an amount is treated as accruing to a person under paragraph 23(7) or (8).

(2) The relevant fund manager must notify the person of the matters mentioned in sub-paragraph (1)(a), (b) or (c).

(3) The notification—

(a) must be in writing, and

(b) must be given within the period of 30 days beginning with the relevant time.

(4) If this paragraph applies as result of sub-paragraph (1)(a) or (b), "the relevant time" means the time at which the deemed disposal is made.

(5) If this paragraph applies as result of sub-paragraph (1)(c), "the relevant time" is the time at which the amount is treated as accruing.

26 (1) A person who fails to comply with paragraph 25 is liable to a penalty not exceeding £3,000.

(2) If—

(a) there is a failure to comply with that paragraph, and

(b) there are two or more persons who are the relevant fund managers each of whom is subject to the duty to notify under that paragraph,

the total amount of the penalties to which those managers (taken together) are liable is not to exceed £3,000.

(3) If a person becomes liable to a penalty under this paragraph, an officer of Revenue and Customs must—

(a) assess the penalty, and

(b) notify the person.

(4) The assessment must be made within the period of 12 months beginning with the day on which an officer of Revenue and Customs first becomes aware that the person has failed to comply with paragraph 25.

(5) A person may, by notice, appeal against a decision of an officer of Revenue and Customs that a penalty is payable under this paragraph.

(6) Notice of appeal under this paragraph must specify the grounds of appeal.

(7) Notice of appeal under this paragraph must be given—

(a) within 30 days after the penalty was notified to the person,

(b) to the officer of Revenue and Customs who notified the person.

(8) A penalty under this paragraph must be paid before the end of the period of 30 days beginning with—

(a) the day on which the person was notified of the penalty, or

(b) if notice of appeal against the penalty is given, the day on which the appeal is finally determined or withdrawn.

Temporary period during which applicable exemption conditions not met

27 (1) This paragraph applies if—

(a) an election under paragraph 12 has been made in respect of a qualifying fund or qualifying company ("Q"),

(b) Q ceases at any time ("the relevant time") to meet the applicable exemption conditions otherwise than as a result of the vehicle or appropriate entity ceasing to be UK property rich (see paragraph 12(2)(c) or (3)(b)),

(c) the election would (but for this paragraph) have, accordingly, ceased to have had effect under paragraph 20 from the relevant time,

(d) the relevant fund manager expects Q to meet the applicable exemption conditions within 30 days, and

(e) Q does meets those conditions within 30 days.

(2) The failure by Q to meet the applicable exemption conditions is to be ignored for the purposes of this Part of this Schedule.

(3) In this paragraph any reference to Q meeting the applicable exemption conditions within 30 days is to Q meeting those conditions before the end of the period of 30 days beginning with the day on which the relevant time falls.

(4) This paragraph does not apply on more than four occasions in any period of 12 months.

28 (1) This paragraph applies if—

(a) an election under paragraph 12 has been made in respect of a qualifying fund or qualifying company,

(b) but for this paragraph, the election would, as a result of paragraph 20, have ceased to have effect from a particular time for all purposes of this Part of this Schedule ("the relevant time"),

(c) the relevant fund manager expects the failure to meet the applicable exemption conditions to last for a temporary period, and

(d) at the end of the temporary period, the qualifying fund or qualifying company does meet those conditions.

(2) It is to be assumed that, for the purposes of any provision of this Part of this Schedule other than paragraph 22, the qualifying fund or qualifying company continues to meet the applicable exemption conditions during the temporary period.

(3) Accordingly—

(a) a deemed disposal occurs under paragraph 22 by reference to the failure to meet the applicable exemption conditions, but

(b) subject to that, the election continues to have effect during the temporary period.

(4) A period is not to be regarded as a temporary period for the purposes of this paragraph if it is longer than a period of 9 months beginning with the relevant time.

(5) This paragraph does not apply if paragraph 27 applies.

29 (1) This paragraph applies if paragraph 28 has applied in relation to a qualifying fund or qualifying company on one or more occasions.

(2) Paragraph 23(8) has effect as if, for the words from "at—" to the end, there were substituted "when the relevant fund is wound up."

Steps taken by relevant fund manager to wind up relevant fund

30 (1) This paragraph applies if—

(a) an election under paragraph 12 has been made in respect of a qualifying fund or qualifying company,

(b) but for this paragraph, the election would, as a result of paragraph 20, have ceased to have effect from a particular time ("the relevant time") for all purposes of this Part of this Schedule, and

(c) the relevant time occurs at a time when the relevant fund manager is taking steps with a view to the disposal of all of the assets of the relevant fund so that it can be wound up.

(2) It is to be assumed that, for the purposes of any provision of this Part of this Schedule other than paragraph 22, the qualifying fund or qualifying company continues to meet the applicable exemption conditions until the relevant fund is wound up.

(3) Accordingly—

(a) a deemed disposal occurs under paragraph 22 by reference to the failure to meet the applicable exemption conditions, but

(b) subject to that, the election continues to have effect until the relevant fund is wound up.

Deemed disposals of UK land by companies previously owned by fund

31 (1) This paragraph applies if—

(a) an election under paragraph 12 has been made in respect of a qualifying fund or qualifying company ("Q"),

(b) Q, or a company covered by the election, disposes of all of its rights and interests in another company ("C") which is UK property rich, and

(c) C is covered by the election.

(2) C is deemed for the purposes of this Act—

(a) to have sold, at the relevant time, the appropriate proportion of every qualifying asset the actual disposal of which by C would be a direct or indirect disposal of UK land, and

(b) to have reacquired the appropriate proportion of the asset immediately after the relevant time,

at its market value at the relevant time.

(3) In the case of a disposal, a company is "covered by the election" for the purposes of this paragraph if the disposal is one to which paragraph 16 applies where the election concerned is the one referred to in this paragraph.

(4) For the purposes of this paragraph "the appropriate proportion" of an asset is equal to whatever would be, for the purposes of paragraph 16, the appropriate portion of any gain if it is assumed—

(a) that C had sold the asset at the relevant time, and

(b) that the total consideration for that sale was such that it results in a gain of £100 accruing to C.

(5) For the purposes of this paragraph, an asset is a "qualifying asset" if, throughout the period of one year ending with the day on which the disposal of the asset is made, the asset has been held by C or any other company covered by the election or by Q.

(6) In this paragraph "the relevant time" means the time immediately before the disposal of all the rights and interests in C.

Deemed disposals of UK land by company or fund ceasing to be qualifying etc

32 (1) This paragraph applies if—

(a) an election under paragraph 12 has been made in respect of a qualifying fund or qualifying company ("Q"),

(b) the election has had effect for a continuous period of at least five years, and

(c) either the election ceases to have effect (otherwise than in disqualifying circumstances) or the relevant fund manager starts to take steps with a view to the disposal of all of the assets of the relevant fund so that it can be wound up.

(2) Q is deemed for the purposes of this Act—

(a) to have sold, at the relevant time, every asset the actual disposal of which by Q would be a direct or indirect disposal of UK land, and

(b) to have reacquired the asset immediately after the relevant time,

at its market value at the relevant time.

(3) In the case of any asset covered by the election for 12 months and held by a company at the relevant time, the company is deemed for the purposes of this Act—

(a) to have sold, at the relevant time, the appropriate proportion of the asset, and

(b) to have reacquired the appropriate proportion of the asset immediately after the relevant time,

at its market value at the relevant time.

(4) For the purposes of sub-paragraph (3) an asset held by a company at the relevant time has been "covered by the election for 12 months" if, assuming the asset were disposed of at the relevant time, the disposal would have been one to which paragraph 16 applied by reference to the election.

(5) For the purposes of sub-paragraph (3) "the appropriate proportion" of an asset is equal to whatever would be, for the purposes of paragraph 16, the appropriate portion of any gain if it is assumed—

(a) that the company had sold the asset at the relevant time, and

(b) that the total consideration for that sale was such that it results in a gain of £100 accruing to it.

(6) For the purposes of this paragraph the election ceases to have effect in "disqualifying circumstances" if—

(a) it ceases to have effect as a result of a notice of revocation under paragraph 15(5)(a) in a case where a designated officer of Revenue and Customs is of the opinion that there have been at least three serious breaches of provision made by or under paragraph 15 during the period for which the election has had effect, or

(b) it ceases to have effect as a result of a notice of revocation under paragraph 18(1).

(7) In this paragraph "the relevant time" means the time immediately before—

(a) the election ceases to have effect, or

(b) the relevant fund manager starts to take steps with a view to the disposal of all or the assets of the relevant fund so that it can be wound up.

(8) For the purposes of this paragraph an election made under paragraph 12 in respect of Q is taken to be the same election as one made at a subsequent time in respect of another qualifying fund or qualifying company ("A") if, at the subsequent time, Q is wholly owned by A.

Exemption for disposals by companies wholly owned by certain investors

33 (1) This paragraph applies if an election under paragraph 12 has been made in respect of a qualifying fund or qualifying company.

(2) If—

(a) a participant in the relevant fund disposes of a unit in the relevant fund,

(b) the participant is a company which is wholly owned by one or more investors to which this paragraph applies, and

(c) the participant is not a collective investment vehicle,

any gain accruing on the disposal is not a chargeable gain.

(3) Nothing in paragraph 21 is to result in a deemed disposal of an asset held by any investor to which this paragraph applies other than an insurance company.

(4) Each of the following is an investor to which this paragraph applies—

(a) any person who is a qualifying institutional investor within the meaning of Schedule 7AC (substantial shareholding exemption),

(b) a company carrying on life assurance business where, immediately before the disposal, its right or interest in the participant is an asset which, applying the rules in section 138 of the Finance Act 2012, is wholly matched to a liability of its life assurance business that is not BLAGAB,

(c) a company carrying on long-term business none of which is BLAGAB where, immediately before the disposal, its right or interest in the participant is an asset held for the purposes of its long-term business, and

(d) a qualifying fund or qualifying company in respect of which an election under paragraph 12 has effect.

(5) In this paragraph "BLAGAB" means basic life assurance and general annuity business.

Disapplication of paragraph 3A of Schedule 7AC: qualifying institutional investors

34 (1) This paragraph applies if—

(a) a gain or loss accrues to a company ("the investing company") which has ordinary share capital owned by one or more qualifying institutional investors,

(b) some of the gain or loss is not chargeable or allowable as a result of paragraph 16(3), and

(c) some or all of the ownership of the qualifying institutional investors in the investing company is through the company which is Q for the purposes of paragraph 16(3).

(2) The ownership of the qualifying institutional investors in the investing company is to be ignored for the purpose of applying the exemption conferred by paragraph 3A of Schedule 7AC so far as the ownership is through Q.

(3) In this paragraph "qualifying institutional investors" has the same meaning as in Schedule 7AC.

(4) Paragraph 3B of Schedule 7AC (meaning of "ownership") applies for the purposes of this paragraph as it applies for the purposes of paragraph 3A of that Schedule.

Relationship between rules in this Part and REIT rules in Part 12 of CTA 2010

35 (1) Nothing in this Part of this Schedule is to exempt so much of any qualifying REIT gain as accrues on a disposal made by a company which is, or is a member of, a UK REIT.

(2) A chargeable gain is a "qualifying REIT gain" so far as—

(a) the gain is not a chargeable gain as a result of section 535 or 535A of CTA 2010, and

(b) the gain is not one falling to be exempted as a result of the application of either of those sections following a notice given under section 586(1) or 587(1) of that Act (venturing group).

(3) In this paragraph "UK REIT" has the same meaning as in Part 12 of CTA 2010.

36 (1) This paragraph applies if—

(a) a gain accrues on a disposal made by a company ("the JV company") which is a member of a group UK REIT,

(b) the gain is one falling to be exempted as a result of the application of section 535 or 535A of CTA 2010 following a notice given under section 586(1) or 587(1) of that Act (venturing group),

(c) the principal company of the group UK REIT that gave the notice is covered by an election made under paragraph 12 in respect of a qualifying fund, and

(d) the JV company is also covered by the election.

(2) The amount of the gain accruing to the JV company which is not a chargeable gain as a result of the operation, by reference to the election, of the rules in this Part of this Schedule—

(a) is found by first taking the two steps mentioned below (which require the application of each of the exemption rules without regard to the other), and

(b) once those two steps are taken, is so much of the amount found by the first step as exceeds the amount found by the second step.

(3) The first step is, ignoring the effect of Part 12 of CTA 2010, to apply the rules in this Part of this Schedule that operate by reference to the election to identify the amount of the gain which (but for this paragraph) would not be chargeable.

(4) The second step is, ignoring the effect of this Part of this Schedule, to apply the rules in Part 12 of CTA 2010 that operate in relation to the group UK REIT to identify the amount of the gain accruing to the JV company which falls to be exempted as mentioned in sub-paragraph (1)(b).

(5) In the case of a disposal, a company is "covered by an election made under paragraph 12" for the purposes of this paragraph if the disposal is one to which paragraph 16 applies where the election concerned is the one referred to in this paragraph.

(6) In this paragraph "group UK REIT" has the same meaning as in Part 12 of CTA 2010.

Separate application of exemptions under this Schedule and elsewhere

37 (1) If—

(a) a person disposes of a right or interest in a company on which a gain or loss accrues, and

(b) proportions of the gain or loss are not chargeable or allowable as a result of the operation of any relevant exemption provision,

each relevant exemption provision is to work separately (without regard to the other) in relation to each proportion of the gain or loss to which the relevant exemption provision applies.

(2) Accordingly—

(a) each relevant exemption provision is to operate by reference to the whole of the gain or loss (ignoring the effect of the other relevant exemption provision), and

(b) the total proportion of the gain or loss which is not chargeable or allowable is the total of the proportions separately found (but not so as to exceed the whole amount of the gain or loss).

(3) Each of the following is a "relevant exemption provision" for the purposes of this paragraph—

(a) any provision made by this Part of this Schedule,

(b) any provision made by paragraph 3A of Schedule 7AC, and

(c) any provision made by Part 12 of CTA 2010.

(4) This paragraph is subject to paragraphs 34 to 36.

Meaning of meeting "the applicable exemption conditions"

38 (1) For the purposes of Part of this Schedule a qualifying fund "meets the applicable exemption conditions" at any time if, at that time—

(a) it is a collective investment vehicle, and

(b) it meets the entitlement conditions set out in paragraph 12(2).

(2) For the purposes of Part of this Schedule a qualifying company "meets the applicable exemption conditions" at any time if, at that time, it meets the entitlement conditions set out in paragraph 12(3).

Meaning of "the relevant fund" and "the relevant fund manager"

39 (1) In this Part of this Schedule "the relevant fund"—

(a) in the case of an election in respect of a qualifying fund under paragraph 12, means the collective investment vehicle concerned, and

(b) in the case of an election in respect of a qualifying company under paragraph 12, means the collective investment scheme which wholly (or almost wholly) owns that company.

(2) In this Part of this Schedule "the relevant fund manager", in the case of an election in respect of a qualifying fund or qualifying company under paragraph 12, means the manager of the relevant fund.

Meaning of "wholly owned" or "wholly (or almost wholly) owned"

40 (1) For the purposes of this Part of this Schedule a collective investment scheme, or a person or persons together, wholly owns or own a company at any time if the scheme, or person or persons together, has or have a 100% investment in the company at that time.

(2) Whether a scheme, or person or persons together, have a 100% investment in a company at any time is determined—

(a) by applying a modified version of the rule in paragraph 9 of Schedule 1A, and,

(b) in the case of a collective investment scheme, on the assumption that it is a person.

(3) The reference here to a modified version of the rule in paragraph 9 of Schedule 1A is to the rule in that paragraph as it has effect without regard to paragraph 10 and as if in sub-paragraph (1) of paragraph 9 the following modifications were made—

(a) for the opening words substitute "A person or persons together ("P") has or have a 100% investment in a company ("C") if all of the following conditions are met—",

(b) omit paragraph (a),

(c) in each of paragraphs (b), (c) and (d), for "25% or more" substitute "100%", and

(d) for the "or" at the end of paragraph (c) substitute "and".

41 (1) For the purposes of this Part of this Schedule a collective investment scheme or person wholly (or almost wholly) owns a company at any time if—

(a) the scheme or person wholly owns the company at that time, or

(b) the scheme or person has a 99% investment in the company at that time.

(2) Whether a scheme or person has a 99% investment in a company at any time is determined—

(a) by applying a modified version of the rule in paragraph 9 of Schedule 1A, and,

(b) in the case of a collective investment scheme, on the assumption that it is a person.

(3) The reference here to a modified version of the rule in paragraph 9 of Schedule 1A is to the rule in that paragraph as it has effect without regard to paragraph 10 and as if in sub-paragraph (1) of paragraph 9 the following modifications were made—

(a) omit paragraph (a),

(b) for "25%", in each place, substitute "99%", and

(c) for the "or" at the end of paragraph (c) substitute "and".

Meaning of "designated HMRC officer"

42 In this Part of this Schedule "designated HMRC officer" means an officer of Revenue and Customs who has been designated by the Commissioners for Her Majesty's Revenue and Customs for the purpose of revoking elections under paragraph 12.

PART 5

REPORTING AND PAYMENT

Reporting by collective investment vehicles

43 (1) The Treasury may by regulations make provision for managers of collective investment vehicles to elect to provide information to an officer of Revenue and Customs in respect of any participant in the vehicle who holds units the disposal of which would constitute an indirect disposal of UK land.

(2) The regulations may specify circumstances in which the provision of information or documents in accordance with the regulations is taken to satisfy obligations of the participant (or anyone else) to provide information or documents to an officer of Revenue and Customs.

(3) The regulations may be framed so as to apply to obligations of a description specified in the regulations.

Withholding of amounts on account of capital gains tax

44 (1) The Treasury may by regulations make provision for managers of collective investment vehicles to elect to meet the liability to capital gains tax or corporation tax in respect of indirect disposals of UK land made by any participant in the vehicle.

(2) The regulations may make provision for a simplified calculation of the tax liability of the participant in respect of those disposals.

(3) The regulations may make provision authorising the manager of a collective investment vehicle (or anyone else of a description specified in the regulations) to deduct an amount on account of capital gains tax from amounts that would otherwise be receivable by the participant.

(4) The regulations—

(a) may provide for the times at which amounts deducted on account of capital gains tax are to be paid to Her Majesty's Revenue and Customs, and

(b) may set out the extent to which those payments meet the liability of the participant to capital gains tax or corporation tax in respect of any indirect disposal of UK land.

General

45 (1) Regulations under this Part of this Schedule—

(a) may make different provision for different purposes, and
(b) may make supplementary, incidental, consequential or transitional or saving provision.

(2) Regulations under this Part of this Schedule may make provision having effect in relation to times before the regulations are made.

PART 6

GENERAL

Meaning of "close company", "qualifying investor" and "direct or indirect participator"

46 (1) This paragraph has effect for the purposes of the provisions of this Schedule which apply this paragraph (or to which this paragraph is applied).

(2) Whether a company is "a close company" is determined in accordance with the rules in Chapter 2 of Part 10 of CTA 2010 but subject to the following modifications—

(a) section 442(a) (non-UK resident companies) is to be treated as omitted,
(b) section 444 (companies involved with non-close companies) is to be treated as omitted,
(c) section 447(1)(a) (shares in quoted companies beneficially held by non-close companies) is to be treated as omitted, and
(d) for the purposes of any attribution under section 451(4) (rights of a person's associates to be attributed to the person etc in determining "control") the rights and powers of a person ("A") are not to be attributed to another person ("P") merely because A is a partner of P.

(3) A "qualifying investor" means—

(a) a person who is within any of section 528(4A)(a), (b), (c), (i) or (j) of CTA 2010 where, if the collective investment vehicle mentioned in the provision concerned is a company, it meets the non-close condition or, if not, the vehicle meets the genuine diversity of ownership condition,
(b) a person who is within any other provision of section 528(4A) of that Act, or
(c) a qualifying fund or qualifying company in respect of which an election under paragraph 12 has effect.

(4) For the purposes of sub-paragraph (3)(a) a collective investment vehicle meets the genuine diversity of ownership condition at any time if, at that time—

(a) it meets conditions A to C of regulation 75 of the Offshore Funds (Tax) Regulations 2009, or
(b) it meets the condition in regulation 75(5) of those Regulations,

and those Regulations apply for the purposes of this sub-paragraph as if any collective investment vehicle which is not an offshore fund were regarded as an offshore fund.

(5) For the purposes of sub-paragraph (3)(a) a company meets the non-close condition at any time if, at that time, it—

(a) is not a close company, or
(b) is a close company but only because it has a qualifying investor as a direct or indirect participator,

applying the provisions of this paragraph for the purposes of this sub-paragraph.

(6) A person is a "direct participator" if the person is a participator for the purposes of Part 10 of CTA 2010 (see section 454).

(7) A person is an "indirect" participator in a company if the person has a share or interest in the capital or income of the company through another body corporate or other bodies corporate.

(8) The reference here to having a share or interest in the capital or income of a company through a body corporate is to be read as follows.

(9) Suppose that 3 or more bodies corporate are ordered in a series such that each body in the series (other than the last) has a share or interest in the capital or income of the body immediately below it in the series.

(10) If B is a body that is below, but not immediately below, A in the series, A is said to own a share or interest in the capital or income of B through each body corporate that is between A and B in the series.

(11) A person is regarded for the purposes of sub-paragraphs (7) to (10) as having a share or interest in the capital or income of a company if the person would be a participator in the company as a result of section 454(2) of CTA 2010.

Other definitions

47 (1) In this Schedule—

"double taxation arrangements" means arrangements having effect under section 2(1) of TIOPA 2010,

"interest in UK land" is to be read in accordance with section 1C,

"the manager", in relation to a collective investment vehicle, means—

(a) any person who is the manager of the property that is the subject of or held by the vehicle, or

(b) any other person who has, or is expected to have, day-to-day control of that property, and

"prospectus", in relation to a collective investment vehicle, means any document (however described) which is made available to investors and which sets out descriptions of the investments to be made, or intended to be made, by the vehicle.

(2) For the purposes of this Schedule—

(a) a reference to a direct disposal of UK land is to a disposal of an interest in UK land, and

(b) a reference to an indirect disposal of UK land is to a disposal of an asset deriving at least 75% of its value from UK land.

(3) For this purpose the reference to a disposal of an asset deriving at least 75% of its value from UK land is to be read in accordance with Part 2 of Schedule 1A.

Power to make provision in relation to UK property rich collective investment vehicles etc

48 (1) The Treasury may by regulations make provision for the purposes of any provision of this Act in relation to—

(a) collective investment vehicles that are UK property rich, or

(b) investments made (directly or indirectly) by collective investment vehicles in companies that are UK property rich.

(2) Among other things, the regulations—

(a) may amend any provision made by this Schedule, or

(b) may disapply any provision made by or under this Act or provide for any provision made by or under this Act to have effect with modifications specified in the regulations.

(3) The regulations may make provision having effect in relation to times before the regulations are made.

(4) The regulations—

(a) may make different provision for different purposes, and

(b) may make supplementary, incidental, consequential or transitional or saving provision.

PART 7

TRANSITIONAL PROVISION

Elections for transparency under paragraph 8

49 (1) This paragraph applies in the case of an offshore collective investment vehicle to which paragraph 8 applies which was constituted before 6 April 2019.

(2) Paragraph 9(1)(c) has effect as if it permitted the election under paragraph 8 to be made before 6 April 2020.

(3) The election is to have effect in relation to disposals made on or after 6 April 2019 (so that paragraph 8(2) has effect subject to this sub-paragraph).

(4) If a person is a participant in the vehicle on 6 April 2019—

(a) the making of an election under paragraph 8 is not to be regarded as being a disposal of the person's units in the vehicle, and

(b) any question arising for the purposes of this Act, in relation to a disposal on or after 6 April 2019 of the person's units in the vehicle, is to be determined as if the election under paragraph 8 had had effect in relation to all times on or after the vehicle's constitution.

Elections under paragraph 12 and information about disposals by participants

50 Nothing in paragraph 14 requires information about disposals made before 6 April 2019."

PART 2

CONSEQUENTIAL AMENDMENTS

TMA 1970

22 In TMA 1970, after section 8B insert—

"8C Returns so far as relating to capital gains tax

(1) This section applies if—

(a) the amount of chargeable gains accruing to a person in a tax year does not exceed the annual exempt amount for the year applicable to the person under section 1K of the 1992 Act,

(b) the total amount or value of the consideration for all chargeable disposals of assets made by the person in the year does not exceed four times that annual exempt amount,

(c) the person is not a remittance-basis individual for the year, and

(d) a notice under section 8 or 8A is given to the person requiring information for the purpose of establishing the amount in which the person is chargeable to capital gains tax for the year.

(2) If the person makes a statement confirming the matters set out in subsection (1)(a) to (c), the statement constitutes sufficient compliance with that requirement.

(3) For the purposes of this section every disposal is a "chargeable disposal" other than—

(a) a disposal on which any gain accruing is not a chargeable gain, and

(b) a disposal to which section 58 of the 1992 Act applies (spouses and civil partners).

(4) For the purposes of this section an individual is "a remittance-basis individual" for a tax year if—

(a) section 809B of ITA 2007 applies to the individual for the year, or

(b) paragraph 2 of Schedule 1 to the 1992 Act applies in relation to any gains that are treated as accruing to the individual in the year as a result of paragraph 1 of that Schedule."

TCGA 1992

23 TCGA 1992 is amended as follows.

24 In section 16 (computation of losses), omit subsection (3).

25 (1) Section 25 (non-residents: deemed disposals) is amended as follows.

(2) In subsection (3A), for paragraph (b) substitute—

"(b) on ceasing to carry on the trade the asset is disposed of in circumstances in which section 139 or 171 applies."

(3) In subsection (7), for the words from "the disposal—" to the end substitute "the disposal would be chargeable to capital gains tax under section 1A(3)(a) or to corporation tax under section 2B(3)."

26 For section 25ZA substitute—

"25ZA Postponing gain or loss under section 25(3): interests in UK land

(1) This section applies if an interest in UK land is deemed to have been disposed of under section 25(3) by a person at any time.

(2) The gain or loss that, but for this subsection, would have accrued to the person at that time is not to accrue at that time.

(3) But, on a subsequent disposal by the person of the whole or part of the interest in UK land, the whole or a corresponding part of the gain or loss is treated as accruing on the subsequent disposal.

(4) This gain or loss is in addition to any gain or loss that actually accrues on the subsequent disposal.

(5) A disposal to which section 171 (transfers within a group) applies does not count as a subsequent disposal for the purposes of this section.

(6) A person may elect for a disposal deemed to have been made under section 25(3) to be excluded from the operation of this section.

(7) An election made by a company must be made within 2 years after the day on which the deemed disposal occurs.

(8) In this section "interest in UK land" has the meaning given by section 1C."

27 (1) Section 48A (unascertainable consideration) is amended as follows.

(2) In subsection (1), for paragraph (a) substitute—

"(a) a person ("P") has made a disposal ("the original disposal") on which a relevant non-resident gain or relevant non-resident loss accrued,".

(3) In subsection (2)—

(a) in the opening words, for the words from "condition A" to "the receipt of the ascertained consideration—" substitute "P is not UK resident for the tax year in which the ascertained consideration is received (as determined for the purposes of Chapter 1 of Part 1)—", and

(b) in paragraph (c), in step 2, for "NRCGT gain or loss, ATED-related gain or loss" substitute "relevant non-resident gain or relevant non-resident loss".

(4) After subsection (6) insert—

"(7) In this section—

"relevant non-resident gain" means—

(a) a gain that falls to be dealt with by section 1A(3) because the asset disposed of is within paragraph (b) or (c) of that subsection, or

(b) a gain that falls to be dealt with by section 1A(1) in accordance with section 1G(2) because the asset disposed of is within section 1A(3)(b) or (c), and

"relevant non-resident loss" means an allowable loss accruing on a disposal which, had a gain accrued instead, would have been a relevant non-resident gain."

(5) The amendments made by this paragraph have effect where the ascertained consideration is received on or after 6 April 2019, but, subject to the following modifications, in a case where the original disposal was made before that date.

(6) In that case, section 48A of TCGA 1992—

(a) has effect without the amendments made by sub-paragraphs (2) and (3)(b), and

(b) has effect as if, in step 3 in subsection (2)(c) of that section, for "(of the type appropriate to the computation)" (in both places) there were substituted "(of a kind most closely corresponding to that accruing on the original disposal)".

28 In section 59 (partnerships), in subsections (2)(b), (3) and (4), for "capital gains of the partnership" substitute "chargeable gains of the partnership".

29 (1) Section 62 (death: general provisions) is amended as follows.

(2) In subsection (2A)—

(a) in paragraph (a), for "section 10A" substitute "section 1M", and

(b) for paragraph (b) substitute—

"(b) relevant non-resident gains (see subsection (11))."

(3) In subsection (2AA), for "allowable NRCGT losses (see section 57B and Schedule 4ZZB)" substitute "relevant non-resident losses (see subsection (11))".

(4) After subsection (10) insert—

"(11) In this section—

"relevant non-resident gain" means—

(a) a gain that falls to be dealt with by section 1A(3) because the asset disposed of is within paragraph (b) or (c) of that subsection, or

(b) a gain that falls to be dealt with by section 1A(1) in accordance with section 1G(2) because the asset disposed of is within section 1A(3)(b) or (c), and "relevant non-resident loss" means an allowable loss accruing on a disposal which, had a gain accrued instead, would have been a relevant non-resident gain."

(5) The reference to relevant non-resident gains in section 62(2A)(b) of TCGA 1992 (as substituted by sub-paragraph (2)(b)) includes NRCGT gains as defined by section 57B of, and Schedule 4ZZB to, that Act.

(6) The reference here to section 57B of, and Schedule 4ZZB to, TCGA 1992 is to those provisions as they had effect before their repeal by this Schedule.

30 (1) Section 79B (attribution to trustees of gains of non-resident companies) is amended as follows.

(2) In subsection (1), for "section 13" substitute "section 3 (see section 3B)".

(3) In subsection (2), for "section 13" substitute "section 3".

(4) In subsection (3)—

(a) for "section 13(2)" substitute "section 3", and
(b) for "section 13(9)" substitute "section 3(7)".

(5) In subsection (4), for "section 13(9)" substitute "section 3(7)".

31 For section 80A substitute—

"80A Postponing gain or loss under section 80(2): interests in UK land

(1) This section applies if—

(a) an interest in UK land is deemed to have been disposed of under section 80(2) by trustees of a settlement at any time, and
(b) the trustees make an election under this subsection.

(2) The gain or loss that, but for this subsection, would have accrued to the trustees at that time is not to accrue at that time.

(3) But, on a subsequent disposal by the trustees of the whole or part of the interest in UK land, the whole or a corresponding part of the gain or loss is treated as accruing on the subsequent disposal.

(4) This gain or loss is in addition to any gain or loss that actually accrues on the subsequent disposal.

(5) In this section "interest in UK land" has the meaning given by section 1C."

32 In section 85A (transfers of value: attribution of gains to beneficiaries and treatment of losses)—

(a) in subsection (2A), for "any section 2(2) amount" substitute "any section 1(3) amount", and
(b) in subsection (3), for "section 2(2) amount" (in both places) substitute "section 1(3) amount".

33 (1) Section 86 (attribution of gains to settlors with interest in non-resident or dual resident settlements) is amended as follows.

(2) In subsection (1)(e), for "section 2(2)" substitute "section 1(3)".

(3) For subsection (4ZA) substitute—

"(4ZA) Where (apart from this subsection) the amount mentioned in subsection (1)(e) would include a chargeable gain or allowable loss to which section 1A(3)(b) or (c) applies (disposals by non-UK residents within the charge to capital gains tax), so much of the gain or loss as would be so included is to be disregarded for the purposes of subsection (1)(e)."

34 (1) Section 86A (attribution of gains to settlor in section 10A cases) is amended as follows.

(2) In subsection (1)(a), for "section 10A" substitute "section 1M(3)".

(3) In subsection (2), for "the section 2(2) amount" substitute "the section 1(3) amount".

(4) In subsection (3), for "section 10A" substitute "section 1M(3)".

(5) In subsection (4)(a), for "the section 2(2) amount" substitute "the section 1(3) amount".

(6) In subsection (6), for "section 10A" substitute "section 1M(3)".

(7) In subsection (7), for "the section 2(2) amount" (in both places) substitute "the section 1(3) amount".

(8) In subsection (8)(c), for "section 10A" substitute "section 1M(3)".

(9) In the title, for "in section 10A cases" substitute "where temporarily non-resident".

35 (1) Section 87 (non-UK resident settlements: attribution of gains to beneficiaries) is amended as follows.

(2) In subsection (2), for "the section 2(2) amount" substitute "the section 1(3) amount".

(3) In subsection (4)—

(a) in the opening words, for "The section 2(2) amount" substitute "The section 1(3) amount", and

(b) in paragraph (a), for "section 2(2)" substitute "section 1(3)".

(4) In subsection (5), for "The section 2(2) amount" substitute "The section 1(3) amount".

(5) For subsection (5A) substitute—

"(5A) Where (apart from this subsection) the amount mentioned in subsection (4)(a) would include a chargeable gain or allowable loss to which section 1A(3)(b) or (c) applies (disposals by non-UK residents within the charge to capital gains tax), so much of the gain or loss as would be so included is to be disregarded for the purposes of determining the section 1(3) amount."

(6) In subsection (5B), for "the section 2(2) amount" substitute "the section 1(3) amount".

36 In section 87A (section 87: matching), for "the section 2(2) amount" (in each place) substitute "the section 1(3) amount".

37 In section 87B (section 87: remittance basis), for subsection (2) substitute—

"(2) The chargeable gains are chargeable gains accruing on the disposal of an asset situated outside the United Kingdom."

38 In section 87J (relevant parts of payment from which onward gift derive), in subsections (2) and (5), for "the section 2(2) amount" substitute "the section 1(3) amount".

39 In section 87N (sections 87 and 87A: disregard of payments to migrating beneficiary), in subsection (2)(d)(i) and (ii), for "the section 2(2) amount" substitute "the section 1(3) amount".

40 In section 87P (sections 87 and 87A: temporary migration after payment disregarded), in subsection (1)(e)(i) and (ii), for "the section 2(2) amount" substitute "the section 1(3) amount".

41 In section 88 (gains of dual settlements), in subsections (2) and (3)(a) and (b), for "section 2(2)" substitute "section 1(3)".

42 In section 89 (migrant settlements, etc), in subsection (2), for "the section 2(2) amount" substitute "the section 1(3) amount".

43 In section 90 (sections 87 and 89(2): transfers between settlements), in subsection (3) (in both places) and subsections (5) and (10)(b), for "the section 2(2) amount" substitute "the section 1(3) amount".

44 In section 91 (increase in tax payable under section 87 or 89(2), in subsection (1)(a), for "the section 2(2) amount" substitute "the section 1(3) amount".

45 In section 96 (payments by and to companies), in subsection (9A)(a), for "section 10A" substitute "section 1M".

46 Omit section 100A (exemption for certain EEA UCITS).

47 In section 103KC (carried interest: foreign chargeable gains), for "a foreign chargeable gain within the meaning of section 12" substitute "a chargeable gain accruing on the disposal of an asset situated outside the United Kingdom".

48 In section 103KE (carried interest: avoidance of double taxation), in subsection (8)(b), for "section 2(2)(b)" substitute "section 1(3)(b)".

49 (1) Section 139 (reconstruction involving transfer of business) is amended as follows.

(2) In subsection (1A)—

(a) in paragraphs (a) and (b), omit "or NRCGT assets", and

(b) in the sentence after paragraph (b), for the words from "and would by virtue of" to "purposes" substitute "chargeable to corporation tax as a result of section 2B(3) or (4)".

(3) Omit subsection (1AA).

50 In section 140A (transfer or division of UK business), in subsection (2), for "section 10B" substitute "section 2B(3)".

51 (1) Section 140E (merger leaving assets within UK tax charge) is amended as follows.

(2) In subsection (5)(b), for "section 10B" substitute "section 2B(3)".

(3) In subsection (6)(b), for "section 10B" substitute "section 2B(3)".

52 In section 159 (non-residents: roll-over relief), in subsection (4), for the words from "the disposal—" to the end substitute "the disposal would be chargeable to capital gains tax under section 1A(3)(a) or to corporation tax under section 2B(3)."

53 For section 159A substitute—

"159A Disposals of interests in UK land by non-residents: roll-over relief

(1) This section applies in a case where—

(a) the old assets that are disposed of are interests in UK land, and

(b) a chargeable gain accruing on the disposal would (apart from section 152) be within the charge to tax because of section 1A(3)(b) or 2B(4)(a).

(2) Section 152 applies only if the new assets that are acquired are interests in UK land.

(3) In this section—

(a) "interest in UK land" has the meaning given by section 1C,

(b) "the old assets" and "the new assets" have the same meaning as in section 152,

(c) any reference to a disposal of the old assets includes a disposal of an interest in them,

(d) the reference to the acquisition of the new assets includes the acquisition of an interest in them or entering into an unconditional contract for their acquisition."

54 (1) Section 161 (appropriations to and from trading stock) is amended as follows.

(2) In subsection (1), for "subsections (3) to (3ZB)" substitute "subsection (3)".

(3) Omit subsections (3ZA) and (3ZB).

(4) In subsection (3A), omit "or (3ZA)".

55 (1) Section 165 (relief for gifts of business assets) is amended as follows.

(2) In subsection (7A)(a), for "non-resident CGT disposal" substitute "direct or indirect disposal of UK land which meets the non-residence condition".

(3) In subsection (7B), for "references to "chargeable NRCGT gain"" substitute "references to "so much of any gain accruing on the disposal as falls to be dealt with as mentioned in subsection (7D)(a) or (b)"".

(4) In subsection (7C), for ""the chargeable NRCGT gain" substitute ""so much of the gain mentioned in subsection (7B)".

(5) After that subsection insert—

"(7D) For the purposes of subsections (7A) to (7C) a disposal is a "direct or indirect disposal of UK land which meets the non-residence condition" if it is—

(a) a disposal on which a gain accrues that falls to be dealt with by section 1A(3) because the asset disposed of is within paragraph (b) or (c) of that subsection, or

(b) a disposal on which a gain accrues that falls to be dealt with by section 1A(1) in accordance with section 1G(2) because the asset disposed of is within section 1A(3)(b) or (c)."

56 (1) Section 167A (gifts of UK residential property interests to non-residents) is amended as follows.

(2) In subsection (1)—

(a) in the opening words, for "of a UK residential property interest" substitute "of an asset within section 1A(3)(b) or (c)", and

(b) for paragraph (b) substitute—

"(b) on the assumption that the disposal is a direct or indirect disposal of UK land which meets the non-residence condition (whether or not that is the case), that gain would be a relevant gain (see subsections (6) and (7))."

(3) In subsection (3)—

(a) in the opening words, for "non-resident CGT disposal" substitute "direct or indirect disposal of UK land which meets the non-residence condition",

(b) in paragraph (a), for ""chargeable NRCGT gain"" substitute ""relevant gain"",

(c) in paragraph (b), for ""chargeable NRCGT gain"" substitute ""relevant gain"", and

(d) in paragraph (c), for ""the chargeable NRCGT gain" substitute ""the relevant gain".

(4) In subsection (4)—

(a) in the opening words, for "the interest in UK land" substitute "the asset within section 1A(3)(b) or (c)", and

(b) for paragraph (b) substitute—

"(b) (if that would not otherwise be the case) is to be treated as a relevant gain."

(5) For subsection (6) substitute—

"(6) For the purposes of this section, a disposal is a "direct or indirect disposal of UK land which meets the non-residence condition" if it is—

(a) a disposal on which a gain accrues that falls to be dealt with by section 1A(3) because the asset disposed of is within paragraph (b) or (c) of that subsection, or

(b) a disposal on which a gain accrues that falls to be dealt with by section 1A(1) in accordance with section 1G(2) because the asset disposed of is within section 1A(3)(b) or (c).

(7) For the purposes of this section, a "relevant gain" means so much of any chargeable gain accruing on a disposal as falls to be dealt with as mentioned in subsection (6)(a) or (b)."

(6) In the title, for "UK residential property interests" substitute "direct or indirect interests in UK land".

57 For section 168A substitute—

"168A Postponing held-over gain: interests in UK land

(1) This section applies if—

(a) an interest in UK land is deemed to have been disposed of under section 168(1) by a transferee at any time, and

(b) the transferee makes an election under this subsection.

(2) The held-over gain (within the meaning of section 165 or 260) that, but for this subsection, would have accrued to the transferee at that time is not to accrue at that time.

(3) But, on a subsequent disposal by the transferee of the whole or part of the interest in UK land, the whole or a corresponding part of the held-over gain is treated as accruing on the subsequent disposal.

(4) This gain is in addition to any gain or loss that actually accrues on the subsequent disposal.

(5) In this section "interest in UK land" has the meaning given by section 1C."

58 In section 169N (amount of entrepreneurs' relief: general), in subsection (4B), for "Section 4" substitute "Section 1H".

59 In section 169VK (cap on investors' relief for disposal by an individual), in subsection (3), for "Section 4" substitute "Section 1H".

60 In section 169VL (cap on investors' relief for disposal by trustees of a settlement), in subsection (4), for "Section 4" substitute "Section 1H".

61 (1) Section 171 (transfers within a group: general provisions) is amended as follows.

(2) In subsection (1A), in the second sentence, for the words from "and would" to the end substitute "chargeable to corporation tax as a result of section 2B(3) or (4)."

(3) After subsection (1A) insert—

"(1B) If—

(a) company A is deemed under section 25(3) to have previously disposed of the asset, but

(b) no gain or loss accrued on that deemed disposal as a result of section 25ZA(2),

that deemed disposal is to be ignored in applying subsection (1) of this section in relation to company B."

(4) In subsection (2), omit paragraph (ba).

62 In section 171A (election to reallocate gain or loss to another member of the group), for subsection (2) substitute—

"(2) In determining for the purposes of subsection (1)(c) whether subsection (1) of section 171 would have applied, it is to be assumed that subsection (1A)(b) of that section read—

"(b) that—

(i) at the time of the disposal, company B is resident in the United Kingdom, or carrying on a trade in the United Kingdom through a permanent establishment there, or

(ii) the asset is a chargeable asset in relation to company B immediately after the time of the disposal.""""

63 In section 171B (election under section 171A: effect), in subsection (5), for the words from "and would by virtue of" to the end substitute "chargeable to corporation tax as a result of section 2B(3) or (4)."

64 In section 175 (replacement of business assets by members of a group), in subsection (2AA), for "section 10B" substitute "section 2B(3)".

65 (1) Section 179 (company ceasing to be member of group: post-appointed day cases) is amended as follows.

(2) In subsection (3B)(c), for "section 13(2)" substitute "section 3".

(3) In subsection (10A)(a), for the words from "and would by virtue of" to "purposes" substitute "chargeable to corporation tax as a result of section 2B(3) or (4),".

66 Omit section 187A (deemed disposal under section 185: ATED-related gains and losses).

67 For section 187B substitute—

"187B Postponing gain or loss under section 185(2): interests in UK land

(1) This section applies if an interest in UK land is deemed to have been disposed of under section 185(2) by a company at any time.

(2) The gain or loss that, but for this subsection, would have accrued to the company at that time is not to accrue at that time.

(3) But, on a subsequent disposal by the company of the whole or part of the interest in UK land, the whole or a corresponding part of the gain or loss is treated as accruing on the subsequent disposal.

(4) This gain or loss is in addition to any gain or loss that actually accrues on the subsequent disposal.

(5) A company may elect for a disposal deemed to have been made under section 185(2) to be excluded from the operation of this section.

(6) The election must be made within 2 years after the day on which the deemed disposal occurs.

(7) In this section "interest in UK land" has the meaning given by section 1C."

68 Omit sections 188A to 188K (and the italic heading before section 188A).

69 (1) Section 190 (tax recoverable from another group company or controlling director) is amended as follows.

(2) In subsection (2), for paragraph (b) substitute—

"(b) that the gain is chargeable to corporation tax as a result of section 2B(3) or (4)."

(3) In subsection (3)(b), for the words from "gain forms" to "10B" substitute "taxpayer company was not resident in the United Kingdom at the time when the gain accrued".

70 (1) Section 199 (exploration or exploitation assets: deemed disposals) is amended as follows.

(2) In subsection (2), for "in respect of whom the residence condition (see section 2(1A)) is not met" substitute "who is not UK resident for a tax year (as determined for the purposes of Chapter 1 of Part 1)".

(3) In subsection (6), for paragraphs (a) and (b) substitute "would be chargeable to capital gains tax or corporation tax as a result of section 1A(3)(a) or 2B(3)".

71 In section 210A (insurance companies: ring-fencing of losses), in subsection (1), for "Section 8(1)" substitute "Section 2A(1)".

72 In section 222A (determination of main residence: non-resident CGT disposals), in subsection (1), for paragraph (b) substitute—

"(b) the disposal is—

(i) a disposal on which a residential property gain (as defined by Schedule 1B) accrues which is chargeable to capital gains tax because of section 1A(3)(b), or

(ii) a disposal on which a loss accrues but is one which, had a gain accrued, would be within sub-paragraph (i)."

73 (1) Section 222B (non-qualifying tax years) is amended as follows.

(2) In subsection (2), for "a non-resident CGT disposal" substitute "a disposal falling within section 222A(1)(b) (non-resident disposals)".

(3) In subsection (10), for "Section 11(1)(a)" substitute "Section 271ZA(2)".

74 (1) Section 223 (amount of relief) is amended as follows.

(2) In subsection (7), in paragraph (b), for "an NRCGT gain chargeable to capital gains tax by virtue of section 14D" substitute "a residential property gain (as defined by Schedule 1B) which is chargeable to capital gains tax because of section 1A(3)(b)".

(3) In subsection (7A), for "paragraph 9 of Schedule 4ZZB applies by virtue of sub-paragraph (1)(b) of that paragraph" substitute "paragraph 8 or 14 of Schedule 4AA applies".

75 In section 228 (conditions for relief: supplementary), in subsection (6), for the words from ", and either" to "section 10B" substitute "chargeable to capital gains tax or corporation tax on gains".

76 (1) Section 260 (gifts on which inheritance tax is chargeable etc) is amended as follows.

(2) In subsection (6ZA)(a), for "non-resident CGT disposal" substitute "direct or indirect disposal of UK land which meets the non-residence condition".

(3) In subsection (6ZB), for "a reference to "chargeable NRCGT gain"" substitute "a reference to "so much of any gain accruing on the disposal as falls to be dealt with as mentioned in subsection (6ZD)(a) or (b)"".

(4) In subsection (6ZC), for ""the chargeable NRCGT gain" substitute ""so much of the gain mentioned in subsection (6ZB)".

(5) After that subsection insert—

"(6ZD) For the purposes of subsections (6ZA) to (6ZC) a disposal is a "direct or indirect disposal of UK land which meets the non-residence condition" if it is—

(a) a disposal on which a gain accrues that falls to be dealt with by section 1A(3) because the asset disposed of is within paragraph (b) or (c) of that subsection, or

(b) a disposal on which a gain accrues that falls to be dealt with by section 1A(1) in accordance with section 1G(2) because the asset disposed of is within section 1A(3)(b) or (c)."

77 (1) Section 261ZA (gifts of UK residential property interests to non-residents) is amended as follows.

(2) In subsection (1)—

(a) in the opening words, for "of a UK residential property interest" substitute "of an asset within section 1A(3)(b) or (c)", and

(b) for paragraph (b) substitute—

"(b) on the assumption that the disposal is a direct or indirect disposal of UK land which meets the non-residence condition (whether or not that is the case), that gain would be a relevant gain (see subsections (6) and (7))."

(3) In subsection (3)—

(a) in the opening words, for "non-resident CGT disposal" substitute "direct or indirect disposal of UK land which meets the non-residence condition",

(b) in paragraph (a), for ""chargeable NRCGT gain"" substitute ""relevant gain"", and

(c) in paragraph (b), for ""the chargeable NRCGT gain" substitute ""the relevant gain".

(4) In subsection (4)—

(a) in the opening words, for "the interest in UK land" substitute "the asset within section 1A(3)(b) or (c)", and

(b) in paragraph (b)—

(i) for "a chargeable NRCGT gain" substitute "a relevant gain", and

(ii) for "a non-resident CGT disposal" substitute "a direct or indirect disposal of UK land which meets the non-residence condition".

(5) In subsection (5)(b)(i)—

(a) for "a non-resident CGT disposal" substitute "a direct or indirect disposal of UK land which meets the non-residence condition", and

(b) for "the chargeable NRCGT gain" substitute "the relevant gain".

(6) For subsection (6) substitute—

"(6) For the purposes of this section, a disposal is a "direct or indirect disposal of UK land which meets the non-residence condition" if it is—

(a) a disposal on which a gain accrues that falls to be dealt with by section 1A(3) because the asset disposed of is within paragraph (b) or (c) of that subsection, or

(b) a disposal on which a gain accrues that falls to be dealt with by section 1A(1) in accordance with section 1G(2) because the asset disposed of is within section 1A(3)(b) or (c).

(7) For the purposes of this section, a "relevant gain" means so much of any chargeable gain accruing on a disposal as falls to be dealt with as mentioned in subsection (6)(a) or (b)."

(7) In the title, for "UK residential property interests" substitute "direct or indirect interests in UK land".

78 In section 261C (meaning of "the maximum amount" for purposes of section 261B), in subsection (2)(b), for "section 3(1)" substitute "section 1K(1)".

79 In section 261E (meaning of "the maximum amount" for purposes of section 261D), in subsection (2)—

(a) in paragraph (a), for "section 2(2)" substitute "section 1(3)", and

(b) in paragraph (b), for "section 3(1)" substitute "section 1K(1)".

80 In section 263ZA (former employees: employment-related liabilities), in subsection (5)—

(a) in paragraph (b), for "section 2(2)" substitute "section 1(3)", and

(b) in paragraph (c), for "section 3(1)" substitute "section 1K(1)".

81 In section 271B (branch or agency treated as UK representative), in subsection (2), for "under section 10" substitute "as a result of section 1A(3)(a)".

82 In section 279A (deferred unascertainable consideration: election for treatment of loss), in subsection (7)(b), for "section 10A" substitute "section 1M".

83 (1) Section 279B (provisions supplementary to section 279A) is amended as follows.

(2) In subsection (1)(b)(ii)—

(a) for "section 2(2)" substitute "section 1(3)", and

(b) for "section 3" substitute "section 1K".

(3) In subsection (7), for "section 10A(2)" substitute "section 1M".

(4) In subsection (8)(a) and (b), for "section 10A(2)" substitute "section 1M".

84 (1) Section 279C (effect of election under section 279A) is amended as follows.

(2) In subsection (3), for "section 2(2)(a)" substitute "section 1(3)(a)".

(3) In subsection (4)—

(a) for "section 2(2)" substitute "section 1(3)", and

(b) omit "(read, where appropriate, with section 2(4)(a))".

(4) In subsection (5), for "section 2(2)(b)" substitute "section 1(3)(b)".

(5) In subsection (6)—

(a) in the opening words, for "section 2(2)(b)" substitute "section 1(3)(b)", and
(b) in paragraph (c), for "section 10A" substitute "section 1M".

85 (1) Section 279D (elections under section 279A) is amended as follows.

(2) In subsection (6)(c), for "section 2(2)(a)" substitute "section 1(3)(a)".

(3) In subsection (7), for "section 2(2)(b)" (in both places) substitute "section 1(3)(b)".

86 In section 287 (orders and regulations etc), in subsection (4), for "3(4)" substitute "1L(2)".

87 (1) Section 288 (interpretation) is amended as follows.

(2) In subsection (1) omit—

(a) the definition of "ATED-related",
(b) the definition of "non-resident CGT disposal",
(c) the definition of "NRCGT gain",
(d) the definition of "NRCGT group",
(e) the definition of "NRCGT loss", and
(f) the definition of "relevant high value disposal".

(3) In subsection (8), in the Table, in the entry relating to "branch or agency", for "s 10(6)" substitute "s 1B(5)".

88 In Schedule 4A (disposal of interest in settled property etc), in paragraph 6(1), for "met the residence condition set out in section 2(1A)" substitute "was UK resident for the tax year (as determined in accordance with Chapter 1 of Part 1 of this Act)".

89 (1) Schedule 4C (transfers of value: attribution of gains to beneficiaries) is amended as follows.

(2) For "the section 2(2) amount" or "the section 2(2) amounts", in each place, substitute "the section 1(3) amount" or "the section 1(3) amounts" respectively.

(3) In paragraph 1A(3), for "meets the residence condition set out in section 2(1A)" substitute "is UK resident for the tax year (as determined in accordance with Chapter 1 of Part 1 of this Act)".

(4) In paragraph 4—

(a) in sub-paragraph (2), for "section 2(2)" substitute "section 1(3)", and
(b) for sub-paragraph (3) substitute—

"(3) Where (apart from this sub-paragraph) the chargeable amount mentioned in sub-paragraph (2) would include a chargeable gain or allowable loss to which section 1A(3)(b) or (c) applies (disposals by non-UK residents within the charge to capital gains tax), so much of the gain or loss as would be so included is to be disregarded for the purposes of determining the chargeable amount."

(5) In paragraph 6(1)(b), for "section 10A" substitute "section 1M".

(6) In paragraph 12(1)(a) and (5), and in the italic heading before paragraph 12, for "section 10A" substitute "section 1M".

(7) In paragraph 12A(1) and (5), and in the italic heading before paragraph 12, for "section 10A" substitute "section 1M".

90 (1) Schedule 5 (attribution of gains to settlors with interest in non-resident or dual resident settlements) is amended as follows.

(2) In paragraph 1(1), for "section 3" substitute "section 1K".

(3) In paragraph 1(2)(a), for "section 2(2)" substitute "section 1(3)".

(4) In paragraph 1(3)—

(a) in paragraph (b), for "section 13" substitute "section 3", and
(b) in the second sentence—
  (i) for "Subsections (12) and (13) of section 13" substitute "Section 3B(1) to (3)", and
  (ii) for "that section" substitute "section 3".

91 In Schedule 7A (restriction on set-off of pre-entry losses), in paragraph 6(1)(c) and (d), for "section 8(1)" substitute "section 2A(1)".

92 In Schedule 7AC (exemptions for disposals by companies with substantial shareholdings), in paragraph 3(2)(c)(ii), for the words from "would" to "purposes" substitute "would be chargeable to corporation tax as a result of section 2B(3) or (4)".

93 In Schedule 7C (relief for transfers to Schedule 2 share plans), in paragraph 8—

(a) in paragraph (a), for "under section 2(1)" substitute "as a result of section 1A(1)", and

(b) in paragraph (b), for "under section 10(1)" substitute "as a result of section 1A(3)(a)".

IHTA 1984

94 IHTA 1984 is amended as follows.

95 In Schedule A1 (non-excluded overseas property), in paragraph 8(3)—

(a) in the definition of "interest in UK land", for the words from "the meaning" to the end substitute "the same meaning as it has for the purposes of section 1A(3)(b) of the 1992 Act (see section 1C of that Act);",

(b) in the definition of "dwelling", for the words from "the meaning" to the end substitute "the same meaning as it has for the purposes of Schedule 1B to the 1992 Act;", and

(c) in the definition of "contract for an off-plan purchase", for the words from "has the meaning" to the end substitute "means a contract for the acquisition of land consisting of, or including, a building, or part of a building, that is to be constructed or adapted for use as a dwelling."

FA 2005

96 FA 2005 is amended as follows.

97 (1) Section 32 (non-UK resident vulnerable persons: amount of relief) is amended as follows.

(2) In subsection (3), in the definitions of "TLVB" and "TLVA", omit "for the purposes of section 3 of TCGA 1992".

(3) After that subsection insert—

"(3A) For the purposes of this section "the vulnerable person's taxable amount for the tax year" means the amount on which that person would be chargeable to capital gains tax for the tax year if no account were taken of section 1K of TCGA 1992."

98 (1) Schedule 1 (non-UK resident vulnerable persons: interpretation) is amended as follows.

(2) In paragraph 3—

(a) in sub-paragraph (1)(a), for "for the purposes of section 3 of TCGA 1992" substitute "(as defined by section 32(3A))",

(b) in sub-paragraph (1)(b), for "for the purposes of that section" substitute "(as defined by section 32(3A))",

(c) in sub-paragraph (2)—

(i) in paragraph (a), for "section 2(2)(b)" substitute "section 1(3)(b)", and

(ii) omit paragraph (b) (together with the "and" before it).

(3) In paragraph 7—

(a) in sub-paragraph (1)(b), for "subsection (3) of that section" substitute "section 1E(2) of that Act", and

(b) in sub-paragraph (2), for "section 10A" substitute "section 1M".

ITA 2007

99 ITA 2007 is amended as follows.

100 In section 641 (accrued income profits and losses: trustees of a disabled person's trusts), in subsection (4), in the definition of "disabled person's trusts", for "paragraph 1(1) of Schedule 1" substitute "paragraph 3 of Schedule 1C".

101 In section 643 (accrued income profits and losses: non-residents), in subsection (5), for "section 10(6)" substitute "section 1B(5)".

102 In section 809F (remittance basis: effect on what is chargeable), in subsection (4), for "section 12 of TCGA 1992" substitute "paragraph 1 of Schedule 1 to TCGA 1992".

103 In section 809G (claim for remittance basis: effect on allowances etc), in subsection (3), for "section 3(1A)" substitute "section 1K(6)".

104 In section 809K (introduction to rules on remittance of income and gains), in subsection (1), for paragraph (e) substitute—

"(e) Schedule 1 to TCGA 1992 (UK resident individuals not domiciled in UK)."

105 In section 809VK (retention of funds to meet CGT liabilities), for subsection (5) substitute—

"(5) The highest potential CGT rate is the highest rate specified in section 1H of TCGA 1992 (regardless of the type of the chargeable gain or, if P is an individual, the rate of income tax at which P's income is chargeable)."

106 (1) Section 809YD (chargeable gains accruing on sales of exempt property) is amended as follows.

(2) In subsection (1)(c)(ii), for "section 13" substitute "section 3".

(3) In subsection (3), for "section 12 of TCGA 1992" substitute "paragraph 1 of Schedule 1 to TCGA 1992".

(4) In subsection (5)(a)—

(a) for "section 10A" substitute "section 1M", and
(b) for "the year of return" substitute "the tax year that consists of or includes the period of return".

(5) In subsection (7)—

(a) in the opening words, for "fell within the definition of foreign chargeable gains in section 12(4) of that Act" substitute "accrued on the disposal of a foreign asset (within the meaning of Schedule 1 to TCGA 1992)", and
(b) for paragraphs (a) to (d) substitute—

"(a) section 1M,
(b) section 3D, and
(c) Schedule 1."

(6) In subsection (8), for "section 14A(2)" substitute "section 3D(2)".

107 In section 809Z7 (meaning of "foreign income and gains" etc), in subsection (5), for the words from "are the foreign" to the end substitute "are the chargeable gains accruing to the individual in that year on the disposal of foreign assets (within the meaning of Schedule 1 to TCGA 1992)".

CTA 2009

108 CTA 2009 is amended as follows.

109 In section 2 (charge to corporation tax), omit subsection (2A).

110 (1) Section 5 of CTA 2009 (territorial scope of charge to corporation tax) is amended as follows.

(2) In subsections (1), (2A) and (3), for "chargeable to corporation tax" substitute "chargeable to corporation tax on income".

(3) In subsection (2), for "within the charge to corporation tax" substitute "within the charge to corporation tax on income".

(4) After subsection (4) insert—

"(5) The territorial scope of the charge to corporation tax on chargeable gains is given by section 2B of TCGA 1992."

111 In section 18A (exemption for profits or losses of foreign permanent establishments), after subsection (2A) insert—

"(2B) Profits and losses are not to be left out of account as mentioned in subsection (2) so far as, if the company were non-UK resident, they would be gains or losses accruing on disposals of assets within section 2B(4)(a) or (b) of TCGA 1992 (interests in UK land or other assets deriving at least 75% of their value from UK land)."

112 (1) Section 19 (chargeable profits) is amended as follows.

(2) In subsection (1), after "applies" insert "for the purposes of the charge to corporation tax on income".

(3) In subsection (3)—

(a) at the end of paragraph (a), insert "and", and
(b) omit paragraph (c).

(4) After subsection (3) insert—

"(4) For the purposes of the charge to corporation tax on chargeable gains accruing to the company, see section 2B(3) of TCGA 1992.

(5) That subsection provides (among other things) that the gains are chargeable to corporation tax only so far as they are attributable to the permanent establishment in accordance with sections 20 to 32 of this Act."

CTA 2010

113 CTA 2010 is amended as follows.

114 In section 533 (financial statements: supplementary), after subsection (1) insert—

"(1A) The profits and gains of the UK property rental business of a non-UK member of the group are to be treated as if they were profits and gains of a UK resident member of the group for the purposes of a financial statement under section 532(2)(a)."

115 After section 535 insert—

"535A Gains: disposals of rights or interests in UK property rich companies

(1) This section applies if—

(a) a company ("A") which is, or is a member of, a UK REIT disposes of an asset, and

(b) the asset consists of a right or an interest in a company ("B") which is UK property rich.

(2) The appropriate proportion of a gain accruing to A on the disposal is not a chargeable gain.

(3) The asset disposed of is regarded for the purposes of section 550 as used for the purposes of A's property rental business to an extent equal to the appropriate proportion.

(4) In the case of a non-UK member of a group UK REIT, this section has effect as if any reference to property rental business of the member were to its UK property rental business.

(5) In relation to a disposal of a right or interest in B—

(a) B is "UK property rich" for the purposes of this section if the disposal would be regarded for the purposes of Schedule 1A to TCGA 1992 as a disposal of an asset deriving at least 75% of its value from UK land, and

(b) any reference in this section to "the appropriate proportion" is to the proportion that, at the beginning of the accounting period in which the disposal is made, the value of B's relevant PRB assets bears to the total value of B's assets.

(6) For the purposes of subsection (5)(b)—

(a) "the value of B's relevant PRB assets" means the value of B's assets deriving (directly or indirectly) from assets used for the purposes of UK property rental business,

(b) B's assets are to be valued in accordance with section 533(1)(d), and

(c) if the asset disposed of was acquired after the beginning of the accounting period, it is to be assumed that an accounting period began on the day on which the disposal is made.

(7) Any reference in this section to the disposal of a right or interest in B includes the disposal of a right or interest in an offshore collective investment vehicle (a "relevant fund")—

(a) to which paragraph 8 of Schedule 5AAA to TCGA 1992 applies, but

(b) in relation to which an election under that paragraph has not been made.

(8) In the case of a disposal which is, as a result of subsection (7), a disposal of a right or interest in B, the value of B's relevant PRB assets for the purposes of subsection (5)(b) is taken to be—

(a) the value of B's assets that are used for the purposes of UK property rental business, plus

(b) the value of B's assets deriving indirectly from assets held by a relevant fund that are used for the purposes of UK property rental business.

(9) This section is to be read as if it were contained in TCGA 1992.

(10) Apart from subsection (7) of section 535, nothing else in that section applies in relation to a disposal to which this section applies.

(11) This section does not apply to a gain—

(a) if sub-paragraph (3) of paragraph 3A of Schedule 7AC to TCGA 1992 applies in relation to the gain (no chargeable gain accruing on disposals of certain shares by qualifying institutional investors), or

(b) so far as sub-paragraph (4) of that paragraph applies to reduce the amount of the gain.

535B Section 535A: use of pre-April 2019 residual business losses or deficits

(1) In determining the amount of a gain accruing to a company which is not to be a chargeable gain as a result of section 535A, any pre-April 2019 residual business losses or deficits which—

(a) have not been deducted from (or taken into account in calculating) other profits or gains (of any kind) of the company or any other person, and

(b) have not previously been deducted under this subsection,

may be deducted from the gain.

(2) For this purpose "pre-April 2019 residual business losses or deficits" means—

(a) allowable losses accruing on disposals made before 6 April 2019, or

(b) deficits or other losses for accounting periods ending before that date,

which would otherwise have been deducted from (or taken into account in calculating) profits or gains (of any kind) accruing to residual business of the company.

(3) If an accounting period (a "straddling period") begins before and ends on or after 6 April 2019—

(a) so much of the straddling period as falls before that date, and so much of it as falls on or after that date, are to be treated as separate accounting periods, and

(b) if it is necessary to apportion an amount for the straddling period to the two separate accounting periods, it is to be apportioned—

(i) on a time basis according to the respective length of the separate accounting periods, or

(ii) if that would produce a result that is unjust or unreasonable, on a just and reasonable basis."

116 In section 547 (funds awaiting reinvestment), at the end insert—

"(6) This section also applies to proceeds held in cash by a company on a disposal of an asset so far as section 535A secures that the appropriate proportion of a gain or loss accruing on the disposal is not a chargeable gain or allowable loss."

117 In section 550(3) (attribution of distributions), after "section 535" insert "or 535A".

118 (1) Section 556 (disposal of assets) is amended as follows.

(2) After subsection (3) insert—

"(3A) Subsection (3B) applies in the case of a company ("C") which is, or is a member of, a UK REIT if—

(a) one or more properties acquired (directly or indirectly) by a relevant UK property rich company have been developed since acquisition,

(b) the cost of the development exceeds 30% of the fair value of the property (determined in accordance with international accounting standards) at entry or at acquisition, whichever is later,

(c) C disposes of any of its rights or interests in the relevant UK property rich company,

(d) the disposal is made within the period of 3 years beginning with the completion of the development, and

(e) if C is a member of a UK REIT, the disposal is not to another member of the UK REIT.

(3B) If this subsection applies, section 535A is not to apply in relation to so much of the amount of a gain accruing on the disposal as relates to the property which has been developed.

(3C) For the purposes of subsection (3A)—

(a) a company is a "relevant UK property rich company" if, as a result of section 535A, any part of a gain accruing to C on a disposal of a right or interest in the company would not be a chargeable gain, and

(b) a relevant UK property rich company acquires property "indirectly" if property is acquired by someone other than the relevant UK property rich company and the property is taken into account in determining the value of the assets of the relevant UK property rich company."

(3) In subsection (7), for "Section 535 is" substitute "Sections 535 and 535A are".

119 In section 582 (early exit), in subsection (3)(b), for "or 535(1)" substitute ", 535(1) or 535A".

PART 3

COMMENCEMENT AND TRANSITIONAL PROVISIONS ETC

120 (1) The amendments made by this Schedule have effect—

(a) for the purposes of capital gains tax, for the tax year 2019–20 and subsequent tax years, and

(b) for the purposes of corporation tax, for accounting periods beginning on or after 6 April 2019.

(2) The amendments made by this Schedule also have effect for the purposes of corporation tax in relation to disposals made on or after 6 April 2019 (whether in their application to accounting periods beginning on, and ending on or after, that date or to later accounting periods).

121 (1) This paragraph applies to—

(a) allowable NRCGT losses accruing to a person before 6 April 2019, and

(b) ring-fenced ATED-related allowable losses accruing to a person before that date,

so far as they have not been deducted under section 2B, 8(1)(b)(ii), 14D or 188D of TCGA 1992 (as those provisions have effect before the amendments made by this Schedule) from chargeable gains accruing before that date.

(2) If losses to which this paragraph applies accrued to a company, they are deductible in accordance with section 2A(1) of TCGA 1992 as if they had accrued to the company while it was within the charge to corporation tax.

(3) If losses to which this paragraph applies accrued to any other person, they—

(a) are deductible in accordance with section 1(3) of TCGA 1992, and

(b) are to be treated for the purposes of section 1E of TCGA 1992 as if they accrued on a disposal of assets that were within section 1A(3) of that Act.

(4) In this paragraph—

(a) the reference to allowable NRCGT losses is to be read in accordance with Schedule 4ZZB to TCGA 1992 (as that Schedule has effect before its repeal by this Schedule), and

(b) the reference to ring-fenced ATED-related allowable losses is to be read in accordance with section 2B of that Act (as that section has effect before its repeal by this Schedule).

122 The Treasury may by regulations make any transitional provisions or savings that they consider appropriate in connection with the coming into force of any provision made by this Schedule.

123 (1) This paragraph applies where this Schedule re-enacts in TCGA 1992 (with or without modification) an enactment contained in TCGA 1992 repealed by this Schedule.

(2) The repeal and re-enactment does not affect the continuity of the law.

(3) Any subordinate legislation or other thing which—

(a) has been made or done, or has effect as if made or done, under or for the purposes of the repealed provision, and

(b) is in force or effective on 5 April 2019,

has effect in relation to times after that date as if made or done under or for the purposes of the corresponding provision of TCGA 1992.

(4) Any reference (express or implied) in any enactment, instrument or document to a provision of TCGA 1992 is to be read as including, in relation to times, circumstances or purposes in relation to which the corresponding repealed provision had effect, a reference to that corresponding provision.

(5) Any reference (express or implied) in any enactment, instrument or document to a repealed provision of TCGA 1992 is to be read as including, in relation to times, circumstances or purposes in relation to which the corresponding provision has effect, as or (as the context may require) as including a reference to that corresponding provision.

(6) The generality of this paragraph is not to be affected by specific transitional, transitory or saving provision made elsewhere by this Schedule.

(7) This paragraph has effect instead of section 17(2) of the Interpretation Act 1978.

124 The Treasury may by regulations make such provision as they consider appropriate in consequence of the provision made by this Schedule.

125 (1) The Treasury may by regulations make provision, in relation to a case in which they consider that a provision of this Schedule changes the effect of a provision of TCGA 1992 that is re-enacted by this Schedule, for the purpose of returning the effect of the law to what it would have been if this Act had not been passed.

(2) The power conferred by this paragraph may not be exercised on or after 6 April 2022.

126 (1) This paragraph applies to regulations made under paragraph 124 or 125.

(2) The regulations may amend, repeal or revoke any provision made by or under—

(a) this Schedule, or
(b) any other provision of the Taxes Acts (within the meaning of section 118(1) of TMA 1970).

(3) The regulations may, if made before 6 April 2020, contain provision (however expressed) for securing that the provision made by the regulations has effect in accordance with paragraph 120 (commencement) as it were included in the amendments made by this Schedule.

(4) The regulations may contain incidental, supplemental, consequential or transitional provision or savings.

COMMENTARY ON SCHEDULE 1

TCGA 1992, Pt 1

Scope

Sections 1–3G replace the current ss 1–14H, creating a new Part 1 of TCGA 1992. New Part 1 is arranged in three chapters:

Chapter 1	The charge on individuals and companies, and the charge on non-UK residents (ss 1–1O, replacing ss 1–4BB, 10, 10A, 10AA, 14B and 14D–14H)
Chapter 2	The charge on companies (ss 2–2G, replacing ss 8 and 10B)
Chapter 3	The attribution of gains from non-resident companies (ss 3–3G, replacing ss 13, 13A, 14 and 14A)
Section 3A	Now included as TMA 1970, s 8C
Section 11	Is included as new ss 271ZA and 271ZB
Section 12	Has been rewritten as new TCGA 1992, Sch 1
Sections 14B and 14D–14H	Non-resident CGT disposals, have been replaced by ss 1A–1G

New TCGA 1992, Pt 1 is now in typical 're-write style' meaning that several new sections do the work that was previously done by one, however it is relatively clearly written and easy to follow. The legislation has been rewritten to accommodate the taxation of non-UK resident persons making disposals of interest in UK land, and simplify the alignment of the new and existing rules. The Government has stated that: 'apart from the changes to implement this measure the provisions are a re-statement of the existing law and make no change to the way the existing provisions work'. Appropriate changes have also been made to Corporation Tax Act (CTA) 2009 to include non-UK resident companies.

This commentary focuses on the new parts of the legislation dealing with the CGT charge on non-residents' disposals of UK land, and the charge on UK residents' disposals of residential property from 6 April 2020, introduced in Sch 1. Where an existing section is clearly reproduced (albeit in re-write language), no analysis has been included.

Commencement provisions: para 120

The amendments in Sch 1 have effect:

- for the purposes of CGT, for 2019/20 and subsequent tax years, and
- for the purposes of corporation tax, for accounting periods beginning on or after 6 April 2019, and
- in relation to corporation tax, for disposals made on or after 6 April 2019 (irrespective of when the relevant accounting period commences).

The CGT charge on non-residents: new TCGA 1992, ss 1A–1D, 2B

TCGA 1992, ss 1A and 2B deal with the territorial extent of CGT and the corporation tax charge on gains. Section 2B(3) mirrors s 1A(3)(a) and s 2B(4) mirrors s 1A(3)(b) and (c).

A person who is non-resident for a tax year is chargeable to CGT or corporation tax on chargeable gains accruing in the tax year on:

- the disposal of assets situated in the UK that have a relevant connection to the person's UK branch, agency or permanent establishment and are disposed of at a time when the person has that branch, agency or permanent establishment (s 1A(3)(a), s 2B(3))
- assets not within (a) that are interests in UK land (s 1C, s 2B(4)(b)), and
- assets (wherever situated) not within s 1A(3)(a) or (b) that derive at least 75% of their value from UK land where the person has a 'substantial indirect interest' in that land (s 1D, s 2B(4)(c) and Sch 1A).

Section 1B replicates old s 10, and s 2C old s 10B, defining assets with a relevant connection to a UK branch, agency or permanent establishment (chargeable under s 1A(3)(a) or s 2B(3)). Sections 1C and 1D introduce definitions of:

- non-UK residents disposing of an 'interest in UK land', and
- non-UK residents' assets deriving 75% of their value from UK land

Each is chargeable under s 1A(3)(b) and (c), or 2B(4), respectively. An 'interest in UK land' is defined as an estate, interest, right or power in or over land in the UK, or the benefit of an obligation, restriction or condition affecting the value of an estate, interest, right or power in or over land in the UK, other than an excluded interest.

The following interests are 'excluded interests':

- any interest or right held for securing the payment of money or the performance of any other obligation (not including rentcharges, feu duties or any payment mentioned in s 56(1) of the Abolition of Feudal Tenure (Scotland) Act 2000),
- a licence to use or occupy land; a tenancy at will or an advowson, franchise or manor, and
- such other categories as may be specified from time to time in regulations made by the Treasury.

The grant of an option by a person binding the person to dispose of an interest in UK land is regarded as a disposal of an interest in UK land by the person for the purposes of s 1A(3)(b).

'Franchise' means a grant from the Crown such as the right to hold a market or fair, or the right to take tolls, and 'land' includes buildings and structures, and land under the sea or otherwise covered by water.

Non-resident companies, unit trusts and other non-partnership collective investment schemes that do not elect for transparency or exemption will be taxed at the corporation tax rate (19%, reducing to 17% on 1 April 2020), while individuals and other entities will be taxed at CGT rates (10% and 20% for commercial property disposals, 18% and 28% where the property is residential).

Allowable losses: new TCGA 1992, ss 1E, 1F, 1G

The **only** allowable capital losses that can be deducted from gains arising from non-resident disposals of UK property (within s 1A(3)) are losses arising from transactions that would have been within s 1A(3) or s 2B(4) had they been gains. In addition, for individuals, losses arising on non-resident disposals of UK property can only be carried back on death against relevant non-resident gains, by virtue of re-written TCGA 1992, s 62(2A) and new s 62(11). The restrictions that apply for CGT do not apply for corporation tax. For corporation tax purposes any losses are treated in the same way as any other allowable loss. Any unused ATED-related CGT or NRCGT losses in the periods to 5 April 2019 can be carried forward and allowed in the same way as any other brought forward allowable loss.

In split years, gains made by individuals in the overseas part of the year are only taxable if they are within TCGA 1992, s 1A(3) (non-resident disposal of UK property) and individuals can only use losses against gains accruing in the overseas part of the tax year if the losses themselves accrued on the disposal of assets within s 1A(3)(b) or (c), or assets that would be within s 1A(3)(b) or (c) if they did not have a relevant connection to the individual's UK branch or agency.

Section 1A(3) losses accruing in the overseas part of the year can however be used against gains arising in the UK part of the year.

Allowable losses arising from non-resident disposals of UK property are also blocked from being deducted from any gains treated as accruing to an individual as a result of:

- section 87 (non-resident settlements – attribution of gains to beneficiaries)
- section 87K (non-resident settlements – attribution of gains to onward gift recipient)
- section 87L (non-resident settlements – cases where the settlor is liable following an onward gift)
- section 89(2) (UK resident settlements – later capital payments matched with gains for years when trustees were non-resident), and
- Gains treated as accruing on return from a period of non-residence where they would otherwise have been charged on a settlor under s 86.

Losses arising on transactions in UK property are not allowable if, had a gain accrued instead, the gain would not have been chargeable to CGT. TCGA 1992, s 16 (computation rules) and s 16A (capital loss TAAR) continue to apply, as they do to all capital losses.

NRCGT and ring-fenced ATED losses: Sch 1, para 121

Where allowable NRCGT losses or ring-fenced ATED-related allowable losses accrued before 6 April 2019, so far as they have not already been deducted under TCGA 1992, ss 2B, 8(1)(b)(ii), 14D or 188D (as those sections were in effect up to 5 April 2019), they are deductible:

- for a company, under s 2A(1) as if they had accrued to the company while it was within the charge to corporation tax, and
- for any other person, under s 1(3), and
- will be treated for the purposes of s 1E as if they accrued on a disposal of assets that were within s 1A(3).

For individuals and other non-corporates, references to allowable NRCGT losses must be read in accordance with TCGA 1992, Sch 4ZZB (as it stood prior to repeal), and to ring-fenced ATED-related allowable losses, in accordance with s 2B (as it stood prior to repeal).

No intention to change existing law: Sch 1, para 125

Up to 5 April 2022, the Treasury has reserved the power to make regulations for the purpose of returning the effect of the law to what it would have been if the re-write of TCGA 1992 had not been passed.

TCGA 1992, SCH 1A: ASSETS DERIVING 75% OF VALUE FROM UK LAND AND SUBSTANTIAL INDIRECT INTERESTS

New TCGA 1992, Sch 1A governs whether an asset derives 75% of its value from UK land and whether a person has a ‘substantial indirect interest’ in UK land for the purposes of ss 1A(3)(c) or 2B(4)(b). Schedule 1A is divided into four parts:

- paras 1–2 deal with various introductory matters and definitions
- paras 3–7 deal with whether an asset derives 75% of its value from UK land
- paras 8–10 deal with whether a person has a substantial indirect interest in UK land, and
- para 11 deals with anti-avoidance

An asset derives at least 75% of its value from UK land if:

- the asset consists of a right or an interest in a company, and
- at the time of the disposal, at least 75% of the total market value of the company’s qualifying assets derives (directly or indirectly) from interests in UK land.

Assets deriving 75% of their value from UK land

Sch 1A, para 3

‘Qualifying assets’ are all of the assets of the company other than any asset that is matched to a related party liability (except where that asset is itself an interest in UK land). A liability for these purposes includes a contingent liability (such as one arising as a result of the giving of a guarantee, indemnity or other form of financial assistance).

Sch 1A, para 4

An asset is treated as being matched to a related party liability if the asset consists of a right under a transaction (for example, a right under a loan relationship or derivative contract), the right entitles the company to require another person to meet a liability arising under the transaction, and the other person is a 'relevant person' in tracing the market value of the company's assets.

A person is relevant to the market value tracing exercise if the person has assets that would be taken into account in the tracing exercise, or the person has obligations in relation to the holding of assets comprised in a trust or other arrangement that would be taken into account in that exercise, or if the other person is a related party of the company on the day of the disposal.

Whether a person is a related party of the company is determined in accordance with CTA 2010, s 356OT (but ignoring the 'six months' condition in s 356OT(4)). There are exceptions for interests in UK land used for trading purposes (para 5) and certain disposals of rights or interests in connected companies (para 6).

Market value may be traced through any number of companies, partnerships, trusts and other entities or arrangements but is not traced through normal commercial loans (as defined by CTA 2010, ss 158(1)(b) or 159(4)(b)) this is modelled on the tracing provisions in CTA 2010, s 356OR (para 3(2)).

It is irrelevant whether the law under which a company, partnership, trust or other entity or an arrangement is established is the law of any part of the UK or otherwise, the tracing exercise will be unaffected (para 3(3)).

The legislation requires the assets held by the company, partnership, trust, other entity or arrangement to be attributed to the shareholders, partners, beneficiaries or other participants at each stage 'in whatever way is appropriate in the circumstances' (para 3(4)). Where a number of entities are disposed of in one arrangement, their assets will be aggregated to establish whether the 75% test is met.

UK land used for trading purposes: Sch 1A, para 5

Land may be excluded from the calculation of whether 75% or more of a company's market value derives from UK land if it is reasonable to conclude that – to the extent that the market value of the company's qualifying assets derives (directly or indirectly) from interests in UK land:

- all of the interests in UK land are used for trading purposes, or
- all of the interests in UK land would be used for trading purposes if low-value non-trade interests in UK land were ignored.

An interest in UK land is 'used for trading purposes' if (and only if), at the time of the disposal it is being used in, or for the purposes of, a qualifying trade, or has been acquired for use in such a trade. HMRC gives the example of a non-UK resident disposing of shares in a retailer which owns a significant number of shops as qualifying for relief under para 5. This should mean that most investments by non-resident investors in UK retail and hospitality businesses are exempt, however HMRC has said that it does not extend to the infrastructure sector.

A trade is a 'qualifying' trade if:

- it has been carried on by the company, or by a person connected with the company, on a commercial basis with a view to the realisation of profits throughout the period of one year ending with the time of the disposal, and
- it is reasonable to conclude that the trade will continue to be carried on (for more than an insignificant period of time) on a commercial basis with a view to the realisation of profits.

For these purposes, 'low-value non-trade interests in UK land' means interests in UK land:

- which are not used for trading purposes, and
- the total market value of which is, at the time of the disposal, no more than 10% of the total market value at that time of the other interests in UK land that are used for trading purposes.

The para 5 test applies at the company level, so where a land-holding subsidiary is involved, para 5 may exempt a sale of shares in the subsidiary. However, the trading exemption is not carried 'up the chain' to parent companies.

Example:

Bosphorus Ltd is the overseas holding company of the B group of companies. Bosphorus has assets worth £12m. In the year to 31 March 2020, its subsidiaries are:

Arcadia Ltd – (incorporated on 1 October 2019) owns and operates three luxury hotels in the UK (£5m)
Argosy Ltd – a property investment company with a portfolio of UK commercial properties (£5m) and
Athene Ltd – a UK trading company (£2m)

Bosphorus Ltd disposes of 10% of its shares in each subsidiary on 31 March 2020. On 31 March 2020, 75% of Bosphorus Ltd's qualifying assets derived from UK land, so it will be within the charge to CGT under s 2B(4).

Had Bosphorus Ltd waited until 1 October 2020 to make the disposal, it would no longer have met the 75% test, as Arcadia Ltd would have met the para 5 test for UK land used for trading purposes, and could have been excluded from the market value calculation.

Exceptions for certain disposals: Sch 1A, para 6

Where there are two or more disposals of rights or interests in companies and those disposals are linked with each other, and some (but not all) of the disposals would be disposals of assets deriving at least 75% of their value from UK land, para 6 gives relief in some circumstances.

If, when the assets were aggregated so that one of the companies was deemed to hold all of the assets of the others, a disposal of a right or interest in it would not be a disposal of an asset deriving at least 75% of its value from UK land, then none of the 'linked' disposals will be regarded as disposals within TCGA 1992, s 1A(3)(c).

A disposal of a right or interest in a company is regarded as 'linked' with a disposal of a right or interest in another company if:

- the disposals are made under the same arrangements
- by the same person or by persons connected with each other
- either to the same person or to persons connected with each other, and
- in the case of each disposal, the person making the disposal is connected (TCGA 1992, s 286) with the company in which the right or interest is disposed of.

For these purposes 'connection' is measured immediately before the arrangements are entered into and, for the purposes of considering related party liabilities (para 4), each of the other companies in which rights or interest are disposed of is assumed to be a related party of the company on the day of the disposal. The test in s 286 is modified, with ss 286(2) and (8) being limited to direct lineal ancestors and descendants of the person or their spouse or civil partner, and s 286(4) relating to partners (and partners' spouses) being ignored.

Example:

Bosphorus Ltd sells 10% shareholdings in both Arcadia Ltd and Argosy Ltd (each now worth £6m), in March 2021, to Colchis Ltd.

These are linked disposals. Both Arcadia and Argosy hold UK property, so Bosphorus Ltd is potentially within the charge on disposals of UK land. However, Arcadia has now been trading as an hotelier for over a year, and therefore meets the trading test in para 5.

When looking at the two subsidiaries in aggregate though, Bosphorus Ltd is treated as owning £12m of UK land assets, of which only 50% qualify for the trading exemption. Since the non-trade assets are more than 10% of the assets deemed to be held by Bosphorus Ltd (see low value interests, above), the 75% test is met and the transaction falls within s 2B(4)(b).

Substantial indirect interests in UK land

Basic rule: Sch 1A, para 8

Where a person disposes of an asset consisting of a right or an interest in a company, and the 75% test is met, the person has a 'substantial indirect interest' in

UK land if, at any time in the period of two years ending with the time of the disposal, the person has a 25% investment in the company (ignoring 25% interests held for brief periods only: the legislation refers to the 25% interest only being held for an 'insignificant' proportion of the two years, and HMRC has suggested it would regard 10% as insignificant in these circumstances).

Meaning of '25% investment': Sch 1A, paras 9, 10

A person has a 25% investment in a company if they possess or are entitled to acquire 25% or more of the voting power in the company, or they would receive 25% or more of the proceeds in the event of a disposal of the whole of the equity of the company, or they would be entitled to receive more than 25% of income distributions to shareholders, or they would be entitled to 25% or more of the assets on a winding-up

'Equity' for these purposes is defined as all shares in the company, excluding restricted preference shares (as defined in CTA 2010, s 160), plus all loan capital, except for normal commercial loans (as defined in CTA 2010, ss 158(1)(b) or 159(4)(b)).

'Shares' in the company are defined as including stock, and any other interests of the members. Where the company does not have share capital, the rules will apply to members' interests (but with the definitions of normal commercial loans and restricted preferences shares in CTA 2010 modified accordingly).

References to 'receipt of any proceeds, amount or assets' include direct or indirect receipts, and their direct or indirect application for the person's benefit. It is irrelevant whether that receipt or application is at the time of a disposal, distribution, winding-up, or other circumstance, or at a later time.

The connection provisions can cause traps for the unwary here:

Example

Where a person (Athena Ltd) which is directly or indirectly owned by other persons (Colchis Ltd and Diomedes Ltd), either directly receives any proceeds, amounts or assets, or any such amounts are directly or indirectly applied by or for Athena Ltd's benefit, there is an indirect receipt or indirect application of that percentage of the proceeds, amount or assets for the benefit of Colchis Ltd and Diomedes Ltd as well, although the usual carve out for normal commercial loans applies.

The percentage of the equity in Athena Ltd directly or indirectly owned by Colchis Ltd and Diomedes Ltd is determined using the rules in CTA 2010, ss 1155–1157.

For persons who are members of partnerships, the 'proceeds, amount or assets' of the person includes the person's share of the proceeds, amount or assets of the partnership (apportioned between partners on a just and reasonable basis).

For these purposes, a person will be taken to have all of the rights and interests of any person connected with them (subject to the usual carve out for normal commercial loans) (para 10). The connection test in TCGA 1992, s 286 is modified, with ss 286(2) and (8) being limited to direct lineal ancestors and descendants of the person or their spouse or civil partner, and s 286(4) relating to partners (and partners' spouses) being ignored.

The 25% test doesn't apply to collective investment vehicles, so if a vehicle derives 75% of its value from UK land, either the vehicle will be within the charge, or its investors will be within the charge irrespective of the size of their interest in the vehicle (but subject to the availability of elections under Sch 5AAA).

Anti-avoidance: Sch 1A, para 11

The normal anti-avoidance rules for CGT continue to apply, but in addition HMRC has power to counteract any arrangements the main purpose, or one of the main purposes, of which is to obtain a tax advantage (relating to CGT or corporation tax) for the person as a result, wholly or partly, of:

- any provision of Sch 1A applying or not applying (para 11(1)(a)), or
- double taxation arrangements having effect where the advantage sought is contrary to the object and purpose of the double taxation arrangements (para 11(1)(b))

The tax advantage will, as usual, be counteracted by the making of such adjustments as are 'just and reasonable' and may be made (whether by an officer of HMRC or the person concerned) by way of an assessment, the modification of an assessment, amendment or disallowance of a claim, or otherwise.

If the non-resident person does not pay any of the tax found to be due, there are provisions enabling HMRC to charge UK resident companies in the same group. In common with most 're-write' anti-avoidance legislation, 'tax advantage' is widely defined as 'relief or increased relief from tax, repayment or increased repayment of tax, avoidance or reduction of a charge to tax or an assessment to tax, avoidance of a possible assessment to tax, deferral of a payment of tax or advancement of a repayment of tax, and avoidance of an obligation to deduct or account for tax'.

CGT will only be chargeable on disposals of or by UK property rich entities if the tax treaty with the vendor's country of residence gives taxing rights to the UK for this type of disposal. Not all of the UK tax treaties currently in force include such a clause, so we are likely to see a gradual replacement of all the treaties that do not give taxing rights to the country where real estate is located. The anti-forestalling rules have prevented new structures being set up to take advantage of such treaties.

The counteraction has effect in a treaty shopping case (a case within para 11(1)(b)) regardless of TIOPA 2010, s 6(1). Affected arrangements are those entered into on or after 22 November 2017 in a 'treaty shopping case', and on or after 6 July 2018 in any other case.

'Arrangements' includes any agreement, understanding, scheme, transaction or series of transactions (whether or not legally enforceable), and 'double taxation arrangements' means arrangements that have effect under TIOPA 2010, s 2(1).

TCGA 1992, SCH 1B: RESIDENTIAL PROPERTY GAINS

Schedule 1B is only ten paragraphs long, and deals with the definition of 'residential property' for the purposes of the charge on UK residents.

While non-resident persons are broadly chargeable on all disposals of UK property, residential or commercial, UK residents will need to make in year returns of CGT (see FA 2019, Sch 2) on UK residential property disposals only, from 6 April 2020. Schedule 1B contains the relevant definitions.

For the purposes of TCGA 1992, Pt 1, Ch 1, a 'residential property gain' means 'so much of a chargeable gain accruing to a person on a disposal of residential property as is, in accordance with Sch 1B, para 2, attributable to that property'.

Attribution of gain to residential property: Sch 1B, para 2

Paragraph 2 largely deals with attributing the correct value to the residential property gain, where there has been mixed use of the land to which the disposal relates on one or more days in the applicable period. The gain will be adjusted, on a 'just and reasonable basis', to take account of the mixed use on that day or days.

There is mixed use of land on any day on which the land consists of one or more dwellings, and also other land.

If the disposal is of an interest in land subsisting under a contract for the acquisition of land consisting of or including a building that is to be constructed or adapted for use as a dwelling, that land is taken to consist of or include a dwelling throughout the applicable period (beginning with the day on which the person making the disposal acquired the interest in land being disposed of or, if later, the day from which the interest in land became chargeable, and ending with the day before the day on which the disposal occurs).

For the purposes of para 2, an interest in land 'became chargeable':

- for disposals of UK land by non-residents (or by an individual overseas during the overseas part of a split year), from 6 April 2015, and
- in any other case (disposals of residential property by UK residents), from 31 March 1982.

If the interest in land disposed of by the person results from interests in land acquired by the person at different times, the person is regarded for these purposes as having acquired the interest disposed of at the time of the first acquisition, mirroring TCGA 1992, s 222(7) (and ss 222A–226) (principal private residence relief). Paragraph 4 defines an interest in land, in the same terms as s 1C.

What constitutes 'a disposal of residential property': Sch 1B, para 3

A disposal of residential property occurs if a person disposes of an interest in land, where:

- the land consisted of or included a dwelling at any time falling on or after the date on which the applicable period begins
- the interest in land subsisted for the benefit of land that consisted of or included a dwelling at any time falling on or after that date, or
- the interest in land subsists under a contract for the acquisition of land consisting of or including a building that is to be constructed or adapted for use as a dwelling.

However, no account is taken of the status of the land at any time falling on (or after) the day on which the disposal is made when evaluating this.

Dwellings: Sch 1B, paras 5, 6, 7

These provisions are familiar from the repealed TCGA 1992, Sch B1, para 4(4) dealing with UK residential property interests (drawn from the ATED definition in FA 2013, s 112 which in turn is based on the SDLT definition in FA 2003, s 116). A building is regarded as a dwelling at any time when it is used, or is suitable for use, as a dwelling, or it is in the process of being constructed or adapted for use as a dwelling (and, in each case, it is not an institutional building). Land that at any time is, or is intended to be, occupied or enjoyed with a dwelling as a garden or grounds (including any buildings or structures on it) will be taken to be part of the dwelling at that time.

Institutional buildings are not dwellings. A building is an institutional building if:

- it is used as residential accommodation for school pupils,
- it is used as residential accommodation for members of the armed forces,
- it is used as a home or other institution providing residential accommodation for children,
- it is used as a home or other institution providing residential accommodation with personal care for persons in need of personal care because of old age, disability, past or present dependence on alcohol or drugs or past or present mental disorder,
- it is used as a hospital or hospice,
- it is used as a prison or similar establishment,
- it is used as a hotel or inn or similar establishment,
- it is otherwise used, or suitable for use, as an institution that is the sole or main residence of its residents,
- it falls within Housing Act 2004, Sch 14, para 4 (buildings in England or Wales occupied by students and managed or controlled by educational establishment) or any corresponding provision in Scotland or Northern Ireland,
- it is student accommodation, incorporating at least 15 bedrooms, is purpose-built, or is converted, for occupation by students, and is occupied by students on at least 165 days (accommodation will be regarded as occupied by persons as students if they occupy it wholly or mainly for undertaking a course of education (otherwise than as school pupils)).

A building will continue to be treated as suitable to be used as a dwelling, even if it has become temporarily unsuitable for such use. The only exception is if the temporary unsuitability results from accidental damage (caused by circumstances beyond the control of the person disposing of the building, so convenient 'accidents' or suspicious fires will not qualify for relief) to the building, and the damage results in the building becoming unsuitable for use as a dwelling for a period of at least 90 consecutive days (not including the day of disposal or any time after disposal).

The exception does not apply if the damage occurs in the course of work done during alterations (including partial demolition) to the building, that itself involves, or could be expected to involve, making the building unsuitable for use as a dwelling for at least 30 consecutive days.

If the exception applies, work done in the 90 day period to restore the building to suitability for use as a dwelling does not count as 'constructing or adapting the building for use as a dwelling'.

Unsuitability for use as a dwelling is not regarded as being 'temporary' if a person disposes of an interest in land on which a building subsists that has been suitable for use as a dwelling, and as a result of 'qualifying works', the building has, at or before the time of completion of the disposal, either ceased to exist or become unsuitable for use as a dwelling. In that case, the building will be regarded as unsuitable for use as a dwelling throughout the whole period of the works (this period is defined as 'when the works were in progress, plus such period (if any) ending immediately before the start of the works throughout which the building was, for reasons connected with the works, not used as dwelling').

Example

In the recent (SDLT) case of *PN Bewley Ltd v HMRC* [2019] UKFTT 0065, the company had purchased a run-down bungalow which had not at that stage been renovated, because undertaking the necessary works would have released asbestos. HMRC sought to impose additional rate SDLT.

HMRC contended that the property either was a dwelling, or was suitable to be used as one, and did not accept the considerable evidence presented that the only thing that could be done with the building was to completely demolish it and start again from scratch.

The FTT held in this instance that the property was derelict and not 'suitable for use as a dwelling' at the time it was purchased. Because of this, non-residential SDLT rates applied and the taxpayer actually got a refund.

Comparing non-resident CGT (NRCGT), had Aeneas Ltd, an offshore person, purchased such a property and later proceeded with the demolition of it, disposing of the land in (say) May 2019, then for CGT purposes, you would expect the building to be regarded as unsuitable for use as a dwelling throughout Aeneas Ltd's entire period of ownership, including the periods before demolition commenced (the reasons the building could not be used as a dwelling being the dilapidation of the property and the presence of asbestos, both of these reasons being 'directly connected to the works', i e the demolition).

'Qualifying works' are those where planning permission or development consent is required for the works, or for any change of use with which they are associated, and has been granted (whether before or after completion), and the works are carried out in accordance with the permission or consent.

If during any time when qualifying works are in progress, other work takes place for which planning permission or development consent should have been obtained, but wasn't (or anything else is being done in contravention of a condition or requirement attached to a planning permission or development consent relating to the building, including putting it to an alternative use where permission or consent is required, but has not been granted), then the 'period of works' does not include times when the unapproved works were carried out, or the periods of alternative use.

A building is regarded as ceasing to exist from the time when either it has been demolished completely to ground level, or it has been demolished to ground level except for a single facade (or a double facade if it is on a corner site) the retention of which is a condition or requirement of planning permission or development consent.

The completion of a disposal of an interest in land is regarded as occurring at the time of the disposal, or if the disposal is under a contract which is completed by a conveyance, transfer or other instrument, at the time when the instrument takes effect. Completion is normally the final step in the legal process of transferring ownership of property – the point at which the purchase price for the property is paid, the transfer is dated and the principal obligations of the parties under the contract for sale are discharged.

TCGA 1992, SCH 4AA: RE-BASING FOR NON-RESIDENTS IN RESPECT OF UK LAND HELD ON 5 APRIL 2019

Schedule 4AA is split into five parts:

- para 1 is an introduction to the rebasing provisions and when they will apply,
- paras 2–5 deal with direct and indirect disposals where the person becomes chargeable on 6 April 2019, and 2019 rebasing,
- paras 6–11 deal with direct disposals of assets held before 6 April 2015 that were fully chargeable before 6 April 2019 and 2015 rebasing,
- paras 12–15 deal with direct disposals of assets that were partly chargeable before 6 April 2019, and how rebasing should be dealt with, and

- paras 16–22 deal with companies with UK land becoming UK resident after 6 April 2019, or persons with UK land becoming non-resident after 6 April 2019, and other sundry matters.

2019 rebasing (Sch 4AA, Pts 1 and 2)

The 2019 rebasing rules apply on the first occasion on which a person disposes of an asset that the person held on 5 April 2019, where the disposal is a direct or indirect disposal of UK land, and the disposal is made by a non-resident or a UK resident in the overseas part of a tax year (para 2). It can also apply to non-UK resident companies holding UK land and becoming resident in the UK after 5 April 2019.

A disposal is a 'direct disposal of UK land' if it is a disposal of an interest in UK land, and a disposal by a person is an 'indirect disposal of UK land' if it is a disposal of an asset (other than an interest in UK land) deriving at least 75% of its value from UK land where the person has a substantial indirect interest in that land, for example disposing of shares in a company that holds UK land.

A disposal is made by a non-resident or a UK resident in the overseas part of a tax year if it is:

- a disposal on which a gain accrues that falls within TCGA 1992, s 1A(3)(b) or (c), or
- a disposal on which a gain accrues that is chargeable in accordance with TCGA 1992, s 1G(2) (gains accruing in the overseas part of a split year) because the asset disposed of is within s 1A(3)(b) or (c), or
- a disposal on which a gain accrues that falls to be dealt with by TCGA 1992, s 2B(4) (the corporate equivalent to s 1A(3)(b) and (c)), or
- a disposal of an asset on which a gain does not accrue but which, if a gain had arisen, would be dealt with within TCGA 1992, s 1A or s 2B.

The 2019 rebasing rules apply for all indirect disposals of UK land, direct disposals of UK land that were not fully residential before 6 April 2019, and direct disposals of UK land by persons who were not chargeable before 6 April 2019, on the first disposal of a relevant asset on or after that date.

A direct disposal of UK land made by a person was 'not fully residential before 6 April 2019' if in the period beginning with the day on which the person acquired the interest in land being disposed of (or, if later, 6 April 2015) and ending with 5 April 2019, there was no day on which the land disposed of consisted of or included a dwelling.

If the disposal is of an interest in land subsisting under a contract for the acquisition of land that, at any time before 6 April 2019, consisted of or included a building to be constructed or adapted for use as a dwelling (determined in accordance with Sch 1B), the disposal is taken to be fully residential before that date.

A disposal is made by a person who was not chargeable before 6 April 2019 if, immediately before that date, the person was a company which was not a close company, or a widely-marketed scheme, or a company carrying on life assurance business (as defined in FA 2012, s 56) where the interest in UK land was, immediately before that date, held for the purpose of providing benefits to policyholders in the course of that business (para 2(1)(c)).

The question as to whether a company was 'a closely-held company' prior to 6 April 2019 will be determined in accordance with TCGA 1992, Sch C1, Pt 1 (repealed by FA 2019); but if the company is a 'divided company' within the meaning of TCGA 1992, s 14G (as it stood before repeal), and the company would not otherwise be regarded as a closely-held company, the company will be regarded as close if:

- the gain or loss accruing on the disposal is primarily or wholly attributable to a particular division of the company, and
- if that division were a separate company, that separate company would be a closely-held company.

A company is a 'divided company' for these purposes if – prior to 6 April 2019 – under the law under which the company is formed, the company's articles of association, or other document regulating the company, or under arrangements entered into by or in relation to the company:

- some or all of the assets of the company were available primarily, or only, to meet particular liabilities of the company, and
- some or all of the members of the company, and some or all of its creditors, had rights primarily, or only, in relation to particular assets of the company.

References to a 'division' in this context are to an identifiable part of a company that carries on distinct business activities and to which particular assets and liabilities of the company are primarily or wholly attributable.

A person is a 'widely-marketed scheme' if the person is:

- a scheme within the meaning of s 14F (as it stood before its repeal on 5 April 2019), i e a unit trust scheme, a company which is an open-ended investment company within Financial Services and Markets Act 2000, s 262, or a company incorporated under foreign law which is the equivalent of an open-ended investment company, *and*
- condition A or B is met:

  Condition A is that the scheme is a widely-marketed scheme throughout the relevant ownership period.

  Condition B is that:
  - an investor in the scheme is an offshore fund, an open-ended investment company or an authorised unit trust (the feeder fund)
  - the scheme is a widely-marketed scheme throughout the alternative period, after taking into account the scheme documents relating to the feeder fund, and the intended investors in the feeder fund, and
  - the scheme and the feeder fund have the same manager.

In determining whether or not a person falls into either of these categories, arrangements will be ignored if the main purpose (or one of the main purposes) of them is to secure a tax advantage as a result of the person not being a closely-held company or the person being a widely-marketed scheme.

Re-basing to 5 April 2019: Sch 4AA, para 3

In calculating the gain or loss accruing on the disposal, the assumption is made that the asset was sold and immediately reacquired on 5 April 2019, at its market value on that date, with neither a gain or loss arising.

Election for retrospective basis of calculation: Sch 4AA, para 4

It is possible to elect for para 3 not to apply. However, for indirect disposals of UK land, where a loss accrues on the disposal, the loss will not be an allowable loss.

Calculation of residential property gain if retrospective basis election made: Sch 4AA, para 5

If a person makes an election under para 4 in respect of a disposal on which a gain accrues, and it is necessary to determine, in accordance with Sch 1B, how much of the gain is a residential property gain, Sch 1B, para 2 has effect as though para 2(5) and (6) were omitted, and that 'the applicable period' was defined as follows:

> 'The applicable period' means the period beginning with the day on which the person acquired the interest in land being disposed of or, if later, 31 March 1982, and ending with the day before the day on which the disposal is made.

2015 rebasing (Sch 4AA, Pt 3)

Sch 4AA, para 6

- Para 6 *does not* apply to direct disposals of UK land made by persons who were not chargeable before 6 April 2019, as such persons could apply the 2019 rebasing rules.
- Para 6 *does* apply to any direct disposal of UK land where the person held the interest in the UK land being disposed of throughout the period beginning with 6 April 2015 and ending with the disposal, and the disposal was fully residential before 6 April 2019.

For this purpose a direct disposal of UK land made by a person is 'fully residential before 6 April 2019' if, on every day in the period between 6 April 2015 and 5 April 2019, the land to which the disposal relates consisted of a dwelling (within the definitions above).

If the disposal is of an interest in land subsisting under a contract for the acquisition of land that, at any time between 6 April 2015 and 5 April 2019, did not consist of 'a building to be constructed or adapted for use as a dwelling', the disposal is not treated as 'fully residential' before 6 April 2019.

Re-basing to 5 April 2015: Sch 4AA, para 7

In calculating the gain or loss accruing on the disposal, the assumption is made that the asset was sold and immediately reacquired on 5 April 2015, at its market value on that date, with neither a gain or loss arising, subject to any election being made under one of (and only one of) para 8 or para 9. Elections need to be made on an asset by asset basis. Since re-basing applies only to the first disposal after 6 April 2019, excellent records will be needed, to ensure that all appropriate elections are made.

Example:

Aries, a non-resident individual, acquired an interest in UK land on 6 April 2013 for £300,000 and disposed of it on 5 April 2020 for £500,000

Its value on 5 April 2015 was £360,000

No election is made under para 8 or para 9 for 2015 rebasing

Chargeable gain (500,000 – 360,000) = £140,000

(Note, had Aries been a non-resident company, indexation allowance would have been available from 5 April 2015 under Sch 4ZZB.)

Election for retrospective basis of calculation: Sch 4AA, para 8

It is possible to elect for para 7 not to apply, in which case gains or losses will be calculated in the normal way taking in the entire period from acquisition to disposal.

Election for straight-line time apportionment: Sch 4AA, para 9

Alternatively, a person may make an election for para 7 not to apply, and for the gain or loss accruing on the disposal to be apportioned so that only the post-5 April 2015 proportion of it is treated as accruing on the disposal.

The ‘post-5 April 2015 proportion’ is worked out on a strict time basis, comparing the days of ownership on or after 6 April 2015 with the total number of days the asset has been owned (or from 31 March 1982, if the asset was acquired before that date).

Example (continued):

Interest in UK land acquired on 6 April 2013 for £300,000 and disposed of on 5 April 2020 for £500,000

Election made under para 9 for straight line apportionment

Total number of days in the post-5 April 2015 ownership period: 1,827

Total number of days in the entire ownership period: 2,557

Chargeable gain (1,827/2,557 × £200,000) = £142,901

This is more than the gain calculated under 2015 rebasing (para 6), so a para 9 election would not be made.

Calculation of residential property gain where election made for retrospective basis: Sch 4AA, para 10

If a person makes an election under para 8 in respect of a disposal on which a gain accrues, and it is necessary to determine, in accordance with Sch 1B, how much of the gain is a residential property gain, Sch 1B, para 2 has effect as though para 2(5) and 2(6) were omitted, and instead ‘the applicable period’ was defined as follows:

> ‘The applicable period’ means the period beginning with the day on which the person acquired the interest in land being disposed of or, if later, 31 March 1982, and ending with the day before the day on which the disposal is made.

Calculation of residential property gain where election made for straight line apportionment: Sch 4AA, para 11

If a person makes an election under para 9 in respect of a disposal on which a gain accrues, and it is necessary to determine, in accordance with Sch 1B, how much of the gain is a residential property gain, Sch 1B, para 2 has effect as though para 2(5) and 2(6) were omitted, and instead ‘the applicable period’ was defined as follows:

> ‘The applicable period’ means the period beginning with 6 April 2015, and ending with the day before the day on which the disposal is made.

Re-basing to both 5 April 2015 and 5 April 2019 (Sch 4AA, Pt 4)

Sch 4AA, para 12

TCGA 1992, Sch 4AA, Pt 4 applies to any direct disposal of UK land if neither Pt 2 (direct or indirect disposals of UK land held on 5 April 2019) nor Pt 3 (direct disposal of fully residential UK land where the person held the interest in the UK land being disposed of throughout the period beginning with 6 April 2015, and ending with disposal) applies to the disposal, and the interest in UK land being disposed of was not a post-April 2015 asset (ie acquired after that date) that was 'fully residential' (within the definitions above) before 6 April 2019.

Sch 4AA, para 13

In calculating the gain or loss accruing on disposal an assumption is made that:

- the asset was sold and immediately reacquired on 5 April 2015 (unless it was acquired after that date), at its market value on that date, *and also*
- that it was sold and immediately reacquired on 5 April 2019, at its market value on that date.

The gain or loss accruing on the deemed sale on 5 April 2019 (which brings into charge the four years between those dates, only) is treated as accruing on the eventual disposal (in addition to the gain or loss that actually accrues on the actual disposal). It is possible to elect for this rebasing calculation not to apply.

Election for retrospective basis of calculation: Sch 4AA, para 14

If more beneficial, the person may make an election for para 13 not to apply, in which case gains or losses will be calculated in the normal way taking in the entire period from acquisition to disposal.

Calculation of residential property gain where retrospective calculation election made: Sch 4AA, para 15

If a person makes an election under para 8 (retrospective basis) in respect of a disposal on which a gain accrues, and it is necessary to determine (in accordance with Sch 1B) how much of the gain is a residential property gain, para 2, Sch 1B has effect as though para 2(5) and (6) were omitted, and 'the applicable period' is defined as follows:

> 'The applicable period' means the period beginning with the day on which the person acquired the interest in land being disposed of or, if later, 31 March 1982, and ending with the day before the day on which the disposal is made.

Miscellaneous (Sch 4AA, Pt 5)

Companies with UK land becoming UK resident after 5 April 2019: Sch 4AA, para 16

Where a company becomes UK resident after 5 April 2019, and makes a direct or indirect disposal of UK land after that date, and any of paras 2–15 would have applied to the disposal but for the fact that it occurred at a time when the company was resident in the UK then paras 2–15 (as appropriate, depending on the dates of ownership, etc) are taken to apply, so that relevant gains will be charged. This allows companies moving onshore after 5 April 2019 to take advantage of rebasing as well.

Trustees with UK land ceasing to be UK resident after 5 April 2019: Sch 4AA, para 17

In any case where the trustees of a settlement cease to be UK resident after 5 April 2019 and afterwards, the trustees dispose of an asset held by them on that date, and the disposal is a direct or indirect disposal of UK land, none of the rebasing provisions in Sch 4AA will apply to the disposal.

The asset that is disposed of is excepted from the application of TCGA 1992, s 80(2) (deemed disposal and reacquisition at market value of assets, on trustees ceasing to be resident in the UK), so no 'exit gain' is deemed to arise, but CGT on an eventual disposal is calculated without any market value uplift at any point.

Companies with UK land ceasing to be UK resident after 5 April 2019: Sch 4AA, para 18

In any case where a company ceases to be UK resident after 5 April 2019, and after that date the company disposes of an asset held by it on that date, and the disposal is a direct or indirect disposal of UK land, none of the rebasing provisions in Sch 4AA apply to the disposal.

The asset that is disposed of is excepted from the application of TCGA 1992, ss 185(2) and 185(3) (deemed disposal of assets on company ceasing to be resident in UK) so no 'exit gain' is deemed to arise, but tax on an eventual disposal is calculated without any market value uplift at any point.

Wasting assets: Sch 4AA, para 19

When calculating the gain or loss accruing to a person in a case where 2019 rebasing (para 3), 2015 rebasing (para 7) or 2015 and 2019 rebasing (para 13) are applicable, it may in some cases be necessary to decide whether the asset disposed of is a wasting asset. In that case, the original acquisition date is to be used, not the deemed date arising from the rebasing.

Capital allowances: Sch 4AA, para 20

In calculating a gain or loss where the rebasing provisions apply (to 5 April 2015 or 5 April 2019 or both), the deemed acquisition cost (market value at the relevant date) is substituted for actual cost for the purposes of looking at any adjustments under TCGA 1992, ss 41 and 47 (restriction of losses by reference to capital allowances and renewals allowances and wasting assets qualifying for capital allowances).

Making elections under Sch 4AA: Sch 4AA, para 21

All the elections available under Sch 4AA *must* (regardless of TMA 1970, s 42(2)) be made by being included in a relevant return (or amendments to it) relating to the disposal in question (either a CGT return within Sch 2, FA 2019, or the self-assessment tax return where appropriate).

Any election made in a CGT return (under FA 2019, Sch 2) may subsequently be revoked in an ordinary tax return (or amendments to it) delivered on or before the filing/due date. Subject to that, any Sch 4AA election will be irrevocable.

TCGA 1992, SCH 5AAA: COLLECTIVE INVESTMENT VEHICLES

Schedule 5AAA is split into seven parts:

- paras 1–3 contain an introduction and key definitions
- paras 4–7 deal with the 'basic' rules
- paras 8–11 deal with the transparency election
- paras 12–42 deal with elections for exemption
- paras 43–45 deal with reporting and payment
- paras 46–48 cover general definitions, and
- paras 49–50 deal with transitional provisions

The legislation is aimed at collective investment vehicles (CIVs) that are 'UK property rich'. Broadly, a CIV is 'UK property rich' if 75% or more of its gross asset value derives from UK land, as defined in new TCGA 1992, s 1C. Schedule 5AAA applies to:

- collective investment schemes (CISs) (Financial Services and Markets Act 2000, s 235)
- alternative investment funds (AIFs) (Alternative Investment Fund Managers Regulations 2013, reg 3)
- companies that are UK real estate investment trusts (UK REITs) (CTA 2010, Pt 12), or
- companies that are resident outside the UK and meet the 'property income condition'.

These are collectively referred to throughout Sch 5AAA as CIVs.

For non-resident companies, the 'property income condition' is that:

- it is not a close company or, if it is a close company, only because it has a 'qualifying investor' as a direct or indirect participator,
- at least half of its income is 'property income from long-term investments', and
- it distributes all, or substantially all, of its property income from long-term investments and does so on an annual basis, and it is not liable to tax on that income under the law of any territory in which it is resident.

Throughout TCGA 1992, Sch 5AAA:

- 'Property income from long-term investments' means income deriving from direct or indirect investments in land, or estates, interests or rights in or over land, which are made on a long-term basis.
- 'Participator' means – in relation to a CIS or an AIF – a person who takes part in the arrangements constituting the scheme or AIF, whether by becoming the

owner of the property that is the subject of the arrangements or undertaking, or in relation to a company, a shareholder in the company.

- 'Unit' means in the case of a CIS or an AIF, the rights or interests (however described) of the participant in the scheme or AIF, or in the case of a company, a share in the company.

Key expressions (Sch 5AAA, Pt 1)

Meaning of 'offshore CIV': Sch 5AAA, para 2

The default treatment for non-resident CIVs is that they are companies for the purposes of TCGA 1992, so they will be treated as persons and chargeable to corporation tax on their gains under new s 2B.

The majority of the rules applicable to companies will also apply to CIVs but the deeming provisions do not treat CIVs as having ordinary share capital, so they will not be able to rely on any provisions that require ownership of ordinary share capital to access reliefs (eg CIVs will not be able to rely on provisions that require any relationship established between a parent and subsidiary, or as common subsidiaries of a parent, for group reliefs, etc). The default treatment is subject to the availability of elections for transparency or exemption. CIVs investing in UK land are vehicles for collective investment, and are not regarded as trading entities.

Throughout TCGA 1992, Sch 5AAA 'offshore collective investment vehicle' means:

- collective investment vehicles constituted as bodies corporate, resident outside the UK ('body corporate' does not include LLPs for these purposes, as s 59A will apply to treat trading LLPs as transparent partnerships for the purposes of TCGA 1992 – except where a liquidator has been appointed – references to partnerships in the text below include references to transparent LLPs, which will also be transparent for income tax by reason of ITTOIA 2005, s 863),
- collective investment vehicles under which property is held on trust for participants where the trustees of the property are non-resident, or
- collective investment vehicles constituted by other arrangements that create rights in the nature of co-ownership where those arrangements take effect as a result of the law of a territory outside the UK

Meaning of a CIV being 'UK property rich': Sch 5AAA, para 3

Whether a CIV is 'UK property rich' at a given time is determined by applying the rules in TCGA 1992, Sch 1A, Pt 2, on the assumption that:

- (if it would not otherwise be the case) the vehicle is treated as a company, and
- a disposal is made, at that time, of a right or interest in that company.

If the above notional disposal by the CIV would be regarded as a disposal of an asset deriving at least 75% of its value from UK land, the vehicle is regarded for the purposes of Sch 5AAA as being UK property rich at that time.

If a disposal by a company would be regarded for the purposes of Sch 1A (which includes comprehensive tracing provisions) as a disposal of an asset deriving at least 75% of its value from UK land, the company is regarded for the purposes of Sch 5AAA as being UK property rich at that time.

Basic rules (Sch 5AAA, Pt 2)

Offshore CIVs: Sch 5AAA, para 4

CIVs that are partnerships or LLPs remain transparent for gains.

For offshore CIVs which are not companies (and which are not partnerships), the rules affecting disposals of UK land by non-residents will apply as though the vehicle is a company, and the rights of the participators are shares in that company (unless the CIV has elected for transparency, so that its individual members will each be chargeable on any underlying gains).

Paragraph 4 applies to a CIV to which s 103D (tax transparent funds) applies but does not affect the operation of the rules set out in TCGA 1992, s 103D(4) to (9) (calculation of gains on disposal of units etc), or s 103DA (share pooling etc). However, where para 4 applies to a CIV, TCGA 1992, s 99 (application of TCGA 1992 to unit trust schemes) does not apply to the scheme.

Units in CoACS treated as shares in a company: Sch 5AAA, para 5

Units in authorised contractual schemes which are co-ownership schemes (CoACS), where units are treated as assets under TCGA 1992, s 103D (tax transparent funds), are treated for the purposes of Sch 1A as if they were shares in a company. UK CoACS will however continue not to be treated as being persons, and so will not be liable to tax on their disposals.

Interests in UK CoACS are treated as though they were shares for non-UK resident investors purely for the purposes of considering whether those investors hold an interest in a UK property rich asset.

Disposals by non-UK residents: Sch 5AAA, para 6

If a person disposes of an asset that derives at least 75% of its value from UK land (determined in accordance with Sch 1A, Pt 2), and the disposal has an 'appropriate connection' (see below) to a CIV, for the purposes of ss 1A(3)(c) or 2B(4)(b) (disposals by non-UK residents of assets deriving 75% of value from UK land), the person is treated as having a 'substantial indirect interest' in the UK land at the time of the disposal (no 25% de minimis applies).

Non-UK resident CIVs which are UK property rich are treated as companies, and interests in them as shares, which means that disposals by non-resident investors in such entities will be chargeable in the same way as a disposal of an interest in a UK property rich company (in accordance with Sch 1A).

Non-resident investors in CIVs that are UK property rich are considered to have a 'substantial indirect interest' in UK land (within Sch 1A, para 8), so they will be chargeable on gains on disposals of an interest in a UK property rich CIV regardless of their level of investment in the CIV – they cannot benefit from the < 25% ownership exemption (Sch 1A, Pt 3). This is the case both for investment in non-UK CIVs, and in UK resident CIVs such as UK REITs and property AIFs.

Non-resident investors in companies that are not CIVs but that derive at least half their market value from one or more CIVs (so that the entity cannot be UK property rich without reference to those CIVs) are considered to have a substantial indirect interest in UK land and will also not benefit from the < 25% ownership exemption.

CIVs, and companies that are UK property rich and at least 50% invested in one or more CIVs, are also considered to have a substantial indirect interest in UK land when disposing of a UK property rich company. This includes (but is not limited to) situations where a partnership CIV is invested in a company.

Non-resident investors will not be considered to have a substantial indirect interest in UK land where they are investing in a CIV that meets 'genuine diversity of ownership' conditions or where the CIV meets the non-close condition, provided that the CIV is being marketed with a policy of not investing more than 40% in UK land.

Even if there is a disposal of a UK property rich company by a CIV that meets either of these conditions, the investors will not be considered to have a substantial indirect interest in UK land. This does not however apply where the disposal is by a partner in a CIV that is a partnership.

A disposal has an appropriate connection to a CIV if the asset disposed of consists of a right or interest in either:

- a CIV, or
- a company at least half of whose market value derives from its being a direct or indirect participant in one or more CIVs.

A disposal has an 'appropriate connection' to a CIV (unless it meets the exclusions in para 7) if:

- the vehicle is constituted by two or more persons carrying on a trade or business in partnership, and
- the disposal is made by a person as a participant in the vehicle, or
- the vehicle is a company and the disposal is made by it, or
- a company (which is not the vehicle) makes the disposal, and the vehicle, and one or more other CIVs that are UK property rich, have a 50% investment in the company making the disposal.

Example:

Diomedes Ltd and Mr Keres are non-UK resident and each own 50% of the Leontius fund.

Leontius is a CIV that owns a property rich company (more than 75% of its gross asset value deriving from UK land) and has not made any elections.

Diomedes Ltd and Mr Keres dispose of 50% of their holdings in Leontius (which is UK property rich by reason of its underlying company) to a UK investor.

Both Diomedes Ltd and Mr Keres will be treated as having 'substantial indirect interests', and will need to return their share of the gain on the disposal.

A person has a 50% investment in a company if they possess or are entitled to acquire 50% or more of the voting power in the company, or they would receive 50% or more of the proceeds in the event of a disposal of the whole of the equity of the company, or they would be entitled to receive more than 50% of income distributions to shareholders, or they would be entitled to 50% or more of the assets on a winding-up.

'Equity' for these purposes is defined as all shares in the company, excluding restricted preference shares (as defined in CTA 2010, s 160), plus all loan capital, except for normal commercial loans (as defined in CTA 2010, ss 158(1)(b) or 159(4)(b)).

'Shares' in the company are defined as including stock, and any other interests of the members. Where the company does not have share capital, the rules will apply to members' interests (but with the definitions of normal commercial loans and restricted preferences shares in CTA 2010 modified accordingly).

References to receipt of any proceeds, amount or assets include the direct or indirect receipt of the proceeds, amount or assets, and the direct or indirect application of the proceeds, amount or assets for the person's benefit, and it is irrelevant whether the receipt or application is at the time of the disposal, distribution, winding-up, or other circumstance, or at a later time.

Rights of connected parties are not taken into consideration in applying the 50% test.

For this purpose each collective investment scheme in the structure is regarded as if it were a single person.

CIVs expected to have no more than 40% investment in UK land: Sch 5AAA, para 7

Where a disposal would otherwise have an appropriate connection to a CIV, it will not be treated as having an appropriate connection if, at the time of the disposal, the vehicle meets:

- the 'non-UK real estate condition', and
- the 'genuine diversity of ownership condition' or, if the vehicle is a company, the 'non-close condition'.

Where a company (which is not the CIV) makes the disposal, and the CIV, and one or more other CIVs that are UK property rich, have a 50% investment in the company making the disposal, provided the CIV is a partnership, the non-close condition will be met provided the company itself meets the non-close condition.

A vehicle will meet the non-UK real estate condition at any time if, by reference to the prospectus for the vehicle, no more than 40% of the expected market value of the vehicle's investments is intended to derive from investments consisting of:

- interests in UK land, or
- rights or interests in companies which are UK property rich.

A vehicle will meet the genuine diversity of ownership condition at any time if:

- it meets conditions A to C in Offshore Funds (Tax) Regulations 2009, reg 75, or
- it meets the condition in the Offshore Funds (Tax) Regulations 2009, reg 75(5).

The Offshore Fund (Tax) Regulations apply for the purposes of para 7 as if any CIV which is not an offshore fund were to be regarded as an offshore fund.

A company meets the non-close condition at any time if, at that time, it:

- is non-close, or
- is a close company but only because it has a 'qualifying investor' as a direct or indirect participator.

A qualifying investor means, for the purposes of TCGA 1992, Sch 5AAA:

- a person who is within any of CTA 2010, ss 528(4A)(a), (b), (c), (i) or (j) where, if the CIV mentioned in the provision concerned is a company, it meets the non-close condition or, if not, meets the genuine diversity of ownership condition,

- a person who is within any other provision of CTA 2010, s 528(4A), or
- a qualifying fund or qualifying company in respect of which an election under para 12 has effect.

Elections for transparency (Sch 5AAA, Pt 3)

If a transparency election is made, it will treat the offshore CIV as a partnership for the purposes of CGT, ensuring that the investors are taxed on disposals of the underlying assets of the partnership.

The election is only available to CIVs that are income transparent. A CIV that has made a para 8 election will be treated as transparent for the purposes of NRCGT, so its investors (whether UK or non-UK resident) will be treated as if they had always owned an interest in the CIV's underlying property and – if they are tax exempt in the UK – they will be able to benefit from the relevant exemptions. Any taxable subsidiary entities below the CIV (including companies) will however be unaffected by the transparency election and would remain subject to NRCGT unless they can make an election themselves – this needs to be borne in the mind in the context of structures in which CIVs (such as JPUTs and GPUTs) are 'layered'.

Transparency will probably be inappropriate for CIVs that have regular changes of investors, as these changes are likely to trigger regular disposals of other investor's interests in the underlying assets (SP D12, para 4).

Election for CIV to be treated as partnership: Sch 5AAA, para 8

The manager of an offshore CIV which is UK property rich, and is transparent for income tax purposes (other than by reason of being a partnership) may make an election for the vehicle to be treated for the purposes of TCGA 1992, TMA 1970 and any provision of CTA 2009 and CTA 2010, so far as they relate to the taxation of chargeable gains, as if it were to be regarded as a partnership.

Under the election for exemption, the CIV remains a person and notionally chargeable to CGT on its gains. The election exempts the CIV from the tax that would be due on the gains calculated, as the investors are already chargeable on their gains on disposals of interests in the CIV. The election is likely to be used mainly by widely held funds with large structures, particularly where the investors are exempt and wish to prevent tax charges in the fund itself that will impact on their investment returns.

The election has effect whether or not the vehicle would, without the election, be regarded as a person chargeable to CGT or corporation tax on chargeable gains.

Whether or not an offshore CIV is regarded as being UK property rich will be determined by reference to the prospectus for the vehicle (on the assumption that investments will be made in accordance with the prospectus).

A CIV is 'transparent for income tax purposes' if any sums which form part of the income of the vehicle:

- paid to UK resident participants would be chargeable to income tax, or
- if any of that income is derived from assets within the UK, would be so chargeable had the assets been outside the UK.

Elections should be made by the fund manager, but the fund manager must have the consent of all of the investors in the fund at the time of making the election. The election must be made within 12 months of the CIV first acquiring a direct interest in UK land or an asset that is UK property rich. In the case of a fund existing at 6 April 2019, the election must be made by 5 April 2020.

Before the CIV makes an election, it remains opaque and chargeable on gains arising from its own disposals. Non-resident investors chargeable to CGT will therefore, at that stage, not be within the rules for 30 day reporting and payments on account (FA 2019, Sch 2) in respect of a disposal by the CIV. The election for transparency has retrospective effect (for example, an election made on 5 April 2020 in respect of a fund which existed on 5 April 2019 will cover the whole of 2019/20), so that once it is made, a disposal by the CIV will become chargeable on the investor.

In that case, the investor's 30-day time limit for reporting and paying tax on any gain begins on the day the election for transparency is sent to HMRC, rather than the normal time limits (FA 2019, Sch 2, para 11).

Once the election has been made the normal 30-day time limit for submitting the CGT return and paying the CGT payment on account applies to future disposals. The normal rules for the 30-day reporting and payment on account apply to all disposals by the investors themselves, regardless of whether the CIV is transparent (a disposal of underlying property) or opaque (a disposal of an interest in the fund itself).

The consent of the investors to making an election can be assumed where it has been made clear to them that they are buying an interest in a fund that intends to make a transparency election. An election will have retrospective effect to cover any disposals by the CIV from commencement of the non-resident capital gains rules on 6 April 2019, or if the CIV is formed after that date, from the date it is formed.

The CIV will need either to be UK property rich at the time of the election, or to have published scheme documents at that time clearly stating the intention of the CIV to invest predominantly in UK land.

If the investors in the CIV change, or it ceases to be 75% UK property rich, it will remain a partnership for gains.

There will be no need to make a new election or provide the consent of the new investors (who should instead be made aware of this within the scheme documentation when they acquire an interest in the CIV). If an election is made neither TCGA 1992, s 99 (unit trust schemes) nor s 103D (tax transparent funds) apply in relation to the vehicle.

Conditions relating to elections: Sch 5AAA, para 9

An election under para 8 is irrevocable. It has effect only if the participants in the vehicle at the time at which it is made have consented to the making of the election. The election must be made by notice given to an HMRC officer, and must be made before the end of the period of 12 months beginning with the relevant acquisition date (so, for vehicles that either held UK land on 6 April 2019, or had published a prospectus by that date showing the intention to do so, by 5 April 2020).

Units in CIVs held by life insurance companies: Sch 5AAA, para 10

If a transparency election under para 8 has effect in relation to an offshore CIV, it will be treated as having no effect in relation to any units in the vehicle that are held by an insurance company for the purposes of its long-term business, which continue to be dealt with under existing rules.

Relationship to re-basing rules under Sch 4AA for non-UK residents: Sch 5AAA, para 11

Where a non-resident investor has an interest in a CIV at 6 April 2019 and the CIV makes an election for transparency, the investor's rebasing date for the purposes of Sch 4AA, when making a disposal of any underlying assets of the CIV, will be 6 April 2019, regardless of whether the asset itself would have a different rebasing date if it had always been held directly.

Under TCGA 1992, Pt 3, Ch 3 UK resident investors will already be treated as having an interest in the CIV as a separate asset for the purposes of capital gains. Investors holding an interest in the CIV as an asset who are deemed, as a result of a para 8 election, to hold an interest in the underlying assets (including UK resident investors under current rules) will be treated as always having held the underlying assets in that way for the purposes of calculating the gain.

Statement of Practice D12 will be relevant in calculating any gain or loss when the investor or the CIV makes a disposal. There is no deemed disposal on the making of the election, and no need to substitute market value for base cost as a consequence of the disposal.

For non-UK resident investors, funds falling within both TCGA 1992, s 103D(1)(b) (offshore tax transparent funds) and Sch 5AAA, will be treated as companies and interests held in them treated as shares in a company. If a fund within s 103D(1)(b) is UK property rich (TCGA 1992, Sch 1A), a disposal of an interest in that fund will be a disposal of an interest in a UK property rich asset.

For non-UK resident investors, units in a CoACS (TCGA 1992, s 103D(1)(a)) will be treated as being shares in a company for the purposes of considering whether the indirect disposal rules in Sch 1A apply.

Funds falling into both TCGA 1992, s 103D(1)(b) and Sch 5AAA will be taxable as persons themselves and liable to corporation tax if they make disposals of interests in UK land, whether or not they are UK property rich.

The funds themselves are already required to report to HMRC, and must meet tests meaning they will be widely held. Where a CIV is treated as a company, even though Sch 5AAA applies, the calculation rules in s 103D(4)–(9) and the share pooling rules in s 103DA remain in force.

Exemptions (Sch 5AAA, Pt 4)

Eligible CIVs that meet qualifying conditions and which undertake to report annually to HMRC can make an election that provides exemption for the CIV itself and for entities in which it has at least a 40% investment. The CIV must be UK property rich. Unlike the transparency election, investor approval is not required, and the making of an exemption election is at the discretion of the manager of the CIV.

The election can also be made by a CIV which is a partnership (based in any jurisdiction, including the UK), in respect of one or more companies that it owns at least 99% of and which are UK property rich – it may also be made by a UK CoACS in respect of one or more companies that it owns at least 99% of provided that the CoACS is UK property rich. Companies invested in by the partnership or CoACS cannot themselves be CIVs, but may be resident anywhere.

In *all* cases – other than where the CIV is a partnership or a CoACS – the CIV making the election must be non-UK resident.

The entities in which the CIV has an interest may be UK or non-UK resident and can be either bodies corporate, or companies, because of the default treatment of non-UK resident CIVs. The exemption only covers direct or indirect disposals of UK land.

It is possible for a UK partnership CIV or a CoACS which has a structure of UK resident companies under it to make the election.

The CIV must have an investment of at least 40% in an entity for that entity to benefit from exemption. Where the investment is less than 100% the gain or loss is exempted in proportion to the level of investment the electing CIV has in the entity.

The CIV must meet qualifying conditions for the election to have effect. If the circumstances of the CIV change so that it does not meet the conditions, this will trigger a deemed disposal and reacquisition of the interests of the investors. In some circumstances any gains triggered by the deemed disposal will be brought into charge immediately, and in others the gain will not come into charge until the investors receive funds from the CIV, the CIV winds up, or a period of three years elapses (whichever is earliest – see below).

The election for exemption is not available to all AIFs, only to non-resident companies that are the equivalent of UK REITs (some of which may not be AIFs). All CISs are in scope. Regardless of whether a CIV is within the exemption regime or not, the investors remain taxable under first principles on any disposal of an interest in a CIV that is itself a UK property rich entity.

Exemption for qualifying offshore CIV that is UK property rich: TCGA 1992, Sch 5AAA, paras 12, 13

An election may be made for a CIV to be exempt from corporation tax on chargeable gains accruing to it on all direct and indirect disposals of UK land, if each of the following entitlement conditions is met:

- the vehicle is offshore,
- the vehicle is a company (or is deemed to be a company),
- the vehicle is UK property rich,
- the vehicle meets all of the qualifying conditions set out in para 13, and
- if the vehicle is an AIF, it would also meet the definition of a CIV for another reason.

An election may be made in respect of a company (irrespective of where the company is resident) which is not a CIV if each of the following conditions is met:

- the company is wholly (or almost wholly) owned by a CIS which is a partnership or a CoACS (ignoring s 103D for the purposes of the test),
- the appropriate entity is UK property rich, and
- the company meets all of the qualifying conditions set out in para 13.

The 'appropriate entity' in the condition above means:

- in cases where the CIS is constituted by two or more persons carrying on a trade or business in partnership: the company, and

- in cases where the CIS is constituted by a CoACS: the CoACS.

If an election is made in respect of a CIV, it is referred to as 'a qualifying fund' (and any reference to a qualifying fund after the election is made – even after it ceases to have effect – is read as a reference to the arrangements, undertaking or company which met the definition of a CIV when the election was made).

If an election is made in respect of a company which is not a CIV the company is referred to as 'a qualifying company' (and any reference to a qualifying company, in relation to any time after the election is made (even after the election ceases to have effect), is read as a reference to the company).

Qualifying conditions for para 12 and information to be provided to HMRC: TCGA 1992, Sch 5AAA, paras 13–15

A CIV will meet the qualifying conditions at any time if:

- it is a CIS and meets the genuine diversity of ownership condition,
- it is a company and it meets the recognised stock exchange condition and the non-close condition, or
- it is a CIV (of any kind) and it meets the UK tax condition and the non-close condition.

A company which is not a CIV meets the qualifying conditions at any time if either:

- the company meets the UK tax condition and the non-close condition, or
- the CIS which wholly (or almost wholly) owns the company meets the genuine diversity of ownership condition.

A CIS will meet the genuine diversity of ownership condition at any time if, at that time:

- it meets conditions A to C in Offshore Funds (Tax) Regulations 2009, reg 75, or
- it meets the condition in reg 75(5) of those Regulations.

The Offshore Fund (Tax) Regulations apply for the purposes of para 7 as if any CIV which is not an offshore fund were to be regarded as an offshore fund.

A company meets the recognised stock exchange condition at any time if:

- it has ordinary share capital, and
- the shares forming part of its ordinary share capital are regularly traded on a recognised stock exchange.

A company meets the non-close condition at any time if it:

- is not a close company, or
- is a close company but only because it has a qualifying investor as a direct or indirect participator.

A company meets the UK tax condition at any time if, on the assumption that all of the shares in it were disposed of for their market value at that time, the person making the election reasonably considers that, as a result solely of double taxation arrangements, no more than 25% of the total proceeds would fall to be left out of account for the purposes of TCGA 1992.

To meet this test the manager of the CIV must reasonably believe that, should all of the assets of the fund be liquidated and the proceeds returned to investors at that point, no more than 25% of the total value returned would not be subject to UK tax in the hands of the investors because of the allocation of taxing rights under double tax treaties.

This percentage must be calculated with regard to the holdings of all of the investors in the fund, including exempt investors and taxable UK resident investors. So where a manager can be sure that more than 75% of the investors are UK residents and/or exempt investors, they can meet the condition.

In the majority of cases for funds already existing at 6 April 2019, the manager will have no reason to know the tax residence of its investors. The manager is not required to obtain additional information in order to perform a test of this condition, but if they are aware of the tax residence of their investors for other reasons – such as for due diligence, the common reporting standard, or anti money laundering procedures, then HMRC's advice is that they should use the information they hold in order to establish whether the condition is passed.

Sch 5AAA, para 14

An election under para 12 has effect only if it is accompanied by information (specified by an HMRC officer) about disposals made by participants in the relevant fund at any time in:

- the period of two years ending with the day before the day on which the election is made, or
- if shorter, the period beginning with the constitution of the relevant fund and ending with the day before the day on which the election is made.

Information is not required to accompany the election if it has already been provided to an HMRC officer (in the specified form) and the election sets out the occasions on which the information has been provided. The CIV is expected to take 'reasonable care' in ensuring its reports are correct and complete, and HMRC may punish serious breaches by revoking the election.

No information is required to be provided for periods prior to 6 April 2019.

HMRC has said that it will consider there to have been a serious breach where the CIV reports incorrect information with respect to the disposals by any investor who is taxable and:

- holds a 25% or greater interest in the CIV, or
- the value of whose investment in the CIV is £1 million or greater.

A designated HMRC officer can also revoke an election if the information provided is consistently incorrect to a significant degree, and in particular if it is incorrect with regard to information on the disposals by investors.

Sch 5AAA, para 15

Elections under para 12 have effect subject to conditions as to the provision of information or documents as specified by an HMRC officer. The required information and documents must be provided to an HMRC officer within 12 months from the end of the period of account.

HMRC's conditions as to the provision of information or documents may include:

- conditions relating to the participants in the relevant fund, and
- conditions requiring certain information or documents.

A designated HMRC officer can revoke a para 12 election if, in the officer's opinion, there has been a breach of any provision without a reasonable excuse, but can also (whether or not designated) waive a breach even where there is no reasonable excuse if, in the officer's opinion (and having regard to all the circumstances), the breach is regarded as insignificant.

An HMRC officer may also allow an extension to the time limit where there is a reasonable excuse. If an extension is agreed then the election remains valid and there is no deemed disposal and reacquisition.

The circumstances which an HMRC officer is able to consider in determining whether or not a breach is insignificant include the number and seriousness of previous breaches.

If a period of account would otherwise be longer than 12 months, the period of account must be treated for these purposes as split into more than one period of account, with the first deemed period of account being 12 months long, and any subsequent deemed period of account starting when the previous deemed period of account ends. The time limit will be 12 months after the end of the deemed 12 month period. The time limit for the provision of information for the following period will be 12 months from when the actual accounting period ends.

Example:

> The Artemis Fund, which was set up in 2016, makes up accounts to 31 March each year until 31 March 2020. Its next period end is 31 December 2021.
>
> Artemis' manager makes a para 12 election and all relevant returns and information are submitted to HMRC for periods up to 31 March 2020 (due date 31 March 2021).
>
> For the following period (1 April 2020 to 31 December 2021), Artemis' manager is required to make two returns of information, the first by 31 March 2022, and the second by 31 December 2022.
>
> Assuming Artemis' accounting reference date remains 31 December, reports will be due annually by 31 December thereafter.

Exemption for direct or indirect disposals of UK land by persons in which fund invests: Sch 5AAA, para 16

If an election under para 12 has been made in respect of a qualifying fund or qualifying company, and the fund or company is UK property rich by reference (wholly or partly) to particular interests in UK land, and a person other than the qualifying fund or company makes a disposal at a time when the election has effect:

- For direct disposals where immediately before the disposal, the qualifying fund or company has a 40% investment in the person making the disposal, the appropriate proportion (between 40% and 100% depending on the interest of the CIV in the person) of any gain accruing to the person on the disposal is not a chargeable gain.
- For indirect disposals of UK land in a case where the interests in UK land in question consist of or include any of the relevant UK property, and immediately before the disposal, the qualifying fund or company has a 40% investment in the company in question, the appropriate proportion (between 40% and 100%) of any gain accruing to the person on the disposal is not a chargeable gain.

The 'appropriate proportion' is the proportion of the consideration for the disposal that forms part (directly or indirectly) of the assets of the qualifying fund or company bears to the total consideration for the disposal.

Example

CIV para 12 exemption election			**0% chargeable in CIV**
UK property rich structure – underlying companies held in following proportions by the qualifying fund or qualifying company:			
Co 1 40%	40% exempt	sells land	60% chargeable in Co 1
Co 2 50%	50% exempt	sells land	50% chargeable in Co 2
Co 3 60%	60% exempt	sells land	40% chargeable in Co 3
Co 4 70%	70% exempt	sells land	30% chargeable in Co 4
Co 5 80%	80% exempt	sells land	20% chargeable in Co 5
Co 6 100%	100% exempt	sells land	0% chargeable in Co 6

A person has a 40% investment in a company if they possess or are entitled to acquire 40% or more of the voting power in the company, or they would receive 40% or more of the proceeds in the event of a disposal of the whole of the equity of the company, or they would be entitled to receive more than 40% of income distributions to shareholders, or they would be entitled to 40% or more of the assets on a winding-up.

'Equity' for these purposes is defined as all shares in the company, excluding restricted preference shares (as defined in CTA 2010, s 160), plus all loan capital, except for normal commercial loans (as defined in CTA 2010, ss 158(1)(b) or 159(4)(b)).

'Shares' in the company are defined as including stock, and any other interests of the members. Where the company does not have share capital, the rules will apply to members' interests (but with the definitions of normal commercial loans and restricted preferences shares in CTA 2010 modified accordingly).

References to receipt of any proceeds, amount or assets include the direct or indirect receipt of the proceeds, amount or assets, and the direct or indirect application of the proceeds, amount or assets for the person's benefit, and it irrelevant whether the receipt or application is at the time of the disposal, distribution, winding-up, or other circumstance, or at a later time. Rights of connected parties are not taken into consideration in applying the 40% test.

If an HMRC officer considers that the operation of this para would otherwise result in the total relief available exceeding 100% of the gain, the officer can make such adjustments to the appropriate proportion of a gain accruing to any person as they consider just and reasonable to prevent that result.

Making the election and period for which it has effect: Sch 5AAA, para 17

An election under para 12 must be made by the relevant fund manager, and specify the day from which it is to have effect (it will have effect in relation to disposals on or after the day specified). It is possible to specify any date up to 12 months prior to the election being made, but if the fund wishes the election to take effect more than 12 months before the date of election, consent from HMRC is required.

For funds in existence on 6 April 2019, who want their election to apply from that date, the election must therefore be made by 5 April 2020.

The election must provide the name and address of the CIV making the election, and the names and addresses of entities included in its structure and the level of interest the CIV making the election has in them. HMRC will be providing forms with which to make elections, in due course.

Revocation of elections: Sch 5AAA, paras 18, 19

In addition to cases where HMRC revokes an election for breaches of the conditions (para 15), a designated HMRC officer may revoke an election under para 12, in order to safeguard the public revenue. To do so, the HMRC officer must give notice to the relevant fund manager, stating the grounds for revocation. The fund manager has a right of appeal within 30 days from the date that notice of revocation is given.

Where an appeal proceeds to Tribunal, the Tribunal is specifically enjoined that it may *only* allow the appeal if it is satisfied that a designated HMRC officer could not reasonably have been satisfied there were grounds for revocation.

The fund manager can revoke a para 12 election by giving notice to an HMRC officer, specifying the day from which the election is to cease to have effect. It is possible to specify a date that falls before the day on which the notice is given but only if an HMRC officer consents.

Qualifying fund or company ceasing to meet applicable exemption conditions: Sch 5AAA, para 20

Where a para 12 election has been made in respect of a qualifying fund or qualifying company, and the qualifying fund or company ceases to meet the applicable exemption conditions, the election ceases to have effect from the time that the conditions ceased to be met, in relation to disposals made at or after that time.

There are provisions dealing with temporary lapses in para 27 (temporary periods of no more than 30 days during which certain of the applicable exemption conditions not met), para 28 (temporary periods of no more than nine months during which applicable exemption conditions not met), and para 30 (steps taken by relevant fund manager to wind up relevant fund).

Elections: summary of conditions

Transparency	Exemption
CIV must be non-resident	CIV must be non-resident, unless it is a partnership or CoACS
CIV must be income tax transparent (eg a properly constituted JPUT or GPUT)	Income transparency not required
Must be UK property rich or have set out intention to be UK property rich in prospectus	CIV or company it 99%+ owns must remain UK property rich
	Available to CISs and companies equivalent to UK REITs
	If CIV is an AIF it must be a CIV on another basis to be eligible, eg being a CIS

Transparency	**Exemption**
	Exemption election can be made by a non-resident (non-CIV) company owned at least 99% by a UK property rich CIV that is a partnership or CoACS i e made by an offshore company holding UK property on behalf of a UK property rich CIV partnership or CoACS
Investors can be tax resident anywhere	Investors can be tax resident anywhere
	Entities in structure can be tax resident anywhere
Unlike the exemption election, there is no diversity of ownership requirement	Must meet a genuine diversity of ownership or 'non-close' requirement
	Permits CIV to be owned directly or indirectly by a small number of qualifying institutional investors and still be treated as 'non-close', and
	Requires the CIV to have less than 25% of its investors in countries that remove the UK's taxing rights over gains
Transparency election is irrevocable	Election revocable by fund manager or HMRC
Every investor in the CIV at the time the election is made must consent to the making of the election (or it must be clear from the prospectus that the CIV intends to elect), and	Investor consent not required
Election for existing CIV must be made within 12 months of 6 April 2019	Election must be made by 5 April 2020 for funds existing at 5 April 2019, will have retrospective effect for up to 12 months before date made
	A CIV will be treated as exempt from UK tax on direct and indirect disposals of UK property
Subsidiary entities below a CIV won't benefit from CGT exemption, but can make own transparency elections	Any entities owned by the CIV will also be exempt from UK tax on direct and indirect disposals of UK property (on a proportionate basis between 40% and 100% but CIV must own at least 40% of underlying entity)
Investors treated as owning underlying assets and chargeable on disposals under SP D12	NRCGT will only be applied on disposals at investor level so, if investors are tax exempt in the UK, they will be able to benefit from exemption
	Feeder companies into the CIV will also be exempt from NRCGT if they are wholly owned by certain qualifying institutional investors
25%+ substantial indirect interest requirement is disapplied in relation to disposals of interests in all CIVs	25%+ substantial indirect interest requirement is disapplied in relation to disposals of interests in all CIVs
Investors holding < 25% interests CIVs will be within scope of NRCGT indirect charge, unless otherwise tax exempt, if disposal is of UK property rich company and connected to collective investment, and investor is non-resident	Investors holding < 25% interests CIVs will be within scope of NRCGT indirect charge, unless otherwise tax exempt, if disposal is of UK property rich company and connected to collective investment, and investor is non-resident
The 25% indirect interest requirement may still apply where the CIV is only temporarily UK property rich, if so:	The 25% indirect interest requirement may still apply where the CIV is only temporarily UK property rich, if so:

Transparency	Exemption
the fund will need to meet a genuine diversity of ownership or non-close test, and be targeting UK property investments of no more than 40% of fund gross asset value in its prospectus or other fund documents	the fund will need to meet a genuine diversity of ownership or non-close test, and be targeting UK property investments of no more than 40% of fund gross asset value in its prospectus or other fund documents

The effect of ceasing to meet the qualifying conditions is summarised in the following table produced by HMRC.

Summary of information relating to ceasing to meet qualifying conditions or breaching reporting requirements

Breach of requirements within that time	When exemption is withdrawn	When deemed disposal of investors' interests arises	When gains on a deemed disposal are charged
Ceasing to meet the applicable exemption conditions	At the point the CIV ceases to meet at least one of the conditions (1), (2)	Immediately before the point when the CIV ceases to meet at least one of the conditions (3)	As the value is paid to the investors, or if earlier three years from the deemed disposal or when the fund is wound up (4)
Making payment of value not taxable in the UK	The exemption continues	Immediately before the point the payment is made, and the reacquisition is immediately after	As the value is paid to the investors, with the balance at winding up
Election is revoked by HMRC or the CIV	When notice is given	Immediately before the exemption ceases	At the point the deemed disposal arises

(1) Where the CIV anticipates meeting the condition again within nine months, the exemption is maintained for that period providing the condition is met again

(2) The exemption is maintained where the CIV manager is actively in the process of winding up the fund.

(3) Where the CIV anticipates meeting the condition again within 30 days, there is no deemed disposal.

(4) The three year countdown is turned off where the fund meets the conditions again within nine months of the breach.

Deemed disposals: payments not otherwise taxable where value derived from direct or indirect disposals of UK land: Sch 5AAA, para 21

Paragraph 21 deals with cases where a para 12 election has been made and a participant in the relevant fund is entitled to receive an amount which represents, in substance, value derived (directly or indirectly) from a direct disposal of UK land or from the UK land component of an indirect disposal of UK land, and the amount is regarded as being of a revenue nature and does not fall to be taken into account for the purposes of income tax or corporation tax on income.

The effect of the para 12 election is to exempt gains in both the fund and structure, so the regime is designed to ensure that the return of value to investors is made in a form that is taxable in the UK.

If the CIV, particularly in the case of corporate funds, pays dividends to investors that represent value deriving from gains on UK land, the value of those gains will not be represented in the asset held by the investors when they subsequently make a disposal of their interests.

Therefore, para 21 provides that if the CIV makes a return of value, in the form of income, to investors (representative of gains on disposals of UK land) there is a deemed disposal and reacquisition of the investors' interests in the CIV. An example would be that the fund paid a dividend that in part represented the capital value derived from selling a company that was UK property rich.

The deemed disposal occurs immediately before the payment is made and the deemed reacquisition immediately after.

The payment must not otherwise be liable to UK tax in the hands of the investor for the rule to be triggered, and the deemed disposal is only in respect of the investors to whom the rule applies – so for example where a payment is made in the form of an income distribution to all investors but some investors have paid tax on that distribution, those investors would not be affected by the rule.

Any tax payable on gains arising from the deemed disposal is not due until funds are actually paid to the investor, with any untaxed balance left coming into charge when the fund winds up. The payment itself is a trigger for this (and for the applicable reporting and payment time limits under FA 2019, Sch 2). The para 12 election continues to have effect despite the payment.

'The UK land component' of an indirect disposal of UK land means the interests in UK land taken into account in determining whether the disposal is an indirect disposal of UK land.

Deemed disposal if election ceases to have effect: Sch 5AAA, para 22

If a para 12 election has been made in respect of a qualifying fund or qualifying company and it ceases to have effect:

- In the case of an election made in respect of a qualifying fund, each participant in the relevant fund is deemed to have sold its units in the relevant fund immediately before the election ceases to have effect, and immediately reacquired those rights and interests at market value, at the same time.
- In the case of an election made in respect of a qualifying company, each participant in the relevant fund is deemed to have sold its rights and interests in the company before the election ceases to have effect, and immediately reacquired those rights and interests at market value, at the same time.

Gains accruing on disposals under para 21 or para 22: Sch 5AAA, para 23

If a disposal of an asset is deemed to have been made by a person at any time under paras 21 and 22, as a result of a qualifying fund or qualifying company ceasing to qualify, any gain accruing to the person on the disposal is treated as accruing to the person in accordance with the rules set out in para 23.

If, at the time of the deemed disposal (or subsequently) the person actually disposes of a unit in the relevant fund, or receives an amount of a kind mentioned in para 21(1) (payments otherwise not taxable), the appropriate portion of the deemed gain is treated as accruing to the person at the time of the actual disposal, or the time of the receipt.

If some of the deemed gain has accrued on one or more previous occasions, the appropriate portion is restricted so that, when added to the appropriate portion or portions on the previous occasion or occasions, it does not exceed 100%.

In determining the appropriate proportion, so much (if any) of the consideration for the actual disposal or the amount of the receipt as exceeds the amount of the deemed gain will be ignored.

In the case of a disposal under para 21, the remainder of the deemed gain is treated as accruing to the person (unless the whole amount has already accrued) when the relevant fund is wound up.

In the case of a disposal under para 22 (on the revocation of an election by HMRC or the CIV), the remainder of the deemed gain is treated as accruing to the person (unless the whole amount has already accrued, or been paid out on winding up of the fund) at the end of the period of three years beginning with the time of the deemed disposal.

Relief for expenses in the case of deemed disposals under para 21 or para 22: Sch 5AAA, para 24

If a disposal is deemed to have been made by a person as a result of paras 21 or 22, the person is treated for the purposes of TCGA 1992, s 38(1)(c) as having incurred incidental costs of making the deemed disposal, equal to the notional costs of disposal (being the costs the person would reasonably have expected to have incurred if the deemed sale under para 21 or 22 had been an actual sale, and which would have been allowable under s 38(1)(c) if there had been an actual sale).

Notification to participants in relation to deemed disposals under para 21 or para 22: Sch 5AAA, paras 25, 26

Where a disposal is deemed to have been made by a person under para 21, or under para 22, as a result of an otherwise untaxed payment being made or the revocation of an election, so that a chargeable gain is treated as accruing under para 23(7) or 23(8) the relevant fund manager must notify the person, in writing, within the period of 30 days beginning with the time the deemed disposal is made or the amount is treated as accruing.

Failure to comply incurs a penalty of up to £3,000 per fund, payable within 30 days from either notification that the penalty is due, or – if appealed – 30 days from when the appeal is finally determined.

The penalty must be assessed by an HMRC officer and must be notified to the fund manager(s) concerned by HMRC within 12 months beginning with the day the officer first becomes aware that the person has failed to comply with para 25. It is possible to appeal against penalties, under para 26, within 30 days.

Temporary period during which applicable exemption conditions not met: Sch 5AAA, paras 27–29

Paragraph 27, the 30 day relief, takes precedence over para 28.

Paragraph 27: If an election under para 12 has been made in respect of a qualifying fund or a qualifying company, and the qualifying fund or company ceases to meet the applicable exemption conditions (other than as a result of the vehicle or appropriate entity ceasing to be UK property rich, which would normally result in the withdrawal of 'qualifying status' under para 20), but the relevant fund manager expects the qualifying fund or company to meet the conditions again within 30 days (and the conditions actually are met within 30 days), then the qualifying fund or company is treated as not losing its qualifying status. This relief cannot be given on any more than four occasions in any 12 month period and does not apply if the CIV ceases to be UK property rich. There is no deemed disposal and reacquisition for the investors, provided the 30-day limit is not breached.

Paragraph 28: If an election under para 12 has been made in respect of a qualifying fund or qualifying company and as a result of para 20 (failing to meet any of the conditions, including UK property richness), the election would cease to have effect, but the fund manager expects the failure to meet the exemption conditions only to last for a temporary period (and at the end of the temporary period – not exceeding nine months – the qualifying fund or qualifying company actually does meet the conditions again), the qualifying fund or qualifying company is treated as continuing to meet the exemption conditions during the temporary period. If the fund fails to meet the qualifying conditions again, then it is treated as non-qualifying from the date the conditions first ceased to be met.

However, where the fund manager is relying on para 28 to maintain qualifying status (ie for periods of 31 days up to nine months), a deemed disposal occurs under para 22 (with each participant in the fund or company being deemed to dispose of and immediately reacquire their holdings at market value at the time the conditions ceased to be met) because there has been a failure to meet the applicable exemption conditions. Subject to that however, the election will be treated as continuing to have effect during the temporary period.

The deemed disposal is treated as occurring immediately before the CIV ceases to be UK property rich as a question of fact, rather than when the CIV becomes aware that it is no longer UK property rich. HMRC has said that it expects that CIVs meeting the conditions for the exemption election would regularly value their assets and would know within a reasonable timeframe following the point where the CIV was no longer UK property rich.

When an election ceases to have effect (because the conditions are no longer met, or the election is revoked) there is a deemed disposal and reacquisition of all of the investors' interests in the CIV immediately before the point the election ceases to have effect. Other than where an election is revoked, any tax payable on gains arising from the deemed disposal will not be due until either funds are actually paid to the investor in respect of their interest in the fund, a period of three years elapses from the deemed disposal, or the fund winds up.

Paragraph 29: Where a CIV meets one of the tests again after a deemed disposal and reacquisition, the three year time limit is switched off. This means that any deemed gain will only be chargeable when an investor receives funds from the CIV on its winding up. If afterwards, the CIV again ceases to meet that condition again, there is another deemed disposal and reacquisition, and the normal rules (including the three year rule) apply once again.

Steps taken by relevant fund manager to wind up relevant fund: Sch 5AAA, para 30

Where the manager of the CIV is actively winding the fund up, the para 12 exemption continues to have effect even where the conditions are not met.

A deemed disposal occurs under para 22 by reference to any failure during this period to meet the applicable exemption conditions, but subject to that, the election continues to have effect until the relevant fund is wound up.

Deemed disposals of UK land by companies previously owned by fund: Sch 5AAA, para 31

This para ensures that where a CIV disposes of an underlying company that is property rich, it is treated as making a gain based on the proportion of the notional gain on UK property held within the subsidiary, which would otherwise be exempt due to the para 12 election in place.

It applies where a fund has made a para 12 election that covers one or more of its 40% owned underlying companies: if the qualifying fund or qualifying company disposes of all of its rights and interests in the underlying company which is UK property rich (and is covered by the election), the qualifying fund or company is deemed to have sold the appropriate proportion of every qualifying asset (the actual disposal of which by the qualifying fund or company would be a direct or indirect disposal of UK land) and to have immediately reacquired the appropriate proportion of the asset, at its market value at the relevant time (the time of the disposal) creating a reportable gain in the qualifying fund or qualifying company.

'The appropriate proportion' of a qualifying asset is equal to what would be, for the purposes of para 16, the appropriate portion of any gain if it is assumed that the underlying company sells the asset at the relevant time, and that the total consideration for that sale is such that it results in a gain of £100 accruing to the underlying company (so, if the CIV has a 40% interest in the underlying company, the notional gain of £100 would be apportioned 40% – £40 – to the CIV). This seems a somewhat clumsy way of dealing with this, but in effect, if the CIV or one of its underlying entities sells a UK property rich company out of the structure and it has benefitted from exemption while in the structure, there is a deemed gain on the UK property element leaving the structure.

An asset is a 'qualifying asset' if, throughout the period of one year ending with the day of the disposal, the asset has been held by the qualifying fund or company, or by any other company covered by a para 12 election.

Deemed disposals of UK land by company or fund ceasing to be qualifying: Sch 5AAA, para 32

Paragraph 32 applies in a similar way to para 31, where a fund ceases to have exemption because the fund manager applies to revoke it, or it is being wound up, to ensure that accrued gains within the CIV and within any of its underlying entities are brought into account.

It applies where an election under para 12 has been in effect for a continuous period of five years in respect of a qualifying fund or qualifying company, and the election ceases to have effect (but not where it ceases in 'disqualifying circumstances' which involve HMRC unilaterally revoking the election) or the relevant fund manager starts to take steps with a view to the disposal of all of the assets of the relevant fund so that it can be wound up.

The qualifying fund or qualifying company is deemed to have sold every asset (the actual disposal of which by the qualifying fund or company would be a direct or indirect disposal of UK land), and to have immediately reacquired it, at its market value at the relevant time creating a reportable gain in the qualifying fund or qualifying company.

In the case of any asset of an underlying company of the qualifying fund or company, which has been covered by a para 12 election for at least 12 months (ending on the date the election was revoked or the fund manager takes steps with a view to winding up the fund), the company is deemed to have sold the appropriate proportion of the asset, and to have immediately reacquired it, at its market value at the relevant time.

'The appropriate proportion' of an asset is equal to whatever would be, for the purposes of para 16, the appropriate portion of any gain if it is assumed that the company had sold the asset at the point immediately the election ceased to have effect, and that the total consideration for that sale is such that it results in a gain of £100 accruing to it (so, if the CIV has a 60% interest in the underlying company, the notional gain of £100 would be apportioned 60% to the CIV). In effect, if the CIV ceases to have exemption, so do its underlying entities and, provided those entities have benefitted from exemption for at least 12 months while in the structure, there is a deemed gain on the UK property element from which exemption is withdrawn.

An election ceases to have effect in 'disqualifying circumstances' if:

- it ceases to have effect as a result of a notice of revocation under para 15(5)(a) in a case where a designated HMRC officer is of the opinion that there have been at least three serious breaches of the para 15 conditions during the period for which the election has had effect, or
- it ceases to have effect as a result of a notice of revocation under para 18(1) (revocation by an HMRC officer to safeguard the public revenue).

'The relevant time' means the time immediately before the election ceases to have effect, or the relevant fund manager starts to take steps with a view to the disposal of all the assets of the relevant fund so that it can be wound up.

For the purposes of para 32, where a qualifying fund or qualifying company is wholly owned by a second qualifying fund or qualifying company and the first fund makes an election under para 12, if the second fund makes an election at a later date it will be treated as being the same election i e as though qualifying status dated from the time the first election was made, and revocation of one would imply revocation of both.

Exemption for disposals by companies wholly owned by certain investors: Sch 5AAA, para 33

If an election under para 12 has been made in respect of a qualifying fund or qualifying company and a participant in the relevant fund disposes of a unit in the relevant fund, where the participant is a company which is wholly owned by one or more of the following and is not itself a CIV, any gain accruing on the disposal is not a chargeable gain:

- any person who is a qualifying institutional investor within the meaning of TCGA 1992, Sch 7AC (substantial shareholding exemption)
- a company carrying on life assurance business where, immediately before the disposal, its right or interest in the participant is an asset which, applying the rules in FA 2012, s 138 is wholly matched to a liability of its life assurance business that is not basic life assurance and general annuity business (BLAGAB)
- a company carrying on long-term business – none of which is BLAGAB – where, immediately before the disposal, its right or interest in the participant is an asset held for the purposes of its long-term business, and
- a qualifying fund or qualifying company in respect of which an election under para 12 has effect.

Paragraph 21 will not result in a deemed disposal of an asset held by any of the above investors, unless the investor is an insurance company.

This means that qualifying institutional investors (TCGA 1992, Sch 7AC, para 3A), will be able pass down their exemption, immunity, or non-taxable status with respect to gains to wholly owned companies that are invested in the CIV making the election.

A company that directly invests in the CIV that is making the election will be exempt on any gains arising from a disposal of an interest in the CIV, providing that all of the participators in the company would themselves not be liable to tax on the gain by reasons of exemption or immunity.

Disapplication of para 3A, Sch 7AC: qualifying institutional investors: Sch 5AAA, para 34

If a gain or loss accrues to a company which has ordinary share capital that is:

- owned by one or more qualifying institutional investors (defined in Sch 7AC), and

- some of the gain or loss is not chargeable or allowable as a result of para 16(3), and
- some or all of the ownership of qualifying institutional investors in the investing company is through the company which is the qualifying fund or qualifying company for the purposes of para 16(3).

The ownership of the qualifying institutional investors in the investing company is ignored for the purpose of applying the substantial shareholding exemption conferred by Sch 7AC, para 3A to the extent that ownership is through a qualifying fund or qualifying company.

Relationship between rules in Sch 5AAA and REIT rules in CTA 2010, Pt 12: Sch 5AAA, para 35

None of the TCGA 1992, Sch 5AAA, Pt 4 exemptions operate to exempt any qualifying REIT gain accruing on a disposal made by a company which is itself, or is a member of, a UK REIT.

A chargeable gain is a 'qualifying REIT gain' if the gain is not a chargeable gain as a result of CTA 2010, ss 535 or 535A, and the gain is not exempt as a result of either of those sections following a notice given under CTA 2010, ss 586(1) or 587(1) (venturing groups).

Sch 5AAA, para 36

- where a gain accrues on a disposal made by a joint venture company which is a member of a group UK REIT, and
- the gain is exempt as a result of CTA 2010, ss 535 or 535A following a notice given under CTA 2010, ss 586(1) or 587(1), and
- the principal company of the group UK REIT that gave the notice is covered by an election made under para 12 in respect of a qualifying fund, and
- the joint venture company is also covered by the election.

The amount of the gain accruing to the joint venture company which is *not* a chargeable gain is found by looking at two steps (which apply each of the exemption rules without regard to the other):

Step 1 – Ignoring the effect of CTA 2010, Pt 12, apply the rules in Sch 5AAA, Pt 4 that operate by reference to the election to identify the amount of the gain which would not be chargeable.

Step 2 – Ignoring the effect Sch 5AAA, apply the rules in CTA 2010, Pt 12 that operate in relation to the group UK REIT to identify the amount of the gain accruing to the joint venture company which would be exempt.

The exempt amount is the amount by which the first step is greater than the second.

Separate application of exemptions under Sch 5AAA and elsewhere: Sch 5AAA, para 37

Subject to the rules in paras 34–36, where a person disposes of a right or interest in a company on which a gain or loss accrues, and parts of the gain or loss are, respectively, either not chargeable or allowable as a result of the operation of any relevant exemption (relevant provisions are those in Sch 5AAA, Pt 4, Sch 7AC, para 3A and CTA 2010, Pt 12), each provision works separately (without regard to the others) in relation to the part of the gain or loss to which it applies.

What this means is that you look at each potential exemption separately, by reference to the whole gain or loss (ignoring the effect of any other potentially relevant exemptions), and then add together the parts of the gain or loss which are either not chargeable or not allowable, arising from each calculation (but subject to a maximum of 100% of the gain or loss).

Priority of exemptions

A company may derive exemption from being owned by a qualifying fund or company, or from being owned by qualifying institutional investors, or because it is a UK REIT. Where more than one exemption might apply with respect to the same investor, the order of priority is Sch 7AC, then CTA 2010, Ch 12 (REITs), and then exemption as a qualifying fund or company under Sch 5AAA, para 12. HMRC has said in its guidance that where different investors provide separate exemptions to a joint venture company, the exemptions may add together but may not exceed the total of the gain or loss.

Meaning of meeting 'the applicable exemption conditions': Sch 5AAA, para 38

- A qualifying fund 'meets the applicable exemption conditions' at any time if it is a CIV, and it meets the entitlement conditions set out in para 12(2).
- A qualifying company 'meets the applicable exemption conditions' at any time if at that time, it meets the entitlement conditions set out in para 12(3).

Meaning of 'the relevant fund' and 'the relevant fund manager': Sch 5AAA, para 39

- 'The relevant fund' in the case of an election in respect of a qualifying fund under para 12, means the CIV concerned, and for an election in respect of a qualifying company under para 12, means the CIS which wholly (or almost wholly) owns that company.
- 'The relevant fund manager', in the case of an election in respect of a qualifying fund or qualifying company under para 12, means the manager of the relevant fund.

Meaning of 'wholly owned' or 'wholly (or almost wholly) owned': Sch 5AAA, para 40

A CIS, or a person or persons together, wholly owns a company at any time if the scheme, or those persons together, has a 100% investment in the company (in the case of a CIS, on the assumption that it is a person).

A 'person or persons together' have a 100% investment in a company if they would receive 100% or more of the proceeds in the event of a disposal of the whole of the equity of the company, or they would be entitled to receive more than 100% of income distributions to shareholders, and they would be entitled to 100% or more of the assets on a winding-up.

'Equity' for these purposes is defined as all shares in the company, excluding restricted preference shares (as defined in CTA 2010, s 160), plus all loan capital, except for normal commercial loans (as defined in CTA 2010, ss 158(1)(b) or 159(4)(b)).

'Shares' in the company are defined as including stock, and any other interests of the members. Where the company does not have share capital, the rules will apply to members' interests (but with the definitions of normal commercial loans and restricted preferences shares in CTA 2010 modified accordingly).

References to receipt of any proceeds, amount or assets include the direct or indirect receipt of the proceeds, amount or assets, and the direct or indirect application of the proceeds, amount or assets for the person's benefit, and it irrelevant whether the receipt or application is at the time of the disposal, distribution, winding-up, or other circumstance, or at a later time. Rights of connected parties are not taken into consideration in applying the 100% test.

Sch 5AAA, para 41

A CIS or person 'almost wholly owns' a company at any time if the scheme or person wholly owns the company, or the scheme or person has a 99% investment in the company (in the case of a CIS, on the assumption that it is a person).

A 'person or persons together' have a 99% investment in a company if they would receive 99% or more of the proceeds in the event of a disposal of the whole of the equity of the company, or they would be entitled to receive more than 99% of income distributions to shareholders, and they would be entitled to 99% or more of the assets on a winding-up

'Equity' for these purposes is defined as all shares in the company, excluding restricted preference shares (as defined in CTA 2010, s 160), plus all loan capital, except for normal commercial loans (as defined in CTA 2010, ss 158(1)(b) or 159(4)(b)).

'Shares' in the company are defined as including stock, and any other interests of the members. Where the company does not have share capital, the rules will apply to members' interests (but with the definitions of normal commercial loans and restricted preferences shares in CTA 2010 modified accordingly).

References to receipt of any proceeds, amount or assets include the direct or indirect receipt of the proceeds, amount or assets, and the direct or indirect application of the proceeds, amount or assets for the person's benefit, and it irrelevant whether the receipt or application is at the time of the disposal, distribution, winding-up, or other circumstance, or at a later time. Rights of connected parties are not taken into consideration in applying the 99% test.

'Designated HMRC officer': Sch 5AAA, para 42

A 'designated HMRC officer' means an HMRC officer who has been designated by the Commissioners for HMRC for the purpose of revoking elections under para 12.

Reporting and Payment (Sch 5AAA, Pt 5)

Reporting by CIVs: Sch 5AAA, para 43

The Treasury may make regulations requiring managers of CIVs to provide information to an HMRC officer in respect of any participant in the vehicle who holds units, the disposal of which would constitute an indirect disposal of UK land. Those regulations may set out circumstances in which the provision of information or documents will be taken to satisfy the obligations of the participant (or anyone else) to provide information or documents to an HMRC officer. HMRC has set out different rules for CIVs first set up before, or on or after, 1 June 2019.

For CIVs set up on or after 1 June 2019

The report should contain the information listed below. The report should be accompanied by a statement that the CIV meets the qualifying conditions for the period the report covers, or in the case of a report where the exemption is not being claimed for the period, the conditions that are met (HMRC has said that there is no legislative significance to 1 June 2019. The date was chosen to allow for a period of time after the rules come into force.)

Information in respect of the CIV making the election and entities in its structure
Name and address of the CIV making the report (the 'top-level' entity)
Total value of disposals by the top-level entity in the period (or £Nil)
Overall gain or loss on disposals (if appropriate)
Name and address of entities in the structure under the top-level entity which are covered by the exemption, and for each of the entities:
The percentage interest the top-level entity holds in them
The total value of their disposals
Overall capital gain or loss on their disposals

Information in respect of the investors in the CIV making the election
First name and surname or company name of all investors, and for each of those investors so reported:
Their address
Their UK capital gains tax unique taxpayer reference (if held)
Their UK corporation tax unique taxpayer reference (if held)
The total value of their disposals
Their overall capital gain or loss (if this is calculable)
Whether the investor is not liable to UK tax on the disposals by reason of exemption, immunity, or other similar status (if held)

For the total value of disposals, the CIV must report on the basis of information it can reasonably be expected to obtain given the terms of its agreement with the investor and the information it has available. HMRC expects that this would at the least be any redemptions made by the investor in respect of their interest in the top-level entity, but in some cases may be secondary market transactions where the CIV's agreement with the investor would mean this information is available.

CIVs set up before 1 June 2019

Established CIVs may be restricted in disclosing personal information about their investors under their local information law, and not have terms in their agreement with the investors that allows them to override those restrictions.

To the extent that they are prevented from providing information to HMRC for legal or regulatory reasons, or because of the contractual impediments of their agreement with the investors, there are easements to what is required to be reported in respect of the investors.

In general, provision of information is subject to reasonable excuse. If an existing CIV – set up without being able to take account of these requirements – legally cannot obtain information pertaining to an investor because of existing agreements or local law or regulations, it is reasonable that they are not able to supply that information to HMRC.

All information in respect of the CIV making the election itself and entities in its structure must still be reported.

Subject to the above, the following information regarding the investors must always be supplied in the report.

First name and surname, or company name of investors who have disposed of an interest in the CIV in the period covered, and for each of those investors so reported:
Their address
Their UK capital gains tax unique taxpayer reference (if held)
Their UK corporation tax unique taxpayer reference (if held)
The total value of their disposals
Their overall capital gain or loss (if this is calculable)
Whether the investor is not liable to UK tax on the disposals by reason of exemption, immunity, or other similar status (if held)

The other information in respect of the remaining investors must also be supplied where there is no legal, regulatory, or contractual restriction on the CIV doing so.

Withholding on account of CGT: Sch 5AAA, para 44

The Treasury may make regulations requiring managers of CIVs to meet the liability to CGT or corporation tax in respect of indirect disposals of UK land made by any participant in the vehicle. This may require a simplified calculation of the tax liability of the participant, as the fund manager will not have access to all the relevant information in order to do so.

Regulations may also authorise the manager of a CIV to deduct an amount on account of CGT from amounts that would otherwise be receivable by participants, and state when such amounts must be paid to HMRC, and the extent to which those payments meet the liability of the participant to CGT or corporation tax in respect of any indirect disposal of UK land.

General (Sch 5AAA, Pt 6)

Meaning of 'close company', 'qualifying investor', 'direct or indirect participator' and other definitions: Sch 5AAA, paras 46, 47

The non-close test is based on CTA 2010, ss 528(4) and 528(5), which apply to UK REITs.

A CIV is close if it is controlled by five or fewer participators. If the non-close test would be failed only because of the inclusion of 'qualifying investors', then the CIV is not regarded as close for these purposes. Unlike the test in s 528, the non-close test for the exemption election allows a look-through of immediate investors to establish whether control is ultimately established through institutional investors.

The look-through is only through bodies corporate however. For example a company which is a direct investor in the CIV could count toward the level of control held by qualifying investors if it were itself owned by sufficient qualifying investors, but a partnership between qualifying investors could not.

Whether a company is 'a close company' is determined in accordance with the rules in CTA 2010, Pt 10, Ch 2, but subject to the following amendments:

- CTA 2010, s 442(a) (non-UK resident companies treated as non-close) is ignored,
- CTA 2010, s 444 (companies involved with non-close companies) is ignored,
- CTA 2010, s 447(1)(a) (shares held by non-close companies) is ignored, and
- for the purposes of any attribution under CTA 2010, s 451(4) (rights of a person's associates to be attributed to the person in determining 'control') the rights and powers of a person are not to be attributed to another person merely because one is a partner of the other.

A 'qualifying investor' for the purpose of the 'non-close test' means:

- a person who is within any of CTA 2010, ss 528(4A)(a), (b), (c), (i) or (j) (authorised unit trusts (UK and overseas); open ended investment companies or their overseas equivalents; limited partnership collective investment schemes; UK REITs or their overseas equivalents where, if the CIV concerned is a company, it meets the non-close condition or, if not, the vehicle meets the genuine diversity of ownership condition),
- a person who is within any other provision of CTA 2010, s 528(4A), or
- a qualifying fund or qualifying company in respect of which an election under para 12 has effect.

A CIV meets the genuine diversity of ownership condition at any time if, at that time:

- it meets conditions A to C, Offshore Funds (Tax) Regulations 2009, reg 75, or
- it meets the condition in Offshore Funds (Tax) Regulations 2009, reg 75(5). The Regulations apply for the purposes of this test as if any CIV which is not an offshore fund were regarded as an offshore fund.

A company meets the non-close condition at any time if, at that time, it:

- is not a close company, or
- is a close company but only because it has a qualifying investor as a direct or indirect participator.

A person is a 'direct participator' if the person is a participator for the purposes of CTA 2010, Pt 10 (s 454), including:

- persons who possess, or are entitled to acquire, share capital or voting rights in the company
- loan creditors of the company
- persons who possess a right to receive or participate in distributions of the company or any amounts payable by the company (in cash or in kind) to loan creditors by way of premium on redemption
- persons who are entitled to acquire such a right, and
- persons who are entitled to secure that income or assets (whether present or future) of the company will be applied directly or indirectly for the person's benefit.

A person is an 'indirect' participator in a company if the person has a share or interest in the capital or income of the company through another body – or bodies – corporate.

Example:

> Two investors, both of which are CIVs, each own 50% of Patroclus Ltd. Patroclus Ltd owns 75% of Orestes Ltd. Orestes Ltd owns 100% of Canopus Ltd. Canopus Ltd owns 50% of Sarpedon Ltd, which owns UK land. The investors are both qualifying funds. Each investor will be treated as having a share as an indirect investor in Sarpedon Ltd. The CIV will be regarded as non-close.

Transitional provision (Sch 5AAA, Pt 7)

Elections for transparency under para 8: Sch 5AAA, para 49

Paragraph 49 applies in the case of an offshore CIV which was constituted before 6 April 2019, and to which para 8 (transparency) applies. In that case, the election will have effect in relation to all disposals made on or after 6 April 2019.

For investors holding an interest in the CIV as an asset and, after the fund makes a para 8 election, holding an interest in the underlying assets of the CIV (including UK resident investors under the current rules) the underlying assets will be deemed to have been always held directly, for the purposes of calculating the gain.

DESTINATION TABLE

TCGA 1992	**After FA 2019 amendment**
Part I, CGT and Corporation Tax on Chargeable Gains	
General	Chapter 1
1 The charge to tax	1 CGT (individuals and companies)
2 Persons and gains chargeable to CGT, and allowable losses	1A Territorial scope; 1E; 1G
2A Taper relief … repealed by FA 2008	…
10 Non-resident with UK branch or agency	1B Non-UK residents: UK branch or agency
New	1C Non-UK residents: disposing of an 'interest in UK land'
New	1D Non-UK residents: assets deriving 75% of value from UK land etc
10A(5)	1E Losses deductible only when within scope of tax etc
10A(4)	1G Gains accruing to UK resident individuals in split years
2B Persons chargeable to CGT on ATED-related gains	Replaced by ss 1–1G
2C 'Relevant high value disposal'	Replaced by ss 1–1G
2D 'The threshold amount'	Replaced by ss 1–1G
2E Restriction of losses	Replaced by ss 1–1G
2F Tapering relief for gains	Replaced by ss 1–1G
3 Annual exempt amount	1K Annual exempt amount
3(3)	1L Increasing annual exempt amount to reflect increases in CPI
3A Reporting limits	TMA 1970, s 8C
4 Rates of CGT	1H The main rates of CGT
4A Section 4: special cases	1I Income taxed at higher rates or gains exceeding unused basic rate band
4(6)	1J Section 1I: definitions and other supplementary provisions
4B Deduction of losses etc in most beneficial way	1F Allowable losses to be used in most beneficial way etc
10A	1M Temporary non-residents
10AA	1N Section 1M(1): assets acquired in temporary period of non-residence
	1O Interpretation
4BA Rates, and use of unused basic rate band, in certain cases	1J Section 1I: definitions and other supplementary provisions
4BB Residential property gain or loss	Replaced by ss 1–1G

5 Accumulation and discretionary settlements … repealed by FA 1998	…
6 Other special cases … repealed by FA 2008	…
7 Time for payment of tax … repealed by FA 1995	…
Corporation tax	Chapter 2
8(1) and 8(2)	2 Corporation tax on chargeable gains
8(1) and 8(2)	2A Company's total profits to include chargeable gains
8(1), 8(2), 10B	2B Territorial scope of charge to corporation tax on chargeable gains
10B	2C Non-UK resident company with UK permanent establishment
8(3) Application of CGT principles in calculating gains and losses	2D Application of CGT principles in calculating gains and losses
8(4) References to income tax or Income Tax Acts in case of companies	2E References to income tax or Income Tax Acts in case of companies
8(5) Interaction of CGT and corporation tax	2F Interaction of CGT and corporation tax
8(6) Assets of a company vested in a liquidator	2G Assets of a company vested in a liquidator
Residence, etc	Chapter 3
9 Residence, including temporary residence … repealed FA 2013	…
10 Non-resident with UK branch or agency	1B Non-UK residents: UK branch or agency
10A Temporary non-residents	1M
10AA s 10A: supplementary	1E and 1N
10B Non-resident company with UK permanent establishment	2B(3), 2C
11 Visiting forces and official agents	271ZA Visiting forces and staff of designated allied headquarters
	271ZB Official agents of Commonwealth countries or Republic of Ireland etc
12 Non-UK domiciled individuals to whom remittance basis applies	Replaced by Sch 1
13 Attribution of gains to members of non-resident companies	3 Gains attributed to UK resident individuals etc
13A Section 13(5): interpretation	3A Gains connected to avoidance or foreign activities etc
	3B Participators and their interests
	3C Prevention of double UK taxation

14 Non-resident groups of companies	3F Non-resident groups of companies
14A Section 13: non-UK domiciled individuals	3D Non-UK domiciled individuals
	3E Temporary non-residents
	3G Supplementary provisions
UK residential property: non-resident CGT	
14B Meaning of 'non-resident CGT disposal'	Replaced by ss 1–1G; Sch 1B
14C Meaning of 'disposal of a UK residential property interest'… repealed by FA 2016	…
14D Persons chargeable to CGT on NRCGT gains	Replaced by ss 1–1G
14E Further provision about use of NRCGT losses	Replaced by ss 1–1G
14F Persons not chargeable under s 14D if a claim is made	Replaced by ss 1–1G
14G s 14F: divided companies	Replaced by ss 1–1G
14H s 14F: arrangements for avoiding tax	Replaced by ss 1–1G
Part II General provisions relating to computation of gains and acquisitions and disposals of assets	
16(3) (capital losses – residence condition)… repealed by FA 2019	…
16ZB Individual who has made election under s 16ZA: foreign chargeable gains remitted in tax year after tax year in which accrue … repealed by FA 2019	…
16ZC Individual who has made election under s 16ZA and to whom remittance basis applies … repealed by FA 2019	…
16ZD Section 16ZC: supplementary … repealed by FA 2019	…
New	25ZA
New	36A Re-basing in relation to direct or indirect disposals of UK land – '2019 re-basing'
New	48A(7) Definition of 'relevant non-resident gain'
57A Computation of gains and losses: relevant high value disposals … repealed by FA 2019	…

57B Computation of gains and losses: NRCGT disposals … repealed by FA 2019	…
57C Computation of gains and losses: disposals of residential property interests … repealed by FA 2019	…
New	62(11) Definition of 'relevant non-resident gain'
Part III Individuals, partnerships, trusts and collective investment schemes etc	
New	80A Postponing gain or loss under s 80(2): interests in UK land
100A exemption for certain EEA UCITS … repealed by FA 2019	…
New	103DB UK property rich collective investment vehicles etc
Part V Transfer of business assets, entrepreneurs' relief and investors' relief	
New	159A Disposals of interests in UK land by non-residents: roll-over relief
New	165(7D) Definition of 'direct or indirect disposal of UK land which meets the non-residence condition'
New	167A(6) Definition of 'direct or indirect disposal of UK land which meets the non-residence condition'
New	167A(7) Definition of 'relevant gain' in s 167A
New	168A Postponing held-over gain: interests in UK land
New	171(1B) (deemed disposals)
Part VI Companies, Oil, Insurance etc	
187A Deemed disposal under s 185: ATED-related gains and losses … repealed by FA 2019	…
New	187B Postponing gain or loss under s 185(2): interests in UK land
188A (and the heading 'Pooling of NRCGT gains and losses')… repealed by FA 2019	…
188B Meaning of 'NRCGT group'… repealed by FA 2019	…
188C Transfers within an NRCGT group … repealed by FA 2019	…
188D Person chargeable to capital gains tax on NRCGT gains accruing to members of an NRCGT group … repealed by FA 2019	…

188E Further provision about group losses … repealed by FA 2019	…
188F Companies becoming eligible to join an NRCGT group … repealed by FA 2019	…
188G Company ceasing to be a member of an NRCGT group … repealed by FA 2019	…
188H The responsible members of an NRCGT group … repealed by FA 2019	…
188I Joint and several liability of responsible members … repealed by FA 2019	…
188J The representative company of an NRCGT group … repealed by FA 2019	…
188K Interpretation of sections 188A to 188J … repealed by FA 2019	…
Part VII Other Property, Businesses, Investments etc	
New	222A(1)(b) (relevant residential property gain or loss)
New	260(6ZD) Defining 'direct or indirect disposal of UK land which meets the non-residence condition'
New	261ZA(6) Defining 'direct or indirect disposal of UK land which meets the non-residence condition'
Minor consequential amendments have been made throughout TCGA 1992, to change legislative references, etc, which are not discussed further here.	
Schedules to Taxation of Capital Gains Act 1992	
Sch A1 Application of taper relief … repealed by FA 2008	…
Sch B1 Disposals of UK residential property interests … repealed by FA 2019	…
Sch BA1 Disposals of non-UK residential property interests … repealed by FA 2019	…
Sch C1 Section 14F: meaning of 'closely-held company' and 'widely-marketed scheme'… repealed FA 2019	…
Sch 1 Application of exempt amount and reporting limits in cases involving settled property … repealed by FA 2019	…
New	Sch 1 UK resident individuals not domiciled in UK

New	Sch 1A Assets deriving 75% of value from UK land
New	Sch 1B Residential property gains
Replacing old Sch 1	Sch 1C Annual exempt amount in cases involving settled property
Sch 2 Assets held on 6 April 1965 – unchanged	
Sch 3 Assets held on 31 March 1982 – unchanged	
Sch 4 Deferred charges on gains before 31 March 1982 – unchanged	
Sch 4ZZA Relevant high value disposals: gains and losses … repealed by FA 2019	…
Sch 4ZZB NRCGT disposals … repealed by FA 2019	…
Sch 4ZZC Disposals of residential property interests: gains and losses … repealed by FA 2019	…
Sch 4ZA Sub-fund settlements – unchanged	
Sch 4A Disposal of interest in settled property: deemed disposal of underlying assets – consequential amendments	
New	Sch 4AA Re-basing for non-residents in respect of UK land etc held on 5 April 2019
Sch 4B Transfers of value by trustees linked with trustee borrowing – unchanged	
Sch 4C Transfers of value: attribution of gains to beneficiaries – consequential amendments	
Sch 5 Attribution of gains to settlors with interest in non-resident or dual resident settlement – consequential amendments	
Sch 5A Settlements with foreign element: information – unchanged	
Sch 5AZA Meaning of 'scheme of reconstruction – unchanged	
Sch 5AA Meaning of 'scheme of reconstruction' – unchanged	
New	Sch 5AAA UK property rich collective investment vehicles etc
Sch 5B Enterprise investment scheme: re-investment – unchanged	

Sch 5BA Enterprise investment scheme: application of taper relief … repealed by FA 2008	…
Sch 5BB Seed enterprise investment scheme: Re-Investment – unchanged	
Sch 5C Venture capital trusts: deferred charge on re-investment … repealed by FA 2004	…
Sch 6 Retirement relief etc … repealed by FA 1998	…
Sch 7 Relief for gifts of business assets – unchanged	
Sch 7ZA Entrepreneurs' relief: 'trading company' and 'trading group' – unchanged	
Sch 7ZB Investors' relief: disqualification of shares – unchanged	
Sch 7A Restriction on set-off of pre-entry losses – consequential amendments	
Sch 7AA Restrictions on setting losses against pre-entry gains … repealed by FA 2006	…
Sch 7AB Roll-over of de-grouping charge: modification of enactments … repealed by FA 2011	…
Sch 7AC Exemptions for disposals by companies with substantial shareholding – consequential amendments	
Sch 7AD Gains of insurance company from venture capital investment partnership – unchanged	
Sch 7B Modification of Act in relation to overseas life insurance companies … repealed by SI 2006/3271, reg 43	…
Sch 7C Relief for transfers to Sch 2 share plans – consequential amendments	
Sch 7D Share schemes and share incentives – unchanged	
Sch 8 Leases – unchanged	
Schedule 8A Foreign currency bank accounts … repealed by FA 2012	…
Sch 8B Hold-over relief for gains re-invested in social enterprises – unchanged	

Sch 10 Consequential amendments – unchanged	
Sch 11 Transitional provisions and savings – unchanged	
Other enactments	
New	TMA 1970, 8C Returns so far as relating to CGT
New	CTA 2009, 18A(2B)
New	CTA 2010, s 535A Gains: disposals of rights or interests in UK property rich companies
New	535B Section 535A: use of pre-April 2019 residual business losses or deficits

SCHEDULE 2

RETURNS FOR DISPOSALS OF UK LAND ETC

Section 14

PART 1

RETURNS AND PAYMENTS ON ACCOUNT: DISPOSALS OF UK LAND ETC

Disposals to which Schedule applies

1 (1) This Schedule applies for the purposes of capital gains tax to—

(a) any direct or indirect disposal of UK land which meets the non-residence condition (whether or not a gain accrues) and which is made on or after 6 April 2019, and

(b) any other direct disposal of UK land on which a residential property gain accrues and which is made on or after 6 April 2020,

but this Schedule does not apply to excluded disposals.

(2) A disposal is an excluded disposal if—

(a) it is a disposal on which, as a result of any of the no gain/no loss provisions, neither a gain nor a loss accrues,

(b) it is the grant of a lease for no premium to a person not connected with the grantor under a bargain made at arm's length,

(c) it is a disposal made by a charity, or

(d) it is a disposal of any pension scheme investments.

(3) The Treasury may by regulations amend sub-paragraph (2).

(4) See also paragraph 9 for a case where a disposal which would have been within sub-paragraph (1)(b) if a gain had accrued is treated, for certain purposes, as if it were a disposal to which this Schedule applies.

2 (1) A disposal is a "direct or indirect disposal of UK land which meets the non-residence condition" if it is—

(a) a disposal on which a gain accrues that falls to be dealt with by section 1A(3) of TCGA 1992 because the asset disposed of is within paragraph (b) or (c) of that subsection,

(b) a disposal on which a gain accrues that falls to be dealt with by section 1A(1) of that Act in accordance with section 1G(2) because the asset disposed of is within section 1A(3)(b) or (c), or

(c) a disposal of an asset on which a gain does not accrue but which, had a gain accrued, would fall to be dealt with as mentioned in either of the preceding paragraphs of this sub-paragraph.

(2) A disposal is "any other direct disposal of UK land on which a residential property gain accrues" if the disposal is a disposal on which a residential property gain accrues where—

(a) the land in question is in the United Kingdom, and

(b) the gain falls to be dealt with by section 1A(1) or (3)(a) of TCGA 1992,

and the disposal does not fall within sub-paragraph (1).

(3) This paragraph applies for the purposes of this Part of this Schedule.

Obligation to deliver a return to officer of Revenue and Customs

3 (1) If a person makes a disposal to which this Schedule applies, the person—

(a) must make a return in respect of the disposal, and

(b) must deliver the return to an officer of Revenue and Customs on or before the 30th day following the day of the completion of the disposal.

(2) If—

(a) a person makes two or more disposals to which this Schedule applies, and

(b) the disposals are made in the same tax year with the same completion date,

the person must make and deliver a single return with respect to the disposals.

(3) This paragraph is subject to—

(a) paragraph 4 (residential property gain accruing but no payment on account required),
(b) paragraph 5 (ordinary tax return already delivered etc), and
(c) paragraph 10 (disposal in case of a collective investment scheme).

4 (1) If—

(a) a person makes a disposal to which this Schedule applies as a result of paragraph 1(1)(b), and
(b) the person would not be liable under paragraph 6 to pay an amount on account of the person's liability to capital gains tax for the tax year concerned,

the person is not required to make or deliver a return under this Schedule in respect of the disposal.

(2) In determining whether sub-paragraph (1)(b) applies, it is to be assumed that the person is required to make a return under this Schedule in respect of the disposal.

5 (1) A person is not required to make or deliver a return under this Schedule in respect of a disposal if the filing date for the return would otherwise fall on or after—

(a) the date on which the person has delivered to an officer of Revenue and Customs the person's ordinary tax return containing a self-assessment that takes account of the disposal, or
(b) the date on or before which the person has (by notice) been required to deliver to an officer of Revenue and Customs the person's ordinary tax return for the tax year concerned.

(2) For the purposes of sub-paragraph (1)(a), a self-assessment does not take account of the disposal if the amount of capital gains tax that is self-assessed is less than the amount that would be payable under paragraph 6 if the person were required to make and deliver a return under this Schedule in respect of the disposal.

Obligation to make a payment on account of capital gains tax

6 (1) This paragraph applies if—

(a) a person is required to make a return under this Schedule in respect of any disposal, and
(b) as at the filing date for the return, an amount of capital gains tax is notionally chargeable on the person (as determined in accordance with paragraph 7).

(2) The person is liable to pay that amount on account of the person's liability to capital gains tax for the tax year concerned so far as that amount has not already become payable as a result of any previous return under this Schedule in respect of a disposal in that period.

(3) The amount is payable on the filing date for the return.

(4) For cases where there are repayments of amounts previously paid on account of capital gains tax, see paragraphs 8 and 9.

Calculation of an amount of capital gains tax notionally chargeable

7 (1) This paragraph applies for determining the amount of capital gains tax (if any) which is notionally chargeable on a person as at the filing date for a return.

(2) The amount of capital gains tax notionally chargeable on the person as at that date is the amount of that tax for which the person would be liable for the tax year concerned, ignoring, for this purpose, the following disposals—

(a) disposals which have a completion date later than the completion date of the disposal in respect of which the return is made (but see sub-paragraph (3)), and
(b) disposals on which gains accrue but which are not disposals to which this Schedule applies.

(3) A disposal on which a loss accrues is not to be ignored under sub-paragraph (2)(a) if the time at which the disposal is made (as determined under section 28 of TCGA 1992) falls on or before the completion date of the disposal in respect of which the return is made.

(4) For provision relevant to the operation of this paragraph, see paragraphs 14 and 15 (making of assumptions, reasonable estimates etc).

Repayments of amounts previously paid on account of capital gains tax

8 (1) This paragraph applies if—

(a) a person makes and delivers a return under this Schedule in respect of a disposal,
(b) the person has previously paid amounts on account of the person's liability to capital gains tax for the tax year concerned, and
(c) the amounts exceed the amount of capital gains tax notionally chargeable on the person as at the filing date for the return.

(2) The excess is repayable to the person on the filing date for the return.

(3) In determining the total amount of payments that have, at any time, been made on account of a person's liability to capital gains tax for a tax year, account must be taken of amounts already repaid under this paragraph.

9 (1) If—

(a) a person makes a disposal on which an allowable loss accrues, and
(b) had a gain accrued instead, the disposal would have been one to which this Schedule applies as a result of paragraph 1(1)(b),

the person may make and deliver a return under this Schedule in respect of the disposal for the purpose of securing the application of paragraph 8.

(2) Accordingly, the disposal is treated for that purpose as if it were a disposal to which this Schedule applies.

(3) This paragraph does not apply in respect of a disposal if the filing date for the return which the person would otherwise be entitled to make and deliver falls on or after the date mentioned in paragraph 5(1)(a) or (b).

Collective investment schemes to which Sch 5AAA to TCGA 1992 applies

10 (1) A person is not required to make or deliver a return under this Schedule in respect of a disposal if—

(a) the disposal has an appropriate connection to a collective investment scheme for the purposes of paragraph 6 of Schedule 5AAA to TCGA 1992, and
(b) the person would not be liable under paragraph 6 of this Schedule to pay an amount on account of the person's liability to capital gains tax for the tax year concerned.

(2) In determining whether sub-paragraph (1)(b) applies, it is to be assumed that the person is required to make a return under this Schedule in respect of the disposal.

11 (1) This paragraph applies if—

(a) an election under paragraph 8 of Schedule 5AAA to TCGA 1992 (election for CIS to be treated as partnership for purposes of Act) has effect in respect of an offshore collective investment scheme (within the meaning of that Schedule),
(b) a disposal is made of property that is the subject of the scheme,
(c) the disposal is made before the day on which this election is made, and
(d) a person is required to make a return under this Schedule in respect of the disposal.

(2) The disposal is treated for the purposes of this Part of this Schedule as if it completed on the day on which the election is made.

12 (1) This paragraph applies if—

(a) a disposal is deemed to have been made by a person as a result of paragraph 21 or 22 of Schedule 5AAA to TCGA 1992 (qualifying offshore CIS etc), and
(b) the person is required to make a return under this Schedule in respect of the disposal.

(2) If the disposal is one to which paragraph 23 of that Schedule applies (gains treated as accruing when value received)—

(a) a disposal to which this Schedule applies is treated as being made by the person on each occasion on which any part of the gain is treated as accruing to the person under that paragraph, and
(b) the time at which that disposal is treated as completing is the time at which the part of the gain is treated as so accruing to the person or, if later, the time at which the required notification is given to the person.

(3) If the disposal is not one to which paragraph 23 of Schedule 5AAA to TCGA 1992 applies, it is treated for the purposes of this Part of this Schedule as if it completed on the day on which the required notification is given to the person.

(4) In this paragraph "the required notification" means notification under paragraph 25 of Schedule 5AAA to TCGA 1992 in relation to the disposal deemed to have been made as a result of paragraph 21 or 22 of that Schedule.

(5) In determining for the purposes of sub-paragraph (1)(b) whether a person is required to make a return under this Schedule in respect of the disposal the effect of paragraphs 4, 5 and 10 is ignored.

Effect of s 144(2) or 144A(2)(b) of TCGA 1992 when asset sold on exercise of option

13 (1) This paragraph applies if—

(a) an option is granted binding the grantor to sell an asset and the grant of the option is a disposal to which this Schedule applies, and

(b) the option is then exercised so that, as a result of section 144(2) or 144A(2)(b) of TCGA 1992, the grant of the option is treated as the same transaction as the sale.

(2) Despite section 144(2) or 144A(2)(b) of TCGA 1992, the grantor remains subject to the obligations under this Schedule in relation to the grant of the option.

(3) In this paragraph references to sale are to be read in accordance with section 144(6) of TCGA 1992.

Making of assumptions, reasonable estimates etc

14 (1) If, in determining whether a disposal is one to which this Schedule applies—

(a) a question arises as to whether a provision of TCGA 1992 applies, and

(b) the determination of the question requires account to be taken of times after the completion of the disposal,

it is to be assumed that the provision does apply if, at the time of the completion of the disposal, it is reasonable to expect that it will apply.

(2) For the purposes of this Schedule it is to be assumed that a person has made a claim or election or given a notice if, at the time of the completion of the disposal in respect of which a return is required to be made under this Schedule, it is reasonable to expect that one will be made or given.

(3) Nothing in sub-paragraph (2) is to be read as affecting—

(a) any requirement imposed by or under any Act for a claim, election or notice to be made or given in a particular way or by a particular time, or

(b) any other provision made by or under any Act that is concerned with the making or giving of the claim, election or notice.

(4) If—

(a) a person is required to make and deliver a return under this Schedule, and

(b) having regard to the person's knowledge and all other relevant circumstances, it is reasonable to make an estimate of a qualifying matter,

the person may make a reasonable estimate of that matter in the return.

(5) For this purpose "qualifying matter" means—

(a) anything that is relevant to the application of section 1I of TCGA 1992,

(b) the value of anything, or

(c) the value of amounts to be apportioned to anything.

15 (1) This paragraph applies if a person is required to make and deliver a return under this Schedule in respect of a disposal and, at any time after the completion of the disposal—

(a) it becomes reasonable to expect that, by reference to the person's residence, a provision of TCGA 1992 will apply,

(b) it becomes reasonable to conclude that a provision of TCGA 1992 conferring a relief applics in relation to the disposal,

(c) matters relevant to the application of section 1I of TCGA 1992 become known, or it becomes reasonable to make a different estimate of those matters, where an estimate of those matters was used in the return, or

(d) the value of anything, or of any amount to be apportioned to anything, becomes known where an estimate was used in the return.

(2) The person may (but need not) assume, for the purposes of this Schedule—

(a) that there is an additional disposal to which this Schedule applies,
(b) that the additional disposal completed at the later time by reference to which this paragraph applies, and
(c) that the additional disposal is in all other respects a replication of the actual disposal.

(3) In determining the amount of capital gains tax notionally chargeable as at the filing date for a return in respect of the additional disposal, the actual disposal is ignored.

Contents of return

16 A return under this Schedule—

(a) must contain information of a description specified by an officer of Revenue and Customs (and different descriptions of information may be specified for different cases), and
(b) must include a declaration by the person making it that the return is, to the best of the person's knowledge, correct and complete.

Interpretation

17 (1) In this Part of this Schedule—

"the filing date", in relation to a return in respect of a disposal, means the date on or before which the return in respect of the disposal must be delivered to an officer of Revenue and Customs,
"lease" has the meaning given by paragraph 10 of Schedule 8 to TCGA 1992,
"ordinary tax return" means a return under section 8 or 8A of TMA 1970,
"pension scheme investments" means investments held for the purposes of a registered pension scheme or an overseas pension scheme (and expressions used in this definition have the same meaning as they have in section 271(1A) of TCGA 1992),
"premium" has the meaning given by paragraph 10 of Schedule 8 to TCGA 1992,
"residential property gain" has the meaning given by Schedule 1B to TCGA 1992, and
"the tax year concerned", in relation to a disposal, means the tax year in which the disposal is made.

(2) In this Part of this Schedule the "completion" of a disposal is regarded as occurring—

(a) at the time of the disposal, or
(b) if the disposal is under a contract which is completed by a conveyance, transfer or other instrument later than the time of the disposal, at the time when the instrument takes effect.

(3) This Part of this Schedule has effect as if it were included in TCGA 1992.

PART 2

NOTIFICATION OF CHARGEABLE AMOUNTS, AMENDMENTS OF RETURNS, ENQUIRIES ETC

Requirement to notify HMRC of amounts chargeable to tax

18 (1) A person is not required to give a notice under section 7 of TMA 1970 merely by reference to a chargeable gain accruing on a disposal if—

(a) the person delivers a return under this Schedule in respect of the disposal, and
(b) the return is delivered before the end of the notification period within the meaning of that section.

(2) But sub-paragraph (1) does not apply if the amount of capital gains tax notionally chargeable on the person as at the filing date for the return (as determined in accordance with paragraph 7) is less than the amount of capital gains tax for which the person is liable for the tax year concerned.

Amendments of returns

19 (1) The amendment provisions applicable to ordinary tax returns apply in relation to returns made by a person under this Schedule as they apply in relation to ordinary tax returns, but subject to the following limitations or other modifications.

(2) An amendment is permitted only so far as the return under this Schedule could, when originally delivered, have included the amendment by reference to things already done.

(3) A person may not make an amendment of a return under this Schedule in respect of a disposal at any time on or after—

(a) the date on which the person has delivered to an officer of Revenue and Customs the person's ordinary tax return containing a self-assessment that takes account of the disposal, or

(b) the date on or before which the person has (by notice) been required to deliver to an officer of Revenue and Customs the person's ordinary tax return for the tax year concerned.

(4) If a person is not required to deliver an ordinary tax return for the tax year concerned, the person may not make an amendment of a return under this Schedule more than 12 months after the last day for delivery of an ordinary tax return.

(5) For the purposes of this paragraph "the amendment provisions applicable to ordinary tax returns" means sections 9ZA and 9ZB of TMA 1970.

Enquiries

20 (1) The enquiry provisions apply in relation to returns made by a person under this Schedule as they apply in relation to ordinary tax returns, but subject as follows.

(2) If the person is required to deliver an ordinary tax return for the tax year concerned, the time allowed for giving a notice of enquiry into a return under this Schedule is the same as that allowed for giving a notice of enquiry into the ordinary tax return.

(3) If the person is not required to deliver an ordinary tax return for the tax year concerned, the time allowed for giving a notice of enquiry into a return under this Schedule is determined on the assumption that the person was required to deliver an ordinary tax return for that year and that it was delivered at the later of—

(a) the last day for delivery of an ordinary tax return, and

(b) the day on which the return under this Schedule was delivered.

(4) If there is an enquiry into a return under this Schedule—

(a) nothing in paragraph 8 requires any repayment to be made before the day on which the enquiry is completed, but

(b) the officer of Revenue and Customs concerned may, at any time before that day, make the repayment, on a provisional basis, to such extent as the officer thinks fit.

(5) If—

(a) a notice of enquiry ("the main enquiry notice") is given at any time into an ordinary tax return for a tax year, and

(b) a notice of enquiry into a return under this Schedule has not been given, on or before that time, in respect of a disposal to which this Schedule applies which is made in that tax year,

the main enquiry notice is also taken to constitute a notice of enquiry into the return under this Schedule in respect of the disposal.

(6) If—

(a) a final closure notice ("the main closure notice") is given at any time which completes an enquiry into an ordinary tax return for a tax year, and

(b) a final closure notice of an enquiry into a return under this Schedule has not been given, on or before that time, in respect of a disposal to which this Schedule applies which is made in that period,

the main closure notice is also taken to constitute a final closure notice of the enquiry into the return under this Schedule in respect of the disposal.

(7) For the purposes of this paragraph "the enquiry provisions" means sections 9A and 28A of TMA 1970 and the other provisions of that Act so far as they relate to those sections.

(8) Nothing in this paragraph is to be read as affecting the operation of the enquiry provisions in relation to ordinary tax returns.

Amendments of returns during enquiry etc

21 (1) For other provisions which, as a result of paragraph 19 and 20, are relevant to returns made by a person under this Schedule, see sections 9B and 9C of TMA 1970.

(2) In the case of Schedule 3ZA to TMA 1970 (date by which payment to be made after amendment or correction of self-assessment)—

- (a) paragraph 1(2) of that Schedule has effect as if the reference to section 59B(3) and (4) of TMA 1970 included a reference to paragraph 7 of this Schedule, and
- (b) the other provisions of that Schedule have effect in accordance with the provision made elsewhere by this Part of this Schedule (see, in particular, paragraph 24(3)).

(3) For provisions of that Schedule relevant to returns made by a person under this Schedule, see—

- (a) paragraph 2 (amendment of return by taxpayer),
- (b) paragraph 3 (correction of return by HMRC),
- (c) paragraph 4 (jeopardy amendment by HMRC), and
- (d) paragraph 5 (amendment of return by closure notice).

Revenue determinations

22 (1) The Revenue determination provision applicable to ordinary tax returns applies in relation to returns made by a person under this Schedule as it applies in relation to ordinary tax returns, but subject to the following modifications.

(2) The modifications are that—

- (a) any reference to being given a notice is to be read as a reference to being required to deliver a return under this Schedule,
- (b) any reference to the filing date is to be read as a reference to the filing date within the meaning of this Part of this Schedule (but see paragraph (e)),
- (c) any reference to the amounts to be determined is to be read as a reference to the amount of capital gains tax which is notionally chargeable on a person as at the filing date for a return under this Schedule,
- (d) any reference in any enactment to the purposes for which a determination is to have effect is to be ignored, and
- (e) the determination may not be made after the end of the period of 3 years beginning with the last day for delivery of an ordinary tax return.

(3) If—

- (a) a determination is made as a result of this paragraph, but
- (b) it is then superseded by a return made under this Schedule,

any amount which, as a result of the supersession, is payable or repayable under paragraph 6 or 8 is to be payable or repayable on the filing date for the return.

(4) For the purposes of this paragraph "the Revenue determination provision" means section 28C of TMA 1970.

Discovery assessments

23 (1) A return made by a person under this Schedule is treated for the purposes of the discovery provisions as if it were an assessment required to be included as part of the person's ordinary tax return (whether or not the person is actually required to deliver an ordinary tax return).

(2) References in the discovery provisions to an ordinary tax return for a tax year include a return under this Schedule made in respect of a disposal for the tax year concerned.

(3) For the purposes of this paragraph "the discovery provisions" means section 29 of TMA 1970 and the other provisions of that Act relating to that section.

Interpretation

24 (1) Expressions have the same meaning in this Part of this Schedule as they have in Part 1 of this Schedule (see paragraph 17).

(2) For the purposes of this Part of this Schedule any reference to the last day for delivery of an ordinary tax return is to 31 January in the tax year following the tax year concerned.

(3) A return made by a person under this Schedule is to be treated for the purposes of any provision made by or under TMA 1970 as if it contained a self-assessment of an amount of capital gains tax.

PART 3

CONSEQUENTIAL AMENDMENTS

Amendments of TMA 1970

25 (1) TMA 1970 is amended as follows.

(2) Omit section 7A (disregard of certain NRCGT gains for purposes of section 7).

(3) Omit sections 12ZA to 12ZN (NRCGT returns) and the italic heading before those sections.

(4) In section 28A (completion of enquiry into personal or trustee return)—

- (a) in subsection (1), omit "or 12ZM", and
- (b) in the heading, omit "or NRCGT return".

(5) Omit section 28G (determination of amount notionally chargeable where no NRCGT return delivered).

(6) In section 29 (assessment where loss of tax discovered), omit subsection (7)(a)(ia).

(7) Omit section 29A (non-resident CGT disposals: determination of amount which should have been assessed).

(8) In section 34 (ordinary time limit of 4 years), omit subsection (1A).

(9) In section 42 (procedure for making claims etc), in subsection (11)(a)—

- (a) omit "12ZB", and
- (b) after "12AA of this Act" insert "or a return under Schedule 2 to the Finance Act 2019".

(10) After section 59A insert—

> **"59AZA Payments on account of capital gains tax: disposals of land etc**
>
> For provision requiring payments to be made on account of capital gains tax, see Schedule 2 to the Finance Act 2019."

(11) Omit section 59AA (non-resident CGT disposals: payments on account of capital gains tax).

(12) In section 59B (payment of income tax and capital gains tax: assessments other than simple assessments)—

- (a) in subsection (1)(b), for "or 59AA of this Act" substitute "of this Act or under Schedule 2 to the Finance Act 2019", and
- (b) omit subsection (2A).

(13) In section 59BA (payment of income tax and capital gains tax: simple assessments), in subsection (2)(b), for "or 59AA" substitute "of this Act or under Schedule 2 to the Finance Act 2019".

(14) In section 107A (relevant trustees), in subsection (2)(b)—

- (a) omit ", 59AA", and
- (b) after "59B of this Act" insert "or under Schedule 2 to the Finance Act 2019".

(15) In section 118 (interpretation), omit the definition of "NRCGT return".

(16) In Schedule 3ZA (date by which payment to be made after amendment or correction of self-assessment)—

- (a) in paragraph 1(1), omit "or an advance self-assessment (see section 12ZE(1))",
- (b) in paragraph 1(2), omit "59AA(2) or",
- (c) in paragraph 2(1), omit "or an amendment of an advance self-assessment under section 12K (amendment of NRCGT return by taxpayer)",
- (d) in paragraph 2(3), omit "or 12ZN(3)" and "or advance self-assessment",
- (e) in paragraph 3(1), omit "or 12ZL" and "or NRCGT return", and
- (f) in paragraph 5(1), omit "or advance self-assessment".

Amendments of other Acts

26 (1) TCGA 1992 is amended as follows.

(2) In section 222A (determination of main residence: disposals by non-residents)—

(a) in subsection (6)(a), for "the NRCGT return" substitute "the return under Schedule 2 to the Finance Act 2019", and

(b) in subsection (7)(a), for "an NRCGT return" substitute "a return under Schedule 2 to the Finance Act 2019".

(3) In section 223A (amount of relief: disposals by non-residents), in subsection (3)(b), for "the NRCGT return" substitute "the return under Schedule 2 to the Finance Act 2019".

27 (1) Schedule 24 to FA 2007 (penalties for errors) is amended as follows.

(2) In paragraph 1(4), in the entry relating to capital gains tax, in the second column, for "section 12ZB of TMA 1970 (NRCGT return)" substitute "Schedule 2 to FA 2019".

(3) In paragraph 21C, for "section 59AA(2) of TMA 1970 (non-resident CGT disposals: payments on account of capital gains tax)" substitute "Schedule 2 to FA 2019".

28 (1) Schedule 36 to FA 2008 (information and inspection powers) is amended as follows.

(2) For paragraph 21ZA and the italic heading before it substitute—

> *"Application of paragraph 21 in case of returns under Schedule 2 to FA 2019*
>
> **21ZA** (1) For the purposes of paragraph 21 any reference to the making by a person of a return under section 8 or 8A of TMA 1970 includes the making by the person of a return under Schedule 2 to FA 2019.
>
> (2) In the application of paragraph 21 in relation to a return under Schedule 2 to FA 2019, the return is to be treated as if it required a self-assessment of an amount of capital gains tax.
>
> (3) For the purposes of paragraph 21, the definition of "the notice of enquiry" in its application to a return under Schedule 2 to FA 2019 needs to be read in the light of the provision made by paragraph 20 of that Schedule."

29 (1) Schedule 55 to FA 2009 (penalty for failure to make returns etc) is amended as follows.

(2) In the table in paragraph 1(5), in item 2A, in the third column, for "NRCGT return under section 12ZB of TMA 1970" substitute "Return under Schedule 2 to FA 2019 (other than one made under paragraph 9 or 15 of that Schedule)".

(3) Schedule 55 to FA 2009, as amended by this paragraph, is taken to have come into force for the purposes of returns under this Schedule on the day on which this Act is passed.

30 (1) Schedule 56 to FA 2009 (penalty for failure to make payments on time) is amended as follows.

(2) In paragraph 1, in the Table, after item 3A insert—

"3B	Capital gains tax	Amount payable under paragraph 6 of Schedule 2 to FA 2019 where not included in a return under section 8 or 8A of TMA 1970	The date falling 30 days after 31 January in the tax year following the one in which the disposal was made"

(3) In paragraph 3(1)(a), after "3" insert ", 3B".

(4) In paragraph 5(3) of Schedule 11 to F(No 3)A 2010 (which amends paragraph 3(1)(a) of Schedule 56 to FA 2009), after "3" insert (in both places) "3B".

(5) Schedule 56 to FA 2009, as amended by this paragraph, is taken to have come into force for the purposes of returns under this Schedule on the day on which this Act is passed.

Late payment interest

31 So far as relating to amounts that are payable (or repayable) as a result of a requirement under this Schedule, sections 101 to 103 of FA 2009 (late payment interest on sums due to HMRC etc) come into force on 6 April 2019.

Commencement

32 (1) The amendments made by this Part of this Schedule have effect in relation to disposals made on or after 6 April 2019.

(2) But section 12ZG of TMA 1970 (cases where advance self-assessment not required) continues to have effect in relation to disposals made on or after that date but before 6 April 2020; and that section has effect in relation to those disposals—

(a) as if references to an NRCGT return were to a return under this Schedule, and

(b) as if references to section 12ZE(1) of TMA 1970 were to paragraph 6 of this Schedule.

COMMENTARY ON SCHEDULE 2

Schedule 2 (as introduced by s 14) is intended to be read as though it forms part of the Taxation of Capital Gains Act (TCGA) 1992. References in the text are to FA 2019, Sch 2 unless otherwise stated. References to TCGA 1992 are references to it as amended by FA 2019, Sch 1.

Introduction

It is going to be vital to raise client awareness of these changes as soon as possible, to avoid the imposition of penalties (and potentially PI claims) due to accidental defaults – it is unfortunately still often the case that clients do not tell their agent about in-year property transactions until after the end of the tax year – expecting these to be reflected on their self-assessment tax returns, if at all. Under the current NRCGT regime, there is an exemption from payment at the 30 day point where the vendor is already in the UK self-assessment system and makes a claim to pay the tax due at the normal self-assessment tax return deadline. This option will be withdrawn from 6 April 2020, as from this date all disposals of UK residential property, including disposals by UK residents, will be brought within this system.

If clients fail to tell their agent about relevant transactions, late filing and late payment penalties will be incurred (as we have seen with the recent spate of cases concerning non-resident CGT penalties, which have by no means all gone in favour of the appellant) and, if their agent has not forewarned them of these changes, the client's natural reaction will be to blame the agent. One point to note is that TCGA 1992, s 3A (reporting limits) has been moved to TMA 1970, s 8C.

This commentary will cover the types of transactions that are impacted by new TCGA 1992, Sch 1, and what the relevant filing and payment obligations will be.

Relevant disposals: paras 1, 2

Schedule 2 applies to all direct or indirect disposals of UK land which meet 'the non-residence condition' whether or not there is a gain, from 6 April 2019 (para 1(1)(a)) and will apply to any other direct disposal of UK land on which a residential property gain accrues from 6 April 2020 (para 1(1)(b)).

A disposal is a 'direct or indirect disposal of UK land which meets the non-residence condition' if it is:

- A disposal within TCGA 1992, s 1A(3)(b) or (c) or s 2B(4)(a) or (b) (non-UK residents disposing of assets situated in the UK that have a relevant connection to the person's UK branch or agency, or assets – wherever situated – that derive at least 75% of their value from UK land where the person has a substantial indirect interest in that land), or
- A disposal which is within TCGA 1992, s 1A(3)(b) or (c) as a result of TCGA 1992, s 1G(2) (gains accruing to an individual in the overseas part of a split tax year), or
- A loss-making disposal which, had a gain accrued, would have been dealt under TCGA 1992, s 1A(3)(b) or (c) (para 2(1)).

A disposal is 'any other direct disposal of UK land on which a residential property gain accrues' if the disposal is a disposal on which a residential property gain accrues, where the land is in the UK and the gain is chargeable under TCGA 1992, s 1A(1) or s 1A(3)(a) and the disposal does not fall within para 2(1) (para 2(2)).

Requirement to make returns: paras 3, 4, 5

If a relevant disposal is made, then the vendor is required to make a return to HMRC within 30 days of *completion* of the transaction, subject to some limited exceptions.

- For disposals falling within para 1(1)(a) (relevant non-resident disposals, defined in para 2(1)) returns are required whether a gain or loss arises.
- For disposals falling within para 1(1)(b) (other direct disposals of UK land, defined in para 2(2)), returns are only required where a gain arises, but a return may be made for a loss (provided it would have been within para 1(1)(b) if it were a gain), so that excessive payments on account already made for that tax year can be reclaimed (para 9(1)).
- For disposals under para 1(1)(b) that do not give rise to a liability to make a CGT payment on account, no return is required (para 4). This may arise where – on the latest in-year recalculation under para 7 – the payments already made in the year to date cover the expected CGT liability for the year.

The legislation also introduces the concept of 'ordinary tax returns' which are, respectively, either the income tax self-assessment or corporation tax self-assessment returns for the tax year concerned. Paragraph 5 deals with exceptions to the requirement to file a Sch 2 return – para 5(1)(a) states that if the filing date for a CGT return falls on or after the filing date for the person's 'ordinary tax return' containing a self-assessment that takes account of the disposal, then no further return is required, provided that the amount of CGT that is self-assessed in that return is the same as, or more than, the amount that would be payable under para 6 if the person were required to make a CGT return in respect of the disposal instead.

Example

The filing deadline for Hector's 2020/21 tax return is 31 January 2022. That return will reflect his CGT position for 2020/21. Hector completes a para 1(1)(b) transaction on 4 April 2021. A CGT return would normally fall due on 4 May 2021.

However, Hector is extremely organised: he collates all his 2020/21 information, sends it to his agent, and his self-assessment for 2020/21 is submitted to HMRC on 30 April 2021, incorporating the para 1(1)(b) transaction on the CGT pages of the self-assessment return.

Provided that the amount of CGT self-assessed in the tax return is the same as, or more than, the amount Hector would have paid under FA 2019, Sch 2, para 6, then no CGT return need be made on 4 May 2021.

Paragraph 5(1)(b) has the same effect where the chargeable person is a company. Both situations are likely to be rare in practice.

Multiple disposals with the same completion date: para 3

Where two or more disposals are made in the same tax year and with the same completion date, then a single return must be made, dealing with both disposals (para 3(2)). This is going to require a certain amount of adjustment for advisers, who are used to focusing on contract dates rather than completion. Now we need to do both – the completion date is relevant for gains, but the contract date determines whether losses are included on the CGT return (and which CGT return) or not. It will be important going forward to track completion dates carefully, as working out the correct combination of returns is likely to be complex until we all get used to the rules.

Example

Paris makes two para 1(1)(b) gains. Exchange of contracts takes place on different dates, but for both, the completion date is 30 August 2020. He also makes a loss (which would have been within para 1(1)(b) if it had been a gain) with an exchange date of 15 September and a completion date of 28 September 2020.

Paris must make two separate Sch 2 returns. The first (due by 29 September 2020) reflects all his relevant gains with the same completion date. The other return, relating to his loss, is due by 28 October 2020.

If Paris had exchanged contracts on his loss-making transaction before the completion date on the para 1(1)(b) gains, he would have been able to take account of the loss when calculating his CGT payment on account.

Requirement to make payments on account: paras 6, 7, 30, 31

If a person is required to make a CGT return under para 3(1) in respect of a disposal and at the filing date for the return, an amount of CGT (calculated in accordance with para 7) is notionally chargeable on them, they are liable to pay that amount as a payment on account of their CGT liability for the tax year (less any amounts already paid as a result of previous Sch 2 returns for the same tax year).

The amount of CGT 'notionally chargeable' on the person at the return date is the amount of CGT that the person would be due to pay in the tax year of disposal, ignoring disposals with a completion date after the completion date of the disposal the return is required for, and ignoring disposals not covered by Sch 2.

Disposals 'not covered by Sch 2' are:

- For 2019/20, disposals that aren't 'non-resident disposals' of UK land
- From 2020/21, disposals by UK resident individuals of non-residential UK property or of other assets which are not land, and disposals by non-residents of other assets which are not UK land
- Disposals specifically excluded by para 1(2) (see *excluded disposals* below).

Example

Ajax is UK resident and owns a large residential property portfolio. He also has a carried interest in a US LLP, and buys and sells shares throughout the year.

On 7 April 2020 he realises carried interest gains of £100k. On 6 April 2020 he exchanges contracts for – and on 30 April 2020 he completes on – the sale of a residential property for £500k, making a gain of £100k.

On 5 May 2020 he exchanges contracts to sell another UK residential property and completes on 15 May, making a loss of £50k.

Ajax's first residential property CGT return is due on 30 May 2020. The loss-making disposal on 5 May will not be included, since the contract date (TCGA 1992, s 28) falls after the completion date of the earlier transaction. (It would not be ignored (see para 7(2)(a)) if the contract date fell on or before the completion date of the disposal in respect of which the return is to be made).

He is required to ignore the loss-making transaction on 5 May in calculating the CGT payment on account and CGT of £28k is due on 30 May 2020 (however, see below). The carried interest disposal is also ignored as this is not a disposal covered by Sch 2.

The due date for payment is the same as the filing date for the CGT return, 30 days from completion of the relevant disposal (para 6(3)). FA 2009, Sch 56 (penalty for failure to make payments on time) applies to Sch 2 returns from 12 February 2019 (Royal Assent to Finance Bill 2019). New category '3B' is inserted in the table in Sch 56, para 1, by para 30. In addition, FA 2009, ss 101–103 (late payment interest on sums due to HMRC) apply to amounts payable (or repayable) under Sch 2 with effect from 6 April 2019 (para 31).

Example (continued)

Ajax is within para 1(1)(b) and is only required by paras 6 and 7 to make returns and payments on account for direct disposals of UK land on which a residential property gain accrues. Since the 5 May 2020 sale is loss-making, technically no return is required.

However, para 9(1) applies in situations where the loss-making transaction would have been within para 1(1)(b) had a gain arisen on it, and allows a return to be made (by 4 June 2020) for the purpose of obtaining a refund of CGT already paid on account for the year.

Para 7(3) makes clear that losses can only be factored into the calculation of the CGT payment on account where the contract date (given by TCGA 1992, s 28) for the loss-making transaction is before the completion date for the gain being reported, so it remains to be seen whether in the example above, HMRC would accept both returns on 30 May 2020 together with a payment on account of £14k, or whether it would in practice insist that the client pay £28k on 30 May and later refund the £14k overpayment.

Repayments: paras 8, 9

Where, during a tax year, a person has made previous Sch 2 returns and payments on account of CGT and on a later para 1(1) disposal in the same year, the recalculated CGT is less than the total previously paid, the excess is repayable. In effect, these rules will leave a fluctuating CGT 'account' with HMRC which may need to be either topped up, or partially repaid numerous times throughout the year depending on the frequency of the client's property transactions.

Excluded disposals: para 1(2)

Virtually all disposals of UK land (whether residential or commercial) by non-UK resident persons are subject to the new rules in FA 2019, Sch 1 from 6 April 2019. The requirements are extended to UK resident persons for residential disposals, from 6 April 2020. There are limited exceptions, which mirror the current exceptions in TMA 1970, s 12ZBA relating to elective NRCGT returns. These are as follows:

(1) disposals where, as a result of any of the no gain/no loss provisions, neither a gain nor loss accrues
(2) the grant of a lease for no premium to a person who is unconnected with the grantor under a bargain made at arm's length
(3) disposals made by charities, or
(4) disposals of any pension scheme investments.

(1) The no gain/no loss provisions for the purposes of TCGA 1992 are set out in full in TCGA 1992, s 288(3A). These include:

- Disposals between spouses or civil partners (TCGA 1992, s 58)
- Disposals on company reconstructions (TCGA 1992, s 139)
- Disposals of UK businesses to non-resident companies in exchange for shares (TCGA 1992, s 140A)
- Transfers of UK businesses via intra-group transfers (TCGA 1992, s 171)
- Exchanges of interests in land (TCGA 1992, ss 248A–248E)
- Gifts to charities (TCGA 1992, s 257)
- Charities becoming absolutely entitled to settled property (TCGA 1992, s 257(3))
- Gifts and other transactions involving heritage property (TCGA 1992, s 258).

(2) TCGA 1992, Sch 8, para 2(1) makes clear that where the payment of a premium is required under a lease of land (or is part of the terms under which a lease of land is granted), there is a part disposal of the freehold or other asset out of which the lease is granted. The exception from the Sch 2 reporting obligations only applies to grants of leases where there is no premium. The grantee must also be unconnected with the grantor and it must have been an arm's length deal for the reporting exception to apply.

(3) A gain is not a chargeable gain if it accrues to a charity and is applied for charitable purposes (TCGA 1992, s 256(1)).

(4) Neither is a gain accruing to a person on a disposal of investments held for the purposes of a registered pension scheme or an overseas pension scheme chargeable (TCGA 1992, s 271(1A)), and such disposals are also excluded from the Sch 2 reporting requirement.

Collective investment schemes: paras 10, 11, 12 (new Sch 5AAA, TCGA 1992)

No returns are required under Sch 2 provided the disposal has an 'appropriate connection' to a collective investment vehicle (para 6, Sch 5AAA) *and*, if the calculation required by Sch 2, para 6 was carried out, no CGT payment on account would be payable.

Paragraphs 10–12 mainly deal with deemed dates of completion, where this would otherwise be unclear due to the various collective investment vehicle elections and revocation events.

- Where an election is made under Sch 5AAA, para 8 (to treat a collective investment scheme as transparent), para 11 treats the completion date for all relevant disposals where the transaction date (presumably the date given by TCGA 1992, s 28) pre-dates the date of the election, as being the date of the election, allowing the transparency election to have effect.
- Para 12 allocates deemed dates of completion in cases where a disposal is deemed to have been made under Sch 5AAA, para 21 or 22 (ceasing to meet conditions for exemption or revocation of exemption), where the person is required to make a return under Sch 2.

- If the disposal is within Sch 5AAA, para 23 (gains treated as accruing when value received) a disposal is treated as being made by the person on each occasion that any part of the gain is treated as accruing to them (a proportion of any deemed disposals will come into charge on occasions when the person has made an actual disposal of units or shares). Completion is treated as occurring when the part of the gain is treated as accruing or, if later, the time at which the required (para 25, Sch 5AAA) notification is given. If para 23, Sch 5AAA does not apply, completion is deemed to take place on the day notification under para 25, Sch 5AAA is given to the person making the gain.

The CIV transparency election (Sch 5AAA, para 8) has retrospective effect, so that a disposal by the CIV earlier in the tax year will nevertheless become chargeable on the investor rather than the CIV. The deemed completion dates in para 10 mean the investor's 30-day time limit for reporting and paying tax on any gain begins on the day the transparency election is sent to HMRC, rather than the actual completion date of the disposal (the normal 30-day time limit applies to disposals that complete after the date an election has been made).

The normal rules for the 30-day reporting and payment on account provisions will apply for any disposal by the investors themselves, regardless of whether the CIV is transparent (treated as a disposal of underlying property) or opaque (a disposal of an interest in the fund itself).

Options: para 13

Where an option is exercised, the grant of the option and the transaction entered into by the grantor in fulfilment of his obligations under the option are treated for CGT purposes as a single transaction (TCGA 1992, s 144(2)):

- If the option binds the grantor to sell, the consideration for the option is part of the consideration for the sale, and
- If the option binds the grantor to buy, the consideration for the option is deducted from the cost of acquisition incurred by the grantor in buying in pursuance of his obligations under the option.

Paragraph 13 ensures that, notwithstanding TCGA 1992, s 144(2), the grantor of an option remains subject to the obligation to make returns and CGT payments on account under Sch 2 in relation to the grant of the option. On the subsequent sale, consideration treated as received for the option is disregarded in calculating the amount chargeable. This rule is unchanged from the pre- 2019/20 NRCGT system.

This will also be relevant where deals 'fail' and deposits are forfeited, which is treated as a disposal of an asset (the option to sell) by the recipient of the deposit and the amount forfeited is treated as the consideration received by him. In such cases, the vendor will make a gain on the deemed date of grant of the option (the date of receipt of the deposit funds), and if this is in connection with property within para 1(1), a Sch 2 return must be made within 30 days. This is likely to be problematic where a deal fails more than 30 days after the deposit was paid. It is not clear how HMRC will approach this in practice.

Estimates and assumptions: para 14

The legislation recognises the complexities of estimating a person's CGT position before the end of the tax year in question, so para 14 provides:

- Where some question arises as to whether a provision of TCGA 1992 might apply to a tax year (ie elections or claims for relief that might be made), but ascertaining that requires you to have regard to periods after the completion of the disposal, then it can be assumed that the provision *does* apply if it is 'reasonable to do so' at the time of the completion of the disposal.
- It will be assumed that a person has made any relevant claim or election or given any notice at the time of the completion of the disposal (for which the Sch 2 return is required) provided that it is reasonable to expect that it will be made or given.
- Where a person is required to make and deliver a return under Sch 2, it will be reasonable for them to make an estimate of a 'qualifying matter' in the return (having regard to the person's knowledge and all other relevant circumstances). A qualifying matter for these purposes is anything that is relevant to the application of TCGA 1992, s 1I (income taxed at higher rates or gains

exceeding unused basic rate band), the value of anything, or the value of amounts to be apportioned to anything.

Replacement returns: para 15

Paragraph 15 basically allows the substitution of an updated return, with better estimates, actual figures instead of estimates, or claiming reliefs, if in the interim it has become apparent that a relief should apply. It states that, at any time after the completion of a disposal where the conditions below apply, the person may (but is not *required* to) make a new CGT return taking into account the presumed relief, election or claim. In determining the amount of CGT notionally chargeable at the filing date for the new return, the new circumstances are substituted for the original.

The conditions are:

- where it becomes reasonable to expect that, by reference to the person's residence status, a provision of TCGA 1992 will apply, or
- it becomes reasonable to conclude that a provision of TCGA 1992 conferring a relief applies in relation to the disposal, or
- matters relevant to the application of TCGA 1992, s 1I (income taxed at higher rates or gains exceeding unused basic rate band) become known, or it becomes reasonable to make a different estimate of those matters, where an estimate of those matters was used in the original return, or
- the value of anything, or of any amount to be apportioned to anything, becomes known where an estimate was used in the original return.

The lack of compulsion in para 15 is a valuable addition, otherwise – for clients who indulge in multiple property transactions each year – agents would be under constant pressure to revise and resubmit returns, which are, it must be remembered, only interim estimates of the CGT payable and tax due, and will continue to be finalised in the self-assessment return (the 'ordinary tax return' as it is referred to in the legislation) each year, after the full facts are known in any event.

Administration: paras 16, 17, 24, 32

Paragraph 16 includes the usual proviso that a CGT return must include a declaration by the person making it that the return is – to the best of the person's knowledge – correct and complete, and must contain such information as is specified from time to time by an HMRC officer. Paragraph 17 contains relevant definitions and is to be treated as though it forms part of TCGA 1992. Paragraph 24 deals with interpretation, incorporating the definitions in para 17.

TMA 1970, s 12ZG (cases where advance self-assessment not required) continues in force in relation to disposals made on or after 6 April 2019 but before 6 April 2020, as if references to a NRCGT return were to a Sch 2 return, and as if references to TMA 1970, s 12ZE(1) (NRCGT return to include advance self-assessment) were to para 6.

Notification of chargeable amounts and amendments to returns: para 18

There is no requirement to make a TMA 1970, s 7 or FA 1998, Sch 18, para 2 notification in respect of a person solely because a gain within para 1(1) has been made (provided that a timely Sch 2 return and payment has been made in respect of it), unless the amount of CGT notionally chargeable on the person at the filing date for the return (determined in accordance with para 7) is less than the amount of CGT for which the person is liable for the tax year concerned (para 18).

The amendment provisions applicable to ordinary tax returns (TMA 1970, ss 9ZA, 9ZB and FA 1998, Sch 18, paras 15, 16) apply in relation to Sch 2 returns in the same way as they apply in relation to ordinary tax returns, subject to the following limitations (para 19):

- An amendment is only permitted so far as the return could, when originally delivered, have included the amendment by reference to things already done.
- A person cannot make an amendment to a Sch 2 return in respect of a disposal at any time on or after:
  - The date on which the person has delivered to an officer of HMRC the person's 'ordinary' tax return containing a self-assessment that takes account of the disposal, or

   - The date on or before which the person has (by notice) been required to deliver to HMRC the person's ordinary tax return for the tax year concerned.
- If a person is not required to deliver an ordinary tax return for the tax year concerned, they cannot make an amendment of a Sch 2 return more than 12 months after the last day for delivery of an ordinary tax return.

Example

Helen makes a number of para 1(1) gains in 2021/22 and submits Sch 2 returns and payments on the relevant due dates.

Helen's 2021/22 self-assessment return is submitted to HMRC on 25 November 2022. She cannot amend any of her 2021/22 Sch 2 returns after 25 November 2022.

Menelaus receives a notice to file a self-assessment for 2020/21 on 4 January 2022. He must file the return by 3 April 2022, and can no longer amend any 2020/21 Sch 2 returns after that date.

Pandarus makes para 1(1)(b) gains during 2021/22, submits the relevant Sch 2 returns and pays all the CGT due. He has no other income or gains in that year so there is no requirement for him to submit a self-assessment return. He can submit amendments to his Sch 2 returns for 2021/22 up until 31 January 2024 (ie one year after the last possible filing date for a 2021/22 self-assessment tax return).

Enquiries, amendments and determinations: paras 19–22

The enquiry provisions are broadly identical to those for ordinary tax returns (TMA 1970, ss 9A–9C FA 1998, Sch 18, Pt IV), subject to the following:

- If the person is required to deliver an ordinary tax return for the tax year concerned, the Sch 2 return enquiry time limit is the same as for giving a notice of enquiry into the ordinary tax return
- If the person is not required to deliver an ordinary tax return for the tax year concerned, the time allowed for giving a notice of enquiry into a return under Sch 2 is determined on the assumption that the person was required to deliver an ordinary tax return for that year and that it was delivered on the later of the last day for delivery of an ordinary tax return, and the day on which the relevant Sch 2 return was delivered.

Example

Pandarus's para 1(1)(b) gain arises on 30 March 2022. He submits the relevant Sch 2 return and pays all the CGT due on 29 April 2022.

The last day for delivery of a self-assessment return for 2021/22 is 31 January 2023, which is later than the Sch 2 return due date, therefore HMRC can enquire into his Sch 2 return up until 31 January 2024. (He can also submit amendments to his Sch 2 returns for 2021/22 up until 31 January 2024, since he was not required to file a self-assessment return for the year – see above).

If there is an enquiry into a Sch 2 return, there is no requirement for HMRC to make repayments before the completion of the enquiry, but an HMRC officer may, before the enquiry concludes, make a repayment on a provisional basis to such extent as the officer thinks is appropriate.

Where a notice of enquiry is given into an ordinary tax return for a tax year, and notice of an enquiry into a Sch 2 return in respect of a relevant disposal in that tax year has not been given, the main enquiry notice is also taken to constitute a notice of enquiry into the Sch 2 return.

Where a final closure notice is given relating to the ordinary tax return for a tax year, but no final closure notice relating to the Sch 2 return has been given, the main closure notice is also taken to constitute a final closure notice of the enquiry into the Sch 2 return.

The ordinary rules relating to Revenue determinations (TMA 1970, s 28C) apply to Sch 2 returns, subject to minor modifications:

- References to notices and to filing dates are to be taken to include references to Sch 2 returns and notional CGT payments and 'amount to be determined' refers to the amount of CGT notionally chargeable at the filing date.
- A determination may not be made after the end of the period of three years

beginning with the last day for delivery of an ordinary tax return (three years from 31 January following the end of the year of assessment or four years after the company year end).

- If a determination is made and is then superseded by submission of a Sch 2 return, any amount payable or repayable as a result is payable or repayable on the filing date for the Sch 2 return.

Discovery assessments: para 23

A Sch 2 return is treated for the purposes of the discovery provisions as if it were an assessment required to be included as part of the person's ordinary tax return (whether or not they are actually required to deliver an ordinary tax return) and references in the discovery provisions to an ordinary tax return for a tax year include any Sch 2 returns in respect of disposals for the tax year concerned.

Consequential amendments: paras 25–29

Provision	Amendment
TMA 1970	
s 7A (disregard of certain NRCGT gains for purposes of s 7)	Omitted
s 12ZA–12ZN (NRCGT returns) and preceding italic heading	Omitted
s 28A (completion of enquiry into personal or trustee return)	Omit references to 'NRCGT return'
s 28G (determination of amount notionally chargeable where no NRCGT return delivered)	Omitted
s 29(7)(a)(ia) (assessment where loss of tax discovered)	Omitted
s 29A (non-resident CGT disposals: determination of amount which should have been assessed)	Omitted
s 34(1A) (ordinary time limit of 4 years)	Omitted
s 42(11)(a) (procedure for making claims etc)	Omit references to 'NRCGT return'
New s 59AZA payments on account of CGT: disposals of land, etc	For provision requiring CGT payments on account, see Sch 2
s 59AA (non-resident CGT disposals: payments on account of CGT)	Omitted
s 59B(2A) (payment of income tax and CGT: assessments other than simple assessments)	Omitted & references to Sch 2 inserted
s 59BA(1)(b) (payment of income tax and CGT: simple assessments)	References to Sch 2 inserted
s 107A(2)(b) (relevant trustees)	References to Sch 2 inserted
s 118 (interpretation)	Omit references to 'NRCGT return'
Sch 3ZA	Omit references to ss 12ZA–12ZN and NRCGT
TCGA 1992	
ss 222A(6)(a) & 222A(7)(a) (determination of main residence: disposals by non-residents)	References to Sch 2 inserted

s 223A(3)(b) (amount of relief: disposals by non-residents)	References to Sch 2 inserted
FA 2007	
Sch 24, para 1(4),	References to Sch 2 inserted
para 21C	References to Sch 2 inserted
FA 2008	
New Sch 36, para 21ZA	References to Sch 2 inserted
FA 2009	
Sch 55, para 1(5) (table), (penalty for failure to make returns)	References to Sch 2 inserted with effect from 12 February 2019
Sch 56, para 1(4) (table), (penalty for failure to make payments)	References to Sch 2 inserted with effect from 12 February 2019

SCHEDULE 3

OFFSHORE RECEIPTS IN RESPECT OF INTANGIBLE PROPERTY

Section 15

1 ITTOIA 2005 is amended as follows.

2 (1) Section 574 (overview of Part 5) is amended as follows.

(2) In subsection (1) after paragraph (a) insert—

"(aa) Chapter 2A (offshore receipts in respect of intangible property),".

(3) In subsection (2) at the end insert "(but see section 608X)".

3 (1) Section 576 (priority between Chapters within Part 5) is amended as follows.

(2) The existing provision becomes subsection (2) of that section.

(3) Before that subsection insert—

"(1) Any income, so far as it falls within Chapter 2 (receipts from intellectual property) and Chapter 2A (offshore receipts in respect of intangible property), is dealt with under Chapter 2."

4 After section 608 insert—

"Chapter 2A

Offshore Receipts in Respect of Intangible Property

Charge to tax on offshore receipts in respect of intangible property

608A Charge to tax on UK-derived amounts

(1) This section applies if—

(a) at any time in a tax year, a person is not UK resident and is not resident in a full treaty territory, and

(b) UK-derived amounts arise to the person in the tax year.

(2) Income tax is charged on the UK-derived amounts.

(3) See—

sections 608D to 608H for the meaning of expressions used in this section;
sections 608J to 608N for exemptions from the charge under this section.

(4) References in the Tax Acts to income from a source in the United Kingdom include UK-derived amounts.

608B Income charged under section 608A

Tax is charged under section 608A on the full amount of the UK-derived amounts arising in the tax year.

608C Person liable for tax under section 608A

The person liable for any tax charged under section 608A is the person receiving or entitled to the UK-derived amounts.

608D Meaning of residence

(1) This section applies for the purposes of this Chapter.

(2) A person is "resident" in a territory if, under the laws of the territory, the person is liable to tax there—

(a) by reason of the person's domicile, residence or place of management, but

(b) not in respect only of income from sources in that territory or capital situated there.

(3) Where—

(a) a person is resident in a territory outside the United Kingdom generally for the purposes of the laws of the territory or for particular purposes under those laws, and

(b) the laws of the territory have no provision for a person to be resident there for tax purposes,

the person is "resident" in the territory.

608E Meaning of "full treaty territory"

(1) For the purposes of this Chapter a territory is a "full treaty territory" if—

(a) double taxation arrangements have been made in relation to the territory, and

(b) the arrangements contain a non-discrimination provision.

(2) In subsection (1) "non-discrimination provision", in relation to double taxation arrangements, means a provision to the effect that nationals of a state which is a party to those arrangements (a "contracting state") are not to be subject in the other contracting state to—

(a) any taxation, or

(b) any requirement connected with taxation,

which is other or more burdensome than the taxation and connected requirements to which nationals of that other contracting state in the same circumstances (in particular with respect to residence) are or may be subjected.

(3) In subsection (2) "national", in relation to a contracting state, includes—

(a) an individual possessing the nationality or citizenship of the contracting state, and

(b) a legal person, partnership or association deriving its status as such from the laws in force in that contracting state.

608F Meaning of "UK-derived amount" and "UK sales"

(1) For the purposes of this Chapter an amount is a "UK-derived amount" if—

(a) it is an amount (whether of a revenue or capital nature) in respect of the enjoyment or exercise of rights that constitute any intangible property, and

(b) the enjoyment or exercise of those rights (or of any rights derived, directly or indirectly, from those rights) enables, facilitates or promotes UK sales (directly or indirectly).

(2) It does not matter whether the amount relates to UK sales in the tax year mentioned in section 608A or any other tax year.

(3) In this Chapter "UK sales" means any services, goods or other property—

(a) provided in the United Kingdom, or

(b) provided to persons in the United Kingdom.

608G Section 608F: apportionment of amounts

(1) This section applies where—

(a) a person receives or is entitled to an amount in respect of the enjoyment or exercise of rights that constitute any intangible property, and that enjoyment or exercise enables, facilitates or promotes UK sales and other sales, or

(b) a person receives or is entitled to an amount in respect of—

(i) the enjoyment or exercise of rights that constitute any intangible property, where that enjoyment or exercise enables, facilitates or promotes UK sales, and

(ii) anything else.

(2) The amount is to be regarded for the purposes of this Chapter as constituting a UK-derived amount to such extent as is just and reasonable.

(3) In a case within subsection (1)(a) it is to be presumed, unless the contrary is shown, that the proportion of the amount that is just and reasonable is—

$X / (X + Y)$

where X is the value of UK sales and Y is the value of other sales.

608H Meaning of "intangible property"

(1) In this Chapter "intangible property" means any property except—

(a) tangible property,

(b) an estate, interest or right in or over land,

(c) a right in respect of anything within paragraph (a) or (b),

(d) a financial asset,

(e) a share or other right in relation to the profits, governance or winding up of a company, or
(f) any property of a prescribed description.

(2) In this section—

"financial asset" has the meaning given by section 806 of CTA 2009;
"prescribed" means prescribed by regulations made by the Treasury.

608I Application of Chapter to certain partnerships

(1) This section applies where, under the laws of a full treaty territory, a partnership is regarded for tax purposes as an entity separate and distinct from the partners.

(2) If the partnership is resident in the full treaty territory at any time, each of the partners is treated for the purposes of this Chapter as resident in the territory at that time.

(3) Section 608D(2) applies for the purposes of determining whether the partnership is resident in the territory at any time (references there to a person being read as references to the partnership).

(4) Nothing in this section affects the application of section 848 (firm not to be regarded as entity separate and distinct from partners) or any other provision of Part 9 (partnerships) to this Chapter.

Exemptions

608J Exemption where limited UK sales

(1) Section 608A does not apply in relation to a person for a tax year if the total value of the person's UK sales in that tax year does not exceed £10,000,000.

(2) Where—

(a) a person (A), or a person connected with A, receives or is entitled to an amount (whether of a revenue or capital nature), and
(b) the amount relates (wholly or in part, and directly or indirectly) to the provision of services, goods or other property constituting UK sales,

the UK sales are regarded for the purposes of subsection (1) as A's UK sales.

608K Exemption where business undertaken within territory of residence

(1) Section 608A does not apply in relation to a person ("the relevant person") for a tax year if—

(a) the relevant person is resident in a territory throughout the tax year,
(b) all (or substantially all) relevant activity in relation to relevant intangible property is, and has at all times been, undertaken in that territory,
(c) there is no relevant connection between relevant intangible property and a related person, and
(d) the person makes a claim under this section.

(2) For the purposes of this section intangible property is "relevant" if any UK-derived amount arising to the person in the tax year relates to it.

(3) In subsection (1)(b) "relevant activity", in relation to relevant intangible property, means anything done (by any person)—

(a) for the purpose of creating, developing or maintaining any of the relevant intangible property; or
(b) for the purpose of generating, for the relevant person, amounts (whether of a revenue or capital nature) that relate, wholly or in part and directly or indirectly, to the enjoyment or exercise of rights that constitute any of the relevant intangible property.

(4) For the purposes of subsection (1)(c) there is a "relevant connection" between relevant intangible property and a related person if any relevant intangible property—

(a) has been transferred (directly or indirectly) from a person related to the relevant person,
(b) derives (directly or indirectly) from anything so transferred, or
(c) derives (directly or indirectly) from intangible property held by a person related to the relevant person.

(5) See section 608T for the meaning of two persons being "related".

608L Exemption where foreign tax at least half of UK tax

(1) Section 608A does not apply in relation to a person for a tax year if—

(a) the person is resident in a territory outside the United Kingdom in that year,

(b) the amount of tax ("the local tax amount") which is paid in the territory in respect of UK-derived amounts arising in the tax year is at least half of the corresponding UK tax, and

(c) the local tax amount is not determined under designer tax provisions.

(2) See section 608M for provisions about the local tax amount.

(3) "The corresponding UK tax" means the amount of income tax that would be charged under this Chapter in respect of UK-derived amounts arising in the tax year, calculated on the following basis—

(a) section 608A applies in relation to the UK-derived amounts, and

(b) the person is not entitled to any relief or allowance for the tax year.

(4) "Designer tax provisions" means provisions which appear to the Commissioners to be designed to enable persons to exercise significant control over the amount of tax which they pay in respect of UK-derived amounts.

608M Section 608L: the local tax amount

(1) This section applies for the purposes of section 608L.

(2) Where an amount of tax is paid in the territory in respect of—

(a) UK-derived amounts arising in the tax year, and

(b) other amounts,

the amount of tax is to be apportioned between the amounts mentioned in paragraph (a) and paragraph (b) on a just and reasonable basis.

(3) Where—

(a) in the territory any tax falls to be paid in respect of UK-derived amounts arising in the tax year,

(b) under the laws of the territory, a repayment of tax, or a payment in respect of credit for tax, is made to any person, and

(c) that repayment or payment is directly or indirectly in respect of the whole or part of the tax mentioned in paragraph (a),

the local tax amount is to be reduced by the amount of that repayment or payment (but this is subject to subsections (4) and (5)).

(4) Subsection (5) applies if the repayment or payment mentioned in subsection (3)(b) is in respect of—

(a) the tax mentioned in subsection (3)(a), and

(b) other tax.

(5) The amount of the repayment or payment is to be apportioned between the tax mentioned in subsection (3)(a) and the other tax on a just and reasonable basis, and the reduction under subsection (3) is limited to the amount apportioned to the tax mentioned in subsection (3)(a).

(6) Any reduction under subsection (3) is to be undertaken after any apportionment under subsection (2).

608N Exemptions: further provision

(1) The Treasury may by regulations—

(a) amend this Chapter for the purpose of creating additional exemptions;

(b) amend any exemption for the time being in force.

(2) "Exemption" means a total or partial exemption from the charge under this Chapter.

(3) The regulations may confer a power to make subordinate legislation or confer a discretion on any person.

(4) The regulations may make retrospective provision, except insofar as they impose or increase taxation.

(5) A statutory instrument containing regulations under this section may not be made unless a draft of the instrument has been laid before and approved by a resolution of the House of Commons.

Recovery of tax from person in same control group

608O Notice requiring payment from person in same control group as taxpayer

(1) This section applies where—

(a) an amount of income tax has been assessed on a person ("the taxpayer") for a tax year by virtue of this Chapter, and

(b) the whole or any part of that amount, or of any interest on that amount, is unpaid at the end of the period of 6 months after the relevant date.

(2) A designated officer may give a notice to a relevant person requiring that person, within 30 days of the giving of the notice, to pay any unpaid tax and interest.

(3) The notice must state—

(a) the amount of income tax and interest that remains unpaid,

(b) the date when the income tax first became payable, and

(c) the relevant person's right of appeal.

(4) A notice under this section may not be given more than 3 years and 6 months after the relevant date.

(5) In this section "relevant person" means any person who was in the same control group as the taxpayer at any time in the tax year (see section 608S for the meaning of being in the same "control group").

(6) In this section "the relevant date" means—

(a) in relation to an amount of income tax determined under section 28C of TMA 1970, the date on which the determination was issued;

(b) in relation to an amount of income tax under a self-assessment in a case where the taxpayer's return under section 8 or 8A of TMA 1970 was delivered after the last day for delivering it in accordance with that section, the date on which the return was delivered;

(c) in any other case, the date the amount mentioned in subsection (1)(a) became due and payable.

(7) A notice may be given anywhere in the world, to any relevant person (whether or not UK resident).

(8) In this section—

"assessment": any reference to an amount of income tax that has been assessed on a person includes an amount of income tax that has been determined under section 28C of TMA 1970 in relation to the person;

"designated officer" means an officer of Revenue and Customs who has been designated by the Commissioners for the purposes of this Chapter.

608P Payment notice: effect

(1) This section applies where a notice under section 608O is given to a person.

(2) For the purposes of the recovery from the person of any unpaid tax and interest (including interest accruing after the date of the notice), the person is treated as if—

(a) the amount of income tax assessed as mentioned in section 608O(1)(a) had been assessed on the person,

(b) that amount became due and payable when the tax mentioned in section 608O(1)(a) became due and payable, and

(c) any payments made in respect of the amount mentioned in section 608O(1)(a) (or in respect of interest on that amount) had been made in respect of the amount treated as assessed by virtue of paragraph (a) of this subsection (or in respect of interest on that amount).

(3) Nothing in subsection (2) gives the person a right to appeal against the assessment mentioned in section 608O(1)(a) (or against any assessment treated as made by virtue of subsection (2) of this section).

(4) Any appeal by the taxpayer against the assessment mentioned in section 608O(1)(a) does not affect the liabilities arising by virtue of the giving of the notice.

608Q Payment notice: appeals

(1) This section applies where a notice under section 608O is given to a person.

(2) The person may appeal against the notice, within the period of 30 days beginning with the date on which it is given, on the ground that the person is not a relevant person (as defined by section 608O).

(3) Where an appeal is made, anything required by the notice to be paid is due and payable as if there had been no appeal.

(4) Section 56 of TMA 1970 (payment of tax where further appeal) applies in relation to any further appeal against the notice, but the relevant court or tribunal may, on the application of Her Majesty's Revenue and Customs, direct that section 56(2) does not apply to anything required by the notice to be paid.

(5) A direction may be given if the relevant court or tribunal considers it necessary for the protection of the revenue.

(6) In this section "relevant court or tribunal" has the same meaning as in section 56 of TMA 1970.

608R Payment notice: effect of making payment etc

(1) This section applies where a notice under section 608O is given to a person.

(2) A person who pays an amount in pursuance of the notice may recover that amount from the taxpayer.

(3) In calculating the person's income, profits or losses for any tax purposes—

(a) a payment in pursuance of the notice is not allowed as a deduction, and
(b) the reimbursement of any such payment is not regarded as a receipt.

(4) Any amount paid by the person in pursuance of the notice is to be taken into account in calculating—

(a) the amount unpaid, and
(b) the amount due by virtue of any other notice under section 608O relating to the amount unpaid.

(5) Similarly, any payment by the taxpayer of any of the amount unpaid is to be taken into account in calculating the amount due by virtue of the notice (or by virtue of any other notice under section 608O relating to the amount unpaid).

Meaning of "control group" and "related person"

608S Control groups

(1) Two persons are in the same control group at any time if—

(a) they are consolidated for accounting purposes for a period which includes that time,
(b) one of them has a 51% investment in the other at that time, or
(c) a third person has a 51% investment in each of them at that time.

(2) Two persons are consolidated for accounting purposes for a period if—

(a) their financial results for the period are required to be comprised in group accounts,
(b) their financial results for the period would be required to be comprised in group accounts but for the application of an exemption, or
(c) their financial results for the period are in fact comprised in group accounts.

(3) In this section "group accounts" means accounts prepared under—

(a) section 399 of the Companies Act 2006, or
(b) any corresponding provision of the law of a territory outside the United Kingdom.

(4) For the meaning of having a 51% investment, see section 608U.

608T Related persons

(1) Two persons are "related" at any time if—

(a) at that time—

(i) they are in the same control group,
(ii) one of them has a 25% investment in the other, or
(iii) a third person has a 25% investment in both of them, or

(b) at any time in the period of 6 months beginning or ending at that time—

(i) one of them directly or indirectly participates in the management, control or capital of the other, or
(ii) a third person directly or indirectly participates in the management, control or capital of both of them.

(2) See—

section 608S for the meaning of being in the same "control group";
section 608U for the meaning of having a 25% investment;
section 608V for the meaning of direct or indirect participation in the management, control or capital of a person.

608U Meaning of "51% investment" and "25% investment"

(1) A person (P) has a 51% investment in another person (C) if any of the following apply—

(a) P possesses or is entitled to acquire more than half of the voting power in C;
(b) in the event of a disposal of the whole of the equity in C, P would receive more than half of the proceeds;
(c) in the event that the income in respect of the equity in C were distributed among the equity holders in C, P would receive more than half of the amount so distributed;
(d) in the event of a winding-up of C or in any other circumstances, P would receive more than half of C's assets which would then be available for distribution among the equity holders in C in respect of the equity in C.

(2) A person (P) has a 25% investment in another person (C) where any paragraph of subsection (1) would apply if in that paragraph for "more than half" there were substituted "at least a quarter".

(3) Section 464(2) to (11) and section 465 of TIOPA 2010 apply for the purposes of subsections (1) and (2) of this section.

(4) In the application of section 464(10) of TIOPA for the purposes of subsection (1), the reference to a "25% investment" is to be read as a "51% investment".

608V Meaning of direct or indirect participation in management, control or capital

(1) This section applies for the purposes of section 608T.

(2) A person is directly participating in the management, control or capital of another person at a particular time only if section 157 of TIOPA 2010 so provides.

(3) A person is indirectly participating in the management, control or capital of another person at a particular time only if section 159 or 160 of TIOPA 2010 so provides.

General

608W Anti-avoidance

(1) This section applies if a person has entered into any arrangements the main purpose, or one of the main purposes, of which is to obtain a tax advantage for the person as a result (wholly or partly) of—

(a) anything not being subject to the charge under section 608A, or
(b) any provisions of double taxation arrangements having effect in a case where the advantage is contrary to the object and purpose of the provisions.

(2) The tax advantage is to be counteracted by the making of such adjustments as are just and reasonable.

(3) The adjustments may be made (whether by an officer of Revenue and Customs or the person) by way of an assessment, the modification of an assessment, amendment or disallowance of a claim, or otherwise.

(4) Where this section applies by virtue of subsection (1)(b), the counteraction has effect despite section 6(1) of TIOPA 2010.

(5) In this section "tax advantage" includes—

(a) relief or increased relief from tax,
(b) repayment or increased repayment of tax,
(c) avoidance or reduction of a charge to tax or an assessment to tax,

(d) avoidance of a possible assessment to tax,
(e) deferral of a payment of tax or advancement of a repayment of tax, and
(f) avoidance of an obligation to deduct or account for tax.

608X Interaction with other general provisions

(1) This section applies where section 608A applies in relation to a person for a tax year (or would apply, if the following provisions of this section applied).

(2) Part 6 (exempt income) does not apply in relation to UK-derived amounts arising to the person in the tax year.

(3) For the purposes of calculating the person's liability to income tax for the tax year—

(a) Chapter 1 of Part 14 of ITA 2007 (limits on liability to income tax of non-residents) does not apply in relation to UK-derived amounts arising to the person in the tax year;
(b) accordingly, the person's liability is the sum of—
(i) the person's liability as regards UK-derived amounts (with that Chapter not applying), and
(ii) the person's liability as regards anything else (with that Chapter applying, to the extent it would otherwise apply).

608Y Appeals against assessments

(1) This section applies where a person ("the taxpayer") makes an appeal in relation to an amount of income tax charged on the taxpayer under section 608A.

(2) Section 55(3) to (8A) of TMA 1970 (application for postponement of payment of tax pending appeal) do not apply in relation to the tax charged (and no agreement as to the postponement of payment of any of that tax, or of interest on it, may be made).

(3) In the case of a further appeal, the relevant court or tribunal (as defined by section 56 of TMA 1970) may, on the application of Her Majesty's Revenue and Customs, direct that section 56(2) of TMA 1970 does not apply to the tax charged.

(4) A direction may be given if the relevant court or tribunal considers it necessary for the protection of the revenue.

(5) Nothing in this section applies in relation to a liability arising as a result of the giving of a notice under section 608O.

Interpretation: general

608Z Interpretation of Chapter: general

In this Chapter—

"arrangements" includes any agreement, understanding, scheme, transaction or series of transactions (whether or not legally enforceable);
"the Commissioners" means the Commissioners for Her Majesty's Revenue and Customs;
"control group" has the meaning given by section 608S;
"double taxation arrangements" means arrangements that have effect under section 2(1) of TIOPA 2010;
"full treaty territory" has the meaning given by section 608E;
"intangible property" has the meaning given by section 608H;
"related": references to two persons being related are to be read in accordance with section 608T;
"resident": references to being resident in a territory are to be read in accordance with section 608D;
"UK-derived amount" has the meaning given by section 608F;
"UK sales" has the meaning given by section 608F."

5 In section 873(3) (procedure for orders and regulations) before paragraph (c) insert—

"(ba) section 608N (offshore receipts in respect of intangible property),".

6 (1) TIOPA 2010 is amended as follows.

(2) In section 157(1) (direct participation)—

(a) omit the "and" at the end of paragraph (d);
(b) at the end of paragraph (e) insert ", and

(f) section 608T of ITTOIA 2005."

(3) In section 159(1) (indirect participation: potential direct participant)—
 (a) omit the "and" at the end of paragraph (d);
 (b) at the end of paragraph (e) insert ", and
 (f) section 608T of ITTOIA 2005."

(4) In section 160(1) (indirect participation: one of several major participants)—
 (a) omit the "and" at the end of paragraph (d);
 (b) at the end of paragraph (e) insert ", and
 (f) section 608T of ITTOIA 2005."

7 The amendments made by this Schedule have effect for the tax year 2019–20 and subsequent tax years.

8 In section 608W of ITTOIA 2005 (inserted by paragraph 4 of this Schedule) the reference to arrangements is to arrangements made on or after 29 October 2018.

9 The Treasury may by regulations make such amendments of the Tax Acts as they consider appropriate in consequence of any of the preceding provisions of this Schedule.

10 The Treasury may by regulations amend Chapter 2A of Part 5 of ITTOIA 2005 (inserted by paragraph 4 of this Schedule).

11 Regulations under paragraph 10 may—
 (a) make any provision that could be made by an Act;
 (b) make incidental, supplementary, consequential or transitional provision or savings.

The consequential provision that may be made includes provision amending any Act (or any instrument under an Act).

12 Regulations under paragraph 10 may not make provision having effect before 29 October 2018.

13 No regulations under paragraph 10 may be made after 31 December 2019.

14 A statutory instrument containing (whether alone or with other provision) regulations under paragraph 10 may not be made unless a draft of the instrument has been laid before and approved by a resolution of the House of Commons.

COMMENTARY ON SCHEDULE 3

Section 15 introduces Sch 3 which contains provisions imposing a new income tax charge on offshore receipts in respect of intangible property. The rules are complex yet targeted in scope, with the aim of applying UK income tax solely to foreign IP owners with low taxation and low substance.

The new legislation is a product of a consultation process which began in December 2017 titled 'Royalties Withholding Tax'. The consultation was part of a broader discussion around the taxation of digital businesses and linked to the OECD's Action 1 output regarding the tax challenges of the digital economy. The stated policy aim of the new legislation is to tackle erosion of the UK tax base via intra-group licensing arrangements that achieve an artificially low effective tax rate.

A key point to note is that the measure introduced in Sch 3 is no longer a withholding tax, but a direct income tax charge on a non-UK resident company. The rules are inserted in ITTOIA 2005 as Chapter 2A, ss 608A–Z, such that they directly follow Chapter 2 (which concerns other matters where a UK income tax charge is levied in relation to intellectual property receipts).

ITTOIA 2005, s 608A provides the broad scope of the new measures: that 'UK derived amounts' will be taxable for persons who are (at any time during the tax year), resident in a jurisdiction that is not a 'full treaty territory'. The person receiving such amounts will then be liable to UK income tax on those amounts.

ITTOIA 2005, ss 608D and E provide further clarification of residence and a 'full treaty territory' for these purposes. A 'full treaty territory' is any jurisdiction with which the UK has a double tax treaty that contains the non-discrimination clause. This of course means that only a minority of jurisdictions across the globe are within the scope of the measures. The UK has the largest treaty network in the world and looks to include a non-discrimination clause in the majority of those treaties. Jurisdictions that fall within the scope of the measures are therefore, in the main, those that could be considered a 'tax haven'. There are some notable exceptions though: to take an example, the UK does not have a tax treaty with Brazil. Other jurisdictions without a full treaty with the UK are likely to be mainly developing countries.

ITTOIA 2005, ss 608F–H contain details on how to define and quantify a 'UK derived amount'. The essence of these subsections is to define these amounts in a broad sense – capturing any intangible property receipts that somehow link to revenues derived from UK persons, or based on UK activities. Intangible property is again defined broadly, to encompass all property except those items that have been listed as excluded. The law provides that amounts should be attributed to UK sales based on a just and reasonable apportionment, with the default position being an apportionment based on overall sales.

There are several important points to note here. Firstly, the definition of intangible property is broader than the definition contained in CTA 2009, s 712 which UK tax practitioners will be familiar with. Therefore, there may be types of property which are within the scope of the measures that would not be intangible assets for UK corporation tax purposes. The amounts which are within scope in relation to such intangibles is also defined broadly – it is not only royalty payments in respect of IP that are within the scope of the measures, but also IP disposal gains and other payments in relation to IP transfers.

The reference to a just and reasonable apportionment, and a sales fraction being the default position in defining such an apportionment, mirrors the 2016 royalty withholding tax and diverted profits tax changes. Further, sales as a driving force for the tax charge appears again in the definition of a UK derived amount. Taxpayers and HMRC will need to give due thought to appropriate mechanisms to apportioning their intangible property receipts between UK derived amounts and other amounts, considering the weight that the legislation places on sales.

In general, IP rights provide protection against infringement by other parties. Payments in respect of IP are then made in respect of activities which would otherwise infringe upon those rights, if not for a license or other arrangement in respect of the rights. Sales figures may therefore not always be an appropriate reasonable measure to understand why payments in respect of IP exploitation are made. Payments in respect of customer distribution rights over IP may easily be traced to sales figures. Payments in respect of manufacturing know-how, for example, may be more reasonably placed to the location of the manufacturing site (and not to location of sales activities). However, given the reference in the new law to direct or indirect enablement, facilitation or promotion of UK sales, we can expect HMRC's focus and default position to be an apportionment of sales figures, even where some of those activities occur in different accounting periods to the recognition of the sales.

ITTOIA 2005, s 608I ensures that partnerships which are treated as opaque for overseas tax purposes and resident in a full treaty territory are outside the scope of the new measures in line with ITTOIA 2005, s 608D.

ITTOIA 2005, ss 608J–N contain exemptions which, subject to meeting conditions, would render a non-resident fully outside the scope of the charge.

ITTOIA 2005, s 608J is an exemption based on quantum of UK sales – which is set at £10m. Sales of all connected persons must be aggregated, hence there is no need for the IP owner to also be a customer facing entity in respect of all sales. This exemption is included such that only large groups are within the scope of the measure. Given the pairing of these measures with the introduction of Digital Services Tax in targeting the tax challenges of the digital economy, the £10m threshold is noteworthy when compared to the £25m proposed threshold for Digital Services Tax in HMT's consultation document.

It should be noted that the £10m threshold is not a requirement for turnover in a UK resident company, but in relation to any UK sales. The legislation contains no requirement for a group to have any corporate tax presence in the UK – merely that sales are made to UK persons or provided in the UK. It is of course feasible that groups without a UK tax presence could fall within the scope of the measures.

No claim is required in respect of ITTOIA 2005, s 608J, such that there is no requirement to act placed on small and medium sized businesses.

ITTOIA 2005, s 608K is an exemption based on genuine business activity. A company is exempt from the charge where development, enhancement, maintenance and exploitation occurs, in the main, in the country of residence (and always has done). The section is drafted narrowly such that only those groups with genuine IP related activities offshore may meet the exemption. Subsection (4) reinforces that those IP activities must always have taken place in the relevant jurisdiction, with the IP not having been transferred in from a related person. Related persons is defined at s 608T.

A claim is required in respect of ITTOIA 2005, s 608K. We can expect HMRC to carefully consider the facts of any claim submitted given the narrow drafting.

ITTOIA 2005, s 608L is an exemption based on a comparison of the actual tax suffered on UK derived amounts, and the UK income tax that would have been suffered on the same amounts under these provisions. Where the actual tax suffered is at least 50% of the comparable UK tax charge, the exemption may apply. No theoretical exemption or allowance is given to the UK comparable, hence a straight 20% calculation is deemed (based on the current basic rate of income tax). Subject to specific adjustments to the tax base in the overseas jurisdiction, this broadly provides a 10% tax rate benchmark for the exemption.

Only local tax suffered in the jurisdiction of relevance is considered in ITTOIA 2005, s 608L. Third country withholding taxes or CFC charges are not considered, and the rules do not consider a credit mechanism for any taxes suffered on the same amounts. While certain overseas jurisdictions may give credit for any UK tax suffered on the same amounts, others may not. It is also plausible that the same profits could ultimately be subject to both the new income tax charge, and a Diverted Profits Tax charge. There is certainly the risk of double taxation on that basis. A lack of a crediting mechanism is likely not to be an omission on the UK legislator's part, but intentional given the nature of the provisions in tackling avoidance by use of low-tax, low-substance IP owners.

No claim is required in respect of ITTOIA 2005, s 608L, such that there is no requirement to act placed on groups with an adequately taxable IP owner. This is likely to deal with the issue created by s 608E in that Brazil and other developing jurisdictions without a full treaty with the UK could be within the scope of the measures. Sections 608E and 608L together should ensure that only low tax jurisdictions where the risk of avoidance is heightened are within the scope of the measures.

ITTOIA 2005, ss 608O–R contain notice and enforcement provisions. Section 608O enforces joint and severable liability on any entity within the same control group as the entity subject to the charge. In practice this means that HMRC can, where possible, collect the tax due from a UK resident company in the same group. Control group is defined at ITTOIA 2005, s 608S.

ITTOIA 2005, s 608T contains an anti-avoidance provision which applies a just and reasonable counteraction to certain arrangements which have a main purpose of obtaining a tax advantage. That tax advantage must be as a result of either avoiding the charge to income tax contained in these measures, or artificially obtaining the benefits of a treaty such that the exclusion for full treaty jurisdictions applies. No particular exclusion from the anti-avoidance rule is included for a genuine commercial restructuring. Groups looking to unwind a low-tax low-substance structure, i e to transfer IP rights to a jurisdiction with a higher tax rate and/or more appropriate IP related activities occurring will need to consider this section carefully, perhaps including open dialogue with HMRC on their interpretation of the measure.

SCHEDULE 4

AVOIDANCE INVOLVING PROFIT FRAGMENTATION ARRANGEMENTS

Section 16

Introduction and overview

1 (1) This Schedule contains provision about countering the tax effects of certain arrangements ("profit fragmentation arrangements").

(2) Profit fragmentation arrangements involve the following parties—

(a) a person resident in the United Kingdom ("the resident party"),

(b) an overseas person or entity ("the overseas party") who is not resident in the United Kingdom, and

(c) an individual (a "related individual") who is—

(i) the resident party,

(ii) a member of a partnership of which the resident party is a partner, or

(iii) a participator in a company which is the resident party.

(3) An "overseas person or entity" means—

(a) a person abroad within the meaning given by section 718 of ITA 2007, or

(b) a company, partnership, trust or other entity or arrangements established or having effect under the law of a country or territory outside the United Kingdom (regardless of whether it has legal personality as a body corporate).

(4) Paragraphs 2 to 6 deal with the definition of profit fragmentation arrangements.

(5) Paragraph 7 deals with the adjustments which must be made to counteract the effects of such arrangements.

(6) Other provisions of this Schedule—

(a) deal with double taxation and the tax treatment of reimbursement payments (paragraphs 8 and 9), and

(b) deal with interpretation and commencement (paragraphs 10 to 12).

Profit fragmentation arrangements

2 (1) Arrangements are "profit fragmentation arrangements" if—

(a) provision has been made or imposed as between the resident party and the overseas party by means of the arrangements ("the material provision"),

(b) as a result of the material provision, value is transferred from the resident party to the overseas party which derives directly or indirectly from the profits of a business chargeable to income tax or corporation tax (see paragraph 3),

(c) the value transferred is greater than it would have been if it had resulted from provision made or imposed as between independent parties acting at arm's length, and

(d) any of the enjoyment conditions are met in relation to a related individual (see paragraph 4).

(2) But arrangements are not "profit fragmentation arrangements" if—

(a) the material provision does not result in a tax mismatch for a tax period of the resident party (see paragraphs 5 and 6), or

(b) it is not reasonable to conclude that the main purpose, or one of the main purposes, for which the arrangements were entered into was to obtain a tax advantage.

(3) For the purposes of sub-paragraph (1)(a) provision made or imposed as between a partnership of which the resident party is a member and the overseas party is to be regarded as provision made or imposed as between the resident party and the overseas party.

Transfer of value deriving directly or indirectly from a business

3 (1) In determining whether value deriving directly or indirectly from a business is transferred from the resident party to the overseas party, account is to be taken of any method, however indirect, by which—

(a) any property or right is transferred or transmitted, or
(b) the value of any property or right is enhanced or diminished.

(2) Sub-paragraph (1) applies in particular to—

(a) sales, contracts and other transactions made otherwise than for full consideration or for more than full consideration,
(b) any method by which any property or right, or the control of any property or right, is transferred or transmitted by assigning—
(i) share capital or other rights in a company,
(ii) rights in a partnership, or
(iii) an interest in settled property,
(c) the creation of an option affecting the disposition of any property or right and the giving of consideration for granting it,
(d) the creation of a requirement for consent affecting such a disposition and the giving of consideration for granting it,
(e) the creation of an embargo affecting such a disposition and the giving of consideration for releasing it, and
(f) the disposal of any property or right on the winding up, dissolution or termination of a company, partnership or trust.

(3) Value may be traced through any number of individuals, companies, partnerships, trusts and other entities or arrangements.

(4) The property held by a company, partnership, trust or other entity or under any arrangements must be attributed to the shareholders, partners or members, beneficiaries or other participants at each stage on a just and reasonable basis.

The enjoyment conditions

4 (1) The enjoyment conditions are met in relation to a related individual if—

(a) it is reasonable to conclude that some or all of the value transferred as a result of the material provision relates to something done by, or any property or purported right of, the individual, and
(b) either of the conditions in sub-paragraph (2) is met.

(2) The conditions are that—

(a) under the arrangements—
(i) the value transferred, or part of it, is so dealt with by any person as to be calculated at some time to enure for the benefit of the individual,
(ii) the value transferred, or part of it, operates to increase the value of any assets which the individual holds or are held for the benefit of the individual,
(iii) the individual receives or is entitled to receive any benefit provided or to be provided out of the value transferred or part of it,
(iv) the individual may become entitled to the beneficial enjoyment of the value transferred, or part of it, if one or more powers are exercised or successively exercised (and for those purposes it does not matter who may exercise the powers or whether they are exercisable with or without the consent of another person), or
(v) the individual (whether acting alone or together with any other person) is able in any manner to control directly or indirectly the application of the value transferred or part of it, or
(b) it is reasonable to conclude that the individual (whether acting alone or with any other person) procured the transfer of value from the resident party to the overseas party in such a way as to avoid the conditions in paragraph (a) being met.

(3) In determining whether the conditions in sub-paragraph (2)(a) are met in relation to an individual and the value transferred as a result of the material provision, all benefits which may at any time accrue to a person as a result of the value being transferred must be taken into account, irrespective of—

(a) the nature or form of the benefits, or
(b) whether the person has legal or equitable rights in respect of the benefits.

(4) For the purposes of sub-paragraphs (2) and (3), references to an individual include a reference to any person connected with that individual and, for the purposes of this paragraph, section 993 of ITA 2007 (meaning of "connected") has effect but as if—

(a) subsection (4) of that section were omitted, and

(b) members of a partnership in which the individual is also a member were not "associates" of the individual for the purposes of sections 450 and 451 of CTA 2010 ("control").

(5) For the purposes of sub-paragraph (4), an individual is treated as connected with a person or entity if—

(a) the individual or a person connected with the individual (whether acting alone or with any other person)—

(i) is able to secure that the person or entity acts in accordance with the wishes of the individual or any person connected with the individual,

(ii) is able to acquire rights which would enable the individual or any person connected with the individual to secure that the person or entity acts in accordance with the wishes of the individual or any person connected with the individual, or

(iii) is able to exercise significant influence over the person or entity (whether or not as a result of a legal entitlement of the individual or any person connected with the individual), or

(b) the person or entity can reasonably be expected to act, or typically acts, in accordance with the wishes of the individual or a person connected with the individual.

Tax mismatch

5 (1) The material provision results in a tax mismatch for a tax period of the resident party if—

(a) in that period, in relation to a relevant tax, it results in one or both of—

(i) an increase in the expenses of the resident party for which a deduction is taken into account in calculating the amount of the relevant tax payable by the resident party, or

(ii) a reduction in the income of the resident party which would otherwise have been taken into account in calculating the amount of the relevant tax payable by the resident party,

(b) it is reasonable to conclude that—

(i) the resulting reduction in the amount of the relevant tax which is payable by the resident party exceeds the resulting increase in relevant taxes payable by the overseas party for the period corresponding to the tax period, and

(ii) the overseas party does not meet the 80% payment test, and

(c) the results described in paragraphs (a) and (b)(i) are not exempted by sub-paragraph (5).

(2) In this Schedule references to "the tax reduction" are to the amount of the excess mentioned in sub-paragraph (1)(b)(i).

(3) It does not matter whether the tax reduction results from the application of different rates of tax, the operation of a relief, the exclusion of any amount from a charge to tax, or otherwise.

(4) "The 80% payment test" is met by the overseas party if the resulting increase in relevant taxes paid by that party as mentioned in sub-paragraph (1)(b)(i) is at least 80% of the amount of the resulting reduction in the amount of the relevant tax payable by the resident party.

(5) The results described in sub-paragraph (1)(a) and (b)(i) are exempted if they arise solely by reason of—

(a) contributions paid by an employer under a registered pension scheme, or overseas pension scheme, in respect of any individual,

(b) a payment to a charity,

(c) a payment to a person who, on the ground of sovereign immunity, cannot be liable for any relevant tax, or

(d) a payment to an offshore fund or authorised investment fund—

(i) which meets the genuine diversity of ownership condition (whether or not a clearance has been given to that effect), or

(ii) at least 75% of the investors in which are, throughout the accounting period, registered pension schemes, overseas pension schemes, charities or persons who cannot be liable for any relevant tax on the ground of sovereign immunity.

(6) In this paragraph and paragraph 6, where the overseas party does not have an actual period for the purposes of relevant taxes which coincides with the tax period of the resident party—

(a) references to the corresponding period of the overseas party in relation to that tax period are to a notional period of that party for the purposes of relevant taxes that would coincide with that tax period, and

(b) such apportionments as are just and reasonable are to be made to determine the income or tax liability of that party for that corresponding period.

(7) In this paragraph—

"relevant tax" means—

(a) income tax,

(b) corporation tax on income,

(c) a sum chargeable under section 269DA of CTA 2010 (surcharge on banking companies) as if it were an amount of corporation tax,

(d) a sum chargeable under section 330(1) of CTA 2010 (supplementary charge in respect of ring fence trades as if it were an amount of corporation tax), or

(e) any non-UK tax on income, and

"tax period", in relation to a resident party, means—

(a) a tax year, or

(b) if the resident party is a company, an accounting period of that party.

Tax mismatch: resulting reduction and resulting increase

6 (1) For the purposes of paragraph 5, the resulting reduction in the resident party's liability to a relevant tax for a tax period is—

$A \times TR$

where—

A is the sum of—

(a) if there are expenses within paragraph 5(1)(a)(i), the lower of the amount of expenses and the amount of the deduction mentioned in that provision, and

(b) any reduction in income mentioned in paragraph 5(1)(a)(ii), and

TR is the rate at which, assuming the resident party has profits equal to A chargeable to the relevant tax for the tax period, those profits would be chargeable to that tax.

For this purpose, the rate at which those profits would be chargeable to that tax for that period is the highest rate at which that tax would be chargeable for that period if those profits were added to the resident party's total income.

(2) For the purposes of paragraph 5(1)(b) and (4), the resulting increase in relevant taxes payable by the overseas party for the period corresponding to the tax period is any increase in the total amount of relevant taxes that would fall to be paid by that party (and not refunded) assuming that—

(a) the overseas party's income for that period, in consequence of the material provision were an amount equal to A,

(b) account were taken of any deduction or relief (other than any qualifying deduction or qualifying loss relief) taken into account by the overseas party in determining that party's actual liability to any relevant taxes in consequence of the material provision, and

(c) all further reasonable steps were taken—

(i) under the law of any part of the United Kingdom or any country or territory outside the United Kingdom, and

(ii) under double taxation arrangements made in relation to any country or territory,

to minimise the amount of tax which would fall to be paid by the overseas party in the country or territory in question (other than steps to secure the benefit of any qualifying deduction or qualifying loss relief).

(3) The steps mentioned in sub-paragraph (2)(c) include—

(a) claiming, or otherwise securing the benefit of, reliefs, deductions, reductions or allowances, and

(b) making elections for tax purposes.

(4) For the purposes of this paragraph, any withholding tax which falls to be paid on payments made to the overseas party is (unless it is refunded) to be treated as tax which falls to be paid by that party (and not the person making the payment).

(5) For the purposes of this paragraph, an amount of tax payable by the overseas party is refunded if and to the extent that—

(a) any repayment of tax, or any payment in respect of a credit for tax, is made to any person, and

(b) that repayment or payment is directly or indirectly in respect of the whole or part of the amount of tax payable by the overseas party,

but an amount refunded is to be ignored if and to the extent that it results from qualifying loss relief obtained by that party.

(6) Where some or all of the overseas party's income is treated for the purposes of a relevant tax charged under the law of a country or territory outside the United Kingdom as the income of a person or persons other than the overseas party, in paragraph 5 and this paragraph—

(a) references to that party's liability to any tax (however expressed) include a reference to the liabilities of that person or those persons to the relevant tax,

(b) references to any tax being payable by that party (however expressed) include a reference to the relevant tax being payable by that person or those persons, and

(c) references to loss relief obtained by that party include a reference to loss relief obtained by that person or those persons,

and sub-paragraph (4) applies to that person or any of those persons as it applies to that party.

(7) In this paragraph—

"qualifying deduction" means a deduction which—

(a) is made in respect of actual expenditure of the overseas party,

(b) does not arise directly from the arrangements,

(c) is of a kind for which the resident party would have obtained a deduction in calculating that party's liability to any income tax or corporation tax had that party incurred the expenditure in respect of which the deduction is given, and

(d) does not exceed the amount of the deduction that the resident party would have so obtained,

"qualifying loss relief" means any means by which a loss might be used for tax purposes to reduce the amount in respect of which the overseas party is liable to tax on the profits of a business, and

"relevant tax" has the same meaning as in paragraph 5.

Adjustments required to be made in relation to arrangements

7 (1) Adjustments must be made so as to counteract the tax advantages that would (ignoring this Schedule) arise from profit fragmentation arrangements.

(2) The adjustments—

(a) must relate to the expenses, income, profits or losses of the resident party for the tax period in which value is transferred as a result of the material provision,

(b) must be based on what the value transferred would have been if it had resulted from a provision made or imposed as between independent parties acting at arm's length, and

(c) must be just and reasonable.

(3) References in this paragraph to "the resident party" are references to the resident party at the time at which the material provision is made or imposed.

Double taxation

8 (1) This paragraph applies where—

(a) the resident party has paid a relevant tax by virtue of the application of paragraph 7,

(b) at any time, the resident party or another person pays—

(i) a further amount of the relevant tax, or

(ii) an amount of non-UK tax corresponding to the relevant tax, and

(c) the result is a double payment of tax calculated by reference to the same income or profits.

(2) In order to avoid the double payment of tax, the resident party may make a claim in writing for one or more consequential adjustments to be made in respect of the tax paid mentioned in sub-paragraph (1)(a).

(3) On a claim under this paragraph an officer of Revenue and Customs must make such of the consequential adjustments claimed (if any) as are just and reasonable.

(4) The amount of any consequential adjustments must not exceed the lesser of—

(a) the tax paid by the resident party as mentioned in sub-paragraph (1)(a), and

(b) the tax paid as mentioned in sub-paragraph (1)(b).

(5) Consequential adjustments may be made—

(a) in respect of any tax period,

(b) by way of an assessment, the modification of an assessment, the amendment of a claim or otherwise, and

(c) despite any time limit imposed by or under any enactment.

Reimbursement payments ignored for tax purposes

9 In calculating income, profits or losses for any tax purposes, no account is to be taken of any amount which is paid (directly or indirectly) by a person for the purposes of meeting or reimbursing the cost of tax charged on the resident party by virtue of the application of paragraph 7.

Treatment of a person who is a member of a partnership

10 (1) This paragraph applies where a person is a member of a partnership.

(2) Any references in this Schedule to the expenses, income, profits or losses of, or to the adjustment of the expenses, income, profits or losses of, the person includes a reference to the person's share of the expenses, income, profits or losses of, or adjustment of the expenses, income, profits or losses of, the partnership.

(3) For this purpose "the person's share" of an amount is determined by apportioning the amount between the members of the partnership on a just and reasonable basis.

Other defined terms

11 In this Schedule—

"arrangements" includes any scheme, agreement, understanding, transaction or series of transactions (whether or not legally enforceable),

"authorised investment fund" means—

(a) an open-ended investment company within the meaning of section 613 of CTA 2010, or

(b) an authorised unit trust within the meaning of section 616 of that Act,

"business" includes any trade, profession or vocation,

"employer" has the same meaning as in Part 4 of FA 2004 (see section 279(1) of that Act),

"genuine diversity of ownership condition" means—

(a) in the case of an offshore fund, the genuine diversity of ownership condition in regulation 75 of the Offshore Funds (Tax) Regulations 2009 (SI 2009/3001), and

(b) in the case of an authorised investment fund, the genuine diversity of ownership condition in regulation 9A of the Authorised Investment Fund (Tax) Regulations 2006 (SI 2006/964),

"material provision" has the same meaning as in paragraph 2,

"non-UK tax" has the meaning given by section 187 of CTA 2010,

"offshore fund" has the same meaning as in section 354 of TIOPA 2010 (see section 355 of that Act),

"the overseas party" has the meaning given by paragraph 1(2),

"overseas pension scheme" has the same meaning as in Part 4 of FA 2004 (see section 150(7) of that Act),
"participator" has the same meaning as in Part 10 of CTA 2010 (see section 454 of that Act),
"partnership" includes an entity established under the law of a country or territory outside the United Kingdom of a similar character to a partnership, and "member" of a partnership is to be construed accordingly,
"related individual" and "the resident party" have the meanings given by paragraph 1(2),
"tax advantage" includes—

(a) relief or increased relief from income tax or corporation tax,
(b) repayment or increased repayment of income tax or corporation tax,
(c) avoidance or reduction of a charge or an assessment to income tax or corporation tax,
(d) avoidance of a possible assessment to income tax or corporation tax,
(e) deferral of a payment of tax or advancement of a repayment of tax, and
(f) avoidance of an obligation to deduct or account for tax,

"tax period" has the meaning given by paragraph 5(7),
"the tax reduction" has the meaning given by paragraph 5(2), and
"trust" includes arrangements—

(a) which have effect under the law of a country or territory outside the United Kingdom, and
(b) under which persons acting in a fiduciary capacity hold and administer property on behalf of other persons,
and "beneficiaries", in relation to such arrangements, is to be construed accordingly.

Commencement

12 This Schedule has effect—

(a) for income tax purposes, in relation to any value transferred on or after 6 April 2019 as a result of a material provision, and
(b) for corporation tax purposes, in relation to any value transferred on or after 1 April 2019 as a result of a material provision.

COMMENTARY ON SCHEDULE 4

Schedule 4 introduces new anti-avoidance provisions targeted at 'profit fragmentation arrangements'. These provisions are introduced following a government consultation on how to directly tackle avoidance schemes which are designed to move UK profits outside of the UK. The Government's stated intention is to prevent UK traders and professionals from avoiding UK tax by arranging for UK business profits to accrue to entities resident in territories where significantly lower tax is paid than in the UK. Where other existing anti-avoidance provisions apply (for example, the transfer pricing rules set out in TIOPA 2010, Pt 4), Sch 4 only applies to arrangements to the extent that any tax advantage remains after such other provisions have been applied. If Sch 4 applies, just and reasonable adjustments must be made to any expenses, income, profits or losses that are taxable or relievable (as applicable) in the UK so as to counteract any tax advantage that would (but for Sch 4) arise from the profit fragmentation arrangements.

Paragraph 1

Paragraph 1 gives and introduction and overview of Sch 4.

Sub-paragraph (1): introduces Sch 4.

Sub-paragraph (2): defines the parties that must be involved in profit fragmentation arrangements in order for the provisions to apply. These parties are referred to in Sch 4 as 'the resident party', 'the overseas party' and 'a related individual'.

Sub-paragraph (3): defines an 'overseas person or entity' (relevant to the definition of 'the overseas party' set out in sub-para 1(2)).

Sub-paragraphs (4) to (6): introduce the remaining paragraphs of Sch 4.

Paragraph 2

Paragraph 2 defines 'profit fragmentation arrangements'.

Sub-paragraph (1) sets out the four conditions that must be satisfied for arrangements to fall within the definition of 'profit fragmentation arrangements'. The first condition requires the existence of a 'material provision' (as defined). The second condition requires that, as a result of the material provision, there is a transfer of value from the resident party to the overseas party and that value must derive directly or indirectly from the provision of a business chargeable to UK income tax or corporation tax. Further provisions relating to this second condition are set out in para 3 (discussed below). The third condition requires that the value transferred is greater than it would have been if the provision had been made or imposed between independent parties acting at arm's length. The fourth condition requires that at least one of the 'enjoyment conditions' set out in para 4 is met in relation to a related individual.

Sub-paragraph (2) includes two carve-outs from the definition of 'profit fragmentation arrangements'. Firstly, the definition does not apply to arrangements where the material provision does not result in a tax mismatch for a tax period of the resident party. The concept of a tax mismatch is addressed in para 5. Secondly, the definition does not apply where it is not reasonable to conclude that the main purpose, or one of the main purposes, for which the arrangements were entered into was to obtain a tax advantage.

Sub-paragraph (3) provides that where the resident member is a member of partnership, that partnership is effectively treated as transparent and any provision made or imposed between the partnership and an overseas party is treated as a provision made or imposed between the resident member and the overseas party.

Paragraph 3

Paragraph 3 explains how to determine whether there is a transfer of value deriving directly or indirectly from a business for the purposes of the second condition in para 2 (set out in sub-para 2(1)(b)).

Sub-paragraph (1): account should be taken of any direct or indirect method by which any property or right is transferred or transmitted or by which the value of any property or right is enhanced or diminished. This sub-para is deliberately broad and is intended to catch any manner in which value is transferred.

Sub-paragraph (2): gives particular examples of transactions, provisions and methods by which value may be transferred. These examples are not an exhaustive list and circumstances that are not covered by this sub-para may still be caught by sub-para 2(1)(b).

Sub-paragraph (3): provides that value may be traced through any number of persons, entities or arrangements.

Sub-paragraph (4): requires that any property held by an entity under any arrangements must be attributed to the participants in that entity at each stage on a just and reasonable basis. This may be in proportion to the participant's directly held shares or membership interests, but will take into account beneficial entitlement or ownership.

Paragraph 4

Paragraph 4 sets out the 'enjoyment conditions' which must be met in relation to a related individual for the purposes of the fourth condition in para 2 (set out in sub-para 1(2)(d)). It also explains how to determine whether the enjoyment conditions are met.

Sub-paragraph (1): the enjoyment conditions are met if it is reasonable to conclude that some or all of the value transferred relates to something done by, or any property or purported right of, the related individual and either of the conditions under sub-para (2) is met.

Sub-paragraph (2)(a): sets out the first enjoyment condition. The first condition will be met if the related individual is able to benefit from, enjoy or control the value transferred or part of it in one or more of the circumstances set out in sub-paras 2(a)(i) to (v).

Sub-paragraph (2)(b): sets out the second enjoyment condition. The second condition is essentially a catch-all provision aimed at any arrangements where it is reasonable to conclude that the transfer of value was procured in such a way as to avoid the first enjoyment condition applying.

Sub-paragraph (3): all benefits accruing to a person as a result of the value transferred must be taken into account in determining whether the enjoyment conditions are met.

Sub-paragraphs (4) and (5): extend the definition of a related individual to include certain connected persons. The definition of connected is a modified version of the definition set out in ITA 2007, s 993. In effect, this means that the enjoyment condition will be satisfied if a related individual (as defined in para (1)) does not satisfy the enjoyment conditions, but one or more persons connected to the related individual (for example, a spouse or certain family members) is able to enjoy the value transferred or part of it as set out in sub-para (2).

Paragraph 5

Paragraph 5 expands on the carve-out set out in sub-para 1(2) for arrangements where the material provision does not result in a tax mismatch. The carve-out should be considered in relation to each tax period of a resident party. Broadly, it must be reasonable to conclude that the provision results in an increase in overseas tax payable by the overseas party which is less than 80% of the reduction in UK tax payable by the resident party.

Sub-paragraph (1): sets out three conditions that must met for a tax mismatch to arise. Broadly, the conditions will be met if: (a) the material provision results in an increase in deductible expenses or a decrease in taxable income of the relevant party for UK tax purposes in the relevant tax period; (b) it is reasonable to conclude that any resulting reduction in UK tax payable by the resident party for the tax period exceeds any resulting increase in non-UK tax payable by the overseas party for a corresponding period (the amount of any such excess being 'the tax reduction'), and the 80% payment test is not met by the overseas party (see sub-para (4) below); and (c) the exemption set out in sub-para (5) does not apply. Note, the terms 'resulting reduction' and 'resulting increase' are defined in para 6.

Sub-paragraph (2): defines 'the tax reduction'.

Sub-paragraph (3): para 5 applies to any 'tax reduction' howsoever it arises.

Sub-paragraph (4): defines 'the 80% payment test'. The test will be met if the increase in tax paid by the overseas party is at least 80% of the amount of the reduction in tax payable by the resident party.

Sub-paragraph (5): a reduction in tax payable as a result of the circumstances described in sub-para (1)(a) and (b)(i) is exempted if it arises solely by reason of a payment or contributions described in this sub-para (including, for example, a payment to a charity).

Sub-paragraph (6): applies a notional period where the overseas party does not have an actual period which coincides with the tax period of the resident party.

Sub-paragraph (7): defines 'relevant tax' and 'tax period'.

Paragraph 6

Paragraph 6 sets out how to calculate a 'resulting reduction' and a 'resulting increase' for the purposes of para 5.

Sub-paragraph (1): sets out a formula which must be applied to calculate the resulting reduction in the resident party's liability to tax for a tax period.

Sub-paragraphs (2) and (3): set out how to calculate the resulting increase in the overseas party's liability to tax for the period corresponding to the tax period.

Sub-paragraph (4): in calculating any resulting reduction or resulting increase, any withholding tax on payments made to the overseas party should be treated as tax paid by the overseas party (unless it is refunded).

Sub-paragraph (5): defines a refund of tax payable by the overseas party.

Sub-paragraph (6): explains how paras 5 and 6 apply where the overseas party's income is treated as the income of another person(s) for tax purposes in an overseas territory. This may be particularly relevant where the overseas party is a partnership or any other transparent or hybrid entity.

Sub-paragraph (7): defines qualifying deduction, qualifying loss relief and relevant tax (terms used in sub-paras (1) and (2) above).

Paragraph 7

Paragraph 7 sets out the adjustments required to be made in relation to profit fragmentation arrangements in order to counteract any tax advantages that would otherwise arise from the arrangements.

Sub-paragraph (1): gives a broad authority to make any adjustments required so as to counteract tax advantages arising from profit fragmentation arrangements.

Sub-paragraph (2): sets out how adjustments must be made and requires that adjustments are made on a just and reasonable basis. 'Just and reasonable basis' is not defined.

Sub-paragraph (3): limits the application of para 7 to the resident party who is party to the arrangements at the time the material provision is made or imposed.

Paragraph 8

Paragraph 8 applies to ensure that amounts taxed as a result of the application of Sch 4 are not taxed more than once.

Sub-paragraph (1): applies para 8 where the resident party has paid tax under Sch 4, the resident party or another party pays further tax (in the UK or an overseas territory) and the further tax results in tax being pad twice by reference to the same income or profits.

Sub-paragraph (2): allows the resident party to claim one or more consequential adjustments to tax paid as a result of Sch 4.

Sub-paragraph (3): provides for HMRC to make consequential adjustments as are just and reasonable following a claim under sub-para (2).

Sub-paragraph (4): limits any consequential adjustments to the lesser of the amount of tax paid by the resident party under Sch 4 or the further tax paid as mentioned in sub-para (1)(b).

Sub-paragraph (5): gives broad authority for consequential adjustments to be made in respect of any tax period and despite any time limit imposed by any enactment.

Paragraph 9

Paragraph 9 states that any amount paid by a person to reimburse the resident party for tax charged as a result of Sch 4 should be ignored for the purposes of calculating income, profits or losses for any tax purposes.

Paragraph 10

Paragraph 10 sets out how Sch 4 applies to a person who is a member of a partnership.

Sub-paragraphs (1) and (2) explain that expenses, income, profits or losses of a person, or adjustment thereto, include the person's share of expenses, income, profits or losses of the partnership, or adjustments thereto.

Sub-paragraph (3) states that a 'person's share' will be determined on a just and reasonable basis for the purposes of sub-para (2).

Paragraph 11

Sets out other defined terms used in Sch 4.

Paragraph 12

Schedule 4 has effect for income tax purposes in relation to any value transferred on or after 6 April 2019 and for corporation tax purposes in relation to any value transferred on or after 1 April 2019.

SCHEDULE 5

NON-UK RESIDENT COMPANIES CARRYING ON UK PROPERTY BUSINESSES ETC

Section 17

PART 1

EXTENSION OF SCOPE OF CHARGE

1 Section 5 of CTA 2009 (territorial scope of charge to corporation tax) is amended as follows.

2 In subsection (2) (circumstances in which non-UK resident company is within the charge)—

(a) omit "or" at the end of paragraph (a), and

(b) after paragraph (b) insert ",

(c) it carries on a UK property business, or

(d) it has other UK property income."

3 After subsection (3) insert—

"(3A) A non-UK resident company which carries on a UK property business is chargeable to corporation tax on income on all its profits that are—

(a) profits of that business, or

(b) profits arising from loan relationships or derivative contracts that the company is a party to for the purposes of that business.

(3B) A non-UK resident company which has other UK property income is chargeable to corporation tax on income on all its profits that—

(a) consist of that income, or

(b) are profits arising from loan relationships or derivative contracts that the company is a party to for the purposes of enabling it to generate that income."

4 In subsection (4) for "(2A) and (3)" substitute "and (2A) to (3B)".

5 After subsection (4) insert—

"(5) In this Part "other UK property income" means income dealt with by any of the following Chapters of Part 4—

(a) Chapter 7 (rent receivable in connection with a UK section 39(4) concern);

(b) Chapter 8 (rent receivable for UK electric-line wayleaves);

(c) Chapter 9 (post-cessation receipts arising from a UK property business)."

PART 2

SUPPLEMENTARY & CONSEQUENTIAL AMENDMENTS

FA 1998

6 (1) Paragraph 2 of Schedule 18 to FA 1998 (duty to give notice of chargeability) is amended as follows.

(2) After sub-paragraph (1) insert—

"(1A) But a company is not required to give notice under sub-paragraph (1) in respect of an accounting period if for the period —

(a) all the income on which it is chargeable to tax consists of payments on which it bears income tax by deduction, and

(b) the company has no chargeable gains."

(3) In sub-paragraph (2) for "The notice" substitute "A notice required to be given under this paragraph".

FA 2004

7 After section 55 of FA 2004 insert—

"55A Section 55: exception to duty to give notice

(1) A company is not required to give notice under section 55 of the beginning of an accounting period if it reasonably expects that—

(a) all the income on which it will be chargeable to corporation tax for the period will consist of payments on which it bears income tax by deduction, and

(b) it will have no chargeable gains for the period.

(2) Subsection (3) applies if—

(a) by reason of subsection (1) a company is not required to give notice under section 55 of the beginning of an accounting period ("the unreported period"), and

(b) a subsequent accounting period immediately follows the end of the unreported period.

(3) The subsequent accounting period is to be treated for the purposes of section 55 as if it does not immediately follow the end of a previous accounting period.

(4) If by reason of subsection (1) ceasing to apply a company becomes subject to the duty to give notice under section 55 of the beginning of an accounting period the notice must be given not later than three months after the date on which it becomes subject to that duty."

ITTOIA 2005

8 In Part 3 of ITTOIA 2005 (property businesses), omit section 362 (effect of company starting or ceasing to be within charge to income tax in respect of UK property business).

ITA 2007

9 In section 5 of ITA 2007 (income tax and companies) in paragraph (b) for the words from "the income" to the end substitute "it is chargeable to corporation tax in respect of the income, or would be so chargeable but for an exemption."

CTA 2009

10 CTA 2009 is amended as follows.

11 In section 3 (exclusion of charge to income tax) in subsection (1)(b) (non-UK resident companies) for the words from "and—" to the end substitute "and it is chargeable to corporation tax in respect of the income, or would be so chargeable but for an exemption".

12 In section 18A (exemption for profits or losses of foreign permanent establishments) in subsection (2A) for the words from ", or would" to the end substitute "or, if the company were non-UK resident, would be—

(a) profits or losses of the company's trade of dealing in or developing UK land (see section 5B),

(b) profits or losses of the company's UK property business,

(c) profits consisting of the company's other UK property income, or

(d) profits or losses arising from loan relationships or derivative contracts that the company is a party to for the purposes of its UK property business or for the purposes of enabling it to generate other UK property income."

13 In section 19 (chargeable profits) for subsection (2A) substitute—

"(2A) But the company's "chargeable profits" do not include—

(a) profits of a trade of dealing in or developing UK land (see section 5B),

(b) profits of a UK property business,

(c) profits consisting of other UK property income, or

(d) profits arising from loan relationships or derivative contracts that the company is a party to for the purposes of its UK property business or for the purposes of enabling it to generate other UK property income."

14 In section 289 (effect of company starting or ceasing to be within charge to corporation tax) in subsection (1) for "a property business" substitute "an overseas property business".

15 (1) Section 301 (calculation of non-trading profits and deficits from loan relationships: non-trading credits and debits) is amended as follows.

(2) In subsection (1) for "as follows" substitute "in accordance with subsections (4) to (7)".

(3) After subsection (1) insert—

"(1A) But in the case of a non-UK resident company the only non-trading credits and non-trading debits to be used are those in respect of loan relationships that the company is a party to for a purpose mentioned in section 5(3A)(b) or (3B)(b)."

16 In section 333 (company with loan relationship ceasing to be UK resident) in subsection (2)—

(a) after "owed" insert "—

(a) ", and

(b) at the end insert ",

(b) for the purposes of the company's trade of dealing in or developing UK land,

(c) for the purposes of the company's UK property business, or

(d) for the purposes of enabling the company to generate other UK property income (within the meaning given by section 5(5))."

17 (1) Section 334 (non-UK resident company ceasing to hold loan relationship for UK permanent establishment) is amended as follows.

(2) In the heading, for "UK permanent establishment" substitute "section 333(2) purposes".

(3) In subsection (1) for the words from "the purposes" to "United Kingdom" substitute "section 333(2) purposes".

(4) In subsection (3)(b) for "the purposes of the permanent establishment" substitute "section 333(2) purposes".

(5) After subsection (4) insert—

"(5) An asset or liability ceases to be held or owed for section 333(2) purposes if and in so far as—

(a) it ceases to be held or owed for any purposes mentioned in section 333(2), and

(b) on doing so, it does not begin or continue to be held or owed for any of the other purposes so mentioned."

18 In section 574 (non-trading credits and debits to be brought into account under Part 5) after subsection (2) insert—

"(2A) But in the case of a non-UK resident company subsection (2) applies only in relation to those credits or debits in respect of derivative contracts that the company is a party to for a purpose mentioned in section 5(3A)(b) or (3B)(b)".

19 In section 609 (company with derivative contract ceasing to be UK resident) in subsection (2)—

(a) after "owed" insert "—

(a) ", and

(b) at the end insert ",

(b) for the purposes of the company's trade of dealing in or developing UK land,

(c) for the purposes of the company's UK property business, or

(d) for the purposes of enabling the company to generate other UK property income (within the meaning given by section 5(5))."

20 (1) Section 610 (non-UK resident company ceasing to hold derivative contract for UK permanent establishment) is amended as follows.

(2) In the heading, for "UK permanent establishment" substitute "section 609(2) purposes".

(3) In subsection (1) for the words from "the purposes" to "United Kingdom" substitute "section 609(2) purposes".

(4) In subsection (3)(b) for "the purposes of the permanent establishment" substitute "section 609(2) purposes".

(5) After subsection (4) insert—

"(5) A right or liability ceases to be held or owed for section 609(2) purposes if and in so far as—

(a) it ceases to be held or owed for any purposes mentioned in section 609(2), and

(b) on doing so, it does not begin or continue to be held or owed for any of the other purposes so mentioned."

21 (1) Section 697 (derivative contracts with non-UK residents: exceptions) is amended as follows.

(2) For subsection (2) substitute—

"(2) Section 696 does not apply if NR—

(a) is chargeable to corporation tax or income tax in respect of income arising from the derivative contract (or would be if there were any such income), and

(b) is a party to the derivative contract otherwise than as agent or nominee of another person."

(3) In subsection (6) omit the definition of "relevant entity" and ", and" immediately before it.

22 In section 746 ("non-trading credits" and "non-trading debits") in subsection (2) for paragraph (b) substitute—

"(b) section 793A (effect of election to reallocate charge within group),".

23 (1) Section 792 (reallocation of charge within group) is amended as follows.

(2) Omit subsection (5).

(3) In subsection (6) for "makes further provision" substitute "sets out further requirements".

(4) After subsection (6) insert—

"(6A) Section 793A makes provision about the effect of elections under this section."

(5) In subsection (8) after "793" insert ", 793A".

24 (1) Section 793 (further requirements about elections under section 792) is amended as follows.

(2) In subsection (1) for "or (3)" substitute ", (3), (3A) or (3B)".

(3) In subsection (3), in the words before paragraph (a), after "if" insert "subsection (2) does not apply and"

(4) After subsection (3) insert—

"(3A) This subsection applies if neither of subsections (2) and (3) apply and at the relevant time—

(a) B carried on a trade of dealing in or developing UK land, and

(b) B was not exempt from corporation tax in respect of profits of that trade because of arrangements that have effect under section 2(1) of TIOPA 2010.

(3B) This subsection applies if none of subsections (2), (3) and (3A) apply and at the relevant time—

(a) B carried on a UK property business, and

(b) B was not exempt from corporation tax in respect of the income of its UK property business because of arrangements that have effect under section 2(1) of TIOPA 2010."

25 After section 793 insert—

"793A Effect of election under section 792

(1) This section applies if an election is made under section 792.

(2) If subsection (2) of section 793 applies to B the gain, or the part specified in the election, is treated as if it had accrued to B at the relevant time as a non-trading credit for the purposes of Chapter 6 (how credits and debits are given effect).

(3) If subsection (3) of section 793 applies to B the gain, or the part specified in the election, is treated—

(a) as if it had accrued to B at the relevant time as a non-trading credit for the purposes of Chapter 6, and

(b) as if it had accrued in respect of an asset held for the purposes of a permanent establishment of B in the United Kingdom.

(4) If subsection (3A) of section 793 applies to B the gain, or the part specified in the election, is treated for the purposes of Chapter 6 as if it had accrued to B at the relevant time as a credit in respect of an asset held for the purposes of B's trade of dealing in or developing UK land.

(5) If subsection (3B) of section 793 applies to B the gain, or the part specified in the election, is treated for the purposes of Chapter 6 as if it had accrued to B at the relevant time as a credit in respect of an asset held for the purposes of B's UK property business."

26 In section 795 (recovery of charge from another group company or controlling director) in subsection (4) omit the words from "but" to "establishment".

27 In section 863 (asset becoming chargeable intangible asset), in subsection (1)(b)—

(a) after "held" insert "—

(i) ", and

(b) after "establishment," insert—

"(ii) for the purposes of a trade carried on by the company of dealing in or developing UK land,

(iii) for the purposes of a UK property business carried on by the company, or

(iv) for the purposes of enabling the company to generate other UK property income (within the meaning given by section 5(5)),".

CTA 2010

28 CTA 2010 is amended as follows.

29 (1) Section 9 (non-UK resident company preparing return of accounts in currency other than sterling) is amended as follows.

(2) For subsection (1) substitute—

"(1) This section applies if a non-UK resident company within the charge to corporation tax prepares its return of accounts for a period of account in a currency other than sterling (the "accounts currency")."

(3) In subsection (4) omit from "of its" to "United Kingdom".

30 In section 107 (group relief: restriction on losses etc surrenderable by non-UK resident) in subsection (1) for "company" (in the second place it occurs) to the end substitute "company within the charge to corporation tax".

31 In section 188BI (group relief for carried-forward losses: restriction on surrender of losses made when non-UK resident) in subsection (1) for "company" (in the second place it occurs) to the end substitute "company within the charge to corporation tax".

TIOPA 2010

32 Part 10 of TIOPA 2010 (corporate interest restriction) is amended as follows.

33 (1) Section 415 (qualifying net group-interest expense: interpretation) is amended as follows.

(2) In subsection (1) for paragraph (b) substitute—

"(b) either—

(i) the condition in subsection (1A) is met, or

(ii) any of the conditions in subsection (2) is met in relation to the guarantee, indemnity or other financial assistance in question"."

(3) After subsection (1) insert—

"(1A) The condition is that—

(a) the member in question is a company that has not been UK resident at any time before 29 October 2018,

(b) the financial assistance in question is provided before that date, and

(c) the financial assistance in question is in respect of a loan relationship, derivative contract or relevant arrangement or transaction (within the meaning of section 382(4)) to which the member in question is a party for the purposes of its UK property business."

34 In section 438 (exemption for interest payable to third parties etc) after subsection (5) insert—

"(5A) For the purposes of subsection (4) a guarantee, indemnity or other financial assistance in favour of the creditor is also ignored if—

(a) it is provided before 29 October 2018,
(b) the company concerned has not been UK resident at any time before that date, and
(c) the amount concerned is in respect of a loan relationship, derivative contract or relevant arrangement or transaction (within the meaning of section 382(4)) to which the member in question is a party for the purposes of its UK property business."

PART 3

COMMENCEMENT AND TRANSITIONAL PROVISIONS

Commencement

35 This Schedule comes into force on 6 April 2020 ("the commencement date").

Transitional provisions

36 Where a period of account of a company begins before and ends on or after the commencement date, it is to be assumed for the purposes of the amendments made by this Schedule—

(a) that the period ("the straddling period of account") consists of two separate periods of account—
  (i) the first beginning with the date on which the straddling period of account begins and ending with 5th April 2020, and
  (ii) the second beginning with the commencement date and ending with the date on which the straddling period of account ends, and
(b) that separate accounts have been drawn up for each of those separate periods in accordance with generally accepted accounting practice.

37 (1) This paragraph applies if—

(a) in a tax year ending before the commencement date a company makes a loss in a UK property business that is within the charge to income tax,
(b) relief for the purposes of income tax is not given to the company for an amount of the loss ("the unrelieved amount"), and
(c) on the commencement date the UK property business ceases to be within the charge to income tax and comes within the charge to corporation tax as a result of section 5(3A) of CTA 2009.

(2) Relief for the purposes of corporation tax is given to the company under this paragraph for the unrelieved amount.

(3) For this purpose—

(a) the unrelieved amount is carried forward to post-commencement accounting periods of the company (for so long as the company continues to carry on the UK property business), and
(b) the profits of any such accounting period that are mentioned in sub-paragraph (4) are to be reduced by the unrelieved amount (so far as that amount cannot be used under this paragraph to reduce the profits of an earlier period).

(4) The profits are—

(a) profits of the UK property business, and
(b) profits arising from loan relationships or derivative contracts that the company is a party to for the purposes of that business.

(5) In this paragraph "post-commencement accounting period" means an accounting period ending after the commencement date.

38 (1) This paragraph applies if—

(a) in the tax year 2019–20 a non-UK resident company is a partner in a firm which—
  (i) carries on a trade, and
  (ii) has untaxed income or relievable losses from a UK property business, and

(b) accordingly, the company is treated under section 854 of ITTOIA 2005 as having a notional business for the tax year.

(2) The basis period for the notional business for the tax year is taken to end with 5th April in that tax year (if it would not otherwise do so).

(3) In this paragraph "untaxed income" has the meaning given by section 854(6) of ITTOIA 2005.

39 (1) This paragraph applies if—

(a) on or after the commencement date a loss arises in connection with a loan relationship of a company,

(b) the loss is wholly or partly referable to a time before the commencement date ("the pre-commencement time"), and

(c) had the loss arisen at the pre-commencement time it would have been brought into account in accordance with Part 3 of ITTOIA 2005 in calculating the profits of the UK property business of the company.

(2) Section 327 (disallowance of imported losses etc) does not apply in relation to so much of the loss as is referable to the pre-commencement time.

40 (1) This paragraph applies for an accounting period ("the loss period") of a non-UK resident company beginning on or after the commencement date if—

(a) apart from this paragraph, a loss arising in connection with a derivative contract of the company would by reason of this Schedule fall to be brought into account in accordance with Part 7 of CTA 2009,

(b) the loss is wholly or partly referable to a time before the commencement date when the derivative contract was not subject to corporation tax, and

(c) had the loss arisen at that time it would not have been brought into account in accordance with Part 3 of ITTOIA 2005 in calculating the profits of the UK property business of the company.

(2) The amounts brought into account for the loss period in accordance with Part 7 of CTA 2009 must be such as to secure that none of the loss referable to that time is treated as arising in the loss period or any other accounting period of the company.

(3) For the purposes of this section a loss is referable to a time when a contract is not subject to corporation tax so far as, at the time to which the loss is referable, the company would not have been chargeable to corporation tax on any profits arising from the contract.

(4) If the company was not a party to the contract at the time to which the loss is referable, subparagraph (3) applies as if the reference to the company were a reference to the person who at that time was in the same position as respects the contract as is subsequently held by the company.

(5) An amount which would be brought into account in accordance with Part 7 of CTA 2009 in respect of a derivative contract apart from this paragraph is treated for the purposes of section 699(1) of CTA 2009 (amounts brought into account under Part 7 excluded from being otherwise brought into account) as if it were so brought into account.

(6) Accordingly, that amount must not be brought into account for corporation tax purposes as respects the derivative contract either in accordance with Part 7 of CTA 2009 or otherwise.

41 (1) This paragraph applies for an accounting period ("the relevant period") of a non-UK resident company beginning on or after the commencement date if—

(a) a profit arising in connection with a loan relationship or derivative contract of the company ("the first instrument") falls by reason of this Schedule to be brought into account in the relevant period in accordance with Part 5 or Part 7 of CTA 2009,

(b) an amount of the profit ("the profit amount") is referable to a time before the commencement date when the first instrument was not subject to corporation tax,

(c) had the profit arisen at that time it would not have been brought into account in accordance with Part 3 of ITTOIA 2005 in calculating the profits of the UK property business of the company,

(d) at that time the first instrument and another loan relationship or derivative contract ("the second instrument") were in a hedging relationship with one another, and

(e) an amount of a loss ("the loss amount") arising in connection with the second instrument would (apart from this paragraph) be prevented by reason of paragraph 40 or section 327 of CTA 2009 from being brought into account in the relevant period accordance with Part 5 or Part 7 of CTA 2009.

(2) So much of the loss amount as does not exceed the profit amount may be brought into account in the relevant period in accordance with Part 5 or Part 7 of CTA 2009.

(3) For the purposes of sub-paragraph (1) the first instrument and the second instrument are in a hedging relationship with one another in so far as one of them is intended to act as a hedge of the company's exposure to changes in the fair value of the other.

(4) In a case where the first instrument and the second instrument are in a hedging relationship with one another to a limited extent, subsection (2) has effect in relation to so much of the loss amount as is just and reasonable having regard to the extent of that hedging relationship.

(5) For the purposes of this paragraph a profit is referable to a time when the first instrument is not subject to corporation tax so far as, at the time to which the profit is referable, the company would not have been chargeable to corporation tax on any profits arising from the instrument.

(6) If the company was not a party to the first instrument at the time to which the profit is referable, subparagraph (5) applies as if the reference to the company were a reference to the person who at that time was in the same position as respects the instrument as is subsequently held by the company.

42 (1) Where—

(a) before the commencement date a company is chargeable to income tax on the profits of its UK property business,
(b) on the commencement date the company becomes chargeable to corporation tax on the profits arising from a derivative contract that it is a party to for the purposes of its UK property business, and
(c) there is a tax asymmetry in relation to the derivative contact,

the amounts to be brought into account in respect of the derivative contract for the purposes of Part 7 of CTA 2009 are to be adjusted in such manner as is just and reasonable having regard to the tax asymmetry.

(2) For the purposes of subparagraph (1) there is a tax asymmetry in relation to the derivative contract if—

(a) fair value amounts arising in relation to the derivative contract are brought into account in calculating for the purposes of income tax the profits or losses of the company's UK property business for tax years ending before the commencement date, but
(b) by reason of regulation 9 of the Disregard Regulations, fair value amounts arising in relation to the contract are not brought into account for the purposes of Part 7 of CTA 2009 for accounting periods of the company beginning on or after the commencement date.

(3) In this paragraph—

"fair value amount" means an amount representing a change in the fair value of a derivative contract which is recognised in determining a company's profit or loss for a period of account in accordance with generally accepted accounting practice;
"the Disregard Regulations" means the Loan Relationships and Derivative Contracts (Disregard and Bringing into Account of Profits and Losses) Regulations 2004 (SI 2004/3256).

43 (1) This paragraph applies if—

(a) an amount representing a change in the fair value of a derivative contract is recognised in determining a company's profit or loss for a period of account beginning before the commencement date, and
(b) the amount would have been brought into account in calculating for the purposes of income tax the profits or losses of the company's UK property business for a tax year ending before the commencement date but for its having been treated as an amount of a capital nature.

(2) In determining the amounts the company is to bring into account for the purposes of Part 7 of CTA 2009 for an accounting period beginning on or after the commencement date—

(a) the derivative contract is to be treated as being one in relation to which an election has effect under regulation 6A of the Disregard Regulations, and

(b) if regulation 7 or 8 of those Regulations applies in relation to the derivative contract, the amount referred to in subparagraph (1) is to be treated for the purposes of regulation 10 of those Regulations as being an amount that has previously been excluded from being brought into account for the purposes of Part 7 of CTA 2009 by regulation 7 or 8 (as the case may be).

(3) In this paragraph—

"the Disregard Regulations" means the Loan Relationships and Derivative Contracts (Disregard and Bringing into Account of Profits and Losses) Regulations 2004 (SI 2004/3256);

"recognised" means recognised in accordance with generally accepted accounting practice.

44 (1) This paragraph applies if—

(a) before 1 January 2015 a company measures a relevant derivative contract at fair value,

(b) on the commencement date the company comes within the charge to corporation tax by reason of this Schedule, and

(c) the first relevant period of the company begins on or after the commencement date.

(2) The company is to be treated for the purposes of regulation 6A of the Disregard Regulations as if it was a new adopter.

(3) In this paragraph—

"the Disregard Regulations" means the Loan Relationships and Derivative Contracts (Disregard and Bringing into Account of Profits and Losses) Regulations 2004 (SI 2004/3256), and

"the first relevant period" and "relevant derivative contract" have the meaning given by regulation 6A(5) of the Disregard Regulations.

45 (1) This paragraph applies if on the commencement date—

(a) an asset held by a non-UK resident company for the purposes of its UK property business becomes a chargeable intangible asset in relation to the company by reason of the business coming within the charge to corporation tax, or

(b) an asset held by a non-UK resident company for the purposes of enabling it to generate other UK property income becomes a chargeable intangible asset in relation to the company by reason of that income coming within the charge to corporation tax.

(2) Part 8 of CTA 2009 applies as if—

(a) the company had acquired the asset immediately on the commencement date, and

(b) had done so for its accounting value at that time.

(3) In this paragraph—

"accounting value" and "chargeable intangible asset" have the meaning they have in Part 8 of CTA 2009, and

"other UK property income" has the meaning it has in Part 2 of CTA 2009.

46 (1) An election under section 792 of CTA 2009 (reallocation of degrouping charge within a group) may not be made if—

(a) subsection (3A) of section 793 applies to B, and

(b) the relevant time is before 5 July 2016.

(2) An election under section 792 of CTA 2009 may not be made if—

(a) subsection (3B) of section 793 applies to B, and

(b) the relevant time is before the commencement date.

(3) In this paragraph references to "B" and "the relevant time" must be read in accordance with section 792 of CTA 2009.

47 (1) This paragraph applies if—

(a) before the commencement date a company incurs expenditure for the purposes of a UK property business it is about to carry on,

(b) the company begins to carry on the business on or after the commencement date, and

(c) when the company begins to carry on the business it is non-UK resident.

(2) Subsection (7) of section 1147 of CTA 2009 (which enables a company to obtain relief for expenditure on contaminated or derelict land incurred prior to carrying on a UK property business) does not apply in relation to the expenditure.

48 Where on the commencement date—

(a) a non-UK resident company ceases to be within the charge to income tax and comes within the charge to corporation tax by reason of this Schedule, and

(b) an accounting period of the company begins in accordance with section 9(1)(a) of CTA 2009,

the Corporation Tax (Instalment Payments) Regulations 1998 (SI 1998/3175) do not have effect in relation to that accounting period.

49 (1) This paragraph applies if on or after 29 October 2018 a company enters into an arrangement the main purpose or one of the main purposes of which is to secure for any person a tax advantage related to the coming into force of this Schedule.

(2) The tax advantage is to be counteracted by means of adjustments.

(3) The adjustments may be made (whether by an officer of Revenue and Customs or the person who would obtain the tax advantage) by way of an assessment, the modification of an assessment, an amendment or disallowance of a claim, or otherwise.

(4) In this paragraph—

"arrangement" includes any agreement, understanding, scheme, transaction or series of transactions (whether or not legally enforceable),

"tax advantage" has the meaning given by section 1139 of CTA 2010.

50 (1) This paragraph applies if—

(a) a company enters into an arrangement of a kind mentioned in paragraph 49(1),

(b) the arrangements are effected by taking only ordinary commercial steps in accordance with a generally prevailing commercial practice,

(c) the tax advantage that the arrangements secure is the benefit of a relief expressly conferred by Part 10 of TIOPA 2010 (corporate interest restriction), and

(d) securing that tax advantage is wholly consistent with the policy objectives of that Part.

(2) If the arrangement is entered into on or after 29 October 2018, the tax advantage is not to be counteracted by means of adjustments under paragraph 49.

(3) In addition, the tax advantage is not to be counteracted by means of adjustments under section 461 of TIOPA 2010 irrespective of the date on which the arrangement was entered into.

COMMENTARY ON SCHEDULE 5

This Schedule will bring non-UK resident corporate landlords carrying on a UK property rental business (or receiving certain other UK property income) within the scope of corporation tax, with effect from 6 April 2020.

The Government has, in recent years, made significant changes to the taxation of UK property in the hands of non-UK resident persons. Non-UK resident companies carrying on a UK property rental business (whether residential or commercial) are currently charged to income tax on their UK property income, capped at the basic rate of 20% (ITA 2007, s 11). Under the Non-resident Landlord Scheme ('NRLS'), tenants and letting agents can be required to deduct tax from rental income paid to non-resident landlords. Non-resident landlords can apply under the NRLS for approval to receive their rental income with no tax deducted, provided they meet certain criteria.

The corporation tax code contains a number of rules not found in the income tax code – including, notably, the loan relationship and derivative contract regimes in CTA 2009, Pts 5 and 7, the rules restricting use of carry forward losses in CTA 2010, Pt 7ZA, and the corporate interest restriction rules in TIOPA 2010, Pt 10. The Government's policy objective in charging non-UK resident corporate landlords to corporation tax is stated as being to 'deliver more equal tax treatment for UK and non-UK resident companies in receipt of similar income, and take steps to prevent those that use this difference to reduce their tax bill on UK property through offshore ownership' (for further reading, see the HMRC policy paper titled 'Corporation Tax: UK property income of non-UK resident companies', published on 29 October 2018). Whilst non-UK resident corporate landlords will benefit from a reduction in headline tax rates from 20% income tax to (with effect from 1 April 2020) 17% corporation tax, they will need to take account of corporation tax rules which have not previously applied under the income tax code. For example, leveraged non-UK resident corporate landlords may find that interest payments which were fully tax deductible under the income tax code become restricted under the corporation tax code.

Readers should note that the extension of corporation tax to non-UK resident corporate landlords does not, at the time of writing, affect the NRLS. Despite being brought within the scope of corporation tax, non-UK resident corporate landlords will still be required to register for gross payment status under the NRLS or otherwise suffer tax deductions from their rental income.

Readers should also note the changes in Schedule 1 (Chargeable gains accruing to Non-residents etc) to FA 2019, which bring non-UK resident corporate landlords within the scope of corporation tax on all UK property gains with effect from 6 April 2019. Taken together, FA 2019 Schedule 1 and Schedule 5 mean that non-UK resident corporate landlords will be fully within corporation tax in respect of both UK property income and gains with effect from 6 April 2020.

Part 1—Extension of scope of charge

Paragraph 2 is the key change which widens the territorial scope of the charge to corporation tax for non-UK resident companies (CTA 2009, s 5(2)) to include non-UK resident companies carrying on a UK property business or with other UK property income.

Paragraph 3 introduces new charging provisions as CTA 2009, ss 5(3A) and 5(3B). Under these subsections, non-UK resident corporate landlords will be chargeable to corporation tax on UK property business profits (i e rental income), certain 'other UK property income' (for the definition of which, see para 5), and also profits arising from loan relationships or derivative contracts which the corporate is party to for the purpose of that property business or enabling it to generate that other UK property income. Non-UK resident corporate landlords will be chargeable in accordance with ordinary corporation tax principles, subject to the rest of this Schedule.

Paragraph 5 inserts CTA 2009, s 5(5) as the definition of 'other UK property income', namely those categories of income charged under CTA 2009, Pt 4, Chs 7 to 9 (inclusive), for example rent receivable for UK electric-line wayleaves.

Part 2—Supplementary and consequential amendments

As a general comment, a number of the changes in Part 2 of this Schedule seek to equalise the tax treatment between UK resident corporate landlords on the one hand, and non-UK resident corporate landlords brought within the extended scope of corporation tax on the other hand. Some of the changes recognise that those non-UK corporates will be brought within the scope of corporation tax even though they are neither UK resident nor trading through a UK permanent establishment.

Readers should be aware that, as a number of the changes widen the scope of rules which currently only apply to non-UK resident companies trading through a UK permanent establishment, those changes may also be relevant to non-UK resident companies carrying on a trade of dealing in or developing UK land (which have been chargeable to corporation tax under CTA 2009, s 5(2A) since July 2016, whether or not trading through a UK permanent establishment).

Paragraph 6 amends the rule in FA 1998, Sch 18, para 2, which requires a company to notify HMRC of its chargeability to corporation tax for an accounting period within 12 months of the end of that period (assuming the company has not already received a 'paragraph 3 notice' from HMRC to deliver a corporation tax return). This para removes the duty to notify HMRC of chargeability to corporation tax if all of the company's income bears income tax by deduction, and it has no chargeable gains in the period. For example, this could apply to a non-UK resident corporate landlord that has not registered for gross payment status under NRLS (see introductory comments at the start of this Schedule for an explanation of the NRLS).

Paragraph 7 makes a similar change to para 6, but this time in relation to the rule which requires a company to notify HMRC when it first comes within the charge to corporation tax (FA 2004, s 55), which will be relevant to non-UK resident corporate landlords being switched from income tax to corporation tax. This paragraph inserts FA 2004, s 55A as an exception from the duty to give notice where all of the company's income bears income tax by deduction, and it has no chargeable gains in the period.

Readers should also note the comments in the HMRC policy paper, which indicate that HMRC will write to non-UK resident corporate landlords during summer 2019 to give them new corporation tax reference numbers, and that this will be regarded as notification to HMRC of chargeability to corporation tax.

Paragraph 8 omits ITTOIA 2005, s 362 to prevent a capital allowances disposal event arising as a result of non-UK resident corporate landlords ceasing to be within the charge to income tax.

Paragraphs 9 to 11 provide that non-UK resident companies are excluded from income tax in relation to income which is chargeable to corporation tax (or would be chargeable but for an exemption), e g non-UK resident corporate landlords within the extended scope of corporation tax on UK property income.

In order to retain full taxing rights over UK property, para 12 amends the 'foreign branch exemption' in CTA 2009, s 18A so that it cannot include the new categories of profit brought within corporation tax.

Paragraph 13 excludes the new categories of profit brought within corporation tax from being chargeable profits attributable to a UK permanent establishment, as those profits will instead be chargeable to corporation tax under the extended CTA 2009, s 5. HMRC does not however intend this to affect the exclusion from the NRLS for rental income attributable to a UK permanent establishment and chargeable to corporation tax (see the Taxation of Income from Land (Non-residents) Regulations 1995, reg 8(3)).

Paragraph 14 addresses the same concern as para 8, this time by amending CTA 2009, s 289 so that a non-UK resident company carrying on a UK property business is not deemed to commence that business when it starts to be within the charge to corporation tax (which could otherwise trigger a capital allowances disposal event). CTA 2009, s 289 will continue to apply to a company carrying on an overseas property business which comes within the charge to corporation tax.

Paragraph 15 relates to the change made by para 3 which brings non-UK resident companies within the charge to corporation tax on profits from loan relationships which the company is party to for the purpose of a UK property business or to enable it to generate other UK property income. This paragraph inserts new CTA 2009, s 301(1A) to make clear that the only non-trading debits and credits to be brought into account are those in respect of loan relationships entered into for the aforementioned purposes.

Paragraphs 16 amends CTA 2009, s 333 to prevent migration exit charges applying to loan relationships which will remain within the scope of corporation tax where a company ceases to be UK resident, e g loan relationship assets held for the purpose of a company's UK property business. Paragraph 17 makes an equivalent amendment to the deemed realisation rule in CTA 2009, s 334, which otherwise applies where a non-UK resident company ceases to hold a loan relationship for the purpose of a UK permanent establishment.

Paragraph 18 inserts new CTA 2009, s 574(2A), which has the same purpose as the change made by para 15 but instead in relation to derivative contract (rather than loan relationship) non-trading debits and credits.

Paragraphs 19 and 20 make equivalent changes to the derivative rules as paras 16 and 17 do for the loan relationship rules, by amending the deemed realisation provisions in CTA 2009 ss 609 and 610.

Paragraph 21 includes a new exception in CTA 2009, s 697, so that the rule in CTA 2009, s 696 does not apply to non-UK residents brought within the extended scope of corporation tax in respect of a derivative contract. The rule in CTA 2009, s 696 can otherwise prevent net debits equivalent to 'notional interest' payments to non-UK residents from being brought into account.

Paragraphs 22 to 25 amend the rules in relation to reallocation of intangible fixed asset ('IFA') degrouping charges within a group. A degrouping charge can arise where an IFA is transferred on a tax neutral basis between group companies, and the transferee company subsequently leaves the group within six years of the transfer whilst still holding the relevant asset.

Currently, it is only possible to reallocate an IFA degrouping charge to a company which is either UK resident or carrying on a trade through a UK permanent establishment and not exempt from corporation tax in respect of that permanent establishment pursuant to a double tax treaty. Paragraph 24 inserts new CTA 2009, ss 793(3A) and 793(3B) so that companies within the extended scope of corporation tax (and not exempt under a double tax treaty) can elect to receive IFA degrouping charges. This change will apply to companies carrying on a trade of dealing in or developing UK land as well as companies carrying on a UK property business.

Paragraph 26 widens HMRC's power under CTA 2009, s 795(4) so that it can recover unpaid IFA degrouping charges from controlling directors of all liable non-UK resident companies, i e not just non-UK resident companies carrying on a trade through a UK permanent establishment, but also those carrying on a trade of dealing in or developing UK land or companies carrying on a UK property business.

Paragraph 27 widens the rule in CTA 2009, s 863, which deems an asset previously outside the IFA regime as being acquired for accounting value when it first becomes a 'chargeable intangible asset' (being where a gain on realisation of that asset would require a credit to be brought into account under the IFA regime). The rule is extended to include intangible assets held for the purpose of carrying on a trade of dealing in or developing UK land, as well as carrying on a UK property business or generating other UK property income.

Paragraph 29 amends the computational rule in CTA 2010, s 9 which applies where a non-UK resident company carrying on a trade through a UK permanent establishment prepares its accounts in a currency other than sterling. The amended rule will apply to all non-UK resident companies within the charge to corporation tax.

Paragraph 30 amends the rule in CTA 2010, s 107 which restricts losses surrenderable by non-UK resident companies. The amended rule will apply to all non-UK resident companies within the charge to corporation tax (not just those trading in UK land or carrying on a trade through a UK permanent establishment). This change should be read in conjunction with FA 2019, s 24 (Group relief etc: meaning of 'UK related' company), which extends group relief to all non-UK resident companies within the charge to corporation tax.

Paragraph 31 makes a similar amendment to that in para 30 but this time in relation to the restriction on surrender of carried-forward losses by non-UK resident companies, such that it will apply to all non-UK resident companies within the charge to corporation tax.

Paragraph 33 amends the corporate interest restriction rules by providing a form of grandfathering for financial assistance in place before 29 October 2018 (the relevance of this date being that the change was first included in the draft legislation published on 29 October 2018 following technical consultation, not the original 6 July 2018 draft). Under TIOPA 2010, s 466, certain guarantees, indemnities and other financial assistance provided by parties related to the debtor can result in the debtor and creditor being treated as related parties such that the loan relationship is disregarded when calculating net group-interest expense for the purpose of the group ratio. TIOPA 2010, s 415 already contains grandfathering for certain financial assistance provided before 1 April 2017 (the effective date of the corporate interest restriction rules). Paragraph 33 inserts new TIOPA 2010, s 415(1A) so that the related party deeming rule will not apply to financial assistance provided before 29 October 2018 in respect of a loan relationship or derivative contract which the company is party to for the purpose of its UK property business, provided also that the company had never been UK tax resident before 29 October 2018.

Paragraph 34 makes a similar amendment to para 33 but this time in relation to the public infrastructure exemption (which can be relevant to non-UK corporate landlords that are 'qualifying infrastructure companies'). Broadly, interest payments made by qualifying infrastructure companies to unrelated parties can be exempt from the deductibility restriction. This paragraph inserts new TIOPA 2010, s 438(5A) so that financial assistance provided before 29 October 2018 can be disregarded in determining whether the exemption applies (again, provided the relevant company was never UK resident before 29 October 2018).

Part 3—Commencement and transitional provisions

As a general comment and as referred to in HMRC's policy paper, a number of the changes in Part 3 of this Schedule are intended to ensure that (following the switch from income tax to corporation tax) a non-UK resident corporate landlord's income is neither taxed twice nor left out of account, and that its expenses are relieved only once.

Paragraph 35 provides that this Schedule will come into force on 6 April 2020.

Paragraph 36 applies where an affected company has a period of account beginning before and ending after the commencement date of 6 April 2020 (which, in practice, will apply to many non-UK resident corporate landlords). Non-UK resident corporate landlords currently submit paper income tax returns (form SA700) for the income tax year ending 5 April. Following the switch to corporation tax, non-UK resident corporate landlords will need to file an online form CT600 (using iXBRL and with iXBRL tags) in respect of corporation tax accounting periods.

Accordingly, a company's actual period of account will be deemed to end on 5 April 2020 (with the profits subject to income tax and included in the final income tax return), with a new period of account deemed to commence on 6 April 2020 (with profits thereafter being subject to corporation tax). Apportionment between the two deemed periods of account will be on a time basis under CTA 2010, s 1172.

For example, if a company has a 31 December actual period of account, the 2020 period would be split into:

- a period of account commencing 1 January 2020 and deemed to end on 5 April 2020 – profits or losses within the scope of income tax; and
- a period of account commencing 6 April 2020 and ending 31 December 2020 – profits or losses within the scope of corporation tax.

Where a company's actual period of account ends on 31 March 2020, it is understood that HMRC will treat that period as ending on 5 April 2020, with the new period deemed to commence on 6 April 2020 (to avoid a small stub period between 1 April and 5 April).

Paragraph 37 provides grandfathering of unused property losses incurred whilst the non-UK resident corporate landlord was within the income tax regime. Any such losses are automatically carried forward to reduce the profits (subject to corporation tax) of the UK property business in the first available accounting period, in priority to carried forward corporation tax losses, and provided the property business is still carried on by the same company.

It should be noted that grandfathered income tax property losses do not become corporation tax losses, and so will not be subject to the usual rules applying to corporation tax losses such as carry forward restrictions and ability to group relieve.

Paragraph 38 applies to non-UK resident companies which are treated as having a notional business under ITTOIA 2005, s 854 by virtue of being a partner in a firm carrying on a trade and which has untaxed income or relievable losses from other sources (including from a UK property business).The basis period of the notional business will be deemed to end on 5 April 2020 for income tax purposes.

Paragraph 39 applies where a loan relationship loss arises after 6 April 2020, but the loss is wholly or partly referable to the period before 6 April 2020. Under CTA 2009, s 327, certain 'imported' loan relationship losses are disallowed if they are referable to a time when the relationship was outside the scope of corporation tax – e g non-UK resident companies which migrate their tax residence to the UK whilst 'pregnant' with losses. As it is not intended that the switch to corporation tax should disallow loan relationship losses previously deductible under income tax, this paragraph dis-applies CTA 2009, s 327 where the relevant loss would have previously been brought into account under income tax in calculating the UK property business profits.

Paragraph 40 introduces a rule similar to CTA 2009, s 327 (see comment on para 39 above) but for derivative contract losses. If a non-UK corporate landlord has a derivative contract loss pre-6 April 2020 which would be brought into account under corporation tax but would not have previously been brought into account under income tax, then the loss which is referable to the pre-6 April 2020 period is disallowed for corporation tax purposes. However, if the loss would have been allowed under income tax, then it can be brought into account for corporation tax.

Paragraph 41 applies where a non-UK resident corporate landlord has hedged a loan or derivative before 6 April 2020 and where any profit on the loan relationship/derivative contract, and loss on the hedging relationship, would not have been brought into account under income tax. Without this paragraph, the profit on the loan relationship/derivative contract could be brought into account for corporation tax purposes, whilst the loss on the hedging relationship could be disallowed under CTA 2009, s 327 (see commentary on para 39) or para 40 above as being pre-commencement losses not brought into account under income tax. Accordingly, this paragraph allows the loss on the hedging relationship to be brought into account, up to the amount of the profit on the loan relationship/derivative contract.

Paragraph 42 deals with the situation where there is a 'tax asymmetry' as a result of profits arising from a derivative contract coming within the scope of corporation tax on 6 April 2020, and so potentially subject to the Disregard Regulations (SI 2004/3256), which do not apply to companies within income tax. The tax treatment of derivative contracts under corporation tax broadly follows the accounting treatment. As such, fair value movements can result in volatility in taxable profits and so the Disregard Regulations allow companies to elect to disregard fair value movements in relation to derivatives that are part of a hedging relationship. Non-UK resident corporate landlords will be able to use the Disregard Regulations following the switch to corporation tax, subject to the modifications in this Schedule.

Tax asymmetry could arise where a non-UK resident corporate landlord is already bringing fair value movements on its derivative contracts into account for income tax purposes, and following the switch to corporation tax that landlord elects to disregard fair value movements on existing derivative contracts. In that circumstance, just and reasonable adjustments are to be made over the remaining term of the derivative contract in order to achieve tax symmetry.

Paragraph 43 deals with potential asymmetries where fair value movements in a derivative contract have not previously been brought into account for income tax purposes as a result of being capital in nature. In that circumstance, the non-resident corporate landlord will be deemed to have made an election under regulation 6A of the Disregard Regulations in order to maintain consistent tax treatment for the derivative contract.

Paragraph 44 applies to non-UK resident corporate landlords which measured a derivative contract at fair value before 1 January 2015 and come within corporation tax for the first time by reason of this Schedule. Under regulation 6A of the Disregard Regulations, the timing of when elections have effect depends on whether or not the company is a 'new adopter'. A new adopter is defined in the Disregard Regulations as 'a company which measures a relevant derivative contract at fair value for the first time *on or after* [emphasis added] 1st January 2015'.

This paragraph extends new adopter status to non-UK resident corporate landlords which have measured a derivative contract at fair value before 1 January 2015.

Paragraph 45 applies where an asset becomes a chargeable intangible asset following the switch to corporation tax, and treats that asset as having being acquired for accounting value as at 6 April 2020 (see also commentary on para 27).

Paragraph 46 relates to IFA degrouping charges (see commentary on paras 22 to 25 in relation to the widening of these rules to non-UK resident companies), and provides that an IFA degrouping charge cannot be reallocated to a non-UK resident company where the relevant degrouping event took place before the non-UK resident company was brought within corporation tax (ie before 5 July 2016 for non-UK resident companies trading in UK land, or 6 April 2020 for non-UK resident companies carrying on a UK property business).

Paragraph 47 provides that expenditure incurred by a non-UK resident corporate landlord before 6 April 2020 in relation to a UK property business it commences on or after that date will not be eligible for contaminated land relief under CTA 2009, Pt 14, Ch 2. Relief may still be available under CTA 2009, s 1147 for expenditure on contaminated or derelict land incurred on or after 6 April 2020.

Paragraph 48 provides that non-UK resident companies coming within the charge to corporation tax as a result of this Schedule will not be subject to the corporation tax instalments regime for their first tax accounting period commencing 6 April 2020.

Paragraph 49 is a targeted anti-avoidance rule aimed at arrangements to secure a 'tax advantage' in relation to the coming into force of this Schedule. 'Tax advantage' is widely drawn and takes its meaning from CTA 2010, s 1137 including, for example, a relief from tax, a repayment of tax and a reduction of tax. HMRC will be able to counteract such advantages through adjustments such as amending or disallowing claims. This paragraph has effect from 29 October 2018 (the date it was published, having not been included in the 6 July 2018 consultation draft).

Paragraph 50 is another provision included following the technical consultation, and provides that tax advantage arrangements entered into from 29 October 2018 will not be counteracted by the para 49 targeted anti-avoidance rule if they are to secure the benefit of a relief under the corporate interest restriction rules, and they are effected by taking only ordinary commercial steps in accordance with generally prevailing commercial practice. Guidance will be helpful in clarifying what HMRC considers to be 'commercial' for this purpose.

SCHEDULE 6
DIVERTED PROFITS TAX

Section 18

Introduction

1 Part 3 of FA 2015 (diverted profits tax) is amended as follows.

Calculation of taxable diverted profits

2 (1) Section 82 (calculation of taxable diverted profits in section 80 or 81 case: introduction) is amended as follows.

(2) In subsection (3) for "(9)" substitute "(10)".

(3) In subsection (7) (when the "actual provision condition" is met) in paragraph (a) omit "(ignoring Part 4 of TIOPA 2010 (transfer pricing))".

(4) After subsection (7) insert—

> "(7A) For the purposes of subsection (7)(a) ignore any adjustment that is required to be made to the results of the material provision under Part 4 of TIOPA 2010 (transfer pricing)."

(5) After subsection (9) insert—

> "(10) "Diverted profits" of the relevant company for the accounting period means an amount—
>
> (a) in respect of which the company is chargeable to corporation tax for that period by reason of any adjustment required to be made to the results of the material provision under Part 4 of TIOPA 2010 (transfer pricing), and
>
> (b) which, in a case where section 81 applies, is attributable (in accordance with sections 20 to 32 of CTA 2009) to UKPE"."

3 In section 83 (section 80 or 81 cases where no taxable diverted profits arise) omit subsection (2).

4 In section 84 (section 80 or 81: calculation of profits by reference to the actual provision) in subsection (2) for the words from "the amount (if any)" to the end substitute "an amount equal to so much of the diverted profits of the company for the accounting period as are not taken into account in an assessment to corporation tax included before the end of the review period in the company's company tax return for that accounting period."

5 (1) Section 85 (section 80 or 81: calculation of profits by reference to the relevant alternative provision) is amended as follows.

(2) In subsection (4) for paragraph (a) (but not the "and" immediately after it) substitute—

> "(a) so much of the diverted profits (if any) of the company for the accounting period as are not taken into account in an assessment to corporation tax included before the end of the review period in the company's company tax return for that accounting period,".

(3) In subsection (6) (meaning of "the notional additional amount")—

(a) in the words before paragraph (a) omit "the amount by which",

(b) in paragraph (a) before "amount" insert "additional",

(c) at the end of paragraph (a) for "exceeds" substitute "less", and

(d) in paragraph (b)(i) for the words from "the application" to the end substitute "any adjustment required to be made to the results of the material provision (whether under Part 4 of TIOPA 2010 (transfer pricing) or otherwise),".

(4) After subsection (6) insert—

> "(7) In calculating the additional amount mentioned in paragraph (a) of subsection (6) no account is to be taken of any adjustment required to be made to the results of the material provision under Part 4 of TIOPA 2010 or otherwise."

6 (1) Section 88 (calculation of taxable diverted profits in section 86 case: introduction) is amended as follows.

(2) After subsection (5A) insert—

"(5B) In calculating the notional PE profits no account is to be taken of any adjustment within subsection (5C).

(5C) An adjustment is within this subsection if—

(a) it is an adjustment required to be made under Part 4 of TIOPA 2010 to the results of any provision made or imposed between the foreign company and the avoided PE,

(b) it is taken into account in an assessment to corporation tax included in a company tax return of the avoided PE, and

(c) the time when it is first taken into account as mentioned in paragraph (b) is after the end of the review period."

(3) In subsection (9)(a) omit "(ignoring Part 4 of TIOPA 2010 (transfer pricing)".

(4) After subsection (9) insert—

"(9A) For the purposes of subsection (9)(a) ignore any adjustment that would be required to be made to the results of the material provision under Part 4 of TIOPA 2010 in calculating what would have been the notional PE profits for the accounting period."

7 After section 111 insert—

"111A Adjustment required to be made to the material provision

A reference in section 82 or 88 to an adjustment required to be made under Part 4 of TIOPA 2010 (transfer pricing) to the results of any provision includes a reference to an adjustment required to be made under any other enactment to the results of the provision if and to the extent that, but for that other enactment, the adjustment would have been required to be made under that Part."

8 The amendments made by paragraphs 2 to 7 have effect in relation to accounting periods beginning on or after 29 October 2018.

Extension of period for issuing a preliminary notice

9 (1) Section 93 (preliminary notice) is amended as follows.

(2) In subsection (5) (period for issuing a notice) for the words from ", a preliminary notice" to the end substitute "—

(a) a preliminary notice may not be issued in respect of an accounting period on the basis that section 80 or 81 applies more than six months after the last day on which an amendment of the company tax return for the accounting period could be made, and

(b) a preliminary notice may not be issued in respect of an accounting period on the basis that section 86 applies more than 24 months after the end of that accounting period."

(3) After subsection (5) insert—

"(5A) For the purposes of subsection (5)(a) no account is to be taken of any exception to paragraph 15(4) of Schedule 18 to FA 1998 (period for amending a company tax return)."

(4) The amendments made by this paragraph do not have effect in relation to a preliminary notice if the period during which it may be issued (but for the amendments) expires before this Act is passed.

Relief from corporation tax

10 (1) After section 100 insert—

"100A Relief from corporation tax

(1) This section applies where a charging notice or supplementary charging notice is issued to a company for an accounting period and any of the following events occurs—

(a) the period of 30 days mentioned in subsection (2) of section 102 ends without notice of an appeal against the notice being given in accordance with that subsection,

(b) an appeal against the notice is finally determined otherwise than by the notice being cancelled, or

(c) an appeal against the notice is withdrawn.

(2) The company is not chargeable to corporation tax for the accounting period in respect of any amount within subsection (3).

(3) An amount is within this subsection if—

(a) the company failed before the end of the review period to take the amount into account in an assessment to corporation tax included in the company tax return for the accounting period, and

(b) that failure gave rise to, or to any of, the taxable diverted profits in respect of which the notice imposes a charge to diverted profits tax."

(2) The amendment made by this paragraph has effect in relation to accounting periods beginning on or after 1 April 2015.

Extension of the review period

11 (1) In section 101 (HMRC review of charging notice)—

(a) in subsection (2) (meaning of "review period") for "12 months" substitute "15 months", and

(b) in subsection (13) (events that bring the review period to an end early) for "12 months" substitute "15 months".

(2) The amendments made by this paragraph do not have effect in relation to a review period that, but for the amendments, expires before 29 October 2018.

Extension of period for amendment of company tax return

12 After section 101 insert—

"101A Amendment of CT return during review period: section 80 or 81 case

(1) This section applies where a charging notice is issued to a company by reason of section 80 or 81 applying in relation to it for an accounting period.

(2) At any time during the first 12 months of the review period, the company may amend its company tax return for the accounting period so as to reduce the taxable diverted profits arising to it in the accounting period.

101B Amendment of CT return during review period: section 86 case

(1) This section applies where a charging notice is issued to a company ("the foreign company") by reason of section 86 applying in relation to it for an accounting period.

(2) At any time during the first 12 months of the review period, the avoided PE may amend a company tax return made by it so as to reduce the taxable diverted profits arising to the foreign company in the accounting period."

COMMENTARY ON SCHEDULE 6

The diverted profits tax (DPT) was introduced in 2015 with the aim of counteracting contrived arrangements used by large groups (typically multinational enterprises) which erode the UK tax base. Since the rules were introduced, it has become clear that a tax planning opportunity was still available and so FA 2019 contains legislation that closes this opportunity. Before these amendments, it was possible to amend a company's tax return for corporation tax purposes after the DPT review period had ended and the DPT time limits had expired. There has also been concern that in certain circumstances profits that are subject to DPT may also be subject to corporation tax (i e a double tax charge could arise) and so it has been clarified that this is not the case. FA 2019 also modifies certain mechanics relating to DPT, namely extending the review period (the period during which HMRC and the taxpayer company are encouraged to work collaboratively to determine the amount of diverted profits) and the time period for which a company has a right to amend its corporation tax return.

The amendments relating to the closure of the tax planning opportunity have effect for accounting periods beginning on or after 29 October 2018 (budget day, when the amendments were announced). The new FA 2015, s 100A (which clarifies that there is no double tax charge to both DPT and corporation tax) has effect for accounting periods beginning on or after 1 April 2015 (the date on which DPT was introduced) and so is deemed to have always had effect as it is a wholly relieving provision. The mechanistic changes apply from Royal Assent, but there are also specific provisions where the relevant period expires before 29 October 2019 or Royal Assent (as applicable – see below for details).

Sub-paragraphs 2(3) and (4) alter the structure of FA 2015, s 82(7)(a) (the actual provision condition) so that it can be read in conjunction with new FA 2015, s 111A (see below).

Sub-paragraph 2(5) inserts a new definition of 'diverted profits' and paragraph 3 deletes the old definition. The new definition refers to an adjustment required under TIOPA 2010, ss 146–217 (Pt 4) (transfer pricing) rather than the application of that part.

Paragraph 4 amends FA 2015, s 84 as the (new) definition of diverted profits now applies to this section.

Sub-paragraph 5(2) amends FA 2015, s 85(4) to bring the calculation in line with the new definition of diverted profits.

Sub-paragraphs 5(3) and (4) amend FA 2015, s 85(6) and insert new FA 2015, s 85(7) to ensure that all adjustments (not just transfer pricing adjustments) are ignored when calculating the notional additional amount.

Paragraph 6 amends FA 2015, s 88 to make clear that, when the notional PE profits are calculated, no account should be taken of any adjustment to any provision made or imposed between the foreign company and the avoided PE if those adjustments are not taken into account in the avoided PE's company tax return before the end of the review period. This section is now also read in conjunction with new FA 2015, s 111A (see below).

Paragraph 7 inserts new FA 2015, s 111A which provides that a reference to a transfer pricing adjustment in FA 2015, ss 82 and 88 also includes an adjustment under any other enactment if but for that enactment an adjustment would have been required under the transfer pricing rules.

Paragraph 9 amends FA 2015, s 93 to change the preliminary notice period from 24 months after the end of the accounting period in cases where FA 2015, s 80 or 81 apply, provided that period (prior to these amendments) had not expired on 12 February 2019.

Paragraph 10 inserts new FA 2015, s 100A, which is deemed to have had effect since DPT was first introduced, to clarify that the same profits cannot be subject to both DPT and corporation tax.

SCHEDULE 7

PAYMENT OF CGT EXIT CHARGES

Section 22

CGT exit charge payment plans

1 In TMA 1970, after section 59BA insert—

"59BB CGT exit charge payment plans

Schedule 3ZAA contains provision for the payment in instalments of capital gains tax to which liability arises by virtue of section 25 or 80 of the 1992 Act."

2 After Schedule 3ZA to TMA 1970 insert—

"SCHEDULE 3ZAA

CGT EXIT CHARGE PAYMENT PLANS

Section 59BB

Introduction

1 (1) This Schedule makes provision for certain persons who are liable to pay an exit charge under section 25 or 80 of the 1992 Act to agree with HMRC to pay the charge in instalments.

(2) An agreement under this Schedule is called a "CGT exit charge payment plan".

Eligibility

2 (1) This paragraph applies where a person resident in an EEA state outside the United Kingdom is liable to pay an exit charge for a tax year by virtue of section 25(1) or (3) of the 1992 Act (deemed disposals by non-residents).

(2) The person is eligible to enter into a CGT exit charge payment plan in relation to any one or more of the assets to which the exit charge relates if—

(a) at the time of the event giving rise to the exit charge, the person had a right to freedom of establishment, or

(b) at any time after that event, the person carries on a trade in an EEA state other than the United Kingdom through a branch or agency and the asset or assets is or are—

(i) used in or for the purposes of that trade, or

(ii) used or held for the purposes of the branch or agency.

3 (1) This paragraph applies where the relevant trustees of a settlement are liable to pay an exit charge for a tax year by virtue of section 80 of the 1992 Act (charge on ceasing to be resident in the UK).

(2) The relevant trustees are eligible to enter into a CGT exit charge payment plan in relation to any one or more of the assets to which the exit charge relates if—

(a) at the time the trustees of the settlement ceased to be resident in the United Kingdom for the purposes of that section, they had a right to freedom of establishment,

(b) immediately before that time, the trustees of the settlement used the asset or assets for an economically significant activity carried on in the United Kingdom, and

(c) immediately after that time, those trustees—

(i) become resident in another EEA state for the purposes of the 1992 Act, and

(ii) use the asset or assets for an economically significant activity carried on there.

Tax to which a plan relates

4 (1) A CGT exit charge payment plan may relate to—

(a) the whole of the exit charge attributable to the asset or assets to which the plan relates (the "deferrable exit charge"), or

(b) only part of the deferrable exit charge.

(2) In this Schedule—

"deferred exit charge" means the amount of the exit charge to which a plan relates;

"taxpayer", in relation to a plan, means the person eligible under paragraph 2 or 3 to enter into the plan.

(3) For the purposes of this Schedule the exit charge attributable to an asset is such proportion of the exit charge as any gain accruing to the taxpayer in respect of the asset by virtue of section 25(1) or (3) or 80 of the 1992 Act in the tax year bears to the total gains to which the exit charge relates.

Payment by instalments

5 A CGT exit charge payment plan must provide for the deferred exit charge to be payable in 6 equal instalments where—

(a) the 1st instalment is due on the day on which payment of the exit charge is (apart from the plan) due and payable under section 59B, and

(b) the other 5 instalments are due one on each of the first 5 anniversaries of that day.

Entering into a plan

6 (1) To enter into a CGT exit charge payment plan, the taxpayer must apply to HMRC.

(2) An application for a CGT exit charge payment plan must—

(a) be made on or before the date specified in section 59B as the date by which the exit charge is payable, and

(b) contain details of all the matters which are required by this Schedule to be specified in the plan.

(3) A CGT exit charge payment plan is entered into when—

(a) the taxpayer agrees to pay the deferred exit charge, and any interest on it, in accordance with the plan, and

(b) an officer of Revenue and Customs agrees to accept payment of the deferred exit charge in accordance with the plan.

(4) A CGT exit charge payment plan is void if—

(a) an event giving rise to the exit charge is part of arrangements the main purpose of which, or one of the main purposes of which, is to defer the payment by the taxpayer of the exit charge, or

(b) any information furnished by the taxpayer in connection with the plan does not fully and accurately disclose all facts and considerations material to the decision of the officer of Revenue and Customs to accept payment in accordance with the plan.

Contents of a plan

7 (1) If the taxpayer is eligible under paragraph 2, a CGT exit charge payment plan must specify—

(a) the EEA state in which the person entering into the plan is resident, and

(b) if the person has ceased to carry on a trade in the United Kingdom through a branch or agency there, the date on which the person ceased to do so.

(2) If the taxpayer is eligible under paragraph 3, a CGT exit charge payment plan must specify—

(a) the date on which the trustees of the settlement became not resident in the United Kingdom for the purposes of section 80 of the 1992 Act, and

(b) the EEA state in which those trustees became resident.

(3) A CGT exit charge payment plan must specify—

(a) the amount of the exit charge which, in the taxpayer's opinion, the taxpayer is liable to pay under section 25 or (as the case may be) section 80 of the 1992 Act in respect of the tax year, and

(b) the amount of the deferred exit charge.

(4) A CGT exit charge payment plan may contain appropriate provision regarding security for HMRC if an officer of Revenue and Customs considers that there would be a serious risk to collection of any amount of deferred exit charge without it.

Effect of a plan

8 (1) This paragraph applies where a CGT exit charge payment plan is entered into by the taxpayer.

(2) The deferred exit charge remains due and payable under section 59B (payment of income tax and capital gains tax: assessments other than simple assessments).

(3) However, the Commissioners for Her Majesty's Revenue and Customs—

(a) may not seek payment of any of the deferred exit charge otherwise than in accordance with the plan, and

(b) may make repayments in respect of any of the deferred exit charge paid, or any amount paid on account of the deferred exit charge, before the plan is entered into.

(4) The deferred exit charge carries interest in accordance with Part 9 as if the plan had not been entered into; and each time a payment is made under the plan, it is to be paid together with any interest payable on it.

(5) The taxpayer is liable to penalties for late payment of the deferred exit charge only if the taxpayer fails to make payments in accordance with the plan (see item 3C of the Table at the end of paragraph 1 of Schedule 56 to the Finance Act 2009).

(6) Any of the deferred exit charge which is for the time being unpaid may be paid at any time before it becomes payable under the plan together with interest payable on it to the date of payment.

(7) If—

(a) the taxpayer becomes bankrupt under the law of England and Wales or Northern Ireland or the taxpayer's estate is sequestrated under the law of Scotland,

(b) an event corresponding to an event in paragraph (a) occurs under the law of an EEA state outside the United Kingdom, or

(c) the taxpayer becomes resident in a country or territory that is not an EEA state,

the outstanding balance of the deferred exit charge is payable on the date on which the next instalment would otherwise have been due under the plan.

Supplementary

9 If, for the purposes of any double taxation arrangements, a person is treated at any time as resident in a territory other than an EEA state, the person is also to be treated as resident there at that time for the purposes of this Schedule.

10 In this Schedule—

"deferrable exit charge" has the meaning given by paragraph 4(1)(a);

"deferred exit charge" has the meaning given by paragraph 4(2);

"double taxation arrangements" means arrangements made by two or more territories with a view to affording relief from double taxation;

"economically significant activity" has the meaning given by section 13A(4) of the 1992 Act (reading references to a company as references to trustees);

"exit charge" means—

(a) for the purposes of paragraph 2, any amount of capital gains tax which a person is liable to pay for a tax year which the person would not be liable to pay if gains arising by virtue of section 25 of the 1992 Act in the tax year were ignored;

(b) for the purposes of paragraph 3, any amount of capital gains tax which the relevant trustees are liable to pay for a tax year which they would not be liable to pay if gains arising by virtue of section 80 of the 1992 Act in the tax year were ignored;

"right to freedom of establishment" means a right protected by—

(a) Article 49 of the Treaty on the Functioning of the European Union, or

(b) Article 31 of the EEA agreement;

"taxpayer" has the meaning given by paragraph 4(2);

"trade" includes a profession or vocation."

Penalties

3 (1) Schedule 56 to FA 2009 (penalty for failure to make payments on time) is amended as follows.

(2) In the Table at the end of paragraph 1, after entry 3B insert—

"3C	Capital gains tax	Amount payable under a CGT exit charge payment plan entered into in accordance with Schedule 3ZAA to TMA 1970	The later of— (a)the date falling 30 days after the date specified in section 59B of TMA 1970 as the date by which the amount is due to be paid, and (b)the date on which the amount is payable under the plan."

(3) In paragraph 3(1)(a), after "3B" insert ", 3C".

4 In section 107A of TMA 1970 (relevant trustees), in subsection (3)(c)(i), after "1," insert "3C,".

5 In paragraph 5(3) of Schedule 11 to F(No 3)A 2010 (penalties for failure to make payments on time), omit "items 1, 3" in both places.

CT exit charge payment plans

6 (1) In sections 59FA, 109B and 109E of and Schedule 3ZB to TMA 1970 (including any headings of, and in, those provisions)—

(a) for "an exit charge payment plan", in each case it occurs, substitute "a CT exit charge payment plan",

(b) for "exit charge payment plan", in each case where it occurs without "an" before it, substitute "CT exit charge payment plan" (but this does not apply to paragraph 10(2A) or 11(1) of Schedule 3ZB to TMA 1970 as respectively inserted and substituted by Schedule 8 to this Act), and

(c) for "exit charge payment plans" in each case it occurs, substitute "CT exit charge payment plans".

(2) In Schedule 56 to FA 2009 (penalties), in the Table at the end of paragraph 1, in entry 6ZA, in the third column, for "an exit charge payment plan" substitute "a CT exit charge payment plan".

Commencement

7 The amendments made by paragraphs 1 and 2 have effect in relation to amounts of capital gains tax which a person is liable to pay by virtue of section 25(1) or (3) or 80 of TCGA 1992 in relation to events occurring on or after 6 April 2019.

COMMENTARY ON SCHEDULE 7

Paragraphs 1 and 2 add new provisions to TMA 1970, allowing for the payment of CGT exit charges in interest bearing instalments, in the following situations provided specified conditions are met:

(1) The TCGA 1992, s 25 (Non-residents: deemed disposals) charge. Broadly, TCGA 1992, s 25 applies where a non-UK resident individual trades in the UK through a branch or agency and one of the following occurs:

  (a) A chargeable asset (or assets) used in the UK trade is taken outside of the UK. In such cases there is a deemed disposal of the asset or assets taken outside of the UK. The disposal is deemed to have taken place immediately before the time that the asset became situated outside of the UK for proceeds equal to the market value at that time.

  (b) The trade ceases. All of the chargeable assets that were used in the trade are deemed to have been disposed of immediately before the time that the trade ceased for proceeds equal to the market value at that time.

(2) The TCGA 1992, s 80 (Trustees ceasing to be resident in UK) charge. The provisions of TCGA 1992, s 80 mean that the trustees are treated as if they had disposed of all the chargeable assets within the trust for proceeds equal to the market value immediately before the emigration.

The legislation was introduced as a result of the finding against the UK by the Court of Justice of the European Union (CJEU) in the case of *Trustees of the P Panayi Accumulation & Maintenance Settlements* (C-646/15, [2017] STC 2495).

The CJEU held that:

- the imposition of an exit charge was acceptable where the residence of a trust shifted to another Member State but the provisions had to be proportionate; and
- TCGA 1992, s 80 was not proportionate as the tax payable as a result of the exit charge could not be deferred.

Finance Act 2019 amended the legislation, since the UK was still part of the EU and still had to abide by EU law. At the time of writing there is considerable uncertainty over Brexit. If a deal between the UK and the EU is agreed the UK may have to abide by EU treaty provisions for some time and this may also have been in the minds of the legislators. It is arguable whether the changes made go far enough to make the legislation compatible with treaty freedoms (see the discussion at the end of this commentary).

Paragraph 1 inserts new TMA 1970, s 59BB which introduces new Sch 3ZAA (CGT Exit Charge Payment Plans) into TMA 1970. Paragraph 2 inserts new Sch 3ZAA into TMA 1970.

New TMA 1970, Sch 3ZAA

The actual charging legislation is unchanged and the default position is that the whole of the CGT on deemed TCGA 1992, s 25 and s 80 gains remains payable in accordance with TMA 1970, s 59B. However, new TMA 1970, Sch 3ZAA (CGT exit charge payment plans) allows the taxpayer to apply to HMRC to enter into a CGT exit charge payment plan ('CGT ECPP') with respect to all or part of the CGT due.

Under the CGT ECPP the tax due is divided into six instalments (TMA 1970, Sch 3ZAA, para 5):

- the first instalment being due on the normal s 59B payment date; and
- the next five instalments (with interest at the standard rate – see TMA 1970, Sch 3ZAA, para 8(4)) being due on each of the first five anniversaries of that date.

Provided the tax and interest is paid in accordance with the CGT ECPP no penalties are due.

The application for a CGT ECPP must be made on or before the date the CGT on the deemed gain is payable (TMA 1970, Sch 3ZAA, para 6(2)).

TMA 1970, Sch 3ZAA, para 10 provides various definitions for the purposes of the schedule.

Eligibility

TMA 1970, Sch 3ZAA, paras 2 and 3 sets down strict eligibility criteria which taxpayers must meet in order to be able to enter into CGT ECPPs. Para 2 applies where TCGA 1992, s 25 is in point and para 3 applies where TCGA 1992, s 80 is in point.

Broadly to qualify for a CGT ECPP:

- At the time of the deemed disposal the taxpayer must have had the right to freedom of establishment. Freedom of establishment is defined in para 10 as a right protected by Article 49 of the Treaty on the Functioning of the European Union or Article 31 of the EEA agreement.
- The movement must be to an EEA jurisdiction:
  - For TCGA 1992, s 25, at any time after the deemed disposal the person must carry on a trade in an EEA state, other than the UK, through a branch or agency and the asset or assets must be: (i) used in or for the purposes of that trade; or (ii) used or held for the purposes of the branch or agency.
  - For TCGA 1992, s 80 immediately before the deemed disposal the trustees must use the asset(s) for an economically significant activity carried out in the UK and immediately after that time: (i) the trust becomes resident in another EEA state (residence being determined by TCGA 1992, s 69); and (ii) the trustees use the asset(s) for an economically significant activity carried on in the other EEA state. Para 10 defines 'economically significant activity' in accordance with TCGA 1992, s 13A(4) but reading references to a company as references to a trustees.

The entire tax liability remains due and payable under TMA 1970, s 59B. However, provided none of the events in TMA 1970, Sch 3ZAA, para 8(7) take place, HMRC is only permitted to seek payment in accordance with the terms of the ECPP. Where a para 8(7) event occurs the outstanding CGT balance and interest will be due in full on the next instalment date. The para 8(7) events are as follows:

- The taxpayer becomes bankrupt under the law of England and Wales or Northern Ireland.
- The taxpayer's estate is sequestrated under the law of Scotland.
- An event corresponding to bankruptcy/sequestration occurs under the law of an EEA state outside of the UK.
- The taxpayer becomes resident in a jurisdiction outside of the EEA. Note that TMA 1970, Sch 3ZAA, para 9 specifies that for the purposes of the provisions a person will be deemed to be resident in a jurisdiction outside of the EEA if that person is dual resident and the non-EEA jurisdiction is treated as the jurisdiction of residence for the purposes of the application of a double tax treaty arrangement.

The CGT ECPP may relate to either the entire CGT due as a result of the relevant exit charges (that is TCGA 1992, s 25 and s 80 as discussed above) or only part of the CGT due (TMA 1970, Sch 3ZAA, para 4).

Entering into an CGT ECPP and the contents of the plan

TMA 1970, Sch 3ZAA, para 6 sets down the terms under which a person meeting the para 2 or para 3 criteria can enter into a CGT ECPP. As mentioned, the taxpayer must apply to HMRC prior to the CGT becoming due.

The application must provide the details of all the information that TMA 1970, Sch 3ZAA, para 7 states must be specified in the CGT ECPP. This information is set down in the following paragraphs.

Where TCGA 1992, s 25 imposes the exit charge (such that the para 2 eligibility conditions apply) the plan must specify:

- which EEA state the person entering into the plan is resident in; and
- if the person has ceased to carry on a trade in the UK through a branch or agency there, the date on which the person ceased to do so.

Where TCGA 1992, s 80 imposes the exit charge (such that the para 3 eligibility conditions apply) the plan must specify:

- the date on which the trust became non-UK resident for the purposes of TCGA 1992, s 80; and
- the EEA state in which the trust became resident.

For all taxpayers entering into CGT ECPPs the plan must specify:

- The amount of the CGT exit charge under TCGA 1992, s 25 or s 80 for the tax year.
- The amount of the CGT exit charge to which the plan will relate (referred to as 'the deferred exit charge').

A taxpayer wanting to enter into a CGT ECPP will have to provide security if the HMRC Officer considers it too risky to enter into the instalment plan otherwise. Where security is provided this must be detailed on the fact of the plan.

For the CGT ECPP to be entered into it requires:

- agreement by the taxpayer to the instalment plan (including interest); and
- an HMRC officer agreeing to accept payment of the exit charge in accordance with the terms of the instalment plan.

The taxpayer can at any time make early payments of the tax due together with the interest payable on it up until the date of payment (TMA 1970, Sch 3ZAA, para 8(6)).

Commencement: para 7

As mentioned, paras 1 and 2 are the main provisions inserting the new legislation with respect to CGT ECPPs into TMA 1970. Paragraph 7 is the commencement provision for these paras. It states that the legislation has effect in relation to events occurring on or after 6 April 2019. This raises an EU law issue. We know from the *Panayi* case that the relevant UK legislation prior to 6 April 2019 was contrary to EU law. As such, since the freedom of establishment (and free movement of capital) have direct effect consideration should be given to filing in line with EU law rather than the conflicting legislation.

Consequential amendments

Paragraphs 3 to 5 make consequential changes with respect to penalties (the table at the end of FA 2009, Sch 56, para 1 has been extended), so that the penalty provisions also apply to late payment under CGT ECPPs.

Paragraph 6 makes consequential changes so that the existing exit charge payment plan legislation for corporates (amended by FA 2019, Sch 8) is clearly differentiated from CGT exit charge payment plans. Now for corporates the exit charge payment plans are always referred to as CT exit charge payment plans.

Is the new legislation compatible with EU Law?

The following bullet points highlight some key issues for advisers to consider:

- There is nothing in the *Panayi* decision to suggest that the CJEU would have made a different decision on freedom of capital grounds. Since freedom of capital has the potential to apply to non-EEA jurisdictions the narrow nature of the legislation could be challenged.
- In the context of TCGA 1992, s 80 and trustees the definition of 'economically significant activity' given by the legislation is arguable contrary to EU law generally and the *Panayi* decision in particular.
- The changes could be said to be insufficient to make the UK legislation proportionate. There is still a dry tax charge and the CGT ECPPs are just fixed instalment plans with HMRC's standard rate of interest applying on all instalments made after the standard TMA 1970, s 59B due date.

SCHEDULE 8

CORPORATION TAX EXIT CHARGES

Section 23

PART 1

CT EXIT CHARGE PAYMENT PLANS

1 Schedule 3ZB to TMA 1970 (CT exit charge payment plans) is amended as follows.

2 In paragraph 1 (circumstances in which plan may be entered into: company ceasing to be resident in UK)—

(a) in subparagraph (1)(b) for "another" substitute "a relevant",
(b) in subparagraph (5) for "an" substitute "a relevant",
(c) in subparagraph (6) for "other" substitute "relevant", and
(d) in subparagraph (7) at the end insert ";

"relevant EEA state" means an EEA state that is—

(a) a member of the European Union, or
(b) a party to an agreement with the United Kingdom that provides for mutual assistance equivalent to that provided for by Council Directive 2010/24/EU of 16 March 2010 concerning mutual assistance for the recovery of claims relating to taxes."

3 (1) Paragraph 4 (circumstances in which plan may be entered into: non-UK resident companies with UK permanent establishments) is amended as follows.

(2) In subparagraph (4) (meaning of "PE qualifying event")—

(a) omit "and" at the end of paragraph (b), and
(b) after paragraph (c) insert ", and

(d) immediately after the event—

(i) the asset or liability is held or owed by the company for the purposes of a permanent establishment of the company in a relevant EEA state, or
(ii) the asset or liability is held or owed by the company otherwise than for the purposes of a permanent establishment of the company and the company is resident in a relevant EEA state."

(3) In subparagraph (6)—

(a) for "and" substitute ",", and
(b) after ""eligible company"" insert "and "relevant EEA state"".

4 In paragraph 8(1) (entering into a plan)—

(a) in paragraph (a) for the words from "the standard" to the end substitute "paragraphs 11 to 14", and
(b) in paragraph (c) for "paragraphs 10 to 12" substitute "paragraph 10".

5 (1) Paragraph 10 (contents of plan) is amended as follows.

(2) In subparagraph (1)(b) before "EEA state" insert "relevant".

(3) After subparagraph (2) insert—

"(2A) In either case a CT exit charge payment plan entered into by a company must specify requirements as to the ongoing provision of information by the company to Her Majesty's Revenue and Customs in relation to the exit charge assets and liabilities."

(4) In subparagraph (3) for paragraph (c) substitute—

"(c) the amount of ECPP tax attributable to each exit charge asset or liability."

(5) Omit subparagraphs (4) and (5).

6 For paragraphs 11 to 17, and the italic heading before those paragraphs, substitute—

"The payment method

11 (1) Where a CT exit charge payment plan is entered into the ECPP tax is due in 6 instalments of equal amounts as follows—

(a) the first instalment is due on the first day after the period of 9 months beginning immediately after the end of the migration accounting period, and

(b) the other 5 instalments are due one on each of the first 5 anniversaries of that day.

(2) But see paragraphs 12, 13 and 14 for circumstances in which all or part of the outstanding balance of the ECPP tax becomes due otherwise than by those instalments.

All of outstanding balance due

12 (1) Where an event mentioned in subparagraph (2) occurs, the outstanding balance of the ECPP tax is due on the date on which the next instalment of that tax would otherwise have been due.

(2) The events are—

(a) the company becoming insolvent or entering administration,

(b) the appointment of a liquidator,

(c) an event under the law of a country or territory outside the United Kingdom corresponding to an event specified in paragraph (a) or (b),

(d) the company ceasing to be resident in a relevant EEA state and, on so ceasing, not becoming resident in another relevant EEA state, or

(e) the company failing to pay any amount of the ECPP tax for a period of 12 months after the date on which the amount becomes due.

All of outstanding balance attributable to particular exit charge asset or liability due

13 (1) This paragraph applies where—

(a) a trigger event occurs in relation to an exit charge asset or liability during the instalments period, and

(b) a trigger event has not previously occurred in relation to that asset or liability during that period.

(2) A trigger event occurs in relation to a TCGA or trading stock exit charge asset or an intangible exit charge asset if the company—

(a) disposes of the asset, or

(b) ceases to hold the asset for the purposes of a business carried on by the company in a relevant EEA state and, on so ceasing, does not begin to hold it for the purposes of another such business.

(3) A trigger event occurs in relation to a financial exit charge asset or liability if the company—

(a) ceases to be a party to the loan relationship or derivative contract in question, or

(b) ceases to be a party to the loan relationship or derivative contract in question for the purposes of a business carried on by the company in a relevant EEA state and, on so ceasing, does not begin to be a party to it for the purposes of another such business.

(4) On the occurrence of the trigger event an amount of the ECPP tax is due.

(5) The amount due is—

$(A - B) \times (O / T)$

Where—

"A" is the amount of ECPP tax attributable to the exit charge asset or liability (see paragraph 10(6)),

"B" is the amount of ECPP tax that has previously become due under paragraph 14 by reason of a partial trigger event occurring in relation to the exit charge asset or liability,

"O" is the amount of ECPP tax that is outstanding at the time of the trigger event, and

"T" is the amount of ECPP tax.

(6) In this paragraph and paragraph 14 "the instalments period" means the period—

(a) beginning immediately after—

(i) the company ceases to be resident in the United Kingdom (in the case of a Part 1 company), or

(ii) the occurrence of the PE qualifying event in respects of the asset or liability concerned (in the case of a Part 2 company), and

(b) ending with the day on which the final instalment of the ECPP tax is due under paragraph 11.

Part of outstanding balance attributable to particular exit charge asset or liability due

14 (1) This paragraph applies if—

(a) a partial trigger event occurs in relation to an exit charge asset or liability during the instalments period, and

(b) a trigger event has not previously occurred in relation to that asset or liability during that period.

(2) A partial trigger event occurs in relation to a TCGA or trading stock exit charge asset if the company disposes of part (but not all) of the asset.

(3) A partial trigger event occurs in relation to a financial exit charge asset or liability if there is a disposal of a right or liability under the loan relationship or derivative contract in question which amounts to a related transaction (as defined in section 304 or 596 of CTA 2009 as the case may be).

(4) A partial trigger event occurs in relation to an intangible exit charge asset if there is a transaction which results in a reduction in the accounting value of the asset but not in the asset ceasing to be recognised in the company's balance sheet.

(5) On the occurrence of the partial trigger event an amount of the outstanding ECPP tax is due.

(6) The amount due is the amount that is just and reasonable having regard to the amount that would have been due had a trigger event occurred in relation to the exit charge asset or liability instead.

(7) In this paragraph "trigger event" has the same meaning as in paragraph 13."

7 In Schedule 56 to FA 2009 (penalty for failure to make payments on time) in paragraph 4 (amount of penalty in respect of certain late payments) in subparagraph (1) for "item 5, 6 or 6ZZA" substitute "any of items 5 to 6ZA".

8 The amendments made by paragraphs 1 to 6 have effect in relation to accounting periods ending on or after 1 January 2020.

COMMENTARY ON SCHEDULE 8, PART 1

Postponement of corporation tax exit charges

If a company ceases to be UK resident a corporation tax exit charge can arise, whereby the company is deemed to dispose of certain assets thus triggering gains or credit subject to corporation tax. This charge can be postponed either under the 'instalment method' or the 'realisation method' if the company migrates to an EEA member state. There are similar rules where a company that is not resident in the UK carries on a trade in the UK through a permanent establishment.

Definition of 'relevant EEA state'

The existing rule applies where a company ceases to be resident in the UK and becomes resident in another EEA state. That rule is now amended to refer to a 'relevant EEA state', meaning either a member of the EU or an EEA country that is party to an agreement providing for mutual assistance for the recovery of claims relating to taxes, equivalent to EU Directive 2010/24/EU. A similar change is made to the exit charge rules for companies not resident in the UK but which are carrying on a trade in the UK through a permanent establishment.

Repeal of realisation method

Under current rules, a company can choose whether to pay the excess charge in instalments or under the 'realisation method', the latter being a mechanism allowing capital gains tax to be paid either when an asset is actually disposed of by the company or ten years after the migration event. Under the new rule, only the 'instalment method' will be available. This requires the corporation tax exit charge payment to be made in six equal instalments, the first payment being nine months and one day after the end of the accounting period in which the migration occurs, followed by five annual instalments thereafter.

Under the instalment method a payment of the outstanding balance of tax becomes immediately payable if the company becomes insolvent, enters into administration or appoints a liquidator or if there is an equivalent event under the law of an EU state other than the UK, or if the company ceases to be resident in the EEA. To this list is now added a requirement to pay the full outstanding balance of any tax due if the company fails to pay an instalment for 12 months after the date on which that instalment becomes due.

A new rule is introduced to require payment of some or all of the postponed charge if there is a 'trigger event' in relation to certain assets. There is a trigger event relating to a chargeable asset, trading stock or an intangible fixed asset if the company disposes of the asset or ceases to hold that asset for the purposes of the business carried on by the company in a relevant EEA state. A trigger event occurs in relation to a financial asset or liability if the company ceases to be a party to the relevant loan relationship or derivative contract or ceases to be a party to that loan relationship derivative contract for the purposes of a business carried on by the company in a relevant EEA state. The effect of this provision is to trigger the immediate payment of an amount of corporation tax equivalent to the unpaid deferred amount specific to that individual asset or liability, subject to a reduction if there has been a partial trigger of liability in respect of that asset previously.

Partial trigger events occur when only part of an asset or loan relationship or derivative contract right or liability is disposed of or, for an intangible fixed asset, if there is a transaction which results in a reduction in the accounting value of the assets but not in that asset ceasing to be recognised. In the case of partial trigger events, there is no formula, we are simply told that the amount of outstanding tax to be paid immediately is to be calculated on a 'just and reasonable' basis, taking into account the payment that would have been required had a trigger event occurred, instead.

The above changes take effect for accounting periods ending on or after 1 January 2020. The notes to the Finance Bill remind us that the migration of the UK resident company will generally trigger the end of an accounting period.

Late payment penalties

Payments under the instalment method regime are brought within the penalty regime of FA 2009, Sch 56, para 4. This means that a failure to make a payment at the correct time carries a 5% late payment penalty, with a further 5% penalty if the tax is paid more than three months late and another 5% penalty if it is paid more than nine months late.

There is no commencement date for this change as Schedule 56 comes into force on an appointed day but no date has yet been appointed!

PART 2

REPEAL OF CERTAIN POSTPONEMENT PROVISIONS

9 (1) Section 187 of TCGA 1992 (postponement of charge on deemed disposal under section 185) is repealed.

(2) The following amendments have effect in consequence of that repeal.

(3) In section 185(1) of TCGA 1992 (deemed disposal of assets on company ceasing to be resident in UK) for "and section 187 apply" substitute "applies".

(4) In Schedule 3ZB to TMA 1970 (CT exit charge payment plans)—

- (a) in paragraph 2(3) (meaning of "exit charge provisions" in Part 1) omit paragraph (b), and
- (b) in paragraph 3 (interpretation: exit charge assets and liabilities)—
  - (i) in subparagraph (2)(a) omit ", (b)", and
  - (ii) in subparagraph (2)(c)(ii) omit "or (b)".

(5) The amendments made by this paragraph have effect in relation to a company in a case where section 185 of TCGA 1992 applies to the company by reason of its ceasing to be resident in the United Kingdom on or after 1 January 2020.

10 (1) Sections 860 to 862 of CTA 2009 (postponement of gain on deemed realisation under section 859) are repealed.

(2) The following amendments have effect in consequence of that repeal.

(3) In section 859 of CTA 2009 (asset ceasing to be chargeable intangible asset: deemed realisation at market value) omit subsection (3).

(4) In Schedule 3ZB to TMA 1970 (CT exit charge payment plans)—

(a) in paragraph 2(3) (meaning of "exit charge provisions" in Part 1)—

(i) at the end of paragraph (e) insert "and", and

(ii) omit paragraph (g) and the "and" immediately before it, and

(b) in paragraph 3 (interpretation: exit charge assets and liabilities) in subparagraph (2)(c)(i) omit "or (g)".

(5) The amendments made by this paragraph have effect in relation to a company in a case where section 859 of CTA 2009 applies to the company by reason of its ceasing to be resident in the United Kingdom on or after 1 January 2020.

COMMENTARY ON SCHEDULE 8, PART 2

Repeal of TCGA 1992, s 187

Part 2 of Schedule 8 repeals TCGA 1992, s 187. This provision disapplied the corporation tax charge on emigration of a UK resident company if it was at least a 75% subsidiary of another company which remained resident in the UK.

There are a small number of consequential amendments as a result of the repeal.

This applies to companies that ceased to be UK resident or after 1 January 2020.

PART 3

TREATMENT OF ASSETS SUBJECT TO EU EXIT CHARGES

11 (1) After section 184I of TCGA 1992 insert—

"Assets subject to EU exit charges

184J Asset subject to EU exit charge on becoming chargeable asset

(1) This section applies if—

(a) an asset becomes a chargeable asset in relation to a company by reason of an event specified in subsection (2), and

(b) on the occurrence of that event the company becomes subject to an EU exit charge in relation to the asset.

(2) The events are—

(a) the company becoming resident in the United Kingdom, and

(b) in the case of a company that is not resident in the United Kingdom, the asset beginning to be held for the purposes of a trade carried on by the company in the United Kingdom through a permanent establishment.

(3) The company is to be treated for the purposes of this Act as if it had acquired the asset for its market value at the time it became a chargeable asset in relation to the company.

(4) For the purposes of this section an asset is a "chargeable asset" in relation to a company at any time if any gain on its disposal by the company at that time would be chargeable to corporation tax.

(5) "EU exit charge" means a charge to tax under the law of a member State in accordance with Article 5(1) of Directive (EU) 2016/1164 of the European Parliament and of the Council of 12 July 2016 laying down rules against tax avoidance practices that directly affect the functioning of the internal market."

(2) The amendment made by this paragraph has effect in relation to assets that become chargeable assets on or after 1 January 2020.

12 (1) Part 8 of CTA 2009 (intangible fixed assets) is amended as follows.

(2) In section 863 (asset becoming chargeable intangible asset) after subsection (2) insert—

"(3) But subsection (2)(b) is subject to section 863A."

(3) After section 863 insert—

"863A Asset becoming chargeable intangible asset: EU exit charge

(1) This section applies if—

(a) an asset becomes a chargeable intangible asset in relation to a company by reason of an event specified in section 863(1)(a) or (b), and

(b) on the occurrence of that event the company becomes subject to an EU exit charge in respect of the asset.

(2) This Part applies as if the company had acquired the asset for its market value at the time it became a chargeable intangible asset in relation to the company.

(3) "EU exit charge" means a charge to tax under the law of a member State in accordance with Article 5(1) of Directive (EU) 2016/1164 of the European Parliament and of the Council of 12 July 2016 laying down rules against tax avoidance practices that directly affect the functioning of the internal market."

(4) The amendments made by this paragraph have effect in relation to assets that become chargeable intangible assets on or after 1 January 2020.

COMMENTARY ON SCHEDULE 8, PART 3

Assets becoming chargeable

Part 3 of Schedule 8 makes provision for assets becoming chargeable assets when a company becomes resident in the United Kingdom or starts to carry on a trade in the UK through a permanent establishment. If an asset becomes a chargeable asset of the company as a result of such an event, and the company has been subject to an exit charge under the law of another EU member state, the chargeable asset is treated as if it had been acquired by the company for market value at the date it became a chargeable asset in relation to the company.

This rebases chargeable assets that are brought into the UK due to a company migration or the commencement of a trade in the UK.

This provision applies where the company has been subject to an exit charge in another EU member state on or after 1 January 2020.

A similar change is made in respect of intangible fixed assets.

This change applies in relation to assets that become chargeable intangible assets of the company on or after 1 January 2020.

SCHEDULE 9

INTANGIBLE FIXED ASSETS: RESTRICTIONS ON GOODWILL AND CERTAIN OTHER ASSETS

Section 25

1 Part 8 of CTA 2009 (intangible fixed assets) is amended as follows.

2 In section 711 (overview of Part) in subsection (8) after paragraph (f) (but before the following "and") insert—

"(fa) Chapter 15A (debits in respect of goodwill and certain other assets),".

3 In section 715 (application of Part to goodwill) in subsection (2) for the words from "section 816A" to the end substitute "Chapter 15A (debits in respect of goodwill and certain other assets))."

4 In section 746 ("non-trading credits" and "non-trading debits") in subsection (2) for paragraph (ba) substitute—

"(ba) sections 879C(3), 879I(3), 879K(5) and 879O(3)(b) (debits in respect of goodwill and certain other assets treated as non-trading debits),".

5 Omit section 816A (restrictions on goodwill and certain other assets).

6 After section 879 insert—

"Chapter 15A

Debits in Respect of Goodwill and Certain other Assets

Introduction

879A Introduction

(1) This Chapter contains special rules about the debits to be brought into account by a company for tax purposes in respect of relevant assets.

(2) In this Chapter "relevant asset" means—

(a) goodwill in a business or part of a business,

(b) an intangible fixed asset that consists of information which relates to customers or potential customers of a business or part of a business,

(c) an intangible fixed asset that consists of a relationship (whether contractual or not) between a person carrying on a business and one or more customers of that business or part of that business,

(d) an unregistered trade mark or other sign used in the course of a business or part of a business, or

(e) a licence or other right in respect of an asset within any of paragraphs (a) to (d).

Requirement to write down at a fixed rate

879B Requirement to write down at a fixed rate

(1) This section applies if a company acquires or creates a relevant asset on or after 1 April 2019.

(2) The company is to be treated as having made an election under section 730 to write down the cost of the asset for tax purposes at a fixed rate.

(3) In its application in relation to the asset, section 731 (writing down at fixed rate: calculation) has effect as if in subsection (1)(a) for "4%" there was substituted "6.5%".

(4) The Treasury may by regulations amend subsection (3) so as to alter the percentage substituted for 4%.

Restrictions on debits: pre-FA 2019 relevant assets

879C Restrictions on debits: pre-FA 2019 relevant assets

(1) This section applies in respect of a relevant asset of a company if it is a pre-FA 2019 relevant asset.

(2) No debits in respect of the asset are to be brought into account by the company for tax purposes under Chapter 3 (debits in respect of intangible fixed assets) or Chapter 15 (adjustments on change of accounting policy).

(3) Any debit in respect of the asset that is brought into account by the company for tax purposes under Chapter 4 (realisation of intangible fixed assets) is treated for the purposes of Chapter 6 as a non-trading debit.

(4) Sections 879D to 879H set out the cases in which a relevant asset of a company is a pre-FA 2019 relevant asset for the purposes of this Chapter.

879D Pre-FA 2019 relevant asset: the first case

For the purposes of this Chapter a relevant asset of a company is a pre-FA 2019 relevant asset if—

(a) the company acquired or created the asset during the period beginning with 8 July 2015 and ending with 31 March 2019, and

(b) the asset was a chargeable intangible asset in relation to the company at any time during the period beginning with 29 October 2018 and ending with 31 March 2019.

879E Pre-FA 2019 relevant asset: the second case

(1) For the purposes of this Chapter a relevant asset of a company ("C") is a pre-FA 2019 relevant asset if—

(a) another company acquired or created the asset during the period beginning with 8 July 2015 and ending with 31 March 2019,

(b) it was a chargeable intangible asset in relation to that other company at any time during the period beginning with 29 October 2018 and ending with 31 March 2019, and

(c) C acquired the asset on or after 1 April 2019 otherwise than in case A or case B from a person who was a related party in relation to C.

(2) Case A is where—

(a) C acquired the asset from a company that was within the charge to corporation tax at the time of the acquisition, and

(b) the asset was not a pre-FA 2019 relevant asset in the hands of that company immediately before the acquisition.

(3) Case B is where C acquired the asset from a person ("the intermediary") who acquired the asset on or after 1 April 2019 from a third person—

(a) who was not at the time of the intermediary's acquisition a related party in relation—

(i) to the intermediary, or

(ii) if the intermediary was not a company, to a company in relation to which the intermediary was a related party, and

(b) who is not, at the time of the acquisition by C, a related party in relation to C.

(4) References in this section to one person being (or not being) a related party in relation to another person are to be read as including references to the participation condition being met (or, as the case may be not being met) as between those persons.

(5) References in subsection (4) to a person include a firm in a case where, for section 1259 purposes, references in this section to a company are read as references to the firm.

(6) In subsection (5) "section 1259 purposes" means the purposes of determining under section 1259 the amount of profits or losses to be allocated to a partner in a firm.

(7) Section 148 of TIOPA 2010 (when the participation condition is met) applies for the purposes of subsection (4) as it applies for the purpose of section 147(1)(b) of TIOPA 2010.

879F Pre-FA 2019 relevant asset: the third case

(1) For the purposes of this Chapter a relevant asset of a company ("C") is a pre-FA 2019 relevant asset if—

(a) the relevant asset was created on or after 29 October 2018,

(b) C acquired the relevant asset on or after 1 April 2019 from a person ("the transferor") who was a related party in relation to C at the time of the acquisition,

(c) the value of the relevant asset derives in whole or in part from another asset ("the other asset"), and
(d) the other asset meets the preserved status condition (see section 879G).

(2) But if only part of the value of the relevant asset derives from the other asset—

(a) the relevant asset is to be treated for the purposes of this Chapter as if it were two separate assets—
(i) one representing the part of the value of the relevant asset that does so derive, and
(ii) the other representing the part of the value of the relevant asset that does not so derive, and
(b) subsection (1) applies only in relation to the separate asset representing the part of the value of the relevant asset that does so derive.

(3) For the purposes of this section the cases in which the value of a relevant asset may be derived from another asset include any case where—

(a) assets have been merged or divided,
(b) assets have changed their nature, or
(c) rights or interests in or over assets have been created or extinguished.

(4) Section 879G supplements this section.

879G The preserved status condition etc

(1) For the purposes of section 879F the other asset meets the preserved status condition if subsection (2) or (3) applies.

(2) This subsection applies if the other asset—

(a) was acquired or created by a company during the period beginning with 8 July 2015 and ending with 31 March 2019, and
(b) was a chargeable intangible asset in the hands of that company at any time during the period beginning with 29 October 2018 and ending with 31 March 2019 when—
(i) that company and C were related parties, or
(ii) that company and the transferor were related parties.

(3) This subsection applies if the other asset was a pre-FA 2019 relevant asset in the hands of a company at any time during the period beginning with 1 April 2019 and ending with the acquisition mentioned in section 879F(1)(b) when—

(a) that company and C were related parties, or
(b) that company and the transferor were related parties.

(4) It does not matter for the purposes of section 879F(1)(a) who created the relevant asset.

(5) Any apportionment necessary for the purposes of section 879F(2) must be made on a just and reasonable basis.

(6) Section 879E(4) to (7) applies for the purposes of section 879F and this section.

(7) Expressions used in this section have the same meaning as in section 879F.

879H Pre-FA 2019 relevant asset: the fourth case

(1) For the purposes of this Chapter a relevant asset of a company is a pre-FA 2019 relevant asset if—

(a) the company acquired the asset on or after 1 April 2019 directly or indirectly in consequence of, or otherwise in connection with, a disposal of a relevant asset by another person, and
(b) the asset disposed of would have been a pre-FA 2019 relevant asset in the hands of the company had the person transferred it to the company at the time of the disposal.

(2) For the purposes of this section it does not matter whether—

(a) the asset disposed of is the same asset as the acquired asset,
(b) the acquired asset is acquired at the time of the disposal, or
(c) the acquired asset is acquired by merging assets or otherwise.

Restrictions on debits: no business or no qualifying IP assets acquired

879I Restrictions on debits: no business or no qualifying IP assets acquired

(1) This section applies in respect of a relevant asset of a company if the company acquires the asset on or after 1 April 2019 otherwise than as part of the acquisition of a business.

(2) This section also applies in respect of a relevant asset of a company if—

(a) the company acquires the asset on or after 1 April 2019 as part of the acquisition of a business, and

(b) the company does not acquire any qualifying IP assets as part of the acquisition of the business for use on a continuing basis in the course of the business.

(3) No debits in respect of the asset are to be brought into account by the company for tax purposes under Chapter 3 (debits in respect of intangible fixed assets) or Chapter 15 (adjustments on change of accounting policy).

(4) Any debit in respect of the asset that is brought into account by the company for tax purposes under Chapter 4 (realisation of intangible fixed assets) is treated for the purposes of Chapter 6 as a non-trading debit.

879J Meaning of qualifying IP asset

(1) In section 879I "qualifying IP asset", in relation to a company, means an intangible fixed asset that meets the following two conditions.

(2) The first condition is that the asset is—

(a) a patent, registered design, copyright or design right, plant breeders' right, or right under section 7 of the Plant Varieties Act 1997,

(b) a right under the law of a country or territory outside the United Kingdom corresponding or similar to a right within paragraph (a), or

(c) a licence or other right in respect of anything within paragraph (a) or (b).

(3) The second condition is that in the hands of the company the asset—

(a) is not to any extent excluded from this Part by Chapter 10, and

(b) is not a pre-FA 2002 asset (see section 881).

(4) The reference in subsection (2)(c) to a licence or other right does not include a licence or other right that permits the use of computer software but does not permit its manufacture, adaptation or supply.

(5) The Treasury may by regulations amend the meaning of qualifying IP asset for the purposes of this Chapter.

Restrictions on debits: acquisition from individual or firm

879K Restrictions on debits: acquisition from individual or firm

(1) This section applies in respect of a relevant asset of a company if—

(a) the company acquires the asset on or after 1 April 2019 directly or indirectly from an individual or firm ("the transferor"),

(b) the related party condition is met, and

(c) the third party acquisition condition is not met.

(2) The related party condition is met if—

(a) in a case where the transferor is an individual, the transferor is a related party in relation to the company at the time of the acquisition;

(b) in a case where the transferor is a firm, any individual who is a member of the transferor is a related party in relation to the company at that time.

(3) The third party acquisition condition is met if—

(a) in a case where the relevant asset is goodwill—

(i) the transferor acquired all or part of the relevant business in one or more third party acquisitions as part of which the transferor acquired goodwill, and

(ii) the relevant asset is acquired by the company as part of an acquisition of all the relevant business;

(b) in a case where the relevant asset is not goodwill—

(i) the transferor acquired the relevant asset in a third party acquisition, and

(ii) the relevant asset is acquired by the company as part of an acquisition of all the relevant business.

(4) No debits in respect of the asset are to be brought into account by the company for tax purposes under Chapter 3 (debits in respect of intangible fixed assets) or Chapter 15 (adjustments on change of accounting policy).

(5) Any debit in respect of the asset that is brought into account by the company for tax purposes under Chapter 4 (realisation of intangible fixed assets) is treated for the purposes of Chapter 6 as a non-trading debit.

879L Meaning of relevant business and third party acquisition

(1) This section applies for the purposes of section 879K(3).

(2) "Relevant business" means—

(a) in a case where the relevant asset is within paragraph (e) of subsection (2) of section 879A, the business or (as the case may be) the part of the business mentioned in the paragraph of that subsection within which the licensed asset falls, and

(b) in any other case, the business or (as the case may be) the part of the business mentioned in the paragraph of that subsection within which the relevant asset falls.

(3) The transferor acquires something in a "third party acquisition" if—

(a) the transferor acquires it from a company ("C") and, at the time of that acquisition—

(i) if the transferor is an individual, the transferor is not a related party in relation to C, or

(ii) if the transferor is a firm, no individual who is a member of the transferor is a related party in relation to C, or

(b) the transferor acquires it from a person ("P") who is not a company and, at the time of that acquisition—

(i) if the transferor is an individual, P is not connected with the transferor, or

(ii) if the transferor is a firm, no individual who is a member of the transferor is connected with P.

(4) But an acquisition is not a "third party acquisition" if—

(a) its main purpose, or one of its main purposes, is for any person to obtain a tax advantage (within the meaning of section 1139 of CTA 2010), or

(b) it occurs during the period beginning with 8 July 2015 and ending with 31 March 2019.

(5) In this section "connected" has the same meaning as in Chapter 12 (see section 842).

Partial restrictions on debits

879M When the partial restrictions apply: qualifying IP assets

(1) Section 879O (the partial restrictions on debits) applies in respect of a relevant asset ("the asset concerned") of a company if—

(a) the company acquires the asset concerned on or after 1 April 2019 as part of the acquisition of a business,

(b) the company also acquires qualifying IP assets as part of the acquisition of the business for use on a continuing basis in the course of the business, and

(c) the amount in subsection (3) is less than 1.

(2) But section 879O does not apply in respect of the asset concerned if either of the following sections applies in respect of it—

(a) section 879C (restrictions on debits: pre-FA 2019 relevant assets);

(b) section 879K (restrictions on debits: acquisition from individual or firm).

(3) The amount is—

$(A \times N) / B$

where—

A is the expenditure incurred by the company for or in connection with the acquisition of the qualifying IP assets mentioned in subsection (1)(b),
B is the expenditure incurred by the company for or in connection with the acquisition of the asset concerned and any other relevant assets acquired with the business, and
N is 6.

(4) The Treasury may by regulations amend the meaning of N.

(5) In this section—

"expenditure" means expenditure that is—

(a) capitalised for accounting purposes, or
(b) recognised in determining the profit or loss of the company concerned without being capitalised for accounting purposes,
subject to any adjustments under this Part or Part 4 of TIOPA 2010;

"qualifying IP asset" has the same meaning as in section 879I (see section 879J).

879N When the partial restrictions apply: acquisition from individual or firm

(1) Section 879O (the partial restrictions on debits) also applies in respect of a relevant asset of a company if—

(a) the company acquires the asset on or after 1 April 2019 directly or indirectly from an individual or firm ("the transferor"),
(b) the related party condition is met,
(c) the third party acquisition condition is met, and
(d) the amount in subsection (6) is less than 1.

(2) But section 879O does not apply in respect of the relevant asset if either of the following sections applies in respect of it—

(a) section 879C (restrictions on debits: pre-FA 2019 relevant assets);
(b) section 879I (restrictions on debits: no business or no qualifying IP assets acquired).

(3) The related party condition is met if—

(a) in a case where the transferor is an individual, the transferor is a related party in relation to the company at the time of the acquisition;
(b) in a case where the transferor is a firm, any individual who is a member of the transferor is a related party in relation to the company at that time.

(4) The third party acquisition condition is met if—

(a) in a case where the relevant asset is goodwill—
 (i) the transferor acquired all or part of the relevant business in one or more third party acquisitions as part of which the transferor acquired goodwill, and
 (ii) the relevant asset is acquired by the company as part of an acquisition of all the relevant business;
(b) in a case where the relevant asset is not goodwill—
 (i) the transferor acquired the relevant asset in a third party acquisition, and
 (ii) the relevant asset is acquired by the company as part of an acquisition of all the relevant business.

(5) Section 879L (meaning of relevant business and third party acquisition) applies for the purposes of this section.

(6) The amount is—

A / B

where—

A is the relevant accounting value of third party acquisitions (see subsections (7) to (9)), and
B is the expenditure incurred by the company for or in connection with the acquisition of the relevant asset that is—

(a) capitalised by the company for accounting purposes, or
(b) recognised in determining the company's profit or loss without

being capitalised for accounting purposes,

subject to any adjustments under this Part or Part 4 of TIOPA 2010.

(7) In a case in which the relevant asset is goodwill, the relevant accounting value of third party acquisitions is the notional accounting value of the goodwill mentioned in subsection (4)(a)(i) ("the previously acquired goodwill").

(8) In a case in which the relevant asset is not goodwill, the relevant accounting value of third party acquisitions is the notional accounting value of the relevant asset.

(9) The "notional accounting value" of the previously acquired goodwill, or the relevant asset, is what its accounting value would have been in GAAP-compliant accounts drawn up by the transferor—

(a) immediately before the relevant asset was acquired by the company, and

(b) on the basis that the relevant business was a going concern.

879O The partial restrictions on debits

(1) Where this section applies in respect of a relevant asset of a company, the following restrictions have effect.

(2) If a debit in respect of the relevant asset is to be brought into account by the company for tax purposes under a provision of Chapter 3 (debits in respect of intangible fixed assets) or Chapter 15 (adjustments on change of accounting policy), the amount of that debit is—

$D \times RA$

where—

D is the amount of the debit that would be brought into account disregarding this section (and, accordingly, for the purposes of any calculation of the tax written-down value of the relevant asset needed to determine D, this section's effect in relation to any debits previously brought into account is to be disregarded), and

RA is the relevant amount (see subsection (6)).

(3) If, but for this section, a debit in respect of any of the relevant assets would be brought into account by the company for tax purposes under a provision of Chapter 4 (realisation of intangible fixed assets), the following two debits are to be brought into account under that provision instead—

(a) a debit determined in accordance with subsection (4), and

(b) a debit determined in accordance with subsection (5), which is to be treated for the purposes of Chapter 6 as a non-trading debit ("the non-trading debit").

(4) The amount of the debit determined in accordance with this subsection is—

$D \times RA$

where—

D is the amount of the debit that would be brought into account under Chapter 4 disregarding this section (and, accordingly, for the purposes of any calculation of the tax written down value of the relevant asset needed to determine D, this section's effect in relation to any debits previously brought into account is to be disregarded), and

RA is the relevant amount (see subsection (6)).

(5) The amount of the non-trading debit is—

$D \times RA$

where—

D is the amount of the debit that would be brought into account under Chapter 4 disregarding this section (but, for the purposes of any calculation of the tax written-down value of the relevant asset needed to determine D, this section's effect in relation to any debits previously brought into account is not to be disregarded), and

TD is the amount of the debit determined in accordance with subsection (4).

(6) In this section the "relevant amount" means—

(a) in a case where this section applies in respect of the relevant asset by reason only of section 879M, the amount in subsection (3) of that section;

(b) in a case where this section applies in respect of the relevant asset by reason only of section 879N, the amount in subsection (6) of that section;

(c) in a case where this section applies in respect of the relevant asset by reason of both section 879M and 879N, the amount found by multiplying the amount in subsection (3) of section 879M by the amount in subsection (6) of section 879N.

Supplementary

879P Date of acquisition of relevant asset

(1) A company that acquires a relevant asset in pursuance of an unconditional obligation under a contract is to be treated for the purposes of this Chapter as having acquired the asset on the date on which the company became subject to that obligation or (if later) the date on which that obligation became unconditional.

(2) An obligation is unconditional if it may not be varied or extinguished by the exercise of a right (whether under contract or otherwise)."

7 (1) The amendments made by this Schedule have effect in relation to accounting periods beginning on or after 1 April 2019.

(2) For the purposes of sub-paragraph (1), an accounting period beginning before, and ending on or after, 1 April 2019 is to be treated as if so much of the accounting period as falls before that date, and so much of the accounting period as falls on or after that date, were separate accounting periods.

COMMENTARY ON SCHEDULE 9

Section 25 introduces Schedule 9, which introduces a new corporation tax deduction at 6.5% a year for goodwill and other 'relevant assets' under very limited circumstances. Broadly, these are:

- The relevant assets must not be 'pre-FA 2019 assets'
- They must be acquired as part of the acquisition of a business or part of a business
- The acquisition should not be from an individual who is a related party in relation to the company or from a partnership where any member is such an individual
- The assets acquired as part of the business acquisition must include 'qualifying IP assets'.

Where the deduction is available, a corporation tax deduction is given at a fixed rate of 6.5% per year, although this rate may be altered by the Treasury by secondary legislation. There does not appear to be any provision whereby a company could choose to disclaim this relief.

The relevant assets must have been acquired on or after 1st April 2019.

Relevant assets

Relevant assets are defined as:

- Goodwill of a business
- Intangible fixed assets consisting of information relating to customers or potential customers of a business
- Intangible fixed assets consisting of a relationship between a person carrying on a business and customers of that business. This does not have to be a contractual relationship
- An unregistered trademark or other sign used in the course of the business
- A licence or other right in respect of any of the above assets.

Pre-FA 2019 relevant assets

The concept of a pre-FA 2019 relevant asset is to ensure that the new deduction only applies where the asset was genuinely acquired or created by a company on or after the 1 April 2019. There are four cases, largely based on provisions already within Part 8 CTA 2009. These are:

- The first case defines a pre-FA 2019 relevant asset as being one that was created or acquired by the company between 8 July 2015 and 31 March 2019, if the asset was a chargeable intangible asset of the company at any time during the period between 29 October 2018 and 31 March 2019. The significance of these dates is that 8 July 2015 is the date on which it was announced that companies would not be able to claim any deduction for the amortisation or impairment of business goodwill acquired from that date, and 29 October 2018 is the date on which it was announced that there would be a new allowance for acquired relevant assets.

- The second case applies where the asset was acquired or created by another company between 8 July 2015 and 31 March 2019, the asset was a chargeable intangible asset in relation to that company in the period between 29 October 2018 and 31 March 2019 and the claimant company acquired the assets from a related party. There are two exceptions to this rule, however:
  - The first is whether the claimant company acquired the asset from a related party company that was within the charge to corporation tax and in whose hands the asset was not a pre-FA 2019 relevant asset
  - The second is where the acquisition is from a related party intermediary (which could be any natural or legal person) who acquire the asset on or after the 1 April 2019 from somebody who was not a related party in relation to the intermediary or to the claimant company.
- In the third case a relevant asset is a pre-FA 2019 relevant asset if the asset was created on or after 29 October 2018, acquired by the company or after 1 April 2019 from a related party and the value of the relevant asset derives wholly or partly from another asset which meets the 'preserved status condition'. The intention of this provision appears to be to prevent the creation of a new assets by, for example, granting a licence or sublicense out of an existing assets which, itself, is a pre-FA 2019 relevant asset. This is borne out by the two ways in which an asset meets the preserved status condition, which are:
  - It was acquired or created by a company between 8 July 2015 and 31 March 2019 and was a chargeable intangible asset in the hands of that company between 29 October 2018 and 31 March 2019, where the company creating or acquiring the asset and the claimant company are related parties or where the person selling the asset to the claimant company is a related party in relation to the company that acquired or created the assets
  - It was a pre-FA 2019 relevant asset of a company from 1 April 2019 to the date of acquisition when the company holding the asset and the claimant company are related parties or where the person selling the asset to the claimant company is a related party in relation to the company that previously held the asset.
- The fourth case for a pre-FA 2019 relevant asset is where the asset is acquired on or after 1 April 2019 in consequence of or in connection with a disposal of a relevant asset by another person but if the asset had been transferred directly to the acquiring company it would have been a pre-FA 2019 relevant asset. This is described in the Explanatory Notes as 'a hypothetical test which identifies situations in which the other pre-FA 2019 cases are circumvented'.

Acquisition from related individuals or partnerships

There is a further restriction in respect of relevant assets acquired on or after 1 April 2019 directly or indirectly from an individual or firm. This applies if an individual transferor is a related party in relation to the company or, if the transferor is a firm, any individual who is a member of that firm is a related party in relation to the company at that time.

This restriction does not apply where the 'third-party acquisition condition' is met, which depends on the nature of the relevant asset:

- Where the relevant asset is goodwill, this condition is met if the transferor individual or firm acquired all or part of the relevant business in third-party transactions as part of which they acquired the goodwill, and the relevant asset is acquired by the claimant company as part of an acquisition of all the relevant business
- Where the relevant asset is not goodwill the transferor individual or firm must have acquired that relevant asset in a third-party acquisition, and the relevant asset must be acquired by the claimant company as part of an acquisition of all the relevant business.

Qualifying IP assets

The new deduction is only available where the asset is acquired on or after 1 April 2019 as part of the business acquisition which also includes the acquisition of qualifying IP assets. These are defined as:

- A patent, registered design, copyright or design right, plant breeders right or right under section 7 of the Plant Varieties Act 1997
- A corresponding or similar right under the law of another country or territory
- A licence or other right in respect of either of the above categories.

A qualifying IP asset must also not be an asset generally excluded from the intangibles regime (such as financial assets rights over tangible assets) and must not be a pre-FA 2002 asset.

Partial restriction of relief

There is a partial restriction on the availability of relief in cases where the value of relevant assets is largely in excess of the value of qualifying IP assets acquired in the business acquisition. The legislation contains a formula (A × N)/B, where A is expenditure on qualifying IP assets, B is expenditure on relevant assets and N is 6, which can be amended by the Treasury by regulations.

The effect of this is that there is a restriction on the tax deduction given in respect of relevant assets if the expenditure on relevant assets is more than six times the expenditure on qualifying IP assets. For example, if expenditure on relevant assets was ten times the expenditure on qualifying IP assets the formula would give 60%, so the 6.5% per annum relief would be restricted by 40%.

There is also a partial restriction of relief where a company acquires a relevant asset from a related individual, or from a firm one of whose members is a related individual, but an allowance is still due because the transferor previously acquired all or part of the relevant asset from a third party. This partial restriction is intended to make sure that the company only gets the tax deduction by reference to the notional accounting value of the relevant asset.

The notional accounting value is the accounting value the relevant asset would have had if GAAP compliant accounts had been drawn up on a going concern basis by the transferor immediately before the acquisition by the claimant company. A formula then divides this notional accounting value by the amount capitalised by the claimant company, or recognised in determining its profit and loss, so that if the company paid more than the notional accounting value for the assets, the restriction will apply. The amount of restriction is given by the fraction. For example, if the notional accounting value is £80 but the company paid and capitalised £100 the formulae gives 80% and only 80% of the 6.5% annual deduction is available.

If there is a debit on realisation of the asset, the amount allowed for trading purposes will be similarly restricted and the excess debit will be treated as a non-trading loss on an intangible fixed assets.

Commencement

As already noted, these provisions only applied to relevant assets acquired on or after 1 April 2019. The legislation strictly also only applies to accounting periods beginning on or after 1 April 2019, but an accounting period straddling this date is to be treated as two separate accounting periods, one ending on 31 March 19 and the other starting on one April 19. As a result, if a company acquires an asset on or after 1 April 2019 in such a straddling accounting period, there will be a restriction in the amount allowed as if the accounting period were less than 12 months.

SCHEDULE 10

CORPORATION TAX RELIEF FOR CARRIED-FORWARD LOSSES

Section 27

Restrictions on deductions from profits

1 CTA 2010 is amended as follows.

2 In section 188DD (group relief for carried-forward losses: claimant company's relevant maximum for overlapping period) omit subsection (4).

3 In section 188ED (group relief for carried-forward losses: claimant company's relevant maximum for overlapping period)—

(a) omit subsection (4), and

(b) in subsection (5) for "(4)" substitute "(3)".

4 In section 269ZB (restriction on deductions from trading profits) in subsection (8) for paragraph (b) substitute—

"(b) any amount specified for the period under section 269ZC(5)(a) (non-trading profits deductions allowance)."

5 In section 269ZC (restriction on deductions from non-trading profits) in subsection (6) for paragraph (b) substitute—

"(b) any amount specified for the period under section 269ZB(7)(a) (trading profits deductions allowance)."

6 (1) Section 269ZD (restriction on deductions from total profits) is amended as follows.

(2) In subsection (2)—

(a) in paragraph (b)—

(i) at the end of sub-paragraph (i) insert "and", and

(ii) omit sub-paragraph (iii) and the "and" immediately before it, and

(b) in the second sentence omit "and section 269ZE".

(3) In subsection (4)(a) after "period" insert "(see section 269ZFA)".

(4) Omit subsection (5).

(5) For subsection (7) substitute—

"(7) Subsection (2) does not apply in relation to a company for an accounting period where the amount given by paragraph (1) of step 1 in section 269ZF(3) is not greater than nil."

7 Omit section 269ZE (restriction on deductions from total profits: insurance companies).

8 After section 269ZF insert—

"269ZFA "Relevant profits"

(1) A company's "relevant profits" for an accounting period are—

(a) the company's qualifying profits for the accounting period, less

(b) the company's deductions allowance for the accounting period (see section 269ZD(6)).

(2) A company's "qualifying profits" for an accounting period are—

(a) the amount given by paragraph (1) of step 1 in section 269ZF(3) in determining the company's qualifying trading profits and qualifying non-trading profits for the accounting period, less

(b) the amount given by paragraph (1) of step 2 in section 269ZF(3) in determining those profits for the accounting period."

9 After section 269ZFA (as inserted by paragraph 8) insert—

"Modifications for certain insurance companies

269ZFB Modifications for certain insurance companies

(1) This section has effect for determining the taxable total profits of a company for an accounting period if the company—

(a) is an insurance company, and

(b) carries on basic life assurance and general annuity business in the period.

(2) A reference in section 269ZD(7) and section 269ZFA(2) to the amount given by a paragraph of a step in section 269ZF(3) is to be read as a reference to the amount that would be so given if—

(a) section 269ZF(4)(a) did not require income referable to a company's basic life assurance and general annuity business to be ignored unless it falls within, and is dealt with under, Part 9A of CTA 2009 by reason of an election under section 931R of that Act, and

(b) section 269ZF(4)(d) required only the policyholders' share of any I-E profit (as determined in accordance with section 103 of FA 2012) to be ignored.

(3) In this section—

"basic life assurance and general annuity business" has the meaning given by section 57 of FA 2012, and

"insurance company" has the meaning given by section 65 of that Act."

10 In section 269ZJ (exclusion of shock losses from restrictions) omit subsection (4).

11 In section 269ZQ (power to amend) in subsection (2)(b) for "124E" substitute "124C".

12 In section 269ZV (group allowance allocation statement: requirements and effects) after subsection (5) insert—

"(5A) In its application in relation to a listed company that is the ultimate parent (see section 269ZZB(3)) of each other company in the group, subsection (5) has effect as if after "the group" in paragraph (b) of the definition of DAP there was inserted "and was not a member of any other group".

13 In section 269CC (restrictions on deductions by banking companies: management expenses etc) in subsection (7) (how to determine "relevant maximum") in Step 1 for "269ZD(5)" substitute "269ZFA".

14 In section 269CN (restrictions on deductions by banking companies: definitions) in the definition of "relevant profits" for "269ZD(5)" substitute "269ZFA".

15 In section 304(7) (certain deductions in respect of losses made in a ring fence trade to be ignored for the purposes of the restriction on deductions from trading profits) in paragraph (b) for "total" substitute "trade".

16 FA 2012 is amended as follows.

17 In section 124 (carry forward of pre-1 April 2017 BLAGAB trade losses against subsequent profits) in subsection (5) omit "(but see also section 124D)".

18 In section 124A (carry forward of post-1 April 2017 BLAGAB trade losses against subsequent profits) in subsection (5) omit "(but see also section 124D)".

19 In section 124C (further carry forward against subsequent profits of post-1 April 2017 loss not fully used) in subsection (6) omit "(but see also section 124D)".

20 Omit sections 124D and 124E (restriction on deductions from BLAGAB trade profits).

Terminal losses: straddling periods

21 For section 45G of CTA 2010 substitute—

"45G Section 45F: accounting period falling partly within 3 year period

(1) This section applies if—

(a) a company ceases to carry on a trade in an accounting period ("the terminal period"), and

(b) a previous accounting period of the company ("the straddling period") falls partly within the period of 3 years ending with the end of the terminal period.

(2) The sum of any deductions under section 45F from the profits of the trade of the straddling period is not to exceed an amount equal to the overlapping proportion of those profits (calculated before making those deductions).

(3) The sum of—

(a) any deductions under section 45F from the profits of the trade of the straddling period, and

(b) any deductions under that section from the total profits of the straddling period in respect of losses made in the trade, must not exceed an amount equal to the overlapping proportion of the total profits of the straddling period (calculated before making those deductions).

(4) The overlapping proportion is the same as the proportion that the part of the straddling period falling within the period of 3 years mentioned in subsection (1)(b) bears to the whole of the straddling period."

Group relief for carried-forward losses

22 CTA 2010 is amended as follows.

23 In section 188BG(3) (types of loss that may not be surrendered by a Solvency 2 insurance company)—

(a) omit "or" at the end of paragraph (b), and
(b) after paragraph (c) insert "or

(d) a BLAGAB trade loss carried forward to the surrender period under section 124A(2) or 124C(3) of FA 2012,".

24 (1) Section 188DD (claimant company's relevant maximum for overlapping period in case of claim under section 188CB) is amended as follows.

(2) In subsection (3)—

(a) for "relevant" (in both places) substitute "qualifying", and
(b) for "section 269ZD(5)" (in both places) substitute "subsection (3A)".

(3) After subsection (3) insert—

"(3A) The claimant company's "qualifying profits" for the claim period are—

(a) the amount given by paragraph (1) of step 1 in section 269ZF(3) in determining the company's qualifying trading profits and qualifying non-trading profits for the period, less
(b) the amount given by paragraph (1) of step 2 in section 269ZF(3) in determining those profits for the period."

25 (1) Section 188ED (claimant company's relevant maximum for overlapping period in case of claim under section 188CC) is amended as follows.

(2) In subsection (3)—

(a) for "relevant" (in both places) substitute "qualifying", and
(b) for "section 269ZD(5)" (in both places) substitute "subsection (3A)".

(3) After subsection (3) insert—

"(3A) The claimant company's "qualifying profits" for the claim period are—

(a) the amount given by paragraph (1) of step 1 in section 269ZF(3) in determining the company's qualifying trading profits and qualifying non-trading profits for the period, less
(b) the amount given by paragraph (1) of step 2 in section 269ZF(3) in determining those profits for the period."

Transferred trades

26 CTA 2010 is amended as follows.

27 In section 357JI (Northern Ireland losses: transfers of trade without a change of ownership) in subsection (2) for the words from the beginning to "that section" substitute "Sections 943A to 944C (which modify the application of Chapter 2 of Part 4) have effect as if the references in those sections".

28 In section 676 (disallowance of trading loss on change in ownership of company: company reconstructions)—

(a) in subsection (2) for the words from "section 944(3)" to "successor company)" substitute "Chapter 1 of Part 22",
(b) in subsection (4)(a) after "45" insert ", 45A, 45B, 303B, 303C or 303D", and
(c) in subsection (4)(b) for "944(3)" substitute "Chapter 1 of Part 22".

29 In section 676AF (restriction on use of carried-forward post-1 April 2017 trade losses)—

(a) the existing provision becomes subsection (1), and
(b) after that subsection insert—

"(2) A loss made by another company ("the predecessor company") in an accounting period beginning before the change in ownership may not be deducted from affected profits of an accounting period ending after the change in ownership under any of the provisions mentioned in paragraphs (a) to (c) of subsection (1) (as applied by virtue of Chapter 1 of Part 22 (transfers of trades))."

30 In section 676BC (disallowance of relief for trade losses)—

(a) in subsection (1) omit "by the company",
(b) in subsection (4), in the words before paragraph (a), after "made" insert "by the company", and
(c) after subsection (4) insert—

"(5) A loss made by another company ("the predecessor company") in an accounting period beginning before the change in ownership may not be deducted as a result of section 45A, 45F or 303C (as applied by Chapter 1 of Part 22 (transfers of trades)) from so much of the total profits of an accounting period of the company ending after the change in ownership as represents the relevant gain."

Deduction buying

31 (1) In section 730C of CTA 2010 (disallowance of deductible amounts: relevant claims)—

(a) in subsection (2) omit paragraph (aa), and
(b) in subsection (3A) for "paragraphs (a) to (e)" substitute "paragraph (a) or (b)".

(2) In Schedule 4 to F(No 2)A 2017 (relief for carried-forward losses) omit paragraph 172.

Commencement

32 (1) The amendments made by this Schedule have effect in relation to accounting periods beginning on or after the relevant date (see subparagraph (3)).

(2) For the purposes of the amendments made by this Schedule, where a company has an accounting period beginning before the relevant date and ending on or after that date ("the straddling period")—

(a) so much of the straddling period as falls before the relevant date, and so much of that period as falls on or after that date, are to be treated as separate accounting periods, and
(b) where it is necessary to apportion an amount for the straddling period to the two separate accounting period, it is to be apportioned—
    (i) in accordance with section 1172 of CTA 2010 (time basis), or
    (ii) if that method would produce a result that is unjust or unreasonable, on a just and reasonable basis.

(3) The "relevant date" is—

(a) 1 April 2017, in relation to the amendments made by paragraphs 24 and 25 of this Schedule,
(b) 6 July 2018, in relation to the amendments made by paragraphs 1 to 11, 13 and 14 and 16 to 20 of this Schedule, and
(c) 1 April 2019, in relation to the other amendments made by this Schedule.

COMMENTARY ON SCHEDULE 10

Section 27 introduces Schedule 10 which makes a series of amendments to the rules relating to carried forward corporation tax losses, which were substantially amended by F(No 2)A 2017. There are 31 separate sets of amendments! There are also three different starting dates for those provisions, two of which are retroactive.

Provisions having effect from 1 April 2017

Paragraphs 24 and 25 of the Schedule provide that the limits on the amount of profits against which group relief for carried forward losses was allowable under CTA 2010, ss 188DD and 188ED are amended. The original legislation stated that the relievable profits were limited to the 'relevant profits' where these were less than the deductions allowance of the company for the period. The revised definition changes the restrictions so that it applies where the 'qualifying profits' are less than the deductions allowance, instead.

The 'qualifying profits' are defined as the 'modified total profits' that are determined by step 1 of CTA 2010, s 269ZF(3) less the amount of in year reliefs such as group relief, determined by step 2 in that subsection.

Provisions having effect from 6 July 2018

Paragraphs 2 and 3 repeal CTA 2010, ss 188DD(4) and 188ED(4). Both provisions refer to a company's relevant maximum group relief for carried forward losses for overlapping periods and the subsections now repealed were adjustments in respect of the special loss for insurance companies. All references are to CTA 2010 unless stated.

A minor drafting error in CTA 2010, s 188ED is also corrected by paragraph 3.

Paragraph 4 amends CTA 2010, s 269ZB(8)(b), the restriction on deductions from trading profits, by removing the reference to BLAGAB (basic life assurance and general annuity business) profits from the restriction.

Paragraph 5 makes an identical amendment to CTA 2010, s 269ZC(6)(b), the restriction on deductions from non-trading profits.

CTA 2010, s 269ZD(2)(b), the restriction on deductions from total profits, is amended by the paragraph 6, which removes reference to BLAGAB trade losses and profits in subsection (2)(b).

Paragraph 6 also repeals CTA 2010, s 269ZD(5), the definition of relevant profits, and amends section 269ZD(7) to omit BLAGAB trade profit from the requirement not to restrict the sum of any relevant deductions where total profits are nil. A new definition of relevant profits is in new CTA 2010, s 269ZFA (see paragraph 8).

Paragraph 7 repeals CTA 2010, s 269ZE, the restriction on deductions from total profits for insurance companies.

Paragraph 8 inserts a new CTA 2010, s 269ZFA, which defines relevant profits for the purposes of CTA 2010, s 269ZD(4)(a). The new definition tells us that a company's 'relevant profits' for an accounting period are the company's qualifying profits less its deductions allowance for the period. These are defined by reference to the amounts given by steps 1 and 2 in section 269ZF(3), exactly as for the amendments made by paragraphs 24 and 25 (above).

Paragraph 9 introduces a new CTA 2010, s 269ZFB, which contains modifications for determining the total taxable profits of insurance companies carrying on basic life insurance and general annuity businesses (BLAGAB) in the period.

Paragraph 10 repeals CTA 2010, s 269ZJ(4), also a measure relevant to BLAGAB trade profits only.

Paragraph 11 makes a minor correction to CTA 2010, s 269ZQ(2)(b).

Paragraphs 13 and 14 amend CTA 2010, ss 269CC and 269CN to refer to the new definition of relevant profits at section 269ZFA.

Paragraph 16 introduces amendments to FA 2012.

Paragraphs 17, 18 and 19 amends FA 2012, ss 124, 124A and 124C to remove references to section 124D (restriction on deductions from BLAGAB trade profits).

Paragraph 20 repeals FA 2012, ss 124D and 124E.

Provisions having effect from 1 April 2019

Paragraph 12 inserts a new provision, CTA 2010, s 269ZV(5A), to prevent a company being allocated a share of the deductions allowance from a group of which it is the ultimate parent if it is also a member of another group.

Paragraph 15 makes a minor correction to CTA 2010, s 304(7) so that the reference to section 45B refers to setting carried forward losses against trade profits, rather than total profits.

Paragraph 21 replaces the existing CTA 2010, s 45G, covering the calculation of relief under section 45F where an earlier accounting period falls partly within the period of three years that ends with the end of the terminal period. A proportionate test is introduced so that, for example, if three months of an accounting period fall into that three-year period, deductions under CTA 2010, s 45F are restricted to 3/12 of the losses of the straddling accounting period.

Firstly, the calculation must be done for losses that, under section 45F, can only be set off against profits of the trade. Then the calculation is made for deductions under section 45F that be used against total profits of the company, but the sum of all deductions cannot exceed the appropriate proportion of the total profits of the straddling period.

Paragraph 22 introduces more amendments to CTA 2010, specific to group relief for carried forward losses.

Paragraph 23 adds a BLAGAB trade loss carried forward under FA 2012, s 124A(2) or s 124C(3) to the types of loss – listed in CTA 2010, s 188BG(3) – that may not be surrendered by a Solvency 2 insurance company.

Paragraph 26 introduces amendments to CTA 2010 rules on transfers of trades.

Paragraph 27 corrects CTA 2010, s 357JI (Northern Ireland losses: transfers of trade without a change of ownership) so that it now refers to sections 943A to 944C, and not to section 944. This updates the references following the amendment of the legislation in F(No 2)A 2017, Pt 22, Ch 1.

Paragraph 28 similarly updates CTA 2010, s 676 (disallowance of trading loss on change of ownership of company: company reconstructions) to include the relevant amendments made by F(No 2)A 2017 and to extend the trading losses that are covered by this provision to include CTA 2010, ss 45A, 45B, 303B, 303C and 303D.

Paragraph 29 amends CTA 2010, s 676AF (restriction on use of carried forward post-1 April 2017 trade losses) to prevent losses transferred to a company following a transfer of trade without a change of ownership, where there is subsequently a change of ownership, from being deducted from affected profits which arise after that change of ownership.

Paragraph 30 amends CTA 2010, s 676BC (disallowance of relief for trade losses) to prevent such losses transferred without a change of ownership prior to a change of ownership of the company being deducted from an amount of total profits that represent a relevant gain arising afterwards.

Paragraph 31 amends CTA 2010, s 730C (disallowance of deductible amounts: relevant claims) to restrict the application of that provision.

Commencement

The commencement dates for the various provisions are highlighted above.

Paragraph 32 also provides that, for each of the relevant dates, if there is an accounting period straddling that date, that accounting period must be treated as being split into an accounting period ending the day before the relevant date and another accounting period starting on the relevant date and ending on the normal accounting period end date.

Any amounts that are to be apportioned should be apportioned on a time basis unless that would give an unjust or unreasonable result, in which case a just and reasonable basis must be used.

SCHEDULE 11

CORPORATE INTEREST RESTRICTION

Section 28

Introductory

1 Part 10 of TIOPA 2010 (corporate interest restriction) is amended as follows.

Tax-interest amounts: amounts capitalised in intangible fixed assets

2 In Chapter 3 (tax-interest amounts), after section 391 insert—

"391A Amounts capitalised in carrying value of intangible fixed assets

In determining for the purposes of this Part whether an amount is a tax-interest expense amount or tax-interest income amount, section 906(1) of CTA 2009 (priority of intangible fixed asset rules) does not apply in respect of any matter which may be brought into account in accordance with Part 5 or 7 of that Act."

Carry forward of interest allowance: new holding company

3 After section 395 insert—

"395A Carry forward of interest allowance: new holding company

(1) This section applies if—

(a) a company ("C") ceases to be the ultimate parent of a worldwide group ("the old group") because of a qualifying takeover, and

(b) another company ("N") becomes the ultimate parent of a worldwide group ("the new group") as a result of the takeover.

(2) For this purpose there is a qualifying takeover if there is a change in the ownership of C which is disregarded for the purposes of Chapters 2 to 6 of Part 14 of CTA 2010 as a result of section 724A of that Act where—

(a) C is the other company referred to as C in that section, and

(b) N is the new company referred to as N in that section.

(3) For the purposes of this Chapter, the interest allowance of the new group is determined as if periods of account of the old group which ended before the beginning of the first period of account of the new group were periods of account of the new group."

Carry forward of excess debt cap: new holding company

4 After section 400 insert—

"400A Carry forward of excess debt cap: new holding company

(1) This section applies if—

(a) a company ("C") ceases to be the ultimate parent of a worldwide group ("the old group") because of a qualifying takeover, and

(b) another company ("N") becomes the ultimate parent of a worldwide group ("the new group") as a result of the takeover.

(2) For this purpose there is a qualifying takeover if there is a change in the ownership of C which is disregarded for the purposes of Chapters 2 to 6 of Part 14 of CTA 2010 as a result of section 724A of that Act where—

(a) C is the other company referred to as C in that section, and

(b) N is the new company referred to as N in that section.

(3) In determining in accordance with section 400 the group's fixed ratio debt cap or group ratio debt cap for its first period of account, its excess debt cap generated in the immediately preceding period of account is taken to be that of the old group for the period of account of the old group ending immediately before the qualifying takeover."

Adjusted net group-interest expense: capitalised interest

5 Section 410 (net group-interest expense), after subsection (5) insert—

"(5A) If, on the assumption that subsections (3) and (5) applied to relevant assets, an amount would, in accordance with subsection (3) or (5), have been treated as included in A or B in subsection (1)—

(a) as an amount attributable to the capitalised expense, or
(b) as an amount attributable to the capitalised income,

none of that amount is to be included in A or B in that subsection."

6 (1) Section 413 (adjusted net group-interest expense) is amended as follows.

(2) In subsection (3)—

(a) in paragraph (a), for "an asset or liability" substitute "a non-financial asset or non-financial liability", and
(b) in paragraph (b), after "an amount that" insert ", in the case of a non-financial asset,".

(3) In subsection (4)—

(a) in paragraph (a), for "an asset or liability" substitute "a non-financial asset or non-financial liability", and
(b) in paragraph (b), after "an amount that" insert ", in the case of a non-financial asset,".

(4) For subsection (5) substitute—

"(5) For the purposes of subsections (3)(a) and (b) and (4)(a) and (b)—

(a) an asset is a "non-financial asset" if it is not a financial asset for accounting purposes or it is a share in a company,
(b) a liability is a "non-financial liability" if it is not a financial liability for accounting purposes or it is in respect of a share issued by a company, and
(c) references to amounts brought into account in determining the carrying value of a non-financial asset or non-financial liability do not include amounts so brought into account as a result of writing off any part of an amount which was itself so brought into account;

and in paragraphs (a) and (b) "share" has the meaning given by section 476(1) of CTA 2009."

7 (1) Section 423 (capitalised interest brought into account for tax purposes in accordance with GAAP) is amended as follows.

(2) After subsection (2) insert—

"(2A) Section 413 has effect, in the case of a GAAP-taxable asset that is a relevant asset, as if—

(a) the definition of "upward adjustment" included so much of its carrying value written down in the group's financial statements for the relevant period of account as is attributable to a relevant expense amount brought into account in the group's financial statements in determining its carrying value, and
(b) the definition of "downward adjustment" included so much of the reduction of its carrying value written down in the group's financial statements for the relevant period of account as is attributable to a relevant income amount brought into account in the group's financial statements in determining its carrying value.

(2B) For the purposes of subsection (2A) it does not matter whether the relevant expense or income amount is brought into account in determining the asset's carrying value in the group's financial statements for the relevant period of account or an earlier period."

(3) In subsection (3), for "But subsection (2)(b) of this section is of no effect where" substitute "But subsections (2)(b) and (2A) of this section are of no effect so far as".

(4) In subsection (4), at the end insert "(and, for the purposes of this subsection, an asset is a GAAP-taxable asset even if an election under section 730 of CTA 2009 is, or could be, made in respect of it)".

Adjusted net group-interest expense: impairment debts and credits and connected companies

8 (1) Section 413 (meaning of "adjusted net group-interest expense") is amended as follows.

(2) In subsection (3)(d)(i)—

(a) for "or 323A" substitute ", 323A, 358 or 359", and

(b) omit "(cases where credits not required to be brought into account)".

(3) In subsection (4)(d)(i)—

(a) after "section 323A" insert "or 354", and

(b) omit "(cases where credits not required to be brought into account)".

Interest allowance (alternative calculation) election: unpaid employees' remuneration

9 After section 424 insert—

"424A Unpaid employees' remuneration

(1) Where an interest allowance (alternative calculation) election has effect in relation to a period of account of a worldwide group, this Chapter applies in relation to the period subject to this section.

(2) The definition of "the group's profit before tax" in section 416(2) has effect as if references to amounts that are recognised in the financial statements of the group for the period, as items of profit or loss, excluded amounts so recognised in respect of employees' remuneration that are not paid before the end of the period of 9 months immediately following the end of the period of account.

(3) If—

(a) an amount is, as a result of subsection (2), excluded from the financial statements of the group for the period of account, and

(b) the amount is paid in a later period of account of the group in relation to which an interest allowance (alternative calculation) election has effect,

the definition of "the group's profit before tax" in section 416(2) has effect as if references to amounts that are recognised in the financial statements of the group for the later period of account, as items of profit or loss, included the amount that is paid in that later period.

(4) Section 1289 of CTA 2009 (unpaid remuneration: supplementary) applies for the purposes of this section as it applies for the purposes of section 1288 of that Act."

Interest allowance (alternative calculation) election: changes in accounting policy

10 (1) Section 426 (changes in accounting policy in cases where interest allowance (alternative calculation) election has effect) is amended as follows.

(2) In subsection (3)—

(a) after "means" insert "the following provisions as modified by subsection (4)", and

(b) after paragraph (a) insert—

"(ab) sections 261 and 262 of that Act (property profits);".

(3) For subsection (4) substitute—

"(4) The provisions mentioned in subsection (3)—

(a) are to have effect for the purposes of this section as if their application were limited to cases where there is a change of accounting policy and as if any election had been made under the provisions, and

(b) are to have effect subject to any modifications necessary for the purposes of this section."

Interest allowance (non-consolidated investment) election

11 In section 427 (group interest and group-EBITDA), after subsection (5) insert—

"(5A) Any increase to be made as a result of subsection (4) or (5) is to be made as part of a single calculation required by section 413(1) or 414(1) (so that the amount produced by that calculation is subject to section 413(2) or 414(2))."

Public infrastructure

12 In section 433 (meaning of "qualifying infrastructure company"), in subsection (5), after paragraph (c) insert—

"(ca) assets held for the purposes of a pension scheme under which benefits are provided to, or in respect of, persons employed for the purpose of the carrying on of qualifying infrastructure activities by the company or another associated qualifying infrastructure company,

(cb) assets in respect of deferred tax so far as attributable to qualifying infrastructure activities carried on by the company or another associated qualifying infrastructure company,".

13 In section 439 (exemption in respect of certain pre-13 May 2016 loan relationships), in subsection (3), after paragraph (b) insert—

", but ignoring amounts that represent the reimbursement of expenses incurred by C or the other company."

Real Estate Investment Trusts

14 (1) Section 452 (Real Estate Investment Trusts) is amended as follows.

(2) In subsection (4), at the end insert "(and, accordingly, the profits mentioned in section 534(1) or (2) of CTA 2010 are not calculated for the purposes of this Part in accordance with section 599 of that Act)".

(3) After subsection (4) insert—

"(4A) An amount charged on the residual business company as a result of section 543 of CTA 2010 (excessive property financing costs) is treated for the purposes of this Part as if it met condition A, B, C or D for the purposes of section 385 (tax-interest income amounts)."

(4) For subsection (5) substitute—

"(5) The allocated disallowance for the property rental business company (if any) for the accounting period—

(a) is to be taken into account in calculating the profits of the property rental business for the purposes of section 530 of CTA 2010 (condition as to distribution of profits), but

(b) must be limited to such amount as secures that neither subsection (3)(b) nor subsection (5) of that section (distribution of profits not required if would result in unlawful distribution) applies."

Interest restriction returns

15 In—

(a) paragraph 1(4)(a) of Schedule 7A (period for appointing a group's reporting company), and

(b) paragraph 2(4)(a) of that Schedule (period for revoking appointment),

for "six months" substitute "12 months".

16 In paragraph 7(5) of Schedule 7A (meaning of "the filing date")—

(a) for paragraph (b) substitute—

"(b) if an appointment of a reporting company under paragraph 4 or 5 has effect in relation to the period of account, the end of the period of 3 months beginning with the day on which the appointment was made,", and"

(b) after that paragraph insert—

"whichever is the later"

17 (1) In paragraph 7 of Schedule 7A (submission of interest restriction returns), after sub-paragraph (5) insert—

"(5A) For an extension of the filing date in the case of a takeover, see paragraph 7A."

(2) After that paragraph insert—

"7A (1) This paragraph applies if—

(a) a period of account ("the affected period") of a worldwide group ("the old group") ends solely as a result of the ultimate parent of the old group becoming a member of a different worldwide group, and

(b) the time at which that happens is within 12 months of the beginning of the affected period.

(2) For the purposes of this Part of this Act the filing date in relation to the affected period of the old group is whichever is the later of—

(a) the date given by paragraph 7(5), and

(b) the end of the period of 24 months beginning with the affected period."

18 In paragraph 20 of Schedule 7A (required contents of interest restriction return: full returns and abbreviated returns), after sub-paragraph (5) insert—

"(5A) In addition to the matters required to be included in an interest restriction return in accordance with sub-paragraph (3) or (5), the return must include such other specified information as may reasonably be required for the purposes of this Part of this Act.

(5B) In sub-paragraph (5A) "specified" means specified in a notice published by Her Majesty's Revenue and Customs (and different information may be specified for different purposes)."

Consequential amendments

19 In section 411 (definitions of "relevant expense amount" and "relevant income amount"), omit subsection (4).

20 In section 494(1) (other interpretation), after "interest restriction return" insert—

""pension scheme" has the meaning given by section 150(1) of FA 2004;".

21 In Part 7 of Schedule 11 (index of defined expressions used in Part 10 of TIOPA 2010), at the appropriate place insert—

"pension scheme (in Part 10)	section 494(1)"

Commencement

22 (1) The amendments made by paragraphs 2, 5 to 11 and 14(2) and (4) have effect in relation to periods of account of worldwide groups that begin on or after 1 January 2019.

(2) In this paragraph "period of account" and "worldwide group" have the same meaning as in Part 10 of TIOPA 2010.

23 The amendments made by paragraphs 3 and 4 have effect in relation to any change in ownership taking place on or after 29 October 2018.

24 Part 10 of TIOPA 2010 has effect, and is to be deemed always to have had effect, with the amendments made by paragraphs 12, 13, 14(3) and 19 to 21.

25 The amendment made by paragraph 17 has effect where the affected period ends on or after 29 October 2018.

26 The amendment made by paragraph 18 has effect in relation to any interest restriction return submitted on or after 1 April 2019.

Transitional provision in case of interest allowance (alternative calculation) elections

27 (1) This paragraph applies if—

(a) an interest allowance (alternative calculation) election has been made before 7 November 2018 with effect in relation to any period of account of a worldwide group ending before that date, and

(b) the election would, but for this paragraph, have been irrevocable as a result of paragraph 16(3)(b) of Schedule 7A to TIOPA 2010.

(2) If the appointment of a reporting company has effect in relation to the first period of account of the group beginning on or after 7 November 2018, the reporting company may revoke the election so that it ceases to have effect in relation to that period of account and subsequent periods of account of the group.

(3) The revocation—

(a) must be made before the end of the period of 3 months beginning with the day on which this Act is passed, and

(b) must be made by notice in writing given to an officer of Revenue and Customs (and, accordingly, paragraph 12(2) of Schedule 7A to TIOPA 2010 does not apply to the revocation).

(4) Expressions used in this paragraph have the same meaning as in Part 10 of TIOPA 2010.

COMMENTARY ON SCHEDULE 11

Schedule 11 makes changes to the corporate interest restriction legislation that was introduced by F(No2)A 2017 and which is now contained in TIOPA 2010, Pt 10.

Paragraph 1 introduces the changes.

Paragraph 2 inserts a new TIOPA 2010, s 391A. This provides that the exclusivity provisions of the intangible fixed assets legislation, which is contained in CTA 2009, Pt 8, will not prevent amounts in respect of a loan relationship or derivative contract that have been included as part of the carrying value of an intangible fixed asset from being treated as tax-interest expense or tax-interest income amounts under the corporate interest restriction legislation. This amendment has effect for periods of account of worldwide groups that begin on or after 1 January 2019 (see para 22).

Paragraph 3 introduces a new TIOPA 2010, s 395A, which provides that unused interest allowance may be carried forward from an old group to a new group where a new holding company is interposed between the existing ultimate parent company and its shareholders. This amendment has effect in relation to a change in ownership that takes place on or after 29 October 2018 (see para 23).

Paragraph 4 introduces a new TIOPA 2010, s 400A, which provides that an excess debt cap amount may be carried forward from an old group to a new group where a new holding company is interposed between the existing ultimate parent company and its shareholders. This amendment has effect in relation to a change in ownership that takes place on or after 29 October 2018 (see para 23).

Paragraph 5 makes an amendment to TIOPA 2010, s 410 to insert a new sub-s (5A), the purpose of which is to ensure that the section works as was originally intended. This new sub-s provides that relevant income amounts and relevant expense amounts that have been capitalised in respect of relevant assets will not be included in the calculation of relevant expense amounts or relevant income amounts in calculating net group-interest expense if such capitalised amounts are amortised to profit or loss. This amendment has effect in relation to periods of account of worldwide groups that begin on or after 1 January 2019 (see para 22).

Paragraph 6 amends TIOPA 2010, s 413, which sets out the calculation of adjusted net group-interest expense, to provide that the adjustments set out therein as regards the carrying value of an asset or liability are limited to non-financial assets and liabilities. In particular, it is intended to make clear that no adjustments will arise in calculating a group's adjusted net group-interest expense in respect of arrangement fees and other expenses that are included in the carrying value of a financial asset or financial liability under an amortised cost basis of accounting. The effect of the amendment is that such amounts will be recognised in arriving at the group's net group-interest expense on the basis that they are reflected in profit or loss in the group's accounts. This amendment has effect in relation to periods of account of worldwide groups that begin on or after 1 January 2019 (see para 22).

Paragraph 7 amends TIOPA 2010, s 423 (capitalised interest brought into account for tax purposes in accordance with GAAP), which sets out how the calculation of a group's adjusted net group-interest expense is modified where the group has made an interest allowance (alternative calculation) election. The intention behind the amendment is to ensure that where profits or losses on relevant assets are recognised for tax purposes on the basis that they are recognised in a company's accounts in accordance with GAAP (GAAP Taxable Asset), for example in the case of an intangible fixed asset, the calculation of the adjusted net group-interest expense includes (by way of an upward or downward adjustment) the amount of any amortisation or write off of relevant expense amounts and relevant income amounts that have previously been capitalised in respect of the asset.

Paragraph 7 also amends TIOPA 2010, s 423 to provide that an intangible fixed asset will be treated as a GAAP Taxable Asset where an election is or could be made under CTA 2009, s 730 to write off the cost of the intangible fixed asset on a straight line basis of 4% per annum. The reference to 'could be' is intended, inter alia, to address the assumption made under TIOPA 2010, s 423(5) that all members of the worldwide group are treated as being within the charge to corporation tax.

The amendments made by para 7 have effect for periods of account of worldwide groups that begin on or after 1 January 2019 (see para 22).

Paragraph 8 makes changes to TIOPA 2010, s 413 (calculation of adjusted net group-interest expense) to provide that when calculating a group's adjusted net group-interest expense:

- an upwards adjustment should be made for any loan relationship release credit which is not included in computing a company's loan relationship profits by virtue of CTA 2009, ss 358 or 359; and
- a downwards adjustment should be made for any loan relationship release debit which is prevented from being brought into account by virtue of CTA 2009, s 354.

These adjustments are intended to align the calculation of adjusted net group-interest expense with the provisions of the loan relationships legislation in circumstances where there is a release of a connected company loan relationship and the counterparty is not a member of the worldwide group. In such cases the release is not eliminated on consolidation and rather is reflected as a relevant expense amount or relevant income amount in arriving at the worldwide group's net group-interest expense and the effect of the amendment is that such release debits or credits will be eliminated in arriving at the group's adjusted net group-interest expense.

The amendments made by para 8 have effect for periods of account of worldwide groups that begin on or after 1 January 2019 (see para 22).

Paragraph 9 inserts a new TIOPA 2010, s 424A, which provides for an additional adjustment to be made to the calculation of group-EBITDA where an interest allowance (alternative calculation) election has been made. New TIOPA 2010, s 424A provides that where such an election has been made, employee remuneration (including provisions in respect thereof) that remains unpaid more than nine months after the end of the relevant period of account is to be excluded from the group's profit before tax as determined for the purposes of TIOPA 2010, s 416. Instead such amounts will be included in calculating the group's profit before tax for the period of account in which they are paid. The intention is to align the calculation of the group's profit before tax with the way in which UK taxable profits would be calculated. This amendment has effect in relation to periods of account of worldwide groups that begin on or after 1 January 2019 (see para 22).

Paragraph 10 amends TIOPA 2010, s 426 (changes in accounting policy where an interest allowance (alternative calculation) election has effect) in two respects.

First, it provides that the change of accounting practice calculation takes into account changes of accounting practice in respect of property business profits.

Secondly, it ensures that only actual changes in accounting practice (as opposed to as a result of a tax provision that requires a particular accounting treatment to be applied) are taken into account for the purposes of the calculation.

The amendments made by para 10 have effect for periods of account of worldwide groups that begin on or after 1 January 2019 (see para 22).

Paragraph 11 amends TIOPA 2010, s 427 (group interest and group-EBITDA) to clarify how adjusted net group-interest expense and qualifying net group-interest expense are to be calculated in cases where an interest allowance (non-consolidated investment) election is made. The amendment makes it clear that any adjustment arising under TIOPA 2010, s 413(4) and (5) (downwards adjustment) is subject to sub-s (1), such that where the calculation produces a negative amount it is treated as being nil. This amendment has effect in relation to periods of account of worldwide groups that begin on or after 1 January 2019 (see para 22).

Paragraph 12 amends TIOPA 2010, s 433 (meaning of qualifying infrastructure company). It amends the definition of qualifying infrastructure assets to include:

- pension scheme assets where the pension scheme is for persons employed for the purpose of the carrying on of qualifying infrastructure activities by the company or another associated qualifying infrastructure company; and
- deferred tax assets to the extent that they are attributable to qualifying infrastructure activities carried on by the company or another associated qualifying infrastructure company.

The amendments made by para 12 are deemed always to have had effect (see para 24).

Paragraph 13 amends TIOPA 2010, s 439, which provides for grandfathering of certain loan relationships to which a qualifying infrastructure company was a party before 13 May 2016. The amendment provides that any reimbursement of expenses is to be disregarded in determining whether the future qualifying infrastructure receipts test set out in TIOPA 2010, s 439(1)(b) is satisfied. The amendment made by para 13 is deemed always to have had effect.

Paragraph 14 makes a number of amendments to TIOPA 2010, s 452 (Real Estate Investment Trusts).

Paragraph 14(2) provides that CTA 2010, s 599 (calculation of profits) is disapplied in determining the amounts of a REIT that should be included in the corporate interest restriction calculations. The intended effect is that any interest or other financing amounts that are included in the REIT property business profits are treated as if they are brought into account under CTA 2009 Pt 5 (loan relationships legislation) and thus are subject to the corporate interest restriction rules. This amendment has effect for periods of account of worldwide groups that begin on or after 1 January 2019 (see para 22).

Paragraph 14(3) inserts a new TIOPA 2010, s 452(4A), which provides that where an amount is charged to corporation tax under CTA 2009, s 543, as a result of the REIT's interest cover ratio falling below 1.25, the amount is to be treated as a tax-interest income amount for the purposes of the corporate interest restriction rules. This is to ensure that the REIT does not suffer an effective double restriction as a result of having high levels of gearing in that particular period. This amendment is deemed always to have had effect (see para 24).

Paragraph 14(4) replaces the existing TIOPA 2010, s 452(5) with a new sub-s (5). This is intended to provide clarification that any interest restriction allocated to the REIT property business profits has effect for the purpose of computing the amount that is required to be distributed by the REIT under CTA 2010, s 530, notwithstanding that the interest and other financing cost may be treated as being brought into account under CTA 2009, Pt 4 (property income) as opposed to Pt 5 (loan relationships) as a result of the application of CTA 2010, s 599. This amendment has effect for periods of account of worldwide groups that begin on or after 1 January 2019 (see para 22).

Paragraph 15 extends the time limit for appointing or revoking the appointment of a reporting company (the company that is responsible for filing interest restriction returns and dealing with other administrative matters on behalf of the worldwide group). The effect of the amendment is that an appointment or revocation will be valid where it is made within 12 months of the end of the relevant period account (as opposed to the previous six months). This amendment takes effect from Royal Assent of FA 2019 (12 February 2019).

Paragraph 16 makes changes to TIOPA 2010, Sch 7A, para 7(5), which defines the filing date for an interest restriction return. The effect of the amendment is that where a group appoints the reporting company more than nine months after the end of the period of account (under the amendment introduced by para 15, the time limit for appointing a reporting company is extended to 12 months after the end of the relevant period of account) this will not extend the time limit for filing an interest restriction return. The existing extended deadline (three months after the appointment of the reporting company) will only apply following this amendment where a reporting company is appointed by HMRC. This amendment has effect from Royal Assent of FA 2019 (12 February 2019).

Paragraph 17 amends TIOPA 2010, Sch 7A, para 7 to provide for an extended deadline for the submission of an interest restriction return where a group ceases to exist because its ultimate parent becomes a member of a new group. In such cases the time limit for filing an interest restriction return is extended to 24 months after the beginning of the period of account in which the takeover occurs, where this is later than the time limit that would otherwise apply, provided that the takeover occurs within 12 months of the start of the period of account. This amendment has effect where the period of account in which the takeover occurs ends on or after 29 October 2018 (see para 25).

Paragraph 18 permits HMRC, by notice, to specify additional information to be included in an interest restriction return. This amendment has effect in relation to any interest restriction return submitted on or after 1 April 2019 (see para 26).

Paragraphs 19 and 20 move the definition of a pension scheme from TIOPA 2010, s 411(4) to TIOPA 2010, s 494(1), which sets out the definitions used the purposes of TIOPA 2010, Pt 10.

Paragraph 21 amends TIOPA 2010, Sch 11, Pt 7 to note that the definition of 'pension scheme' is now included in TIOPA 2010, s 494(1).

Paragraphs 22–26 set out the commencement dates of the various amendments introduced by FA 2019, Sch 10 and these are noted in the commentary above.

Paragraph 27 provides a transitional provision in respect of an interest allowance (alternative calculation election) which permits an election that has been made before 7 November 2018 in respect of a period of account that ended before this date to be revoked (notwithstanding that ordinarily such an election is irrevocable). This is to ensure that a group is not disadvantaged as a result of the amendment introduced by para 9.

SCHEDULE 12

ELIMINATING TAX MISMATCH FOR CERTAIN DEBT

Section 29

Loan relationships with qualifying link

1 After section 352A of CTA 2009 insert—

"352B Eliminating tax mismatch for loan relationships with qualifying link

(1) This section applies if—

(a) section 349 applies in respect of a loan relationship of a company for an accounting period (application of amortised cost basis to connected companies relationships),

(b) the company is a party to another loan relationship ("the external loan relationship") in respect of which that section does not apply for the period,

(c) the external loan relationship is a debtor relationship dealt with in its accounts on the basis of fair value accounting, and

(d) the external loan relationship has a qualifying link with one or more other loan relationships of the company.

(2) For this purpose the external loan relationship has "a qualifying link" with one or more other loan relationships of the company if—

(a) each of those other loan relationships of the company is a loan relationship in respect of which section 349 applies for the accounting period, and

(b) taking those other loan relationships together, the money received by the company under the external loan relationship is wholly or mainly used to lend money under those other loan relationships.

(3) The credits and debits which are to be brought into account for the purposes of this Part in respect of the external loan relationship for the period are to be determined on an amortised cost basis of accounting.

(4) If a company has a hedging relationship between—

(a) a relevant contract ("the hedging instrument"), and

(b) the liability representing the external loan relationship,

it is to be assumed in applying the amortised cost basis of accounting for the purposes of subsection (3) that the hedging instrument has where possible been designated for accounting purposes as a fair value hedge of that loan relationship."

2 In section 465B of CTA 2009 (meaning of "tax-adjusted carrying value"), in subsection (9), after paragraph (k) insert—

"(ka) section 352B (eliminating tax mismatch for loan relationships with qualifying link),".

Commencement and transitional provisions

3 (1) The amendments made by this Schedule have effect for accounting periods beginning on or after 1 January 2019.

(2) An accounting period beginning before and ending on or after 1 January 2019 is to be treated for the purposes of any provision made by this Schedule as if so much of the period as falls before that date, and so much of the period as falls on or after that date, were separate accounting periods.

4 (1) This paragraph applies in relation to an accounting period of a company beginning on 1 January 2019 ("the 2019 period") to bring in credits or debits in respect of a loan relationship which is the external loan relationship for the purposes of section 352B of CTA 2009 so far as they would not otherwise be brought into account.

(2) If there is a difference between—

(a) the tax-adjusted carrying value of the liability representing the external loan relationship at the end of the accounting period of the company ending on 31 December 2018, and

(b) the tax-adjusted carrying value of that liability at the beginning of the 2019 period, a credit or debit (as the case may be) of an amount equal to the difference must be brought into account for the purposes of Part 5 of CTA 2009 for the 2019 period in the same way as a credit or debit which is brought into account in determining the company's profit or loss for that period in accordance with generally accepted accounting practice.

(3) Section 465B of CTA 2009 (meaning of "tax-adjusted carrying value") applies for the purposes of this paragraph as it applies for the purposes of Part 5 of that Act.

Power to amend section 352B of CTA 2009

5 (1) The Treasury may by regulations amend section 352B of CTA 2009.

(2) The power conferred by this paragraph may not be exercised after 31 December 2019.

(3) The regulations may contain incidental, supplementary, consequential and transitional provision and savings.

(4) The consequential provision that may be made by the regulations includes provision amending any provision made by or under any Act.

(5) The regulations may contain retrospective provision.

COMMENTARY ON SCHEDULE 12

Schedule 12 introduces a new CTA 2009, s 352B. This requires the profits and losses arising to a company on a debtor relationship, to which it is a party with an unconnected third party and which is carried at fair value in its accounts, to be determined using an amortised cost basis of accounting where the conditions set out in the section are satisfied. These are that the money borrowed is used wholly or mainly to make loans to companies with which the borrower is connected for the purposes of the loan relationships legislation.

Where the debtor relationship is hedged by a derivative contract and the derivative contract could be treated as being a fair value hedge of the debtor relationship, the company is permitted to revalue the debtor relationship for movements in the value of the risk (typically interest rate movements) that is being hedged by the derivative contract.

CTA 2009, s 352B took effect for accounting periods beginning on or after 1 January 2019. Where an accounting period straddled this date it was split into two deemed periods, with the second period starting on 1 January 2019. Any difference between the tax adjusted carrying value of the debtor relationship at 31 December 2018 and its opening value at 1 January 2019 is required to be brought into account in determining the company's loan relationship profits for its accounting period beginning on 1 January 2019.

The Treasury has a power, by regulation, to amend CTA 2009, s 352B and such amendments may contain retrospective provision.

The new CTA 2009, s 352B is intended, inter alia, to cover a case where a member of a banking or an insurance group raises regulatory capital through borrowing and on lends the borrowed funds wholly or mainly to a member of the same group on broadly the same terms and it is required to account for the on loan on a fair value basis. In such circumstances, typically, it would also account for the debtor relationship at fair value through profit loss. For tax purposes, however, it would be required to determine the profits and losses arising on the on loan using an amortised cost basis of accounting since the on loan would be a connected companies creditor relationship. The effect of CTA 2009, s 352B is to enable the company to apply the same basis for computing the loan relationship profits or losses arising on the two loan relationships.

SCHEDULE 13

ANNUAL INVESTMENT ALLOWANCE: PERIODS STRADDLING 1 JANUARY 2019 OR 1 JANUARY 2021

Section 32

Chargeable periods which straddle 1 January 2019

1 (1) This paragraph applies in relation to a chargeable period which begins before 1 January 2019 and ends on or after that date ("the first straddling period").

(2) The maximum allowance under section 51A of CAA 2001 for the first straddling period is the sum of the maximum allowances that would be found if the following were treated as separate chargeable periods—

(a) so much of the first straddling period as falls before 1 January 2019;
(b) so much of the first straddling period as falls on or after that date.

(3) But, so far as concerns expenditure incurred before 1 January 2019, the maximum allowance under section 51A of CAA 2001 for the first straddling period is what would be the maximum allowance if the modification made by section 32(1) were not made.

Chargeable periods which straddle 1 January 2021

2 (1) This paragraph applies in relation to a chargeable period ("the second straddling period") which begins before 1 January 2021 and ends on or after that date.

(2) The maximum allowance under section 51A of CAA 2001 for the second straddling period is the sum of the maximum allowances that would be found if the following were treated as separate chargeable periods—

(a) so much of the second straddling period as falls before 1 January 2021;
(b) so much of the second straddling period as falls on or after that date.

(3) But, so far as concerns expenditure incurred on or after 1 January 2021, the maximum allowance under section 51A of CAA 2001 for the second straddling period is the maximum allowance, calculated in accordance with sub-paragraph (2), for the period mentioned in paragraph (b) of that sub-paragraph.

Operation of annual investment allowance where restrictions apply

3 (1) Paragraphs 1 and 2 apply for the purpose of determining the maximum allowance under section 51K of CAA 2001 (operation of annual investment allowance where restrictions apply) in a case where one or more chargeable periods in which the relevant AIA qualifying expenditure is incurred are chargeable periods within paragraph 1(1) or 2(1).

(2) There is to be taken into account for that purpose only chargeable periods of one year or less (whether or not they are chargeable periods within paragraph 1(1) or 2(1)), and, if there is more than one such period, only that period which gives rise to the greatest maximum allowance.

(3) Sub-paragraph (4) applies to a chargeable period if—

(a) it is longer than one year, and
(b) any part of the chargeable period is within the period of two years beginning with 1 January 2019.

(4) For the purposes of sub-paragraph (2) the chargeable period (the "relevant period") is to be divided into two periods, as follows—

(a) a chargeable period of one year ending when the relevant period ends, and
(b) a chargeable period consisting of so much of the relevant period as is not within paragraph (a).

(5) Nothing in this paragraph affects the operation of sections 51M and 51N of CAA 2001.

COMMENTARY ON SCHEDULE 13

Section 32 increases the annual investment allowance (AIA) to £1,000,000 with effect for the two-year period from 1 January 2019 to 31 December 2020. This is subject to a number of rules concerning how the AIA is calculated where a person's chargeable period includes the change in rate. Where a business does not have a 31 December year-end, the transitional rules set out in Sch 13 apply.

There are different rules regarding introduction of the temporary rate on 1 January 2019 and its expiry on 1 January 2021. However, in both cases the maximum for the chargeable period is calculated the same way. The period is split into two notional periods, with the first ending immediately before the change in rate. Separate AIAs are calculated for each notional period and then added together to give the maximum AIA for the whole chargeable period.

For periods straddling 1 January 2019 there is another separate AIA limit which is outlined in paragraph 1 of Schedule 13. This applies only to expenditure incurred before 1 January 2019. The maximum AIA that can be claimed for expenditure between the beginning of the chargeable period and 1 January 2019 is what would have been available in the absence of the temporary increase. In other words, for a business with a 12-month chargeable period, the AIA applying for the notional period to 31 December 2018 is £200,000.

For example, a business with a year-end of 31 March 2019 (whether subject to income tax or corporation tax) will have a maximum AIA for the whole period of £400,000 (being 9/12 of £200,000 plus 3/12 of £1,000,000). However, the maximum AIA applying to expenditure in the period from 1 April 2018 to 31 December 2018 is £200,000.

Paragraph 2 of Sch 13 provides for the transitional rules for periods straddling 1 January 2021. There is a limit placed on the notional period beginning 1 January 2021 and ending with the chargeable period end. The maximum AIA for this period is the notional period's separate AIA already calculated. That is, the maximum AIA for the notional period beginning 1 January 2019 is calculated by time apportioning the AIA of £200,000 according to the length of the notional period.

For example, a business with a year-end of 31 March 2021 (whether subject to income tax or corporation tax) will have a maximum AIA for the whole period of £800,000 (being 9/12 of £1,000,000 plus 3/12 of 3/12 of £200,000). However, the maximum AIA applying to expenditure in the period from 1 January 2021 to 31 December 2021 is £50,000 (3/12 of £200,000).

Paragraph 3 then explains how the transitional rules apply in cases where the AIA is shared between companies in a group, individuals with more than one trade or other businesses where a single AIA is shared. These apply the transitional rules above but state that, as the transitional AIA differs according to period end which may differ between businesses under common control, the AIA that applies is the one which gives rise to the greatest maximum AIA. For this purpose, chargeable periods must be one year or less. If there is a longer period, it is notionally curtailed to one year for the purposes of establishing the maximum AIA.

Paragraph 3(5) explicitly states that the special provisions for long chargeable periods provided under CAA 2001, ss 51M and 51N are unaffected by the transitional rules.

SCHEDULE 14

LEASES: CHANGES TO ACCOUNTING STANDARDS ETC

Section 36

PART 1

FINANCE LEASES: AMENDMENTS AS A RESULT OF CHANGES TO ACCOUNTING STANDARDS

1 (1) Part 2 of CAA 2001 (plant and machinery allowances) is amended as follows.

(2) In section 67 (plant or machinery treated as owned by person entitled to benefit of contract, etc), in subsection (2B), for the words from "falls (or would fall)" to the end substitute "—

(a) falls (or would fall) to be treated by that person in accordance with generally accepted accounting practice as a finance lease, or

(b) if that person is a lessee under a right-of-use lease, would fall to be treated in that person's accounts as a finance lease were that person required under generally accepted accounting practice to determine whether the lease falls to be so treated."

(3) In section 70E (disposal events and disposal values), in subsection (2D)(a), after "finance charges" insert ", or interest expenses,".

(4) In section 70YA (changes in accountancy classification of long funding leases)—

(a) in subsection (1)(b), for "or an operating lease" substitute ", an operating lease or a right-of-use lease",

(b) in subsection (4)—

(i) for "or an operating lease" substitute ", an operating lease or a right-of-use lease", and

(ii) for "and (6)" substitute "to (6A)",

(c) in subsection (5)—

(i) omit the "and" at the end of paragraph (a), and

(ii) after paragraph (b) insert "and

(c) the change of classification is not a relevant change of classification.",

(d) in subsection (6)—

(i) omit the "and" at the end of paragraph (a), and

(ii) after paragraph (b) insert "and

(c) the change of classification is not a relevant change of classification.",

(e) after subsection (6) insert—

"(6A) Case 3 is where—

(a) immediately before the relevant time, the lease is a right-of-use lease which is a long funding finance lease, and

(b) at the relevant time, the lease becomes one which—

(i) is not a right-of use lease, and

(ii) falls (or would fall) to be treated in the relevant accounts in accordance with generally accepted accounting practice as not being a finance lease.", and

(f) after subsection (10) insert—

"(11) In this section—

"relevant change of classification" means a change of accountancy classification as a result of the person adopting a different accounting standard or a change to an accounting standard, and

"accounting standard" means any accounting standard issued or recognised by—

(a) the Accounting Standards Board (or successor body), or

(b) the International Accounting Standards Board (or successor body)."

(5) In section 70YI (general definitions), in subsection (1)—

(a) for the definition of "long funding finance lease" substitute—

"“long funding finance lease” means—

(a) in relation to any person, a long funding lease that meets the finance lease test by virtue of section 70N(1)(a), or

(b) in relation to a lessee, a right-of-use lease which is a long funding lease—

(i) that meets the lease payments test in section 70O or the useful economic life test in section 70P, but

(ii) is not a lease that, before a relevant change of classification, was a long funding operating lease;", and

(b) at the appropriate places insert—

"“relevant change of classification” has the meaning given by section 70YA(11);";

"“right-of-use lease”, in relation to a lessee, means a lease in respect of which, under generally accepted accounting practice—

(a) a right-of-use asset falls (or would fall) at the commencement date of the lease to be recognised for accounting purposes in the accounts of the lessee, or

(b) a right-of-use asset would fall to be so recognised but for the lessee granting a sublease of the leased asset,

and, in determining whether a lease falls within paragraph (a) or (b) at any time in an accounting period, it is to be assumed that the accounting policy applied in drawing up the lessee's accounts for the period also applied at the commencement date of the lease;".

(6) In section 228J (anti-avoidance: plant or machinery subject to further operating lease), in subsection (7)—

(a) for paragraph (a) substitute—

"(a) the lease—

(i) falls, under generally accepted accounting practice, to be treated in that person's accounts as a finance lease or loan, or

(ii) if that person is a lessee under a right-of-use lease, would fall to be treated in that person's accounts as a finance lease were that person required under generally accepted accounting practice to determine whether the lease falls to be so treated,", and

(b) in paragraph (b), for the words from "fall" to the end substitute "—

(i) fall, under generally accepted accounting practice, to be treated as a finance lease or loan, or

(ii) if that person is a lessee under a right-of-use lease, would fall to be treated in that person's accounts as a finance lease were that person required under generally accepted accounting practice to determine whether the arrangements fall to be so treated."

2 (1) ITTOIA 2005 is amended as follows.

(2) In section 148G (lessee under long funding finance lease: limit on deductions), in subsection (2), after "finance charges" insert ", or interest expenses,".

(3) After that section insert—

"148GA Lessee under long funding finance leases: right-of-use leases

(1) This section applies if—

(a) for the whole or part of any period of account, a person carrying on a trade, profession or vocation is the lessee of any plant or machinery under a right-of-use lease that is a long funding finance lease,

(b) there is a change in the amounts payable under the lease, and

(c) as a result of the change and in accordance with generally accepted accounting practice—

(i) a remeasurement of the lease liability is shown in the person's accounts for the period of account, or

(ii) a deduction is shown in those accounts other than as an interest expense under the lease or an amount of depreciation, or an impairment, in respect of the right-of-use asset arising from the lease.

(2) In calculating the profits of the person's trade, vocation or profession for the period of account, the amount deducted in respect of amounts payable under the lease (after taking account of any limitation as a result of section 148G) is to be increased or decreased so as to take account of the remeasurement or deduction mentioned in subsection (1)(c).

(3) No adjustment is to be made under subsection (2) if the remeasurement or deduction results in the person being treated by section 70D of CAA 2001 (long funding finance lease: additional expenditure: allowances for lessee) as having incurred further capital expenditure on the provision of the plant or machinery."

3 In section 809BZN of ITA 2007 (finance arrangements: exceptions), after subsection (9) insert—

"(9A) A finance arrangement code does not apply if the arrangement is a right-of-use lease—

(a) under which the relevant person is a lessee, and

(b) which, were that person required under generally accepted accounting practice to determine whether the lease falls to be treated in the accounts of that person as a finance lease or loan, would not fall to be so treated.

(9B) In subsection (9A) "right-of-use lease" has the same meaning as in Part 2 of CAA 2001 (see section 70YI(1) of that Act)."

4 (1) CTA 2010 is amended as follows.

(2) In section 288 (sale and lease-back)—

(a) in subsection (5), for sub-paragraph (a) substitute—

"(a) falls, in accordance with generally accepted accounting practice, to be treated in the accounts of the lessee—

(i) as a finance charge, or

(ii) as an interest expense where any such expenditure would fall to be treated in those accounts as a finance charge if the lessee were required under generally accepted accounting practice to determine whether that expenditure should be so treated,

(aa) if the lease is a right-of-use lease which is a long funding finance lease, falls, in accordance with generally accepted accounting practice, to be treated in the accounts of the lessee as an interest expense, or", and

(b) in subsection (9), for the definition of "long funding operating lease" substitute—

""long funding finance lease", "long funding operating lease" and "right-of-use lease" have the meanings given in Part 2 of CAA 2001 (see section 70YI(1) of that Act),".

(3) In section 331 (meaning of "financing costs" etc)—

(a) in subsection (3), after paragraph (d) insert—

"(da) if the company is the lessee under a right-of-use lease which is a long funding finance lease, any costs falling, in accordance with generally accepted accounting practice, to be treated in the accounts of the company as interest expenses,",

(b) in subsection (4)(a), after "finance charge" insert ", or an interest expense,",

(c) for subsection (6) substitute—

"(6) In this section "finance lease" means a lease which—

(a) under generally accepted accounting practice—

(i) falls (or would fall) to be treated, in the accounts of the lessee or a person connected with the lessee, as a finance lease or loan, or

(ii) is comprised in arrangements which fall (or would fall) to be so treated, or

(b) if the lease is a right-of-use lease—

(i) would fall to be treated in those accounts as a finance lease, or

(ii) is comprised in arrangements which would fall to be so treated,

were the lessee or person connected with the lessee required under generally accepted accounting practice to determine whether the lease falls, or arrangements fall, to be so treated.", and

(d) in subsection (9)—

(i) omit the "and" at the end of the definition of "exchange gains" and "exchange losses", and

(ii) after that definition insert—

""lease" means any arrangements which provide for an asset to be leased or otherwise made available by a person to another person ("the lessee"), and "long funding finance lease", "long funding operating lease" and "right-of-use lease" have the meanings given in Part 2 of CAA 2001 (see section 70YI(1) of that Act)."

(4) In section 377 (lessee under long funding finance lease: limit on deductions), in subsection (3), after "as finance charges" insert ", or interest expenses,".

(5) After that section insert—

"377A Lessee under long funding finance leases: right-of-use leases

(1) This section applies if—

(a) for the whole or part of any period of account, a company is the lessee of any plant or machinery under a right-of-use lease that is a long funding finance lease,

(b) there is a change in the amounts payable under the lease, and

(c) as a result of the change and in accordance with generally accepted accounting practice—

(i) a remeasurement of the lease liability is shown in the person's accounts for the period of account, or

(ii) a deduction is shown in those accounts other than as an interest expense under the lease or an amount of depreciation, or an impairment, in respect of the right-of-use asset arising from the lease.

(2) In calculating the company's profits for the period of account, the amount deducted in respect of amounts payable under the lease (after taking account of any limitation as a result of section 377) is to be increased or decreased so as to take account of the remeasurement or deduction mentioned in subsection (1)(c).

(3) No adjustment is to be made under subsection (2) if the remeasurement or deduction results in the company being treated by section 70D of CAA 2001 (long funding finance lease: additional expenditure: allowances for lessee) as having incurred further capital expenditure on the provision of the plant or machinery."

(6) In section 381 (interpretation of Chapter 2 of Part 9), in subsection (2), for the definition of "long funding finance lease" substitute—

""long funding finance lease" means—

(a) in relation to any person, a long funding lease that meets the finance lease test as a result of section 70N(1)(a) of that Act, or

(b) in relation to a lessee, a right-of-use lease (see section 70YI(1) of that Act) which is a long funding lease—

(i) that meets the lease payments test in section 70O of that Act or the useful economic life test in section 70P of that Act, but

(ii) is not a lease that, before a relevant change of classification (see section 70YA(11) of that Act), was a long funding operating lease;".

(7) In section 437 (interpretation of the sales of lessors Chapters)—

(a) for subsection (4) substitute—

"(4) "Finance lease" means—

(a) in relation to any person, a lease that, in accordance with generally accepted accounting practice, falls (or would fall) to be treated in the accounts of that person as a finance lease or loan, or

(b) in relation to a lessee under a right-of-use lease, a lease that would fall to be treated in the accounts of the lessee as a finance lease if the lessee were required under generally accepted accounting practice to determine whether the lease falls to be so treated.", and

(b) in subsection (6), for "and "long funding operating lease"" substitute ", "long funding operating lease" and "right-of-use lease"".

(8) In section 544 (meaning of "property profits" and "property financing costs"), after subsection (5) insert—

"(5A) In subsection (5) "finance lease" means—

(a) in relation to any person, a lease that, in accordance with generally accepted accounting practice, falls (or would fall) to be treated in the accounts of that person as a finance lease or loan, or

(b) in relation to a lessee under a right-of-use lease, a lease that would fall to be treated in the accounts of the lessee as a finance lease if the lessee were required under generally accepted accounting practice to determine whether the lease falls to be so treated.

(5B) In subsection (5A)(b) "right-of-use lease" has the meaning given in Part 2 of CAA 2001 (see section 70YI(1) of that Act)."

(9) In section 771 (finance arrangements: exceptions), after subsection (9) insert—

"(9A) A finance arrangement code does not apply if the arrangement is a right-of-use lease—

(a) under which the relevant person is a lessee, and

(b) which, were that person required under generally accepted accounting practice to determine whether the lease falls to be treated in the accounts of that person as a finance lease or loan, would not fall to be so treated.

(9B) In subsection (9A) "right-of-use lease" has the meaning given in Part 2 of CAA 2001 (see section 70YI(1) of that Act)."

5 In section 494 of TIOPA 2010 (corporate interest restriction: other interpretation), in subsection (1)—

(a) for the definition of "finance lease" substitute—

""finance lease", in relation to a company or a worldwide group, a lease which—

(a) in accordance with generally accepted accounting practice, falls (or would fall) to be treated, in the accounts of the company or the financial statements of the group, as a finance lease or loan, or

(b) is a right-of-use lease that would fall to be treated in those accounts or financial statements as a finance lease if the company or group were required to determine for accounting purposes whether the lease falls to be so treated;", and

(b) insert at the appropriate place—

""right-of-use lease" means a lease in respect of which, under generally accepted accounting practice—

(a) a right-of-use asset falls (or would fall) at the commencement of the lease to be recognised for accounting purposes in the accounts of the lessee, or

(b) a right-of-use asset would fall to be so recognised but for the lessee granting a sublease of the leased asset,

and, in determining whether a lease falls within paragraph (a) or (b) at any time in an accounting period, it is to be assumed that the accounting policy applied in drawing up the lessee's accounts for the period also applied at the commencement of the lease;".

Commencement

6 (1) The amendments made by this Part of this Schedule have effect in relation to periods of account beginning on or after 1 January 2019.

(2) But, for the purposes of Chapter 7 of Part 10 of TIOPA 2010 (corporate interest restriction: group-interest and group-EBITDA), the amendments made by paragraph 5 have effect in relation to periods of account of a worldwide group (within the meaning given by section 480 of that Act) beginning on or after 1 January 2019.

COMMENTARY ON SCHEDULE 14, PART 1

Section 36 and Schedule 14 implement a package of changes for income tax and corporation tax rules as a result of the adoption of International Financial Reporting

Standard 16 (IFRS 16), for all entities which apply International Financial Reporting Standards (IFRS), or Financial Reporting Standard 101 Reduced Disclosure Framework (FRS 101). The legislation takes effect for periods of account commencing on or after 1 January 2019. There are also amendments to long funding lease rules which are independent of the IFRS 16 changes.

Currently, lessees and lessors are required to make a distinction between finance and operating leases. Where the lessee has substantially all the risks and rewards incidental to the ownership of an asset, it recognises a finance lease asset and liability on its balance sheet. Where the lessee does not have substantially all the risks and rewards incidental to the ownership of the asset, it recognises lease payments as an expense over the lease term and is considered to have an operating lease. This treatment will continue under FRS 102, the main Financial Reporting Standard. The new accounting standard (IFRS 16) will remove the distinction between finance leases and operating leases for a lessee (but not a lessor). Going forward, under IFRS 16, a lessee will recognise all leases on its balance sheet leading to a financial lease liability and a 'right of use' asset (this is apart from certain exempted leases which are short term or of low value).

The FA 2019 changes mean that the existing tax treatment of leased assets, including the capital allowance regime on long funding leases, will be maintained although with some modifications. This is generally done by modifying the legislation wording so that if, under IFRS 16, a lease is treated as a right-of-use lease, the lessee would have to determine whether the lease would have been treated as a finance lease under GAAP had they been required to do so.

Other specific changes to the tax legislation in relation to long funding leases are summarised as follows.

Where there is a change in an accounting standard or a change to an accounting standard a deemed disposal and reacquisition will not occur under CAA 2001, s 70YA when a long funding lease is reclassified as a result. An extra Case 3 situation is also added to CAA 2001, s 70YA where a deemed disposal and reacquisition would apply if the lease is a right-of-use lease and starts to be accounted for as an operating lease.

The definition of long funding finance leases in CAA 2001, s 70YI and CTA 2010, s 381 is updated so that where leases are accounted for under IFRS 16 as right-of-use leases they will all be long funding finance leases as long as they meet the lease payments test or useful economic life tests in CAA 2001, ss 70O and 70P respectively. Any leases which were long funding operating leases before IFRS 16 adoption will have their tax treatment grandfathered.

New sections ITTOIA 2015, s 148GA and CTA 2010, s 377A have been introduced which allow increased or decreased deductions by a lessee using IFRS 16 with a long funding finance lease. The amendments occur when there is a change in the amounts payable under the lease which results in entries in the lessee's accounts for a remeasurement of the lease liability or a deduction which is not interest, depreciation or an impairment. This increased deduction does not apply if the result is enhanced capital expenditure which would be claimed through the depreciation charge.

PART 2

LONG FUNDING LEASES

Amendments to Part 2 of CAA 2001

7 Part 2 of CAA 2001 (plant and machinery allowances) is amended as follows.

Meaning of "short lease"

8 (1) In section 70I ("short lease")—

(a) in subsections (2) and (9)(d), for "5" substitute "7", and
(b) omit subsections (3) to (8).

(2) In section 70YF (the "term" of a lease)—

(a) in subsection (5)(b), for "5" substitute "7",
(b) in subsection (6), for "5" substitute "7", and
(c) omit subsection (7).

(3) In section 220 (allocation of expenditure to a chargeable period), in subsection (4)(c), for "5" substitute "7".

The lease payments test: interest rate implicit in lease

9 (1) Section 70O (the lease payments test) is amended as follows.

(2) In subsection (4), for paragraph (b) substitute—

"(b) if a rate cannot be determined in accordance with paragraph (a), the interest rate implicit in the lease is taken to be 1% above LIBOR."

(3) After that subsection insert—

"(5) For this purpose—

(a) LIBOR means the London interbank offered rate at the relevant time for deposits for a term of 12 months in the applicable currency,
(b) the relevant time is the inception of the lease, and
(c) the applicable currency is the currency in which payments under the lease are payable."

Commencement

10 The amendments made by this Part of this Schedule have effect in relation to leases entered into on or after 1 January 2019.

COMMENTARY ON SCHEDULE 14, PART 2

The long funding lease rules in CAA 2001 ss 70A–70YJ, provide that where a plant or machinery lease is, in substance, a funding lease for the lessee (because the effect of the lease is substantially equivalent to the lessee having borrowed funds to acquire the asset) the lessee is entitled to claim capital allowances on the asset even though they are not the legal owner. The legislative changes ensure that those rules will continue to apply as intended for an IFRS 16 lessee.

The definition of a long funding lease has been simplified so that a lease whose term is less than seven years (previously five years) is short and therefore, by definition, not a long funding lease. The detailed rules for leases between five and seven years which could be deemed to be short have been repealed.

There is also an amendment to the rate of interest used under the lease payments test in the event that the rate implicit in the lease cannot be determined.

These changes take effect for leases entered into on or after 1 January 2019.

PART 3

CHANGES TO ACCOUNTING STANDARDS AND TAX ADJUSTMENTS

Repeal of section 53 of FA 2011

11 (1) In FA 2011, omit section 53 (leases and changes to accounting standards).

(2) The amendment made by this paragraph has effect in relation to periods of account beginning on or after 1 January 2019.

(3) But, for the purposes of Chapter 7 of Part 10 of TIOPA 2010 (corporate interest restriction: group-interest and group-EBITDA), the amendment made by this paragraph has effect in relation to periods of account of a worldwide group (within the meaning given by section 480 of that Act) beginning on or after 1 January 2019.

Transitional provisions following repeal of section 53 of FA 2011: introductory

12 (1) This paragraph and paragraphs 13 to 17 modify the effect of the change of basis provisions in relation to periods of account of a lessee beginning on or after 1 January 2019 if the lease is one—

(a) in respect of which, under generally accepted accounting practice, a right-of-use asset falls (or would fall) to be recognised for accounting purposes in the accounts of the lessee for any period of account (whether beginning before or on or after that date), and
(b) which would not fall to be treated in those accounts as a finance lease if the

lessee were required under generally accepted accounting practice to determine whether the lease would fall to be treated in those accounts as a finance lease.

(2) In this Part of this Schedule, "the change of basis provisions" means—

(a) Chapter 17 of Part 2 and Chapter 7 of Part 3 of ITTOIA 2005 (adjustment income), and

(b) Chapter 14 of Part 3 and sections 261 and 262 of CTA 2009 (adjustment on change of basis).

Cases where asset first recognised for period of account beginning on or after 1 January 2019

13 (1) This paragraph applies if the right-of-use asset falls (or would fall) to be first recognised for accounting purposes in the accounts of the lessee for the first period of account beginning on or after 1 January 2019 ("the first period of account").

(2) Any adjustment income or adjustment expense, or any receipt or expense, treated by any of the change of basis provisions as arising in consequence of a change of accounting policy that results in the right-of-use asset being first recognised for accounting purposes is to be treated as arising over a period ("the spreading period") determined in accordance with the following steps—

Step 1

Find for each lease the amount by which the credits exceed the debits (or vice-versa). For this purpose, the credits and the debits are the amounts which, under generally accepted accounting practice—

(a) are taken to equity as adjustments in the accounts of the lessee for the first period of account, and

(b) are in consequence of the change of accounting policy that results in the right-of-use asset being first recognised for accounting purposes in those accounts.

Step 2

Calculate for each lease the percentage ("the relevant percentage") that—

(a) the amount found under Step 1 for the lease bears to

(b) the total of all amounts found under Step 1 (treating such amounts as positive amounts).

Step 3

Find for each lease the period which results from applying the relevant percentage to the term of the lease that remains unexpired as at the date on which the first period of account begins. For this purpose, the term of a lease is to be determined in accordance with generally accepted accounting practice as it applies for the first period of account.

Step 4

Calculate the sum of all periods found under Step 3.

Step 5

The spreading period is the period equal to the sum calculated under Step 4 beginning with the day on which the first period of account begins.

(3) An amount to be treated as arising in any period falling wholly or partly in the spreading period is to be determined in proportion to the number of days of the period falling within the spreading period.

(4) This paragraph is subject to paragraphs 15 and 16 (transfers of leases and cessation of activities).

Cases where asset first recognised for an earlier period of account

14 (1) This paragraph applies if the right-of-use asset falls (or would fall) to be first recognised for accounting purposes in the accounts of the lessee for a period of account earlier than the first period of account.

(2) The change of basis provisions and this Part of this Schedule have effect—

(a) as if there were a change of accounting policy with respect to the accounts of the lessee for the first period of account, and

(b) as if the right-of-use asset falls (or would fall) to be first recognised for accounting purposes in those accounts.

(3) In this paragraph "the first period of account" has the same meaning as in paragraph 13.

Certain cases where there is a transfer of a lease

15 (1) This paragraph applies if—

(a) before the whole of an amount has been treated by paragraph 13 as arising to the lessee, there is a transfer of a lease or part of a lease from the lessee to another person,

(b) the transferee is connected to the lessee,

(c) immediately after the transfer, the transferee carries on activities the profits of which are chargeable to income tax or corporation tax, and

(d) the transfer is not one where it is reasonable to suppose that the transfer is, or arrangements of which the transfer is part are, designed to avoid tax.

(2) The amount is to continue to be dealt with in accordance with paragraph 13 but is to be treated as arising to the transferee over so much of the spreading period as falls on or after the date on which the transfer takes place.

(3) If, following the transfer, it is necessary to apportion between more than one person an amount treated by paragraph 13 or this paragraph as arising, the apportionment is to be made on a just and reasonable basis.

(4) In this paragraph—

"connected" is to be read in accordance with sections 993 and 994 of ITA 2007 and sections 1122 and 1123 of CTA 2010, and

"the spreading period" has the same meaning as in paragraph 13.

Cases where lessee permanently ceases to carry on activities

16 (1) Sub-paragraph (2) applies if—

(a) before the whole of an amount has been treated by paragraph 13 as arising, the lessee permanently ceases to carry on activities the profits of which are chargeable to income tax or corporation tax, and

(b) the whole of the amount so far as not treated by paragraph 13 as arising is not treated by paragraph 15(2) as arising to a transferee.

(2) The amount so far as not otherwise treated as arising—

(a) is to be treated as arising to the lessee, and

(b) is to be brought into account in calculating the profits of the lessee,

immediately before the cessation.

Application of paragraphs 12 to 16 to lease portfolios

17 (1) This paragraph applies if a lessee, in accordance with generally accepted accounting practice, prepares accounts by reference to a portfolio of leases having similar characteristics rather than by reference to the individual leases.

(2) Paragraphs 12 to 14 and 16 apply to the portfolio (subject to any necessary modifications) in the same way as they apply to a lease.

(3) If there is a transfer of the portfolio (or an individual lease within the portfolio), paragraph 15 applies to the transfer (subject to any necessary modifications) in the same way as it applies to the transfer of a lease.

Corporate interest restriction: changes of accounting policy

18 (1) In section 426 of TIOPA 2010 (changes of accounting policy), in subsection (3), after paragraph (e) insert—

"(f) paragraphs 12 to 17 of Schedule 14 to FA 2019 (transitional provision following the repeal of section 53 of FA 2011) so far as they have effect in relation to adjustments under Chapter 14 of Part 3 of CTA 2009 or sections 261 and 262 of that Act."

(2) The amendment made by this paragraph has effect in relation to periods of account of a worldwide group (within the meaning given by section 480 of TIOPA 2010) beginning on or after 1 January 2019.

Corporate interest restriction: treatment of certain adjustments

19 (1) Sub-paragraph (2) applies if—

(a) an amount is brought into account for corporation tax purposes for a period of account beginning on or after 1 January 2019 as a receipt or expense treated by any of the change of accounting policy provisions as arising to a company which is a lessee,

(b) the receipt or expense is treated as arising to the company in consequence of a change of accounting policy relating to a lease in respect of which the company is the lessee,

(c) under the old accounting policy, the lease fell to be treated as a finance lease in the accounts of the company, and

(d) under the new accounting policy, the lease would fall to be treated as a right-of-use lease in those accounts but for—

(i) the short term of the lease, or

(ii) the low value of the leased asset.

(2) For the purposes of Part 10 of TIOPA 2010 (corporate interest restriction)—

(a) if the amount is brought into account as an expense, "tax-interest expense amount" (see section 382 of that Act) does not include that amount;

(b) if the amount is brought into account as a receipt, "tax-interest income amount" (see section 385 of that Act) does not include that amount.

(3) This paragraph has effect in relation to adjustments to which the financial statements of a worldwide group are treated by section 426 of TIOPA 2010 (changes in accounting policy) as subject in the same way as it has effect in relation to adjustments made under the change of accounting policy provisions by a company and accordingly—

(a) if the amount is brought into account as an expense, "relevant expense amount" (see section 411(1) of that Act) does not include that amount;

(b) if the amount is brought into account as a receipt, "relevant income amount" (see section 411(2) of that Act) does not include that amount.

(4) In this paragraph—

"the change of accounting policy provisions" means Chapter 14 of Part 3 and sections 261 and 262 of CTA 2009 (adjustment on change of basis), and

"right-of-use lease" has the meaning given by section 494 of TIOPA 2010 (other interpretation).

COMMENTARY ON SCHEDULE 14, PART 3

Currently the amount charged to P&L for an operating lease ie rental deductions, is the amount of the tax deduction and no adjustment is generally made for tax purposes. For finance leases the amount treated as the tax deduction on the lease is the finance charge and the depreciation on the asset in the period. On adoption of IFRS 16, under the FA 2019 changes, operating leases will have the same tax treatment as finance leases with the finance charge (interest under IFRS 16) and depreciation being allowable deductions. These amounts will follow what is charged in the accounts, unless statute provides differently, although those amounts may be different under IFRS to the amounts that would have been charged under UK GAAP.

The changes introduced by IFRS 16 were anticipated in 2011 and FA 2011, s 53 required lessees to disregard the accounting changes on leases as a result of IFRS 16 and instead apply historic accounting standards to calculate the tax deductions. This was effectively a holding measure until the impact of leasing changes could be consulted on and, now that the new rules are to be implemented, FA 2011, s 53 is repealed. This now means that the business can follow the IFRS 16 accounts for the relevant tax-deductible amounts as noted above.

Normally the tax treatment of amounts arising as result of a change in accounting practice is to tax or deduct the adjustment which arises in the first period of accounts for which the new basis of accounting is adopted (ITTOIA 2005, Pt 2, Ch 17 and Pt 3, Ch 7; CTA 2009, Pt 3, Ch 14 and ss 261, 262). However, for the change to IFRS 16, the transitional adjustments arising on operating leases will be spread so that the adjustments are recognised over the mean average length of the leases. The steps of the spreading computation are summarised below, and the explanatory notes give the following example:

Step 1

Calculate the net debits and credits brought into account for each lease. The legislation ensures that the net amount includes only amounts recognised in equity which are in consequence of the transition to IFRS 16.

Step 2

Calculate a percentage for each lease ('the relevant percentage') by dividing the amount under Step 1 for that lease by the total amounts for the lessee for all leases found under Step 1 (treating such amounts as positive amounts) and multiplying by 100.

Step 3

Multiply the relevant percentage found under Step 2 by the remaining period outstanding in days of the lease as at the date of transition. The term of a lease is determined in accordance with GAAP.

Step 4

Add together all of the amounts calculated under Step 3. This will result in the weighted average or weighted mean of remaining periods of the leases affected by IFRS 16 transitional accounting adjustments taken to equity.

Step 5

The spreading period is the number of days found under Step 4 beginning with the day on which the first period of account begins.

Example

A lessee adopts IFRS on 1 January 2019.

	Step 1	**Step 2**	**Step 3**
Lease (remaining lease term on IFRS 16 adoption)	Transitional accounting adjustment	Relevant %	Applying relevant % to remaining lease on adoption of IFRS 16
Lease 1 (1,826 days)	£(10,000,000) credit	26.32% (£10M/£38M × 100)	481 (1,826 days × 26.32%)
Lease 2 730 days)	£8,000,000 debit	21.05% (£8M/£38M × 100)	154 (730 days × 21.05%)
Lease 3 (1,826 days)	Nil	Nil	Excluded
Lease 4 (1,461 days)	£20,000,000 debit	52.63% (£20M/£38M × 100)	769 (1,461 days × 52.63%)
Overall	Net £18,000,000 debit	100%	1404 days = Step 4 total

If the lessee has a period of account which runs from 1 January 2019 to 31 December 2019 they would claim as a deduction £4,679,487 (=365/1,404*£18,000,000).

If a business has early-adopted IFRS 16, the above transitional adjustment will be treated as taking place in the first accounting period beginning on or after 1 January 2019. If the lease is transferred to a connected party the spreading will continue in the transferee. On the cessation of the business the remaining amount is brought into account immediately before the cessation.

For the calculation of the corporate interest restriction (CIR), transitional amounts are included in the calculations of group figures for CIR in circumstances where the group has made an interest restriction (alternative calculation) election. Where a lease was a finance lease under the previous accounting standard eg FRS 102 and is not treated as a right-of-use lease under IFRS 16 because it is short term or low value, any transitional amounts are treated as tax-EBITDA amounts and not tax-interest amounts.

SCHEDULE 15

OIL ACTIVITIES: TRANSFERABLE TAX HISTORY

Section 37

PART 1

ELECTION TO TRANSFER TAX HISTORY

Entitlement to make a TTH election

1 This Schedule applies if, on or after 1 November 2018, the OGA gives consent for a company (the "seller") to sell an interest in a UK oil licence to another company (the "purchaser").

2 (1) On or after the licence transfer date, the seller and purchaser may jointly make a TTH election in respect of an interest ("the TTH asset") in a transferred oil field (the "TTH oil field").

(2) A "TTH election" is an election for—

(a) an amount of the seller's ring fence profits (the "total TTH amount") to be treated, in accordance with the provisions of this Schedule, as if it were an amount of the purchaser's profits (instead of the seller's profits), and

(b) a corresponding amount of the seller's adjusted ring fence profits to be so treated for the purpose of Chapter 6 of Part 8 of CTA 2010 (supplementary charge).

COMMENTARY ON SCHEDULE 15, PART 1

The transferable tax history (TTH) rules are implemented by Sch 15 with the aim of facilitating the sale of interests in UK and UK continental shelf oil and gas fields held under licence granted by the Oil and Gas Authority (OGA).

The transferable tax history rules are designed to operate in cases where the buyer may not have paid enough corporation tax and supplementary charge at the time the costs of decommissioning the acquired field assets are incurred to provide effective relief for those decommissioning costs. For companies which have paid tax in the past on ring fence profits, the decommissioning costs can be relieved against such profits. Companies without such history have hitherto been at a disadvantage in comparison when viewed in the context of acquiring interests in oil fields. The effect has been the adoption of commercial arrangements between purchaser and seller which in many cases require the seller to retain obligations extending over many years. By transferring tax history, the rules aim to permit sellers to make a clean break where they would otherwise have retained a liability to bear the costs of decommissioning arising from the interest being sold. For purchasers, the acquisition of tax history to permit tax repayments on losses derived from decommissioning is preferable to having to rely on the seller.

Part 1 sets out the conditions for making a TTH election.

Paragraph 1 restricts the application of the TTH rules to cases where the OGA consents to the sale of a field interest on or after 1 November 2018.

Paragraph 2 permits that in such cases the seller and purchaser, on making a joint election, will be treated as if the purchaser generated an amount of ring fence profits and associated profits subject to the supplementary charge (the 'total TTH amount') and, in conjunction with para 28, had incurred the tax actually paid by the seller on those profits, and the seller will be treated as not having generated those profits or paid the related tax.

The effect is to permit the purchaser to generate tax repayments from decommissioning losses carried back against such profits, and deny the seller the potential for such repayment if it incurs decommissioning expenditure on any of its other assets.

PART 2

THE TOTAL TTH AMOUNT

The total TTH amount

3 (1) The total TTH amount may comprise—

(a) an amount representing the seller's eligible ring fence profits for the reference accounting period, and

(b) amounts representing the seller's eligible ring fence profits for so many of the preceding accounting periods ending on or after 17 April 2002 as the seller and purchaser may determine.

(2) Sub-paragraph (1) is subject to—

(a) paragraph 4 (limits on total TTH amount),

(b) paragraph 11 (consecutive accounting periods), and

(c) paragraph 12 (the transferred profits amount for an accounting period).

(3) See—

(a) paragraph 13 for the meaning of "eligible ring fence profits", and

(b) paragraph 102 for the meaning of "reference accounting period" in relation to the seller.

Limits on total TTH amount

4 The total TTH amount must not exceed the lower of—

(a) the uplifted decommissioning costs estimate in relation to the TTH asset, and

(b) the total amount of the seller's eligible ring fence profits for the period—

(i) beginning with 17 April 2002, and

(ii) ending at the end of the reference accounting period.

The "uplifted decommissioning costs estimate"

5 To determine the "uplifted decommissioning costs estimate" in relation to the TTH asset—

(a) determine the transferred proportion of the net cost amount (see paragraphs 6 and 7),

(b) allocate the relevant proportion of the amount determined under paragraph (a) to the TTH asset (see paragraph 8),

(c) adjust the allocated amount in accordance with paragraph 9, and

(d) double the adjusted amount.

6 (1) The "net cost amount" is the appropriate DSA estimate of the decommissioning costs for the TTH oil field.

(2) A "DSA estimate" is an estimate approved for the purposes of a qualifying decommissioning security agreement.

(3) If there is only one qualifying decommissioning security agreement relating to the TTH oil field, the "appropriate DSA estimate" is the most recent DSA estimate approved for the purposes of that agreement within the relevant period.

(4) If there is more than one qualifying decommissioning security agreement relating to the TTH oil field, the "appropriate DSA estimate" is the lowest of the DSA estimates approved for the purposes of any of those agreements within the relevant period.

(5) For the purposes of sub-paragraphs (3) and (4), the "relevant period" is the period of 12 months ending with—

(a) the date on which the TTH election is made, or

(b) in a case where the hive down condition (see paragraph 56(5)) is met, the date on which the seller and the purchaser cease to be associated with one another.

7 The "transferred proportion" of the net cost amount is the proportion of the decommissioning costs for the TTH oil field that, under the qualifying decommissioning security agreement for the purposes of which the appropriate DSA estimate is approved, is allocated to—

(a) the seller, in the case of an agreement entered into before the sale of the interest in the UK oil licence concerned, or

(b) the purchaser, in the case of an agreement entered into on or after that date.

8 In paragraph 5(b), the "relevant proportion" means—

(a) the proportion that the interest in the TTH oil field which is the TTH asset bears to—

(i) the seller's other interests in the TTH oil field, if paragraph 7(a) applies, or

(ii) the purchaser's other interests in the TTH oil field, if paragraph 7(b) applies, or

(b) if the proportion cannot reasonably be determined in accordance with paragraph (a), such other proportion determined on a just and reasonable basis.

9 (1) To adjust the allocated amount for the purposes of paragraph 5(c)—

(a) disregard the adjustments listed in sub-paragraph (2) made, for the purposes of calculating the net cost amount, in accordance with the terms of the decommissioning security agreement, and

(b) if, in making that calculation in accordance with those terms, the relevant proportion of the estimate of the decommissioning costs is increased by an amount to take account of inflation, disregard the amount (if any) by which the increase exceeds the standard inflation adjustment amount.

(2) The adjustments to be disregarded are—

(a) any discount applied by reference to the period of time expected to elapse before the decommissioning costs are payable in relation to the TTH oil field, and

(b) any adjustment made for the purposes of taking account of the risk that the decommissioning costs for the TTH oil field will exceed the estimate of those costs.

(3) The "standard inflation adjustment amount" means the amount (if any) by which the relevant proportion of the estimate of the decommissioning costs for the TTH oil field would be increased if an adjustment for the purposes of taking account of inflation were made on the basis specified by Her Majesty's Revenue and Customs for the purposes of this paragraph.

10 (1) A "decommissioning security agreement" is an agreement entered into for the purpose of—

(a) determining the costs of decommissioning an oil field, and

(b) providing security for—

(i) the performance of obligations under an abandonment programme for the purposes of section 38A of the Petroleum Act 1998 (whether or not such a programme has been approved at the time the agreement is entered into), or

(ii) the costs of decommissioning plant or machinery which is, or forms part of, a relevant onshore installation.

(2) A decommissioning security agreement is "qualifying" for the purposes of this Schedule if—

(a) the seller is a party to the agreement,

(b) at least one of the parties is not associated with the seller, and

(c) the estimate approved for the purposes of the agreement is a reasonable estimate of the decommissioning costs for the oil field.

(3) In a case where the corporate restructuring condition (see paragraph 56(2)) is met, sub-paragraph (2)(a) has effect as if the reference to the seller were a reference to a party to the third party election (as defined in that paragraph).

(4) In sub-paragraph (1)—

"abandonment programme" has the meaning given by section 29 of the Petroleum Act 1998, and

"relevant onshore installation" has the same meaning as in section 163 of CAA 2001 (see subsection (3C) of that section).

(5) See paragraph 98 of this Schedule and section 271 of CTA 2010 for further provision about the meaning of "associated companies".

Consecutive accounting periods

11 (1) The total TTH amount may not include an amount representing the eligible ring fence profits for a particular accounting period (other than the reference accounting period) unless it also includes an amount representing the eligible ring fence profits for the next following qualifying accounting period.

(2) An accounting period is "qualifying" for the purposes of this Schedule if the seller has eligible ring fence profits for that period.

The transferred profits amount

12 (1) The transferred profits amount for an accounting period, other than the earliest period, must be an amount equal to the amount of the seller's eligible ring fence profits for the period.

(2) The transferred profits amount for the earliest period must be an amount equal to the amount of the seller's eligible ring fence profits for that period, so far as that amount does not exceed the TTH balance for the earliest period.

(3) The "TTH balance" for the earliest period is an amount equal to—

(a) the total TTH amount, less
(b) the transferred profits amounts for each later accounting period.

(4) In this paragraph, "earliest period" means the earliest accounting period for which there is a transferred profits amount.

"Eligible ring fence profits"

13 Ring fence profits of an accounting period are "eligible" for the purposes of a TTH election if, as at the date the TTH election is made—

(a) corporation tax is charged on the profits of that period at the main ring fence profits rate,
(b) neither section 279B nor section 279C of CTA 2010 (marginal relief) applies in relation to the seller in that period,
(c) the seller's liability to corporation tax in respect of the profits has been discharged in full, and
(d) the total TTH amount for any other TTH election made by the seller (whether made with the purchaser or with another person) does not include an amount representing those profits.

14 In determining, for the purposes of this Schedule, the amount of the seller's eligible ring fence profits for an accounting period that falls partly before 17 April 2002, the amount of the seller's eligible ring fence profits for that period is to be reduced by the proportion which the part of the accounting period falling before that date bears to the whole of the accounting period.

COMMENTARY ON SCHEDULE 15, PART 2

Part 2 defines the amount of profits that can be transferred and the source thereof.

Paragraph 3 places limits on the total TTH amount to profits arising in the 'reference accounting period' of the seller and earlier accounting periods ending on or after 17 April 2002; matching the earliest accounting period for which relief can be obtained on a carry-back of ring fence trade losses. Paragraph 3 also imposes limits defined in subsequent paragraphs. The 'reference accounting period' is defined in para 102 as the most recent accounting period for which there are ring fence profits and for which the 'amendment period' of 12 months after the corporation tax return filing date has elapsed.

Paragraph 4 limits the total TTH amount to the lower of the uplifted decommissioning costs estimate of the interest being sold, and a defined amount of the 'eligible ring fence profits' of the seller.

Paragraphs 5–10 define the 'uplifted decommissioning costs estimate' value which is used as a maximum for the profits that can be transferred. The limit to an amount appropriate to the interest being sold is aimed at preventing companies transferring tax history for tax optimisation.

The limit set by para 5 is double the adjusted proportion of the estimated net cost of decommissioning.

Paragraphs 6–10 set out the calculation, based on the industry practice of having a decommissioning security agreement (DSA) for oil fields with multiple owners. A DSA will require security for anticipated decommissioning costs to be posted by persons holding an interest in the oil field. The definition in para 10 aligns with this industry practice, meaning that in practice only in cases where there is a single current owner of a field interest will an issue arise; para 6 requires a DSA estimate from a 'qualifying decommissioning security agreement', which, per para 10 requires non-associated parties. In the absence of another third party, there will not be a qualifying decommissioning security agreement.

Paragraph 6 permits only qualifying decommissioning security agreements to provide the cost estimates. Paragraph 6 takes the lowest of the decommissioning costs estimates approved in DSAs where there are multiple relevant DSAs, or otherwise uses the most recent estimate, and in all cases requires that the estimates are approved in the 12 months prior to the TTH election date, or prior to the date when the seller ceases to be associated with the company being sold in those cases where the transfer is effected by an intra-group transfer of the underlying oil field interest followed by a share sale of the transferee. The amount identified becomes the 'net cost amount'.

Paragraph 6 thereby relies on industry practice that DSAs are updated and approved annually.

Paragraphs 7 and 8 work with para 5 to identify the seller's entire share of the 'net cost amount' for a field and then the part thereof which is proportionately attributable to the interest being transferred. Where the sale of the field has already occurred, the calculation works from the purchaser's ownership shares.

Paragraph 9 adjusts the DSA calculation of decommissioning costs to remove the effect of discounting the costs and also removes the risk factor on cost overruns. Additionally, inflation factors in excess of any HMRC determined standard inflation adjustment will be removed. The restriction to a standard inflation adjustment amount permits HMRC to set such amount.

Paragraphs 11–14 further restrict the profits that can be included in the total TTH amount.

Paragraph 11 defines which profits may comprise the total TTH amount; the election will only be effective in respect of eligible ring fence profits (defined in para 13) for periods prior to the 'reference period' if eligible ring fence profits of consecutive periods are also included in the TTH amount. Loss periods are ignored. The phrasing of 'may not include' is considered to be a restriction.

Paragraph 12 ensures that the transferred profits amount comprises the full amount of profits for the accounting periods, aside from the earliest one from which the balance of transferred profits is taken. In conjunction with paras 11 and 3, this means the history transferred is the whole of the profits from each accounting period working backwards chronologically; there is no element of choice. Given the change in tax rate over time this is important.

Paragraph 13 defines the 'eligible ring fence profits' for transfer, to ensure that tax has already been paid on these at the full corporation tax rate, and the amount has not already been transferred.

Paragraph 14 addresses the cases where the accounting period containing eligible ring fence profits straddles 17 April 2002, the limit to which a ring fence trade loss carry back can be made. A proportional allocation is enforced.

PART 3

EFFECT OF A TTH ELECTION ON THE SELLER

Application of this Part

15 This Part applies if—

(a) the seller and the purchaser have jointly made a TTH election in respect of the TTH asset, and

(b) the TTH election has been approved by an officer of Revenue and Customs (see paragraphs 61 and 62).

Effect of a TTH election: corporation tax

16 (1) Sub-paragraphs (2) and (3) apply if the seller makes a loss in a trade in an accounting period.

(2) For the purposes of section 37(3)(b) of CTA 2010 (including for the purposes of that provision as it has effect under the other trade loss relief provisions), the seller's total profits of a pre-transfer accounting period are treated as being—

(a) the seller's total profits for that period, less

(b) the transferred profits amount for that period.

(3) For the purposes of section 42 of CTA 2010, the seller's profits of a ring fence trade of a pre-transfer accounting period are treated as being—

(a) the seller's ring fence profits for that period, less
(b) the transferred profits amount for that period.

17 The transferred profits amount for an accounting period is to be disregarded for the purposes of the application of any provision of the Corporation Tax Acts by reference to which the seller would (apart from this paragraph) be entitled to relief from, or a repayment of, corporation tax.

18 (1) Paragraphs 16 and 17 are subject to this paragraph.

(2) If, on or after the licence transfer date, the seller's eligible ring fence profits for a pre-transfer accounting period are reduced to an amount which is lower than the transferred profits amount for that period—

(a) the seller is treated as incurring a loss in a ring fence trade, of an amount equal to the difference, for the accounting period, and
(b) paragraph 17 does not apply to the difference.

Effect of a TTH election: supplementary charge

19 Paragraphs 20 and 21 apply in relation to an accounting period for which there is a transferred profits amount.

20 (1) The transferred adjusted ring fence profits amount for the accounting period is to be disregarded for the purposes of any provision of the Corporation Tax Acts by reference to which the seller would (apart from this paragraph) be entitled to a repayment of supplementary charge.

(2) The "transferred adjusted ring fence profits amount" is—

(a) in the case of an accounting period other than the earliest period, the amount of the seller's eligible adjusted ring fence profits for the period;
(b) in the case of the earliest period, an amount equal to the transferred proportion of the seller's eligible adjusted ring fence profits for the period.

21 (1) For the purposes of the application of any provision of Part 4 or Part 8 of CTA 2010 in relation to the seller—

(a) the amount of each ARFP component, or (in the case of the earliest period) an amount equal to the transferred proportion of each ARFP component, for the accounting period is to be disregarded, and
(b) in the case of the earliest period, references in those provisions to an ARFP component for the accounting period are to be treated as references to the retained proportion of that ARFP component for the period.

(2) "ARFP component", in relation to an accounting period, means—

(a) the financing costs for the period that are left out of account for the purposes of the assumption mentioned in section 330(3) of CTA 2010, and
(b) the amount of any reduction of the seller's adjusted ring fence profits by reference to the cumulative total amount of activated allowance for the period under any of the following provisions of CTA 2010—
  (i) section 332E (investment allowance),
  (ii) section 356D (onshore allowance), and
  (iii) section 356JG (cluster area allowance).

(3) See paragraph 17 for provision about disregarding the transferred profits amount for an accounting period.

(4) Sub-paragraph (1) does not apply in relation to the application of any provision for the purposes of determining the seller's eligible adjusted ring fence profits for an accounting period for the purposes of this Schedule.

22 (1) For the purposes of paragraphs 20(2) and 21(1)—

(a) "earliest period" has the meaning given by paragraph 12(4),
(b) the "transferred proportion" is the same as the proportion that the transferred profits amount for the accounting period bears to the seller's ring fence profits amount for the period, and
(c) the "retained proportion" is the same as the proportion that the retained profits amount for the accounting period bears to the seller's ring fence profits amount for the period.

(2) In sub-paragraph (1)(c), "retained profits amount" means the amount of the difference between the amount of the seller's ring fence profits for the earliest period and the transferred profits amount for that period.

(3) For the purposes of this Schedule, adjusted ring fence profits of an accounting period are "eligible" if—

(a) an amount is charged on the profits under section 330(1) of CTA 2010 (supplementary charge in respect of ring fence trades), and

(b) as at the TTH election is made, the seller's liability to tax under that section in respect of the adjusted ring fence profits has been discharged in full.

COMMENTARY ON SCHEDULE 15, PART 3

Part 3 sets out the effect for a seller of a transfer of its profits.

Paragraph 15 makes the first reference to the requirement for HMRC to approve a transfer before it can take effect.

Paragraphs 16–18 ensure transferred profits are effectively removed from the seller's history for the purposes of the trade loss relief provisions of CTA 2010, ss 37 and 42 and incorporates a blanket exclusion of transferred profits from any Corporation Tax Acts provisions for relief or repayment of tax.

However, para 18 applies an exemption to this where the eligible ring fence profits of the seller for a period are reduced to a value below the amount transferred. The difference is characterised as a loss eligible for relief. In this way after transferring an amount of profits, in the unusual situation where the profits are subsequently found to be less, the overall position is maintained as would be expected.

Paragraphs 19–22 address the supplementary charge position of the seller to the same effect, but without provision for any case where the profits are subsequently reduced below the amount transferred. For the earliest period (for which only some of the corporation tax ring fence profits are transferred) there is a proportional transfer of the adjusted ring fence profits subject to the supplementary charge to match the proportion of corporation tax profits transferred.

Paragraph 21 ensures that where the adjusted ring fence profits amount transferred has been reduced by investment allowance, cluster allowance or onshore allowance, the seller loses the entitlement to any further relief from those amounts. In effect having been used to reduce the transferred profits amount, the allowance has been used by the seller and the purchaser does not receive any such allowance.

PART 4

EFFECT OF A TTH ELECTION ON THE PURCHASER

Application of this Part

23 This Part applies if—

(a) the seller and the purchaser have jointly made a TTH election in respect of the TTH asset,

(b) the TTH election has been approved by an officer of Revenue and Customs (see paragraphs 61 and 62),

(c) the winning of oil from the TTH oil field has permanently ceased, and

(d) in a post-acquisition accounting period (the "loss period")—

(i) the purchaser makes a loss in a ring fence trade,

(ii) the loss is a decommissioning loss, and

(iii) the purchaser holds, for the loss period, an activated TTH amount (see Parts 5 and 6).

24 In paragraph 23(d)(ii), "decommissioning loss" means a loss in respect of which—

(a) a claim for relief under section 37 of CTA 2010 is made by the purchaser by virtue of section 39 or 40 of that Act (relief for trade losses: terminal losses and ring fence trades), or

(b) relief is given under section 42 of CTA 2010 (ring fence trades: further extension of period for relief).

Effect of trade loss relief provisions

25 (1) The total activated TTH amount held by the purchaser for the loss period is to be applied in accordance with sub-paragraph (2)(b) or (3)(b).

(2) The purchaser's total profits of a pre-acquisition accounting period are to be treated, for the purposes of section 37(3)(b) of CTA 2010 (including for the purposes of that provision as it has effect under the other trade loss relief provisions) as being the total of—

(a) the amount of the purchaser's total profits for that period, and
(b) if and so far as the loss in respect of which relief is claimed exceeds the amount mentioned in paragraph (a), the activated transferred profits amount for that period.

(3) The purchaser's profits of a ring fence trade of a pre-acquisition accounting period are to be treated for the purposes of section 42 of CTA 2010, as being the total of—

(a) the purchaser's profits of a ring fence trade for that period, and
(b) if and so far as the loss in respect of which relief is claimed exceeds the amount mentioned in paragraph (a), the activated transferred profits amount for that period.

(4) The "activated transferred profits amount" for a pre-acquisition accounting period means the amount allocated to the period under paragraph 44 for the purposes of the application of this paragraph in relation to the loss period.

(5) See paragraphs 38 to 42 for provision about the "total activated TTH amount".

Repayment of supplementary charge

26 (1) This paragraph applies where, in respect of a loss period, an activated transferred profits amount for a pre-acquisition accounting period is to be applied in accordance with paragraph 25(2)(b) or (3)(b).

(2) A repayment of tax to be determined as if—

(a) an amount had been charged under section 330(1) of CTA 2010 in respect of the activated ARFP amount for the pre-acquisition accounting period,
(b) that amount had been charged on, and paid by, the purchaser (instead of the seller), and
(c) the transferred adjusted ring fence profits amount for the pre-acquisition accounting period were recalculated in accordance with paragraph 50.

(3) See paragraph 53 for provision about the "activated ARFP amount".

27 (1) In this Schedule, references to the transferred adjusted ring fence profits amount for a pre-acquisition accounting period of the purchaser are references to—

(a) the transferred adjusted ring fence profits amount (see paragraph 20(2)) for the accounting period of the seller which coincides with the pre-acquisition accounting period of the purchaser, or
(b) if there is no coinciding accounting period of the seller, the overlapping proportion of the transferred adjusted ring fence profits amount for each accounting period of the seller that overlaps with the pre-acquisition accounting period of the purchaser.

(2) The overlapping proportion, in relation to an accounting period of the seller, is the same as the proportion that the part of the seller's accounting period that overlaps with the pre-acquisition accounting period of the purchaser bears to the whole of the seller's accounting period.

Supplementary provision: repayment and enquiries

28 For the purposes of section 59D(2) of TMA 1970 (repayment of excess corporation tax), the following amounts paid by the seller are treated as having been paid by the purchaser—

(a) the amount of corporation tax in respect of an activated transferred profits amount, for a pre-acquisition accounting period, that is applied in accordance with 25(2)(b) or (3)(b), and
(b) the amount of supplementary charge in respect of the transferred adjusted ring fence profits amount for that accounting period.

29 (1) An enquiry under Part 4 of Schedule 18 to FA 1998 into a tax return for the accounting period in which the claim under section 37 of CTA 2010 in respect of a decommissioning loss in a loss period is made (see paragraphs 23 and 24), or an enquiry into the claim under Schedule 1A to TMA 1970, extends to—

(a) the decommissioning expenditure amount attributable to the TTH oil field for any accounting period,
(b) the tracked profit or loss amount attributable to the TTH asset for any accounting period, and
(c) whether a TTH activation event has occurred in relation to the TTH asset.

(2) See Part 5 for provision about "the decommissioning expenditure amount" and a TTH activation event, and paragraphs 64 and 65 for provision about the "tracked profit and loss amount".

COMMENTARY ON SCHEDULE 15, PART 4

Part 4 sets out the purchaser's position regarding the entitlement to repayment of tax and the potential for HMRC enquiry. Repayment of tax in relation to the transferred profits requires the TTH amount to be activated under Part 5.

Paragraphs 23 and 24 set the scope; the provisions apply where a TTH election has been made in respect of a TTH asset, approved by HMRC, and the winning of oil from the TTH oil field has permanently ceased. In such cases where the purchaser makes a 'decommissioning loss' and holds activated TTH, Part 4 will apply.

A 'decommissioning loss' is one that is claimed either as a terminal loss or under the extended carry-back provisions for ring fence trade losses. There is no requirement that the loss is derived from expenditure on decommissioning assets used in relation to the oil field interest that underlies a TTH election.

Paragraph 25 addresses the operation of the corporation tax loss relief rules and ensures the activated transferred profits are treated as the purchaser's profits for the purposes of the loss carry back rules. This will apply in the accounting periods prior to the acquisition of the TTH asset. The rule sets the loss carried back against the activated transferred profits. The rules dictate that the transferred profits are used only after the purchaser's own profits for each respective period. Thus, the loss carry back rules work period-by-period in the normal way, but with additional profits recognised in pre-acquisition periods.

Paragraph 26 applies where para 25 has applied the carried back loss against activated transferred profits. The repayment of supplementary charge is calculated as if the purchaser had paid the tax on the amount of transferred adjusted ring fence profits, and the repayment is triggered by recalculating the adjusted ring fence profits now transferred to the buyer and comparing this to the activated ARFP amount (see para 53).

The recalculation is made in accordance with paras 50–55 and is based on the amount of transferred ring fence profits that generate the repayment from the availability of loss relief under para 25.

Paragraph 27 attributes the transferred adjusted ring fence profits amounts required in calculating repayments to accounting periods of the purchaser using the seller's accounting periods and where these do not align uses a proportional attribution. For the ring fence profits the same effect is imposed at para 45.

Paragraph 28 applies the normal corporation tax rules for repayments.

Paragraph 29 extends HMRC enquiry powers where these are used to enquire into the corporation tax return of the loss period or an enquiry into a claim for relief by repayment made outside the tax return. In each case the enquiry extends to the key elements required for TTH activation.

PART 5

TTH ACTIVATION

TTH activation event

30 (1) A TTH activation event occurs in relation to the TTH asset if—

(a) the winning of oil from the TTH oil field has permanently ceased, and
(b) at the end of a post-acquisition accounting period of the purchaser, the total decommissioning expenditure amount exceeds the total net profits amount.

(2) The "total decommissioning expenditure amount" is the relevant proportion of the total of the decommissioning expenditure amounts (see paragraph 31) attributable to the TTH oil field, in respect of which an allowance or allocation is made to the purchaser, for—

(a) the period mentioned in sub-paragraph (1)(b), and
(b) each preceding accounting period which is a post-acquisition accounting period.

(3) The "total net profits amount" is the aggregate of the tracked profit or loss amounts (see paragraphs 64 and 65) attributable to the TTH asset for—

(a) the period mentioned in sub-paragraph (1)(b), and

(b) each preceding accounting period which is a post-acquisition accounting period.

(4) But if the aggregate of the tracked profit or loss amounts attributable to the TTH asset for the periods mentioned in sub-paragraph (3)(a) and (b) is a negative amount, the total net profits amount is nil.

(5) In this paragraph, "the relevant proportion" means the proportion that the interest in the TTH oil field which is the TTH asset bears to the purchaser's other interests in the TTH oil field or, if the proportion cannot reasonably be determined on that basis, such other proportion determined on a just and reasonable basis.

Decommissioning expenditure amount

31 The "decommissioning expenditure amount" attributable to the TTH oil field for an accounting period, is the total of each of the following amounts attributable to the field for the post-acquisition accounting period—

(a) the special allowance amount,

(b) the post-cessation expenditure amount, and

(c) the restoration expenditure amount.

32 (1) The "special allowance amount" for an accounting period is the amount of a special allowance made under section 164 of CAA 2001 (general decommissioning expenditure incurred before cessation of ring fence trade) for that period.

(2) A special allowance amount is attributable to the TTH oil field so far as the expenditure in respect of which the allowance is made is expenditure incurred on decommissioning plant or machinery brought into use for the purposes of oil-related activities carried on wholly or partly in direct connection with the field.

33 (1) The "post-cessation expenditure amount" for an accounting period is the amount that, under section 165(3)(a) of CAA 2001 (general decommissioning expenditure after ceasing ring fence trade), is allocated to the appropriate pool for that period.

(2) A post-cessation expenditure amount is attributable to the TTH oil field so far as the general decommissioning expenditure in respect of which the amount is allocated is expenditure incurred on decommissioning plant or machinery brought into use for the purposes of oil-related activities carried on wholly or partly in direct connection with the field.

34 (1) The "restoration expenditure amount" for an accounting period is the amount that is treated as qualifying expenditure under section 416ZA of CAA 2001 (ring fence trades: expenditure on site restoration) for that period.

(2) A restoration expenditure amount is attributable to the TTH oil field if the qualifying expenditure is incurred in relation to the field.

35 For the purposes of paragraphs 32(2), 33(2) and 34(2), expenditure for an accounting period is to be apportioned between the TTH oil field and other oil fields (or parts of oil fields) on a just and reasonable basis.

COMMENTARY ON SCHEDULE 15, PART 5

Parts 5 and 6 cover TTH activation. Transferred amounts must be activated to generate repayments, and the rules seek to ensure this occurs only after the production of oil in the relevant oil field has ceased and the TTH asset's decommissioning costs exceed the cumulative net income from the transferred interest. This ensures the TTH rules are used only for the intended purposes.

Paragraph 30 limits activation to cases where the winning of oil has permanently ceased from the TTH asset and at the end of the purchaser's accounting period the total decommissioning expenditure in relation to the TTH asset exceeds the total net profits which are the tracked profits (defined at para 64) aggregated over the period of ownership by the purchaser.

Paragraphs 31–35 define the decommissioning expenditure amount in relation to the availability of particular allowances under the Capital Allowances Act 2001 for decommissioning and restoration expenditure. A just and reasonable apportionment is made where expenditure is not wholly attributable to the TTH oil field interest acquired.

PART 6

ALLOCATION OF ACTIVATED TTH AMOUNT

Application of this Part

36 This Part of this Schedule applies if a TTH activation event occurs in relation to the TTH asset.

37 In this Schedule—

(a) "first activation period" means the first post-acquisition accounting period of the purchaser in which a TTH activation event occurs, and

(b) "post-activation period" means a subsequent accounting period of the purchaser.

"Total activated TTH amount"

38 The "total activated TTH amount" held by the purchaser for a loss period which is the first activation period is the lower of—

(a) the amount by which, at the end of that period, the total decommissioning expenditure amount exceeds the total net profits amount (see paragraph 30), and

(b) the total TTH amount.

39 The "total activated TTH amount" held by the purchaser for a loss period which is a post-activation period is the lower of—

(a) the adjusted activated TTH amount (see paragraphs 40 to 42), and

(b) the closing balance of the total TTH amount for the immediately preceding accounting period (see paragraph 49).

40 (1) This paragraph applies if, in relation to a post-activation period—

(a) the relevant proportion of the decommissioning expenditure amount attributable to the TTH oil field for that period, exceeds

(b) the tracked profit or loss amount attributable to the TTH asset for that period.

(2) The "additional activated TTH amount" for the post-activation period is an amount equal to the excess.

(3) For the purposes of paragraph 39, the adjusted activated TTH amount is the total of—

(a) the closing balance of activated TTH for the immediately preceding accounting period, and

(b) the additional activated TTH amount for the post-activation period.

(4) In this paragraph and in paragraph 41, "relevant proportion" has the same meaning as in paragraph 30(5).

41 (1) This paragraph applies if, in relation to a post-activation period—

(a) the tracked profit or loss amount attributable to the TTH asset for that period, exceeds

(b) the relevant proportion of the decommissioning expenditure amount attributable to the TTH oil field for that period.

(2) The "TTH reduction amount" for the post-activation period is an amount equal to the excess.

(3) If the TTH reduction amount is less than the closing balance amount, the adjusted activated TTH amount for the purposes of paragraph 39 is an amount equal to the difference.

(4) If the TTH reduction amount is equal to, or greater than, the closing balance amount, the adjusted activated TTH amount for the purposes of paragraph 39 is nil.

(5) In this paragraph, references to the "closing balance amount" are references to the closing balance of activated TTH for the accounting period immediately preceding the post-activation period.

42 If neither paragraph 40 nor paragraph 41 applies in relation to a post-activation period, the "adjusted activated TTH amount" for the purposes of paragraph 39 is—

(a) an amount equal to the closing balance of activated TTH for the immediately preceding accounting period, if it is greater than nil, or

(b) nil, if the closing balance of activated TTH for the immediately preceding accounting period is nil or a negative amount.

Allocation of activated TTH to an accounting period

43 Paragraph 44 applies for the purposes of paragraph 25 (effect of trade loss relief provisions in relation to the purchaser).

44 The total activated TTH amount for a loss period is to be allocated, for the purposes of the application of paragraph 25 in relation to that loss period, to pre-acquisition accounting periods of the purchaser as follows—

Step 1

Take the most recent pre-acquisition accounting period for which there is an unused transferred profits amount which is greater than nil.

Step 2

Allocate to that pre-acquisition accounting period an amount equal to the lower of—

(a) the unused transferred profits amount, and
(b) the total activated TTH amount held by the purchaser for the loss period.

Step 3

Allocate to the next most recent pre-acquisition accounting period an amount equal to the lower of—

(a) the transferred profits amount for that period, and
(b) the available activated TTH amount for the loss period.

Step 4

Repeat Step 3 (taking later pre-acquisition accounting periods before earlier ones) until the amount given by paragraph (a) or (b) is nil.

Transferred profits amount for a pre-acquisition accounting period

45 (1) In this Schedule, references to the transferred profits amount for a pre-acquisition accounting period of the purchaser are references to—

(a) the transferred profits amount for the accounting period of the seller which coincides with the pre-acquisition accounting period of the purchaser, or
(b) if there is no coinciding accounting period of the seller, the overlapping proportion of the transferred profits amount for each accounting period of the seller that overlaps with the pre-acquisition accounting period of the purchaser.

(2) The overlapping proportion, in relation to an accounting period of the seller, is the same as the proportion that the part of the seller's accounting period that overlaps with the pre-acquisition accounting period of the purchaser bears to the whole of the seller's accounting period.

"Unused transferred profits amount"

46 (1) This paragraph applies for the purposes of Steps 1 and 2 of paragraph 44.

(2) If the loss period is the first activation period, the reference to the "unused transferred profits amount" for a pre-acquisition accounting period is a reference to the transferred profits amount for that period.

(3) If the loss period is a post-activation period, the reference to the "unused transferred profits amount" for a pre-acquisition accounting period is a reference to the amount equal to—

(a) the transferred profits amount for the pre-acquisition accounting period, less
(b) the total of the amounts applied for the pre-acquisition accounting period in accordance with paragraph 25, for the purposes of the application of that paragraph in relation to the first activation period or an earlier post-activation period.

"Available activated TTH amount"

47 (1) This paragraph applies for the purposes of allocating an amount to a pre-acquisition accounting period under Step 3 of paragraph 44.

(2) The "available activated TTH amount" held by the purchaser for the loss period, is an amount equal to—

(a) the total activated TTH amount for the period, less
(b) the total of the activated transferred profits amounts allocated under paragraph 44 to later pre-acquisition accounting periods.

(3) In sub-paragraph (2)(b) the reference to "later pre-acquisition accounting periods" is a reference to pre-acquisition accounting periods that begin after the period mentioned in sub-paragraph (1).

"Closing balance of activated TTH"

48 (1) The closing balance of activated TTH for the first activation period, or a post-activation period in relation to which paragraph 40, 41(3) or 42 applies, the closing balance of activated TTH for the period is—

(a) the total activated TTH amount held by the purchaser for that period, less
(b) the amount applied in accordance with paragraph 25 for that period.

(2) If paragraph 41(4) applies in relation to a post-activation period, the closing balance of activated TTH for the period is the negative amount determined by deducting—

(a) the TTH reduction amount for that period, from
(b) the closing balance of activated TTH for the immediately preceding accounting period.

"Closing balance of the total TTH amount"

49 The closing balance of the total TTH amount for an accounting period is—

(a) the total TTH amount, less
(b) the total of the amounts (if any) applied in accordance with paragraph 25 for that accounting period and earlier accounting periods.

COMMENTARY ON SCHEDULE 15, PART 6

Paragraphs 36–42 govern the activation of TTH.

Activation occurs to the extent that the total decommissioning exceeds the total net profits until all the transferred profits are activated. The calculation of the adjusted activated TTH amount is made on a period by period basis commencing with the period in which activation first occurs; when production has ceased and the decommissioning expenditure exceeds the net profits. The purpose of these paragraphs is to adjust the activated TTH amount to reflect further decommissioning expenditure, and also any changes to the net profits position, to incrementally increase or decrease on a period by period basis the activated TTH for which relief can be obtained.

The limit is set in paras 38 and 39 by the total activated TTH amount held by the purchaser for each relevant accounting period. The activated amount cannot exceed the transferred amount and will increase period by period where the decommissioning costs exceed the profits. A corrective mechanism is introduced by para 41 to reduce the activated amount in the unusual event of tracked profits in a period exceeding the relevant decommissioning expenditure of the period; the excess is deducted from the brought forward activated amount.

Paragraphs 43, 44 and 46 dictate how the loss relief rules are to work by allocating the activated TTH to transferred profits (see para 25) by allocating activated TTH amounts sequentially in reverse chronological order to periods prior to the acquisition of the TTH asset. This makes the transferred profits 'activated transferred profits' which permits tax repayment to be made.

Paragraph 45 addresses cases where the seller and purchaser do not have coinciding accounting periods from which the transferred profits originate and makes a proportional allocation for overlapping periods.

Paragraphs 46 and 47 allocate the activated TTH to accounting periods, preventing double counting.

Paragraph 48 works in conjunction with paras 38–42 to adjust the total activated TTH amount available as it is reduced from having been used to give relief. It also serves to effect an adjustment arising from a surplus of the net profit over the decommissioning expenses that exceeds the accumulated activated TTH, by permitting the carried forward balance of activated TTH to be a negative value.

Paragraph 49 defines the closing balance of the total TTH amount for the purposes of para 39, to ensure relief is given only once.

PART 7

SUPPLEMENTARY CHARGE: RECALCULATION OF ADJUSTED RING FENCE PROFITS

Recalculation: steps

50 (1) This paragraph applies for the purposes of recalculating the transferred adjusted ring fence profits amount for the pre-acquisition accounting period mentioned in paragraph 26(1) (for the purposes of paragraph 26(2)(c)).

(2) The recalculated transferred adjusted ring fence profits amount for the period is the aggregate of—

(a) the reduced ARFP amount for the pre-acquisition period (see paragraphs 51 and 52), and

(b) the adjusted finance cost amount for the loss period mentioned in paragraph 26(1) (see paragraph 55).

(3) But if the amount given by taking the steps in sub-paragraph (2) is a negative amount, the recalculated transferred adjusted ring fence profits amount is nil.

"Reduced ARFP amount"

51 (1) To determine the "reduced ARFP amount" for a pre-acquisition accounting period—

(a) take the activated ARFP amount for the period, and

(b) reduce that amount by the amount applied, in relation to the loss period mentioned in paragraph 26(1), in accordance with paragraph 25(2)(b) or (3)(b) for the pre-acquisition accounting period.

(2) This paragraph is subject to paragraph 52.

52 (1) This paragraph (instead of paragraph 51) applies if the percentage specified in section 330(1) of CTA 2010 for the pre-acquisition accounting period mentioned in paragraph 26(1) is greater than 20%.

(2) To determine the "reduced ARFP amount" for the pre-acquisition accounting period—

(a) calculate the total of—

(i) the activated ARFP amount for the period, and

(ii) the ARFP uplift amount for the period (see paragraph 54),

(b) reduce the amount given by paragraph (a) by the amount applied, in relation to the loss period mentioned in paragraph 26(1), in accordance with paragraph 25(2)(b) or (3)(b) for the pre-acquisition accounting period.

"Activated ARFP amount"

53 (1) The "activated ARFP amount" for a pre-acquisition accounting period is the amount equal to—

$(A / T) \times ARFP$

where—

A is the amount applied, in relation to the loss period, in accordance with paragraph 25(2)(b) or (3)(b) for the pre-acquisition accounting period,

T is the unused transferred profits amount for that period, and

(2) In sub-paragraph (1), "unused transferred profits amount" has the same meaning as it has for the purposes of Steps 1 and 2 of paragraph 44 (see paragraph 46).

(3) Sub-paragraph (4) applies if, in respect of an earlier loss period—

(a) an activated transferred profits amount for the pre-acquisition accounting period mentioned in paragraph 26(1) is applied in accordance with paragraph 25(2)(b) or (3)(b), and

(b) a corresponding repayment is determined under paragraph 26(2) (an "earlier repayment").

(4) The amount of the transferred adjusted ring fence profits for the pre-acquisition accounting period is treated, for the purposes of sub-paragraph (1), as being reduced by an amount equal to the total of the activated ARFP amounts for that period for the purposes of each earlier repayment.

"ARFP uplift amount"

54 The "ARFP uplift amount" for a pre-acquisition accounting period is the amount equal to—

(SC – 20%) / SC) × A

where—

SC is the percentage specified in section 330(1) of CTA 2010 for the pre-acquisition accounting period, and
A is the amount applied, in relation to the loss period, in accordance with paragraph 25(2)(b) or (3)(b) for the pre-acquisition accounting period.

"Adjusted finance cost amount"

55 The "adjusted finance cost amount" for a loss period is the amount equal to—

(A / L) × FC

where—

A is the amount applied, in relation to the loss period, in accordance with paragraph 25(2)(b) or (3)(b) for the pre-acquisition accounting period,
L is the amount of the decommissioning loss in the loss period (see paragraph 23(d)(i) and (ii)), and
FC is the lower of—

(a) the amount of the financing costs brought into account under section 330(3) of CTA 2010 for the purposes of determining the purchaser's adjusted ring fence profits for the loss period, and
(b) the amount of the purchaser's loss in the ring fence trade for the loss period (see paragraph 23(d)(i)).

COMMENTARY ON SCHEDULE 15, PART 7

Paragraphs 50–55 reduce the profits subject to supplementary charge by, in the first instance, the same value as was used for corporation tax. However, to implement the supplementary charge calculation that excludes finance charges, an adjusted finance cost amount is identified and added to the chargeable profits. This serves the same function as would apply on a carry back claim against a company's own history.

The adjusted finance cost amount is taken from the accounting period for which a loss arose to the purchaser and from which loss relief was available under the TTH rules. Where not all the ring fence loss for the loss period is used to give TTH relief, para 55 pro-rates the identified finance charge to the proportion so used.

Paragraph 52 in conjunction with para 54 matches the CTA 2010, s 330A increase in adjusted ring fence profits for supplementary charge purposes for periods where the supplementary charge rate exceeds 20% to limit relief from expenditure on decommissioning to a maximum of 20% against supplementary charge and applies this for TTH relief.

Paragraphs 51 and 53 ensure there is no duplication of relief and make a proportional allocation in the same ratio as used for ring fence loss set-off where not all the transferred profits of a period generate TTH relief. Paragraph 53 also enforces the same allocation ratios of profits to accounting periods as used for ring fence profits in cases where the accounting periods do not align.

PART 8

TTH ELECTIONS: CONDITIONS AND PROCEDURE

Election conditions: associated companies

56 (1) A TTH election may only be made if—

(a) the seller and purchaser are not associated with one another on the licence transfer date,
(b) the corporate restructuring condition is met, or
(c) the hive down condition is met.

(2) The "corporate restructuring condition" is met for the purposes of a TTH election if —

(a) the seller and purchaser are associated with one another on the licence transfer date, and
(b) either—
(i) a third party election is made in respect of the TTH asset within the permitted period, or
(ii) a hive down election is made in respect of the TTH asset within the permitted period.

(3) For the purposes of sub-paragraph (2)(b)(i)—
(a) a "third party election" is an election made between two companies that are not associated with one another, and
(b) the "permitted period" in relation to a third party election in respect of the TTH asset is—
(i) the period of 90 days ending with the licence transfer date referred to in sub-paragraph (2)(a), or
(ii) the period of 90 days beginning with that date.

(4) For the purposes of sub-paragraph (2)(b)(ii)—
(a) a "hive down election" is an election in respect of which the hive down condition is met, and
(b) the "permitted period" in relation to a hive down election in respect of the TTH asset is the period of 180 days ending with the licence transfer date referred to in sub-paragraph (2)(a).

(5) The "hive down" condition is met for the purposes of a TTH election if the seller and purchaser—
(a) are associated with one another on the licence transfer date, but
(b) before the end of the period of 90 days beginning with that date, the purchaser ceases to be associated with—
(i) the seller, and
(ii) any other company that is associated with the seller.

(6) See paragraph 98 of this Schedule and section 271 of CTA 2010 for further provision about the meaning of "associated companies".

Election conditions: decommissioning relief agreements

57 (1) If the seller is a party to a decommissioning relief agreement, a TTH election may only be made if the agreement provides for the total TTH amount to be disregarded when determining the reference amount.

(2) In this Schedule, "decommissioning relief agreement" and "reference amount" have the meaning given by section 80(2) of FA 2013.

Timing of election

58 (1) A TTH election in respect of a TTH asset may not be made—
(a) before the licence transfer date, or
(b) after the end of the period of 90 days beginning with that date or, if later, 1 June 2019.

(2) Paragraph 3 of Schedule 1A to TMA 1970 (amendment of claims and elections) does not apply in relation to a TTH election (but see paragraph 74 (amounts discovered to be incorrect)).

Content

59 (1) The election must contain such information and declarations as an officer of Revenue and Customs may reasonably require.

(2) The officer may, in particular, require information and declarations as to—
(a) the TTH asset to which the election relates,
(b) the amount of the seller's taxable profits that are represented by the total TTH amount and each transferred profits amount,
(c) the rate of tax chargeable on those taxable profits, and the amount of tax paid,
(d) any decommissioning security agreement which relates to the TTH oil field and the seller, and any estimate of the decommissioning costs for the field determined for the purposes of any such agreement, and

(e) any decommissioning relief agreement to which the seller is a party (see paragraph 57).

Timing of an enquiry: cases where the corporate restructuring condition is met

60 (1) This paragraph applies if—

(a) a TTH election is made, and
(b) the corporate restructuring condition or the hive down condition is met in relation to that election.

(2) Paragraph 5(2)(a) of Schedule 1A to TMA 1970 (power to enquire into claims: time limits) has effect in relation to the election as if the reference in that provision to the day on which the claim was made were a reference to—

(a) in a case where the corporate restructuring condition is met by reference to paragraph 56(2)(b)(i), the day on which the third party election was made;
(b) in a case where the corporate restructuring condition is met by reference to paragraph 56(2)(b)(ii), the day on which the seller and purchaser cease to be associated with one another;
(c) in a case where the hive down condition is met, the day on which the seller and the purchaser ceased to be associated with one another.

COMMENTARY ON SCHEDULE 15, PART 8

Part 8 determines the pre-requisites for making an election to transfer tax history and the procedural aspects.

Paragraph 56 sets out that elections can only be made in one of three circumstances. The rules are aimed at facilitating transfers of tax history between third parties but permit cases where the interest in the oil field is transferred through a corporate vehicle and integrated into a different group of companies.

Paragraph 56(1) therefore only permits elections where the seller and purchaser are not associated at the time of the licence transfer, or alternatively where either the corporate restructuring condition, or the hive down condition is met. The definition of associated is taken from CTA 2010, s 271.

Paragraph 56(2)–(4) sets out that the corporate restructuring condition is met where the seller and purchaser are associated at the time of the licence transfer, but either a third-party election is made within 90 days either side of the licence transfer, or a hive down election is made within 180 days ending with the licence transfer. This permits the TTH to transfer on a licence transfer intra-group where there has been a sale between third parties within 90 days, and also in the case where in the preceding 180 days the licence now being transferred within the group of the new owner was hived down within the vendor group and the recipient corporate vehicle has then left the vendor group within 90 days.

Paragraph 56(5) sets out the hive down condition as an associated party transfer followed by a cessation of association within 90 days. Meeting this condition alone will permit an intra-group TTH transfer, and in conjunction with the foregoing will enable TTH transfers in the most common transfer arrangements.

Where the seller is party to a decommissioning relief agreement para 57 permits TTH elections only where, for the purposes of the agreement, the seller does not retain the benefit of transferred-out tax history. Without this stipulation the seller would potentially be able to draw value from its past tax history, notwithstanding the TTH recipient also being able to do so.

Paragraph 58 determines that a THH election can only be made on or after the licence transfer date and within 90 days of that date, with a transitional provision for early transfers permitting an election prior to 2 June 2019 where this would be later. The TMA 1970, Sch 1A, para 3 rules permitting amendments, including the 12 month amendment period for claimants, are prevented from applying. The rules aim to make elections final and irrevocable, so for planning purposes it is desirable to have the position prepared timeously.

Paragraph 59 stipulates that an election must contain such information as HMRC reasonably require, and in particular this may include details of the asset, the amounts of profits being transferred and the tax rate applicable, the tax paid thereon, the decommissioning security agreement governing the transferred licence interest and the estimate of decommissioning costs prepared for that agreement, and the decommissioning relief agreement of the seller. These last items should allow HMRC to verify the validity of the election with regard to paras 4 and 57.

Paragraph 60 varies the normal time period for HMRC enquiries into claims and elections in the cases where the corporate restructuring condition is met and where the hive down condition is met.

In the cases where the corporate restructuring condition is met, where there is no prior hive down, the date of claim is taken to be the date of the third party election, and where there was a prior hive down the date is taken to be the date there was a cessation of association in regard to the corporate vehicle and the vendor group.

In the cases where the hive down condition alone is met, the date of claim is taken to be the date of cessation of association of the corporate vehicle and the vendor group.

In these cases, for the purposes of the TMA 1970, Sch 1A rules, the rules impose a deemed date of claim to coincide with the effective transfer between third parties, and the enquiry powers run off the deemed date of claim instead of the actual date of any election.

PART 9

TTH ELECTIONS: APPROVAL

Approval notice

61 An officer of Revenue and Customs may approve the TTH election by giving notice in writing (an "approval notice") to the seller and the purchaser.

Deemed approval

62 (1) If no approval notice or enquiry notice is given, in respect of the TTH election, before the end of the period mentioned in paragraph 5(2) of Schedule 1A to TMA 1970 (time limit for opening an enquiry), the election is deemed to have been approved by an officer of Revenue and Customs at the end of that period.

(2) In sub-paragraph (1), the reference to an "enquiry notice" is a reference to a notice under paragraph 5(1) of Schedule 1A to TMA 1970 (intention to enquire into a claim or election).

Conditions of approval

63 The purchaser is required, as a condition of the approval of the election—

(a) to comply with the profit tracking requirements in relation to—

(i) the accounting period in which the interest in a UK oil licence, referred to in paragraph 1, is acquired by the purchaser, and

(ii) each subsequent accounting period; and

(b) to keep and preserve records, in accordance with such requirements as may be specified by an officer of Revenue and Customs, for the purposes of giving effect to this Schedule.

Profit tracking requirements

64 (1) The purchaser complies with the profit tracking requirements in relation to an accounting period if the purchaser's company tax return for the period is accompanied by a statement of the tracked profit or loss amount for the period.

(2) The "tracked profit or loss amount" for an accounting period is the amount of profit or loss that is attributable to the TTH asset, excluding the relevant proportion of the decommissioning expenditure amount attributable to the TTH oil field, for that period.

(3) In sub-paragraph 64(2), "relevant proportion" has the same meaning as in paragraph 30 (see paragraph 30(5)).

65 (1) For the purposes of determining the tracked profit or loss amount for an accounting period—

(a) just and reasonable apportionments are to be made of the receipts, expenses, assets and liabilities of—

(i) the purchaser, and

(ii) any other company that is associated with the purchaser and has an interest in the TTH asset (including an interest in a share in the oil won and saved in the TTH oil field), and

(b) for the purposes of paragraph (a), an officer of Revenue and Customs may require that financing costs for an accounting period are to be apportioned on such basis as the officer may reasonably specify before the beginning of that period.

(2) In this paragraph "financing costs" has the meaning it has for the purposes of section 330 of CTA 2010 (see section 331 of that Act).

Senior tracking officers

66 (1) The purchaser's senior tracking officer must—

(a) take reasonable steps to ensure that the tracked profit and loss amount attributable to a TTH asset for each tracking period is determined in accordance with paragraph 65, and

(b) provide the Commissioners for Her Majesty's Revenue and Customs with a certificate as to compliance with paragraph (a).

(2) For each tracking period, the purchaser must notify the Commissioners for Revenue and Customs of the name of each person who was its senior tracking officer at any time during the period.

(3) The certificate under sub-paragraph (1)(b), and the notice under sub-paragraph (2), must be given—

(a) in the form and manner specified by an officer of Revenue and Customs, and

(b) on or before the filing date for the purchaser's tax return for the tracking period (see paragraph 14 of Schedule 18 to FA 1998).

(4) In this Part, "tracking period", in relation to the TTH asset, means each accounting period in relation to which the purchaser is required under paragraph 63(a) to comply with the profit tracking requirements.

67 (1) The purchaser's "senior tracking officer" is the officer of the purchaser or of an associated company who, in the purchaser's reasonable opinion, has overall responsibility for the purchaser's financial accounting arrangements.

(2) In this section, "officer", in relation to a company, means—

(a) a director,

(b) a manager,

(c) a secretary, and

(d) any other person managing or purporting to manage any of the company's affairs.

68 (1) The senior tracking officer is liable to a penalty of £5,000 if the officer, without reasonable excuse—

(a) fails to comply with paragraph 66(1)(a) at any time in a tracking period, or

(b) fails to provide a certificate in accordance with paragraph 66(1)(b) and (3).

(2) The senior tracking officer is not liable to more than one penalty under paragraph 68(1)(a) in respect of the TTH asset and the same tracking period.

(3) If the purchaser, without reasonable excuse, fails to give a notice in accordance with paragraph 66(2) and (3), the purchaser is liable to a penalty of £5,000.

(4) If (but for this sub-paragraph) more than one person would be liable for a penalty under sub-paragraph 68(1)(a) or (b) in respect of the TTH asset and a tracking period, only the person who became the senior tracking officer latest in the tracking period is liable to such a penalty.

69 (1) Where a senior tracking officer, or the purchaser, becomes liable for a penalty under paragraph 68—

(a) Her Majesty's Revenue and Customs may assess the penalty, and

(b) if they do so, they must notify the person liable for the penalty.

(2) An assessment of a penalty under this Part for a failure in respect of a tracking period may not be made—

(a) more than 6 months after the failure first comes to the attention of an officer of Revenue and Customs, or

(b) more than 6 years after the filing date for the purchaser's tax return for the tracking period (see paragraph 14 of Schedule 18 to FA 1998).

(3) See paragraph 94 for provision about appeals against a penalty under paragraph 68.

70 (1) A penalty under paragraph 68 must be paid—

(a) before the end of the period of 30 days beginning with the date on which the notification under paragraph 69 was issued, or

(b) if a notice of appeal against the penalty is given, before the end of the period of 30 days beginning with the date on which the appeal is determined or withdrawn.

(2) A penalty under this Schedule may be enforced as if it were income tax charged in an assessment and due and payable or, in the case of the purchaser, corporation tax charged in an assessment and due and payable.

COMMENTARY ON SCHEDULE 15, PART 9

Part 9 contains the procedure for approval of an election and the requirements for an election to be approved.

Paragraphs 61 and 62 permit HMRC to approve an election in writing to both the purchaser and seller, and in the absence of an approval or an enquiry by HMRC into the election, it is deemed to be approved once the window for an enquiry closes.

Paragraphs 63 to 67 require, as a condition for approval, that the purchaser will comply with the profit tracking requirements and keep such records as may be required by HMRC.

Paragraph 64 requires the purchaser to submit a computation of the tracked profit and loss; the profit or loss attributable to the TTH asset transferred, excluding decommissioning expenditure. This profit or loss shall include apportionments where required, not only of the purchaser's receipts and expenses, but also those of an associate with an interest in the TTH oil field. This is to prevent manipulation of the tracked profits within a group holding multiple interests in the same licence in different entities. Paragraph 65 specifically permits HMRC to dictate an apportionment of financing costs. It is not clear how often this is likely to occur in practice.

Paragraphs 66 and 67 require the appointment and notification to HMRC of a senior tracking officer for each accounting period for which the company is tracking the profits of the TTH asset. The senior tracking officer has a responsibility to ensure the tracked profits are properly calculated, and must supply a certificate of compliance for each accounting period by the corporation tax filing date for the period. The owner of the relevant licence interest must notify HMRC of the names of the senior tracking officer(s) by the corporation tax filing date.

Penalties are set out under para 68; potential fines of £5000 on the senior tracking officer and £5000 on the holder of the relevant licence interest, in the absence of a reasonable excuse for failure.

Paragraphs 69 and 70 set out the penalties' procedural rules and introduce the appeal rights at para 94. The most notable deviation from normal corporation tax penalty procedures is the time limit for imposing penalties which, per para 69(2), cannot be more than six months after HMRC becomes aware of the failure, and also cannot be more than six years after the filing date for the relevant corporation tax accounting period.

PART 10

TTH ELECTIONS: EFFECTIVE DATE AND WITHDRAWAL

Effective date of a TTH election

71 (1) A TTH election in respect of a TTH asset—

(a) has effect, if it is approved in accordance with paragraph 61 or 62, from the licence transfer date,

(b) continues to have effect indefinitely in relation to seller, and

(c) continues to have effect in relation to the purchaser unless it is withdrawn in accordance with the provisions of this Schedule.

(2) References in this Schedule to the "effective date of a TTH election" are to be construed in accordance with sub-paragraph (1)(a).

Withdrawal of a TTH election by an officer of Revenue and Customs

72 (1) A TTH election ceases to have effect in relation to the purchaser if—

(a) the purchaser, without reasonable excuse, persistently fails to comply with either of the conditions mentioned in paragraph 63, and

(b) an officer of Revenue and Customs gives notice to the purchaser of the withdrawal of the election.

(2) If notice is given under sub-paragraph (1), the TTH election ceases to have effect in relation to the purchaser for the accounting period in which the notice is given and each subsequent accounting period.

(3) A notice given under sub-paragraph (1) does not affect any relief given by reference to paragraph 25 or 26 for a loss period ending before the notice is given.

(4) See paragraph 94 for provision about appeals against a decision to withdraw an election under this paragraph.

COMMENTARY ON SCHEDULE 15, PART 10

Part 10 sets out the period for which a TTH election is effective.

Paragraph 71 provides that a TTH election has effect from the licence transfer date once approved, even where that approval is made or deemed to be made at a later time, and the references to the effective date of an election are references to this licence transfer date. The election has indefinite effect for the seller and will have effect for the purchaser unless withdrawn.

Paragraph 72 permits the withdrawal of an election by HMRC. This action would only affect the purchaser's position going forward. HMRC can withdraw the election where there has been a persistent failure by the purchaser to meet the profit tracking and record keeping requirements of para 63. Withdrawal of an election by HMRC requires a notice from HMRC to the purchaser whereupon the election is ineffective for the accounting period in which the notice is given and all subsequent accounting periods. There is an appeal process for the purchaser, and any relief given for prior periods is unaffected.

PART 11

TTH ELECTIONS: INACCURACIES

Penalties for errors

73 If a document provided for the purposes of making a TTH election contains an inaccuracy which is, or results in, an overstatement of the total TTH amount, Schedule 24 to FA 2007 has effect as if—

(a) the seller (and not the purchaser) is treated as giving the document to Her Majesty's Revenue and Customs,

(b) the inaccuracy is treated (so far as would not otherwise be the case) as leading to a false or inflated claim to repayment of tax, and

(c) "the potential lost revenue" in respect of the inaccuracy is an amount equal to 10% of the amount by which the total TTH amount is overstated.

Amendment of TTH election: amounts discovered to be incorrect

74 (1) This paragraph applies if an officer of Revenue and Customs discovers that a TTH election incorrectly states an amount that affects, or may affect—

(a) the amount which may be applied in accordance with paragraph 25 (effect of trade loss relief provisions), or

(b) the amount of a repayment determined by reference to paragraph 26 (supplementary charge: repayment of tax).

(2) The officer—

(a) may amend the TTH election to correct that amount, subject to paragraph 75, and

(b) must give notice to the purchaser of an amendment under paragraph (a).

(3) But the power to amend the TTH election under this paragraph may only be exercised if, at the time the election was approved (see paragraphs 61 and 62), an officer of Revenue and Customs could not have been reasonably expected, on the basis of the information made available to the officer before that time, to be aware that the amount stated was incorrect.

(4) An amendment under this paragraph may not be made more than 12 months after information that, in the opinion of an officer of Revenue and Customs, justifies the correction of the TTH election, comes to the officer's attention.

(5) An amendment under this paragraph is to be ignored for the purposes of the application of Part 3 of this Schedule (effect of a TTH election on the seller).

(6) If, on or after the licence transfer date, the seller's total profits for a pre-transfer accounting period are reduced, the statement of the total profits (or a statement of an amount determined by reference to the total profits) is not to be regarded as incorrect for the purposes of this paragraph (but see paragraph 18).

(7) See paragraph 94 for provision about appeals against a decision under this paragraph.

75 (1) This paragraph applies if, before the correction under paragraph 74 is made, an activated transferred profits amount for a pre-acquisition accounting period has been applied in accordance with paragraph 25(2)(b) or (3)(b).

(2) An amendment made under paragraph 74(2) may not—

(a) reduce the transferred profits amount for that pre-acquisition accounting period to an amount which is less than the amount that has been applied, in respect of loss periods ending before the determination is made, in accordance with paragraph 25 for the pre-acquisition accounting period, or

(b) reduce the total TTH amount to an amount which is less than the total of the amounts that have been applied in accordance with paragraph 25 in respect of loss periods ending before the determination is made.

COMMENTARY ON SCHEDULE 15, PART 11

Part 11 governs the penalties and procedures where inaccuracies are discovered in a TTH election.

Paragraph 73 ensures the penalty provisions for inaccurate information will apply to documents supplied in making a TTH election, where there is an overstatement of the TTH amount.

Paragraph 74 permits HMRC to amend the TTH election to correct inaccuracies, but this power is limited to cases where at the time the election was approved HMRC could not reasonably have been expected to be aware of the inaccuracy, and also HMRC's amendment must be made not later than 12 months after becoming aware of the inaccuracy. Separately para 74 provides that a post-election change in the seller's pre-transfer profits is not to be regarded as an inaccuracy such that amendment or penalties can apply under the paragraph. In all cases, any amendment has no effect on the seller's TTH position. This means that since amendments only apply to limit the purchaser's potential benefit, the lack of a corresponding adjustment to the seller's position could lead to an overall loss of tax relief.

Paragraph 75 limits the effect of any amendment under para 74; it will not affect claims already made by the purchaser to use transferred profits.

PART 12

CHARGEABLE GAINS

Transferred tax history is not to be regarded as an asset

76 Where the seller and the purchaser jointly make a TTH election in respect of the TTH asset, the transfer of tax history is not to be treated as—

(a) the disposal or acquisition of an asset for the purposes of TCGA 1992, or

(b) the disposal or acquisition of an intangible fixed asset for the purposes of Part 8 of CTA 2009.

Consideration for transferred tax history to be treated as consideration for the licence interest

77 The amount or value of any consideration for the transfer of tax history is to be treated as part of the consideration for the licence interest for the purposes of—

(a) computing the chargeable gain or allowable loss accruing on the disposal (or on any subsequent disposal) of the licence interest (see section 8 of TCGA 1992), and

(b) computing the disposal value of the licence interest, on its disposal, for the purposes of Part 5 of CAA 2001 (mineral extraction allowances).

Market value of the licence interest: value of transferred tax history to be taken into account

78 Any value attributable to the transfer of tax history is to be taken into account in determining the market value of the licence interest for the purposes of—

(a) section 17 of TCGA 1992 (disposals and acquisitions treated as being made at market value);

(b) Part 5 of CAA 2001, if the disposal value of the licence interest for the purposes of that Part is the market value of the licence interest at the time of that disposal (see section 423 of CAA 2001).

Licence swaps: references to disposal include references to transfer of tax history

79 For the purposes of the application of sections 195A to 196 of TCGA 1992 (oil licence swaps) in relation to the disposal of the licence interest by the seller to the purchaser, references in those sections to the disposal are treated as including references to the transfer of tax history.

Interpretation of this Part

80 (1) References in this Part to "the transfer of tax history" are references to—

(a) the seller, in consequence of the TTH election, ceasing to be entitled to take the transferred profits for an accounting period into account for certain corporation tax purposes in the circumstances specified in Part 3 of this Schedule, and

(b) the purchaser, in consequence of the TTH election, acquiring an entitlement, in the circumstances specified in Part 4 of this Schedule, to apply an amount of the transferred profits for the purposes of the trade loss relief provisions and to a corresponding repayment of supplementary charge.

(2) References in this Part to "the licence interest" are references to the interest in a UK oil licence referred to in paragraph 1.

COMMENTARY ON SCHEDULE 15, PART 12

Part 12 governs the chargeable gains treatment, essentially to ensure neutrality.

Paragraph 76 ensures that the TTH is not treated as an asset for the purposes of the chargeable gains rules nor the intangible assets rules on the transfer of the tax history under a TTH election, as defined in para 80.

Paragraph 77 acknowledges that in a licence transfer an amount of value may be attributable to any tax history being transferred and clarifies that such part of the consideration shall be treated as paid for the licence interest for the purposes of chargeable gains and capital allowances rules.

Paragraphs 78 and 79 follow on from para 77, to ensure any value of the transferred tax history is incorporated into the market value of the licence interest used in the calculation of chargeable gains and capital allowances, and the values used in the licence swaps rules in TCGA 1992, ss 195A–196.

PART 13

ONWARD SALE

Application of paragraphs 83 to 90

81 This Part applies if—

(a) the purchaser (referred to in this Part as "the first purchaser") and the seller jointly make a TTH election (the "first TTH election") in respect of an interest (the "first TTH asset") in the TTH oil field,

(b) the first purchaser subsequently sells to another company ("the second purchaser") an interest in a UK oil licence which applies to the area which includes the TTH oil field, and

(c) the first purchaser and the second purchaser jointly make a TTH election (the "subsequent TTH election") in respect of an interest (the "subsequent TTH asset") in the TTH oil field.

82 (1) Sub-paragraph (2) applies if—

(a) the first purchaser has an interest in the UK oil licence referred to in paragraph 1, in addition to the interest in that licence acquired from the seller, and

(b) the UK oil licence referred to in paragraph 81(b) is the same UK oil licence referred to in paragraph 1.

(2) Interests in the licence acquired later by the first purchaser are treated, for the purposes of this Part, as being transferred to the second purchaser before interests in the licence acquired earlier by the first purchaser.

Original TTH amount treated as eligible ring fence profits

83 (1) This Schedule applies, for the purposes of the subsequent TTH election, as if the original TTH amount for all relevant accounting periods were an amount of the first purchaser's eligible ring fence profits for that period.

(2) Sub-paragraph (1) is subject to paragraphs 85 to 88.

(3) In this Part of this Schedule, "relevant accounting period" means a pre-acquisition accounting period of the first purchaser for which there is, immediately before the effective date of the subsequent TTH election, an unused transferred profits amount.

(4) In this Part of this Schedule, references to the "original TTH amount" mean, in relation to a relevant accounting period—

(a) the unused transferred profits amount for that period, or

(b) if the first TTH asset is not the same as the subsequent TTH asset, the relevant proportion of that amount for that period.

(5) For the purposes of sub-paragraph (4)(b), the "relevant proportion" is the proportion that the subsequent TTH asset bears to the first TTH asset or, if the proportion cannot reasonably be determined on that basis, such other proportion determined on a just and reasonable basis.

(6) In this paragraph, references to the unused transferred profits amount for an accounting period are references to—

(a) the transferred profits amount, in relation to the first TTH election, for that period, less

(b) the total of the amounts applied for that period in accordance with paragraph 25, for the purposes of the application of that paragraph in relation to a loss period of the first purchaser.

84 The original TTH amount for each relevant accounting period ceases to be treated, for the purposes of the first TTH election, as a transferred profits amount for that period in relation to the first purchaser.

Original TTH amount transferred before eligible ring fence profits (subject to opt-out)

85 (1) Paragraphs 86 and 87 apply in relation to the subsequent TTH election, subject to sub-paragraph (2).

(2) The first purchaser and the second purchaser may elect, at the time the TTH election is made, that neither paragraph 86 nor paragraph 87 applies in relation to the subsequent TTH election.

86 (1) The total TTH amount may not include an amount representing the first purchaser's eligible ring fence profits for an accounting period unless it also includes an amount representing, in respect of each relevant accounting period, the original TTH amount for that period.

(2) Paragraph 11 (consecutive accounting periods) does not apply in relation to an amount representing an original TTH amount for a relevant accounting period (but see sub-paragraph (3)).

(3) The total TTH amount may not include an amount representing the original TTH amount for a particular accounting period unless it also includes an amount representing the original TTH amount for the next following relevant accounting period.

(4) If the original TTH amount exceeds the total TTH amount, the transferred profits amount for the earliest relevant accounting period must be an amount equal to—

(a) the total TTH amount, less

(b) the transferred profits amount for later relevant accounting periods.

(5) For the purposes of paragraph 12 (the transferred profits amount)—

(a) references to the "earliest period" are to be treated as references to the earliest accounting period for which there is a transferred profits amount by reason of the first purchaser's eligible ring fence profits for that period (and not by reason of an original TTH amount for that period), and

(b) the reference in sub-paragraph (2) to the TTH balance for the earliest period is to be treated as a reference to the TTH balance less the transferred profits amounts for each relevant accounting period.

87 In the application of this Schedule for the purposes of the subsequent TTH election—

(a) in sub-paragraph (2) of paragraph 30 (TTH activation event), the reference to an allowance or allocation made to the purchaser includes a reference to the relevant proportion (within the meaning of paragraph 83(5)) of an allowance or allocation made to the first purchaser;

(b) in paragraph 30(2)(b) and (3)(b), and in paragraph 31 (decommissioning expenditure amount), references to a post-acquisition accounting period of the purchaser include references to a post-acquisition accounting period of the first purchaser;

(c) in paragraph 30(3) as it applies in relation to post-acquisition accounting periods of the first purchaser, the reference to amounts attributable to the TTH asset is to be treated as a reference to the relevant proportion (within the meaning of paragraph 83(5)) of those amounts;

(d) in paragraph 30(5) as it applies for the purposes of determining the total decommissioning expenditure amount in relation to a post-acquisition accounting period of the first purchaser, the reference to the purchaser is to be treated as a reference to the first purchaser;

(e) references in this Schedule to a pre-acquisition accounting period of the purchaser include references to a pre-acquisition accounting period of the first purchaser;

(f) references in paragraphs 83 to 86 and 89 to an amount of the first purchaser's eligible ring fence profits do not includes references to an original TTH amount.

Opt-out under paragraph 85(2): further provision about the application of this Schedule

88 (1) This paragraph applies if—

(a) the first purchaser and the second purchaser make an election under paragraph 85(2) (disapplication of paragraphs 86 and 87), and

(b) in relation to the subsequent TTH election, the total TTH amount exceeds the total amount of the first purchaser's eligible ring fence profits for—

(i) the accounting period which is, at the licence transfer date in relation to the subsequent TTH election, the first purchaser's most recent qualifying accounting period in respect of which the amendment period has ended, and

(ii) each earlier accounting period which is, in relation to the first TTH election, a post-acquisition accounting period of the first purchaser.

(2) In the application of this Schedule for the purposes of the subsequent TTH election—

(a) in sub-paragraph (2) of paragraph 30 (TTH activation event), the reference to an allowance or allocation made to the purchaser includes a reference to the relevant proportion (within the meaning of paragraph 83(5)) of an allowance or allocation made to the first purchaser;

(b) in paragraph 30(2)(b) and (3)(b), and in paragraph 31 (decommissioning expenditure amount), references to a post-acquisition accounting period of the purchaser include references to the accounting periods of the first purchaser mentioned in sub-paragraph (1)(b)(i) and (ii);

(c) in paragraph 30(3) as it applies in relation to the accounting periods of the first purchaser mentioned in sub-paragraph (1)(b)(i) and (ii), the reference to amounts attributable to the TTH asset is to be treated as a reference to the relevant proportion (within the meaning of paragraph 83(5)) of those amounts;

(d) in paragraph 30(5) as it applies for the purposes of determining the total decommissioning expenditure amount in relation to an accounting period of the first purchaser mentioned in sub-paragraph (1)(b)(i) or (ii), the reference to the purchaser is to be treated as a reference to the first purchaser;

(e) in paragraph 83 and in sub-paragraph (1)(b) of this paragraph, references to an amount of the first purchaser's eligible ring fence profits do not include references to an original TTH amount.

Supplementary charge: treatment of transferred adjusted ring fence profits

89 (1) The provisions of this Schedule apply, for the purposes of the subsequent TTH election, as if—

(a) the transferred adjusted ring fence profits amount for each relevant accounting period, or

(b) if the first TTH asset is not the same as the subsequent TTH asset, the relevant proportion of that amount for that period,

were an amount of the first purchaser's eligible adjusted ring fence profits for that period.

(2) For the purposes of sub-paragraph (1)(b), "the relevant proportion" means the proportion that the subsequent TTH asset bears to the first TTH asset or, if the proportion cannot reasonably be determined on that basis, such other proportion determined on a just and reasonable basis.

Tracking

90 (1) This paragraph applies if, after the effective date of the subsequent TTH election, the first purchaser continues to be liable for the decommissioning costs, or for a proportion of the decommissioning costs, for the subsequent TTH asset.

(2) In the application of this Schedule for the purposes of the subsequent TTH election, references to the "purchaser" in paragraph 65 are to be treated, in respect of the period beginning with the effective date of the subsequent TTH election, as including references to the second purchaser.

Sale by the second purchaser or subsequent sale

91 In the case of a sale by the second purchaser, or a subsequent sale, of an interest within paragraph 81(c) in respect of which the parties make a TTH election—

(a) references in paragraph 86 to the original TTH amount are references to the original TTH amount in relation to each election,

(b) amounts in relation to earlier elections are to be applied for the purposes of paragraph 86(1) and (3) before amounts in relation to later elections,

(c) the provisions of paragraph 87 apply in relation to the second purchaser, and each subsequent purchaser, as they apply in relation to the first purchaser, and

(d) in paragraph 90—

   (i) the reference to the first purchaser in sub-paragraph (1) is treated as including a reference to the second purchaser, or a subsequent purchaser, and

   (ii) sub-paragraph (2) applies in relation to each subsequent purchaser as it applies in relation to the second purchaser.

COMMENTARY ON SCHEDULE 15, PART 13

Part 13 contains the rules for onward sales of licence interest after they have been acquired with TTH.

Paragraph 81 sets out that the rules only apply where a purchaser ('the first purchaser') under a TTH election subsequently sells to another company (the 'second purchaser') an interest in the TTH oil field under a TTH election.

Paragraph 82 sets out an order for cases where the first purchaser has acquired interests in the relevant licence subject to a TTH election in stages; more recently acquired interests are treated as sold prior to those acquired earlier.

Paragraphs 83 and 84 allow unused transferred profits acquired by the first purchaser in a TTH election to be transferred onward to the second purchaser of the interest to the extent that relief has not already been given against them. Once transferred to the second purchaser, para 84 ensures they will only give relief to the second purchaser. Where the onward sale does not represent the full interest acquired under a TTH election, a just and reasonable proportion of the TTH profits are transferred.

Paragraphs 85–88 set out the order in which transferred profits are passed on in cases of an onward sale.

There are two options. In the absence of an election under para 85, para 86 ensures that on the transfer to the second purchaser, the transferred profits are taken from the profits acquired by the first purchaser in priority to any profits the first purchaser accrues from its own activities. Paragraph 87 then ensures that in the calculation of the decommissioning costs required to activate TTH, all the expenditures accrued after the first TTH transfer are taken into account. Paragraph 87 also amends the definitions elsewhere in relation to TTH activation and TTH transfer to ensure that a second or subsequent transfer maintains the effect of transfers as intended, without stranding tax history, and taking into account aggregated expenditure on decommissioning.

If an election is made under para 85 the effect of the first TTH election remains in place; the first purchaser will keep the TTH it acquired on the first TTH election. There is no possibility to split the TTH acquired on the occasion of a subsequent TTH election; it is either retained, or passed on in full. Where the first purchaser however passes on TTH to the second purchaser in excess of the profits he has made since the first transfer the rules operate to ensure there is no double counting.

Paragraph 88 also applies where an election under para 85 is made and only a proportion of the TTH asset is being transferred to a second purchaser, to ensure the rules operate as intended in respect of the proportionate transfer.

Paragraph 89 then applies the rules for the purposes of the supplementary charge.

Paragraph 90 applies where the first purchaser retains some decommissioning obligations with respect to the interest transferred with TTH to the second purchaser and requires that in determining how much of that decommissioning expenditure can activate its TTH it needs to take into account the second purchaser's profits from the transferred interest. It is not clear how this could operate in practice and would presumably require appropriate notification provision to be included in the second transfer SPA of expenditure of that transferee in its tracked profits.

Paragraph 91 then ensures the rules work on any subsequent transfer in the same way.

PART 14
SUPPLEMENTARY

Multiple interests in the same oil field

92 (1) This paragraph applies if—

- (a) interests in more than one UK oil licence are sold by the seller to the purchaser at the same time, and
- (b) the seller and the purchaser would be entitled to jointly make a TTH election in respect of more than one interest in the same oil field that falls within both licensed areas.

(2) The seller and purchaser may jointly make a TTH election in respect of all interests in the oil field.

(3) If an election is made in accordance with this paragraph, the interests mentioned in sub-paragraph (2) are to be treated as a single interest for the purposes of this Schedule (and references in this Schedule to "the TTH asset" are to be construed accordingly).

Multiple TTH elections

93 (1) This paragraph applies if, in a loss period, more than one TTH election in respect of the TTH asset has effect in relation to the purchaser.

(2) For the purposes of paragraph 44 (allocation of activated TTH to an accounting period)—

- (a) references to the unused transferred profits amount for an accounting period are to be treated as references to the total of the unused transferred profits amounts for that period in respect of each of the TTH elections, and
- (b) the amount in respect of a later TTH election is to be allocated to an accounting period before the amount which is subject to an earlier TTH election.

Appeals

94 (1) A person may appeal against—

(a) a decision that a penalty under paragraph 68 is payable by that person;
(b) a decision to withdraw a TTH election under paragraph 72;
(c) a decision to amend a TTH election under paragraph 74 (amounts discovered to be incorrect).

(2) Notice of an appeal must be given—

(a) in writing,
(b) before the end of the period of 30 days beginning with the date on which notice of the decision is given, and
(c) to an officer of Revenue and Customs.

(3) Notice of an appeal must state the grounds of appeal.

(4) On an appeal that is notified to the tribunal, the tribunal may—

(a) confirm or cancel the decision, or
(b) in the case of an appeal within sub-paragraph (1)(c), substitute for the decision another decision that an officer of Revenue and Customs had power to make.

(5) If a decision under paragraph 72 (withdrawal) is cancelled, the TTH election is to be treated as having had continuing effect (subject to any further appeal).

(6) Subject to this paragraph and (in the case of an appeal within sub-paragraph (1)(a)) paragraph 70, the provisions of Part 5 of TMA 1970 relating to appeals have effect in relation to appeals under this paragraph as they have effect in relation to appeals against an assessment to corporation tax.

Anti-avoidance

95 (1) If a person enters into arrangements within sub-paragraph (2), an officer of Revenue and Customs may—

(a) amend a TTH election, or
(b) amend or disallow a claim,

to secure that the election or claim has effect as if the arrangements had not been entered into.

(2) Arrangements are within this sub-paragraph if it is reasonable to regard the arrangements as—

(a) designed to secure that an entitlement to a repayment, or an increased repayment, of tax by reason of the application of any provision of this Schedule, arises earlier than would (apart from the arrangements) be the case,
(b) circumventing the intended limits of the provisions of this Schedule on an amount that is relevant for the purposes of determining a repayment of tax by reference to those provisions, or
(c) otherwise exploiting shortcomings in those provisions.

(3) In this paragraph, "arrangements" includes any agreement, understanding, scheme, transaction or series of transactions (whether or not legally enforceable).

96 (1) If relief is given to a person under the trade loss relief provisions by reference to an amount of the seller's ring fence profits which (by reason of the application of the provisions of this Schedule) is treated as if it were an amount of the purchaser's profits, no relief may be given to any other person by reference to the same amount.

(2) If a repayment of supplementary charge is made to a person by reference to an amount of the seller's adjusted ring fence profits which (by reason of the application of the provisions of this Schedule) is treated as if it were an amount of the purchaser's adjusted ring fence profits, no repayment may be made to any other person by reference to the same amount.

COMMENTARY ON SCHEDULE 15, PART 14

Part 14 contains supplementary rules.

Paragraph 92 permits a single TTH election to be made where multiple licence interests are being transferred between the same persons, and the interests are treated as a single TTH asset.

Paragraph 93 allocates TTH available under more than one TTH election where a loss arises for which relief is available from activated TTH. The later TTH election takes priority.

Paragraph 94 permits appeals against penalties imposed on senior tracking officers for failure to meet the requirements to track profits and submit the certification. Appeals are also permitted for penalties imposed for failing to notify HMRC of the senior tracking officer, and against withdrawal of a TTH election or amendment thereof. The usual appeal provisions apply; any appeal must be made in writing within 30 days of the notice of decision.

Paragraph 95 contains certain anti-avoidance powers. HMRC may amend a TTH election or amend or disallow a claim in cases of avoidance; defined as the presence of arrangements that are designed to advance the timing of repayments, or which circumvent the intended limits on repayments or otherwise exploit 'shortcomings' in the legislation. When triggered, the provision allows HMRC to cancel the effect of the arrangements.

Paragraph 96 confirms that relief can only be given to one person in respect of an amount of transferred profits.

PART 15

INTERPRETATION

Introductory

97 The following definitions apply for the purposes of this Schedule.

98 Expressions used in this Schedule that are defined for the purposes of Part 8 of CTA 2010 (oil activities) have the same meaning in this Schedule as in Part 8 of that Act.

"UK oil licence"

99 "UK oil licence" means a licence granted under—

(a) Part 1 of the Petroleum Act 1998, or
(b) the Petroleum (Production) Act (Northern Ireland) 1964 (c 28 (NI)).

"Licensed area" and "transferred oil field"

100 In this Schedule—

(a) references to the "licensed area" are references to the area to which the UK oil licence mentioned in paragraph 1 applies, and
(b) references to a "transferred oil field" are references to an oil field, or such part of an oil field, that falls within the licensed area.

"Licence transfer date"

101 "Licence transfer date", in relation to a TTH election, means the date of completion of the sale of the TTH asset in respect of which the election is made.

The seller's "reference accounting period"

102 (1) The seller's "reference accounting period" is the accounting period which is, at the licence transfer date, the seller's most recent qualifying accounting period in respect of which the amendment period has ended.

(2) The "amendment period", in relation to an accounting period, is 12 months beginning with the filing date for the company tax return for the accounting period.

(3) In this paragraph "filing date" has the same meaning as in Schedule 18 to FA 1998 (see paragraph 14 of that Schedule).

The purchaser's "reference accounting period"

103 (1) The "purchaser's reference accounting period" means—

(a) an accounting period of the purchaser that begins with the same date as, and ends with the same date as, the seller's reference accounting period, or
(b) if no accounting period of the purchaser falls within paragraph (a), the earliest accounting period of the purchaser that overlaps with the seller's reference accounting period.

(2) See paragraph 106 for provision about accounting periods before the purchaser comes within the charge to corporation tax.

The seller's "pre-transfer accounting periods"

104 Each of the following is a "pre-transfer accounting period" of the seller—

(a) the reference accounting period (see paragraph 102), and

(b) each preceding accounting period.

The purchaser's "pre-acquisition accounting periods" and "post-acquisition accounting periods"

105 (1) Each of the following is a "pre-acquisition accounting period" of the purchaser—

(a) the purchaser's reference accounting period, and

(b) each preceding accounting period.

(2) Each of the following is a "post-acquisition accounting period" of the purchaser—

(a) the first accounting period after the purchaser's reference accounting period,

(b) each subsequent accounting period, and

(c) each period which is a notional accounting period for the purposes of section 165 or section 416ZA of CAA 2001.

(3) See paragraph 106 for provision about accounting periods before the purchaser comes within the charge to corporation tax.

Accounting periods before the purchaser comes within the charge to corporation tax

106 (1) This paragraph applies if the date on which the purchaser comes within the charge to corporation tax falls after the end of the seller's reference accounting period.

(2) The provisions of this Schedule have effect as if the purchaser had—

(a) an accounting period of 12 months ending on the day before the purchaser comes within the charge to corporation tax, and

(b) successive accounting periods of 12 months in the preceding period.

"Transferred profits amount" and "activated transferred profits amount"

107 (1) References to the "transferred profits amount" for an accounting period of the seller are references to the amount representing the seller's ring fence profits for that period which forms part of the total TTH amount.

(2) See paragraph 45 for provision about references to the "transferred profits amount" for a pre-acquisition accounting period of the purchaser.

(3) See paragraph 25(4) for provision about the meaning of "activated transferred profits amount".

"Trade loss relief provisions"

108 "Trade loss relief provisions" means 37 to 44 of CTA 2010 (trade losses: carry back relief etc).

COMMENTARY ON SCHEDULE 15, PART 15

Part 15 contains definitions and interpretation. The specialised definitions applied to ring fence trades are used.

Paragraph 106 contains a deeming provision to accommodate cases where a non-resident company comes into charge to UK tax after the end of the seller's reference period. This is needed because the purchaser's reference period is defined by matching to the seller's using accounting periods determined for UK tax purposes. Without para 106 a non-resident would not have such an accounting period.

SCHEDULE 16

ENTREPRENEURS' RELIEF

Section 39

Periods throughout which conditions for relief must be met

1 (1) Chapter 3 of Part 5 of TCGA 1992 (transfer of business assets: entrepreneurs' relief) is amended as follows.

(2) In section 169I (material disposal of business assets)—

(a) in subsections (3), (6) and (7A)(b) and (c), for "1 year" substitute "2 years",

(b) in subsection (4)(a), for "1 year" substitute "2 years",

(c) in subsections (7) and (7B)(b) and (c), for "1 year" substitute "2 years", and

(d) after subsection (7) insert—

"(7ZA) If, in any case where an individual disposes of any shares in a company—

(a) there has been an issue of shares in the company to the individual following a relevant business transfer, and

(b) any of the issued shares constitute, or otherwise form part of, the shares disposed of,

the conditions in subsection (6)(a) and (b) are to be treated as met in any period ending immediately before the transfer throughout which the individual owned the business.

(7ZB) For the purposes of subsection (7ZA), shares have been issued "following a relevant business transfer" if they have been issued wholly or partly in exchange for the transfer of a business as a going concern, together with the whole assets of the business or the whole of those assets other than cash."

(3) In section 169J (disposal of trust business assets)—

(a) in subsection (4), for "1 year" substitute "2 years", and

(b) in subsection (5)(a), for "1 year" substitute "2 years".

(4) In section 169K(4) (disposal associated with relevant material disposal), for "1 year" substitute "2 years".

(5) In section 169O(6) (amount of relief: special provisions for certain trust disposals), for "1 year" substitute "2 years".

(6) In Schedule 7ZA ("trading company" and "trading group"), in paragraph 25 (meaning of "relevant period")—

(a) in sub-paragraph (a), for "1 year" substitute "2 years", and

(b) in sub-paragraphs (b) and (c), for "1 year" substitute "2 years".

Additional requirements relating to the beneficial ownership of companies

2 (1) Chapter 3 of Part 5 of TCGA 1992 (transfer of business assets: entrepreneurs' relief) is amended as follows.

(2) In section 169K(1B) (disposals associated with relevant material disposal), for paragraph (a) (together with the "and" at the end of it) substitute—

"(a) the ordinary shares disposed of constitute at least 5% of the company's ordinary share capital and are shares in the individual's personal company (and section 169S(3A)(a) to (c) apply here but as if the reference to the final day of the period mentioned in section 169S(3A)(a) were to the date of the disposal), and".

(3) In section 169LA (relevant business assets: goodwill transferred to a close company)—

(a) for subsection (1) substitute—

"(1) Subject to subsection (1A), subsection (4) applies if—

(a) as part of a qualifying business disposal, a person ("P") disposes of goodwill directly or indirectly to a close company ("C"), and

(b) immediately after the disposal, P meets any of the personal company conditions in the case of C or any company which is a member of a group of companies of which C is a member.

(1ZA) For the purposes of subsection (1)(b)—

(a) the reference to the personal company conditions is a reference to any of the conditions in 169S(3)(a), (b), (c)(i) or (ii), and

(b) P is taken to have all the rights and interests of any relevant connected person.

(1ZB) For the purposes of subsection (1ZA)—

(a) section 169S(3) is treated as having effect with the omission of the references to "by virtue of that holding",

(b) section 169S(3A)(a) and (b) are to apply for the purposes of section 169S(3)(c)(ii) but as if the reference to the final day of the period mentioned in section 169S(3A)(a) were to the time immediately after the disposal, and

(c) the condition in section 169S(3)(c)(i) is to be read as containing two separate conditions (one relating to profits and the other relating to assets).", and

(b) in subsection (1A)(a), for "subsection (1)(aa)" substitute "subsection (1)(b)".

(4) In section 169S (interpretation of Chapter), for subsections (3) and (4) substitute—

"(3) For the purposes of this Chapter a company is a "personal company" in relation to an individual if—

(a) the individual holds at least 5% of the ordinary share capital of the company,

(b) by virtue of that holding, at least 5% of the voting rights in the company are exercisable by the individual, and

(c) either or both of the following conditions are met—

(i) by virtue of that holding, the individual is beneficially entitled to at least 5% of the profits available for distribution to equity holders and, on a winding up, would be beneficially entitled to at least 5% of assets so available, or

(ii) in the event of a disposal of the whole of the ordinary share capital of the company, the individual would be beneficially entitled to at least 5% of the proceeds.

(3A) In determining whether subsection (3)(c)(ii) applies for the purposes of any provision of this Chapter under which a question arises as to whether or not a company is the individual's personal company at any time in a particular period —

(a) it is to be assumed that (so far as this is not otherwise the case) the whole of the ordinary share capital is disposed of at that time for a consideration equal to its market value on the final day of the period,

(b) it is to be assumed that the amount of the proceeds to which the individual would be beneficially entitled at that time is the amount of the proceeds to which, having regard to all the circumstances as they existed at that time, it would be reasonable to expect the person to be beneficially entitled, and

(c) the effect of any avoidance arrangements is to be ignored.

(3B) For the purposes of subsection (3A)(c)—

(a) arrangements are "avoidance arrangements" if the main purpose of, or one of the main purposes of, the arrangements is to secure that any provision of this Chapter applies or does not apply, and

(b) "arrangements" includes any agreement, understanding, scheme, transaction or series of transactions (whether or not legally enforceable).

(3C) For the purposes of subsection (3) if the individual holds any shares in the company jointly with one or more other persons, the individual is to be treated as the sole holder of so many of them as is proportionate to the value of the individual's share (and references in subsection (3) to the exercise of voting rights or beneficial entitlement are to be read accordingly).

(3D) A modified version of Chapter 6 of Part 5 of CTA 2010 (group relief: equity holders and profits or assets available for distribution) applies for the purposes of subsection (3) reading references to company A as references to the individual.

(3E) The reference here to a modified version of Chapter 6 of Part 5 of CTA 2010 is to the provisions of that Chapter having effect as if—

(a) for the purposes of section 158(1)(b), a person carrying on a business of banking were not a loan creditor of a company in respect of any loan capital or debt issued or incurred by the company for money lent by the person to the company in the ordinary course of that business,

(b) sections 171(1)(b) and (3), 173, 174 and 176 to 181 were omitted, and

(c) any modifications were made as are necessary for the purpose of applying that Chapter as if the individual were company A."

Relief where company ceases to be individual's personal company

3 In Part 5 of TCGA 1992 (transfer of business assets), after Chapter 3 (entrepreneurs' relief) insert—

"Chapter 3A

Entrepreneurs' Relief Where Company Ceases to be Individual's Personal Company

169SB Overview of Chapter

This Chapter makes provision about an individual claiming entrepreneurs' relief in certain cases where relief would otherwise become unavailable because of a company ceasing to be the individual's personal company.

169SC Election by individual where company ceases to be personal company

(1) If the following conditions are met, an individual may elect for this section to have effect.

(2) The first condition is that, as a result of a relevant share issue, the company ceases to be the individual's personal company.

(3) The second condition is that—

(a) if, immediately before the relevant share issue, the individual had made a disposal at their relevant value of all assets consisting of shares in or securities of the company, the disposal would have been a material disposal of business assets, and

(b) if a claim for entrepreneurs' relief had been made in respect of that disposal, a chargeable gain would have been treated by section 169N(2) as accruing to the individual.

(4) Where this section has effect, the individual is to be treated for the purposes of this Act—

(a) as having made a disposal immediately before the relevant share issue of all assets consisting of shares in or securities of the company, and

(b) immediately after that event, as having reacquired those assets,

at their relevant value.

(5) In this section—

"material disposal of business assets" and "personal company" have the same meanings as in Chapter 3 (see section 169S),

"relevant share issue" means an issue of shares by the company where—

(a) the shares are issued by the company for consideration consisting wholly of cash, and

(b) the shares are subscribed, and issued, for genuine commercial reasons and not as part of arrangements the main purpose, or one of the main purposes, of which is to secure a tax advantage to any person, and

"relevant value" means—

(a) in relation to an asset consisting of shares, an amount equal to the consideration that would be apportioned to the asset if, immediately before the relevant share issue, the whole of the issued share capital of the company were sold for a consideration equal to its market value at that time, or

(b) in relation to any other asset, its market value at the time of the relevant share issue.

(6) For the purposes of the definition of "relevant share issue" in subsection (5)—

"arrangements" includes any agreement, understanding, scheme, transaction or series of transactions (whether or not legally enforceable), and "tax advantage" means—

(a) relief or increased relief from tax,
(b) repayment or increased repayment of tax,
(c) the avoidance or reduction of a charge to tax or an assessment to tax, or
(d) the avoidance of a possible assessment to tax,

and for the purposes of this definition "tax" means capital gains tax, corporation tax or income tax.

(7) In this Chapter—

(a) references to "the notional disposal" are references to the disposal mentioned in subsection (4)(a),
(b) references to "the notional gain" are references to the chargeable gain mentioned in subsection (3)(b), and
(c) references to shares in or securities of a company include references to interests in such shares or securities.

169SD Supplementary election to defer gains until subsequent disposal

(1) An individual who makes an election under section 169SC may also elect that, for the purposes of this Act—

(a) no chargeable gain or allowable loss is to be treated as accruing to the individual on the notional disposal, but
(b) a chargeable gain calculated in accordance with this section is to be treated as accruing to the individual on any subsequent disposal by the individual of one or more assets consisting of shares in or securities of the company (in addition to any gain or loss that actually accrues on that disposal).

(2) The chargeable gain treated as accruing to the individual on a subsequent disposal is the amount resulting from the following steps—

Step 1

Attribute the notional gain to each of the classes of shares in or securities of the company which are the subject of the notional disposal.

The attribution must be made, in relation to each class, by reference to the proportion that—

(a) the relevant gains (see section 169N(5)) accruing on the notional disposal in respect of shares or securities within each class bears to
(b) the total amount of relevant gains accruing on the notional disposal.

Step 2

Apportion the amount attributed to each class under Step 1 to the shares or securities of that class which are the subject of the subsequent disposal.

The apportionment must be by reference to the proportion that—

(a) the nominal value of the shares or securities of that class which are the subject of the subsequent disposal bears to
(b) the nominal value of shares or securities of that class which are the subject of the notional disposal.

Step 3

The amount resulting from these steps is—

(a) the total of the amounts apportioned to shares or securities under Step 2, but
(b) excluding, in relation to each class of shares or securities, so much of those amounts as would, together with any chargeable gains treated by this section as accruing on previous disposals of shares or securities of that class, exceed the amount attributed to that class under Step 1.

(3) If the subsequent disposal is a disposal by virtue of section 122, the nominal value of shares of a particular class which are the subject of that disposal is to be treated for the purposes of Step 2 of subsection (2) as being equal to the nominal value of shares of that class as are the subject of the notional disposal.

169SE Application of section 169SD where section 116 applies

(1) This section has effect in any case where a transaction occurs to which section 116 (reorganisations, conversions and reconstructions) applies.

(2) If sections 116(10)(b) and 169SD(1)(b) have effect in relation to a subsequent disposal of the new asset—

(a) there must be calculated the chargeable gain that would have been treated by section 169SD(1)(b) as accruing to the individual if, at the time of the relevant transaction, the old asset had been disposed of immediately before that transaction,

(b) the whole or a corresponding part of the chargeable gain mentioned in paragraph (a) is to be treated as accruing on the subsequent disposal of the whole or part of the new asset (in addition to any gain or loss that actually accrues on that disposal and any chargeable gain treated by section 116(10)(b) as accruing on that disposal), and

(c) on that subsequent disposal, section 115 (exemptions for gilt-edged securities and qualifying corporate bonds) has effect only in relation to any gain that actually accrues and not in relation to any gain which is treated as accruing by virtue of paragraph (b).

(3) In subsection (2) "the new asset", "the old asset" and "the relevant transaction" have the same meanings as in section 116.

169SF Application of section 169SD where sections 127 to 130 apply

(1) This section has effect in any case where a transaction occurs to which sections 127 to 130 (treatment of share capital following a reorganisation) apply by virtue of any provision of Chapter 2 of Part 4.

(2) If a gain is treated by section 169SD(1)(b) as accruing on a subsequent disposal of the new holding and it is necessary to apportion the gain between shares or securities forming part of that new holding, the apportionment must be made in the same proportions as those in which the costs of acquisition of the original shares fall to be apportioned under the provisions of that Chapter.

(3) If subsection (3) of section 128 (consideration given or received by holder) has effect in relation to an individual, the individual is treated for the purposes of section 169SD as making the disposal of the interest in the original shares mentioned in that subsection.

(4) In this section "the new holding" and "the original shares" have the same meanings as in sections 127 to 130 (see section 126).

169SG Elections under sections 169SC and 169SD

(1) An election under section 169SC or 169SD is irrevocable.

(2) An election under section 169SC must be made on or before the first anniversary of the 31 January following the tax year in which the notional disposal is made ("the relevant tax year").

(3) An election under section 169SD may not be made more than 4 years after the end of the relevant tax year.

(4) If—

(a) an individual makes an election under both sections 169SC and 169SD, and

(b) a tax return under the Management Act would not otherwise be required for the relevant tax year,

the individual may make the elections by giving notice on or before the first anniversary of the 31 January following the relevant tax year.

169SH Claims for relief in respect of subsequent disposals

(1) Where, as a result of an election under section 169SD, a chargeable gain is to be treated as accruing on a subsequent disposal, the following rules have effect.

(2) The individual making the subsequent disposal must make a claim for entrepreneurs' relief on or before the first anniversary of the 31 January following the first tax year in which, as a result of the election, the chargeable gain is to be treated as accruing.

(3) The chargeable gain is to be treated for the purposes of section 169N as the amount resulting from a calculation under subsection (1) of that carried out when that chargeable gain accrues and because of the claim mentioned in subsection (2).

(4) If the chargeable gain is a part only of the notional gain, each chargeable gain that subsequently accrues is to be treated for the purposes of section 169N as the amount resulting from a calculation under subsection (1) of that section carried out when that chargeable gain arises and because of the claim mentioned in subsection (2).

(5) In relation to the claim for entrepreneurs' relief in respect of the chargeable gain, the company is to be treated for the purposes of condition A in section 169I(6) as if it were, throughout the period of 2 years ending with the date of the subsequent disposal, the individual's personal company."

Commencement

4 (1) Subject as follows, the amendments made by paragraph 1 of this Schedule have effect in relation to disposals on or after 6 April 2019.

(2) The amendments made by paragraph 1(2)(b), (3)(b) and (4) do not have effect in relation to a disposal where the time at which the business ceases to be carried on is before 29 October 2018.

(3) The amendments made by paragraph 1(2)(c), (3)(a) and (6)(b) do not have effect in relation to a disposal where the date on which the company—

(a) ceases to be a trading company without continuing to be or becoming a member of a trading group, or

(b) ceases to be a member of a trading group without continuing to be a trading company,

is before 29 October 2018.

(4) The amendments made by paragraph 2 of this Schedule have effect in relation to disposals on or after 29 October 2018 but, in the case of a disposal made before 21 December 2018, section 169LA(1ZA)(a) of TCGA 1992 has effect as if the reference to section 169S(3)(c)(ii) of that Act were omitted.

(5) The amendment made by paragraph 3 of this Schedule has effect in relation to relevant share issues (within the meaning given by section 169SC(5) of TCGA 1992) which take place on or after 6 April 2019.

COMMENTARY ON SCHEDULE 16

Schedule 16 makes three important changes to entrepreneurs' relief. Paragraph 1 extends the qualifying period during which the conditions for relief must be satisfied from one to two years. Paragraph 2 tightens the definition of a personal company to ensure that only shares which give an economic entitlement to 5% of more of the value of a company qualify for relief. Paragraph 3 allows individuals to preserve at least an element of relief if they cease to qualify before certain types of disposals.

Paragraph 1: Periods throughout which conditions for relief must be met

Sub-paragraph (1) introduces amendments to TCGA 1992, Pt 5, Ch 3.

Sub-paragraph (2)(a), (b), (c) replace all references to one year in the rules for material disposals of businesses assets with a reference to two years.

Sub-paragraph (2)(d) introduces two new subsections designed to ensure that entrepreneurs' relief is maintained following certain business transfers. New TCGA 1992, s 169I(7ZA) applies where before the disposal of shares there was an issue of shares to that individual following a relevant business transfer and the subsequent disposal was of, or included, shares acquired in that relevant business transfer. Where this test is met the qualifying period can include periods before the transfer during which the individual owned the business. New TCGA 1992, s 169I(7ZB) says that shares are acquired after a qualifying business transfer if they were issued wholly or partly in exchange for the transfer of a business as a going concern together with all of the assets (or all of the assets excluding cash).

The effect of this change is that it will now be possible to 'look through' the incorporation of a business when determining the qualifying period for entrepreneurs relief. Previously there was no ability to look back, with the result that if a business was sold within 12 months of an incorporation no relief was possible. With the extension of the qualifying period to 24 months this could have created significant problems in a number of cases and hence look through will be possible.

Sub-paragraphs (3) to (6) are all minor drafting amendments to ensure that all references in the entrepreneurs' relief legislation to one year are amended to two years.

Paragraph 2: Additional requirements relating to the beneficial ownership of companies

Paragraph 2 tightens up the definition of a personal company for the purpose of entrepreneurs' relief. The existing test simply requires a person to have 5% of the ordinary share capital and 5% of the voting rights in a company. There is no test of economic entitlement. In a surprise announcement in Budget 2018 the Chancellor introduced two further tests, based on entitlement to profits and entitlement to assets in a winding up. The purpose of the change was explained in the Budget note as follows:

> 'this measure ensures that the claimant has a true material stake in business in order to claim entrepreneurs' relief. Having such an interest is characteristic of true entrepreneurial activity (as distinct from simple investment or employment), so the measure ensures that allowable claims are limited to those which are within the spirit of the relief. This is part of the government's policy of supporting enterprise.'

There was broad support for the principle behind this change, because it was accepted that it had been too easy to create share structures which met the strict requirement of the test, but which did not actually give shareholders any meaningful stake in the business. However concerns were expressed that the drafting of the proposed new clauses was too broad and would deny relief in a number of situations – particularly where 'alphabet' share arrangements had been put in place which involved individuals receiving their own class of shares on which differential amounts of dividends could be paid – where there was no policy reason to deny it. The Government responded by tabling an amendment at third reading stage to introduce a simpler, alternative, test based on an individual's share of the actual proceeds of sale. This was widely seen as meeting the concerns raised by commentators while at the same time preserving the policy of restricting relief to cases of genuine economic ownership.

Paragraph 2(1) introduces amendments to TCGA 2992, Pt 5, Ch 3. Because the amendments are set out in the same order as the legislation which they amend they are difficult to follow if read sequentially. The key change is in 2(4), which sets out the new definition of a personal company. Readers are recommended to look at this subsection first and then look at the other subsections.

Paragraph 2(2) applies the revised definition of personal company to cases where there is a disposal associated with a relevant material disposal (eg a disposal of an asset held personally but used by that individual's personal company). The new test is applied at the date of the disposal of shares.

Paragraph 2(3) makes similar alterations to the rules restricting relief on transfers of goodwill to a close company to make them consistent with the new definition of a personal company. A new TCGA 1992, s 169LA(1) is substituted for the existing subsection. This new subsection now makes reference to the revised definition of a personal company. A transfer of goodwill is within the section if it is made to a personal company or any member of a group of which the personal company is a member.

New TCGA 1992, s 169LA(1ZA) states that the restriction applies if the company to which the goodwill is transferred is a personal company under any of the tests in the revised definition. It also specifies the individual making the transfer is taken to have the rights and interests of any relevant connected person (ie a company connected with that individual or trustees connected with him or her).

New TCGA 1992, s 169LA(1ZB) contains a number of further definitions, whose effect is to ensure that the revised definition of personal company is effective in making the legislation work as intended. TCGA 1992, s 169LA(1ZB)(a) states that the words 'by virtue of that holding' in s 169S(3) are to be ignored. This is to ensure that it is not possible to split voting rights from ownership of capital. Without that it might be possible to deliberately fall outside the definition and thus enable entrepreneurs' relief to be claimed on a goodwill transfer. TCGA 1992, s 169LA(1ZB)(b) sets the date on which the test is to be carried out to be the time immediately after the disposal of goodwill. TCGA 1992, s 169LA(1ZB)(c) states that the two conditions in s 169(3)(c)(i) – ie rights to profits and right to a distribution in a winding up are to be treated for these purposes as separate conditions. Again, this is an anti-avoidance measure to ensure that people do not set up structures which deliberately fail the test (say by being entitled to profits in a winding up but not in a distribution) and thus to be able to claim the relief on a goodwill transfer.

Paragraph 2(3)(b) is a minor drafting amendment. Paragraph 2(4) is the substantive section, which introduces the new definition of a personal company.

New TCGA 1992, s 169S(3) replaces the existing definition of a personal company. Subsection (3)(a) and (b) retain the existing tests that an individual must hold at least 5% of the ordinary share capital or the company and by virtue of that holding is able to exercise at least 5% of the voting rights.

New TCGA 1992, s 169S(3)(c) adds the new tests. These are in addition to the existing tests, which still apply, but one or both of the new tests must also be met. The test in s 169S(3)(c)(i) is that the individual must, by virtue of his holding of 5% of the ordinary share capital be entitled either to 5% of the profits available to distribution to equity holders or beneficially entitled to at least 5% of the assets on a winding up. The test in s 169S(3)(c)(ii) is that in the event of a disposal of the whole of the ordinary share capital of the company the individual would be beneficially entitled to at least 5% of the proceeds.

New TCGA 1992, s 169S(3A) sets out how the new (c)(ii) test is to be applied. In looking at whether the test applies during a particular period it is to be assumed that the whole of the ordinary share capital is sold at its market value at the end of that period. This is important because it does not require a valuation to be made at every point in that period. It is then assumed that the proceeds which will be received would be the amount that it would be reasonable to expect the person to be beneficially entitled. This is not an easy provision to understand, but its effect seems to be that if, for example, there are ratchet arrangements in place, the effect of those ratchets can be taken into account. Finally, the effect of any avoidance arrangements are to be ignored.

New TCGA 1992, s 169S(3B) provides that avoidance arrangements are arrangements whose main purpose is to secure that any provision of the entrepreneurs' relief legislation does or does not apply. The reference to the legislation **not** applying may seem odd, but parts of the legislation are anti-avoidance measures (ie the restriction on relief on goodwill transfers) and so arrangements to fall outside those anti-avoidance provisions will also be caught. Arrangements takes its usual wide definition.

New TCGA 1992, s 169S(3C) states that where shares are held jointly an individual is treated as the sole holder of a proportionate part of those jointly held shares for the purposes of the voting rights and beneficial ownership test. This is presumably to stop arrangements under which a large number of individuals between them have a joint holding of 5% of the ordinary share capital and each claim to be able to exercise 5% of the voting rights by virtue of their interest in that holding.

New TCGA 1992, s 169S(3D) – in working out whether or not a person has an appropriate entitlement to distributions or profits in a winding up a modified version of the group relief rules in CTA 2010, Pt 5, Ch 6 (which is where these tests originate) is to be used and references to company A (ie the owner of the shares for group relief purposes) are to be taken to be references to the individual.

New TCGA 1992, s 169S(3E) sets out the modifications required under (3D) above as follows:

(a) A person who carries on a business of banking is not treated as a loan creditor in respect of loan capital or debt lent to the company in the ordinary course of business. Without this rule many bank loans would mean that a company would have no assets in a winding up to distribute to shareholders and thus the test at (3)(c)(ii) would be failed.

(b) Certain specified sections of the group relief rules are not to be taken into account. These are sections mainly dealing with situations such as temporary rights or option arrangements.

(c) Any modifications as are necessary for the purpose of applying the group relief rules as if the individual were company A are to be made. This last is a catch all introduced as part of the late amendment to the Finance Bill referred to at the start of this commentary. It is there to reflect the fact that the unmodified group relief legislation did not really work in the very different context of entrepreneurs' relief. For example, the group relief legislation operates by reference to accounting periods, whereas these have no relevance to an individual's capital gains tax position. It would have been much more satisfactory to produce a specific set of rules to deal with the problem which the Government was trying to solve rather than shoehorn the group relief legislation into the very different context of entrepreneurs' relief. Unfortunately there was not sufficient legislative time to do this and therefore this catch all provision will allow any problems to be dealt with on an ad hoc basis. It is not a particularly satisfactory solution, but it is better than what was originally proposed i e simply to apply the group relief legislation without any modifications at all.

Paragraph 3: Relief where company ceases to be individual's personal company

The third change to entrepreneurs' relief is a relieving measure. Under the original rules the relief is an all or nothing. A person could have qualified for relief for many years but, perhaps through a new funding round, lost entitlement for the last 12 months of ownership and hence forfeited all the relief which was otherwise building up. The case of Mr and Mrs McQuillan (*HMRC v M and E McQuillan* [2017] UKUT 344) was widely reported and undoubtedly was a catalyst for change.

The broad effect of the new provision is that an individual can elect to be treated as making a disposal of shares immediately before a share issue which results in him/her loosing entitlement to relief. This protects relief on that element of the gain, although the gain accruing from that point on to the eventual sale will not be entitled to relief. The individual may also separately elect to defer payment of the tax until the shares are finally disposed of.

Paragraph 3 introduces a new Chapter 3A into TCGA 1992, Pt V. New TCGA 1992, s 169SB introduces the new Chapter.

New TCGA 1992, s 169SC: Election by individual where company ceases to be personal company

TCGA 1992, s 169SC(1) introduces the section and states that an individual may elect for the section to have effect if the conditions are met.

TCGA 1992, s 169SC(2) provides that the first condition is that the company ceases to be an individual's personal company as a result of a relevant share issue. It is important to note that it is only in these limited circumstances that the extension of relief will apply. If a company ceases to be a personal company for any other reason relief will be lost.

TCGA 1992, s 169SC(3) – the second condition is that had the individual made a disposal of all of the shares and securities in the company the disposal would have been a material disposal of business assets and if a claim had been made entrepreneurs' relief would have been available.

TCGA 1992, s 169SC(4) – where the above conditions apply the individual is to be treated as having made a disposal of his or her shares immediately before the relevant share issue of the shares and securities and having then immediately reacquired them. The deemed disposal and reacquisition is treated as taking place at what is described as the relevant value.

TCGA 1992, s 169SC(5) is a definition section. 'Material disposal of business assets' and 'personal company' take their ordinary entrepreneurs' relief definition. A relevant share issue is an issue of shares wholly for consideration in cash and where the subscription is for genuine commercial reasons and not to secure a tax advantage for any person. The relevant value definition is important. For shares the value is taken to be the pro-rata value of the entire issued share capital on a market value sale. So, if the value of the company at the date of the share issue were £1m and the individual concerned held 10% he would be deemed to have disposed of those shares for £100,000 and not the much lower amount which would result from the application of the normal minority basis of valuation. Securities are valued at their market value at the date of the relevant share issue.

TCGA 1992, s 169SC(6) defines arrangements and tax advantage. A typically wide definition is adopted. TCGA 1992, s 169SC(7) is a minor drafting amendment.

New TCGA 1992, s 169SD: Supplementary election to defer gain until subsequent disposal

TCGA 1992, s 169SD(1) allows for a person who has made an election under s 169SC above to make a further election to treat the deemed disposal and acquisition under that section as **not** giving rise to a chargeable gain and instead to calculate the gain in accordance with this section.

TCGA 1992, s 169SD(2) sets out the mechanism for calculating the gain if an election under s 169SD has been made. There are three steps:

Step 1 – Apportion the notional gain on a proportional basis between all classes of shared and securities which are treated as being disposed of under s 169SC. (In most cases where the shares being disposed of are all of a single class this step will not be necessary).

Step 2 – Apportion the amounts determined above to the shares which are subsequently disposed of on a pro rata basis by reference to the nominal value of the shares.

Step 3 – The total gain which is treated as accruing is the total of all amounts under step 2 but it is capped (including any previous disposals) at the total amount of deferred gain attributed to that class of shares and securities.

This provision is not that easy to understand. It seems to be designed to ensure that values cannot be artificially shifted between classes of share to enhance the amount of the deferred gain which would qualify for relief. The explanatory notes to the Finance Bill give the following example:

> 'X made an election under section 169SC to defer her deemed gain of £100,000. £25,000 of that gain related to her 50 class A shares and £75,000 of it related to her 50 class B shares. Step 1 allocates the gain between those shares accordingly.
>
> Step 2 is to apportion the amounts identified under step 1 by reference to the nominal value of the shares or securities which were the subject of the deemed disposal that have actually been disposed of. Example: if X sold 25 of her 50 £1 class A shares, the calculation would be £25,000 (the amount of deemed gain attributed to 50 class A shares above) × (£25/£50) = £12,500

TCGA 1992, s 169SD(3) provides that if the subsequent disposal of shares is a capital distribution under s 122 the nominal value of shares of a particular class under that disposal is treated for the purpose of step 2 as being equal to the nominal value of share of that class which are the subject of the capital distribution. In other words the step 2 amount is the total number of shares and there is no apportionment.

TCGA 1992, s 169SE: Application of s 169SD where s 116 has effect

TCGA 1992, s 169SE(1) introduces the special rules which apply where there is a reorganisation to which s 116 (exchanges involving qualifying corporate bonds) applies.

TCGA 1992, s 169SE(2) provides that where s 116(10)(b) applies, i e the gain on the original disposal is frozen, and election is made under s 169SD(1)(b) to defer the gain until a subsequent disposal, a modified version of the calculation is made. This is done as follows:

(a) The gain which would have been treated as accruing immediately before the share issue is calculated.

(b) The gain (or corresponding part of it) calculated above, is treated as accruing on the disposal (in whole or part) of the new asset. This is in addition to any gain which actually accrues on the disposal and of any chargeable gain which is treated as accruing under s 116(10)(b).

(c) On the subsequent disposal the exemption under s 115 for gilt edged securities and qualifying corporate bonds only applies to any gain which actually accrues and not to any gain treated as accruing under paragraph (b).

The effect of this is to preserve the existing treatment of such exchanges. A frozen gain is still calculated on the exchange for qualifying corporate bonds, but only becomes chargeable when the QCB is actually disposed of. Any gain made on the QCB from the date of the exchange will still be exempt under the normal rules for QCBs.

TCGA 1992, s 169SE(3) is a minor drafting amendment.

TCGA 1992, s 169SF: Application of s 169SD where ss 127 to 130 apply

TCGA 1992, s 169SF(1) states that the section applies where there is a reorganisation (eg a share-for-share exchange) under ss 127 to 130.

TCGA 1992, s 169SF(2) provides that where there is an election to defer a gain under s 169SD(1)(b) and it is necessary to apportion that gain between shares or securities forming part of the new holding (ie the shares which were issued on the original disposal) the apportionment must be made on the same basis that the apportionment of acquisition costs of the original shares is made under the normal reorganisation provisions, ie different valuation methods cannot be used for the different apportionments.

TCGA 1992, s 169SF(3) – if on an exchange an individual receives consideration other than the new shares the individual is treated for the purposes of s 169SD as making a disposal of the original shares. This means that the gain which is treated as arising on the receipt of that consideration is included in the computation of the deferred entrepreneurs' relief gain.

TCGA 1992, s 169SF(4) is a minor definitional section.

TCGA 1992, s 169SG: Elections under ss 169SC and 169SD

TCGA 1992, s 169SG(1) states that an election under either of these two sections is irrevocable.

TCGA 1992, s 169SG(2) provides that an election under s 169SC (election to treat a gain as arising) must be made on or before 31 January in the year following the year in which the notional disposal is made.

TCGA 1992, s 169SG(3) – the time limit for an election under s 169SD is no later than four years after the end of the year in which the notional disposal is made.

TCGA 1992, s 169SG(4) – where a person makes an election under both sections and is not otherwise required to submit a tax return for the year of disposal, he/she can make the election by giving notice in writing to HMRC by 31 January in the year following the year of disposal. If a person only makes an election under s 169SC the effect is that a gain actually arises in the year of disposal and consequently a liability to tax will arise. If the individual is not already within self-assessment there will be a requirement to notify chargeability. It is only if there is an election under s 169SD that no gain will actually arise, hence the need for a mechanism to notify HMRC that the election has been made.

TCGA 1992, s 169SH: Claims for relief in respect of subsequently disposals

TCGA 1992, s 169SH(1) sets out the mechanism of what happens when a person has made an election under s 169SD and there is a subsequent disposal of the shares.

Under TCGA 1992, s 169SH(2) the individual must make a claim for entrepreneurs' relief by 31 January in the year following the year in which the chargeable gain is treated as accruing. (In other words the individual does not need to make a claim for entrepreneurs' relief by reference to the date on which the share issue resulted in the loss of entrepreneurs' relief).

The wording of TCGA 1992, s 169SH(3) is confusing (there seems to be a word missing between 'that' and 'carried' and the words following 'because' appear not to have any relevance). The effect is however tolerably clear. Although the gain is not taxable until the year of the ultimate disposal of the shares, the rates and limits for entrepreneurs' relief applying at the date of the dilution of the holding are to be applied rather than the rates at the date of the ultimate disposal.

TCGA 1992, s 169SH(4) allows further claims to entrepreneurs' relief if there is a part disposal so that subsequent part disposals also benefit from the same treatment.

TCGA 1992, s 169SH(5) deems the company to be the individual's personal company for the two years period ending on the date of the subsequent disposal. This does not mean that entrepreneurs' relief will be available on the element of the gain post dilution, which is calculated in the normal way. It is simply a deeming provision to enable the election to procure to operate as intended.

Paragraph 4: Commencement

The commencement provisions are quite complex because the various strands of the reforms were announced at different times. The basic rule is that provisions of Sch 16 all come into force in relation to disposals on or after 6 April 2019.

The amendments made by Sch 16, para 1(2)(b), (3)(b) and (4) do not apply where the business ceases to be carried on before 29 October 2018. These are provisions dealing with associated disposals within three years of the date of cessation of a business. If the extension of the personal company test to two years applied in relation to these provisions there could be an element of retrospection.

Similarly a further set of amendments as specified do not apply where a company ceases to be a trading company member of a trading group before 29 October 2018. This is again to avoid possible retrospection.

The amendments made by Sch 16, para 2 (definition of a personal company) apply to disposal on or after 29 October 2018. However for disposals made before 21 December TCGA 1992, s 169LA(1ZA)(a) has effect as if the reference to s 169S(3)(c)(ii) were omitted. That is the section which was added at 3rd reading stage to allow for the alternative test of entitlement to proceeds of sale. There is thus a small window between 29 October and 21 December 2018 where relief may not be available which would have been available before or after those dates. For an example of how this might work in practice see 'Happy outcome' by Pete Miller, *Taxation Magazine,* 22 January 2019.

The amendments made by Sch 16, para 3 (dilution of shareholdings) have effect in relation to share issues which take place on or after 6 April 2019.

SCHEDULE 17

VAT TREATMENT OF VOUCHERS

Section 52

1 VATA 1994 is amended as follows.

2 In section 51B—

(a) in the heading, at the end insert "issued before 1 January 2019";
(b) the existing text becomes subsection (1);
(c) after that subsection insert—

"(2) Schedule 10A does not have effect with respect to a face value voucher (within the meaning of that Schedule) issued on or after 1 January 2019."

3 After section 51B insert—

"51C Vouchers issued on or after 1 January 2019

(1) Schedule 10B makes provision about the VAT treatment of vouchers.

(2) Schedule 10B has effect with respect to a voucher (within the meaning of that Schedule) issued on or after 1 January 2019.

51D Postage stamps issued on or after 1 January 2019

(1) The issue of a postage stamp, and any subsequent transfer of it, is a supply of services for the purposes of this Act.

(2) The consideration for the issue or subsequent transfer of a postage stamp is to be disregarded for the purposes of this Act, except to the extent (if any) that it exceeds the face value of the stamp.

(3) The "face value" of the stamp is the amount stated on or recorded in the stamp or the terms and conditions governing its use.

(4) This section has effect with respect to postage stamps issued on or after 1 January 2019."

4 In the heading to Schedule 10A, at the end insert "issued before 1 January 2019".

5 After Schedule 10A insert—

"SCHEDULE 10B

VAT TREATMENT OF VOUCHERS ISSUED ON OR AFTER 1 JANUARY 2019

Section 51C

Meaning of "voucher"

1 (1) In this Schedule "voucher" means an instrument (in physical or electronic form) in relation to which the following conditions are met.

(2) The first condition is that one or more persons are under an obligation to accept the instrument as consideration for the provision of goods or services.

(3) The second condition is that either or both of—

(a) the goods and services for the provision of which the instrument may be accepted as consideration, and
(b) the persons who are under the obligation to accept the instrument as consideration for the provision of goods or services,

are limited and are stated on or recorded in the instrument or the terms and conditions governing the use of the instrument.

(4) The third condition is that the instrument is transferable by gift (whether or not it is transferable for consideration).

(5) The following are not vouchers—

(a) an instrument entitling a person to a reduction in the consideration for the provision of goods or services;
(b) an instrument functioning as a ticket, for example for travel or for admission to a venue or event;
(c) postage stamps.

Meaning of related expressions

2 (1) This paragraph gives the meaning of other expressions used in this Schedule.

(2) "Relevant goods or services", in relation to a voucher, are any goods or services for the provision of which the voucher may be accepted as consideration.

(3) References in this Schedule to the transfer of a voucher do not include the voucher being offered and accepted as consideration for the provision of relevant goods or services.

(4) References in this Schedule to a voucher being offered or accepted as consideration for the provision of relevant goods or services include references to the voucher being offered or accepted as part consideration for the provision of relevant goods or services.

VAT treatment of vouchers: general rule

3 (1) The issue, and any subsequent transfer, of a voucher is to be treated for the purposes of this Act as a supply of relevant goods or services.

(2) References in this Schedule to the "paragraph 3 supply", in relation to the issue or transfer of a voucher, are to the supply of relevant goods or services treated by this paragraph as having been made on the issue or transfer of the voucher.

Single purpose vouchers: special rules

4 (1) A voucher is a single purpose voucher if, at the time it is issued, the following are known—

(a) the place of supply of the relevant goods or services, and
(b) that any supply of relevant goods or services falls into a single supply category (and what that supply category is).

(2) The supply categories are—

(a) supplies chargeable at the rate in force under section 2(1) (standard rate),
(b) supplies chargeable at the rate in force under section 29A (reduced rate),
(c) zero-rated supplies, and
(d) exempt supplies and other supplies that are not taxable supplies.

(3) For the purposes of this paragraph, assume that the supply of relevant goods or services is the provision of relevant goods or services for which the voucher may be accepted as consideration (rather than the supply of relevant goods or services treated as made on the issue or transfer of the voucher).

5 (1) This paragraph applies where a single purpose voucher is accepted as consideration for the provision of relevant goods or services.

(2) The provision of the relevant goods or services is not a supply of goods or services for the purposes of this Act.

(3) But where the person who provides the relevant goods or services (the "provider") is not the person who issued the voucher (the "issuer"), for the purposes of this Act the provider is to be treated as having made a supply of those goods or services to the issuer.

Multi-purpose vouchers: special rules

6 A voucher is a multi-purpose voucher if it is not a single purpose voucher.

7 (1) Any consideration for the issue or subsequent transfer of a multi-purpose voucher is to be disregarded for the purposes of this Act.

(2) The paragraph 3 supply made on the issue or subsequent transfer of a multi-purpose voucher is to be treated as not being a supply within section 26(2).

8 (1) Where a multi-purpose voucher is accepted as consideration for the provision of relevant goods or services, for the purposes of this Act—

(a) the provision of the relevant goods or services is to be treated as a supply, and
(b) the value of the supply treated as having been made by paragraph (a) is determined as follows.

(2) If the consideration for the most recent transfer of the voucher for consideration is known to the supplier, the value of the supply is such amount as, with the addition of the VAT chargeable on the supply, is equal to that consideration.

(3) If the consideration for the most recent transfer of the voucher for consideration is not known to the supplier, the value of the supply is such amount as, with the addition of the VAT chargeable on the supply, is equal to the face value of the voucher.

(4) The "face value" of a voucher is the monetary value stated on or recorded in—

(a) the voucher, or
(b) the terms and conditions governing the use of the voucher.

Intermediaries

9 (1) This paragraph applies where—

(a) a voucher is issued or transferred by an agent who acts in their own name, and
(b) the paragraph 3 supply is a supply of services to which section 47(3) would apply (apart from this paragraph).

(2) Section 47(3) does not apply.

(3) The paragraph 3 supply is treated as both a supply to the agent and a supply by the agent.

10 Nothing in this Schedule affects the application of this Act to any services provided, by a person who issues or transfers a voucher, in addition to the issue or transfer of the voucher.

Composite transactions

11 (1) This paragraph applies where, as part of a composite transaction—

(a) goods or services are supplied to a person, and
(b) a voucher is issued or transferred to that person.

(2) If the total consideration for the transaction is not different, or not significantly different, from what it would be if the voucher were not issued or transferred, the paragraph 3 supply is to be treated as being made for no consideration."

6 In regulation 38ZA(2) of the Value Added Tax Regulations 1995 (SI 1995/2518), in the definition of "cash refund", after "Act" insert "or a voucher falling within Schedule 10B to the Act".

COMMENTARY ON SCHEDULE 17

Schedule 17 creates a new VATA 1994, Sch 10B which provides for the taxation of face-value vouchers issued on or after 1 January 2019, in alignment with EU Council Directive (EU) 2016/1065 which came into effect on the same day and amends Directive 2006/112/EC (the Principal VAT Directive).

The term 'face value voucher' does not include discount vouchers, tickets (for travel, admission to events, etc) or postage stamps.

Face value vouchers fall into two categories:

- A 'single purpose voucher', ie one where:
  - the place of supply of the underlying goods or services is known at the time of issue
  - the VAT liability of the underlying goods or services is known at the time of issue
  - the VAT liability of the underlying goods falls into a single category, ie they are wholly standard-rated, zero-rated, reduced rated or exempt
- A 'multi-purpose voucher', ie a voucher other than a single purpose voucher

The supply of a single purpose voucher is treated as if it were a supply of the underlying goods or services and accordingly in the case of a taxable supply, is subject to VAT at the appropriate rate, giving rise to an output tax liability in the hands of the supplier and (in the case of intermediate supplies) an entitlement to input tax recovery in the hands of the purchaser. Where the person redeeming the voucher for goods or services is not the issuer of the voucher, there is a deemed supply of those goods or services from the redeemer to the issuer.

The issue of a multi-purpose voucher is disregarded at the time of issue (and at any intermediate stage) since the liability of the underlying goods or services is not known at that time. VAT is accounted for on the redemption of the voucher, when the liability crystallises. The consideration in respect of which VAT is due is the price paid for the voucher at the immediately preceding stage if this is known to the redeemer; otherwise, the face value of the voucher.

SCHEDULE 18
VAT GROUPS: ELIGIBILITY

Section 53

PART 1
ELIGIBILITY OF INDIVIDUALS AND PARTNERSHIPS

1 (1) Section 43A of VATA 1994 (groups: eligibility) is amended as follows.

(2) In subsection (1), in the opening words—

(a) for "bodies corporate" substitute "UK bodies corporate";

(b) omit "each is established or has a fixed establishment in the United Kingdom and".

(3) Omit subsections (2) and (3).

(4) At the end insert—

"(4) An individual carrying on a business and one or more UK bodies corporate are eligible to be treated as members of a group if the individual—

(a) controls the UK body corporate or all of the UK bodies corporate, and

(b) is established, or has a fixed establishment, in the United Kingdom in relation to the business.

(5) Two or more relevant persons carrying on a business in partnership ("the partnership") and one or more UK bodies corporate are eligible to be treated as members of a group if the partnership—

(a) controls the UK body corporate or all of the UK bodies corporate, and

(b) is established, or has a fixed establishment, in the United Kingdom in relation to the business.

(6) In this section—

(a) "UK body corporate" means a body corporate which is established or has a fixed establishment in the United Kingdom;

(b) "relevant person" means an individual, a body corporate or a Scottish partnership.

(7) Section 43AZA contains provision for determining for the purposes of this section whether a body corporate, individual or partnership controls a UK body corporate."

2 In that Act, after section 43A insert—

"43AZA Section 43A: control test

(1) This section applies for the purposes of section 43A (and expressions used in this section have the same meaning as in that section).

(2) A body corporate ("X") controls a UK body corporate if—

(a) X is empowered by statute to control the UK body corporate's activities, or

(b) X is the UK body corporate's holding company.

(3) An individual ("Y") controls a UK body corporate if Y would, were Y a company, be the UK body corporate's holding company.

(4) Two or more relevant persons carrying on a business in partnership ("the partnership") control a UK body corporate if the partnership would, were it a company, be the UK body corporate's holding company.

(5) In this section "holding company" has the meaning given by section 1159 of, and Schedule 6 to, the Companies Act 2006."

PART 2
CONSEQUENTIAL AMENDMENTS

VATA 1994

3 VATA 1994 is amended as follows.

4 In section 18A (fiscal warehousing), in subsection (9), for "body corporate which" substitute "person who".

5 (1) Section 43 (groups of companies) is amended in accordance with this paragraph.

(2) In subsection (1), for "bodies corporate" substitute "persons".

(3) In subsection (1AA)—

(a) in paragraph (c)(ii), for "body which" substitute "person who";
(b) in the closing words, for "body" substitute "person".

6 In section 43AA (power to alter eligibility for grouping), in subsection (1), for "section 43A" substitute "sections 43A and 43AZA".

7 (1) Section 43B (groups: applications) is amended in accordance with this paragraph.

(2) In subsection (1), for "bodies corporate, which" substitute "persons, who".

(3) In subsection (2)—

(a) in the opening words, for "bodies corporate" substitute "persons";
(b) in paragraph (a), for "body corporate, which" substitute "person, who";
(c) in paragraph (b), for "body corporate" substitute "person";
(d) in paragraph (d), for "bodies corporate" substitute "persons";

(4) In subsection (3)—

(a) in the opening words, for "bodies corporate" substitute "persons";
(b) in paragraph (b), for "bodies" substitute "persons";

(5) In subsection (5)—

(a) in paragraph (a), for "bodies corporate" substitute "persons";
(b) in paragraph (b), for "body corporate" substitute "person".

8 (1) Section 43C (groups: termination of membership) is amended in accordance with this paragraph.

(2) In subsection (1), for "body corporate" substitute "person".

(3) In subsection (3)(a) and (b) and in the closing words, for "body" substitute "person".

(4) In subsection (4)(a) and (b), for "body" substitute "person".

9 (1) Section 43D (groups: duplication) is amended in accordance with this paragraph.

(2) In subsection (1), for "body corporate" substitute "person".

(3) In subsection (2), for "body which" substitute "person who".

(4) In subsection (3)—

(a) in paragraph (b), for "bodies" substitute "persons";
(b) in the closing words, for "body or bodies" substitute "person or persons".

(5) In subsection (4)(b), for "body" substitute "person".

(6) In subsection (5), for "body" substitute "person".

10 In section 44 (supplies to groups), in subsection (1)(a) and (b), for "body corporate" substitute "person".

11 In section 53 (tour operators), in subsection (2)(d), for "body corporate" substitute "person".

12 In section 97 (orders, rules and regulations), in subsection (4)(ca), for "bodies" substitute "persons".

13 (1) Schedule 9 (exemptions) is amended in accordance with this paragraph.

(2) In Group 14, in Note (13)—

(a) in the opening words, for "body corporate" substitute "person";
(b) in paragraph (a) for "body" substitute "person";
(c) in paragraph (b)—
  (i) for "body corporate, or of any other body corporate which", substitute "person, or of any other person who";
  (ii) for "body, at a time when that body" substitute "person, at a time when that person".
(d) in paragraph (c), for "body corporate" substitute "person".

(3) In that Group, in Note (14), for "body corporate's" substitute "person's".

14 (1) Schedule 9A (anti-avoidance provisions: groups) is amended in accordance with this paragraph.

(2) In paragraph 1(2), for "body corporate" substitute "person".

(3) In paragraph 2—

(a) in sub-paragraph (1)(a), for "body corporate" substitute "person";

(b) in sub-paragraph (2), for "body corporate's" substitute "person's".

(4) In paragraph 3—

(a) in sub-paragraph (1)(a) and (b), for "body corporate" substitute "person";

(b) in sub-paragraph (3), for "body corporate" (in both places) substitute "person";

(c) in sub-paragraph (5), for "body corporate which" substitute "person who".

(5) In paragraph 5—

(a) in sub-paragraph (1)(b)—

(i) for "body corporate which" substitute "person who";

(ii) for "that person" substitute "the person mentioned in paragraph (a)";

(b) in sub-paragraph (2)—

(i) for "body corporate ("the relevant body")" substitute "person ("the relevant person")";

(ii) for "that body or to any body corporate which" substitute "that person or to any person who";

(iii) for "the relevant body" substitute "the relevant person".

(6) In paragraph 6—

(a) in sub-paragraph (7)(b), for "body corporate that" substitute "person who";

(b) in sub-paragraph (11)(b)—

(i) for "body corporate which" substitute "person who";

(ii) for "that person" substitute "the person mentioned in paragraph (a)";

(c) in sub-paragraph (11)(c), for "body corporate which" substitute "person who".

15 (1) Schedule 10 (buildings and land) is amended in accordance with this paragraph.

(2) In paragraph 3—

(a) in sub-paragraph (1), for "body corporate" substitute "person";

(b) in sub-paragraph (2)—

(i) in the opening words (in both places) and paragraph (c), for "body corporate" substitute "person";

(ii) in paragraph (c), for "that body" substitute "that person";

(c) in sub-paragraph (3), for "body corporate" substitute "person ("P")";

(d) in sub-paragraph (4)—

(i) in the opening words, for "The body corporate" substitute "P";

(ii) in paragraphs (a), (aa), (b) and (c), for "the body corporate" substitute "P";

(e) in sub-paragraph (5)—

(i) in the opening words, for "The body corporate" substitute "P" and for "the body corporate" substitute "P";

(ii) in the closing words, for "the body corporate" substitute "P".

(3) In paragraph 4—

(a) in sub-paragraph (1), for "body corporate which" substitute "person ("P") who";

(b) in sub-paragraph (2), for "the body corporate, it" substitute "P, P";

(c) in sub-paragraph (3)(b), for "the body corporate" substitute "P";

(d) in sub-paragraph (3)(c)—

(i) for "the body corporate" substitute "P";

(ii) for "it" substitute "P";

(e) in sub-paragraph (4)(b)—

(i) for "the body corporate" substitute "P";

(ii) for "it" substitute "P";

(f) in sub-paragraph (5), in the opening words—

(i) for "the body corporate" substitute "P";

(ii) for "it" substitute "P";

(g) in sub-paragraph (6)(a)—

(i) for "the body corporate" substitute "P";

(ii) for "its" substitute "P's";

(h) in sub-paragraph (6)(b), for "the body corporate" substitute "P";

(i) in sub-paragraph (7), for "the body corporate" substitute "P".

(4) In paragraph 21—

(a) in sub-paragraph (1)(b)—

(i) for "body corporate" substitute "person";

(ii) for "the body" substitute "the person";

(b) in sub-paragraph (3)(a), for "body corporate which" substitute "person who";

(c) in sub-paragraph (9)(b), for "body corporate which" substitute "person who";

(d) in sub-paragraph (11)(b), for "body corporate which" substitute "person who";

(e) in sub-paragraph (12), in the definition of "relevant group member"—

(i) after "any person" insert "("P")";

(ii) for "body corporate which" substitute "person who";

(iii) for "that person" substitute "P".

(5) In paragraph 35(3), for "body corporate" substitute "person".

COMMENTARY ON SCHEDULE 18

Schedule 18 extends, with effect from a date to be appointed by regulations, the scope of group VAT registration to persons other than corporate bodies. This is as a result of the CJEU decision in *Larentia + Minerva* (Case C108/14) which held that the current limitation was only justified for the purpose of the prevention of evasion or avoidance.

VATA 1994, s 43A is amended to provide that:

- an individual, and one or more 'UK bodies corporate', or
- two or more 'relevant persons' (ie individuals, bodies corporate or Scottish partnerships) carrying on a business in partnership, and one or more UK bodies corporate

may form a VAT group. This is subject to the requirement that the individual or partnership:

- controls the UK body corporate or all of the UK bodies corporate
- is established or has a business establishment in the United Kingdom

The term 'UK bodies corporate' replaces the former 'bodies corporate', but the requirement that the body must be established in the UK or have a fixed establishment in the UK remains.

A new section 43AZA to VATA 1994 replaces the 'control' conditions in s 43A and extends them so that an individual/partnership is deemed to control a corporate body (A) if, were the individual/partnership a corporate body, it would be A's holding company as defined in CA 2006, s 1159 and Sch 6.

Consequential amendments are made to other parts of VATA 1994.

SCHEDULE 19
GAMING DUTY

Section 63

Accounting periods

1 (1) Section 11 of FA 1997 (rate of gaming duty) is amended as follows.

(2) In subsection (2), for "subsection (3)" substitute "subsections (3), (4A) and (4B)".

(3) After subsection (4) insert—

"(4A) Where the gaming duty provisions of this Act have effect in relation to any premises as if accounting periods were periods longer or shorter than six months ("alternative accounting periods") as a result of—

(a) a direction under paragraph 9(1A) of Schedule 1, or
(b) a direction or agreement under paragraph 9(1C) of Schedule 1,

then for the purposes of determining the amount of gaming duty which is to be charged on those premises for that period, the Table in subsection (2) is modified in accordance with subsection (4B).

(4B) Each amount specified in column 1 of the Table is multiplied by—

A / B

where—

A is the number of days in the alternative accounting period directed or agreed, and

B is the number of days in the period that would have been the accounting period in the absence of any direction or agreement (or where the alternative accounting period spans more than one such period, the first of those periods)."

2 (1) Paragraph 9 of Schedule 1 to FA 1997 (accounting periods) is amended as follows.

(2) For sub-paragraph (1) substitute—

"(1) Where the Commissioners and every relevant person so agree, the gaming duty provisions of this Act shall have effect in relation to any premises as if accounting periods for the purposes of those provisions were the periods specified in the agreement, which may be—

(a) periods of six months (beginning on any date);
(b) periods (beginning on any date) which are longer or shorter than six months, but which must be the approximate equivalent of periods of six months in weeks.

(1A) If the Commissioners have reason to believe that the liability in relation to any premises may not be discharged as it falls due from time to time, the Commissioners may direct that periods shorter than six months are to be treated as accounting periods for the purposes of the gaming duty provisions of this Act.

(1B) The Commissioners may direct in relation to any premises that periods beginning on dates other than 1st April and 1st October are to be treated as accounting periods for the purposes of the gaming duty provisions of this Act.

(1C) The Commissioners may by direction or by agreement with every relevant person make transitional arrangements in relation to any premises for periods (whether of six months or otherwise) to be treated as accounting periods for the purposes of the gaming duty provisions of this Act where—

(a) those premises cease to be specified in an entry on the gaming register for any person, or
(b) an agreement under sub-paragraph (1) or a direction under sub-paragraph (1A) or (1B) begins or ceases to have effect.

(1D) The Commissioners must not enter into an agreement under sub-paragraph (1) or give a direction under sub-paragraph (1B) unless they are satisfied that any transitional arrangements which are appropriate for the protection of the revenue have been agreed or directed.

(1E) Any direction under this paragraph continues to have effect until it is withdrawn by the Commissioners (unless otherwise specified in the direction).

(1F) Withdrawal of a direction under this paragraph in relation to any premises does not prevent the giving of further directions in relation to those premises.".

(3) In sub-paragraph (2), for "sub-paragraph (1) above" substitute "this paragraph".

(4) Omit sub-paragraphs (3) and (4).

(5) For sub-paragraph (5) substitute—

"(5) The decisions mentioned in sub-paragraph (6) are to be treated as if they were listed in subsection (2) of section 13A of FA 1994 (customs and excise reviews and appeals: meaning of "relevant decision") and accordingly are to be treated—

(a) as if they were relevant decisions for the purposes mentioned in subsection (1) of that section, and

(b) as if they were ancillary matters for the purposes of section 16 FA 1994 (appeals to a tribunal).

(6) The decisions are—

(a) a decision of the Commissioners to refuse a request for an agreement under sub-paragraph (1) or (1C), or to refuse a request for such an agreement on particular terms,

(b) a decision of the Commissioners to give a direction under sub-paragraph (1A), (1B) or (1C), or to give such a direction in particular terms, or

(c) a decision of the Commissioners not to give a direction under sub-paragraph (1A), (1B) or (1C)."

3 In paragraph 11(2) of Schedule 1 to FA 1997 (regulations), after "of this Act" insert "or paragraph 9 of this Schedule".

Carrying forward of losses

4 In section 11 of FA 1997, for subsection (10) substitute—

"(10) In subsection (8) above the banker's profits from any gaming are—

(a) the value, in money or money's worth, of the stakes staked with the banker in any such gaming, less

(b) the value of the prizes provided by the banker to those taking part in such gaming otherwise than on behalf of a provider of the premises.

(10ZA) Where the gross gaming yield from any premises in an accounting period is a negative amount ("amount X")—

(a) the gross gaming yield for those premises in that accounting period is treated as nil, and

(b) amount X may be carried forward in reduction of the gross gaming yield for those premises for one or more later accounting periods."

Removal of obligation to make payments on account

5 In section 12 of FA 1997 (liability to pay gaming duty) omit subsections (4) and (6).

6 (1) The Gaming Duty Regulations 1997 (SI 1997/2196) are amended as follows.

(2) In regulation 2 (interpretation) omit the definition of "quarter".

(3) Omit regulations 3 to 6 (Part II: payments on account) and the heading before them.

Commencement

7 The amendments made by this Schedule come into force on 1 October 2019.

8 (1) Where there is an agreement under paragraph 9(1) of Schedule 1 to FA 1997 and as a result the period to be treated as the accounting period for any premises is a period beginning on or before 30 September 2019 and ending after 30 September 2019 (a "paragraph 9(1) accounting period"), sub-paragraph (2) applies.

(2) The period to be treated as the accounting period for those premises is instead a period (a "transitional accounting period") beginning on the date specified in the agreement and ending on 30 September 2019.

(3) For the purposes of determining the amount of gaming duty which is to be charged on those premises for the transitional accounting period, the Table in section 11(2) of FA 1997 is modified in accordance with sub-paragraph (4).

(4) Each amount specified in column 1 of the Table is multiplied by—

A / B

where—

A is the number of days in the transitional accounting period, and
B is the number of days in the paragraph 9(1) accounting period.

COMMENTARY ON SCHEDULE 19

Schedule 19 amends the gaming duty in a number of important ways and comes into force on 1 October 2019.

Under the previous legislation, businesses liable to gaming duty were required to file two returns and make payments on account in each six month accounting period after three months. Schedule 19 removes the obligation to make payments on account which will aid cash flow for casino operators.

In addition, Schedule 19 introduces the ability to carry forward losses from one accounting period to offset against gaming duty profits in future periods, which is consistent with other gambling duties such as machine games duty, remote gaming duty and general betting duty. Consequently, this may lead to a reduction in the duty payable by some casinos when compared with the present arrangements.

Schedule 19 also includes provision for non-standard accounting periods which will usually be approximately six months. These non-standard accounting periods can be at the request of taxpayers or directed by HMRC. Where non-standard accounting periods are used, the gaming duty gross gaming yield bands are increased or decreased in proportion to the number of days in the non-standard accounting period in comparison to the number of days in standard periods. For example, if there are fewer days in the non-standard accounting period then the gross gaming yield bands will be lower.

As a minimum these amendments should bring cash flow benefits to the casino sector and for some operators it could lead to real tax savings if they make a loss in any given period.

SCHEDULE 20

TAXATION OF HYBRID CAPITAL INSTRUMENTS

Section 89

PART 1

REVOCATION OF SPECIAL RULES FOR REGULATORY CAPITAL SECURITIES

1 (1) The Taxation of Regulatory Capital Securities Regulations 2013 (SI 2013/3209) are revoked.

(2) In consequence of the revocation made by sub-paragraph (1), the Taxation of Regulatory Capital Securities (Amendment) Regulations 2015 (SI 2015/2056) are revoked.

PART 2

CORPORATION TAX, INCOME TAX AND CAPITAL GAINS TAX

Distributions in respect of hybrid capital instruments

2 At the end of Chapter 12 of Part 5 of CTA 2009 insert—

"Hybrid capital instruments

420A Amounts payable in respect of hybrid capital instruments

(1) This section applies if a loan relationship is a hybrid capital instrument for an accounting period of the debtor.

(2) The Corporation Tax Acts have effect in relation to any person in respect of times in the accounting period as if any qualifying amount payable in respect of the hybrid capital instrument were not a distribution.

(3) An amount is a "qualifying amount" so far as it would not be regarded as a distribution if it is assumed that any provision made by the loan relationship under which the debtor is entitled to defer or cancel a payment of interest under the loan relationship had not been made.

(4) This section also needs to be read together with section 1015(1A) of CTA 2010 (which prevents hybrid capital instruments from being "special securities" as a result of being equity notes)."

3 (1) After section 475B of CTA 2009 insert—

"Meaning of "hybrid capital instrument"

475C Meaning of "hybrid capital instrument"

(1) For the purposes of this Part, a loan relationship is a "hybrid capital instrument" for an accounting period of the debtor if—

- (a) the loan relationship makes provision under which the debtor is entitled to defer or cancel a payment of interest under the loan relationship,
- (b) the loan relationship has no other significant equity features, and
- (c) the debtor has made an election in respect of the loan relationship which has effect for the period.

(2) For the purposes of this section a loan relationship "has no other significant equity features" if under the loan relationship—

- (a) there are neither voting rights in the debtor (ignoring insignificant voting rights in the debtor) nor a right to exercise a dominant influence over the debtor,
- (b) any provision for altering the amount of the debt is limited to write-down or conversion events in qualifying cases, and
- (c) any provision for the creditor to receive anything other than interest or repayment of the debt is limited to conversion events in qualifying cases.

(3) For the purposes of subsection (2)(a)—

- (a) the loan relationship makes provision for "insignificant voting rights in the debtor" if (and only if) the voting rights of any creditor under the loan relationship are limited to one vote exercisable in relation to matters generally affecting the debtor without conferring any special advantage or other right on the creditor, and

(b) "a right to exercise a dominant influence over the debtor" means a right to give directions with respect to the debtor's operating and financial policies with which it is obliged to comply (whether or not they are for the debtor's benefit).

(4) For the purposes of subsection (2)(b) a "write-down event" means—

(a) a permanent release of some or all of the debt, or

(b) a reduction in the amount of the debt (including to nil) in a case where provision is made for the reduction to be temporary (whether on the meeting of conditions or the exercise of a right or otherwise).

(5) For the purposes of subsection (2) a "conversion event" means—

(a) the conversion of the loan relationship into shares forming part of the debtor's ordinary share capital, or

(b) the conversion of the loan relationship into shares forming part of the ordinary share capital of the debtor's quoted parent company.

In paragraph (b) "quoted parent company" has the meaning given by section 164(3) to (7) of CTA 2010.

(6) For the purposes of subsection (2), a loan relationship makes provision for a qualifying case if—

(a) the provision applies only in the event that there is a material risk of the debtor becoming unable to pay its debts as they fall due,

(b) the provision applies only in the event that the value of the debtor's assets is less than the amount of its liabilities, taking into account contingent and prospective liabilities, or

(c) the provision is included in the loan relationship solely because of a need to comply with a regulatory or other legal requirement,

and, in each case, the provision in question does not include a right exercisable by the creditor.

(7) Provision is not to be regarded as failing to meet the condition in subsection (2)(b) merely because, in the case of a write-down event mentioned in subsection (4)(b), it provides for a subsequent increase in the amount of the debt (but not above the original amount).

(8) An election under this section—

(a) is irrevocable,

(b) must be made before the end of the period of 6 months beginning with the day on which the company becomes a party to the loan relationship, and

(c) has effect for the accounting period in which the company becomes a party to the loan relationship and subsequent accounting periods.

(9) But an election under this section has no effect if—

(a) the company is a party to the loan relationship directly or indirectly in consequence of, or otherwise in connection with, any arrangements (within the meaning of section 455C(2)), and

(b) the main purpose of, or one of the main purposes of, the arrangements is to secure a tax advantage for the company or any other person."

(2) In a case where a company became a party to a loan relationship before 1 January 2019, section 475C(8)(b) of CTA 2009 has effect as if the election were required to be made on or before 30 September 2019.

4 In section 1015 of CTA 2010 (meaning of "special securities") after subsection (1) insert—

"(1A) But hybrid capital instruments (within the meaning of section 475C of CTA 2009) are not special securities by reason of meeting condition E."

Loan relationships: credits and debits to be brought into account

5 After section 320A of CTA 2009 insert—

"320B Hybrid capital instruments: amounts recognised in equity

(1) This section applies if in accordance with generally accepted accounting practice, an amount in respect of a hybrid capital instrument relating to any of the matters in section 306A(1) of CTA 2009—

(a) is recognised in equity or shareholders' funds for a period, and
(b) is not recognised in the company's accounts for the period as an item of profit or loss or as an item of other comprehensive income.

(2) The amount is to be brought into account for the period for the purposes of this Part in the same way as an amount which is brought into account as a credit or debit in determining the company's profit or loss for the period in accordance with generally accepted accounting practice.

(3) But this section does not bring into account for the purposes of this Part any exchange gain or loss of the company which is recognised in the company's statement of total recognised gains and losses, statement of recognised income and expense, statement of changes in equity or statement of income and retained earnings."

Normal commercial loans

6 In section 162 of CTA 2010 (meaning of "normal commercial loan") after subsection (1) insert—

"(1B) For those purposes, "normal commercial loan" also includes a hybrid capital instrument (within the meaning of section 475C of CTA 2009)."

Consequential amendments

7 (1) Part 5 of CTA 2009 (loan relationships) is amended as follows.

(2) In section 398 (overview of Chapter 12), in subsection (2)—

(a) omit the "and" at the end of paragraph (d), and
(b) after paragraph (e) insert ", and

(f) section 420A (hybrid capital instruments)."

(3) In section 465(3) (provisions preventing amounts from being distributions), before paragraph (za) insert—

"(zza) section 420A(2) (hybrid capital instruments),".

8 (1) Part 10 of TIOPA 2010 (corporate interest restriction) is amended as follows.

(2) In section 413(6) (adjusted net group-interest expense: "relevant enactment") for paragraph (b) substitute—

"(b) section 320B of CTA 2009 (hybrid capital instruments: amounts recognised in equity)."

(3) In section 415 (qualifying net group-interest expense: interpretation), omit subsection (8).

9 (1) The Loan Relationships and Derivative Contracts (Disregard and Bringing into Account of Profits and Losses) Regulations 2004 (SI 2004/3256) are amended in accordance with this paragraph.

(2) In regulation 2(1) (interpretation)—

(a) after the definition of "fair value profit or loss" insert—

""hybrid capital instrument" has the meaning given by section 475C of CTA 2009;", and

(b) omit the definition of "regulatory capital security".

(3) In regulation 3 (exchange gains or losses arising from liabilities or assets hedging shares etc), in paragraph (5)(c), for "a regulatory capital security" substitute "a hybrid capital instrument".

(4) In regulation 4 (exchange gains or losses arising from derivative contracts hedging shares etc), in paragraph (4A)(c), for "a regulatory capital security" substitute "a hybrid capital instrument".

Commencement for purposes of corporation tax

10 The following have effect for accounting periods beginning on or after 1 January 2019—

(a) the provision made by paragraphs 1 to 4 and 6 so far as relating to corporation tax, and

(b) the amendments made by paragraphs 5 and 7 to 9.

11 An accounting period beginning before and ending on or after 1 January 2019 is to be treated for the purposes of the provision made by this Schedule (other than paragraph 12 or 13) as if so much of the period as falls before that date, and so much of the period as falls on or after that date, were separate accounting periods.

12 (1) This paragraph applies in the case of a security which was a regulatory capital security for the purposes of the Taxation of Regulatory Capital Securities Regulations 2013 immediately before 1 January 2019 (referred to in this Part of this Schedule as a "transitional qualifying instrument").

(2) The revocations made by paragraph 1 do not affect any case where regulation 3(2)(a) or (b), (3) or (3A) of those Regulations would have applied in relation to accounting periods ending on or before 31 December 2023 but for the provision made by paragraph 1.

(3) In a case where sub-paragraph (2) has applied, paragraph 13 makes provision for corporation tax purposes in relation to an accounting period beginning on 1 January 2024 ("the 2024 period") to bring in credits or debits in respect of a transitional qualifying instrument which exists immediately before that date so far as they would not otherwise be brought into account.

(4) For the purposes of this paragraph and paragraph 13, an accounting period beginning before and ending on or after 1 January 2024 is to be treated as if so much of the period as falls before that date, and so much of the period as falls on or after that date, were separate accounting periods.

13 (1) If there is a difference between—

(a) the tax-adjusted carrying value of a transitional qualifying instrument which is an asset or liability at the end of an accounting period ending on 31 December 2023, and

(b) the tax-adjusted carrying value of that instrument at the beginning of the 2024 period,

a credit or debit (as the case may be) of an amount equal to the difference must be brought into account for the purposes of Part 5 of CTA 2009 for the 2024 period in the same way as a credit or debit which is brought into account in determining the company's profit or loss for that period in accordance with generally accepted accounting practice.

(2) For the purposes of this paragraph "tax-adjusted carrying value" is to be construed in accordance with—

(a) section 465B of CTA 2009 (tax-adjusted carrying value in relation to the asset or liability representing a loan relationship), and

(b) section 702 of CTA 2009 (tax-adjusted carrying value in relation to a contract).

(3) Where in the 2024 period, in accordance with generally accepted accounting practice, the rights and liabilities under the transitional qualifying instrument have been treated as divided between—

(a) a loan relationship, and

(b) one or more derivative financial instruments or equity instruments,

the reference in this paragraph to the tax-adjusted carrying value of the transitional qualifying instrument means the sum of the tax-adjusted carrying values for each of those component instruments.

(4) In sub-paragraph (3) "equity instrument" has the meaning it has for accounting purposes.

14 (1) This paragraph applies to a transitional qualifying instrument which qualified as a regulatory capital security as a result of falling within regulation 2(1)(c) or (d) of the Taxation of Regulatory Capital Securities Regulations 2013.

(2) The revocations made by paragraph 1 do not affect the application of regulation 3(2)(c)(i) of those Regulations in a case where the writing down or conversion concerned took place before 1 July 2019.

15 (1) This paragraph applies if—

(a) regulation 3(2)(c)(i) of the Taxation of Regulatory Capital Securities Regulations 2013 applied in relation to a transitional qualifying instrument as a result of the writing down of the principal amount of the security on a temporary basis, and

(b) a credit was, accordingly, not brought into account under Part 5 of CTA 2009.

(2) No debit is to be brought into account under that Part in respect of the writing up of the principal amount of the security in accordance with any regulatory requirements or the provisions governing the security.

Commencement for purposes of income tax and CGT

16 (1) The provision made by paragraphs 1 to 4 has effect for the purposes of income tax in relation to payments made on or after 1 January 2019.

(2) But the revocations made by paragraph 1—

(a) do not affect the application of regulation 6 or 9 of the Taxation of Regulatory Capital Securities Regulations 2013 in relation to payments made before the day on which this Act is passed, and

(b) do not, in the case of a transitional qualifying instrument, apply to payments made before 1 January 2024 in any case where regulation 6 or 9 of those Regulations would have applied but for the provision made by paragraph 1.

17 The revocations made by paragraph 1 have effect for the purposes of capital gains tax in relation to disposals made on or after 1 January 2019.

18 In so far as it relates to the definition of "corporate bond" in section 117(1) of TCGA 1992, the amendment made by paragraph 6 has effect in relation to disposals made on or after 1 January 2019.

Power to amend definition of "hybrid capital instrument"

19 (1) The Treasury may by regulations amend section 475C of CTA 2009.

(2) The power conferred by this paragraph may not be exercised after 31 December 2019.

(3) The regulations may contain incidental, supplementary, consequential and transitional provision and savings.

(4) The consequential provision that may be made by the regulations includes provision amending any provision made by or under any Act.

(5) The regulations may contain retrospective provision.

PART 3

STAMP DUTY AND STAMP DUTY RESERVE TAX

20 A transfer of a hybrid capital instrument (within the meaning of section 475C of CTA 2009) is exempt from all stamp duties.

21 The revocations made by paragraph 1, and the provision made by paragraph 20, have effect—

(a) for the purposes of stamp duty, in relation to instruments executed on or after the day on which this Act is passed, and

(b) for the purposes of stamp duty reserve tax—

(i) in the case of agreements to transfer securities which are not conditional, in relation to agreements made on or after that day, and

(ii) in the case of agreements to transfer securities which are conditional, in relation to agreements where the condition is satisfied on or after that day.

COMMENTARY ON SCHEDULE 20

Schedule 20 introduces new rules relating to 'hybrid capital instruments', and at the same time revokes regulations (SI 2013/3209) which define and determine the tax treatment of 'regulatory capital securities'.

The changes have been prompted primarily by the publication by the Bank of England in June 2018 of a Statement of Policy on its approach to setting minimum requirements for own funds and eligible liabilities (MREL) of banks, such requirements having taken effect on 1 January 2019. This change of approach requires a new way to define the subset of debt instruments with certain equity features that should be taxed as debt, hence the formulation of the hybrid capital instruments rules.

At the same time, the Government has acknowledged that market instruments which bear both equity and debt features are issued by groups in sectors outside banking and insurance, and that these instruments should also be eligible to be taxed as debt. Therefore the hybrid capital instrument rules apply irrespective of the identity of the issuer or the sector it operates in (in contrast with the regulatory capital securities regulations).

In the Government's words, the new rules are intended to 'achieve the policy aims of providing tax certainty, reducing tax volatility, and allowing coupon deductibility for hybrid capital instruments in all sectors, but only so long as they are, in essence, debt instruments.'

Paragraph 1 of the Schedule revokes the regulatory capital securities regulations (SI 2013/3209).

Paragraphs 2 to 6 of the Schedule insert new sections into law or amend existing sections in order to define hybrid capital instruments and determine the tax treatment of such instruments.

Paragraph 2 inserts new CTA 2009, s 420A, which sets out that a 'qualifying amount' in respect of a hybrid capital instrument will not constitute a distribution for the purposes of the Corporation Tax Acts. A 'qualifying amount' is an amount that *would* otherwise have been treated as a distribution as a result of the ability to defer or cancel interest within the terms of the instrument. This new section is required to ensure, in particular, that instruments which contain an interest cancellation term are not treated as 'results-dependent' such that the instrument would constitute a 'special security' under Condition C of CTA 2010, s 1015.

Separately, paragraph 4 amends CTA 2010, s 1015 to make it explicit that hybrid capital instruments are not 'special securities' by virtue of Condition E of that section (the 'equity notes' condition).

Paragraph 3 inserts new CTA 2009, s 475C, which defines 'hybrid capital instrument'. Firstly it is worth noting that the definition only applies to loan relationships. That is, in general an instrument must meet the basic requirements of CTA 2009, s 302 et seq before considering further whether it might be a hybrid capital instrument. The other relevant conditions are:

- The instrument includes provision under which the debtor is entitled to defer or cancel interest payments;
- The instrument has no other 'significant equity features';
- The debtor has made an election to treat the loan relationship as a hybrid capital instrument.

The term 'significant equity features' is defined further. In broad terms, a significant equity feature would be any of:

- Voting rights in the debtor (other than one vote per creditor and no special right or advantage contained within that vote);
- A right to exercise 'dominant influence' over the debtor, being the right to give operating/financial policies direction with which the debtor must comply;
- Provisions in the instrument providing for the alteration of the amount of the debt or the right to receive anything other than interest or repayment of the debt. These are however not considered significant equity features in a number of scenarios. Broadly those scenarios are permanent or temporary debt write-down provisions, or provision for the conversion of the debt into ordinary shares of the debtor or its listed parent – but always only if any such provisions are necessary to comply with a legal or regulatory requirement (eg in the case of banks, MREL rules), or if they only apply on 'triggering' events such as debtor distress or insolvency. In particular, if any such provision in the instrument is a right exercisable by the creditor, it would automatically be a significant equity feature.

The relevant election must be made by the debtor within six months of becoming party to the instrument (or by 30 September 2019 for an instrument to which the debtor was party prior to 1 January 2019), and is irrevocable. There is a tax advantage, purpose-based, anti-avoidance test which, if met, prevents the election being of any effect. HMRC has separately indicated in a Technical Note published on

29 October 2018 that HMRC would not normally consider the choice of debt with these 'hybrid capital' features to indicate a tax advantage purpose. Likewise, the issuance of these instruments to enhance or protect the credit rating of more senior debt instruments would not normally indicate a tax advantage purpose. HMRC has, however, also indicated that it does not intend to give specific clearances on the application of the anti-avoidance rule.

Paragraph 5 inserts new CTA 2009, s 320B. This provides broadly that amounts recognised under generally accepted accounting practice in equity or shareholder's funds in respect of a hybrid capital instrument give rise to loan relationship credits/debits in the same way that amounts recognised as items of profit or loss would. This may apply, for example, where a hybrid capital instrument is accounted for as equity of the issuer, and so coupon payments may be recognised for accounting purposes as if they were dividends. The wording of new CTA 2009, s 320B is comparable to that of CTA 2009, s 321, which was applicable to loan relationships more generally and was repealed by Finance (No 2) Act 2015 (subject to grandfathering). Exchange gains and losses appearing in various statements are excluded from the application of CTA 2009, s 320B.

Paragraph 6 amends CTA 2010, s 162 to include explicit reference to hybrid capital instruments in the definition of 'normal commercial loan' (relevant in assessing who are 'equity holders' of a company in the group relief provisions).

Paragraphs 7 to 9 contain a number of consequential amendments to other provisions, including the Corporate Interest Restriction rules of TIOPA 2010, Pt 10 and the 'disregard regulations' (SI 2004/3256).

Paragraphs 10 to 18 contain detailed commencement and transitional provisions. In general, for corporation tax purposes the hybrid capital instrument rules are applicable to accounting periods of companies beginning on or after 1 January 2019 (with straddling period provisions treating such periods as two notional periods for the purposes of these rules). For income tax purposes they are applicable to payments made on or after this date, and for capital gains tax for disposals made on or after this date.

The main transitional provision is the grandfathering of certain aspects of the tax treatment of instruments which constituted 'regulatory capital securities' under SI 2013/3209 immediately before 1 January 2019:

- One aspect is the collection of rules which ensure that regulatory capital securities are taxed on an amortised cost basis. This grandfathering is applicable up to 31 December 2023, with transitional rules at that point to tax/relieve any differences in the tax-adjusted carrying value of the instrument at that point and what it will be from 1 January 2024 (under the application of the hybrid capital instrument rules).
- Another aspect is the exemption from the duty to withhold income tax on payments made under these instruments, again up to 1 January 2024. It is notable that there is no equivalent withholding exemption contained in the hybrid capital instrument rules. HMRC has confirmed its view in the Technical Note of 29 October 2018 that hybrid capital instruments can, however, still in principle constitute 'quoted Eurobonds' (i e the requirement for an instrument to 'carry the right to interest' would not be failed merely by reason of interest cancellation features).
- There is also grandfathering of the non-taxable treatment of write-downs or conversions of insurance industry regulatory capital securities, where the relevant event happens before 1 July 2019. According to HMRC this 'will allow regulatory authorities time to work with industry to fully consider the impacts of the revocation of [SI 2013/3209] for the insurance and reinsurance industry'.

Paragraph 19 confers powers to HM Treasury allowing for the amendment by regulations of the definition of hybrid capital instrument in new CTA 2009, s 475C, but only if such powers are exercised before 31 December 2019.

Paragraph 20 deals with stamp duty and stamp duty reserve tax. Like regulatory capital securities, the transfer of hybrid capital instruments will be exempt from all stamp duties.

INDEX